Christendom at the Crossroads

The Westminster History of Christian Thought

CHRISTENDOM AT THE CROSSROADS
The Medieval Era

J. A. Sheppard

WESTMINSTER
JOHN KNOX PRESS
LOUISVILLE · KENTUCKY

Scripture quotations from the New Revised Standard Version of the Bible are copyright © 1989 by the Division of Christian Education of the National Council of the Churches of Christ in the U.S.A. and are used by permission.

Scripture quotations from the Revised Standard Version of the Bible are copyright © 1946, 1952, 1971, and 1973 by the Division of Christian Education of the National Council of the Churches of Christ in the U.S.A. and are used by permission.

Book design by Sharon Adams
Cover design by Lisa Buckley

First edition
Published by Westminster John Knox Press
Louisville, Kentucky

This book is printed on acid-free paper that meets the American National Standards Institute Z39.48 standard. ∞

PRINTED IN THE UNITED STATES OF AMERICA

05 06 07 08 09 10 11 12 13 14 — 10 9 8 7 6 5 4 3 2 1

Library of Congress Cataloging-in-Publication Data
Sheppard, James.
 Christendom at the crossroads : the medieval era / James A. Sheppard.—1st ed.
  p. cm.
 Includes bibliographical references and index.
 ISBN 0-664-22813-5 (alk. paper)
 1. Church history—Middle Ages, 600–1500. I. Title.

 BR162.3.S48 2005
 270.3—dc22
                                                              2005042215

Contents

SERIES INTRODUCTION

The Westminster History of Christian Thought series provides a set of resources for the study of the history and development of Christian thought from the period of the early church to the present. The books are designed to be accessible introductory studies. They focus on the issues that were important questions and the theological expressions that emerged during the various eras. Strong attention is also paid to the historical and cultural contexts in which the theology developed. The studies are written by superb teachers who present their work in clear and energetic ways. These experts are committed to enhancing the teaching and learning tasks.

We hope this series will be of help to those who want skilled guidance to the development of Christian thought from the days of early Christianity to contemporary times.

The Publisher

Preface

The Middle Ages is a complicated topic for a number of reasons. First, there is a cast of bizarrely named characters to master. There are figures like Caedwalla, Galswinth, and Theudebert. There are also folks with unusual nicknames: Charles the Bald, Louis the Pious, Pippin the Short, etc. And to make matters worse, there is no good explanation for any of these names. That is to say, nobody seems to know whether or not Charles had hair, what made Louis so pious, or how tall Pippin really was. Second, the fact that Europe was often a fragmented place, overrun by a number of different tribes, makes it hard to keep track of wars, kings, and other customary historical landmarks. Third, when it comes to medieval intellectual achievements, the scholars of the Middle Ages examined with painstaking detail issues for which modern readers have little patience. Yet, the aim of this book is to try to gather up a large chunk of exactly this kind of information and fashion it into a reasonable orientation to the Christian thought of the medieval world. Accomplishing the goal at hand has been something of a team sport, and a lot of people have helped with the endeavor.

Everyone who works in the field of medieval intellectual thought should have access to Dr. Phil Schmidt. He is a trained historian. He has an unbridled passion for proper grammar. He is also an active lay member in his local congregation. This combination of qualities means that when Phil reads a manuscript, the pages get covered with corrections and comments. That is to say, Dr. Phil Schmidt prevents me from saying embarrassing, stupid, boring, or otherwise irrelevant things. I am grateful for Phil's willingness to be annoyed by my constant incorrect usage of the "'s." That having been said, it is likely that I have thwarted Phil's best efforts and found ways to sneak a few errors into the pages that follow. For those blunders, I apologize and take sole responsibility.

Dr. Beth Sheppard also receives credit for helping to shape my work. She is a trained scholar and a wonderful resource for biblical and theological information. She is also my spouse and as such has license to offer criticism in ways that others do not. For example, after the fifth or sixth time of my reading the same passage to her she would say things like, "Stop obsessing and move on," or "That is nice, dear, now say something funny." Beth knows what works. When it came time to plan out chapters, she was there. Drawing from her own experience of taking church history courses in seminary, she was able to tell me what information she wished she would have received. Fitting everything into this little book was not possible, but there are a few unusual twists that are not customarily found in standard church history textbooks.

Special thanks is also due to Don McKim. This particular project and, in fact, the series of which it is a part were born out of my conversations with him. Don understands the mysteries of the publishing world, and without his involvement this book would not exist. He has been my constant e-mail companion, and I am grateful for his support. I am in debt to my boss, President Dick Merriman, who allows me to carve out the time to keep the "academic" in the title academic administrator. All of my faculty colleagues at Southwestern College have been terrific cheerleaders whilst I was bringing this project to its conclusion. Finally, I have enjoyed the love and support of my family, who have encouraged me to write and enjoy the intellectual life since my childhood.

Introduction

Telling the story of the Middle Ages requires an organizing principle. Indeed, over one thousand years of stormy politics, passionate personalities, and meticulous theology all tangled together inevitably means that many things are going to be left unsaid. So a solid plan will help to make sure that most of the important stuff makes its way forward. If that plan happens to have its roots in the Middle Ages too, then so much the better. That is to say, in a book that portrays the Middle Ages as the crossroads between the early church and the Protestant Reformation, it would be helpful to have a signpost that clearly marks the medieval link. One common thread that runs through Christianity is the formula known as the Apostles' Creed. And its simple structure should do nicely for ordering a quick romp through a bit of medieval theology. The creed, in fact, grew out of an ancient Roman affirmation of faith. Around the fourth century, church leaders used it as a handy way to teach new converts the basics of Christianity. By the eighth and ninth centuries, however, the creed became well integrated into worship life and served as a simple statement of belief. Toward the beginning of the thirteenth century, Pope Innocent III made the Apostles' Creed the official statement of the church. Even the sixteenth-century reformers Martin Luther, John Calvin, and Ulrich Zwingli knew the Apostles' Creed. What better marker could there be for connecting the early church with the Protestant Reformation?

In terms of its more immediate practicality, the Apostles' Creed does have the perfect structure for unpacking the history of medieval theology. It begins with the pronouncement "I believe." Medieval theologians did believe, and they thought about their belief in great detail. Thus, the second chapter of this book is about the various ways in which they chose to express their faith. On the one hand, some medieval people accepted mystical experiences. On the other hand, there were medieval scholars who exercised their faith by applying reason to church teachings. Belief was also expressed in fairly simple and occasionally amusing ways by the laity. In any case, the chapter is a bit of a glimpse into the variety and challenges of claiming Christian belief. The full opening pronouncement of the creed is actually, "I believe in God the Father." So chapter 3 is an examination of the scholastic proofs for the existence of God. Rather than simply present the logic of the various arguments, however, we will try to tackle some tough questions from a historical point of view. A number of books offer detailed analysis of various medieval proofs for the existence of God. Very few books, however, explain why medieval theologians developed the proofs in the first place. Most of the time, the proofs were born out of an educational agenda and were a mechanism teachers used to help students to grow in their Christian faith. With that in mind, the chapter is designed both to clarify the content of a few of the more famous proofs and to show how they fit into preparation for effective ministry.

Following the assertion about belief in God, the Apostles' Creed goes on, "I believe in Jesus Christ, his only Son, our Lord." Although third-century Roman emperors like Decius (c. 249–51) actively persecuted Jesus' early followers, by the fifth century Christ was definitely all the rage. In fact, medieval theologians believed in Christ so much that they spent an incredible amount of time thinking, writing, and preaching about Jesus. Not surprisingly, from the roughly one thousand years of study that medieval scholars inherited, a huge number of issues related to the person and work of Jesus Christ had been identified. For the sake of simplicity, we will focus on only one question about the incarnation: "Would the Word have become flesh if humans had not fallen?" Many other questions could equally serve as a suitable topic, but this one is fun for two reasons. First, it tends to strike right at the core of the Christian faith. That is to say, it is asking about the ultimate purpose for Christ. Medieval scholars rightly saw that this was a tricky question, because whichever way one answered, yes or no, there were serious consequences that had to be addressed. Second, the question affords a good sampling of opinions from a period of over two centuries and offers a glimpse into the rather thought-provoking answers that were proposed from a wide array of theologians.

Where would Jesus be without his mom? Chapter 5 is dedicated to Mary. The creed teaches that Jesus was born of the Virgin Mary but does not say much more about her. Why did Mary have to be a virgin? Was it a necessary condition for preventing the transmission of human sin to the baby Jesus? After a quick word about medieval medicine, our chapter is basically an exploration into the immaculate conception and what being chosen by God meant for

Mary. The Jesus section of the creed ultimately winds up with the line, "He will come again to judge the living and the dead." This line, however, implies that humans must have some degree of free will. That is to say, the necessity for judgment supposes that we are going to make a few "bad" choices. Following out this line, chapter 6 is dedicated to the problem of evil. St. Anselm used the story of the fall of the devil as an anchor for understanding what happens when humans choose in a way that is contrary to the will of God. With a few thoughts about evil out of the way, the next line of the Apostles' Creed offers a glimpse into the medieval desire for church unity. More specifically, the creed states, "I believe in the Holy Spirit." The focus of chapter 7 is on the procession of the Holy Spirit, and the context is the Council of Lyons. The reader is exposed to the theological problems that led to the split between Constantinople and Rome, to the opinions of scholars like Robert Grosseteste and Duns Scotus, and to the political intrigues that led to Pope Gregory's attempt to mend the church.

What is not part of the creed is the contents of the first and the last chapters. Nevertheless, these are important bits of our project because they contain the maps for marking the crossroads. The first chapter introduces some basic terminology, presents a few basic concepts, and explains some of the philosophical developments that help to make sense of the Middle Ages. Similarly, the last chapter leads away from the crossroads and toward the Protestant Reformation. It should be fairly obvious that the changes in the church that took place during the sixteenth century owe a huge debt to the ideas that were developed during the Middle Ages. That is to say, the Protestant Reformation did not just happen magically. Martin Luther was a member of a religious group that got its official start in the thirteenth century, and his theology was conditioned by their doctrines. Also, scholars like John Major, a late medieval Franciscan philosopher, helped to shape the ideas of both John Knox and John Calvin. In short, the first and last chapters, along with a handful of "closer look" boxes that are scattered throughout the entire book, serve as resources for gaining insight into the very broad topic that is called medieval theology.

Time Lines

The dates given for the popes refer to their tenure in office. Dates for monarchs and scholars, however, are indicative of their life spans. If a birthdate is unknown, then the date of death is given.

LEADERS

Fifth Century

Emperor Theodosius II	401–50
Pope Celestine I	422–32
King Attila	d. 453
Pope Leo I	440–61
King Theodoric	453–526
King Clovis I	466–511

Sixth Century

Emperor Justinian	483–565
The Prophet Muhammad	570–632
Pope Gregory I	590–604

Seventh Century

Queen Brunhild	d. 613
King Oswald	605–41

Eighth Century

Charles Martel	d. 741
Emperor Charlemagne	742–814
Pope Hadrian I	772–95
King Louis the Pious	773–840

Ninth Century

Emperor Lothar I	795–855
Emperor Charles the Bald	823–77
King Alfred the Great	849–99

Tenth Century

King Hugh Capet	940–96
King St. Edward	963–78
Emperor Henry II	972–1024

Eleventh Century

King William the Conqueror	1028–87
Emperor Henry IV	1050–1106
Pope Gregory VII	1073–85

Twelfth Century

Emperor Frederick I Barbarossa	1122–90
Pope Innocent III	1198–1216

Thirteenth Century

St. Francis	1182–1226
King Louis IX	1214–70
King Edward I of England	1239–1307
King Philip IV of France	1268–1314
Pope Gregory X	1271–76
Pope Boniface VIII	1294–1303

Fourteenth Century

Pope John XXII	1316–34
Emperor Louis of Bavaria	1283–1347

SCHOLARS

Fifth Century

St. Augustine of Hippo	345–430
St. Patrick	390–460

Sixth Century

Boethius	480–525
Denis the Pseudo-Areopagite	fl. c. 500
St. Isidore of Seville	560–636
St. Benedict of Nursia	480–550

Seventh Century

St. Bede	673–735
St. Willibrord	658–739
St. Boniface	680–754

Eighth Century

Alcuin of York	735–804
St. Benedict of Aniane	750–821

Ninth Century

Hincmar of Reims	806–82
Gottschalk	804–69
John the Scot	810–77

Tenth Century

St. Odo	879–942
St. Dunstan	909–88
Gerbert of Aurillac	940–1003

Eleventh Century

Lanfranc	1005–89
St. Peter Damian	1007–72
Berenger of Tours	1010–88

Twelfth Century

St. Anselm of Canterbury	1033–1109
Peter Abelard	1079–1142
Peter Lombard	1095–1160

Thirteenth Century

Robert Grosseteste	1160–1253
St. Albert the Great	1200–1280
St. Bonaventure	1217–74
Henry of Ghent	1217–93
John Peckham	1225–92
St. Thomas Aquinas	1225–74
Matthew of Aquasparta	1238–1302
Meister Eckhart	1260–1328
John Duns Scotus	1266–1308

Fourteenth Century

William of Ockham	1285–1347
John Buridan	1295–1358
Henry Suso	1295–1360
John Tauler	1300–1361
John Wycliffe	1330–84

Fifteenth Century

Nicholas of Cusa	1401–64
John Major	1467–1550

EVENTS

Fourth Century

Conversion of Constantine the Great	312
Council of Nicaea	325
War between Rome and Persia	360

Fifth Century

Visigoths enter Italy	408
Sack of Rome	410
St. Jerome dies	420
Council of Ephesus	431
Council of Chalcedon	451

Sixth Century

Boethius dies	524
Reign of Pope Gregory I begins	590

Seventh Century

Muhammad's revelations begin	610
Muhammad captures Mecca	630
Reign of King Oswald	633
Arabs capture Jerusalem	636
Synod of Whitby	663

Eighth Century

Battle of Tours	732
Second Council of Nicaea	797
Vikings raid Lindisfarne	793

Ninth Century

Imperial coronation of Charlemagne	800
Coronation of King Alfred of Wessex	871
Coronation of Charles the Bald	875
Viking siege of Paris	885

Tenth Century

Cluny monastery founded	909
King Wenceslas assassinated	929
End of Carolingian dynasty: Hugh Capet crowned	987

Eleventh Century

St. Hugh chosen as Abbot of Cluny	1049
East-West Schism	1054
Battle of Hastings	1066
St. Anselm becomes Archbishop of Canterbury	1093
Crusaders capture Jerusalem	1099

Twelfth Century

Peter Abelard condemned	1141
St. Bernard of Clairvaux dies	1153

Thirteenth Century

The Great Mongol invasion	1240
Second Council of Lyons	1274
Condemnations of philosophy	1277

Fourteenth Century

Unam sanctam	1302
Babylonian Captivity begins	1309
Hundred Years' War	1337–1453
Great Schism in West	1378
John Wycliffe condemned	1380

Fifteenth Century

Council of Constance	1414
Jan Huss dies	1415
Joan of Arc dies	1431
Council of Basle	1431–49

Sixteenth Century

John Major dies	1550

1

At the Crossroads

What's the difference between a monk and a friar? Both were deeply religious people. Both wore burlap robes. Neither, in theory, had many dates with the opposite sex, and they all had bad haircuts. So what's the difference? Technically, there is a huge distinction between monks and friars. First, monks stem from a much older tradition. They were members of a religious order and tended to live in small communities or monasteries that kept them sheltered from the outside world. Medieval monks aimed for spiritual growth, gave up all of their personal property, and spent their days following a strict schedule of reading and prayer.

The roots of this rigorous lifestyle can be traced back to the ancient church and ultimately developed from the writings of St. Anthony, an Egyptian hermit who organized a community of disciples in about 305, and St. Pachomius, who developed his community near the Nile River around 320. Nearly a century later, two monks, St. Jerome (c. 345–420) and John Cassian (c. 360–after 430), made their contributions to the monastic life by both translating and adding to the insights of the ancient hermits. Then, about the middle of the sixth century, an Italian named Benedict of Nursia (c. 480–550) drew freely from these older resources and developed his own rule book that ultimately became the popular guide for both spiritual and administrative life in a monastery. There was a wide range of monastic communities during the Middle Ages, but all of them, in one way or another, tended to follow the Rule of St. Benedict. The one exception to this was the Carthusian order, founded by St. Bruno in 1084. These monks based their lives in part on the Rule of St. Benedict, but they tended to downplay the communal aspect of religious life. More specifically, the Carthusians took a vow of silence, dedicated themselves to several hours of daily prayer, and lived in little individual cells within the monastery.

A second major difference between a monk and a friar is that the friars rarely stayed at home. Rather than live in a monastery, they embarked on wandering ministries and were active primarily in urban areas. Like monks, medieval friars sought God by following Jesus Christ and gave up all of their worldly possessions. The friars, however, also had an additional purpose attached to their lives, such as the pursuit of a work of charity. For example, the Trinitarian order was dedicated to the redemption of captives, and the Crutched friars, so called because of the white cross that was emblazoned on their black robes, devoted their efforts to hospitals. These extra interests meant that friars directly engaged the world. Unlike monks, they were evangelists. They professed the apostolic life—the life of the apostles of Jesus as it was expressed in the New Testament—and actively undertook missions of service to the poor. Undoubtedly the two most important orders of friars during the Middle Ages were the Franciscans and the Dominicans. St. Francis (c. 1182–1226) actually named the first group the Minorites because he wanted his followers to have a permanent reminder that the members should not strive for positions of distinction. So too the correct name for the Dominicans is the Order of Preachers; the name stems from the work that Dominic of Caleruega (c. 1174–1221), their founder, thought was important. In any case, both the Franciscans and the Dominicans produced some of the most famous scholars, poets, diplomats, and explorers of the medieval period.

So why study monks and friars? Because they stand at the crossroads between the early church and the Reformation period. More specifically, the monks and the friars were largely responsible for both creating and preserving the history of the Christian church between the years 312 and about 1530. Or, to put it another way, the monks and friars were some of the major players between the time of Constantine the Great's Christian conversion and Martin Luther's break with Rome. This is not to say that studying the monks and friars always provides a perfect picture of the Middle Ages. Sometimes the historical account gets messy because the monks and friars themselves were given to a bit of exaggeration.

For instance, a monk named Bede (c. 673–735) is one of the best resources for the history of the English people. At one point in his account, however, he tells the story of the miraculous healings that took place at the site of King Oswald's death in Shropshire. King Oswald himself was a wonderfully pious Christian king, but he fell in a fierce battle against the pagan King Penda of Mercia. Shortly after Oswald's death, people discovered that the dust from the spot where the king had died could be mixed with water and drunk to the benefit of healing the sick. And the medicinal qualities were quite handy for pets too. When a horse happened to collapse in pain, the rider waited to see if the animal would live or die. According to Bede, the horse was foaming at the mouth, and it rolled in pain. But when it rolled onto the spot where King Oswald died, the pain stopped and the horse got up, fully recovered. Suffice to say that such incredible healings do not appear to be quite so frequent in modern-day Shropshire.

Despite the little distortions in the historical record, a narrow focus on monks and friars can also yield an odd picture because it hides other significant people. Bishops, priests, lay people, kings, queens, and many others all helped to shape the church. Nevertheless, even with the minor flaws that come with taking a close look at a small group within a vast and complicated European medieval society, the simple fact is that the information medieval monks and friars oversaw contained highly detailed explanations for many issues that are still at the heart of Christian intellectual life. In short, to understand the works of the monks and friars is to grasp a central part of Christianity.

MEDIEVAL CONTRIBUTIONS

Saying that the work of monks and friars is a central part of Christianity is a pretty bold thing to do. Nevertheless, the claim has merit. The weight of the assertion is perhaps a bit hard to recognize, because medieval theology is often dismissed as being concerned with only "the number of angels that can dance on the head of a pin." But even that rather uncomplimentary assessment owes something to the Middle Ages. Most of the time the disco scenario is wrongly attributed to the thirteenth-century Dominican friar St. Thomas Aquinas. But it was probably his followers in the seventeenth century who first raised the question about dancing angels. For his part, St. Thomas asked all kinds of other questions about angels. For instance, he wanted to know whether or not they move and if they know material things. Thomas also questioned what kind of bodies angels have. He asked these questions because he wanted to know more about the spiritual world. His angels, however, never boogied. Rather, St. Thomas's angels served many other functions. Their various roles had been defined by Origen (c. 184–254), and then they had been systematically classified by the Greek Christian writer Denis the Areopagite sometime around 500. In short, St. Thomas's angels were rooted in Scripture, inherited from the early church, given greater definition, and passed on to later generations.

Just as St. Thomas's angels were rooted in the early church and shaped in the Middle Ages, so too were several church doctrines. For instance, the monks and friars recognized that if someone thought carefully about scriptural passages that describe the annunciation—Luke 1:26–38, for instance, where the angel announces the conception of a Messiah—the role of the Virgin Mary could create an awful theological snare. The troublesome line of reasoning goes something like this: Mary was a human being, and that meant that she should have passed on to Jesus the sin of Adam and Eve. But Jesus was perfect and was completely without sin. So does that mean that Mary too was perfect and had no sin to pass to her son? If Mary did not have a sinful nature, then Jesus could not have been the universal redeemer. That is, without the stain of sin, Mary would not need to be saved. That is absurd! Jesus was sent to save *everyone*. So, how do the pieces fit together? In the twelfth century, two monks named Eadmer and Anselm wrangled over the problem of what to do about Mary. There was no clear-cut winner in the debate, but St. Anselm argued that Mary did in fact have the stain of original sin, and his view became fairly well accepted. Toward the end of the following century, however, a Franciscan friar named John Duns Scotus reconsidered the question and decided that Mary was without sin from the moment of her conception. Although Scotus's explanation was highly controversial, more than five hundred years later it became the generally accepted interpretation.

Questions about Mary are usually questions about Jesus in disguise. And Christology is something else that grew out of the Middle Ages. Various church councils gathered throughout the Middle Ages in order to sort out the best explanations for understanding the person and nature of Jesus Christ. There were so many councils, in fact, that it is impossible to recount them all here. Rather, a quick snapshot of the top four that provided the framework in which most theologians worked will do. Although the monks and the friars were major players during the Middle Ages, they did not hold center stage at the church councils. Most of the action centered on bishops, emperors, and other leaders. Some monks, such as John Cassian, did occasionally weigh in with their opinions. Others actually triggered the need for a council because they asked enormously thorny questions. But, in general, the majority of monks preferred to keep to themselves and leave the business of church politics well enough alone.

The first major church council met at the dawn of the Middle Ages about 325 in Nicaea. The Emperor Constantine called the gathering, which in itself is extraordinary, because prior to his reign Roman emperors famously spent their time hassling Christians. Constantine, however, came to power under the Christian symbol and was much more tolerant of the Christian community than his predecessor had been. In any case, the council convened in order to deal with a range of issues, such as how to determine the correct date for Easter and what to do with Christians who had abandoned their faith in order to escape Roman abuses. The hot topic for the conference, however, centered on

A CLOSER LOOK

Bishops and monks were not two distinct groups. In fact, several monks held positions of importance within the church hierarchy. The most famous was St. Augustine, who was both a monk and the bishop of Hippo, in north Africa. The patron saint of France, St. Martin of Tours, also a monk, was elected bishop about 371. St. Adalgar of Bremen was a monk at Corvey but became the archbishop of Sundrold of Mainz toward the end of the ninth century. And in 724, when King Charles's nephew Hugh was elected abbot of Fontenelle, he was already serving as the archbishop of Rouen and the bishop of both Bayeux and Paris. Much later, in 1294, a monk named Peter Morrone was elected bishop of Rome. And that means that Peter was the pope!

Further Reading: P. Brown, *Augustine of Hippo* (Berkeley 1969).

the ideas of an Alexandrian priest named Arius. Arius thought that Christ was a creature who was inferior to God. Alexander, the bishop of Alexandria, was hugely offended by the idea. For Alexander, Christ existed eternally with God the Father. Sorting out the problem wasn't easy either, as each side had powerful arguments against the other's position. For instance, it seemed to Arius that Alexander was advocating for the existence of more than one God. That was hardly suitable for a Christian position. Alexander was convinced that Arius was denying the divinity of Christ. What kind of Christian could do that? After some rousing debate, the council sided with Alexander, voted to condemn Arius's position, and hammered out a mutually agreeable understanding of the relationship between God and Jesus Christ. The formula that they developed became known as the Nicene Creed.

Shortly after the reign of Constantine, the power of the Roman Empire began to fade. Germanic tribes had entered Italy and in 410 had managed to conquer Rome. In a manner of speaking, the empire had lost its luster. And, as a matter of course, the second council, which was held at Ephesus in 431, was a tasteless event. The barbarian invasions caused disarray in nearly every aspect of life, including the church. In the absence of stability and control, the council at Ephesus became a fairly unsavory gathering. In large part this was because the outcome was determined more by political intrigue than by genuine debate and judgment. The council itself was the result of a dispute between two intractable views about the person of Jesus Christ. Nestorius, the patriarch of Constantinople, argued that Christ's divine nature should be kept apart from his human nature. In strong opposition, Cyril of Alexandria and a handful of Egyptian monks argued that the two natures were completely united. Eventually, both positions were submitted to Pope Celestine I (c. 422–32) for consideration. Rather than simply recognize and silence the two disputing parties, however, Celestine mistakenly thought that he was being presented with a formal appeal from the East—a natural conclusion to draw since Rome possessed as much prestige as both Alexandria and Constantinople. As such, he requested additional guidance on the matter from both Cyril and John Cassian. Indecorously operating with a stacked deck, Celestine acted to condemn Nestorius's position. To make matters more interesting, Cyril was then directed to carry out an excommunication order against Nestorius.

At about that same time, Cyril had managed to secure support from the politically inept but well-meaning Eastern Emperor Theodosius II, who then called another council at Ephesus to decide the issue. Nestorius's supporters, however, were slow in coming to the meeting. After waiting a few weeks, and despite several protests lodged by various bishops, the council convened and Nestorius's ideas were condemned. When the other participants finally arrived, they discovered that Nestorius had lost the fight without having an opportunity to defend himself. They lodged a protest against the proceedings, but it went largely went unnoticed. Consequently, they held their own council meeting and excommunicated Cyril. Taking his turn in the struggle, Cyril and his supporters met again and reaffirmed their first decision against Nestorius. They also condemned the participants of the council that excommunicated Cyril. Rather than permit this rather embarrassing behavior to continue, Theodosius arrested both Cyril and Nestorius and forced them to reconcile. He also declared that the decision from the first council meeting was the official, and final, word on the matter.

The Council of Nicaea settled the question of whether Jesus was God. The Council of Ephesus, despite the political scheming, seemed to go some way toward answering the question of how Jesus could be both God and human. But the theology that came out of Ephesus was not absolutely conclusive. Rather than suppose, as Nestorius had, that the divine and human natures should be kept separate, a monk named Eutyches took an extreme position and wagered that the human aspects of Jesus were absorbed into the divine. On balance with events of the other councils, Flavian, archbishop of Constantinople, objected to Eutyches' position on the grounds that it ran the risk of suggesting that Christ's human suffering on the cross was only apparent. Since Eutyches' position appeared to diminish the work of Christ, Flavian condemned the monk, along with his ideas. Eutyches appealed to Pope Leo I (c. 440–61), but the pontiff responded by siding with Flavian. Eventually, the conflict grew to involve the entire church, and Emperor Theodosius called for yet another council to be held in the city of Ephesus in 449.

At the gathering, despite the enormous weight of Pope Leo and Flavian against them, the council chose to reinstate Eutyches. Naturally, the pope and others were deeply offended by the reversal of their decision, but Theodosius had apparently received quite a lot of gold for his trouble and now considered the matter closed. The matter reopened, however, when the emperor fell off of his horse and died. His sister Pulcheria, an open-minded individual who was quite familiar with the theological controversies, gained control of the empire. A much better leader than her brother, she recognized that his council of 449 was a deeply unsatisfying event. Consequently, at Pope Leo's urging, she called another council at Chalcedon, which met in 451. At that meeting, both Eutyches and the actions of the council that met in 449 were condemned. Then the council drew up a definition of faith that brought the church back in line with the moderate decision that had been reached at Ephesus in 431.

With the natures of Christ sorted out, theology bumped along quietly until the fourth council was needed. It met in Constantinople in 681, to consider a teaching that was very similar to Eutyches' position. The issue was not whether Christ's human nature was absorbed by the divine, but whether the divine will actually took the place of the human will in Christ. This idea, called monothelitism, had a fairly strong following, with a few notable champions, including Pope Honorius (625–38). By 678, or roughly eight popes later, a Sicilian monk who had been elected to the papacy led a four-year reign that effectively ended the view that the will of Christ was exclusively divine. Pope Agatho (678–81) was an able administrator. Before sending his representatives to Constantinople to debate whether or not Christ had both a divine and human will, he held special meetings in Milan, England, and Rome. The upshot of those meetings was a united front against the monothelite position. So, with most of the West upholding the doctrine that Christ did in fact have two distinct wills, Agatho sent his representatives to Constantinople, where the emperor Constantine IV had called a general council. By the end of the meeting in 681, monothelitism was condemned and Pope Honorius, who had been dead for roughly forty-three years, was excommunicated. Pope Agatho's work was decisive, but he never saw the fruit of his labor. He died before the council could announce the official position that Christ had two wills.

The collective decisions of these and other councils had a lasting, albeit mixed, impact on the church. On the one hand, the councils did not have the power to change the theology of the popular culture. Arianism continued to find support through most of the Germanic tribes. For instance, Theodoric the Ostrogoth (c. 493) decreed that all churches be handed over to the Arians. The Vandals, also Arians, happily persecuted Catholics in North Africa. After the Visigoths defeated the Romans in 410, they settled in Spain. From about 415 until the conversion of their King Ricared in 589 they remained Arians. Even the Burgundians, the barbarian tribe that lived in Gaul (France), practiced the Arian faith until the early sixth century. The monothelite heresy too enjoyed a life that ranged well beyond the dictates of the councils. For example, the emperor Heraclius issued his famous statement *Ekthesis* about 639. The provision of that document was that Christ had two natures and two persons but only one will. Again, in 650 Pope Martin I was forced to condemn the heresy. By the fifteenth century Pope Eugene IV signed agreements with Armenian Monophysites and Mesopotamian Nestorians. That having been said, the councils were effective in terms of church governance. They set a precedent as the locus of power for the direction of the Christian community, and they set the limits of what could be considered proper theology. In fact, by the close of the Middle Ages, the councils were viewed as the necessary tools that could undermine the absolute authority of the papacy and reform the church.

MEDIEVAL POLITICS

In addition to the monks and friars, political rulers had an important role in shaping the Middle Ages, especially in the sense that they often drove the action that either required theological justification or elicited a theological response. Although it is virtually impossible to sum up the entirety of the political history of the Middle Ages in the space of a few paragraphs, two key concepts, combined with a few examples, are sufficient to give a flavor of the various maneuverings that took place.

The first is the two-swords theory, the separation of the spiritual and earthly powers. The "two swords" label was derived mostly from Luke's Gospel. Just prior to Jesus' capture, the apostles indicated their willingness to use two swords in order to resist arrest. Jesus, however, rejected the call to arms. When Peter used his sword a bit later to cut off the ear of the servant of a high priest, Jesus ordered that the sword be put away, healed the ear of the servant, and surrendered to the authorities.[1] Rather than accept this story at face value, medieval commentators viewed the tale of Jesus' capture as an opportunity to find deeper meaning in Scripture. In particular, they saw the two swords as highly symbolic. One sword, in the words of Pope Gregory VII (1073–85), represented the sword of the divine word. The other sword stood for the power exercised by a king. Although there were various other interpretations associated with the two swords, the imagery eventually became a standardized way to express the relation of the powers of the church and the state.

One of the most famous instances of a political sword fight between priest and king is the war between King Philip IV of France and Pope Boniface VIII. The trouble began when Philip needed money to pay for an expensive war against England. In order to make ends meet, he began to tax church property. The French clergy, not at all happy about the king's policy of raiding the church piggy banks, complained to the pope. Pope Boniface responded to their pleas by issuing a formal document, *Clericis Laicos*, that forbid the king to tax the church. Rather than submit to the authority of the pope, however, Philip imposed trade sanctions on Rome and prohibited anyone from taking gold or silver out of France. This move cut directly into Pope Boniface's funding. The pope countered by issuing another official document, *Ineffibilis*, in which he claimed the right to supervise the king. The document had no effect on the king, and the policy of taxing the French churches continued. As the conflict escalated, both Pope Boniface and King Philip called special councils to have each other condemned. The fight continued and was basically ended when Pope Boniface died from natural causes on October 12, 1303. Nevertheless, even in one of Boniface's best-known bids to assert supremacy over temporal powers, *Unam Sanctam*, he referred to the two swords and tried to claim them both as instruments that belong to the church.

The other key concept that is helpful for grappling with medieval thought is the notion of feudalism. In very general terms, feudalism is the form of government that characterized the Middle Ages. It is, however, a very imprecise word. On the one hand, "feudalism" is a term of convenience that was invented well after the Middle Ages to describe the various ways in which people related to each other. In fact, an average medieval person would have had absolutely no idea what the word "feudalism" meant. Rather, a medieval vassal, or landholder, would simply know his obligations. That is to say, people lived their lives in a kind of social structure that was supported by their promise of loyalty to each other. On the other hand, the word "feudalism" is ambiguous because the radical changes in the nature of leadership were so dynamic that one term cannot adequately represent them all.[2] For instance, it is hard to have an even comparison between the barbarian King Clovis I (481–511), who secured his kingdom with the help of a loose group of warlords, and the reign of King Louis IX (1226–70), who used a professional army to gain profit both for his own kingdom and for God. What is consistent in the use of the term "feudalism," however, is that it refers to a type of class system in which a king rules with the support of a military class who are bound to their lords by oaths.

Some medievalists occasionally identify a third layer of society below the level of the kings and the knights when using the term "feudalism." This last group is the serfs, a working class who spent most of their time farming. In the strict sense, they are not involved with feudalism. They were not a free people and consequently were not really in the position to promise their support to anyone. Rather, the word "manorialism" is better suited to describe their lives, because it refers to the relationship between a landowner and his peasants. Serfs, to be blunt, were property. They could no more pledge loyalty to a king than could a garden trowel. Feudalism is about an oath of fidelity that establishes a clear relationship of dependence between king and subject. When Charlemagne became emperor in 800, for example, he expected every freeman over the age of twelve to swear obedience. His subjects had to promise to serve God, to respect both royal and church properties, including serfs, and to answer calls to war.

These two key concepts, the two swords and feudalism, are important frameworks within which most medieval theology was constructed. In some cases, the reactions of the monks and friars in light of the political climate are easy to see. For instance, a great deal of William of Ockham's (1285–1347) theology is clearly aimed at criticizing the political policies of Pope John XXII (1316–34). Thus, as will be seen in the last chapter, Ockham was caught up in a call for the pope to submit to the temporal sword. Other times, the agendas are much more subtle. For example, the way in which the Dominican theologian Jean de Pouilly passionately defended the traditional understanding of the immaculate conception has caused some modern scholars to suppose that he may have been casting a vote for King Philip the Fair's policies against Pope Boniface. In any case, medieval theologians frequently responded to economic, social, and political change. The rise of a new king, the formation of a new religious order, heresies, and newfound nationalism were all forces that shaped the Christian theology of the Middle Ages.

CONTINENTAL KINGS

Not only did the leaders set the pace for medieval society, but the reigns of the kings can be a particularly good way to mark off the periods of the Middle Ages. In the medieval West, with which our work is mostly concerned, there were essentially three groups of kings: the Merovingians, the Franks, and the Capetians. The first group in particular grew out of the chaos that resulted from the tribal invasions and the subsequent collapse of Rome. The Merovingian kings were barbarians themselves; their exact origin, however, is unclear. On the one hand, some early historians took great pains to establish the notion that the Merovingians descended from the Trojans. They probably did this because the Merovingians saw the golden age of Rome as an ideal and wanted others to believe that they were part of a noble race. On the other hand, some medieval histories contain a Merovingian genealogy that suggests a supernatural origin. More specifically, a barbarian queen apparently went swimming and met a sea monster. The consequence of the encounter was that she became pregnant with Merovich, who grew up to become the founder of the dynasty.[3] Neither legend is realistic, although the first is at least slightly more credible.

In any case, there is very little that is elegant about the Merovingian dynasty or their period, roughly 450–750. Merovingian family lineages and correlating political intrigues are complicated and, at times, shocking. For instance, another barbarian queen, Fredegund, allegedly murdered one of her stepsons and then drove the other to suicide, in order to ensure that her own children would inherit the kingdom. Such violent behavior was common for the Merovingians. Nevertheless, the Merovingians were the first glimmers of a new centralized state in which the monks often provided stability and support.

At least three Merovingian kings are worthy of note. The first of the great Merovingian kings was Clovis I (c. 481–511). In part, his popularity stems from the fact that he was very good at war, defeating several of the other tribes that were in Gaul or what is now known mostly as France. By conquering so many warlords, Clovis ended up establishing the largest state since the fall of Rome. The rest of his magnitude appears to have come from historians who portrayed him as the ideal orthodox Christian warrior king. By most accounts Clovis married Chlothild, the daughter of a Burgundian king, from the Rhone valley. She apparently tried to convert Clovis to Catholic Christianity but failed. A short time later, however, Clovis was engaged in a campaign against the Alamans, a group that settled around the upper Rhine. Upon his victory, Clovis became baptized. With the newfound fervor of a recent convert, Clovis set out to engage the Arian, and consequently heretical, Visigoths. In the end, the Visigothic King Alaric II was killed, and his territories too were ceded to Clovis. By the accounts handed down, Clovis converted directly from paganism to orthodox Christianity. There are hints in the sources, however, that he was an Arian before his fight with the Visigoths. In any case, the image of King Clovis set the standard for the following generations of medieval kings.

The second Merovingian king who merits comment is Theudebert. After Clovis died, his kingdom was divided among his sons. Not too surprisingly, both this new generation of barbarian kings and the one following set out aggressively to expand their territories. For example, when Clovis's son Chlodomer died in 524, his children were sent to their grandmother Chlothild. Rather than allow the children to grow up and inherit their father's lands, however, their uncles decided that the kingdom would be better divided between them. So they gave Chlothild a choice: either send her grandchildren to a monastery to become monks, or let them be killed. She chose the latter option. When the same two uncles united against Theudebert, they found that the elimination of their opponent was not so easily gained. Theudebert was an accomplished military leader. In fact, he too was particularly good at war. His skill in battle became so well known that the Byzantines worried that he would actually attack Constantinople, the best protected city of the medieval world. Suffice to say that Theudebert won the respect of several bands of people. He was imperial in his method and Christian in his persona. He successfully defended his kingdom and managed to extend it from France to northern Italy.

The third illustrious Merovingian king was Dagobert I. The chroniclers did not hold Dagobert in quite the same esteem as Theudebert. The Frankish historians did a much better job of pointing out where Dagobert was manipulated into battles by his advisors. Nevertheless, Dagobert was a strong warrior, like the other barbarian kings mentioned. Dagobert, however, was also serious about the church. He was an avid supporter of the abbey of St. Denis in north Paris. And he provided both money and land to support a religious group associated with a saint that Dagobert thought provided him with special protection. Regardless of his murky motives for supporting the church, Dagobert also befriended and supported the Aquitanian evangelist St. Amandus. Working under the protection of the most powerful barbarian king, Amandus played a large role in spreading a very strict form of Irish monasticism throughout Europe by establishing approximately eight monasteries. He also served as the godfather to King Dagobert's illegitimate son. Why Amandus was chosen for the family honor is not at all certain. It likely was a step toward ensuring a smooth transition of power; in the event of Dagobert's death, Amandus would have served as an advisor to the prince until he was old enough to control his kingdom.

Feudalism played a key role in the second set of kings that defined part of the Middle Ages. The Arnulfings (sons of Arnulf) were an Austrasian family who served as mayor of the palace to the Merovingians. That is to say, they were the primary managers of the kingdom and they were the descendants of Arnulf, the seventh-century bishop of Metz. As mayors of the palace or chief operating officers, the Franks had the power to dispense both titles and offices in exchange for pledges of loyalty. To put it another way, they exacted the role of the feudal lord by accepting oaths of loyalty and then rewarding their new allies with gifts of land and status. As the Merovingian kingdom declined due to its own inefficiency and internal strife, the Arnulfings steadily gained a following of vassals. When they had amassed enough power, the Arnulfings overthrew the Merovingians and became the kings of the Franks. The transition between dynasties did not happen immediately, however; the process of transferring power took just over one hundred years. Nevertheless, once the Arnulfings had established themselves, they ruled continuously from about 750 to 987.

The new line of leadership began when Pippin I deposed Childeric III. The first great ruler to emerge from the Arnulfing family, however, was Pippin's illegitimate son: Charles Martel, or Charles the Hammer. Charles's rise to power was both slow and steady. When Pippin II died, the control of the kingdom shifted to his grandsons: Theudoald and Arnulf. Unfortunately, as a bastard Charles was prevented from holding a share of the kingdom. To be sure that he did not interfere with royal plans, he was imprisoned. Charles eventually escaped and spent his time building a small following. Meanwhile, skirmishes with rebels preoccupied his stepbrothers and eroded their power. At one point, the rebels had formed an alliance with the Frisians, a small kingdom in the northwest of France, and they both attacked and defeated Charles's small army. In 717, however, Charles fought the Frisian alliance again, but this time he was the victor. Immediately following the battle Charles went to his stepmother and persuaded, perhaps threatened, her to support his authority. She agreed. Thus Charles had secured the platform upon which he could build his kingdom. Charles continued to engage his nemesis Ragamfred, the rebel leader, in both physical wars and strategic political positioning. For instance, when they fought by using the church as a weapon Ragamfred bribed monks away from their former allegiances, while Charles extended his influence by gaining the support of various bishops. In any case, by 723 Ragamfred and his band of rebels were defeated, and Charles was the undisputed ruler of the Frankish kingdom. Even with his kingdom secured, Charles continued to fight his way to greater dominance. He attacked and subdued the Alamans, the Saxons, and the Bavarians, all of whom had previously been under Merovingian control. In 733, in his most famous battle, he defeated the Arab army at Poitiers and forced them back to Spain.

Charles Martel's grandson was Charlemagne, the greatest of the Frankish kings. Since much more will be said about him later, it is worth noting the importance of his son Louis the Pious (c. 773–840).[4] Louis was one of the great Frankish kings. First, he was, as his nickname might suggest, an avid church reformer. Second, Louis revived the role of the papacy in the selection of the emperor. Third, he basically established the rule of primogeniture, the custom of passing an inheritance to the eldest son. That having been said, Louis was Charlemagne's third son. When Louis was two years old, Pope Hadrian crowned him the king of Aquitaine. Although he began to learn the business of being a king almost from birth, it does not appear that Louis spent much time with his father. Rather, he grew up under the watchful eyes of Charlemagne's loyal supporters. When Louis did become old enough to rule his kingdom, he, along with his close friend Benedict of Aniane, took as part of his mission the reform of monastic life. Louis is credited with having repaired, built, and economically supported several monasteries.

In 810 Louis's brother Pippin died and in the following year his other brother, Charles. Louis became the sole heir to his father's empire. On October 5, 816, Pope Stephen IV both anointed and crowned Louis. The event clearly demonstrated Louis's alliance with the church. It was also the first time that a pope anointed an emperor. Shortly after his installation, Louis set out to extend his program of church reform throughout the empire. For example, he required bishops to give up their military roles and expected all Frankish monastic houses to implement, follow, and memorize the rule of St. Benedict. Louis's program of shaping the church into a unified institution was successful. But his plans to transfer power to his sons were not equally so. Louis rightly understood that the Merovingian practice of dividing kingdoms equally among sons led to squabbling and some of the worst expressions of greed. Consequently he chose to change the practice by passing his title to Lothar, his oldest son. No matter how noble his intentions, the plan failed. Louis's other sons fought for their share of the kingdom and enlisted the support of the nobility, who simply could not comprehend what the emperor had hoped to accomplish.

The coronation of Hugh Capet in 987 marks the end of the Arnulfings and the rise of the Capetians, a line of kings that lasted until the early fourteenth century. On two counts Hugh stands in sharp contrast to the other kings mentioned so far. First, he gained his major victories more by diplomacy than by the power of the sword. This is not to suggest that he was less of a warrior than his predecessors; Hugh was in fact quite good at killing people. It is just that he was better at talking than skewering. Second, Hugh was not necessarily a pathbreaking leader. Rather he held fewer territories than his predecessors, and his reign as king was essentially a continuation of the poor policies from the previous weakened monarchy. Nevertheless, Hugh's election as king did signify the end of rule by a single dynasty, and for that he must be recognized.

By most counts Hugh was pious and fairly affable, but there were occasions where Hugh's temper became evident. For instance, before he received the crown, he supported Lothar in the western Frankish king's struggle with Otto II, the king of the east Franks. When peace was arranged between the two leaders, Hugh appears to have withdrawn his support from Lothar. When Lothar died in 986, the kingdom naturally passed to his son, Louis. The new king was interested in pursuing his father's policies. And his first order of business was to discipline Adalbero, the archbishop of Reims, for supporting the Ottonians against his father. Louis, however, died before he had the chance to punish the powerful archbishop. The death of Louis naturally raised the question as to who should be the new king. Although there is no clear evidence, most historians suspect that Adalbero and Gerbert of Aurillac, later Pope Sylvester II, engineered the election of the duke of the Franks, Hugh Capet. The rest of the story amounts to Hugh's continued struggle with the Ottonians and his amazing luck in avoiding death at the hands of his enemies.

The Capetian dynasty may have started slowly, but it did eventually gather strength. By 1226, Louis IX had strengthened the power and prestige and consequently raised the profile of the crown.[5] Assessing Louis's reign is not easy, however. On the one hand, he was a strong ruler who more or less enjoyed popular support. On the other hand, he has been criticized for overrelying on advisors and making poor strategic decisions. Perhaps the worst decisions associated with Louis relate to his participation in two crusades. In his first campaign, he followed the disastrous advice of his brother, Robert of Artois. Louis was captured by Muslims and was forced to pay a large ransom for the release of both himself and his army. The second campaign was worse. King Louis, sick and weak before he even left for battle, was supposed to go to Palestine but changed his mind at the last minute and went to Tunis instead, because he had hopes that the sultan there would convert to Christianity. After a brief battle in Tunis, Louis decided to wait for his brother, Charles of Anjou. But disease spread throughout the army and killed several soldiers, including the king himself. Prior to these military failures, St. Louis, with the careful guidance of his mother, Blanche of Castile, fended off internal attacks from the barons. Louis also did much to encourage the growth of the mendicant, Franciscan and Dominican, friars. And the king certainly did not hesitate to use these new religious groups to root out heretics and non-Christians throughout France. Louis's piety can seem brutal at times; nevertheless, in the eyes of his contemporaries he was the staunch enemy of the infidel and a great patron of the church. And in his grandson, Philip IV, mentioned above, the French crown would find one of its best expressions of leadership.

INTELLECTUAL CURRENTS

So far, we have touched on several fairly broad points. First, both monks and friars were key players in understanding medieval Christianity. Second, the period called the Middle Ages covers a huge span of time that forms the crossroads between the early church and the Protestant Reformation. Third, medieval theologians built upon the ideas that they inherited from the early church as they crafted the defining theological structure of Christianity. Fourth, the medieval political landscape can be a hugely complicated place. The final point left to make is that there were several medieval theologians who, by dint of their academic interests, made incredible intellectual discoveries by examining ideas from outside of the Christian tradition. These additional resources opened new lines of thought and provided the extra material needed for what would become the most powerful intellectual synthesis in Christian history.

Playing with Plato

Of all the resources that were external to the Christian tradition, Plato (427–347 BC), the ancient Greek philosopher, probably had the single greatest influence on medieval thought. In particular, his understanding of forms, exemplars or ideas that constitute ultimate reality, became an anchor for many medieval theologians. The basic notion of the forms grew out of the social and political turmoil that characterized Plato's ancient Greece. As Greek society descended into chaos, Plato began to wonder if there was any stable truth beyond the world of visible things. His answer was that such a truth did exist. Individual things were the mere reflections of their form or blueprint, and, he supposed, the exemplar could be grasped only by a perfect intelligence. The upshot of this is a kind of hierarchy of being. Things in the world that come into existence and then pass away are on the low end of the scale. Forms, the patterns that make things in the world what they are, are on the high end. Plato's philosophy does include much greater detail, but the two essential ingredients, forms and the hierarchy of things, were fused into Christianity and carried through the Middle Ages.

Plotinus (205–70) and St. Augustine (354–430) were largely responsible for bringing Platonic philosophy into medieval Christendom. Of the two, Augustine was the more popular. Plotinus too had an enormous impact on the development of Christian thought, but he has been sadly neglected by historians for many reasons, not the least of which is his inability to present his ideas clearly. What Plotinus did was unintentionally borrow elements from other Greek schools of thought and fold them into his understanding of Plato. The result was a fully developed theory that there is a supreme mind at the head of the hierarchy of being. The One, as Plotinus calls it, was removed from all other kinds of beings. It was the highest principle of reality, beyond thought and language, and completely self-sufficient. Below the One is the *nous*, that is, the divine mind, which contains the world of ideas. The third and lowest member is the Soul, the intermediary between the world of forms and the world of individual things. According to Plotinus, all individual souls participate in the Soul's ability to think. Moreover, since the One, *nous*, and Soul are really all the same thing and since all individuals are connected to the Soul, all of the different levels in the hierarchy create a single, unified whole. It is not too much of a stretch to see how a philosophy that touts three distinct persons who are one and the same would be seductive to a school of thought that holds to the Christian doctrine of the Holy Trinity. Making such a connection, however, would be a bit wide of the mark. As a concept, the Trinity is older than Plotinus. In fact, the term first appears in the writings of the Greek theologian Theophilus of Antioch (180).

What Plotinus did do for Christianity, however, was create a framework in which Plato's forms easily became the thoughts in the mind of the divine.

Just over one hundred years after the death of Plotinus, St. Augustine, a native of North Africa, traveled to Milan. While there, he met Bishop Ambrose and was exposed to a spiritual interpretation of Scripture. Augustine grew curious and the following summer started to read the works of Plotinus. He was absolutely amazed by his discoveries. Augustine had grown up under the influence of the Manicheans, a sect that believed that being made in the image of God meant that the divine had skin, hair, and teeth, just like a human being. Plotinus offered a very different view. In fact, the idea that God might not have a fleshly body had never really occurred to Augustine. Plotinus had managed to show that God was not bound by physical limitations. Being able to think of God as a spiritual substance was incredibly liberating for Augustine. He left the Manicheans for the faith that Ambrose preached. As Augustine dug deeper into the philosophy of scholars like Plotinus, he found a fatal flaw. The followers of Plato rightly understood God as an abstract being, but they missed the fact that the word of God had become flesh. This one blind spot, Augustine supposed, was due to their failure to be humble. After a brief dalliance with the writings of St. Paul, St. Augustine declared himself to be a Christian and set out to become a servant of God. In the process, Augustine wrote several philosophical sermons, letters, and books. And, in many cases, the lessons that he learned from Plotinus and other followers of Plato shaped the views that he passed on to future generations.

St. Augustine's fusion of Plotinus and Christianity was all the rage throughout the Middle Ages. A great number of scholars served to transmit what Augustine wrote to later generations. For example, Isidore of Seville (560–636) produced a grand collection of St. Augustine's theological opinions. A bit later, Hugh of St. Victor (1096–1141) used St. Augustine's ideas as vehicles for developing his own thoughts. So too Peter Lombard's four-volume collection of quotes derived mostly from Augustine became standard reading in European universities from the twelfth century until the sixteenth century.

The Age of Aristotle

Plato and his followers were not the only threads of Greek thought to be woven into medieval Christian theology. Aristotle also had an enormous impact. Rather than find ultimate truth in forms or ideas, Aristotle found truth in the physical world. That is to say, Aristotle thought that physical objects in the world invade the senses and cause thoughts. And, as the human mind catalogs its different encounters with the world, it discovers what things are. To put it in slightly more technical terms, the mind discovers the essences of things. So knowledge and truth are derived from human experience of the world, rather than discovered at the top of a hierarchy of being.

Anicius Manlius Torquatus Severinus Boethius, or just Boethius, was the main transmitter of Aristotle's works into the Middle Ages.[6] But Boethius (480–525) was not devoted exclusively to Aristotle. Rather, he was a Christian who was keen to translate into Latin everything that both Plato and Aristotle wrote. Boethius, like most Christians of his day, gravitated toward Plato, but Boethius was eclectic and suspected that the two ancient Greek philosophers might actually agree on several important points. His plan to find the harmony in their thought, however, was rudely interrupted when he was accused of treason, imprisoned, and ultimately executed. More specifically, Boethius served as the Master of Offices for the emperor. The position made him a powerful civil servant who served as the link between the Gothic ruler Theodoric and his court, but he soon became enmeshed in a political snare. A senator had been accused of treason for writing letters of appeal to the emperor Justinian in Constantinople. Boethius apparently defended the senator and in no time at all was himself accused of the same crime. That is to say, he was accused of expressing a desire to be liberated from Gothic rule. The Senate failed to defend him, and Boethius was sentenced to death.

Prior to receiving his death sentence, however, Boethius did manage to translate several of Aristotle's logical writings into Latin. These works, along with Boethius's commentaries on them, became standard reading in schools until the thirteenth century. But Aristotle was not always readily received by the Christian community. In part this was because much of what he wrote clashed with church doctrine. For instance, Aristotle maintained that the world was eternal. Yet the Christian view is that God is eternal and that the world is created. Again, Aristotle thought that the soul was a metaphysical abstraction. The church, by contrast, preferred a soul that is more of an entity which survives the physical body after death. Conflicts such as these prevented Aristotle from catching on with many medieval scholars. Plato, in fact, held first place in philosophy from the time of Charlemagne through the thirteenth century. When Aristotle did gain popularity, however, it was the translations and commentaries of Boethius that served as the main sources for accessing Aristotle's philosophy when it was employed in service to the church.

The Arabic Influence

Given the six-century span between the lives of Christ and Muhammad, it may be difficult to believe that Islam had an impact on the formation of Christian theology. About the middle of the seventh century Muhammad, an Arab merchant with a penchant for religious zeal, began the Islamic era. The start of his movement was hard fought, but it did catch on, and by 632, the date of Muhammad's death, most of Arabia was in Muslim hands. Under the guidance of new leadership, Muslim armies had managed to conquer Syria, Damascus, and Jerusalem. By 640, they had invaded Egypt and started to march along the northern coast of Africa. Finally, in the early part of the eighth century, a band of Muslims had crossed the Strait of Gibraltar and sacked most of Spain. They would have kept going, but the Muslim general, Abd-ar-Rahman, and his army were defeated by the Frankish King Charles Martel in 733 at the battle of Poitiers (France). The reason for calling attention to the rise of Islam is not so much to marvel at the speed of the Islamic conquest but to note that during the seventh and eighth centuries many centers of Christian influence were not controlled by Christians. And, since Aristotle's writings usually entered the West through Spain, it should not be at all surprising that when they finally did arrive in western Europe, they came complete with Islamic commentaries.

Although there were several fascinating Islamic philosophers, two are particularly noteworthy because of the great impact of their work on Christian theology. The first was Abu Ali al-Husain Ibn Sina or, in its Latin form, Avicenna. He was born in 980 in a village near Bukhara, northern Persia. His family eventually moved to Bukhara, and Avicenna received a solid private education in subjects like writing and logic. Avicenna was undoubtedly a good student, and quite proud of his accomplishments. In fact, in his autobiography he brags about his gifted intellect. More specifically, by the age of ten he had completed his study of the Qur'an and turned his attention to physics and medicine. By his sixteenth birthday, he had attained the standing of a well-respected medical

---

A CLOSER LOOK

Islam, much like Christianity, was subject to various intellectual movements from within. And its theologians, like those of Christendom, inherited their ideas from the classical world. For example, al-Razi worked out a system of thought that owed much to Plato. Similarly, al-Ghazali made a considerable effort to attack Neoplatonic ideas that were advanced by his Muslim predecessors. What the range of opinions among medieval theologians illustrates, however, is that there is no unified body of knowledge which can properly be called Islamic thought. Islamic scholars disagreed about many of the answers to difficult theological questions. Muslim scholars even fell into different camps. For example, the group that tried to fuse Greek thought with Muslim doctrine was called the Mu'tazilites.

Further Reading: M. Fakhry, *A History of Islamic Philosophy* (New York 1983)

authority. When he turned eighteen, Avicenna had mastered all subjects available to him with the exception of metaphysics. He does admit being frustrated by the subject, but he found a commentary written by al-Farabi that finally enabled him to make sense of the discipline. Eventually Avicenna found himself working as a court physician in the service of the Muslim nobility. He served in several different courts and rarely stayed long in any one place. In part this may have been because he was constantly looking for new challenges. It may also have been because he feared persecution for some of his religious opinions. In any case, his character is a matter of some mystery. By most accounts, he was passionate about wine and women, both of which are strictly regulated in the Islamic faith. He was also a devoted Muslim who died only after repenting of his sins, donating all of his cattle, and freeing his slaves. Regardless of his ambiguous behavior, Avicenna was a brilliant scholar, and his reflections on metaphysics served as the foil for the insights of scholars like the Franciscan theologian John Duns Scotus. Other claims that Avicenna made, such as his thesis that "only one thing is made by one cause," became a problematic proposition for Christian theologians who were convinced that God was the single cause of all things. In any case, Avicenna was one of the greatest transmitters of Neoplatonic philosophy into the Latin West.

The second important Islamic philosopher was named Abu-l-Waldi ibn Rushd, or Averroës (1126–98). His family were well-educated, respected members of the intellectual community in Muslim Spain. Averroës himself received a solid education and excelled at medicine, language studies, and theology. In 1169 he was introduced to a caliph or chief named Abu Ya'qub, who had a strong interest in philosophy. Apparently the meeting was a bit unsettling, because as soon as the two men were introduced, Abu Ya'qub asked Averroës whether he thought the world was eternal. Since Averroës was smart enough to realize that the question was a hotly debated theological topic, he was reluctant to answer. That is to say, Averroës did not want to offend the ruler. Nonetheless, Abu Ya'qub had reasons for asking. He enjoyed philosophy but was unable to read the works of Aristotle, because they were written in Greek. His hope was that Averroës was enough of a talented philosopher to translate the books. Exactly what Averroës answered is unclear, but it must have been a pretty good response, because Averroës both got the job and was awarded a post as the religious judge of Seville. A bit later, Averroës returned to Cordova and served as the chief judge, just as others in his family had. For the most part, he continued to have a fairly normal career.[7] However, it seems that much larger political circumstances unfolded in such a way that, for a brief period, both Averroës and philosophy in general fell out of fashion. The interruption lasted only a short time, however, and after an interlude of about ten years, he was allowed to continue his study of philosophy.

Averroës's commentaries on Aristotle's philosophy became quite famous. In fact, his works had an enormous impact on the Christian theologians of the Middle Ages. Or, to put it more brashly, because of his incredible ability to comment on texts, to offer insights into thorny philosophical questions, and to separate what Aristotle wanted to say from what Muslim doctrine thought he should have said, Averroës is more important than Avicenna. Moreover, Averroës also had a larger following in the West. Thirteenth-century theologians such as Albert the Great, St. Thomas Aquinas, and Giles of Rome both used and criticized Averroës's writings. Among the more extreme defenders of Averroës, one can count Siger of Brabant and Boethius of Sweden (Dacia). In the following century, John of Jandun and the Englishman John Baconthorp continued to find insight in Averroës's philosophy. Despite this great following, many of Averroës's ideas were considered by church authorities to be a danger to the Christian faith. For instance, Averroës disagreed with Avicenna regarding the number of things that can come from a single cause. This placed Averroës closer to the Christian understanding of God's creative activity, but the way in which Averroës finished his explanation of creation would appear quite foreign to a believing Christian. Certainly Averroës's most problematic opinion was his thesis that there is only one intellect for the whole human race. Again, this was disconcerting for Christians, because it amounted to saying that although there is life after death, there cannot be any form of personal immortality. Finally, the church recognized the danger in Averroës's work in that it raised the issue of whether or not religious faith was in tension with human reason. By 1270, thirteen of his theories were condemned.

The Great Christian Synthesis

It is tempting to describe medieval theology as the outcome of having put Plato and Aristotle in a blender. The resulting concoction is an inglorious mixture of intellectual initiative. Such an assessment would be shortsighted, however. The history, philosophy, personalities, and politics that form medieval theology came together in a way that reveals the best of a long-running human struggle to understand the divine. Generally speaking, medieval scholars were unique champions of the Christian faith. They were careful with their craft. For instance, medieval theologians never would have asked themselves, "What would Jesus do?" For an intensely religious medieval scholar, a question like that implies that one knows how God would respond to a given situation. So the only safe answer would be one that was found in Holy Scripture. With that in mind, the character of medieval theology is inspiring but modest. Medieval theologians tried not to be too original and rarely welcomed risky explanations. For example, when a monk named Paschasius Radbertus (790–860) declared that the bread and wine at communion were transformed into the flesh and blood of Christ that was born of the Virgin Mary, he was sharply attacked in favor of a more spiritual interpretation by Ratramnus and Rabanus Maurus. Similarly, when Gottschalk of Orabis (800–870) taught a view of double predestination (God predetermines who goes to heaven and who goes to hell), he was declared a heretic and imprisoned in a monastery. Suffice to say, there were serious consequences for straying outside the bounds of commonly accepted church teaching.

In short, medieval theologians worked hard to conceal their originality. They were nevertheless creative in their use of sources. Later scholars like St. Bonaventure and St. Thomas Aquinas developed highly detailed theories for some remarkably difficult theological questions by reflecting on a full range of sources. Plato and Aristotle were very important, but so were the church fathers, Holy Scripture, the decisions of church councils, and the insights of earlier theologians. Some modern scholars, most notably Etienne Gilson, have referred to the synthesis of these sources as a kind of Christian philosophy that puts God as the ultimate reality. This is perhaps true of the theologians of the thirteenth and fourteenth centuries. But there is such a great variety of opinions among medieval theologians that grouping them into a single school of thought is difficult if not impossible. What medieval theologians did have in common, however, is their quest to find clarity in the Christian faith. They viewed their reflections as a means for preparing for wisdom. They sought deeper meaning in Holy Scripture. They hoped to gain insight into the mysteries of the faith. And they struggled to understand what it meant to be created in the image of God.

QUESTIONS FOR DISCUSSION

1. What role does politics have in shaping popular religion today?
2. Are philosophy and theology compatible disciplines?
3. Does the influence of Greek, Roman, and Islamic thought on the evolution of church doctrine invalidate Christian claims?
4. How does the life of a medieval monk or friar differ from the career of a modern clergyperson?

2

I Believe

Medieval theology declined in the sixteenth century. When the Reformers declared *sola scriptura* (by Scripture alone), they did more than provide a battle cry for a protest against the Roman Catholic Church. They signified the rise of biblically based theology and the eclipse of the golden age of philosophical theology. This change was not the start of a new faith, however. Belief in the Judeo-Christian God is common to both types of theology. But biblical theology was a completely different way to both explore and express the Christian faith. Without too much detail, the difference between the two approaches to the Christian faith consists in their assumptions. In a more biblically based theology the primary assumption is that a faith in the truth of Holy Scripture is both necessary and sufficient for a believer to know the divine. That is to say, the Bible holds the assurance that what human beings need to know about God is contained within its pages. By contrast, while philosophical theology stresses the Bible as its foundation, it also tries to make good use of the natural human ability to reason. So philosophical theology involves a kind of interdependence between Scripture and reason. Scripture contains God's truth, but reason helps the believer to understand that truth in more profound ways. Reason enables a believer to grasp God by way of such things as definitions and commonsense experience, but the faith found in the Bible perfects what the mind alone is not able to understand about the divine.

MARVELOUS MYSTICISM

The balance between reason, revelation, and experience has never been formulaic in Christian theology. That is to say, there is no recipe for faith, like one part Scripture, two parts reason, and a dash of experience lead to greater insights into the divine. In fact, some medieval theologians rejected reason completely. Others emphasized personal experience over Scripture or reason. The majority of the pages that follow are dedicated to exploring the philosophical theology of the Middle Ages. The bulk of the work is focused on theologians who tried to apply reason to the basics of church doctrine. Before rushing off to conquer some of the more systematic expressions of the Christian faith, however, a word or two must be said about mysticism, for a couple of reasons. First, although they were not a dominant school of thought, the mystics had an enormous impact on later periods. For instance, the mysticism that grew out of the German Rhineland informed a movement which became known as the Brethren of the Common Life. Their view, more or less the idea that the soul of a believer could directly make contact with God, contained a seed that eventually weakened the authority of the church hierarchy and helped to pave the way for the Reformation. Second, not everyone in the Middle Ages thought that taking a rational approach to faith was such a jolly good idea. Philosophical theology gave rise to several of the more tightly conceived explanations of the Christian faith. But, some thought that the aim of theology should be a personal, immediate communion with the divine, that God is found in contemplation and adoration, not argument and axiom. If speculation is the aim of the philosophical theology, then devotion marks the mystic.

One of the charter members of medieval mysticism was St. Bernard of Clairvaux. In the hands of some modern historians, Bernard has been characterized as a mystic who stood opposed to the intellectual insights offered by philosophically trained theologians. This is in part due to some of his disputes

---

A CLOSER LOOK

The Holy Bible was the most studied book during the Middle Ages. In fact, commenting on Scripture was a primary activity in both the monastic cloister and in the university. The preferred mode of interpretation, however, was not literal. Rather, medieval scholars pursued a multifaceted approach to Scripture, a method of interpretation, used by both St. Augustine and John Cassian, in which each biblical passage reveals a variety of meanings. More specifically, a good medieval commentator was able to actively identify a historical, an allegorical, a mystical, and a moral message in a single biblical reference. Sometimes scholars could find additional meanings. In any case, this broad approach to Holy Scripture was the standard interpretive device that was used well into the early part of the Protestant Reformation.

Further Reading: B. Smalley, *The Study of the Bible in the Middle Ages* (Notre Dame 1978).

with the great philosophers and logicians like Gilbert de la Porrée (c. 1080–1154) and Peter Abelard (c. 1079–1142). Yet Bernard was not an anti-intellectual. He was born near Dijon, France, in 1090,[1] son of a knight and the third of seven children. As a child he received a typical liberal arts education in grammar, rhetoric, and logic. Shortly after his mother died in 1112, Bernard and his brothers joined the white monks, the Cistercian order, in their new monastery at Citeaux. The lifestyle there was recognized as the strictest form of the Benedictine monasticism, and Bernard displayed a keen ability to follow the rule. Eventually, he was asked to start his own monastic house, which he, along with twelve companions, did at Clairvaux. Throughout the rest of his life, Bernard spent an enormous amount of energy trying to curtail what he saw as threats to the faith. This included a variety of entanglements with the Benedictine abbot Peter the Venerable (c. 1092–1156), condemnations of the works of philosophers like Peter Abelard, and serving as the official preacher for the Second Crusade against the Muslims. In all of these activities, St. Bernard proved himself to be incredibly well read and an astute intellectual powerhouse. Despite his wide-ranging knowledge, however, he believed that it was the mystery of the incarnation, not the discoveries made through reason, which helps us to uncover what is at the core of Christianity.

Without shortchanging Bernard then, it is safe to say he thought that speculating about God is quite different from loving God. To be more precise, there is a distinct mystical quality to St. Bernard's writings in which loving God is a type of knowledge. That mystical quality is best illustrated throughout his sermons on the Song of Songs. According to St. Bernard, love is the central concept, and it is symbolized by a kiss. Of course Bernard does not mean a literal kiss. That kind of smooching was a sport for the fickle in the minds of medieval theologians. Rather, Bernard is thinking of the opening line of the Song of Songs, where Solomon cries out "O that you would kiss me with the kisses of your mouth!" (1:1 RSV).[2] In this case, according to Bernard, the kiss is meant figuratively, and the line conveys a human desire to be filled with the joy that comes from being united in love with the divine. Now the link between the human soul and God is the Holy Spirit. With that in mind, Bernard further expands his understanding of the kiss to include the persons of the Trinity. More specifically, Bernard views the kiss as a metaphor for the Holy Spirit, which is produced by the loving activity that is shared between the Father and the Son. Christ then gives the kiss to his bride, which is the church. The upshot of all this kissing is that Christ unites the bride to the Father through the Holy Spirit. So mystical union with God is simply an extension of the love that binds the persons of the Holy Trinity. Through the action of the Holy Spirit, human beings can have an intense, personal experience of the divine in which love becomes understanding. The extent to which Bernard's explanation for a mystical encounter with the divine influenced later generations is not absolutely clear. Nevertheless, there are some shadows of his theology in the Franciscan views of the person of Christ and the Holy Spirit. The explanation of those ideas, however, will have to wait for chapters 4 and 6.

St. Bernard's theology relies more heavily on Scripture and the experience of love than on reason. In addition to St. Bernard, there were other mystics, many of whom were women. Like most mystics, they tended to begin with an experience of visions and dreams as the port of entry into greater faith. St. Catherine of Siena (c. 1347–80) is probably the best-known among them. In her theology, Catherine became legendary for her mystical marriage to Christ—a union that gave her the courage to carry her love for him into the world. In the course of her spiritual journey, Catherine came to believe that she had been united with Christ through marriage. When she was twenty years old, she had the vision in which the Lord appeared to her. He placed a ring on her finger and pronounced them wed. According to Catherine, the ring was a diamond circled with four pearls. She thought this meant that her faith should be like the diamond but that her intentions, thoughts, words, and actions should remain pure like the pearls. Only Catherine herself could see the ring, but it was always visible to her when she thought of Christ. And, as his bride she was now obligated to help others through acts of charity.

A short time after her union with Christ a small group of disciples, many of whom were Dominicans, gathered around Catherine with the hope of gaining some spiritual direction. These devoted followers proved to be very valuable later in Catherine's life. In fact, they actually saved her life. Catherine was fairly outspoken and, not having much social status, managed to offend some fairly powerful people. When she was summoned to explain herself to church authorities, however, her popularity was so great that the Dominican friars gave her official protection and appointed one of their own, a friar named Raimondo di Capua, to watch over both her and her followers. Moreover, Catherine needed a bit of safeguarding. Although she was not particularly motivated by politics, her activities of charitably engaging the world naturally spilled over into public affairs. On one occasion, she found herself supporting a religious crusade against the Turks. On another occasion, Catherine went on a diplomatic mission to Pope Gregory XI. The Italian wars had made it unsafe for the pope to stay in Rome, and ever since the struggle between Pope Boniface VIII and King Philip, the pontiff had been a French political pawn. Catherine, however, had another vision, in which the pope returned to Italy. So the point of her trip was to urge the pope to make peace with the Italian state of Florence and come home to Rome. The problems in Italy were absolutely huge, however, and by dabbling in these affairs Catherine stood a good chance of gaining some very powerful enemies. Yet it was her intense personal experience of the divine that led her to confront the most powerful people in Europe.

There were several other famous women mystics named Catherine during the Middle Ages. For example, St. Catherine of Genoa (c. 1447–1510) grew up in the midst of turbulent Italian politics. Yet she found peace through a direct personal experience of divine love, and the focus of her message is the tireless and all-embracing goodness of God. So too, St. Catherine of Bologna (c. 1413–63) gained a deeper appreciation for the divine through her mystical vision. She wrote in the Franciscan tradition and became famous for her vision in which the Virgin Mary appeared to her and placed the newborn Christ in her arms. Fortunately, not every famous female mystic was named Catherine. There were others. Hildegard of Bingen (c. 1098–1179), Juliana of Liège (c. 1191–1258), and Teresa of Avila (c. 1515–82) also had mystical encounters with the divine. Like St. Bernard, many of these mystics focused their attention on the experience of the love of Christ. The English abbess Julian of Norwich (c. 1342–1416?) too viewed Christ as central to her theology, but Julian differed from many of the other women mystics in that she taught that her experience contained an element that is universal. That is to say, despite the fact that Julian had an intense personal experience with the divine, she was convinced that it could be understood by others. Julian was a mystic who used reason! She began with a focus that is mainly on God's love as understood through the sacrifice of Christ. But Julian had sixteen visions or "showings," as she calls them, that she describes in great clarity for everyone to understand. Although the showings are far too detailed to recount here, a chunk of her first showing will serve nicely for illustrating how Julian's faith stimulated a desire for a deeper intellectual knowledge of the love of God.[3]

Julian begins by expressing her desire for three things: a greater understanding of the passion of Christ, a bodily sickness that would prepare her ultimately to draw nearer to God, and God's gifts of the wounds of Christ. By her own account, Julian's desires were met through active prayer and contemplation. She explains that, in preparation for her visions, she became quite ill. The condition must have been horrible indeed. According to Julian, the top half of her body went limp and her breathing became shallow. Then, in an instant, all of the pain was gone, and she was restored to health. Julian interpreted this miraculous cure as the first of three graces that she would receive during the course of her vision. The second grace that came to her was the immediate impulse to pray to be filled with a feeling for the passion of Christ. As answer to her prayer she received both a bodily vision and a spiritual vision. In the first, she saw Christ's head bleeding from the crown of thorns. Then, in the spiritual vision, she saw God's familiar love. She describes holding a little ball, about the size of a hazelnut, in the palm of her hand. Although she did not immediately know what it was, she soon discovered that it is everything that is created. Julian marveled at the small size of creation. It could become lost so easily, but she learned that it continues to exist because God made it, loves it, and continues to preserve it.

The small size of creation is important. On the one hand, Julian explains that the entirety of creation was so little because she saw it in relation to God. On the other hand, Julian is keen to stress that God wishes to be known and that human beings are to find rest in the divine. Souls that become too preoccupied with created things can never come to know true wisdom and love. As Julian explains it, those who occupy themselves with earthly business do not experience rest in God, because they love and seek something that is mostly insignificant. So the smallness of creation is a kind of metaphor that helps Julian to explain that all created things are beneath God and that they are not sufficient for sustaining human beings. In short, Julian understands that God's love is all-embracing, but that it can be shared with humans only when they make themselves completely available to the love that is grasped through the contemplative union with the divine.

Another slightly different, although wide-ranging, theologian with a distinct mystical component to his theology was John Eckhart (c. 1260–1328). Eckhart was born in Germany. He joined the Dominican order in Erfurt and went to school in Cologne. The university at Cologne perhaps is not as well known as the universities of Paris and Oxford, but in the thirteenth century it was a tremendous hub of theological activity. Albert the Great (d. 1280) taught there, and his form of Christian Platonism became an important force in shaping the theology of the Dominicans. Also between 1268 and 1281 William of Moerbeke was working in Cologne and was busy translating Greek theological works into Latin. In any case, John Eckhart benefited at least indirectly from the contributions of these scholars, and by 1293 he was lecturing on theology in the Dominican study house, St. Jacques, at the University of Paris. John continued to faithfully serve the Dominican friars, and by 1311 he was awarded the title "Meister" or Master of theology at Paris. It is by this title, Meister Eckhart, that he is most commonly known.

In addition to being fairly skilled at offering tightly reasoned explanations of the faith, Meister Eckhart was also a gifted preacher. His popularity was further aided by the fact that he frequently delivered sermons in German rather than Latin. Because they could actually understand what he was saying, the German sermons were particularly well received by non-Latin-speaking groups of Dominican and Cistercian nuns. In terms of his mystical theology, however, Eckhart's ideas required quite a bit more translation and explanation than normally would be due to a typical Sunday sermon. That is to say, Meister Eckhart's thought is obscure. Rather than focus upon the person of Jesus Christ as the inspiration for his theology like any of the St. Catherines, Meister Eckhart taught that God the almighty could be found directly through contemplation. Moreover, his radical penchant for the kind of thinking that was inspired by Plotinus, as opposed to the more doctrinal approach of St. Bernard, both distinguished him as a mystic and got him into trouble with the church authorities. In 1325 the archbishop of Cologne, Henry of Virneberg, ordered an investigation into Eckhart's writings, and in the following year Meister Eckhart's teachings were condemned. The condemnation did not stand without a challenge, however. The mystic scholar made an appeal to the pope, but before his case could be heard, Meister Eckhart died. Eckhart probably did not do anything theologically unusual. The real problem was his habit of phrasing his thoughts in fairly obscure language. For instance, in some cases he refers to God as the "negation of negation," which means, of course, that God is a positive agent. A careless reader, however, might quickly conclude from such a turn of phrase that Eckhart was putting God in a very bad light.

In the broadest terms, Meister Eckhart tries to explain the relations between God and creation through a Neoplatonic framework. He sees God as beyond the human understanding of existence. God is unbounded, inexpressible in human terms, and completely unrestrained. In short, God is the absolute One. Saying that God is beyond being distinguishes Meister Eckhart from many of the other philosophical theologians of his day. Other theologians, such as Thomas Aquinas, had read Exodus 3:14, where God is revealed as the great "I am." Since God named himself in the nominative singular form of the verb "to be," they took "being" as their starting point. For Eckhart, however, thought is above being, and the wisdom that is God is without end. For most medieval theologians, God is a being who knows, but for Meister Eckhart, knowing is what makes God a being. And the focus on the unity of the divine drives the mystical component of his theology. That is, Eckhart thinks that humans cannot truly be said to have either unity or existence, because those are proper only to the divine. Creatures are only an expression of the richness contained within the divine, and they are called beings only according to the extent that they participate in God. Since there is a real unity of humans and God, one can access the divine by means of deep contemplation. We realize our union with God by looking beyond the world and by recognizing the divine spark that is within us.

THE PLACE OF FAITH AND REASON

One way to divide the roughly one thousand years of the Middle Ages (c. 500–1500) is to say that in the first half of the period theologians were content

A CLOSER LOOK

Several later medieval theologians wrote a great deal about the tension between faith and reason. The issue became much more pronounced in the later Middle Ages, when Aristotle's writings were reintroduced into the West. For instance, the Paris theologian Siger of Brabant (1240–81) became famous for his strict adherence to Averroës's commentaries on Aristotle. The fact that he would not twist Aristotle to fit better with Christian doctrine led him to be accused of heresy. So too John of Jandun (1285–1328) was painted as a radical follower of Aristotle and viewed philosophy as separate from theology. In 1277, Pope John XXI ordered the bishop of Paris, Stephen Tempier, to study the teachings of the faculty at the University of Paris. The result of the action was a formal condemnation of 219 theses that supposedly ran contrary to church dogma. In short, the commission built a fence between the reason taught by Aristotle and the faith taught by the church.

Further Reading: J. Wipple, *Mediaeval Reactions to the Encounter between Faith and Reason* (Milwaukee 1995).

to build a deposit of faith. They collected the writings of the early church fathers, reflected upon Scripture, and tried to adhere to the traditions of the church. By contrast, in the later half of the period, scholars were more willing to try to combine resources in new ways in order to ask speculative questions. Rather than seek the anchors that affirmed the Christian faith, later scholars incorporated more reason into their theology as they began to wonder about the divine. The reintroduction of ancient philosophy and the access to Islamic sources in the later half of the Middle Ages further intensified the need for Christians to clarify the relationship between faith and reason. This is not to say that early theologians were blissfully ignorant about God. They too asked serious questions and explored critical issues. But in general the early Middle Ages were more a time for mission ministry than for scholarly inquiry. For instance, when St. Patrick was sixteen years old, he was kidnapped by Irish pirates and spent the next six years of his life working in captivity. After a rousing escape, Patrick returned home to England. He started training for Christian ministry and eventually set out to serve as a missionary to the Irish. A lot of fantastic legends surround the life of Patrick, such as the doubtful account of him using a clover to teach the doctrine of the Trinity. The point of introducing him here is that, even in the mid to late fifth century, various European peoples were not practicing, orthodox Christians. So the workload of able Christians tended toward that of conversion rather than reflection.

There were other great ministers in the early Middle Ages. For example, Wilfrid of York (c. 634–709) spent a year preaching in Frisia, northern England, while making his way to Rome. John the Scot (c. 810–77) too was a wandering minister. John, however, traveled from Ireland to the court of Charles the Bald, king of France. Although he did not have an appointment in a church, he did work in the palace school. John is an interesting figure because his writings can be viewed as a kind of foreshadowing of the discussion about the place of faith and reason in Christian thought. He could read Greek and was able to use a combination of early church fathers such as Gregory of Nyssa (c. 330–95), Maximus the Confessor (c. 580–662), and Denis the Pseudo-Areopagite (c. 500) in order to create a much more speculative theology. In the process of studying and translating these authorities, John appears to have realized that what the church fathers wrote was their own interpretation or reasoned explanation of what was revealed in Scripture. Since each of these authorities relied on his or her own native reason to explain the faith, John determined that it was entirely appropriate to challenge what they thought, because the conclusions reached by the church fathers were not final. He thought that there was little danger in challenging those conclusions in his own court of reason.

Almost fifty years ago, a French historian named Etienne Gilson offered the best explanation for how John the Scot dealt with faith and reason.[4] Gilson sees John as proposing three stages. First, for the period between the fall of Adam and Eve and the coming of Christ, human knowledge of the truth was limited to what could be known about the world. The second stage began with Christ. Knowledge of the truth of God became much more certain at this point because it was revealed in Scripture. It does, however, take an act of faith to accept the truth as God has revealed it. In this sense, faith precedes reason. As Gilson notes, John views faith as a kind of mechanism that enables reason to develop knowledge of the divine. To put it another way, faith is a condition of intellectual knowledge. John's third stage is yet to come. It involves the doctrine of the beatific vision in which faith is completely replaced by a direct knowledge, because human beings will have a face-to-face encounter with God. John the Scot essentially proposes a kind of journey to God in which the entire human history moves toward a complete grasp of the divine. For now, however, human beings must be content to allow faith to lead them toward a greater awareness.

THOMAS AQUINAS

It would be easy to suppose that faith stands opposed to reason. St. Paul warns his readers not to fall prey to philosophy or empty deceit. The early Christian writer Tertullian is famous for asking, "What has Athens to do with Jerusalem?" by which he meant to imply that the philosophy of Plato and Aristotle should have nothing in common with the church. To take these warnings as permission to completely shun reason, however, would be painfully short-sighted. What these and other authorities were trying to say is that one should not adopt the teachings of any particular philosophical school at the expense of Christian teaching. St. Paul and Tertullian were not suggesting that Christians should stop thinking altogether. Rather, they were indirectly raising a question as to the place that reason should hold in the Christian belief system. As the writings of Aristotle and others gradually became reintroduced into thirteenth-century western Europe, the need to sort out exactly where reason had its foothold for the believer intensified. Aristotle, in particular, had developed a very detailed philosophy that both fit well with common sense and provided reasonable explanations for many things in the world. But none of his explanations were loose enough to allow for the creative activity of the Judeo-Christian God. So, conceding that faith and reason are completely intertwined, the challenge was to nail down the exact role that reason could play in enabling believers to understand the content of their faith.

The thirteenth-century Dominican friar Thomas Aquinas, about whom much more will be said later, is a good representative of a later medieval thinker who clearly taught that a Christian cannot have at the same time both belief and knowledge about an object. Yet Thomas also was not compelled simply to dismiss reason in favor of blind acceptance of revelation. When St. Thomas considered an act of faith, he did so on the assumption that thought is somehow integrated into the project. His starting question, in fact, is whether believing is thinking with assent.[5] That is to say, does an act of believing as a Christian require both the understanding and acceptance of certain ideas that cannot be grasped by the light of natural reason? Thomas's answer is a carefully crafted yes. It is carefully crafted because "to think" can be understood in three different ways. First, it can be taken in a very general way to refer to any act of consideration. Second, it can be construed more narrowly to mean the process of inquiry that precedes a conclusion. Thomas explains that thinking in this sense is the movement of the mind while deliberating but not yet in possession of the truth. Within this definition Thomas finds his third sense: the process by which one puts together an exact notion of a particular object.

Now St. Thomas is pretty sure that if the expression "thinking with assent" is used in the first sense, it does not apply to religious belief. This kind of thinking is what we humans do even when considering information that is known to be a hard-nosed fact. The second sense of "thinking with assent," however, completely expresses what it means to believe. The human intellect can engage in a variety of actions in which it does not hold an absolute conviction. For instance, one might have an unformed thought without any inclination as to the correctness of the particular matter. This, according to Thomas, describes what we mean by the word "doubt." So too the human intellect might be motivated toward accepting a particular idea. When that happens, the mind is properly said to "suspect." A person also might formulate an opinion. In this case, Thomas thinks that we are basically clinging to one side of an issue out of fear of the other side. Belief is a bit of both worlds. That is to say, belief involves a firm conviction just as if thinking about a hard-nosed fact. But belief does not have the kind of clarity that comes with such thinking. In this sense it agrees more with doubts, suspicions, and opinions. Because belief involves thinking with assent, it is different from all other kinds of thinking.

Now this would all seem to raise the question of whether St. Thomas has reversed the order of faith and reason that is found in the writings of John the Scot. That is to say, does reason come before faith? If it does come before faith, does that fact somehow lessen the importance of faith? The short answer is no to both questions. What St. Thomas wants to say is that all of our actions are meritorious if the grace of God motivates our free will. This is especially true with regard to giving our assent to faith. Human reason then can stand in a twofold relationship to the will. First, it can come before an act of the will, in which case our faith would be diminished. To illustrate the point, imagine being magically transported back to Cremona, Italy, about 1197. There on the streets we see a man giving money to a poor person; it is St. Homobonus. How lucky we are to actually see the patron of tailors and cloth workers engaging in one of his many good works! As we follow Homobonus down the road and watch him extend a helping hand to others, we begin to realize that he is not motivated to help others out of a sense of pity. St. Homobonus is willing to help anybody. He has a strong understanding of charity. Just as it is noble for Homobonus to act out of his understanding of charity, as opposed to a feeling of pity, so too it is better to have faith in God on the basis of divine authority, as opposed to reason. Faith founded on reason is diminished, just as good works born out of pity are lesser than those from a conscious act of charity. And St. Thomas is pointing out that when reason dictates whether one chooses to say yes to God, there is a decrease in the value of the religious faith.

The other way that reason can relate to the will of a believer is to follow it. St. Thomas explains that when a person has the will to believe, that person will love the truth that is believed. And the believer will take to heart whatever reasons can be found to support the belief. In this way, Thomas thinks that reason actually supports faith. Because St. Thomas defines faith as thinking with assent, it makes sense to suppose that a faith with at least a few intelligent, well-formed thoughts behind it will be better than one without such content. For Thomas, the ideas help to remove obstacles to faith, because they help to show that what one is accepting is at least possible.

MEDIEVAL FAITH

After this brief look at the methods of some of the great medieval teachers, the question, How did average people in medieval society express their faith? presents itself. There is no one clear answer. In some cases the Christian faith was expressed through simple popular beliefs. Other, more grounded expressions of the faith came through ceremonies and rituals. And, of course, religious life was certainly shown through play. The lessons the theologians taught were designed mostly for the people charged with the responsibility to ensure that all of the religious activities, with the possible exception of cultural expressions, retained some sacred quality. The best way to do that was to apply rational explanations to otherwise authoritative teachings of the church.

Most medieval people did not speak Latin. This fact has contributed somewhat to the misconception that medieval society was largely illiterate. This is simply not true. Many people could read and write in their own language, English or French, for example. With the rise of a merchant class, there were increasingly detailed records of goods and services, along with a rapidly expanding vocabulary. Latin was the language of the church, used mostly by the trained clergy and the nobility for important matters. Yet the use, or rather the abuse, of Latin by common people betrays something of the superstitious nature of the medieval mind. For example, the phrase "hocus pocus" is a medieval invention, or, more precisely, a medieval goof. When attending the Eucharist, non-Latin-speaking congregation members heard the priest say, "Hoc est meum corpus," which means "This is my body." Not fully grasping the nuances of the mass, people were able to surmise that once the words were spoken, everyone should expect something magical and good to happen. That is why there are accounts of people stealing communion bread from the churches, saying, "Hocus pocus," in their best imitation of the priest, and burying the morsel in their gardens with the hope of a better harvest.

Another account is of a woman who put chewed-up bread from the mass in her beehive in order to keep her bees from dying. Empowered by the body of Christ, the bees built a complete chapel, including bell tower and altar, out of a honeycomb and then began buzzing loudly in praise of God.[6] Bread in fact created many problems for the superstitious. There are accounts, for instance, of entire villages turning out with whatever could be used as a suitable weapon for killing demons in the forest. The belief in demons was real. The moldy rye used to bake the bread that people ate produced a real hallucination, but the bodies of the dead demons were never found.

Religion saturated medieval culture. Every person was acutely aware of God's presence and power. Therefore, they kept a constant lookout for the perilous pleasures that could creep in from the smallest of activities. For instance, St. Thomas warned his students about the dangers in using makeup. Women's painting themselves, he thought, was a form of counterfeit that can lead to a sin of deception. It can also lead to much more serious sins when it is applied in contempt of God.[7] Despite the general pietistic paranoia, a good bit of religious life for common people was expressed through church rituals such as marriage. And much like modern religious life, there was often no pure theological motive in the minds of the laity. That is to say, medieval religious rituals were a mixture of pragmatic and ecclesiastical concerns.

Medieval marriage is a complicated affair because so much of it was tied into the culture of the feudal system. Nevertheless, the Christian liturgical marriage began to emerge at the beginning of the twelfth century. The first step in the marriage process was for the priest to make sure that both the prospective bride and the prospective groom actually wanted to get married. Among the nobility especially, there were all kinds of reasons for marriage. Many of the unions were strategically motivated to ensure peace between kingdoms or to guarantee birthrights. The priest also did his best to make sure that the future couple was not already related. The church had very strict rules against picking fruit from the family tree. Once the necessary homework was done, the rite of marriage was accomplished through a two-step process. First, the bride became a *sponsa*. This initial step was essentially a secular arrangement in which the right and duty to protect the bride was transferred to the groom. Second, after an indeterminate period of time, the *nuptiae* took place. This was the stage of the marriage in which the union between the bride and the groom became absolutely binding in the eyes of the church. It was not always the case that the two steps were completed.

For instance, the future Capetian King Louis VI in 1105 was joined to a little girl named Lucienne as a means for reconciling warring factions around Paris. Lucienne, however, was not of an age to be eligible for phase two of the marriage process. So Louis elected to transfer her care and feeding to another member of his court and to seek a more suitable bride.[8] In a sense, Louis was born a bit too late. That is to say, had the situation occurred earlier in history, he might have avoided complications with the church. But around the start of the twelfth century, marriage actually became a sacrament. So, rather than simply focus on an exchange of oaths to establish the marriage bonds, the clergy had managed to incorporate more spiritual elements into the ceremony. And this meant that Louis had to make a special appeal to the Council of Troyes (1107) in order to annul his obligations to little Lucienne. The marriage was no longer just a matter of a promise shared between two parties. It was now a contract before God and sanctioned by the church.

Religious life also permeated play in medieval society. Just as with modern society, people had a wide range of recreational activities. They told stories of chivalrous knights, sang songs, went to plays, wrote poems and music. Some people in the Middle Ages even gambled. One slightly different activity was the celebration of feast days, special days specifically set aside to celebrate some aspect of the church. On most occasions people were expected to attend a mass and avoid work that might get in the way of worship. In a manner of speaking, feast days were a church-sanctioned bank holiday that afforded the opportunity to relax. Feast days included Sundays, a traditional day of rest. Another was the feast of All Saints (November 1), which took root when Pope Gregory IV ordered its universal observance in the mid-ninth century. Christmas too was a popular feast day. Because that celebration came with a bit of leisure time, St. Francis was able in 1223 to organize the first live manger scene in the Italian town of Greccio. Feast days were not always important occasions, however. One of the more flamboyant celebrations was the feast of fools, or the feast of asses. This holiday was basically a spoof, a time when riotous and often saucy behavior was allowed in the church. To make the affair even greater fun, people exchanged feudal status for the festival. For instance, the people chose a "pope of fools" from the lower clergy; that person then served as the master of ceremonies for the remainder of the celebration. In some areas of France, the festival actually involved an ass. At first, the introduction of a donkey into the church was probably meant to be serious. Donkeys played an important role in the story of the flight from Egypt, and even Jesus rode into town on one. Nonetheless, the church service grew in the spirit of fun, and eventually congregation members were, among other silly behavior, invited to bray like donkeys at certain key points in the worship service. There is no doubt that the feast of fools and the feast of asses got a bit out of hand. They began as early twelfth-century celebrations; by the mid-fourteenth century the Council of Basle had suppressed them. The church council, like the others before it, did not, however, have enough weight to eliminate the feast of fools completely. The animal party continued throughout various towns for several years following.

In addition to wild parties, people who lived during the Middle Ages also enjoyed good stories. But even the popular entertainment was tied to the church. For example, the *Song of Roland* is a splendid, and at the same time grim, tale of a valiant knight who fought and died for the king. Because of his incredible heroism the knight was received into heaven. What is interesting about the story, however, is the way that the author weaves his religious fervor through the narrative. The background for the story is simply one of Charlemagne's battles. In 778, when he was returning from a war in northern Spain and his troops were crossing the Pyrenees, the Gasgons attacked his rear guard. The onslaught was horrible, and few members of the rear guard survived. Since the anonymous author of the story lived during the twelfth century, a few of the details from the battle were changed to suit the new generation. First, rather than point to the Basque people of France as the enemy, the author chose to portray the battle as one against the Muslims. Second, the author made sure that his fiercely enviable characters bluntly state opinions such as Christians are right and pagans are wrong. Third, an archbishop was given a role in which he is pious, wise, compassionate, and great in battle. Finally, despite making a serious tactical error that led to the devastating loss, the gallant knight Roland is triumphantly received into heaven by a couple of archangels. Add up all of the changes, and, voilà! the people who undertake a crusade for the good of the church are the ultimate action heroes.

Medieval society enjoyed virtually every kind of story. That is to say, in addition to adventure, people in the Middle Ages heard tales of romance, drama, and mystery. They also had comedy. Probably the most famous comedy was written by an Italian named Dante Alighieri (c. 1265–1321). In fact, his story became known as *The Divine Comedy*. The gist of the story is that Dante himself goes on a tour of the afterlife. On his journey through hell, purgatory, and heaven he meets several famous characters who are either being punished or being rewarded for their lives on earth. Hell is shaped like a funnel with nine levels, each reserved for a particular sin, such as lust or treachery, and each with its own bizarre punishment. The deeper one goes into the funnel, the worse the sins are. The very bottom is reserved for the devil. Dante placed Pope Innocent III near the bottom of hell. Their encounter is amusing because the pope is stuck upside down with his head in a tube. His punishment also includes flames that burn the soles of his feet. Pope Innocent gets excited when he hears Dante's voice, because he mistakenly believes that his time of punishment is over and that Pope Boniface VIII has come to take his place.

Dante takes the opportunity to continue poking fun at the papacy even in purgatory, an island mountain with seven ledges. Just as in hell, each level is reserved for people who need to work out their sinful disposition. So, for example, when entering the area reserved for people who turned away from God in favor of material wealth, Dante meets Pope Hadrian V. Since the pope had set his eyes on so many shiny things during his lifetime, his punishment is to lie face down and stare at the dust. Despite the pope's curious physical position, however, he and Dante are able to have a brief conversation. After learning that the church hierarchy does not apply in the afterlife, Dante moves along the incredibly crowded ledge, only to meet Hugh Capet. Through Dante's brilliant execution of satire, Hugh ends up condemning all of the kings that issued forth from his dynasty. That is to say, he laments the bloodthirsty greed of all the Philips and Louis who reigned between 1060 and 1300. Hugh also reveals more of the terrible things that the French kings did in order to gain their power. For example, he points to Charles of Anjou, the brother of

King Louis IX, who defeated and beheaded Conrad, king of Jerusalem. Dante even draws on a rumor that Charles poisoned St. Thomas Aquinas as yet another instance of the joy of killing that was rife among the nobility.

Dante ultimately leaves purgatory and travels to paradise. His guide for this section of the trip is St. Bernard of Clairvaux. Paradise is a pretty heady place; that is, Dante finds that heaven is a place for intellectuals. He discusses both Christian doctrine and the latest scientific concepts with a range of characters. He also learns that different degrees of joy are awarded in heaven. Not all good souls are treated equally. Rather, they are stationed on various heavenly bodies according to their reward. For instance, on the moon, or at the low end of the scale, he meets a nun and an empress, who both took vows as nuns but were forced to break their promises to God because of demands for political marriages. So, although they were faithful, they were not absolutely pure. On the highest end, what Dante calls the Empyrean, heaven is like a rose, with the souls of the blessed arranged like petals and God at the center. Then, because a direct experience of God is outside of the human ability to describe, Dante simply explains that he became keenly aware of God's universal love. Thus, *The Divine Comedy* ends with a kind of joyous affirmation of the beatific vision.

In short, the people who lived during the Middle Ages had full lives. They worked hard, but they also took breaks that were built around life in the church. Much like people in modern society, medieval folks attended worship and practiced their religious beliefs at home. Their books and games were often centered in the church. They read theology, reflected on Scripture, and felt the presence of a God who loves and cares for humanity. They also found themselves in awe of the divine mystery—an irresistible mystery that begged for explanation.

QUESTIONS FOR DISCUSSION

1. What are some of the benefits of mysticism? What are some of the benefits of rational theology? Is one approach better than the other?
2. If religious life permeated medieval society through plays, literature, and special occasions, what are some of the ways that Christianity is expressed in modern society? Are there any connections between medieval and modern practices?

3

In God the Father

For some modern minds, grasping medieval philosophical theology is difficult because theologians engaged in wildly speculative discussions about the nature of God. Why waste all of that mental energy when everything that a believer needs to know is found in Scripture? Were it possible to resurrect a medieval theologian, and perhaps a Medieval Latin interpreter, our newly revived visitor would probably say something to the effect that Scripture is not always immediately clear. Worse, Scripture is silent about many things in our world. For instance, Jesus clearly ate loaves and fishes. But what did he think about flummery? Since flummery was a fourteenth-century dessert made mostly from the scum that forms on top of oat meal, probably Jesus never actually ate it. But would he have enjoyed it? Did he even like loaves and fishes? It seems like a minor detail, but there is no answer in Scripture for what Jesus' favorite food was. In the same way that Scripture does not reveal what Jesus actually enjoyed eating, it fails to unveil many other things about God. For the medieval scholar, this realization was disconcerting, because being a Christian meant constantly trying to understand as much about the divine as is humanly possible.

That having been said, thinking about God in practiced ways did not really begin until after Charlemagne (c. 742–814) started his educational reforms toward the end of the eighth century. Of course there were bright spots of intellectual activity before Charlemagne's restructuring. For instance, Gregory of Tours (c. 538–94) produced his multivolume history of the Franks, and St. Benedict wrote his monastic rule. Yet Charlemagne's demand for better education helped to pave the way for the evolution of a variety of different schools. The monastic schools were the earliest and most influential of these institutions. Famous monasteries such as Monte Cassino and Bec had fantastic libraries and served as a home to some of the best writers and translators. Desideridus (c. 1027–87), who later became Pope Victor III, was the abbot of Monte Cassino; under his care the ancient medical texts of Hippocrates and Galen were translated from Arabic into Latin. Lanfranc and Anselm, who are discussed in greater detail later, were unquestionably the most renowned scholars of their age. They earned their reputations by teaching in the cloisters at Bec.

Cathedral schools developed roughly between 1050 and 1200. They were, as their name implies, attached to the church cathedrals. Although these schools did not build a particularly solid reputation for quality, they did produce a number of great scholars. Cathedrals throughout France, in cities like Loan and Rheims, became well known for theological studies. Other schools, such as one at Chartres, excelled at studies of Plato. It was at Paris, however, that the seeds for the proper university were sown. In addition to Notre Dame, the cathedral school, some scholars were permitted to establish their own houses for study. Thus Peter Abelard founded a school on the left bank of the Seine River, Mont Ste. Geneviève, where he taught the new way of thinking that was found in the works of Aristotle. Similarly another famous logician, Adam Balsham, began taking students near Petit Pont. By the twelfth century these smaller schools began to form themselves into proper organizations. At the dawn of the thirteenth century they evolved into universities. These schools provided the training ground for some of the most impressive insights to come out of the twelfth and thirteenth centuries. Great masters like St. Bonaventure and St. Thomas Aquinas taught in these environments and devised lessons that prepared students to unveil the truths of Christian doctrine which were otherwise hidden from uninformed believers.

FROM PROOFS TO PREACHING

Both sermons and speeches rely on human language as the vehicle for communication. Yet most medieval students were taught that a sermon differed from a speech on a couple of counts. Speeches could be about almost anything, but a sermon was specifically designed to be an expansion of the witness that is found in Scripture. Aspiring clergy were also taught that sermons differed from speeches in terms of the authority under which the presentation was made. That is to say, speeches were usually delivered by permission of a human authority such as a king. A sermon, by contrast, was presented under the authority of God. In fact the primary ingredient for effective preaching was that the sermon carried with it the confidence that it was communicating the things of God. So it is not at all surprising that four of the greatest medieval teachers—St. Anselm, St. Thomas Aquinas, St. Bonaventure, and John Duns Scotus—took great pains to steady the convictions of those charged with the responsibility of generating enthusiasm for Scripture. By developing solid logical arguments that demonstrated the existence of the divine, these scholars hoped to firmly fix the Christian faith within a new generation of ministers. The logical arguments that they devised are the so-called "proofs for God."

Anselm, Aquinas, Bonaventure, and Scotus are good representatives of how medieval scholars worked out their proofs for the existence of God, but it would be unfair to create the impression that their ideas form a harmonious, unified system of thought. Anselm was separated from Aquinas and Bonaventure by almost two hundred years, and the differing historical periods give a slightly different color to their respective projects. That is to say, Anselm, Aquinas, and Bonaventure were all reacting to the needs of the dynamic social world in which they lived. For Aquinas and Bonaventure, this meant responding to the emergence of a literate merchant class, understanding new sciences and philosophies in light of Christian doctrine, and shifting the church away from a hierarchical power structure. In short, their underlying curriculum was geared toward social reform. By contrast, the aim of Anselm, who spent most of his life in a Benedictine monastery, was contemplation. The logical exercises that he devised were meant both to help students integrate intellectual activity into their devotional life and to develop their skills for inquiry. Consequently, a big part of Anselm's agenda was committed to teaching a kind of meditation in which students came to recognize the interchange between themselves and the divine.

There are still other significant differences between Anselm, Aquinas, and Bonaventure. For example, when St. Anselm worked out his proof for God, he was following a Benedictine practice that can be traced back through St. Benedict, the patriarch of Western monasticism, to John Cassian, who basically developed the rules for monastic life, and finds its roots in the great Alexandrian biblical critic, Origen. In like fashion, Aquinas and Bonaventure followed their own historical paths and drew from earlier sources. Church doctors such as St. Augustine and St. John of Damascus certainly had a tremendous impact on the two friars, but Aquinas and Bonaventure also made good use of St. Anselm's writings. To illustrate even sharper contrasts, the work of Aquinas has a distinctly philosophical taste, flavored with an obvious enthusiasm for Aristotle; Anselm and Bonaventure, however, were more suspicious of the value that rational philosophy could bring to Christianity. In any case, all of the different lines of influence add up to the single point that medieval scholars are a key part of a long and varied Christian tradition of thinking about God.

ST. ANSELM (1033–1109)

Since there is not a clear-cut consensus among the medieval scholars about how to develop a rational understanding of the divine, taking each representative in turn is perhaps the best way to unpack their respective proofs for God. Since Anselm set the stage for the other two, it makes sense to start with him. Anselm was an Italian from Aosta, the border area of Italy and Switzerland. According to one legend, when Anselm was a young boy, he dreamt that he had climbed to the top of the Alps to visit with God. Along his way to meet with the Almighty, however, Anselm noticed that some maidens were neglecting their work, and, presumably out of some unusually strong sense of piety, he decided to report the infraction to the king. Fortunately for the maidens, the king turned out to be an incredibly gracious person, and his presence was so impressive that Anselm forgot about the charges that he had intended to make. Apparently undaunted by his sudden lapse in memory, Anselm continued to enjoy the king's hospitality and managed to fill himself with very tasty bread before setting off for home. Upon waking from his dream, Anselm maintained that he had been in heaven and that he had eaten at the Lord's Table.[1]

St. Anselm did in fact travel over the Alps. He did not do so to spy on lazy maidens, however. Rather, he went to meet the brilliant theologian and most trusted counselor of William the Conqueror, Lanfranc of Pavia. Under this accomplished scholar's guidance, Anselm began studying in the Benedictine monastery at Bec in 1059 and in the following year took monastic vows. Three years later, Anselm himself had earned a reputation as an extremely able person and was chosen to supervise the monastery. His administration proved to be very popular and ultimately led to a glorious thirty-three-year monastic career. Anselm's quiet life as a monk ended in 1093, however, when the son of William the Conqueror, King William Rufus, named him as the archbishop of Canterbury. Anselm reluctantly accepted the new job, but, as it turned out, the arrangement was not a particularly happy one. In fact, the remainder of Anselm's career as a church leader is a twisted little tale of turbulent politics over various issues such as whether the money collected from all of the churches under the rule of Canterbury should be appropriated by the king and whether Urban II could be rightly recognized as a legitimate pope.

Despite his chaotic and often violent term as archbishop, Anselm still managed to write some delightful books. Most of his writings, in fact, were the result of conversations in the monastic cloisters and were intended for young students of theology. For instance, an earlier piece, the *Proslogion* (1078–79), contains his celebrated proof for the existence of God and reflects something of Anselm's concern to teach others. The word *Proslogion* means a conversation with the idea of bringing something into the open. On the one hand, Anselm's chat is with God. As he notes in his opening prayer, "I desire to understand in some measure thy truth, which my heart believes and loves. For I do not seek to understand in order to believe, but I believe in order to understand. For this too I believe, that, 'unless I believe, I shall not understand.'"[2] So, by engaging in a discussion with the divine, St. Anselm is demonstrating how he tried to bring greater clarity to his own religious faith. On the other hand, Anselm is engaging in a direct conversation with his students. Through the dialogue that is shared between an author and a reader, Anselm intends to provide his students with a means for enlightening atheists, for whom revelation is meaningless.

Since he spent the majority of his life in a Benedictine monastery, Anselm probably did not know too many atheists. Nevertheless, he had good reasons to tend to his students' needs. There was a dangerous temptation in medieval European culture to think that ancient philosophy might hold some promise for shedding light on the mysteries of the faith. Rather than permit his students to become confused by the use of reason in other approaches that, at best, could only express a part of God's existence, such as being good or being unlimited, Anselm attempted to establish the Christian belief in God by reason alone. Indeed, only Christianity held the possibility of providing a picture of God simple enough to offer a universally available insight that only a numbskull would deny. As Anselm explains:

> Even the fool, then, must be convinced that a being than which none greater can be thought exists at least in his understanding, since when he hears this he understands it, and whatever is understood is in the understanding. But clearly that than which a greater cannot be

thought cannot exist in the understanding alone. For if it is actually
in the understanding alone, it can be thought of as existing also in
reality, and this is greater. Therefore, if that than which a greater cannot be thought is in the understanding alone, this same thing than
which a greater cannot be thought is that than which a greater can be
thought. But obviously this is impossible. Without doubt, therefore,
there exists, both in the understanding and in reality, something than
which a greater cannot be thought.[3]

"That than which a greater cannot be thought" is what Anselm thinks people
mean when they utter the word "God." This definition is important because
Anselm's strategy is to show his students how to persuade the fool or nonbe-
liever on the basis of principles that are readily accepted. That is to say, he
wants to begin with knowledge that is absolutely certain. And the definition of
God as he presents it is known to be true without recourse to anything other
than reason. It is an abstract fact that everybody knows, just as they accept the
fact that every A is an A and one plus one is the same as two.

Keeping in mind that Anselm is working from an assumption that he supposes will be acceptable to any reasonable person, the rest of his argument follows. He explains that the concept of God, as that than which nothing greater
can be thought, must necessarily exist in the mind. Yet such a being is greater
when it exists in physical reality too. That is to say, if one can think of a being
that exists in both the mind and in reality, then there is a being that is greater
than the one that exists only in the mind. Consequently, the greatest of all
objects must exist in reality, because if it were only in the mind, another,
greater object would still be possible. Thus, God must really exist. Anselm was
apparently quite pleased with this line of reasoning. His description of the
emotional satisfaction that accompanied the insight is so vivid, in fact, that Sir
Richard Southern described the proof as "written in a state of philosophical
excitement which (it is probably safe to say) had never before been experienced
so intensely in any Benedictine monastery, and was probably never again to be
repeated in Benedictine history."[4] Sadly, not everyone shared Anselm's enthusiasm. A French contemporary named Gaunilo of Marmoutiers was among
the first to reject Anselm's proof, and almost two hundred years later St.
Thomas Aquinas soundly criticized the work before proposing his own
method for gaining insight into the existence of God.

ST. THOMAS AQUINAS (1225–74)

Like St. Anselm, Thomas Aquinas encountered Benedictine monasticism in
his youth. Thomas's circumstances were quite different, however, and the

cloistered life did not take with him. Given to the Benedictine abbey of Monte Cassino at age five or six, Thomas began learning the elements of piety and grammar. He was taught calligraphy but, judging from his notoriously poor penmanship, was not particularly good at it. Rather, his interests tended toward studying the writings of early church scholars like St. Jerome, St. Gregory, and St. Augustine. By the time that he was fourteen years old, a war forced Thomas, along with the other young monks, to relocate to Naples where they were expected to complete their studies at the imperial university. In Naples Thomas was first exposed to the writings of Aristotle. By 1243 he had developed an interest in the ideal of evangelical poverty, service to the church, and scholarship that was expressed through the Dominican order. Thomas officially joined the Dominicans in April 1244. His mother was apparently displeased with the decision, because she wanted him to become the head of a Benedictine monastery. Nevertheless, he prevailed over his mother's wishes and after a few years' delay began more advanced studies in Cologne. In 1252, Thomas was recommended as a suitable candidate for a doctorate at the University of Paris. He was assigned to Saint-Jacques, the Dominican House in Paris, and in the fall of 1252 he began lecturing on theology. Over the next ten years, Thomas continued to travel and to develop as a scholar. He wrote several books and by about 1263 had compiled a work in which passages from Greek patristic sources were strung together in order to explain various portions of Scripture. The project spurred his interest in the ancient Greek Fathers and led him to revise some portions of the lectures that he eventually published in the form of a theological textbook: the *Summa Theologica*.

Thomas's agenda in writing the *Summa* was thoroughly practical. Unlike St. Anselm, however, he was not so much concerned with demonstrating the truth of the Christian faith by reason alone. Rather, Thomas was compelled to sort out which bits of the faith can be demonstrated by reason and which bits cannot. Reason can make the existence of God obvious, Thomas thought, but in order to justify that claim he had to reckon with statements from earlier Greek theologians such as St. John Damascene (675–749), who taught that the human awareness of God's existence was innate. Thomas also had to challenge St. Anselm's notion that only fools think of God as not existing. That Anselm began with a generally accepted fact about God was troublesome, because it meant that a very distinct knowledge about God is present to all human beings. To say that humans do have some knowledge of the divine is reasonable, but could it really be an exact knowledge? Thomas would want to say that created beings may have an awareness of truth or a natural desire for happiness but that awareness does not necessarily mean they grasp the primal source of truth or happiness. Just as knowing that someone is approaching and knowing that Peter is approaching are different things, so too having an awareness of God is very different from having knowledge of God's existence. So, for St. Thomas, it just would not do to suppose that everybody readily agrees that God is "that than which a greater cannot be thought."

The Argument from Change

Since St. Thomas did not think that Anselm's proof was a very good way to demonstrate God's existence, he decided to try a different approach. He developed five separate arguments that all start from our experience of the world.[5] That is to say, Thomas thinks that it is possible to abstract from what we know about the world and build on a general fact, such as movement. As Thomas himself explains, "it is certain and evident to our senses, that in the world some things are in motion." Now Aquinas assumes that whatever is in motion must be moved by another, because motion is the process in which an object is reduced from potentiality to actuality. The prerequisite for such a reduction is that there must be something else that is already in a state of actuality. This is a fairly obscure way to go about describing motion, but St. Thomas's murky explanation is due mostly to his adoption of Aristotle's scientific vocabulary. In order to clear things up, Thomas offers an illustration of "that which is actually hot, as fire makes wood which is potentially hot, to be actually hot, and thereby moves and changes it." Thus, motion is simply a series involving an active agent working on potential agent. Implicit in the illustration is also the commonsense realization that something cannot be in both states at the same time. Ignited wood cannot be both potentially hot and actually hot at the same time. In more general terms, a thing cannot at exactly the same time be both a mover and the thing that is moved.

Having shown that whatever moves is put into motion by another, Thomas argues that a series of active agents moving potential agents could not go on forever, because in an endless chain there would be no mover that is first. Imagine, for example, an endless line of dominoes where each one falls and knocks over the next. Thomas's point is that this scenario would be impossible because some domino had to be pushed in order to start the chain reaction. Without some primary agent to start the ball rolling, the other dominoes would not fall. Rather, they would continue to stand as individual units with the potential to fall over. Or, as St. Thomas would want to say, one must reject an infinite regress of moved movers, because without some active principle at the start of the entire series, the process could not begin. Something must put the entire series into play, as motion comes about only when subsequent movers are acted upon by another. Whatever it is that first put everything into motion is what St. Thomas thinks everyone understands to be God.

The Argument from Causation

Following much the same pattern of reasoning, Thomas offers a second argument based on the observation of causes and their effects. Relying again on what is known from our experience of the world, Thomas notes that there is an order of efficient causes. By efficient cause he means the force or agent that produces an effect. On the one hand, to Aquinas this means that nothing can be the cause of itself. To say otherwise would be to claim that something is prior to itself, which would be ridiculous. On the other hand, a causal chain is just like a series of moving objects in the sense that it cannot be endless. As St. Thomas explains, "in efficient causes it is not possible to go on to infinity because in all efficient causes following in order, the first is the cause of the intermediate cause, and the intermediate is the cause of the ultimate cause." To remove one cause would destroy the entire chain. As Thomas himself would say, to take away a cause is to take away the effect. So, if there is no first cause among efficient causes, there can be no ultimate or intermediate causes. Since causal chains do appear to exist, it is necessary to admit the existence of a first cause. Whatever that first cause is, everyone understands to be God.

The Argument from Contingency

The third argument that St. Thomas advances is commonly called the argument from contingency, because the crux of the argument is that various things depend upon (are contingent upon) others for their existence. Aquinas does not use the term "contingency," however. Rather, he casts his argument in terms of necessity and possibility, the former meaning "absolutely has to be" and the latter meaning "can be." St. Thomas notes that in nature everything we observe can either exist or not exist. Yet nothing in nature is able to exist all of the time. Indeed, things come into being and then pass away. If everything contains the possibility of not existing, it seems reasonable to suppose that there may have been a time in which nothing existed. If this were true, however, then nothing would exist now, because nonexistent things can be brought into existence only by existing things. Things do exist now, however. So Thomas infers that not all beings are merely possible. There must be at least one necessary thing in existence. Moreover, after examining what he learned about cause and effect, Aquinas is sure that an infinite line of necessary beings that cause other things to exist is impossible. Consequently, he concludes there must be a being that has its own necessity and causes all other things. That being, he thinks, is God.

The Arguments from Excellence and Harmony

The last two arguments that Thomas advances are much less complicated. The fourth proof is from degrees of excellence. Some things are better than others; whatever is maximally best, according to Thomas, would be God. The fifth and final argument, from design, is derived directly from Aristotle's theory that all things in the universe tend toward the end for which they are made. That is to say, Aquinas supposes that everything in nature functions in a particular way and that there is a design which enables each thing to act properly in order to obtain what is best. Even objects that are not possessed with an intellect appear to function according to their design. Noticing this capacity for things to operate correctly leads Thomas to conclude that everything must be directed by some being that has knowledge and determines the action, much in the same way that an arrow is directed to the target by an archer. Not surprisingly, St Thomas insists that whatever the being is that moves nature to its proper end is God.

ST. BONAVENTURE (1217–74)

St. Bonaventure lived at the same time as Thomas Aquinas, and it is likely that they knew each other. The details of St. Bonaventure's early life, however, are not nearly as well documented as the stories about either Anselm or Aquinas. Bonaventure, originally named John Fidanza, was born in 1217 in Bagnoregio, Italy. He does tell us that he became very ill as a child and was restored to health only after his mother, Maria di Ritello, prayed to St. Francis. Exactly how old Bonaventure was when this took place is not particularly clear but since St. Francis died in 1226 it is safe to assume that he was at least nine years old. In any case, John Fidanza, or Bonaventure, as he was commonly called, began his connection to St. Francis well before he joined the Franciscan order in 1243 or 1244.

Upon completing his formative education in 1235, Bonaventure took up studies at the University of Paris. While there he encountered several notable scholars, including Alexander of Hales (c. 1186–1245), who started the Franciscan school at Paris and most likely influenced Bonaventure's decision to join the Franciscan order; John of La Rochelle; and Odo Rigaud. Bonaventure remained at the University of Paris and eventually earned the Franciscan chair of theology. His work of teaching and preaching came to a crashing halt, however, when surrounding political circumstances in Paris spun out of control. The secular clergy, the masters at the University of Paris, had long complained that the mendicant promotion of poverty was subversive and ran contrary to the teachings of the Gospels. To make matters worse, a rather misguided Franciscan named Gerard of Borgo San Donnino, about whom much more will be said in chapter 7, adopted the predictions of a mystic named Joachim of Fiore. When he equated the Franciscans with a poor, barefoot people who were to replace the clergy in Joachim's prophecy, the problems festered. Gerard's interpretation found favor in several quarters that included the minister general of the Franciscan order, John of Parma, but it inflamed the already existing fight between the Franciscans and the secular clergy. The tension in fact became so great that Gerard's works were condemned and John of Parma was forced to resign. Bonaventure was named as the person best suited to lead the Franciscan order; on February 2, 1257, at the age of forty, he was chosen to become the seventh minister general of the order.

Like St. Anselm, Bonaventure continued to rise through the ranks of the church. In 1273 he was elected Cardinal Bishop of Albano, and in the following year Pope Gregory X asked him to help organize the Council of Lyons, the assembly that temporarily restored Christian unity to the church. Like both Anselm and Thomas Aquinas, Bonaventure was an able teacher who cared deeply about helping his brothers to build a solid foundation of faith for their preaching ministry. He wrote several works to that end, but the basic principles of his theology are found in the writings that date from his early university career. This work contains what Bonaventure shared with his students at Paris and his explanation of how proofs for the existence of God can help one to attain certainty about the truth.

When St. Bonaventure considered the proofs for God's existence, he began by laboring under the same question that confronted both St. Thomas and St. Anselm: is the existence of God self-evident? St. Anselm thought that knowledge of God was indeed obvious and that a deeper awareness of the existence could be gained through a little careful reflection. By contrast, St. Thomas, although he thought that human beings have a very basic awareness of God, was sure that confirmation of the divine existence was best gained by analyzing the data gathered from sense experience. Bonaventure too was convinced that God is obvious to everyone but, in classic Franciscan fashion, follows out the feeling of God's presence in nature, wherein each created thing testifies to the divine existence in its own way. Thus there is a sense in which St. Bonaventure would have viewed the approaches of Anselm and Aquinas as perfectly compatible. For Bonaventure, whether one begins with the idea of God or sense perception is irrelevant. The trick is to amass as many proofs as possible in order to show that God is so universally attested that the divine existence cannot seriously be doubted.

In seeking the greatest variety of proof, Bonaventure first considered a famous quote from St. John Damascene: "Certainly nobody is subject to death,

not for whom this is naturally implanted in them, as is the knowledge of God."
(*Nemo quippe mortalium est, cui non hoc ab eo naturaliter insitum est, ut deum esse cognoscat.*) When St. Thomas read this statement, he thought that St. John meant that human beings were endowed with an innate awareness that pretty much guaranteed knowledge of God. St. Bonaventure, by contrast, understood the quote to mean that human beings start with an innate knowledge of God, and although that knowledge may be incomplete, it is nevertheless sufficient for excluding any doubts about the divine existence. To illustrate the point, Bonaventure points out that the desire for happiness is so much a part of the human condition that nobody could doubt whether another person wishes to be happy. Moreover, he supposes that the greatest happiness consists in the highest good, which is God. Since it is impossible for someone to desire something without some kind of prior knowledge of it, some knowledge of God or at least of the highest good must be implanted in the soul.

A second type of proof that helps to confirm what is accepted in faith comes from what is known about the world. Bonaventure essentially thinks, as does St. Thomas, that God's existence can be demonstrated from creatures. Bonaventure, however, has his own reasons for establishing the truth of God's existence from nature. On the one hand, he sees the utility of beginning with what is sensible, because such data is the means by which humans arrive at most of their knowledge. On the other hand, he recognizes that convincing arguments that begin with sensible things show how clearly creatures proclaim God's existence. That is to say, St. Bonaventure thinks that because the sensible world is the mirror of God, by reflecting on perceptible objects the human soul can begin a journey to God. That every creature does in fact attest to God's existence can be shown through ten different claims, many of which echo St. Thomas. For instance, if there is a being that is dependent upon another, there is a being that is not dependent on another, because nothing can bring itself from nonexistence to existence. Thus the reason for bringing things into existence is required in the form of a First Being that is not brought into existence.

Finally, St. Bonaventure appeals to St. Anselm's proof as a means for gaining confirmation of God's existence. God is that than which nothing greater can be thought. But what is such that it cannot be conceived of as nonexistent is truer than something which can be so conceived. Therefore, if God is that than which nothing greater can be conceived, then God cannot be conceived not to be. Bonaventure notes that one could try to object to this on the grounds that some people worship idols and that to conceive of God as an idol is the same as thinking that the deity does not exist. The objection fails, however, because although idolaters have an awareness of God, they also possess an inaccurate idea of the divine. Dealing with those who simply deny the existence of God is a bit more complicated, but like St. Anselm, Bonaventure suggests that one can deny God only out of foolishness or defective reason. Bonaventure is confident that if a person fails to note the existence of God, it is merely because of a lack of careful consideration or an inability to grasp what the word "God" means.

JOHN DUNS SCOTUS (1266–1308)

John Duns Scotus was another Franciscan friar who worked out an astounding proof for the existence of God. But, where St. Bonaventure tried to reconcile the differing opinions by gathering them all together, Duns Scotus found a way to harmonize the spirits of Anselm and Aquinas. Not much is known about Duns Scotus. Originally from Scotland, he was probably born around 1266. Later, he was educated at Oxford and taught both there and at Paris. Around 1308, Duns Scotus died at Cologne. The details surrounding all of these activities, however, are fuzzy, but it is clear that his theological synthesis had an enormous impact on Christian thought. Throughout the Middle Ages, he had a following that was as large as or larger than that of St. Thomas Aquinas. By the time the sixteenth century rolled around, there were so many followers of Duns Scotus that the Reformers called them "Dunces." In fact, if Thomas Cromwell's command that Scripture should be explained literally and not according to Scotus is any indication, the intellectual changes

---

A CLOSER LOOK

Although there are several variations on the proofs for God's existence, no matter which theologians worked out rational demonstrations, the proofs themselves fall into two main categories. The first set is based on an interior awareness of the divine and contains arguments that are based strictly on the meanings of the words that are involved. The other group, based on our knowledge of the world, contains arguments that permit us to reason to God by way of what we have experienced with our senses. St. Anselm's proof reflects the first kind of argument. The second kind is found in Thomas Aquinas's five ways. One alternative to these methods is to follow the complicated road of metaphysics. In this approach, the trick is to begin with really existing entities that are known through the mind and then deduce God. That is to say, knowledge of God is derived from an awareness of abstract entities. The Franciscan theologian John Duns Scotus followed this approach. In every case, the proofs for God's existence are designed to allow others to attain greater certainty about the truth of the Christian faith.

Further Reading: W. Frank and A. Wolter, *Duns Scotus, Metaphysician* (West Lafayette 1995).

that took place during the Protestant Reformation were partly in reaction to Duns Scotus's theology.

Although Duns Scotus may not have been the most popular medieval scholar with the Protestant Reformers, he was definitely one of the bright lights of his day. Much like St. Anselm, he was largely convinced that it is impossible to be ignorant of God. Yet, Scotus took a little different approach to the issue. In contrast to Bonaventure, he did not downplay the importance of rational proof. Also, contrary to St. Thomas, he did not think that demonstrating the existence of a first mover equated to knowing the Supreme Being. What Scotus apparently decided to do was to take the very best ideas from all of these scholars and use them in a way that truly shows there is an infinite being.

St. Bonaventure thought that God's existence is fairly obvious to everyone, but he was not alone. Several other Franciscans agreed with him; they all thought that the Anselmian description of God as the highest being proved the point. Duns Scotus's old teacher, William of Ware, sided with St. Bonaventure. So too did St. Bonaventure's student and the subsequent minister general of the Franciscan order, Matthew of Aquasparta. John Pecham, the man who followed St. Anselm to the see of Canterbury some one hundred and eighty-three years later, thought that God's existence could be grasped through pure intuition. Despite the enormous weight against him, Scotus chose to disagree with all of these outstanding scholars. In fact, he states rather bluntly that St. Anselm never thought the proposition that "God is that than which a greater cannot be conceived exists" is self-evident. Rather, Scotus says that Anselm was interested in posing an argument; in order to grasp the truth of the proposition, one must formulate at least two fairly simple syllogisms:

> A being is greater than any nonbeing.
> Nothing is greater than the highest being.
> Therefore, no highest being is a nonbeing.[6]

And

> Whatever is not a nonbeing is a being.
> The highest is not a nonbeing.
> Therefore, it is a being.[7]

Scotus is claiming that the statement "That than which a greater cannot be conceived is God" is not obviously true. At least it is not visibly true like such statements as "the sun is a star" or "the whole is greater than the part." By noting the two syllogisms, Duns Scotus is showing us that nobody can grasp Anselm's greatest conceivable being without some kind of additional thought process, and on that count, God is not self-evident. Even to begin thinking about Anselm's highest being requires a bit of deduction. The authorities are wrong! The best way to know for certain that God exists is to find arguments that can be tested out in our experience of the world.

Duns Scotus's insistence that knowledge of God should be grounded in experience of the world pretty well dictates the order for the solution that he proposes. First, he must consider the relative properties that an infinite being would have. That is to say, he must think about aspects like being the first cause, being the ultimate end, and having absolute perfection. To do this, Scotus suggests a fairly straightforward three-part procedure. Step one is to show that there is a being that is first in its particular order, for example, the order of perfection. Step two is to prove that such a being would be uncaused. Step three involves demonstrating that a being with the property under consideration actually exists. Once the properties are established, Scotus uses them to begin exploring the existence of the infinite being itself. With the program of study set, Scotus first decides to examine the properties of primacy, finality, and eminence. Second, he shows that only one infinite being can possess those properties.

God the First Cause

Duns Scotus is ready to start exploring the properties of primacy, finality, and eminence. Taking each property in its turn, Scotus constructs a fairly long argument out of three thesis statements for each property. For instance, when he considers whether or not some being is first, he does so by drawing three conclusions: 1. Some being is first. 2. Some being is not caused. 3. Some being exists. The properties of finality and eminence also follow the same pattern. What is remarkable about Scotus's method, however, is that in each case the information that he derives from one conclusion supplies fodder to support the next. Each conclusion is like a rung on a ladder; with each rung, Scotus climbs closer to the top until he eventually reaches the top or, in this instance, God. Climbing a logical ladder to get to God can take one to dizzying intellectual heights, so the first step must be solid. Scotus must keep the academic acrophobes happy, so he takes a tremendous amount of time to show that it is possible for a prime being to exist.

1. Among beings that can produce, one is simply first.

In his first argument for the relative properties of God, Scotus wants to show that there is a first being that gives rise to all others. He begins his argument by supposing that some being is an effect because some being is produced. Scotus then notes that whatever is produced is produced in one of three ways: 1. it is produced by nothing; 2. it is produced by itself; or 3. it is produced by another. Finding out which of the three is correct requires a simple process of elimination. According to Scotus, the first possibility can be ruled out because what is nothing causes nothing. The second possibility can be excluded on the grounds that nothing gives rise to itself. Consequently, the third choice is the only viable option: another produces some being. That would appear to settle the matter. But Scotus rightly suggests that the argument may not be complete just yet. It is possible, he muses, that this "other" is first and that it does produce some being. If so, then the argument for a first being is finished. But if the "other" is simply one in a long line of produced things, then there is still some work to be done. Indeed, if the being in question is the same as all of the other entities, then either another being must produce it, or that being produces its effect by virtue of something else. In short, Scotus would have to account for the existence of whatever produces the producing being. To this objection, Scotus would want to say that the absence of a first being is ridiculous, because the process of beings causing other beings must come to a stop with something that is not produced and from which all other beings ultimately originate. This must be the case, because without a first being, it is impossible to account for the causal series.

Now Duns Scotus was smart enough to realize that insisting on a first being does not make it so. He also knew that two potentially devastating objections could be raised to his argument. The first, and perhaps the more deadly of the two, is that not everybody would agree that a series of causes must come to an end. For example, he notes that one might suggest that sons come from fathers and that such a process may be unending. The point is well taken, but Scotus does not pick up the gauntlet and face the attack directly. Rather, he handles the objection by explaining that causation itself is a pretty slippery concept. In fact, he distinguishes between two types of causes, essentially ordered causes and accidentally ordered causes. The absolutely brilliant part of Scotus's response is that no matter which sense is meant, both lead to the conclusion that an endless series is impossible.

So what is an essentially ordered cause? Allan Wolter and William Frank have explained the notion in terms of a fan that, in order to propel air, requires electrical energy to turn the blade.[8] Similarly, Richard Cross has referred to a medieval illustration in which the efforts of a mother and father combine to create a child.[9] These examples are helpful because they convey the sense that two different causes, that is, electricity and fan blade or mom and dad, combine to create a third cause, either moving air or a baby. Another talented modern medievalist, Rega Wood, has described essentially ordered causes in a way that is probably even more helpful for grasping Scotus's point. She notes that Scotus probably had in mind claims of causes that extend to the celestial sphere.[10] What is terrific about Professor Wood's illustration is that it serves as a reminder that another feature of essentially ordered causes is that each cause is superior, in the sense of being more general and more unlimited than the next.

Accidentally ordered causes differ from essentially ordered causes, but the contrast is fairly straightforward. Father Bernardine Bonansea has pointed out that Scotus himself lists three ways to distinguish between them.[11] First, in an essentially ordered series the secondary cause depends on the prior cause for its act of causation. By contrast, in accidentally ordered causes the second cause may depend on the first for its existence but it does not require the first cause in the generation of its own causality. Second, a higher cause is considered to be more perfect and to exert a superior form of causality on the lesser cause in matters of essential causation. Such a relation of superior causes, however, does not obtain with regard to accidental causation. Finally, the third difference is that all essentially ordered causes work together to produce an effect. Accidental causes work independently and act in succession with regard to their effects.

Both essentially and accidentally ordered causation are important to Scotus's argument, because after he considers them from various points of view he is able to determine that, in either case, an infinite series is impossible. In the case of essentially ordered causes, Scotus himself actually proposes five different arguments to establish his contention that they must have an end. Rather than lose sight of the larger issue, that is, proving that some being must simply be first, a brief explanation of the first argument will do. Scotus begins by explaining that in any given series there must be a cause that is external to the series. If no external cause is present, then the series in question would be either groundless or contradictory. That is to say, in an essentially ordered series, "cause" is synonymous with "effect" because each member of the series depends upon a preceding member for its causation. When the members of the series are viewed in the context of an endless series, the final outcome is absurd. On the one hand, if there is no cause that is external to a series then that series must depend upon an uncaused effect and would be groundless. On the other hand, if the series was infinite, it would depend on a cause that is its own effect, which is a contradictory notion. Since neither option makes much sense, Scotus reasons, a series of essential causes must have a terminus.

The possibility of an infinite accidentally ordered series fares no better than an infinite essentially ordered series. In fact, Scotus wagers that an accidentally ordered series cannot exist unless it is first grounded in an essentially ordered series. In making this point clear, Scotus begins by recalling the fact that in an accidentally ordered series, each cause takes place one after the other so that what follows stems in some way from what came before. Yet, a succeeding cause does not depend upon a preceding one for its causality. That is to say, a subsequent cause is effective whether the proceeding cause exists or not. For instance, Scotus explains that a man can beget a child whether or not his own father is still alive. With this basic understanding in mind, it does not appear likely to Scotus that an infinite series of accidentally ordered causes is possible. In fact, he notes that the only way that such a series could result is if the accidentally ordered series depended upon something of infinite duration. A succession of new beings is conceivable only in terms of something permanent that is not a part of the series. Scotus supposes that all of the components of an accidentally ordered series are of the same nature, and since none of them can be coexistent with the whole series without changing their place in the causal chain, something else must exist prior to the succession. The whole series of accidentally ordered causes depends upon an outside superior cause, for without it no causal series could exist.

Having demonstrated that there are good grounds for supposing that a causal chain must have an end, Scotus is able to turn his attention to the second potentially devastating objection to his argument that some thing is capable of producing an effect and thus something is an efficient cause. The problem in this case is that it would appear that Scotus's argument begins with a contingent proposition rather than a necessary one. That is to say, Scotus begins by supposing that some being is an effect, therefore assuming the existence of something caused. Scotus, however, escapes this objection by constructing his proof on the possibility of such events as motion and cause because he understands that once they are ascertained beyond doubt, they become necessary truths.[12]

2. The simply first efficient cause is uncausable.

Through his fairly long analysis of the various types of causal chains, Scotus rather skillfully demonstrated that some being must be first. His analysis also provided the key for proving a second conclusion, namely, that the first cause is not caused. The grounding for this claim relies on the argument that an infinite regress is impossible in an essentially ordered causal series.[13] Put in slightly different terms, if Scotus's claim that an essentially ordered series always comes to an end is right, then it is an inescapable fact that the first cause is uncaused. Yet, what would happen if somebody flat out denied the possibility of an essentially ordered series? If that happened, Scotus's argument would not work well at all. His point that an essentially ordered series cannot go on forever is the foundation for showing that the first cause is not caused. Without an essentially ordered series the claim that some being is not caused has no chance for success. Scotus recognized this problem and in his later works took steps to fix it. In this version of the argument, however, people who like to quibble about the possibility of infinite series must either reread the first bit about essentially ordered causes until they become convinced or they will have to remain unsatisfied.

One other excellent feature of Scotus's argument for an uncaused first cause that is worth mentioning is that by pairing the first cause with a finite series of essential causes, he can rule out the possibility of the first cause being anything other than an efficient cause. "Final," "material," and "formal" are all types of causes identified by Aristotle. In brief, a final cause is the end or purpose for which something is created. Material cause refers to the stuff from which things come. For example, bronze is the material cause of a statue. Formal cause is what a particular thing is, that is, its essence or nature, such as being a statue of St. Francis. An efficient cause is the source of a first beginning. Since the first cause is an independent, uncaused being that is at the head of an essentially ordered series, Scotus supposes that it must be an efficient cause. The fact that it is an efficient cause rules out the possibility of it being any other type of cause. Something must cause the bronze that causes the statue that is shaped into the form of St. Francis. The other types of causes all need an efficient cause.

3. A first being, existing by itself, actually exists.

Duns Scotus has shown that it is possible for some being to be both first and uncaused. The last step in his discussion about the possibility of a first efficient cause is to show that such a being actually exists. That may seem to be an ambitious task, but Scotus makes short shrift of the work. In fact, most of the material that he needed for the job has already been provided in the first two arguments. As mentioned earlier, one feature of essentially ordered causes is that they are arranged in a kind of hierarchy such that each cause is superior to the one that succeeds it. For Scotus this can be boiled down to mean that some causes are better than others. And, if there is a first cause, which Scotus has just taken great pains to prove, then it must also be the best cause, since no other cause could precede it. The first cause is maximally excellent.

Another important point can be abstracted from the earlier discussion. Scotus has shown that it is possible for some being to exist all by itself. That is to say, he has demonstrated that there is an independent uncaused being. This is a provocative detail for Scotus, because it suggests to him that if it is possible for an uncaused being to exist, then that being must have necessary existence. Although his terminology is a bit obscure, all that he is really trying to say is that it is logically impossible for the first being not to exist. Let's see if that point can be made a bit more clearly. All sorts of things come into being; that is a fact confirmed by our senses. The fact that those things exist is a necessary truth. Even if the world and everything in it suddenly changed into a bizarre alternate reality, or even if everything disappeared altogether, it is still an inescapable fact that such a world can exist. So, the possible things that are known through our senses have a type of necessary existence.

Now, by combining his point that some beings are better than others with his insistence that some being is necessary, Scotus has all of the ingredients that are required for an argument for the existence of a being that looks a bit like St. Anselm's argument for the existence of God. Indeed, although Duns Scotus and St. Anselm differ in their terminology, the content of the two arguments is really quite similar. For instance, St. Anselm begins with "the greatest possible being." What that means is that it is contradictory to think of the greatest being and then think of one that is even greater. That is exactly what Duns Scotus has in mind when he refers to "a thing to whose concept it is repugnant that it depends upon another." Independent existence is what makes a being the greatest. To think of an independently existing being that depends upon another for its existence would be a contradiction that neither Anselm nor Scotus would accept. Independent existence is the crucial concept, and our two scholars also want to point out that that independence implies necessary existence, because there is nothing upon which the first being can depend.

Scotus proves the second property, namely finality, in much the same way that he demonstrates the existence of a first efficient cause. First, he shows that an ultimate end is possible. Second, he demonstrates that it is totally uncaused. Third, he proves that it actually exists. The procedure is quite obviously the same, but a word or two about finality itself should probably be said. When Scotus mentions finality, he is thinking of an Aristotelian notion that every agent acts toward an end. That is to say, there must be a definitive goal for everything that is created. So when Scotus considers the order of finality, he wants to show that there is an utmost goal. "Finality" means an absolutely unqualified end. What would make Scotus think that there is an ultimate end in the first place? Believe it or not, it is the natural outcome of his proof for a first cause. From the facts that it is possible to produce a being and that the produced being is dependent upon an efficient cause, it follows that there must be an end. Saying that there are causes but no ends is the same as saying that the things that are caused happen at random or by chance. A bunch of things without any reason for their existence, however, leads to a fairly unpalatable situation. Indeed, it bars the way to any rational explanation for anything. So Scotus's first proof actually provides the warrant for his claim for an ultimate end.

Duns Scotus's final conclusion is the synthesis of the prior two conclusions, and it too follows the pattern of reasoning that was established in his argument for the first being. Since an end must be better than anything that exists for the sake of it, there must be an order in which some things are better than others. A hierarchy of really good ends, however, cannot go on forever; that is fairly clear from what Scotus said about essentially ordered causal series. So there must be a most perfect being that can have neither an end nor a cause. Indeed, an end would imply that it exists for the sake of another, and a cause suggests that it depends upon another. If either condition obtained, the being in question could not be called most perfect. Finally, just as with the properties of causality and efficiency, Scotus concludes that a most perfect being must actually exist.

At the very end of his discussion about the relative properties, Scotus offers a smashing insight. He points out that any being that has the property of being the first cause will have the other two properties, being an ultimate end and maximal perfection, as well. The properties are integrated! To illustrate, agents act for the sake of an end. Yet, as was just demonstrated, there is nothing for the sake of which the ultimate end could be produced. Hence, the ultimate end is uncaused. So too, for a being to be truly maximally excellent, it must be first. Thinking back to what Scotus had to say about essentially ordered causal series, it seems pretty clear that the first cause will be superior to any cause that follows it. The observation that the three relative properties must inhere in one being is not only a first-rate insight but it also prepares the way for the second part of Scotus's proof for God: the existence of an infinite being.

The Infinite Being

So far, Duns Scotus has worked out a system in which he can say that there is a being that is uncaused, the ultimate end, and maximally perfect. Amazingly, he can also say with great confidence that if a being has one of those properties, it will also have the other two. These are important insights, because they lend well to the second half of Scotus's project: to determine whether or not an infinite being actually exists. To see how the two parts fit, however, requires some insight into what Scotus means by the term "infinite." As it turns out, "infinite" can be applied in a couple of ways. Most of the time, "infinity" means an endless number, but this sense of the term probably is not very useful. The human mind is simply not capable of grasping an infinite number of parts whose infinity is not immediately obvious in any one of its many components. At best, one might suggest that by thinking about the finite, we can figure out what it means for the series to be beyond any finite measure. Another meaning of the term "infinity," however, is perfect simplicity, and it is this usage that Scotus has in mind. Under this flag, if one point can be grasped, then the whole can be understood. Infinity in this second sense means that it is possible to have an endless number of successive parts on the condition that all of the parts exist simultaneously.

To claim there is a being with an infinite number of parts that all exist at the same time seems a bit counterintuitive. Can a being really be infinite? For his part, Duns Scotus thinks that the idea of an infinite being is a rather pleasant notion, actually, the most perfect thing that we can know. Our minds are fine-tuned receivers, and just as we might enjoy listening to a good song, so too we like thinking about an infinite being. In much the same way that we wince when hearing a musician sing off-key, our minds would naturally cringe if the idea of an infinite being were contradictory. That was the brilliance behind St. Anselm's argument. He saw the contradiction that comes from thinking that an unbounded deity does not exist; to think that the Supreme Being exists only in the mind is just too discordant. To make the point clear, Scotus suggests touching up Anselm's work. The highest conceivable being must exist, because if it did not, it would not be the highest. Should there be a question about the matter, one need only to review what was already said about the property of being maximally excellent. Thus, an infinite being that is first in the orders of causation, finality, and eminence exists. Moreover, it is a fact that no rational mind can ignore.

QUESTIONS FOR DISCUSSION

1. How does the medieval use of the word "proof" differ in meaning from the modern sense of the word?
2. The point of the proofs for the existence of God was to apply rigorous reason to church doctrine. How valuable is that exercise today?
3. Is the method of formulating proofs for the existence of God a good way to meditate on the divine? Why or why not?
4. What are some specific ways that Duns Scotus used the ideas of Anselm to propel his proof for God? Where are there shadows of St. Thomas's method in Duns Scotus's proof?
5. Of the methods offered by St. Anselm, St. Thomas, and Duns Scotus, which do you prefer? Why?

4

And in Jesus Christ

Why did the Word become flesh? In modern Christian theology, two related doctrines help to answer this question. The first is the doctrine of the incarnation. In a nutshell, it is the understanding that the divine Word did, in fact, become a human being in the form of Jesus Christ. The second is the doctrine of atonement. The gist of it is that when Adam and Eve disobeyed God, they caused a huge rift between humans and the divine. When Jesus Christ died on the cross, however, God was reunited with his people; or, to put it another way, God and creatures became reconciled. With these two doctrines in mind, the answer to the question at the start of this chapter is simply that the Word became flesh in order to save humanity from sin. Most medieval theologians basically agreed about salvation through Christ. But they did not necessarily treat the incarnation and the atonement as two separate events. Rather, they tended to have a slightly more integrated view of God's activity. In the hands of most medieval theologians, it is impossible to have the atonement without the incarnation. This slightly more holistic view of why the Word became flesh created a framework that allowed for some exciting explanations for what Christ accomplished by entering the world.

Nearly every theologian since the beginning of Christianity has pondered the question about the reasons for the incarnation. The most important of these scholars was, of course, St. Augustine, whose writings contain several different answers to the question. For instance, in his earliest work, he simply says that the divine intellect subjected itself to the humiliation of a fleshly body out of compassion for the souls who had succumbed to error. When writing his famous *Confessions*, St. Augustine simply noted that Christ was a wise and hugely important figure who was born from a virgin. The bishop of Hippo did not elaborate on the role of Christ because he hadn't really thought much about the incarnation, but his brief statement did at least suggest that Christ's presence served as an outstanding moral example. Later in his works, when Augustine was being poetic, he cast Christ as a physician who came to heal the ill, not from disease but from sin. Finally, but not exclusively, St. Augustine described God as being locked in a great cosmic war with the devil. When Satan tried to capture Christ, however, he was defeated by the power of the resurrection and humans were set free. This last image caught on, and the theme of God as warlord made good sense to the Anglo-Saxon mind. Jesus too was rendered as a strong warrior who defeated the devil.

All of Augustine's themes helped to shape the answers that medieval theologians gave when struggling with the mystery of the incarnation. For instance, by the twelfth century, the barbarian concept of God's tough-guy image shifted a bit, and this had an effect on how theologians understood the incarnation. Hugh of St. Victor, a mystical monk living in France, returned to Augustine and supposed that the incarnation was a mechanism intended to refocus humanity. That is to say, he thought that human beings fell in love with the material goods of the secular world and that the incarnation served the purpose of pulling our sight back toward the divine. In Hugh's mind this meant that the incarnation is intimately connected with creation. More specifically, the incarnation is part of a circle that begins with God's creative act but then moves through a process of shaping human beings into the image of God, with the ultimate expression in the incarnation. This basic theory eventually had an enormous impact on thirteenth-century theologians like St. Bonaventure.

On quite a different count, Peter Abelard (1079–1142) considered the purpose of the incarnation to be an example of what people ought to do. The life of Christ was basically an excellent example of how human beings should be prepared to deal with the world around them. God will save humanity through an act of grace. But the fact that God also chose to walk around in the flesh serves as a kind of an instance from which human beings can gain inspiration and faith in the divine. Jesus is a moral paradigm, a living lesson in how to do the right thing for all of humanity to imitate. In Abelard's mind, the reason for the incarnation amounts to a lesson in morality. Peter was frequently outspoken and critical of church teachings and, as such, a very controversial figure during his day. Moreover, his views of the incarnation did not help him fend off his enemies. That is to say, although the basic understanding of a moral lesson being taught through the life of Christ is defensible on scriptural grounds, Peter went too far. He failed to allow for the power of the divine to work through the incarnation. It was in fact his theological teachings combined with his public attempts to interpret Scripture by way of philosophical methods, rather than through the guidance of the church fathers, that ultimately got him into trouble. St. Bernard convicted the Parisian philosopher of trying to censor faith as opposed to following the faith. In 1140 Pope Innocent II formally condemned Peter Abelard's work.

Nevertheless, what all of the medieval incarnation theories, including Peter Abelard's, have in common is that saving humanity is at the heart of the divine initiative. But is that all there is to it? Christ became human in order to save human beings from their sins? Since our salvation and indeed the whole of our eternal life are tied up in the answer to the question, most medieval theologians thought it best to avoid hasty answers. In just thinking about the question itself, two serious problems become evident. First, it seems appropriate to ask whether or not God *had* to save humanity. Did human beings put themselves into a situation that forced God to act a certain way? Can any human, purposely or accidentally, force God to do anything? Second, the salvation explanation seems to imply that human sin caused something good to happen, namely, the incarnation. Does that mean that good things happen when we sin?

A LITTLE BIT OF CONTEXT

There are probably a million reasons why medieval theologians spent their energy trying to demonstrate the reasonableness of Christianity. For instance, since monks and friars were already professing Christians, the exercise of critically examining the purpose and work of Jesus Christ was a way to nurture their religious faith. Another reason was undoubtedly that medieval monks

---

A CLOSER LOOK

Although there were several important monasteries during the Middle Ages, such as Grandmont and Cîteaux, the most famous one was Cluny. Founded in 909 by the Duke of Aquitaine, it quickly became well known for its high standards of monastic life. Under the leadership of St. Odo (927–42) many other monastic houses reformed themselves to be more like the Cluniacs. Their strict observance of the Rule of St. Benedict, combined with their great numbers, made Cluniacs a highly influential force in several reform movements throughout the history of the medieval church. Most notably, they were on the front lines of attempts by Pope Gregory VII to clean up simony (the buying and selling of positions in the church) and to enforce celibacy among the clergy. Throughout the tenth to the twelfth centuries, talented young men such as Gerbert d'Aurillac, who became Pope Sylvester II, and Hermann of Carinthia, a famous translator of Arabic sources, joined Cluny and inspired powerful social and intellectual movements.

Further Reading: H. E. J. Cowdrey, *The Cluniacs and the Gregorian Reform* (Oxford 1970).

were compelled to defend the faith of the church, especially during the late eleventh century, when Europe went to war against Islam in the Crusades. That is to say, medieval leaders saw two ways to fight a war. On the one hand, it was possible to deploy a skilled army that used lethal force. On the other hand, one could deploy the tools of the church. At the time of the First Crusade, Pope Urban II was keenly aware of the power that was attendant in the second option. Before rising to papal office, Urban II was a monk known as Odo of Lagery. He was active in the church at a time when monasteries were rapidly gaining popularity with nearly every segment of society. For instance, even the military class stood ready to perform service for the church. Odo too was a part of the craze. He started his career by studying under St. Bruno, the founder of the Carthusian order, but eventually became a monk at Cluny.

By 1080 Odo had earned a job working directly under Pope Gregory VII, who had managed to get himself into an extraordinarily dangerous conflict with King Henry IV. More specifically, Gregory viewed himself as a kind of church reformer. In yet another good illustration of the tension between the temporal and spiritual powers, he asserted his right to depose all princes. When he decided to end the royal control over the bishops, however, he ended up at loggerheads with the most powerful man in Europe. In any case, the tense controversy with the king led some of Gregory's supporters to abandon him. Odo, however, proved to be both very loyal and a highly skilled diplomat. Eight years later Gregory died and Odo was elected to the papacy. Upon his coronation he took the name Urban II. It was not, however, a smooth transition to power. Clement III, an illegitimate pope whose election was the outcome of the fight between Gregory and King Henry, was in control of Rome, and at least thirteen cardinals stood in full support of his leadership. Urban II inherited a divided house and was forced into the position of having to stabilize the church. By taking a diplomatic approach to most matters Urban ended up gaining control of Rome by 1093. By using a bit of tact he managed to steer clear of the fight between King William II of England and St. Anselm. So too Urban carefully avoided the temptation to comment on the adulterous marriage of King Philip I of France. What Urban could not get with skill, he bought with cash. And with the help of some well-placed bribe money, he managed to secure the rest of the papal possessions. That is to say, for the right price he was able to regain the Lateran Palace and a few castles.

With his position secured, Urban began to focus on the overall health of the church. In 1095 he called a special meeting in which he defrocked both Clement III and the cardinals who supported him. Next, Pope Urban reissued a condemnation of the eucharistic teaching of Berengar of Tours (c. 1010–88). That is to say, Urban touched briefly on the issues of incarnation, atonement,

A CLOSER LOOK

The Crusades played a fascinating role in shaping the church. There were in fact several Crusades that enabled Christians to regain possession of several eastern territories that had been lost to Islam. The First Crusade began in 1095 and led to the capture of Jerusalem. The Second Crusade was launched by Pope Eugene II and was led by King Louis VII of France. The expedition was a miserable failure and ended crusading zeal until 1187. Three years later France, England, and Germany answered a call from Pope Gregory VIII. Although the campaign was not fully successful, the crusaders did recover a large part of the Mediterranean. Disastrous crusades include the Children's Crusade of 1212 and the Fifth Crusade, which played a role in the excommunication of Emperor Frederick II. Despite their questionable success, the Crusades did give rise to new religious orders, for example, the Knights Templar and the Hospitallers. Also, great heroes such as Richard the Lionheart of Robin Hood fame were forged from the wars.

Further Reading: J. Richard, *The Crusades, 1071–1291* (Cambridge 1999).

and redemption when he damned the theological argument that the bread and wine in a communion service did not have to turn into real flesh and blood in order to explain the actual presence of Christ. Nevertheless, the Pope's most notable action was his issuance of a call to all Christian warriors. Urban set out to help the Byzantine emperor Alexius I Comnenus defend the Eastern church against Islam. The First Crusade had begun. Urban's appeal was received with great enthusiasm, as warriors from Italy and France who had reclaimed Spain ten years earlier were again eager to receive papal indulgence in exchange for their work. Over a thousand people took up arms and set out to liberate Jerusalem from the Muslims. Urban was likely a bit surprised by the response. He had neither established a well-organized plan of attack nor thought much about who should go into battle. If Urban was shocked by the turnout, then Emperor Alexius must have been absolutely stunned. He had asked for some help but never imagined that crusading armies would arrive in huge waves. Raymond, count of Toulouse, brought his army from southern France. Hugh of Vermandois, Robert the count of Flanders, Stephen Henry the count of Blois, and Robert the duke of Normandy all came from northern France. Godfrey of Bouillon and his brother Baldwin arrived from the borders of France and Germany. Even Bohemund, who had spent a significant amount of his time attacking the Byzantine Empire, left southern Italy in order to join the fight. Despite the poor planning and rather chaotic nature of the First Crusade, the campaign had surprisingly good luck; on July 15, 1099, the crusaders gained control of Jerusalem.

THE BENEDICTINE VIEW

While chivalrous knights were eagerly wreaking havoc in the east, the monks who remained behind were contributing to the war effort by using their own weapons. More precisely, they were engaging in a kind of spiritual warfare that included carefully crafted arguments that affirmed the correctness of Christianity. For instance, in his letter to Pope Urban II, St. Anselm (see chapter 5) explained that he had written a work that clarified why God became human. In fact, Anselm had a twofold purpose in writing his book. On the one hand, he wanted to help Christians to understand the truth of their faith. On the other hand, he wanted to both refute and provide a reasonable explanation for nonbelievers. Anselm definitely had the Muslims in mind. But he was also concerned about the large Jewish population that flourished in Europe. The first part of his book, he says, contains the objections of the unbelievers who reject Christian claims on the grounds that they are opposed to reason. In the second part of the book Anselm takes on the ambitious task of showing that it is impossible to be saved without Christ.

According to St. Anselm the nonbelievers basically think that Christians dishonor God. They would allege that it is simply inappropriate to hold that God descended into the womb of a woman, grew up just like any other human child, and endured pains like hunger, thirst, crucifixion, and death. But that is exactly what Christians claim. So, in the first part of his work, St. Anselm argues that the unbeliever's criticism is unsound. In fact, it fails to recognize the incredible symmetry of God's activity. That is to say, Anselm thinks that God's actions are perfectly proportionate. Just as death entered into the human race by the disobedience of Adam and Eve, so the obedience of a human should restore people to God. The humanity of Christ does not lessen the majesty of the divine. For Anselm, the humanity is an expression of God's wisdom and justice. So, having rebuffed the sad misunderstanding of the Christian enthusiasm for a deity in the flesh, Anselm turns his attention to the issues of the second half of his book.

Anselm argues that God took on flesh for the express purpose of making amends for the sins of humanity. Briefly put, Anselm reasons that the act of disobedience against God required a payment of perfect obedience. When Adam and Eve wronged God, they obligated humanity to make restitution. Anselm is thinking here of the fairly classical notion of justice, the sense of which is that when a crime is committed, simply returning goods or repairing damage is not sufficient. Rather, the criminal should also pay for having committed the crime in the first place. But making satisfaction for violating the divine will is not an easy trick. On the one hand, human beings and angels cannot offer anything worthy to God, because everything that they have already belongs to God. On the other hand, human beings should not expect God to overlook the offense, because that would put the sinner on an equal footing with the blameless. That would amount to a kind of disorder in God's kingdom. The only way that human beings would be able to meet the demands of divine justice would be for a being that is both fully human and fully divine to make restitution. By being divine, Christ would be able to offer something worthy to God for the payment of the wrong. By being human, Christ would be able to represent human beings adequately. So the incarnation was the only way to save humanity from everlasting punishment. As Anselm would want to say, the incarnation was a necessary action for human redemption.

If St. Anselm's purpose was to show that it was necessary for God to become human in order to rescue mortals, it was his fellow Benedictine Rupert of Deutz (c. 1075–1129) who first considered the issue as contrary to fact. Rupert asked whether God would have come if humans had not sinned. By putting the question in this way, Rupert saw that the focus on salvation from sin might be too narrow. There was, of course, good scriptural evidence for St. Anselm's view. But Rupert also found that passages like Hebrews 2:10 could be used to support the idea that Christ's incarnation is also about the completion of God's creation. With this in mind, it was possible that sin and redemption were not the only motivating factors behind the incarnation. For Rupert, righteousness itself is grounded in the incarnation, whether humans sinned or not. As he put it, "The real question is whether it was in some way necessary for the human race that the God-man should become lord and king of all. Certain it is that the saints and elect would have been born if there was no sin."[1]

Why Rupert chose to find new insights by asking the question about Christ in a slightly different way is not especially clear. He too had a concern about combating other religious claims that rivaled Christianity. But Rupert may have also been trying to straighten out problems within the Christian ranks. For instance, in 1116 a young monk announced that another Anselm, Anselm of Loan, had taught that evil exists because God wills it to happen. Rupert heartily disagreed with this thesis and wrote a response that became hotly disputed. Yet it is possible that while Rupert was arguing against such notions as Anselm's he wanted to make sure that the bad behavior on the part of Adam and Eve did not get transferred illegitimately to God. By putting the incarnation into a much bigger picture of God's creative plan he was able to diminish the importance associated with the role of human evil.

In any case, Rupert of Deutz was in the minority for suggesting that God did not become human just to save us from sin, but he was not alone. Another twelfth-century monk, Honorius of Autun, also thought that there might be reasons beyond human sin that warranted the incarnation. Rather than locate the embodiment of the divine in the broader context of creation, however,

Honorius saw a different problem. If St. Anselm of Canterbury was correct in asserting that Christ had to become human in order to save humanity from the sin of Adam and Eve, then he should be equally committed to saying that something good resulted from human sin. Or worse, a position like St. Anselm's could be taken to suggest that human beings were able to act in such a way that God was forced to redeem them. But that is ridiculous. On purely logical grounds, it would be impossible for a totally helpless creature to force an almighty deity to do anything. So, for Honorius, the incarnation was part of a larger divine plan that enables human beings to participate in the beatific vision.

THE DOMINICAN ANSWER

It is perhaps a mark of his early Benedictine training that when St. Thomas Aquinas considered the question of whether Christ came primarily to save sinners, he too was aware of the danger in supposing that Christ came only to save sinners. That is to say, Thomas was keen to avoid the suggestion that human sin forced God to act in a certain way. In any case, Thomas was able to think of a couple of explanations that seemed to show that human sin was not a major factor in the incarnation. First, Thomas rather boldly states that human nature did not become more capable of grace because of sin. Rather, after having sinned, human beings were still fully capable of receiving the grace of union. For Thomas, the grace of union with the divine is the greatest gift that a human being can receive. In this light, it would not matter whether human beings had sinned. If humans had not sinned, they still would have received grace, because God would not withhold any form of good that humans are capable of receiving. So even if humans had managed not to sin, God still would have become incarnate. A second reason Thomas found to show that sin was not the motivation for the incarnation came from St. Augustine. In one of his lengthier books, Augustine noted that there are many other things to consider in the incarnation besides the forgiveness of sins. For example, through the incarnation human beings are able to journey more faithfully toward God. By taking human form, God was also able to teach humans how high a place in creation they hold. With St. Augustine's observations in mind, one could reasonably hold that God would have become incarnate even if human beings had not sinned.

Like any scholar, St. Augustine's theology evolved as he read and reflected on various scriptural passages. The process of growing in a personal faith can be quite messy at times; so it is not at all surprising that there are occasions when one needs to have a change of mind. St. Thomas probably appreciated this aspect of St. Augustine's personal growth, but in terms of settling the question of whether or not Christ came to redeem sinners, waffling was not particularly helpful. St. Thomas noticed that other parts of Augustine's work contained passages that conflicted with the earlier argument. Specifically, in a meditation about the Gospel of Luke, Augustine flat out stated that the Son of Man came to save what was lost. And when he noticed that 1 Timothy clearly stated that Jesus Christ came into the world to save sinners, St. Augustine decided that Christ did come to take away the sin of the world. In the words of Augustine himself, there is no need for medicine if there are no diseases or wounds. Human sin was the disease, and the Word made flesh was the medicine that saved humanity.

St. Augustine's personal reflections were of no help at all. St. Thomas had to decide which direction to go. Either Christ did come to save humanity, or he did not. After dutifully noting that there were a number of opinions on the matter, Thomas decided that Holy Scripture would be the only accurate guide for getting to the bottom of the issue, because that is where God's will is made known to humans. Throughout Scripture, the sin of the first human being, Adam, is given as the reason for the incarnation. Consequently, it is probably more in line to say that God became flesh as a remedy for sin. Yet God's power is not limited in such a way that even if human beings had not fallen from grace, the incarnation would not have happened. Thomas is certain that whether or not human beings sinned, God could become flesh if he chose to do so.

A FRANCISCAN POINT OF VIEW

The ideas of Rupert and Honorius quietly bumped along for a few years, but by the dawn of the thirteenth century their speculations found new life in the sermons of Robert Grosseteste (c. 1170–1253). An Englishman from Suffolk, he taught for a while at Oxford, where he became quite well-known. About 1229 he became the archdeacon of Leicester, but he resigned after only a few years in order to become a teacher in one of the newly opened Franciscan study houses just outside the walls of Oxford. Although Robert himself never became a Franciscan, he was a great friend of the friars, and when he became the bishop of Lincoln in 1235, he helped to organize the preaching ministries of both the Franciscans and the Dominicans. In his approach to the incarnation Robert, like most Benedictines, thought that Holy Scripture established the fact that the Son of God became flesh in order to save humanity. Yet, like Rupert and Honorius, Robert also thought that there were still greater reasons for the incarnation. There were, in fact, three major reasons why the Word became flesh. First, Christ came to be the head of all creation. The fall of humanity is an important part of the picture, but Robert thought that all of creation was made for Christ. Second, Robert thought that the incarnation was an expression of God's perfect love. Just as love tends to unite a lover with the loved, so too, Robert suggested, God loves his creatures in the highest manner and expresses that love in the personal union of the incarnation. Third, the Word became flesh because the incarnation amounts to the greatest glory of the universe. If God would create lowly creatures like worms and grubs without sin, it makes sense that he would also will the incarnation, which is incomparably better than all other creatures.[2]

About the same time that Bishop Grosseteste was speculating about the reasons behind the incarnation, St. Bonaventure was working out a systematic explanation for why the Word became flesh. Always a careful scholar, Bonaventure began by noting that the word "incarnation" actually has a double meaning. On the one hand, the term, referring to the assumption of flesh, suggests both imperfection and the ability to suffer pain. This sense of the term is in use when one points out the extent to which Christ suffered and died on the cross. When humans speak of the Son of God in this way, it is clear that the incarnation presupposes the redemption of humanity because the sacrifice of Christ is the center of focus. On the other hand, if one crafted a sermon in which the focus fell on the Son of God assuming human nature, the word "incarnation" would not be intended to refer to the liberation of humanity. Rather, Bonaventure thinks that in this second sense, "incarnation" must entail far more than an act of salvation for humans.

Since the reason for the incarnation is clear in the first sense, St. Bonaventure set out to explain why God took on human nature according to the second sense. That is to say, Bonaventure began to explore what the incarnation might mean apart from human salvation. The first order of business was to determine the role of Christ according to nature. Fortunately, most of the raw material that Bonaventure needed for formulating his answer was already available. In Paul's letter to the Colossians, Jesus was described as the "firstborn of all creation." Robert Grosseteste had pointed out that this description was important because it meant that God planned on Christ prior to anything else in creation.[3] The incarnation was predetermined, or to put it in more Aristotelian terminology, Christ was willed first by God, because he was intended to be the end of all creation. Rather than follow the Bishop of Lincoln with complicated terminology for the preexistent Word as the foundation for all creation, however, St. Bonaventure offered a rather simple explanation. Just as the first man was created on the sixth day for the completion of the whole world, so the second man, the complement of the whole world redeemed, should come into existence in the end of ages. In Christ one finds the first principle joined with the last. The incarnation is the unification of God with clay.

To say that Christ is the head of creation is to say that he is the ultimate perfection of nature.

The second bedrock reason to suppose that Christ would have become incarnate even if humanity had not fallen is under the explanation of grace or God's love. On this count, St. Bonaventure advances a theory that implies the absolute primacy of Christ. He explains that in the incarnation, Christ assumes human nature, becomes the head of the church, and binds all of its members with charity. Even if there had not been a case of original sin that required a Christ, the Son of God still would have assumed flesh in order to be the head of the whole church. Christ's being the head of the whole church is independent of the need for redemption from sin. At the same time that Christ becomes the head of the church, he perfects all merit, because all merit depends upon and is bettered by the incarnate Word.

Finally, a third reason for the incarnation apart from human redemption rests in understanding God's glory. According to St. Bonaventure, God is perfectly united with all of creation through the Eucharist, and the completion of both the spiritual and the bodily parts would not occur if the Son of God had not assumed flesh.

BONAVENTURE'S ECHO

St. Bonaventure had two students who became very influential voices in helping to form the Franciscan opinion of the incarnation. The first, an Englishman named John Peckham, after studying at Paris, ended up serving as the archbishop of Canterbury. Throughout his career, John proved to be a vigorous church reformer and a rigorous theologian in his own right. When it came to explaining the reasons behind the incarnation, however, he faithfully followed the teachings of St. Bonaventure. That is, John too was able to see motives for God to become human that ranged well beyond the relief of human misery.

Although John was persuaded by St. Bonaventure's basic three-part explanation for why the Word became flesh, he did not blindly accept the arguments. In fact, he noted that there were several reasons to suppose that Christ would not have come if humans had not sinned. For instance, several passages in the writings of St. Augustine indicated that the only reason that God became incarnate was to save humanity. As Archbishop Peckham noted:

> Augustine, concerning the Word of the Lord: "If man would not have sinned, Christ would not have become incarnate." —Further, in Sermon 9 of the same book: "Christ comes in this world for no other cause than to set sinners free." Further, in Sermon 12: "Neither is the Savior

sought nor would Christ have come unless by shedding his own blood
for his Church he sought destruction." —Further, in Sermon 8: "For
no other cause was the coming of the Lord made unless to make sinners free and to take away death."[4]

All of these bits from the authority of St. Augustine's sermons would seem to
confirm that rescuing human beings from the sins of Adam and Eve was the
purpose behind the incarnation. If St. Augustine's opinion was correct, John
Peckham would have to live with some very unpalatable conclusions. Saying
that Christ had to come into the world because human beings fell from grace
is equal to saying that creatures put God into a situation that forced him to act.
It is strange to think that God absolutely had to come into the world because
of human sin. What about the love and mercy of God? Why couldn't God
decide to become flesh as an act of perfect self-expression?

Ultimately Archbishop Peckham determined that the Son of God did come
to be our redeemer. In addition to our salvation, however, John also sided with
St. Bonaventure in claiming that the full and glorious reward for the entirety
of creation is found in the incarnation. In order to make sense of the passages
found in St. Augustine's work, John suggested that the references must pertain
to the mortal state of Jesus; St. Augustine must have meant that Christ became
mortal in order to counteract the sins caused by humans. On that count alone,
the Son of God should inspire devotion.

ANOTHER ECHO OF BONAVENTURE

Earlier we mentioned that St. Bonaventure had two famous students. The first
was John Peckham and the second was Matthew of Aquasparta (c. 1238–1302).
Matthew, from Todi, Italy, studied at the University of Paris and taught in both
Bologna and Rome. In 1287 Matthew, following in his old teacher's footsteps,
was elected to become the minister general of the Franciscan order; the following year he was made a cardinal. Throughout his career Matthew was heavily involved in politics and even undertook several difficult diplomatic missions
on behalf of Pope Boniface VIII. In his theology, however, Matthew of Aquasparta tended to stick closely to the ideas that he had inherited from St.
Bonaventure, especially with regard to the incarnation. More specifically,
Matthew too thought that the nature, grace, and glory of God were the reasons why the Word became flesh. Like his other Franciscan brothers, Matthew
began by asking whether the Son of God would have become flesh if humans
had not fallen. Before giving his answer, Matthew carefully considered the pros
and cons of the issue. On the negative side of things, he like John Peckham
found suggestions that the only reason the Word united with flesh was to save
sinners. Indeed, Matthew writes:

Augustine, in the sermon, *Concerning the Word of the Lord*, writes that I Tim. I, 15: "The saying is sure and worthy of full acceptance, because Christ came in this world to save sinners, of which I am the first," he says: "If man did not sin, the Son of God would not have come." And there he says that Christ does not come for another cause, unless sinners are saved; therefore, *etc*.[5]

Both Scripture and the words of St. Augustine would seem to confirm that the reason God became incarnate was to blot out sin. Without the corrupting influences of sin, there would be no need for Christ. Despite the weight of these authorities, however, there must be some reason why God assumed human nature.

With St. Augustine's arguments in mind, Matthew offers his own position. He begins, following Bonaventure, by noting that the incarnation can be considered in one of two ways. On the one hand, the assumption of the flesh can be considered to be impassable and immortal. On the other hand, it could be viewed as passable and mortal. If the first way is under consideration, then it is clear that the fall of humanity was the reason for the incarnation. On the other hand, if one is speaking of the immortal Christ, then the Son of God became flesh for other reasons and these, just as St. Bonaventure had argued, are the perfection of nature, grace, and glory.

When Matthew speaks of the perfection of nature, he does not necessarily mean that God is trying to make things better. Rather, he means that God's work is complete. In the incarnation God unites the extremes of spiritual and material existence. Human beings, the last of God's creation according to Genesis, are united with the Word, the beginning principle of all things. The best way to express the completion of creation is through a comparison with a circle in which all of nature comes from God and returns to God. When human beings proceed from, or are apart from, God, their nature is imperfect. When they are reunited with the divine, however, they are completed, because their nature is reattached to God. Thus, the incarnation is the ultimate act of completion.[6] The created order that was once outside of God returns to and is united with God. The action is not motivated by human sin; rather, it is an expression of God's love and constitutes the deepest supreme unification of two extremes.

The second reason that Matthew thinks the incarnation took place relates to the perfection of grace. Following Scripture, Matthew notes passages like Ephesians 1:22 and Colossians 1:18, which clearly indicate that Christ, as the Son of God, is the head of the church. But, Matthew argues, Christ's position as the head of the church is not so much as God but as a human being. Matthew focuses on the human nature of Christ because, like many medieval scholars, he believes that people who do exceptional work for God receive a reward. That is to say, they earn merit. It may seem a bit strange to think that a human being has the right to be rewarded by God. In fact, three centuries later many Protestant Reformers rejected the idea of merit for ordinary mortals. In relation to the work of Christ, however, early church fathers such as St. Augustine, most medieval theologians, and even the Protestant Reformers all accepted the notion that Christ could share his merit with the members of his mystical body. Now Matthew wants to say that the merit awarded to the head of the church would be the same merit awarded to the members, because Christ did not earn the merit for himself, he specifically earned his merit for the members of the church. If abounding and perfect grace is available from the merit of Christ and overflows into the universal church—just as it says in John 1:16, "From his fullness we have all received, grace upon grace"—to complete and perfect grace it is perfectly appropriate for Christ to assume human nature.

Matthew's third argument for the perfection of glory is ultimately derived from the writings of St. Augustine. Moreover, the same explanation can be found, more or less verbatim, in the works of both St. Bonaventure and Robert Grosseteste. The gist of the argument as Matthew presents it is that God wants human beings to be happy. But when human beings were made, they were created with a twofold nature: intellectual and physical. Since the object of true happiness is God, Matthew wants to say that the divine Word had to assume human flesh in order to satisfy both natures. Human beings can begin to grasp God by way of their intellectual nature through contemplation. The physical nature, however, requires a sensible object. Without a bodily object, in this case Jesus Christ, the physical nature of all created human beings would remain unfulfilled. By grasping the Son of God as having assumed flesh, our senses grasp the highest form of happiness. Matthew thinks that this strategy for creating completely satisfied human beings goes some way toward answering the question about the motivation behind the incarnation. Christ would have come even if there had been no sin, because God apparently intended the incarnation as an outcome. The incarnate Word was God's way of achieving human happiness in a way that meshed perfectly with our created natures.

THE WELL-ORDERED JESUS

John Duns Scotus follows along the Franciscan line of thought in the sense that he joined the minority position of Rupert of Deutz. Scotus, however, gives the question of the incarnation a slightly different color. In particular, he argues that the reason that the Word became flesh was born out of God's love for creation. For Scotus, probably more than for any other medieval theologian, the doctrines of the incarnation and the atonement are integrated in such a way that Christ is both the crown and the origin of the physical world. While the majority of medieval scholars supposed that God became human in order to bring about salvation, Scotus taught that the incarnation was an expression of God's overall creative plan. For this reason Scotus finds St. Anselm's explanation deeply unsatisfying. Could the incarnation really be a divine reaction to original sin? Scotus is sure that the Anselmian position is shortsighted, because it amounts to saying that the incarnation was forced rather than a free act of divine initiative. St. Thomas's position is also not quite spot-on. The Scriptures do show that Christ came to save humanity. Nevertheless, if the question is whether Christ would have come if humans had not fallen, then St. Thomas's answer must be a solid no, because humans would not have needed Christ. But that means that God's love is conditional, that human beings receive the highest form of the love of God only if they sin. That is flat out bizarre! Worse, just as Honorius of Autun had feared, it is also equal to claiming that the incarnation was motivated by human action.

In addition to these common objections, Scotus also thinks that the popular view of the incarnation as payment for sin involves a fairly dim view of what it means to be a Christian. More specifically, Scotus notes that if St. Anselm's view is correct, then believing Christians should be happy that Adam and Eve ran afoul of God. By their mistake humanity now has Christ and is saved. Hooray for Adam and Eve! They goofed up and we got Christ! What kind of Christian witness is that? It is unbecoming for anyone to be pleased at another person's misfortune. For a Christian, it is absolutely despicable. Scotus thinks that Christianity requires a great deal of charity on the part of the believer, and that means that everyone should be at least a little troubled by the human failure to love and obey God. St. Anselm's explanation simply cannot be correct, because while it gives a reason for the incarnation, it sacrifices what it means to live as a Christian. It forces believers to give up what it means to be a person of good will. On this count, probably more than any other, Scotus thinks that incarnation must have its ground in something other than human sin.

Scotus wants to say that God did not assume flesh as the result of an occasion or a single event that probably should not have happened. But in order to grasp his approach to Christ, it is important to keep in mind that Scotus envisions a very tidy and rational God. It is also important to get comfortable with two key concepts: intention and action. Intention is easy to explain. Take the act of raising your arm; then subtract the action of raising your arm. What is left? The *intention* to raise your arm. The intention is the same as the purpose or the idea that precedes an activity. The action then is the business of arm raising; the action is the outcome of what somebody means to do. To put it another way, a sculptor who wants to carve out a likeness of Hercules will not be very successful if the intention to do so is lacking. Applying these concepts of intention and action, Scotus thinks that God first intended the incarnation before actually creating anything. Just as an artist foresees the outcome of a sculpture before actually carving a likeness so too, Scotus argues, God planned on the incarnation before the creation of the universe. With this in mind, Scotus supposes that God would have known about the fall of humanity before it happened. The redemption of a sinful people was only a secondary aspect of what God was intending. In fact, it seems safe to say that the creation of human beings with free will, the fall of humanity, and the incarnation were all part of how God intended to go about glorifying creation. So the incarnate Christ was the occasion for demonstrating the depth of the divine love for creation. Rather than concede that greater good resulted from human sin, Christians can recall the love that shows through the sacrifice and respond in kind.

QUESTIONS FOR DISCUSSION

1. What is the difference between the incarnation and the atonement?
2. Did Christ come to rescue humanity or to perfect the order of creation?
3. For some medieval theologians, the rational defense of the incarnation was a spiritual weapon used during the Crusades. Are there modern parallels of fighting wars with faith as opposed to force?

5

Born of the Virgin Mary

Medicine came to medieval Europe in much the same way that philosophy did. The ideas of ancient Greek and Latin authors such as Hippocrates and Galen were transmitted into the Arab culture. Great Islamic commentators like Avicenna made their contributions, and the body of knowledge passed into the hands of monks and friars like Constantine of Africa (d. before 1098). Early conceptions of the human body, especially those linked to human reproduction, were quite fanciful. In part, this was because much of the science was based on observation linked more with philosophical speculation. For instance, physicians who followed Hippocrates developed a bizarre theory about the female uterus. They thought that the human womb was the source of various diseases, and had a tendency to wander throughout the body. It could, for example, drop to the legs and cause a spasm in the big toe. It could also cause mischief when visiting the liver, which it apparently did when it was thirsty.[1] The female anatomy was mystifying indeed, but the male anatomy was equally as perplexing. The ancient writers recognized that semen was definitely an active ingredient for bringing about life. And in the thirteenth century there are accounts of doctors instructing sterile men to pray to St. Bartholomew in order to remedy their condition.[2]

The mingling of theology and medicine in the Middle Ages was in fact quite common. The thirteenth-century Franciscan friar Roger Bacon argued that part of the reason that Adam ate the forbidden fruit was because his bodily elements were slightly imbalanced. If he ate the fruit, he would restore perfect balance and secure immortality. Thus, Adam's original sin could be somewhat explained by malnutrition.[3] But not everyone was completely content to mix the two disciplines. Isidore of Seville (560–636), for example,

77

thought that philosophy treated the soul and medicine treated the body. So too, sometime around 1140, the theologian William of St. Thierry was keen to insist that the spiritual soul was not a physical thing and that neither the beauty nor the dignity of human beings was located in the body.[4] On one side of the coin, William's concern was probably not too serious, because doctors tended to skirt theological issues. They were in fact too busy trying to determine whether or not urine or crushed sheep's lice had any medicinal value. The dangerous overlapping in the disciplines was on the other side of the coin, from the theologians who used medical knowledge in attempts to answer complicated questions. For instance, Thomas Aquinas like many others, took time to speculate about the active and passive powers that enable human generation.

Despite the fusion of medicine and theology over the course of the Middle Ages, there were some distinct shifts in thought and doctrine, due in part to the changes in the foundations of medical knowledge. More specifically, earlier theologians, such as those writing between the fifth and twelfth centuries, followed the best sources of their day, most of which were at least tied to, if not directly derived from, the theories of Hippocrates. By the thirteenth century, however, the introduction of Aristotle into the field of medicine changed the way the human body was understood. As a result, some church doctrines were subjected to revision.

The role of Mary in the story of Jesus is one place where the shift is clearly visible. Theologians like St. Augustine and St. Anselm followed the Hippocratic notions of the body and reproduction. One outcome of their intellectual background was that they believed the physical process for human generation was a vehicle for the transmission of sin after the fall of Adam. Toward the end of the thirteenth century, however, theologians were armed with a better understanding of Aristotle. This change in philosophical outlook afforded theologians like William of Ware and Duns Scotus an opportunity to remove sin from flesh and locate it more in the human soul. Since sin was no longer thought to be genetically transmitted through sex in quite the same way, the picture of the Virgin Mary changed.

THE AMBIVALENCE OF ST. AUGUSTINE

Of all of the earlier theologians to consider how sin might be transmitted from one generation to another, St. Augustine is probably the most important, because he actually engages the question of whether a human could live without sin. About 415 Augustine wrote a work in which he attacked the ideas offered by the Celtic theologian Pelagius. In the context of his larger debate about grace and the human freedom to reject sin, Augustine touches on Mary's sinful nature. Pelagius had argued that many figures from Scripture had led sinless lives; for example, he supposed that Enoch, Abraham, and Jacob were all blameless individuals. So, too, devoted women such as Deborah, Judith, and Esther all avoided sin. St. Augustine certainly shares a reverence for these and other individuals, but he simply cannot accept the claim that they were free to choose a completely blameless life. Throughout his works, Augustine states his opinion rather eloquently. In his commentary on the Psalms, for instance, he candidly states that "Mary, who was of Adam, died for sin, Adam died for sin, and the flesh of the Lord which was of Mary died to put away sin."[5] In his monumental work *The City of God*, Augustine bluntly notes that everyone, without exception, was dead in sin.

Rather than simply stand in opposition to Pelagius, St. Augustine constructs a powerful argument in which he gathers together the best sources in gynecology, logic, and Scripture in order to prove his point. Before starting out on the attack, however, he shows a bit of ambivalence about how the Virgin Mary figures into the equation. Augustine declines to comment on whether or not Mary herself was wrapped in sinful flesh. He excuses her from the debate, because including her would be disrespectful to Christ, but he supposes that Mary would have likely received more than enough grace for overcoming sin on the merit of having borne the Christ child. With Mary at least somewhat removed from the picture, Augustine starts his attack on Pelagius by appealing to Scripture. He rhetorically proposes that we ask all of the holy people from the Bible whether or not they lived a life without sin. How would they answer? Would characters like Samuel and his mother, Anna, answer according to Pelagius's formula? Would the righteous characters actually claim that they were free from sin? Or would they choose to answer using language from John's epistle: "If we say that we have no sin, we deceive ourselves, and the truth is not in us"?

Supposing that the characters from the Bible would in fact choose to express themselves in terms of a higher authority, that is, Holy Scripture, St. Augustine sets his trap. If a character like Isaac acknowledged his sin because he actually had sin, then he would be telling the truth. He was sinful. On the other hand, if Isaac claimed that he did not suffer from the defect of original sin, then, on the basis of the authority of Scripture, he would be exhibiting a form of self-deception. If he claimed to be free from sin but really was not as the passage from John dictates, then the truth certainly would not be in him. So, whether the heroic characters in the Bible would admit it or not, they all suffered from the defect of original sin. Pelagius was wrong! Everybody since the time of Adam suffers from sin. And for Augustine the sin was passed from generation to generation by way of natural descent. Every human being who is born from a womb, wherever it might have been, is infected with sin. To make the point clearly, Augustine explains it this way: human beings do not become justified by imitating the example of Christ. Rather, they are justified in Christ by reason of his grace. So too, humans are not sinners because they followed Adam's example. They are sinners because his penalty permeates human flesh.[6]

Practically speaking, how can Augustine conclude that sin is acquired through natural generation? He does so, in part, on the basis of medical observation. He is sure that human sexuality is of a completely different order from spirituality. When it comes to a sexual impulse, the human body can seem to ignore whatever the soul desires in order to take action. In order to explain that experience, St. Augustine supposes that the bodily independence is the penalty for refusing to go along with the divine plan. From there it is a short step to concluding that the physical sex act was the vehicle for the transmission of sin.[7] All of the generations that followed from Adam and Eve would be stuck with rebellious bodies. What of Mary? She is no exception. Mary was a human and was born of flesh just like any other person. She was born to Joachim and Anne, and thus Mary too descended from Adam and Eve. So Mary's flesh too should have been sinful. On the basis of a rather straightforward medical observation of the human body, St. Augustine could at least reasonably imply that Mary suffered under original sin and was redeemed by Christ just like any other human.

A CLOSER LOOK

Whether or not Mary suffered from the taint of original sin is not usually a question modern Christians ask themselves. Medieval theologians, however, had scriptural grounds for raising the issue. More specifically, when Gabriel the angel greets Mary he says, "Hail, O favored one, the Lord is with you!" (Luke 1:28 RSV). To the monks and the friars this meant that Mary must have been free from sin. Grace and sin are incompatible, and if Mary would have carried the disease of sin from Adam, the angel might have simply said, "Hi, Mary." The later part of Gabriel's salutation required an explanation, and the immaculate conception was the best one offered. In terms of devotion to Mary the popular "Hail Mary" prayer has roots as deep as the eleventh century and received its current form in the fifteenth century.

Further Reading: J. Pelikan, *Mary through the Centuries: Her Place in the History of Culture* (New Haven 1996).

ST. ANSELM

St. Anselm too worried about whether it was possible to avoid the stain of original sin. Unlike St. Augustine, however, St. Anselm is less circumspect in giving his answer. Rather than exempt Mary from the question, Anselm simply concludes that she did in fact suffer from original sin. Anselm kicks off his argument by presenting a dialogue with one of his students.[8] More precisely Dom Boso, one of St. Anselm's friends, somewhat inelegantly asks how God managed to take a human nature without sin from a sinful mass. As Boso goes on to explain, the whole issue of Mary's role in the incarnation is a bit like making unleavened bread from fermented dough. It just is not clear how Christ could be free from sin. Mary was conceived in sin, and her mother was also conceived in her sins. In fact, Boso argues, all of the people since Adam were born into original sin. Anselm gives two responses to Boso's question. The first reply appears to be something of a nonanswer. Anselm notes that once it is accepted that Jesus is God, then there can be no doubt that he was without sin. Moreover, just because there is a lack of understanding on the part of the believer, one should not be surprised that God could have managed to be born of flesh without the accompanying sin. In the same way that God created human nature, he could have restored it to perfection after the fall.

Anselm continues his seemingly wooden answer by further pointing out how much more wonderful God is for having restored a human being to a state of existence before the sin of Adam. More specifically, Anselm explains that when humanity fell, it deserved to be annihilated as a consequence for having sinned directly against God. Rather than lose existence, however, Adam existed either to be punished or to receive the mercy of God. Neither of these options would have been possible if humanity ceased to exist. So Anselm praises God for choosing to rescue humanity rather than obliterating the offenders. Anselm does not pause to weigh the consequences of what he is saying. More precisely, he does not bother to consider the relative merits of instant destruction versus protracted punishment. Instead, he assumes a much more optimistic tone and marvels at the remarkable feat of uniting the human and divine natures in one person. Boso, however, is pretty sharp; he is less than satisfied with Anselm's first answer. He acknowledges the great mystery surrounding the incarnation but pushes Anselm to provide deeper reasons. Anselm needs to offer at least some kind of insight that shows that he has an understanding of the meaning behind the incarnation, or he should remain silent.

But that is exactly what St. Anselm wants. His seemingly superficial answer is a shrewd illustration of exactly the same point that he made in the opening to his proof for the existence of God. That is to say, through his conversation with Boso, Anselm shows the demand for a faith that seeks understanding. Anselm's hollow answer was a lure. And, having now established a certain receptiveness to explore beyond the standard corporate answer, Anselm offers his second, more serious consideration of the matter of Mary. To begin, Anselm asks Boso to imagine a city in which the entire population, with the exception of one person, has committed an offense against the crown so awful that they all deserved to die. The one remaining innocent person, however, decides to reconcile the king with anyone who has confidence in his plan. Capitalizing on his good standing with the king and out of a deep sense of compassion for the people, the innocent member of the community offers to perform a service that will be agreeable to the king. In exchange for that service, the capital offense will be forgiven. The king, in his turn, recognizes the great value in the service that is offered and also knows that it would be impossible for every guilty person to show his or her support for the plan by being present on the day that the service is rendered. So he extends forgiveness to anybody who seeks a pardon through the benevolent action of the innocent person. Moreover, there is a value-added component to the service. The action of the innocent person is so great that the king decides that any person who gives offense after the service is rendered will be forgiven on the conditions that they ask for a pardon and reform their behavior. Thus any guilty person can enter the king's palace for any sin, either before or after the service is rendered, and be considered innocent, provided the individual meets the conditions of the pardon.

Anselm's little story is of course a thinly veiled description of his feudalistic conception of salvation. The people are protected by pledging an oath to the feudal lord, that is, Jesus Christ, in order to receive the grace of the king. For his part, Boso is fine with St. Anselm's illustration. He also understands that the thrust of Anselm's argument is that all people, no matter where they might be located in history, have an opportunity to share in the reconciliation since the time of creation. It really does not matter if a person lives before, at the time of, or after the crucifixion of Christ. What does matter is that people are reclaimed through the service that is provided, just as God intended. More precisely, Boso grasps the idea that Adam and Eve are part of a larger plan leading up to Christ, and it would be wrong to think that just because they lived well before the birth of Christ they were somehow outside of the bounds of God's divine plan. Expanding on Boso's insight, St. Anselm further points out that the first humans must have a stake in the reconciliation, because God created them with the intention of bringing forth all of the human beings who are brought into the heavenly kingdom.

St. Anselm insists that regardless of who the fallen person is, the ability to enter into paradise depends upon the death of Christ. To a large extent, Boso is fine with Anselm's line of reasoning, but there is still a problem, and in raising it, he brings the issue of Mary to its climax. He notes that Anselm still has not answered the question of whether Mary avoided the stain of original sin. On the one hand, if the whole human race is condemned by virtue of its sinful lineage, then it would make sense to claim that Mary too suffered from sin. Since Jesus was born from Mary, he too should have inherited the problem. On the other hand, if the sinful defect is passed on from generation to generation but Jesus was pure, then it would appear that his mother did not have an infection to pass along to her son. Using Anselm's illustration, if Christ is the innocent person, then it would seem to make sense that he gained his exemption from sin by virtue of his mother. Anselm, however, disagreeing with both options, thinks that Mary should be counted among the people who existed before Christ performed his self-sacrifice. Thus she too was made acceptable to God through Christ. With regard to Christ's freedom from sin, Anselm bluntly states without argument that Christ was pure by and through himself. Or, to put it another way, Christ is the reason for his own purity.

THE AGE OF ARISTOTLE

Several medieval scholars following Augustine and Anselm thought that the Virgin Mary was not completely pure. They thought that she inherited the sin of Adam just like any other human being. By about the mid-thirteenth century, however, scholars began to challenge the received view. More specifically, they began to pose new hypotheses that might explain how a break in the transmission of sin could occur between Mary and Jesus. One of the more curious theories was offered by Henry of Ghent. It is perhaps appropriate here, however, to say a bit more about who Henry was. Born in Ghent sometime before 1240, most likely he was from a noble family and educated in the cathedral school at Tournai. By 1273 Henry was serving as the archdeacon of Bruges, and five years later he was also the archdeacon of Tournai. In addition to these titles, Henry was also a successful scholar who taught at the University of Paris and was the regent master of theology 1276–92. He died the following year, but his theology and political activities, such as his appointment to the commission that condemned Averroistic errors in 1277, made him one of the most important intellectual figures of his day. Probably between 1279 and 1281, Henry began incorporating much more of Aristotle's thought into his theology. One place where the ancient Greek philosopher's ideas had an amazing impact was on Henry's understanding of the Virgin Mary.

In a sense, Henry's approach to the question of whether Mary was marked

by original sin is a hodgepodge of physics, medicine, and theology. Starting
with the physics, Henry notes that Aristotle's theory of motion for things
that travel in a straight line suggests a promising framework. Even more
exciting for the physicist is what happens when an object traveling in a
straight line hits something solid. The object bounces back and reverses
direction. It is hard to suppose that Henry becomes wrapped with joy at this
insight. Nevertheless, he is able to find a morsel in the observation that he
can apply to the case of Mary. More specifically, Henry is able to use the
opposing directions of a bouncing object as a means for explaining how Mary
could both have and not have original sin at the same time. To do this, however, he needs to have a practical example to frame his insight. And, he
chooses to illustrate his point by referring to a millstone. Without too much
detail for his otherwise hugely complicated description, Henry suggests that
when used in grinding, a millstone continues its forward rotation, but a bean
dropped on the stone will bounce and travel in the opposite direction. Thus,
when the two objects, bean and millstone, collide, there is a point at which
the opposite directions coincide. To put it another way, the millstone continues moving forward, but the bean moves in reverse. And at the initial
point of contact both directions are present.

What Henry is proposing is a wacky abuse of physics. Nevertheless his
point is clear, and he is able to transfer it to the case of Mary.[9] But this time,
Mary's soul is the bean and her flesh is the millstone. In Henry's account,
when Mary's soul was being created, it started its downward journey. It was
in a state of grace and all was well. When the soul made contact with the
body, however, it bounced upward. Or to put it another way, it changed
direction and entered a state of sin. Just as with the bean and the millstone,
there was the point of initial contact at which both sin and grace were present in Mary. So, on the one hand, the Virgin Mary was free from the stain
of original sin. On the other hand, her flesh carried the same defect as any
other human being that descended from the line of Adam. The whole theory sounds a bit ridiculous but, in light of Henry's understanding of medicine, it makes sense. Henry, like most medieval theologians, thought babies
were formed in a two-part process. First, there was the point at which the
sex cells connected and life began. Second, there was a point at which a soul
was injected into the fetal flesh and the organism officially became human.
Henry is sure that the theological debates centered on Mary's purity relate
to this second stage. Since a soul would smash into the flesh just as with any
child, the coincidence of opposing forces, sin and grace, makes sense. That
is to say, sin and grace can exist at the same time just as forward and reverse
can exist at the same time for a bouncing bean.

THE OPPOSITION

Not too surprisingly, nearly everyone who received Henry's theory thought it was at best very odd. The less generous scholars, such as the Franciscans Godfrey of Fontaine and William of Ware, thought Henry's approach to the Virgin Mary was downright silly. What these scholars found strange in Henry's theory, however, was not his understanding of medical science. They thought that human beings were made in the two stages, just as Henry did. So the bean and the millstone example made perfect sense. What the scholars thought was weird was Henry's claim that two opposites could be contained within the same thing. Henry's theory that grace and sin existed in Mary at the same time was like saying that something that is completely black at the same time is also completely white. Henry's theory was, however, incredibly original, and it certainly ran contrary to the authorities of his day. More specifically, scholars like St. Thomas Aquinas and St. Bonaventure stood in line with St. Anselm and St. Augustine. They all taught that Mary inherited original sin. That is to say, St. Thomas thought that original sin is passed through the generations just as human nature is. And, he thought that the infection of original sin takes place at the point when the soul unites with flesh in the womb of the mother. Once the soul and flesh are united, the child remains in the mother until it is big enough to be born. With that in mind, the question is not so much, did Mary contract original sin? Rather, the issue is, when did she contract original sin?[10]

A bit like Henry of Ghent, St. Thomas is certain that Mary became infected with original sin at the moment her soul animated her flesh. But she was sanctified, or cleansed from the sin, afterwards. St. Thomas was able to explain Mary's corruption without recourse to an analysis of the industrial arts. To Thomas, on the one hand, Mary must have been polluted with sin at animation because she was sanctified. And since sanctification is the process of cleansing the rational soul by means of grace, she would not have been sanctified prior to the infusion of the soul. On the other hand, sanctification must have taken place when her flesh was animated, because only a rational creature can sin. That is to say, Thomas thinks that before a rational soul is injected into the flesh, a body is not accountable for mistakes. So, if Mary had been subject to sanctification prior to animation, she would not have incurred original sin and thus would not have needed Christ to redeem her.[11] St. Bonaventure would have agreed with Thomas. Rather than offer too technical an answer, however, he remained the well-formed pastor. He simply pointed out that one ought to suppose that Mary suffered from original sin rather than risk diminishing the glory of Jesus.

HAIL MARY, FULL OF GRACE!

It would be remiss to discuss the immaculate conception without reference to John Duns Scotus, because Scotus came up with an explanation for Mary that, although not universally accepted in his day, did become official church dogma. Scotus did not simply dream up his version of Mary. Rather, he arrived at his position by reflecting on the opinions of the early church fathers and by allowing himself to be influenced by his teachers. The one teacher who was particularly influential with regard to the immaculate conception was an Englishman named William of Ware (1255?–?). His theology reflects the highly critical spirit that was typical of Oxford theologians. And he was probably one of the first friars to defend the view that Mary was not infected with original sin. More specifically, William took issue with the process of sanctification that was promoted by Henry of Ghent, St. Thomas, and St. Bonaventure. While the scholars influenced by the opinion handed down from St. Augustine taught that the disease of original sin was removed from Mary's flesh at the point when her soul was infused into her body, William offered what he considered to be a more prudent approach. He argued that he would rather be in error by supposing something more wonderful for Mary than make the mistake of diminishing her importance. To that end, William basically claimed that the process of sanctification described by Henry of Ghent and St. Thomas was not appropriate. Mary's flesh, William supposed, was conceived like any other human being, but at the same time that her flesh was formed, it was cleansed by God. The sanctification process was unnecessary, because sanctification is appropriate only for those whose flesh needs to be purified. In short, William taught that because original sin was not an integral part of the human body, God fixed things in Mary in such a way that the entire business of purging sin was irrelevant.

William's views, although interesting in their own right, prompted Scotus to examine the issue of Mary in a new light. For starters, Scotus followed William in thinking that original sin was not a natural disease; that is to say, he did not think that sin was something transmitted from parents to their children through the process of procreation. Rather, original sin is simply a lack of original justice. It is the absence of the supernatural gift that enables the human will to balance the sense appetites.[12] Once original sin was completely disassociated from the procreative acts of parents, Scotus was able to argue that Mary was restored to the state of original justice in a much more subtle way than previously supposed by William. Specifically, Scotus suggested that Mary's debt of original sin was prepaid by the merit of Christ. To put it another way, Scotus thought that the merit that Christ earned in the process of saving humanity was retroactive. Scotus was not blind to the objections to such a view, however. He knew that he needed to reckon with arguments such as the protest that his thesis would diminish the saving work of Christ.

The first, and most potent, objection against which Duns Scotus needed to defend himself was the opinion that the dignity of Christ would be diminished if Mary was viewed as sinless. More precisely, Scotus needed to overcome the objection of scholars like St. Thomas who thought that if Mary had not contracted original sin, then she would not need to be redeemed. If Mary was not saved, then Christ could not be the universal redeemer. Scotus, however, breaks down this objection by challenging the very notion of a redeemer. Scotus points out that Mary was free from sin precisely because Christ was a perfect mediator. A most perfect mediator, he reasons, would have a most perfect act of mediation. A perfect redeemer would intercede in the best way possible, and there is nobody for whom the act of intercession would have gone better than for his own mother. Rather than supposing that Christ liberated everyone in the same way, as St. Thomas's objection might imply, Scotus's argument is spinning on degrees of redemption. It would indeed be the perfect act of salvation if Christ merited enough to preserve Mary from original sin.

A second argument against which Scotus needed to defend himself was the claim that Mary's body was formed and physically constructed from infected seed and therefore shared in the normal punishments encountered by original sinners. That is to say, Mary suffered from thirst and hunger. When she stubbed her toe or met with any other kind of physical injury, it hurt. Had Mary escaped original sin, she would have avoided these kinds of discomforts. On the one hand, Scotus was able to dismiss this argument for its lack of medical respectability. More precisely, Scotus's understanding of Aristotle and medical science meant that he could largely ignore the idea that sin was passed like a disease from parent to child. But even if original sin was passed in this way, Scotus mused, the action of transmission is not the reason why the sin remains in the soul. Indeed, he points out that the infected flesh remains even after the sin is replaced by grace through baptism. So from a biological point of view, there is no good reason to suppose that God could not have chosen to remove the sin from Mary at the moment of her conception. God could have replaced the sin with grace and consequently inoculated Mary's soul against the sins of the flesh. On the other hand, Scotus rejected the argument on the grounds that bodily pains do not prove that Mary suffered original sin. It simply does not follow logically that just because Mary suffered physical pain, she must have had original sin. It could have been the case, for example, that God took away the pain of original sin that was useless to Mary, but God left the physical pains so that Mary could gain her own merit through them.

Scotus carefully considered other arguments that might detract from his thesis that Mary was born without the taint of original sin. In every case, however, the objections were less persuasive than the attempts to liberate Mary from sin. Even Henry of Ghent's wacky theory had slightly more value than the other Augustinian approaches. Scotus recognized Henry's contradictory explanation as nonsense; but to the extent that it suggested that Mary could have been created in a state of sin and then sanctified for the rest of her life, it had some value. In the end, Scotus determined that sorting out Mary's status comes down to a choice of three options. First, a perfect act of redemption could involve the prevention of sin. Second, perhaps Mary was in a state of sin for a moment or two but then was cleansed from the sin. Third, perhaps she was in sin for an extended period but was cleaned up at just the right time. Another way to view the menu of options is to balance the wholesale prevention of original sin, the first option, against an act of satisfaction for original sin, the latter two options. In that light, Scotus supposes that option number one is the best route to go. As Scotus would want to say, it seems probable that the more excellent method should be attributed to Mary.

Ultimately, the strength of Duns Scotus's position was that it alleviated the tension between the role of Christ as universal savior and Mary's human nature. By attributing the prevention of sin to Mary, Scotus was able to show that Mary, like any other human being, needed the grace and redemption that came through Christ. If it had not been for the merit of Christ, in fact, she would have contracted original sin. Thus, in Scotus's system, Mary could be immaculately conceived and Christ could still be her redeemer. Despite the fact that Scotus's argument solved some problems that confounded theologians, it was not readily accepted by everyone in the church; in fact, Scotus's position was quite controversial. For instance, Mary's immaculate conception was popular in areas of northern France and Great Britain but was opposed in Paris. The friars themselves became divided. The Franciscans tended to follow Duns Scotus, but the Dominicans and others remained faithful to Thomas Aquinas. One of the best illustrations of both the national and fraternal tensions playing out can be seen in the actions of Raoul de Hotot and Jean de Pouilly. Raoul was a Norman friar and master of theology in Paris. On December 8, 1308, he delivered a sermon to his brothers in which he defended Scotus's view of Mary. At about that same time, the secular master Jean de Pouilly wrote his opinion in which he urged that the church take action against those who claim that Mary was without sin and treat them as heretics. In any case, the number of Christians willing to support the Franciscan view of Mary grew steadily. By the end of the fourteenth century it was heartily defended in the University of Paris.

QUESTIONS FOR DISCUSSION

1. In what ways is devotion to the Virgin Mary expressed in modern culture?
2. Should Mary be held in higher regard than other biblical figures? Is the role of the Virgin Mary important to Christianity, or is she merely a literary starting point for telling the story of Jesus?
3. Is sin a condition, an infection, or what?

6

To Judge the Living and the Dead

Matthew of Aquasparta was tempted. As the story goes, Pope Boniface VIII sent Matthew on a political mission to Florence, Italy. In theory, the purpose of the trip was to resolve the tension between the Guelphs and the Ghibellines. Matthew was sent to heal a long-standing feud between two powerful groups: the Guelphs, who supported the right of papal supremacy over the crown, and the Ghibellines, who were loyal to the Hohenstaufens, or the royal line of the German Emperor Frederick II, against the pope. Since Matthew was an agent for Pope Boniface, who had a knack for political sword fights (see earlier), it is hard to believe that he was actually in Florence to mediate the dispute. Rather, he was probably there to further the cause of the papal party. So it is not surprising that upon his arrival in Florence a member of the Guelph party presented him with a silver cup that held two thousand silver florins. Matthew gazed at the cup for a long time.[1] What went through his mind? Was he trying to determine the right thing to do? He could accept the money, because that would be polite and would probably help to further his mission. Yet, Matthew's vow of poverty as a Franciscan meant that he could not receive such treasures. Matthew had to make a choice—further diplomacy or keeping his promise.

In a sense, Matthew must have felt that he was in a no-win situation. Yet, at the same time, choosing either option would have been quite noble. People ought to work for peace, and they should try to keep their promises. Ultimately Matthew chose politely to decline the gift. His case, however, illustrates the practical problem that medieval theologians faced when considering matters of judgment. Sometimes human beings are presented with choices where one option is obviously right and the other is definitely wrong. Other times, people confront situations that are not so clear, where it is hard to determine which course of action is the best way to go, because either path could be acceptable. If one option is better than the other and one chooses to take the lesser of the two options, would that choice amount to a form of sin? To put it another way, when weighing a choice between two good options, is it a sin if the alternative chosen is not the best? This kind of ethical pitfall is quite serious, because Christian doctrine is clear that Jesus Christ shall come again to judge the living and the dead. With that in mind, human beings need to make wise choices in order to avoid unfavorable judgments later. Peter Lombard, a twelfth-century theologian who taught at the cathedral school in Paris, set the cornerstone for medieval investigations into human free will and the choices that are made in a world which was created good when he asked the simple question, "How can the will be bad?"

A CLOSER LOOK

The nature and operation of human free will was a huge point of fascination for medieval theologians. In the latter Middle Ages in particular, differing emphases on the will led to different conclusions. For example, the Franciscan school stressed the primacy of the will over the intellect, because they thought that the will's virtue of charity was superior to the intellectual virtue of faith. Dominican scholars, by contrast, reversed the places of the will and the intellect, because reason and truth are what incline the will to act. The most famous free-will puzzle was offered by Jacques Buridan, who supposed that humans must delay choosing between options until the reason reveals the greater good. Without proper information human beings are not able to make a decision. The problem, however, was what to do if presented with two equally good options. In that case, the will would be stuck!

Further Reading: T. Shannon, *The Ethical Theory of John Duns Scotus* (Quincy 1995).

ON THE FALL OF THE DEVIL

How does one choose? That is to say, assuming that God has endowed people with free will, how do we decide to pick anything when confronted with a choice? Do you want an apple or an orange? Choosing here seems easy enough. Pick the one that you want to eat. But is it ever possible to make an incorrect choice? An even more frightening thought, is it possible for a human being to choose evil over good? The early church father Gregory of Nyssa (c. 330–95) played a bit with this latter question and found a fairly original answer.

In his work the "Great Catechism" Gregory explores the idea that evil is nothing. Gregory does not think that evil is an existing thing; rather, when someone refers to evil, they mean that one has departed from a better state. Since God has given human beings free will, when choices are made, they are done so in accordance with what is most pleasing. So Gregory is able to say that evil does not come about because God made it happen. Rather, evil exists because human beings acted recklessly and made choices that were worse in preference to the better.

That seems like a pretty abstract way to go about explaining how humans make the wrong decisions. So Gregory helps to clarify his position by using a story of the tower of Babel. Gregory tells about the creation of an angel of the earth. In our modern language, he tells the story about the devil.

THE DEVIL AS A BACKDROP

When St. Anselm began exploring the operation of the will in relation to right and wrong actions, he found all of the raw material that he needed in St. Gregory's writings. More precisely, Anselm chose to use the story of the fall of the angel Lucifer as a test case for his work. Exactly why Anselm chose to focus on the fall of the devil, as opposed to the sin of Adam and Eve, is a bit of a mystery. It may have been because in Anselm's mind the issues surrounding the first humans categorically belonged in discussions about salvation, and questions about the nature of sin were more properly placed under the flag of conversations about evil. Just as Adam and Eve were handy characters for understanding the motivation behind the incarnation, so Satan was a useful figure for thinking about evil. Some medieval scholars think that Anselm chose to focus on the story of the fall of the devil because speculating about angels was a perfectly normal thing for a medieval theologian to do.[2] This certainly makes sense in light of the fact that so many other medieval theologians spent time reflecting on the nature of angels. For example, St. Denis the Areopagite arranged angels into ranks of celestial hierarchies called choirs. Adalbero of Loan (1030) and Gerard of Cambrai (c. 1051) also wrote about angels and compared their ranks to the structures of the church. Shortly after Anselm wrote, an Englishman named Odo was so influenced by the works of the archbishop of Canterbury that he ended up defining theology as a discipline that involves speculation about God, the angels, and man.

In contrast to the view that the devil was a common theological topic, other medieval scholars suppose that St. Anselm had a much deeper philosophical motive. Anselm noticed that various words such as "nothing," "bad," and "unrighteousness" indicated a lack of something good. With that in mind, Anselm may have thought that getting a better grip on these kinds of negative terms would naturally lead to a better understanding of the positive aspects that come from God.[3] This philosophical explanation certainly would illuminate something of Anselm's genius. But there are also other, more historical reasons that may have prompted Anselm to write about the fall of the devil. First, the story of the fall of the devil, a fairly popular tale, was probably familiar to both St. Anselm and his students. Most notably the story appears in the Townley and Chester plays where Satan waits until God is busy with creation. While the Lord is busy making the world, the devil gives in to an undue sense of pride and sits on God's throne. In still other songs, the story is told in a way that the devil falls because he is rebellious and refuses to worship Adam as God commanded.[4] In any case, these kinds of performances were something like an eleventh-century Hollywood blockbuster. By writing about the fall of the devil Anselm may have been using the story because he wanted to do a bit of popular theology; that is, he wanted his ideas to be expressed in a way that would be accessible to almost anyone.

There is also a chance that Anselm used the story of the fall of the devil because he was thinking it would make sense in the context of the studies that his students were taking. For instance, his students were aware of the writings of Gregory of Nyssa, who used the story in his "Great Catechism." In fact, Gregory spent a great deal of time exploring the idea that evil is nothing. So it might seem reasonable for Anselm to capitalize on the story of the fall of the devil as a consistent vehicle for further explaining to his students what St. Gregory meant by the claim that evil is nothing.

In any case, the story of the fall of the devil provided Anselm with a nifty literary device for exploring issues related to sin and evil. Rather than get sidetracked on whether or not evil is simply a product of a lustful, fleshly existence, focusing on an angel permitted Anselm to reflect on sin in its broadest sense. Although humans have bodies, angels do not. By using an experiment with angels Anselm was able to provide an extended analogy to explain how evil can be an outcome of our free choices, as opposed to a flaw in our design that makes us susceptible to temptations of the flesh. Examining the fall of the devil also helped Anselm avoid pitfalls associated with the interpretation of Scripture. The Bible is pretty clear about how God went about creating Adam and Eve. In speculating about angels, however, Anselm was able to suppose that their creation took place in stages. As illustrated below, this proved to be an invaluable asset to Anselm's argument, because it permits him to focus on the nature of free will.

A CAROLINGIAN INTERLUDE

Earlier, it was mentioned that Anselm's thought process may have been at least partially concerned with developing an analysis of negative terms—terms that do not signify any positive existing thing. In the same way that the story of the fall of the devil may have been handed to Anselm through history, a concern about negative terms also may have come to him through the tradition of exercises that took place in Charlemagne's palace school. Anselm's concern for terms like "evil" and "nothing" is somewhat reminiscent of arguments that some Carolingian scholars confronted several years earlier.[5] Although there were nearly two centuries between Charlemagne's court and St. Anselm, it is nevertheless worth digressing into the argument for negative terms, because getting a solid grasp on the business of positives and negatives is eminently helpful for better understanding the main thrust of Anselm's work, namely, that words like "evil," "darkness," and "nothing" all correspond to a positive reality.

By way of introduction, the palace school came about because King Charles the Great, or Charlemagne, had a deep love of learning. When he coupled that love with his desire for his subjects to have an education, he essentially lifted Europe out of the dismal culture of the preceding Merovingian epoch. The center of Charlemagne's learning initiative was the palace school which served as a kind of incubator for future bishops and abbots. Since Charlemagne was essentially building a culture of enlightenment from scratch, he had to encourage foreign scholars to work in his school, because the local academic talent was lacking. The king's efforts paid off, however. Great talents such as Peter of Pisa, a grammarian, and Theodulf, a Visigoth from Spain, came to engage the intellectual life. After a number of interviews and repeated invitations, the king also enticed to his court an English monk, Alcuin of York, who unquestionably became the lead scholar. In addition to serving as an abbot, building a library, and writing a number of academic works, Alcuin even offered lessons to the king. For instance, on one occasion he dared to point out to Charlemagne that forcing Saxons to be baptized was probably an ill-conceived way to gain reliable converts for the church. In any case, the work of Charlemagne and his small group of scholars quickly began to take root, and by the start of the ninth century most monasteries had developed two distinct schools: an interior school for training monks and an exterior school for providing more secular education.

Alcuin taught several students during his tenure at the palace school. One of his disciples, Fredegis, succeeded his master both as a scholar and as the abbot of St. Martin of Tours. Although very little is known about Fredegis, his letter to Charlemagne entitled "On Nothing and Darkness" did survive. The

letter itself is an explanation of an exaggerated realist position; it explains how
the concepts in our mind correspond perfectly with objects in the world. St.
Anselm will use precisely this philosophical principle to show that the devil
actually chose evil. Fredegis starts his note to the king with the explanation
that he wanted to explore the question, is nothing something or not? At first
blush, the question seems a bit juvenile, but Fredegis is taking a simple case in
order to show how our language can easily mislead us into making bad judgments about the world. On the one hand, it seems to Fredegis that the claim
that nothing exists is the same as saying, "Nothing is something," because the
statement appears to affirm that the thing called "nothing" exists in some way.
On the other hand, the claim that "nothing is not something" would appear
to mean that "nothing" literally is "no thing." This latter position seems to be
a bit dodgy, and Fredegis thinks that he can prove that point by way of both
reason and authority.

First, on the part of reason, Fredegis points out that every definite name
signifies a thing such as wood, a stone, or a man. This would seem to be a fairly
sensible position, because whenever somebody mentions one of these kinds of
names, the thing that is signified by the name immediately comes to mind. So,
for example, when somebody says the word "man," the person hearing the
word understands that it refers to a unified substance in which all individual
men—Aristotle, Plato, and others, for example—participate. On that same
count, because the word "nothing" is a noun, it must work in the same way
that the word "man" does. Just as the word "man" governs all individual men,
so the word "nothing" also has signification and points to the subsistent reality of nothing. To put it another way, "nothing" too is a noun and picks out
the thing that it is meant to signify. On that count, "nothing" must be something. Philosophically speaking, this may appear to be a fairly naive position.
But what Fredegis is proposing is a moderately valid spin of Boethius's earlier
attempt to wrestle with the question of whether or not species and genera are
subsistent entities or merely concepts.

So much for reason; as a second step in his explanation Fredegis appeals to
authority. And he finds significant proof for his position in Holy Scripture.
Accordingly, he notes that those who are instructed in the church "confess with
unwavering faith" that God made the earth and all that is on it, angels and souls
from nothing. In the context of Christian theology, Fredegis's philosophical
project loses some of its silliness because the issue now tacitly raises the question of whether we can understand various aspects of the divine revelation.
With that in mind, Fredegis supposes that no earnest Christian would dare
question the authority of Holy Scripture. Since the Bible clearly states that all
was created from nothing, everyone should readily concede that "nothing" is
truly something of such a great magnitude that the human mind is not able to

grasp it. In fact, Fredegis suggests that it is not at all surprising that human beings are unable to comprehend "nothing." No theologian has ever fully understood the soul or an angel. If these things cannot be fully understood, how could one ever hope to grasp their origin? In short, "nothing" is something, for without the nothing, Scripture would not report that all things were fashioned from it.

Fredegis's argument was not particularly well received by some of his colleagues. What is somewhat surprising, however, is that the criticism came on two fronts. On the one hand, a contemporary named Agobard disapproved of the idea that the human soul was constructed out of an unknown substance called nothing. On the other hand, Agobard also thought that Fredegis was simply out of line in his use of philosophical reasoning. The gist of the complaint was presumably that Fredegis's argument was constructed in a way that was properly entertained in the exterior schools but was illegitimately applied to matters that were reserved for contemplation in the interior schools. Despite Agobard's protests, the application of exaggerated realism to theological questions continued. For instance, Odo of Tournai (d. 1113) used it to explain the transmission of original sin. More specifically, he pointed out that if sin turns out to be a positive infection, then theologians are faced with a nasty problem: each time a new child is born, either God creates a new soul out of nothing and adds a dash of sin, thus making God responsible for sin, or one must deny that God creates individual souls.[6] St. Anselm too was a kind of exaggerated realist. And this becomes especially clear when he makes evil a thing that the devil can choose. Anselm, however, keen to avoid the complication that makes God the author of evil, in his study of angels artfully dodges that problem.

ANSELM'S THOUGHT EXPERIMENT

St. Anselm supposes for the sake of discussion that "nothing" refers to a sort-of-something. To put it another way, Anselm thinks of "nothing" in much the same way as Fredegis. But the reason that St. Anselm thinks that "nothing" is something is because it provides the angels with a real choice. That is to say, if evil is "nothing" in the sense of a nonexistent thing, then it would be impossible for anyone to choose evil. There would be no thing to choose. If both good and evil are things, however, then it makes sense to choose between them. With that little technicality out of the way, Anselm proposes a kind of thought experiment. He asks that we entertain the idea that the angels were created in stages as opposed to being made all at once. The reason for this is that a careful analysis of how an angel is built might reveal some insights into how the angels got off track. Leaving aside the business of how God decided that halos should go above the wings, Anselm zeros in on the addition of the will. Since the angel is still under construction, it has not yet actually made any choices. Rather, Anselm would want to say that the angelic will is still a potential power; it cannot start making choices until God activates it. But here is a key insight! Anselm points out that there must be a difference between a power that comes before an act and the power that accompanies an act. The difference is very subtle. The action of God starting the will is different from the will choosing things once it is empowered to do so. It's a bit like saying that there is a difference between turning on a light and a light bulb illuminating a room.

So, assuming that the will is now active, what exactly does a new angel choose? Here again Anselm discovers another subtle distinction. There is a difference between the will to be happy and the will to be righteous. This distinction is quite handy because it illustrates the wide range of options available to the angel. The distinction also enables Anselm to point out that all of God's gifts are good. The angel is good, the will in the angel is good, and the things that the will might choose are all good. In fact, Anselm thinks that God never authors anything that is evil. But if that is true, how do we end up with sin and evil? Anselm needs only to pull together all of the pieces of his little experiment in order to answer the question. There are two reasons that sin does not come from God. First, God is only the active principle that engages the will, not the author of the actions that flow from the will. Second, the will and everything else that God created is good. So it is reasonable to think that sin or evil must live entirely with the angel. And if there is a distinction between happiness and righteousness, an angel with truly free will could choose to abandon one of these gifts. If the angel chose to preserve happiness at the expense of what is just, then the angel would fall, because it failed to preserve what is right.

So in a sense the devil fell not because of what he did, but because of what he did not do. He failed to act justly. The devil, just like any other angel, had been given the task of willing what is right. When the devil stopped willing in this way, he damned himself. Moreover, because the devil chose not to continue preserving what is right for its own sake, he was open to forms of unrestrained happiness. To make this point, Anselm reflects a bit on his proof for the existence of God. If God truly is that than which nothing greater can be thought, then it would seem to be impossible for the devil to conceive of himself as equal to or greater than God. Giving the devil at least a few points for intelligence, he must have known that he could never be like God. Consequently, Anselm supposes that the devil must have pretended to be God's equal. Perhaps one could even imagine an impetuous childlike devil creeping into a big room, sitting on the throne, and giving commands to imaginary legions while God was away creating the universe. What great fun it must have been to pretend to be the almighty force to which everything owes its existence! Then again, even pretending to be God is an arrogant thing to do! And in this sense, the devil chose to will happiness for himself, as opposed to willing what is right. St. Anselm suggests that preserving a sense of righteousness would have restrained the devil's desire for happiness.

DUNS SCOTUS AND THE DISORDERED DEVIL

The story of the fall of the devil was popular throughout the Middle Ages. In fact, the existing manuscripts reveal that the story was read by every age from the ninth century well up to the fifteenth century. For instance, the story had practical application for early Frankish theologians who were battling Pelagianism. It was woven into the twelfth-century *Historia Scholastica*, a history of the Old and New Testaments, by Peter Comester (whimsically known as Peter the Eater, because he existed on a steady diet of books). Later the fall of the devil appears in several works by the thirteenth-century scholar Robert Grosseteste.[7] Yet another popular thirteenth-century theologian to make use of the story of the fall of the devil was John Duns Scotus. In part, Scotus may have used the story because he was exposed to it during his early education at Oxford. At least this might explain in part why it appears in his theology but is not so much a part of Italian works like those of Thomas Aquinas or Dante. Scotus's use of the fall is striking for several reasons. First, he follows along with and improves upon much of what St. Anselm wrote. Second, he too uses the story to illustrate how free will can be the origin of evil, which is merely a lesser good than the good that human beings ought to choose. Third, the story of the fall of the devil was at least one foil that Scotus used to develop a doctrine of free will that became a root for generations of later scholars such as Molina and John Wesley.

The tone of St. Anselm's approach is that the devil fell because he succumbed to the sin of pride. That is, the devil wanted to be equal to or greater than God. For Scotus, the devil fell because he suffered from the sin of lust. Yet Scotus adopts most of the framework that St. Anselm had already built. Rather than simply rehash Anselm's thought experiment, however, Scotus set out to understand better how the angel's will could act in such a dysfunctional way.[8] It seems to Scotus that there are two acts of the will: to like and to dislike. Both acts are toward something positive, in the sense that in the act of disliking something, the will rejects the distasteful, and in the act of liking, the will accepts what it finds attractive. Furthermore, Scotus notes that there is a twofold aspect to liking. On the one hand, there is love or liking out of a sense of friendship. On the other hand, there is a kind of love that is born out of desire or coveting. In the case of the former, the love is about well-wishing. In the case of the latter, the love is in reference to an object that is desired for self or some other beloved.

Now Scotus is sure that these acts follow a certain order. With regard to like and dislike, he reasons that liking comes first. The rationale for this is that the only reason a person turns away from an object is because it is inconsistent with what the person prefers. That is, people must know what they like before they can dislike. Scotus then tries to illustrate his point by borrowing an example from St. Anselm's work. In the course of his explanation of how the devil managed to abandon justice in favor of being more like God, Anselm tells about a miser. He notes that the devil was like a man who reluctantly parts with his money in order to buy bread. Naturally a miser would want to hoard his money, but in order to have food it is necessary to spend the money. For Duns Scotus, this example presumably explains the point rather well. Disliking the act of spending money, for instance, is visible only in light of liking the act of saving money. With that in mind, Scotus goes on to establish an order between the two kinds of love. Here the love of friendship comes before the love of coveting. In relation of coveting, a friend is only a quasi-end. That is, the reason anything is coveted is because there is someone for whom a particular object is desired. Scotus then notes that since the end is always the first object willed—that is, it is the motive for any action—friendship must precede coveting.

Scotus next notes that the same order would obtain for disordered acts. He does not think that a muddled act of the will could start with dislike, precisely because of the conditions that he described above. So, too, disordered acts of love follow the same sequence that Scotus described for the acts of the will that take place under normal conditions. Then Scotus sets out to explore why the devil fell. He supposes that with respect to the love of friendship, the devil's first inordinate act was one he directed toward one to whom he wished well. In theory, the recipient of that love should have been God, but Scotus rules out the divine as the object of Lucifer's love, for a couple of reasons. First, in terms of friendship, it is not possible to love God too much. Scotus believes that God is so wonderful that any act of love directed toward the divine would be rendered good. Second, Scotus thinks that in an act of friendship love it would be impossible to love an object more than oneself. This must be the case on two points. First, Scotus thinks that human beings have a natural inclination toward themselves, more than toward any other creature. Second, he suspects that friendship is based on oneness in the sense that what is good for a friend has roots in what is good for one's self. At least that is what Scotus believes to be the case from what he had gleaned from Aristotle's philosophy.

So, with these conditions in mind, Scotus concludes that the devil's inordinate act was simply one of self-love, or benevolence toward himself.

Having settled how Lucifer got out of whack with regard to the love of friendship, Scotus moves on to explore how the love of coveting got out of hand. The best explanation that Scotus can find is that Lucifer appears to have coveted too much happiness. To confirm that impression, Scotus formulates four arguments. First, Scotus recalls St. Anselm's distinctions between the affection for justice and the affection for the advantageous. Lucifer's inordinate desire did not come from a sense of justice, because, by definition, no sin can flow from a love for justice. Thus the sin must have come from seeking what was advantageous. As St. Anselm had shown, a will unchecked by a sense of justice will be inclined toward what is most advantageous. On that count, the only thing to rule the will would be an immoderate appetite for happiness.

The second argument is that the sin of covetousness flows from desire. Duns Scotus thinks that any desire boils down to one of three possible motives: justice, utilitarianism, and hedonism. Now obviously the sin could not have been a result of desire inspired by justice, because if the desire was indeed honorable, then sin could not have resulted. Justice is a matter of doing what is right, and sin is a matter of doing what is wrong; they are opposites. The second choice is that of utilitarianism or what is useful. Here again Scotus is able to rule out the motive because nobody first covets what is useful. Rather, they covet whatever it is that necessitates the useful. For example, it would seem pretty odd to suddenly desire a hammer. Such tools are quite useful, but they aren't something that one normally wants unless confronted with a nail that needs to be driven or a large bug that must be squashed. With the first two out of the way, it stands to reason that the devil must have suffered from the love of covetousness that was born from a sense of hedonism. That is, the devil did it because it felt good. As Scotus would put it, the devil sinned by excessively loving his greatest delight.

For his third argument Scotus openly reasons from human beings to angels. He supposes that human beings are hardwired in such a way that the natural desire to satisfy a function requires some previous awareness of what is most in harmony with the power of that function. For example, the sense of sight carries with it an appetite for seeing. And the eye would naturally tend toward seeing the most pleasing object it has ever observed. This is true for the other senses too. The sense of taste involves the inclination to experience what is most savory. Similarly the sense of hearing always includes a disposition for perceiving what is most pleasant to the ear. That seems logical for the exterior senses, but angels do not have bodies and consequently do not perceive things in the same way as human beings. Scotus, however, is not bothered by this, because he thinks that the same reasoning applies to the interior senses. More specifically, the will, which both human beings and angels have, will seek whatever is most pleasing to the mind, if it is unassociated with any other sense. That is, the will wants the happiness that comes from delighting in knowledge of an object. On this count, Lucifer sinned because he willed what he knew was the most pleasant thing of which he could think—he willed to be God.

The final argument that Scotus formulates is slightly reminiscent of the first. It rests again on the importance of tempering the will with a sense of justice. The argument is slightly different, however, because in this case Scotus is pointing out that the will must be balanced between affections. If the will is not balanced by an affection for something else, it will operate as if nothing else will be wanted. Its actions will be one-sided. For instance, if justice is lacking, then the will will act without regard for it. To make the point more concretely, Scotus offers delight as such a thing that is necessary for keeping equilibrium in the will. If somebody were mildly sad, one would not want to become profoundly sad. Rather, our melancholy person would want happiness or something like it. Being delighted is the counterweight to being sad. Without delight, a person would be on the road to becoming absolutely morose.

Considering all four arguments together then, it seems to Scotus that Lucifer's first sin of desire was an act of coveting happiness. The conditions for the wrongful act are threefold. First, the will needs to be unassociated with a sense appetite such as sight or taste. This condition bars the way for the will to be attracted to anything that would naturally incline toward a particular sense. To put it another way, without linking the will to a sense like sight, the will would not covet a vision of what is most pleasing to the eye. Second, the will cannot be checked by justice. Without justice, or what Scotus calls right reason, the will is completely free to follow its own inclinations. Third, Scotus assumes that every cognitive power has a corresponding appetite that delights when the function of that power is satisfied. The will is the appetite of knowledge, and it is satisfied only by knowing the most perfect of knowable objects. Lucifer appears to have been in a state where he met these three conditions, and, Scotus concludes, his sin of coveting stemmed from an immoderate desire for happiness.

Having basically settled where Lucifer went wrong, Duns Scotus sets out to build on St. Anselm's thought. A good bit of the explanation for the fall of the devil relies on the notion of justice. Scotus takes a moment to clarify exactly what that means. Justice can be understood to be infused, acquired, or innate. In the first case, justice resembles what modern theologians call grace and is a free gift from God. Acquired justice, by contrast, is derived from moral experience. It may be helpful to think of infused justice as being supernaturally extended from God to human beings and acquired justice being a natural part of human nature. Innate justice is simply a matter of the will's own free activity. Now, in thinking about St. Anselm's example of an angel who loved what was good without also loving what is just, Scotus believed that such an angel would have no other choice than to covet. Since that is how the angel was constructed, such desirous behavior could hardly be considered sinful. Rather, the angel would simply be doing what it was designed to do. Roughly speaking, the scenario raises a fairly significant theological problem. If the angel could will only what he desired and could not do otherwise, then God would be cruel for punishing the angel. Similarly, if the ability to will justice was a gift from God that the divine never actually gave to the angel, Lucifer could not have sinned. How could the devil be negligent with a tool that he never possessed? With these points in mind Duns Scotus determines that justice must be innate or native to the will. Having an inborn sense of justice would enable the angel to want something both for its own value and for how it might be beneficial. In fact, Scotus would want to say that the affection for justice is the innate liberty in the will that acts as the counterweight to the affection for happiness.

It seems to Scotus that St. Anselm's work supports this interpretation. He notes that sometimes Anselm appears to be speaking of infused justice. In any case, Scotus points out, St. Anselm does at least mention that infused justice can be lost through a mortal sin. Or, to put it another way, the will's sense of justice can be lost in cases of spiritual death. Nevertheless, when St. Anselm distinguished between the affection for justice and the affection for good, he set the stage for illustrating the will as a free expression of intellectual desire. To the extent that it is an expression of an inclination, the will would tend toward what is most advantageous. But as a truly free entity it must be able either to choose what it desires or to restrain itself from following its natural inclination. So Scotus argues that a free will is not bound in every way to seek happiness. Rather, it is bound to moderate choices, to keep the intellect in check by moderating the desire for happiness and tempering that desire with a sense of justice. If the will fails in that function, the end result is sin or a disorderly act.

So how does the will get out of balance such that it would fail to moderate the intellectual desire for what is advantageous? According to Duns Scotus, there are three, and possibly several more, ways in which the failure could occur. First, the will might love the object of happiness more intensely than it deserves. Second, the will might want something before it is ready to be had. That is, the will might act with speed that is inappropriate. Third, the will might want something without having merited it. Scotus was not interested in speculating about which of the three ways led to the sin of Lucifer. But he was certain that one of these ways likely led to the downfall. Either the devil wanted happiness as a good for himself rather than loving it as a good in itself, or he wanted something before God was willing to let him have it, or he wanted to try to earn happiness rather than receive it through the grace of God. Whichever the case, Lucifer's will should have moderated his desire in such a way that the fall did not take place. More concretely, Lucifer should have wanted happiness less for his own sake than for the sake of God. If the devil failed to moderate his desire, then it stands to reason that he sinned.

CANON LAW

At the end of the day, medieval theologians like Anselm and Scotus were worried about making the right choices. They wanted to ensure that every child of God stayed on the right side of the divine commands. Thus it was important to know how the human will worked. People who poorly handled their freedom to choose were considered to be a danger both to themselves and to the others who might be infected by their actions. Both Scripture and the ancient creeds were absolutely clear that failure to will in accordance with the divine commands would inevitably lead to prosecution at the end of time. So the theologian's task of understanding the nature of moral judgment was very serious business. But medieval theologians also understood people. They knew that it was not always possible to count on members of the Christian community to act with charity toward each other. Rather, a society of people living and working in the world required a structure that could ensure stability. To that end, the church devised rules of conduct that were binding for the entire body of Christ. They developed canon law.

Canon law was not simply a power play that a few nobles with large armies imposed on the peasant class. To be sure, at times that is exactly how the canon law was enforced. For instance, during a festival of 1228, a group of students from the University of Paris decided to visit a tavern. After filling themselves with wine they took it upon themselves to argue the price with the owner of the establishment. A barroom brawl ensued. Although the students managed to get in their licks, they were driven away by the innkeeper's neighbors. The next day the students returned with their friends and avenged their loss. After vandalizing the pub and beating both the shopkeeper and his neighbors, the students continued their hostilities in the streets. Before too long, the papal representative in the village complained to the authorities. When Queen Blanche of Castile, the mother of the two-year-old King Louis IX, heard the grievance, she ordered an immediate end to the riot. Then things got ugly! The provost and his mercenary guard arrived in the village. They found the students and attacked. Several of the students were killed in the fight, and the brutal assault shocked the citizenry. Normally orders of excommunication would have been issued for such violent behavior, but the church remained silent.[9] The ecclesiastical inaction was tied to much larger political concerns concerning the relationship between the church and the university. Nevertheless, it was the responsibility of the church to punish the wrongdoers. It is also worth pointing out that well after the riot canon lawyers representing the university were busy trying to win settlements in the Roman courts. So civil claims were also the jurisdiction of the church.

The foundation of canon law is found in Scripture, and early church documents like the *Didache* (pronounced DID-a-kay) provided guidelines for right behavior. The proceedings of the church councils, such as those at Nicaea, Chalcedon, and Ephesus, also became sources for Christian law, by virtue of the authority that was invested in the church. After the fall of Rome, however, canon law was carried out locally. That is, barbarian Europe used canon law in a way that must have been as chaotic as the dynasties. The national churches operated independently, and people were bound by the laws of their own lands. So Burgundians, for example, were held accountable to the Burgundian law, and the Visigoths were subject to Visigothic law.[10] The one form of legislation that eventually did cross local borders was that of the Irish and Anglo-Saxon missionary monks. More specifically, they developed catalogs that contained lists of the various sins that people might commit and the corresponding courses of action that would fit a sinner's needs. The fragmentation of the law basically ended when Charlemagne unified Europe. Working with Pope Hadrian I, he established a basic group of canons that formed the most up-to-date statement of church law.[11] By the middle of the twelfth century, canon law finally started to become a professional discipline. Gratian wrote his defining work in which he gathered texts and explained the various types of law. From Gratian's work canon law started to be studied as a viable academic discipline.[12]

Regardless of its state, splintered or unified, canon law touched the lives of everyone. The church ruled over intensely personal matters. For example, it made provisions for proper marriages and divorce, and legislated over matters such as adultery and prostitution. Personal finance too was subject to the church courts. In addition to dealing with the Arian heresy, the Council of Nicaea also stipulated the rules for charging interest on loans. Medieval canonists continued to uphold that council decision by ensuring that borrowers were not mistreated by a lender. Wills, wages, property, taxes, and rights were all subject to canon law. When conflicts emerged, they were settled in the church courts. This is not to imply that the church dabbled only in the lives of the citizenry, however. Canon law was also binding on corporations, kings, and royal courts, and even touched the papacy. In general, canon lawyers were confident that papal sovereignty was granted by God. This was quite different from the tug-of-war between the arbitrary will of a prince and the will of the people that governed a king. But even the pope had limits; for instance, he was not allowed to change the doctrines of the church that were established by the apostles. In short, canon law governed the elections of the popes and made provisions for removing a bad pope from office when necessary (see chapter 7).

A CLOSER LOOK

Canon law certainly came with its share of complications. Shortly after Charlemagne's death, a series of councils were held with the aim of guaranteeing clerical rights under the law. But without a powerful king like Charlemagne in charge, the increasing political disorder created an environment in which secular leaders were able to accuse the clergy of crimes, attack church property, and either depose or exile bishops. It was in this context that a set of forged canon law documents were written. Exactly who wrote the documents is a mystery, but the author used the pseudonym Isidore Mercator. The forged documents were focused on the protection of the bishops but also touched other aspects of the church, including administrative authority and regulations for the liturgy. Although the documents were a ruse, they became very influential in the life of the church. For instance, Pope Gregory VII used them to orchestrate his church reforms in the mid-eleventh century. In fact, the false decretals continued to influence canon law until a seventeenth-century Calvinist pastor, David Blondel, exposed the fraud.

Further Reading: R. McKitterick, *The Frankish Church and the Carolingian Reforms, 789–895* (London 1997).

SAINTS

This is the point in the book where the saints come marching in. Making saints is one expression of canon law. Since a large number of the monks and friars mentioned throughout the previous chapters bear the title "Saint," it is entirely proper to say a word or two here about the history of sainthood as a legal process. In the early church, sainthood was not a legal matter. Rather, it was a purely theological construct and was usually tied to martyrdom. People whose lives were sacrificed as an inspiring Christian witness to others became saints.

By the fifth and sixth centuries, however, a few problems emerged. On the one hand, as more of barbarian Europe converted to orthodox Christianity, the number of saints grew rapidly. Some of the saints, like Wilfred and Bede, were not persecuted or martyred, but they undertook great preaching missions and built fantastic churches. For their labor they received the title "confessor," which attached to any saint who was not killed in the line of duty.[13] There was still a growing log of martyred saints, particularly those missionaries who tried to convert the Germanic tribes. For example, St. Boniface, who reformed the church just after death of Charles Martel, was martyred in 754. By the eleventh and twelfth centuries, several people were recognized as saints because they had rendered incredible service and had a massive impact on medieval culture. St. Bernard of Clairvaux fits under this flag. So too does St. Hugh of Lincoln, an abbot of Cluny who served as an advisor to nine different popes and helped to organize the First Crusade. The thirteenth-century founders of religious orders like St. Dominic and St. Francis also became recognized for their influence. In short, there were several avenues by which a person could be considered for sainthood, and the number of good candidates continued to grow.

On the other hand, sainthood became a problem, in the sense that there were several false alarms. Since people were permitted to choose their own saints on the basis of a contender's personal reputation, it became difficult to tell exactly who merited the title. Was the saint candidate really martyred, or did the person commit suicide? Did the nominee really make an impact on the life of the church, or was it more a case of a local zealot impressing a small village? In the case of either having too many saints or the wrong ones, the important question was, how can the church judge which applicants are valid? In the earlier periods of medieval history, the common sense way to sort out who should be a saint was to gather a committee and decide. When a church council did not suffice, bishops were asked to determine the status. From about the thirteenth century forward, however, the job of selecting a saint fell under papal control. Most notably Pope Gregory IX is credited with building the legal procedures by which sainthood is established.

By the sixteenth century, the Protestant Reformers rejected canonization, because they did not think the practice was supported by Scripture. Nevertheless, both the Roman Catholic Church and the Eastern Church continued to observe the practice of lifting up the saints as sources of inspiration. And they continued doing so because, in addition to being a legally sanctioned activity, it is an important connection to the history of the Christian community. For instance, these pages are being written on July 15. That means that today is the feast day in celebration of St. Bonaventure. So it is likely that several modern Roman Catholic priests have built their homilies for the day around the life or theology of Bonaventure. July 15 is also reserved for St. David of Munktorp, an eleventh-century missionary from England who worked in Sweden. His accomplishments include building a monastery and responsibility for several baptisms. He entered into the missionary fields because he wanted to be martyred, but the gift of ultimate sacrifice never came his way. He died in old age sometime around 1080.[14] St. David is still on the calendar, however, because his success as a missionary is meaningful to some local churches. Thus another important detail: when a saint's activities are valued by a community, the anniversary of that person's death is added to the church calendar and commemorated every year.

QUESTIONS FOR DISCUSSION

1. Is evil nothing or something? Can human beings choose evil?
2. Assuming that human beings want to choose in accordance with the will of God as opposed to what is beneficial for the self, how does one determine what the will of God is?
3. The story of the fall of the devil is not in the Bible. Are there examples in Scripture that can be used to guide human beings when choosing between two good alternatives?
4. Should the church have a separate set of laws to constrain the wills of believers, or should civil law be derived from divine law? Should divine law have any influence on civil law?

7

In the Holy Spirit

Understanding the medieval approach to the Holy Spirit is a complicated task. This is not because the doctrines associated with the Holy Spirit are tricky. It is also not because of the scarcity of sources dedicated solely to the mystical third person of the Trinity. The difficulty owes to the fact that the Holy Spirit was frequently mired in political wrangling. This is especially true in relation to the perception of the Spirit that was created during the eighth and ninth centuries by figures like Charlemagne and the Byzantine patriarch Photius. The Spirit was shaped by later political devices as well. In the eleventh century, for example, the church in Constantinople and the church in Rome split. In part the breakup was over a difference of opinion about the procession of the Spirit, but the motives for some of the Western theological positions were born out of a strong need to reject Byzantine authority. Later, in the thirteenth century, a reasonable attempt was made at reunification. It was a short-lived union, however. It failed because the merger was built on a fear of military threat, as opposed to a genuine desire for a healed Christian body. The breakup in the on-again, off-again relationship also came about because theologians were simply unable to find a shared understanding of the Holy Spirit. The ugly historical truth is that the third person of the Trinity was frequently invoked throughout the Middle Ages as a weapon to settle disputes about both land and jurisdiction. When kings and emperors wrestled, their national churches became deeply involved in the fights. When the leaders were not dabbling in doctrine themselves, they were triggering the circumstances that forced the church to fortify its teachings of the Holy Spirit.

THE CAROLINGIAN PROBLEM

One way to look at the problem of how to understand the Holy Spirit of the ninth century is to view it as a festering theological issue that came to a head when two Eastern church leaders, Photius and Ignatius, fought for the title patriarch of Constantinople. Photius came to power in 858 after revolutionaries in Constantinople had deposed Ignatius. The transfer of power was messy. Because several people still supported Ignatius, as Photius took office, riots followed. Nevertheless the change was ultimately made, and eventually Photius's enthronement was announced to Pope Nicholas I. Nicholas, however, did not rally to the cause. Rather, he supported Ignatius, partially on the grounds that a layperson should not be installed as a patriarch and partially because he was biased by Ignatius's supporters. A few years later the icy situation grew even colder when the Bulgarian ruler Boris I sent an appeal to Rome. King Boris was upset because Photius had refused to provide a bishop or a patriarch for Bulgaria.

Despite the fact that Bulgaria was well out of Pope Nicholas's protection, he nevertheless agreed to help poor Boris and sent two bishops. Unfortunately, their presence proved to be visibly unhelpful. First, they publicly criticized the Byzantine position. Then, they introduced the Western version of the Nicene Creed, which professes that the Spirit proceeds "from the Father and the Son." Photius was understandably angered by Pope Nicholas's intervention. Bulgaria was under the spiritual jurisdiction of Constantinople, which meant that Nicholas was roaming outside of his yard. The Eastern version of the Nicene Creed differs from the Western account in that the Spirit proceeds "from the Father *through* the Son." Although the difference is quite subtle, there are huge implications for understanding how the various persons of the Trinity relate to one another (see later). So, in the interests of asserting his authority and dealing with the Latin theology, Photius formally condemned all of the Western innovations, especially those related to the Nicene Creed.

Hearing about all of this petty power positioning seems to be a long way to go in order to grasp an understanding of the evolution of the doctrine of the Holy Spirit. Nevertheless, the struggle between Photius and Nicholas points up some serious questions that help to illustrate the emergence of the doctrines before they were actually cemented into Christian culture. For instance, when Pope Nicholas taught the Western form of the creed to the Bulgarians, why didn't the Byzantine emperor Michael III simply march on Rome and punish the pontiff? More importantly, how did the change in the Nicene Creed come about in the first place? This second question is easier to answer, so the better approach is to start with it. Nobody is exactly sure how the Western formulation became ingrained in the life of the Roman church. The change in the creed is visible in the churches of Spain from about the middle of the sixth century onward. The Western wording may have been used earlier, but in any case, it is in the profession used at the Council of Toledo in 589. Spain was unique among the regions of western Europe; there the creed was integrated into the Mass. Apparently the Western form of the Nicene Creed simply became a matter of custom for the Spanish church and from there spread to other regions.

By the time of Charlemagne, about seventy years prior to the Photian dispute, the change had become deeply embedded in the life of the Western church. In fact, it was Charlemagne's wrangling with the Eastern Empress Irene that solidified the phrase "from the Father and the Son" in the West. And, it is also Charlemagne's political and military maneuvering that is the key to answering the other question about the use of force. As Charlemagne was rising in power, Byzantium was declining. The Arab attacks on Constantinople had certainly taken their toll, but the East also had other problems. Most seriously, the iconoclastic controversy had a devastating impact on the Byzantine power base. The very complicated theological dispute about the proper use of religious images created tremendous unrest in the Eastern half of the church, and the violence associated with that storm led to instability in the government.

In 790 Constantine VI forcibly removed his mother, the regent Irene, from power. Six years later, Constantine suffered from a different kind of image problem. He got divorced from his wife. His divorce, coupled with rumors that he was planning to restore iconoclasm, created the perfect atmosphere for Irene to recover her place on the throne. With the help of the imperial guard, she launched a coup and deposed her son. Irene then ordered that Constantine should be blinded, in order to prevent him from ever again seizing power. Although it is hard to imagine, something in the blinding process went horribly wrong, and Constantine died. His death was shocking, and Irene suddenly appeared to be an even more irresponsible ruler. In order to maintain control, she was forced to look for allies wherever she could find them.

Meanwhile, in 773 Charlemagne captured the Lombard capital of Pavia. In the following year, the king paid a visit to Rome and while there promised to restore rightful lands to the papacy. The Empress Irene certainly took notice of the activity. She was concerned to protect her own territories in Italy. Also, Pope Hadrian I was becoming closely attached to Charlemagne in a way that could create both a powerful union and a rival emperor in the West. When Charlemagne and Irene finally came to loggerheads, it was over the restoration of both Rome's territorial jurisdiction and the papal lands. As the patrician of the Romans, Charlemagne felt free to assert himself in both secular and church affairs. At odds with Irene over the disposition of certain lands, Charlemagne set his theologians to the task of pointing out the errors of the Byzantine church wherever possible. For instance, Alcuin of York pointed to the differing versions of the Nicene Creed and noted that Rome had not officially approved the Eastern version. Pope Hadrian had a little better sense of history than Alcuin, however, and was able to demonstrate the orthodoxy of the Eastern form of the creed. Ever persistent, Charlemagne again challenged the Eastern creedal form in 810. This time Theodulf of Orleans devised an appeal to Pope Leo III, Hadrian's successor, which amounted to a request to add the Frankish wording about the procession of the Holy Spirit to the Roman creed. Undoubtedly trying to please the warrior Christian king who enabled him to take office, Pope Leo split the difference. He approved the doctrine implied by the revised Western creed but refused to change the Nicene Creed itself.

The combination of the papacy's increased dependence upon the Frankish crown for protection and Charlemagne's tactic of using the church as a weapon actually enabled the dispute between Pope Nicholas and Photius to take place. A little more than a hundred years after Charlemagne and Irene, Western leaders like Pope Nicholas were fully aware that they did not need Constantinople. Although an Eastern patriarch like Photius wielded an enormous amount of power, so did Frankish emperors such as Louis II and Charles the Bald. So hasty military intervention in areas under their control as a solution to solving theological disputes was a profoundly bad idea. This is not to say that the Frankish kings supported Pope Nicholas. Indeed, his relationship with the nobility was rocky. At the time of his dispute with Photius, however, southern Italy was a turbulent place, and the Western emperor's presence was keenly felt. Rather than go to war, the Eastern emperor Michael III tried to work with Nicholas at the outset of the dispute, but their relations soured when the pontiff lost his patience, excommunicated Photius, and asserted the rights of the Holy See. In any case, the right combination of power, politics, and creedal ingraining set the stage for the formal split between Rome and Constantinople. To put it another way, Nicholas and Photius were simply part of a huge ecclesiastical and political storm that had the Holy Spirit at its center.

A BREAK IN THE CLOUDS

Despite the political intrigue of the late eighth and early ninth centuries, one should not be misled into thinking that theologians thought about the Holy Spirit only as a means to greater political control. There were, in fact, several theologians who gave very serious consideration to the role of the Holy Spirit in God's interaction with human beings. They did it, moreover, without wrecking the structure of the church. In the eleventh century St. Bernard of Clairvaux, for example, provided an elegant explanation of the part that the Spirit plays. Remarkably, Bernard developed his insights in the first work that he ever wrote, "The Steps of Humility and Pride," which was based in part on the twelve steps of humility found in St. Benedict's rule. Bernard's choice to follow Benedict's rule, certainly no accident, may give a hint as to why Bernard wrote the work in the first place. Bernard was in charge of a very popular monastery at Clairvaux. When he opened his Cistercian community, the growth rate was alarming. During his tenure as abbot alone, the monastery acquired sixty-five daughter houses. This meant that Bernard was a busy man, probably a little pressed to provide counsel to every person who wanted to join the simple life of a monk. Bernard's little book, then, served as a clever way for him to provide counsel to the new members of his community.

According to St. Bernard, there are three related degrees of truth: the truth in one's self, the truth in one's neighbor, and the truth in itself. With regard to the first, we look for truth in ourselves when we judge ourselves. People must first possess a genuine sense of empathy in order to form any meaningful relationships with others. Precisely by being able to recognize one's own failings one begins to understand the feelings of others. If we do a good job of reckoning with ourselves, we achieve humility, which is one of Bernard's primary goals. Second, the truth in our neighbors is related to the truth in ourselves. A real understanding of others is gained only by being merciful. And, being merciful presupposes a good, solid sense of one's own misery. Taking the Beatitudes from Jesus' Sermon on the Mount as his backdrop, Bernard points out that people who extend mercy shall receive mercy. On a much broader plane, the mercy that comes from God permits the compassionate, humble person to know the truth itself, which is the third degree. Just to keep things tidy, Bernard finds correlates in the Holy Trinity for each of the degrees of truth. Jesus Christ, the Word, is the truth that works in the human mind. The Holy Spirit endows the will with love, or, as Bernard notes, the Spirit provides the gift of charity that enables a humble person to reach the second stage of love for neighbor. Finally, God the Father receives into glory those people who have been nurtured by the Son and the Spirit.

In the writings of St. Bernard and other eleventh- and twelfth-century theologians, the Holy Spirit is fully integrated into the Trinity. That is, the Spirit is rarely studied by itself. Even when the Holy Spirit became the center of a political storm, the Father and the Son were still part of the conversation. The Holy Spirit is an inseparable part of the Trinity; it is the divine love that makes human beings charitable. Just as words help the mind to discover truth, so too the Word, or Jesus Christ, helps the intellect to know the first truth, that of humility. The Holy Spirit is guide for the second level. It attaches to the will.

That is, Bernard thinks that when the Holy Spirit came to earth, it found the human will in a rotten condition, because it had been infected by the flesh. In a sense, Bernard is driving at roughly the same thing that St. Anselm was when he talked about the will as the mechanism for pursuing happiness (see chapter 5). But there is a major difference between the two thinkers. For Anselm the will is held in check by an innate sense of justice; that is, a source of truth is programmed into the soul. By contrast, St. Bernard is a bit more mystical. In Bernard's framework, the Holy Spirit had to work on the human will until it was able to be merciful and loving. It was the union of the Holy Spirit with the human will that gave rise to charity. That is what enables us to love our enemies. When a soul is conditioned in such a way as to be enlightened by the truth and inflamed by love, it is made acceptable to God. So truth is something that must be both sought and discovered.

Knowing what it is that makes human beings charitable, Bernard offers his famous twelve steps of humility and pride. Rather than list all twelve here, it will be more economical to say a word about each of the three groups into which Bernard divides the steps. The first group of six steps or behaviors is what one can do to keep from showing contempt for others. For example, step two is to not love one's own will. Presumably this would entail accepting the Holy Spirit and the gift of charity that extends to other people. Similarly, step five is to confess one's sins. It is clear from what Bernard said about the truth in one's self that without the confession of sins, genuine compassion for others would be impossible. The second group contains four steps that all relate to avoiding contempt for superiors. Keeping silent until questioned and admitting that one is lesser than others are both required behaviors of this step. Finally, Bernard's third group of two steps is in relation to God. These are always remaining truly humble and speaking in a reasoned, low, voice. For St. Bernard, if one knows the steps that ascend to humility, then one also knows the steps that descend to pride. To put it another way, one can move either toward God or away from God on the same stairway to heaven.

Despite the eloquent theology by scholars like Bernard that teaches Christians to be charitable toward others, the poor relations between the East and the West continued well after the time of Charlemagne. By about 1009, Rome and Constantinople had stopped all meaningful contact. Forty-five years later, the diplomatic affairs became so strained that the church formally split. This is not to say that the church just had a really bad day in 1054. Rather, the break between the East and the West was a continuation of the issues that had been present since Charlemagne squared off with Irene. The problems were in fact so chronic that the impact of the separation between Rome and Byzantium hardly would have been noticed by the people who were living during the period. Several church administrators and imperial politicians were involved in the event, but the Christian community in general probably took little notice of the activity. The church had stalled. The same questions about who should have jurisdiction over Rome and southern Italy had continued.

THE STORM RAGES ON

Although the church continued its bleak march toward disunity, there were some bright spots in the process of dissolving the visible body of Christ. For instance, during the eleventh century some of the more tricky questions, like those related to the procession of the Holy Spirit, had been eased. Pope Leo IX (1049–54) himself had even offered an explanation for the Spirit that defended the orthodoxy of both formulas. What is even more curious about the formal split between Byzantium and Rome is that during the mid-eleventh century the key ingredient for unification emerged: a common enemy. The Normans had been invited into southern Italy in 1016 to serve as mercenaries for one of the Lombard kings. As it turned out, they were very good at their jobs, and in a relatively short period of time they had managed to capture part of the country for themselves. By 1030 they had created their own principality. Sixteen years later they had significantly expanded their territory in southern Italy by capturing most of Apulia and Calabria. This new aggressive threat in an area where the Eastern emperor had limited reach should have proven to be the perfect glue to bond the East and the West. Nevertheless a rather inflexible group of key people who, for various reasons, simply could not see past their own preferences for certain church customs failed to seize the opportunity to unite. More specifically, the patriarch of Constantinople was extremely intolerant of the West, and Pope Leo IX excelled at making regrettable strategic decisions.

Perhaps the worst decision that Leo made was in May 1053. Going against the advice of his chief advisor, Peter Damian, Leo IX thought it would be a good idea to set out on a military campaign to protect his papal state from the marauding Normans. Leo, however, was grossly underprepared for the fight. The pope knew that the papal army was no match for a murderous band of seasoned mercenaries, but his plan was to secure victory upon receiving reinforcements from the Byzantine army. Unfortunately, he was unable to find the much-needed help in time. Without the aid of their allies, the papal army was easily defeated and Leo was captured. Surprisingly, for a murderous band of seasoned mercenaries, the Normans treated Leo very well. Permitted to keep contact with the outside world, he continued to run the affairs of the church through both correspondence and reliance on faithful agents. But the Norman captivity kept him largely out of circulation, so to speak. Leo's stupidity ended up angering virtually every important leader in medieval Christendom. The Byzantine emperor was dismayed by Leo's behavior, because the pontiff's actions amounted to dabbling in an area where Rome had no jurisdiction. The Western emperor Henry III was equally unimpressed with the pontiff's strategic savvy. Without the prospect of a rescue party, Leo remained in captivity for nine months, setting the stage for the final split between East and West. In order to understand the difficulties that compounded the problem, however, something must be said about the other key player who demonstrated remarkable levels of inflexibility and poor judgment: the patriarch of Constantinople, Michael Cerularius.

Just prior to Leo's useless show of force, the Byzantine emperor had enjoyed a string of military victories, making some small gains in southern Italy and reconquering both Syria and Bulgaria. This imperial success translated into a sense of national pride, and the patriarch of Constantinople appears to have grasped something of the patriotic atmosphere. He presented himself as a fiercely anti-Latin clergyman when he shut down the Roman churches in Constantinople in 1053. The catalyst for his action was a letter in which the metropolitan of Bulgaria both defended the Eastern practice of using leavened bread in the Mass and attacked the Latin practices for not observing the same customs. Presumably the recipient of the letter, the bishop of Trani in Apulia, was supposed to carry the complaint to the pope. Because the letter basically accused Rome of breaking the unity of the church, it tacitly questioned the range of the pope's authority.[1] Thus, the relations between the East and West grew even more adversarial. When negotiations between the imprisoned pope and the patriarch, Michael Cerularius, opened, it is difficult to know whether the latter initially intended to treat the pope as an equal or if he was interested in subjugating the pontiff. Whichever was the case, when Cerularius made contact with the papal legates from Rome, he was deeply offended upon hearing Rome's claims of primacy. Consequently Cerularius struck a very public position in which he asserted that Rome and the East would never be united.

Recognizing the immediate political and military needs for a reunion between the churches Leo, still held captive by the Normans, tried to solve the problem with Constantinople by sending his faithful agent and longtime friend Humbert of Moyenmoutier (c. 1000–1061). This proved to be Leo's second fatal mistake. A staunch reformer, Humbert was fanatically opposed to ecclesiastical abuses. He was theologically trained, had a background in Greek, and was skilled in law. A formidable scholar, Humbert was also amazingly stern in matters related to the primacy of Rome. When he arrived in Constantinople, he met with the equally unreasonable Michael Cerularius. The two men sparred with words, each failing to grasp the depth of his own rigidity. Then, on April 19, 1054, Pope Leo IX died. Humbert was out of time. With the death of the pontiff, Humbert probably knew he had lost the legal basis for his role as a negotiator. Worse, he certainly saw that the talks had completely broken down. Rather than retreat and allow the situation either to fester or to deflate with time, Humbert acted quickly. On July 16, 1054, he walked into the Church of the Hagia Sophia and, in front of the entire congregation, placed on the altar an order of excommunication for the patriarch and his supporters. Then Humbert walked out. The give-and-take between the East and the West did not end with Humbert's rash actions. In fact, relations between the Byzantine church and the church in Rome continued to ebb and flow for quite some time afterwards. Nevertheless, 1054 is a turning point in the history of the church and one of the lowest points in the struggle for unity.

There are some ironic points about the separation between the East and the West. First, in the theological sense, the Holy Spirit was a bone of contention. But Christ ordained only one church, and the Spirit is what is supposed to hold it together. In bringing about a division in the church, the key players throughout the ages lost sight of the divine architecture. Second, the Holy Spirit is the agent that makes human souls charitable, but it was precisely the lack of charity among the clergy that led to the disunity. Third, less than five hundred years after Humbert's activities, the Western church would divide again. The division that came in the form of the Protestant Reformation would end up raising one of the more curious questions an historian can ask: since the Christian community had already split once, why didn't the Protestant Reformers seek asylum in the East? The answer to the question is really a matter for sixteenth-century scholars to answer. Whatever the reason, in the run-up to the Protestant Reformation, the Holy Spirit was again invoked in the process of questioning papal sovereignty.

IS THE STORM OVER YET?

Like the works of St. Bernard of Clairvaux, John Duns Scotus's work on the Holy Spirit contains some valuable insights that reveal something of the Western theologian's concern to help bring about greater Christian union. The unifying themes in Scotus's thought are not surprising, however, because he himself lived during a period in which the spirit of reconciliation became an important issue. Yet grasping the tone of that general feeling means having to unpack the circumstances that shaped it. The most important influence on the events that Scotus experienced was the impact of Pope Gregory X (1271–76). Pope Gregory had a strong desire for Christian union, in large part because as a young man he had participated in a Crusade. Having thus seen firsthand what kind of force was required, he knew that joining forces with the East would be the key to liberating holy places like Jerusalem and the rest of Palestine. To that end, when Gregory became pope, he surprised a number of people by immediately proposing a union with the Eastern church. The Byzantine emperor, Michael Palaeologus, agreed, and Gregory arranged for a great council that would bring about both church reform and Christian reunion. In fact, at the Council of Lyons he temporarily put an end to one of the longest running quarrels in church history: whether or not to grant the double procession of the Holy Spirit.

By bringing a general council into play, Gregory enabled scholars to focus on the central theological issue that divided the two empires. More specifically, the Eastern church with its headquarters still in Constantinople clung to its contention that the Holy Spirit proceeds directly from the Father. This rationale permitted theologians to emphasize that everything must come from a single source, which is God. In order to keep the three persons of the Trinity straight, Eastern theologians also argued that the procession of the Holy Spirit is characteristic of its individuality. That is, just as being unbegotten belongs to the Father, and being eternally generated is proper to the Son, so procession marks the Spirit. The church in Rome, by contrast, advocated for a double procession. Following along the lines of what St. Bernard had taught much earlier (see chapter 2), Western theologians argued that the Holy Spirit was produced by the love that is shared between the Father and the Son. The double procession is required to prevent all kinds of strange subordination theories. That is to say, Western theologians thought that the double procession ensures that the Father and the Son are on an equal footing, so no matter how one views the Holy Trinity, there is an absolute coordination or balance among the three persons. Boiled down to the bare bones then, the theological argument between the East and the West was about whether the Father is the only source of the Spirit.

To a certain extent, the fact that the Greek and Latin churches came up with two entirely different theological explanations for how the Holy Spirit is sent into the world is understandable. In part, the problem is rooted in different understandings of Jesus' farewell speech to the disciples in the Gospel of John: "When the Advocate comes, whom I will send to you from the Father, the Spirit of truth who comes from the Father, he will testify on my behalf" (John 15:26). On the one hand, Jesus specifically says that he will send the Spirit. On the other hand, the Lord also clearly says that the Holy Spirit proceeds from the Father. What Jesus does not say is that the Spirit proceeds from both the Father and the Son. Then how does one make sense out of Jesus' role in the sending of the Spirit? Either he sends the Spirit or he does not. Since Scripture is not particularly clear on the point, some kind of reasoned explanation for the faith is warranted. Moreover, on the basis of this scriptural ambiguity, along with an obvious lack of charity by many of the rulers and theologians mentioned above, the different interpretations were refined, expanded, adopted, and publicized throughout the respective empires.

So when Pope Gregory X set out in 1272 to heal the rift that grew out of these differences, he began by summoning the best theologians for his gathering. St. Bonaventure himself set the agenda for the meeting and, during the second session of the council, even preached a sermon on the reunion of the church.[2] Bonaventure's good friend, one of the French king's most trusted advisors, Odo Rigaldi, helped to organize the event and lent his keen intellect to the proceedings. Robert Grosseteste was also a participant, and the sermon that he delivered to the council was so poignant that Duns Scotus both read and quoted it a few years after the meeting concluded. For the Eastern church, Emperor Michael Palaeologus sent his own delegation of fairly impressive representatives. For instance, Germanus III, the ex-patriarch of Constantinople; George Acropolites, an accomplished lay theologian; the archbishop of Nicaea; and a few other notables were also conference participants.[3] In the end, the work of the council went well, and as would be expected with so many gifted scholars in attendance, an agreement between Rome and Constantinople was ultimately reached. The bottom line was that the Greeks embraced Roman doctrines but kept their own statement of faith.

Despite both the willingness to cooperate on the part of the key leaders and the recommendations of some of the most respected theologians in Europe, the work of the Council of Lyons did not endure. It failed because the ultimate motivation for the council was not really a desire to find theological truth; rather, the powers in the East agreed to council because of a legitimate fear of military threat. Michael Palaeologus had recently stabilized his empire after yet another round of unrest. At the same time that the emperor was coming to power in the East, Charles I, count of Anjou, had become the king of Sicily. This meant that the French crown was within striking distance of Constantinople. Eager to prevent an attack on his newly settled empire, Michael hoped that a union between the churches would prevent Charles from launching an attack. To that end, he made the necessary deals with Pope Gregory before the council actually gathered. The Eastern church would agree to the Roman creed with its reference to the double procession of the Holy Spirit, and it would accept the primacy of Rome. In exchange, Pope Gregory would make sure that Charles did not attack Constantinople. Despite the fact that the top tier of the church administration ratified the decisions of the Council of Lyons, the patriarch of the Greek monasteries and a large number of the clergy in the East rejected the terms of the agreement. Simply put, they thought that Rome had received too many concessions. Almost as soon as it was implemented, the great compromise began to erode.

Although there were quite a few dissenting voices in the East, several scholars in the West continued to try to find ways to uphold or reaffirm the church union. For instance, probably about twenty years after the Council of Lyons, Duns Scotus proposed a line of argument that reflected a desire to blend the ideology of the two empires. Scotus ardently believed that the church is the communion of the faithful, and in his attempt to preserve the body of Christ he began a struggle to find clear insights into the person of the Holy Spirit. His study begins with a great sensitivity for the single procession of the Holy Spirit. More specifically, Scotus began by acknowledging that there were several ancient Greek authorities that could be used to support the Greek view of the Spirit proceeding directly from the Father. He noted that John of Damascus taught that the Holy Spirit comes from the Father rather than the Son.[4] The Greeks also argued that the double procession of the Holy Spirit should be ruled out because the teaching is not expressly stated in Scripture. As Scotus observed, "according to the reason of the Greeks: nothing is held as an article of faith unless it is contained in the Gospel, or at least in the New Testament Scripture; but that the Holy Spirit proceeds from the Son is not expressly seen in the New Testament; therefore, etc."[5] This was a curious point, however, because what is testified to in Scripture is codified in the creeds. And Scotus noted that the double procession is defensible as an article of faith. To be sure, the creed states:

Et in Spiritum Sanctum	And in the Holy Spirit,
Dominum et vivificantem,	the Lord and giver of life,
qui ex Patre *Filioque* procedit,	who proceeds from the Father *and the Son,*
qui cum Patre et Filio simul	who with the Father and the Son together
adoratur et conglorificatur;	is adored and glorified,
qui locutus est per Prophetas.	who spoke through the prophets.

How could the church fall apart when the substance of faith is so obvious? The tension between the Greek position and the teachings of the Roman Catholic Church caused Scotus to suspect that the problem related to the double procession of the Holy Spirit may be more a matter of misunderstanding than logical inconsistency. Indeed, the stumbling block could be a simple communication problem. That is, maybe the dispute is more verbal than real. On that count, the reason that the East and the West have a hard time shaking hands is because a matter of wordplay prevents them from getting along.

Among the important theologians at the Council of Lyons were Humbert of Romans, the general of the Dominican order, who urged greater study of

Greek resources, and William of Moerbeke, the famous interpreter and translator of Greek sources. One of the most impressive speeches presented at the gathering, however, came from the bishop of Lincoln, Robert Grosseteste, who apparently helped to resolve the conflict between the East and the West by persuading the delegates to recognize that they were engaged in a battle over words rather than truth. It must have been an impressive speech indeed, as Scotus quoted a substantial portion of it:

> The opinion of the Greeks is that the Holy Spirit is the Spirit of the Son, not proceeding from the Son but only from the Father, nevertheless through the Son; and this opinion is seen to contradict us, because we say that the Holy Spirit is to proceed from the Father and the Son. Yet it so happens that if there are two wise men, one Greek and the other Latin—and each of the two truly are lovers of the truth, and not one's own speech, this violent controversy can be investigated in detail, and it can be shown that in the end, both sides for the controversy itself are not truly real, although it is verbal; otherwise either the Greeks themselves or we Latins truly are heretics. But who hears these authors, such as John Damascene, the Blessed Basil, Gregory the theologian, and Gregory of Nyssa, Cyril and similar Greek fathers, to declare heresy? Who in particular would argue anew the heresy of the Blessed Jerome, Augustine, and Hilary and with similar Latins? Therefore, it truly is that the sayings are not under a declaration of contrary expressions that stand opposed to holy opinion; indeed, in many places it is said (just as this "of this" and so this, "by this" or "from that") in different ways by chance that would suggest to the subtle and discriminating intellect contrary words and not a disagreement of opinion.[6]

Robert Grosseteste was one of the most famous teachers of the thirteenth century, a formidable thinker and an authority on all of the authors that he mentioned. In fact, his translations of their works were used by many subsequent generations. Thus, by quoting him, Scotus may have wanted to remind his readers of the spirit of reconciliation that pervaded the council. But by reproducing a part of Grosseteste's speech, Scotus was also appealing to the wisdom of the one theologian who had peered further than anyone else into the Greek sources.

The main point that Grosseteste was making is pretty clear: the Greeks and the Latins have nothing to argue about. By citing the particular passage from the bishop of Lincoln's speech, Scotus was reminding theologians to observe the difference between real disagreements and pseudodisagreements. Indeed, real disagreements occur when the statements offered by the disputants are logically inconsistent, that is, when the disagreement is one in which it is logically impossible for both positions to be true. For example, "St. Thomas

Aquinas was chubby" and "St. Thomas Aquinas was not chubby" results in a direct conflict. By contrast, pseudodisagreements or apparent disagreements happen when the disputants are talking about the same thing but fail to recognize it. For example, the statement "St. Bonaventure was the Seraphic Doctor" is not logically inconsistent with "John of Fidanza was the Seraphic Doctor," because both statements are in reference to the same person. But two people who don't know much about the great Franciscan theologian could fight about whether John or Bonaventure was the Seraphic Doctor. With that in mind, Scotus is convinced that the problems surrounding the procession of the Holy Spirit are more akin to the latter case: they are centered on a pseudodisagreement.

A LITTLE BIT OF WISDOM

If the dispute between the Greeks in the East and the Latins in the West includes a bit of wordplay, then the next task is to show how the discussion got off track. In doing this, Scotus upholds the Catholic position that the Holy Spirit proceeds from both the Father and the Son.[7] Yet this claim by itself does not help to solve the problem. Rather, getting to the bottom of the issue will require an understanding of how the various persons of the Holy Trinity relate to each other. St. Augustine offers some help on this matter by explaining that the Holy Spirit is produced by the mutual love that is shared between the Father and the Son.[8] As noted above, this implies that the Father and the Son are coequals in producing the Holy Spirit. Medieval scholars generally accepted St. Augustine's explanation, sometimes without seriously considering that it appears to be exactly the opposite of what the Greek church wanted to say. Rather, they were more concerned to maintain the balance between the persons of the Trinity. As Duns Scotus's contemporary, Henry of Ghent, put the matter when considering whether or not two persons could originate from one source,

> [t]his question touches on the controversy concerning the procession of the Holy Spirit. In which it is indeed said that the Holy Spirit does not proceed from the Son; it is said that neither person emanates from a person that is from nothing; it emanates from a remaining one, because these two persons emanating are the Son, who emanates by the mode of nature, and the Holy Spirit, who emanates according to the mode of the will.[9]

So Henry did recognize that that Greek model calls for the Son to proceed from God's intellect and the Holy Spirit to proceed from the will of God. But

Henry did not do much to harmonize the Greek and Latin positions effectively. Rather, he simply pushed on to assert the standard Roman, Augustinian position.

Yet St. Augustine's explanation may not be as straightforward as it appears. In fact, it forces us to acquire a deeper understanding of the persons of the Trinity in the sense that we must recast the problem in terms of whether or not the Son plays a role in the production of the Holy Spirit. Looking at the problem in this way may make it easier to see how the Holy Spirit and the Son relate to each other and to the Father. With this in mind, Scotus, a bit more like the Greek theologians, discusses the pouring out of the Spirit as a process of "spiration." That is to say, he thinks that the Holy Spirit issues forth by an act of will and proceeds from the Father. The Son, by contrast, is begotten from the Father. This means that the Son is generated, as opposed to being willed, from God. In reflecting on these two processes, Scotus supposes that there is a certain order that must obtain between them and that, by better understanding them, we will be in a position to see exactly how the Spirit and the Son relate to each other. What is interesting about his approach, however, is that by arguing for a sequence from generation to spiration, Scotus fell into a genuine dispute with Henry of Ghent, one of his own Western Roman Catholic colleagues.

When Henry of Ghent considered the issue of the Holy Spirit, he forcefully argued that there was no special order between generation and spiration. Roughly, Henry's opinion was that there cannot be an order among these actions because such an arrangement might suggest that the Son and the Spirit do not have the same status. That is, when considering the relationship between the Father and the Son, it is perfectly normal to recognize that the Son is produced from the basic constitution of the Father. In Henry's words, the Father produces the Son by way of his nature. Yet, this does not mean that the Holy Spirit is less consequential because its origin resides in the divine will. It only means that the Son and the Spirit are produced in different ways.[10]

Henry wanted to ensure that all three persons of the Holy Trinity were considered both eternal and equal. A special order between generation and spiration might, Henry feared, imply that the Son existed before the Holy Spirit. Further, by placing an emphasis on the order, one might be suggesting that the persons of the Trinity are the results of different parts of God. For Henry of Ghent, ordering the two relationships of begetting and spirating could threaten the orthodox understanding that God is three in one. In strict opposition to Henry's view, however, Duns Scotus argued that there must be an order and that generation or begetting comes first.

The trick for Duns Scotus is to explain how two different relations can be ordered logically but remain the same in reality. To make this point, he likens the Father, Son, and Holy Spirit to fire, heat, and dryness. More concretely, Scotus notes that heat and dryness are both effects of fire. Yet, the action of drying does not happen unless it is preceded by the action of heating. Obviously things can become dry without the use of heat and Scotus freely admits that point but he wants to say in cases where fire is being used, heat and dryness characteristically operate in sequence. Moreover, he also wants to claim that if a damp object is put next to a fire it will communicate heat and dryness at the same time. Or to put it another way, the dryness is in the heating and the heating is in the dryness.[11]

What Scotus is trying to convey is that fire can produce heat and dryness, just as the Father can produce both the Son and the Holy Spirit. Just as heating is not the same as drying, neither is begetting the same as generating. Heat must produce warmth before the dryness from a fire can occur. In the same light, the Son must be generated before the Holy Spirit spirates. Nevertheless, the warmth that radiates from the heat and the dryness is the same, just as the will of the Father is the same principle in producing the Son and the Holy Spirit.

In general, Scotus thinks that by both bearing in mind the comments offered by Bishop Robert Grosseteste and focusing on the relations between the Father and the Holy Spirit, the dispute between the East and the West can be straightened out. The problem stems from mistaking the will of the Father for the person of the Holy Spirit. This is particularly true in the case of John of Damascus's position when he writes, "We say for the Holy Spirit, from the Father proceeding and in the Son resting."[12] If John of Damascus had been referring to the divine will, the statement would have been right on target, because the will, which is the principle of spiration, is "from the Father in the Son." Indeed, Scotus notes, the Father communicates his will to the Son. And by saying, "resting in the Son," he would not be saying that a new principle proper to the Son is then communicated to the Holy Spirit. Rather, the will rests in the Son until it is passed to the Holy Spirit. Unfortunately, Scotus points out, John of Damascus was talking about the person that is the Holy Spirit and not the will that is spirated. Hence, at least this particular part of the Greek father's work should be disregarded.

Perhaps the more serious objection to the double spiration was the accusation that the Western view is not found in Holy Scriptures, and Scotus does concede this point. Nevertheless, he also argues that the Christian faith contains several truths that are not explicitly found in Scripture. For instance, he notes that the creeds describe Christ descending into hell, which is not taught in the Gospel.[13] It is, however, held as an article of faith and is considered to be an important part of our Savior's victory over death. Also, the sacramental life is not completely spelled out in the Holy Scriptures. As Scotus explains, Christ did not teach everything pertaining to the dispensation of the sacraments. Rather, he said to his disciples, "I have yet many things to say to you, but you can not bear them now; when the Spirit of truth comes, however, it will teach you all the truth."[14] The simple truth is that there are many places in Scripture where the Holy Spirit teaches the disciples, and, Scotus reminds his readers, it is precisely those teachings that have been handed down through the traditions of the church.

A CLOSER LOOK

Devotion to the Holy Spirit was expressed in a variety of ways during the Middle Ages. One of the most impressive movements was started by Peter of Marrone, a Benedictine monk who wanted a more contemplative life. He retreated to the mountains in Marrone, Italy. The disciples who gathered around him became known as Celestines, a religious order that was dedicated to the Holy Spirit. They even adopted a symbol that reflected their enthusiasm: a cross wrapped in an S. When Peter was eighty-five years old, a church council, believing that they had been inspired by the Holy Spirit, elected him to the papacy. Although he was a very poor church administrator, Peter became well known for his protection of the Spiritual Franciscans, a group dedicated to the strict observance of poverty and the age of the Holy Spirit.

Further Reading: *Monks and Nuns, Saints and Outcasts: Religion in Medieval Society; Essays in Honor of Lester K. Little,* ed. S. Farmer and B. Rosenwein (Ithaca 2000).

ANTICIPATING THE AGE OF THE SPIRIT

Besides tampering with the actual structure of the church, there were other occasions to focus on the Holy Spirit. In the mid-thirteenth century several people, mostly Franciscans, prepared for what they thought would be a new epoch in history, the age of the Spirit. Their behavior was something akin to millennial fever. Understanding how such delirium could take root in the middle of a century requires a glimpse into the prophecy that prompted the excitement. The people who were anticipating the new age of the Holy Spirit were following the predictions of a monk named Joachim of Fiore. As a young man, Joachim had traveled to the Holy Land on a pilgrimage. The range of human suffering that he saw along the way changed his life. Upon returning to Sicily, he entered the Cistercian monastery and began working as a lay preacher. Eventually Joachim formally joined the monastery and was ordained in 1168. About nine years later, he was elected abbot. Joachim, however, did not have much interest in administrative life. Rather, he was suited to scholarship, and to that end he asked for permission to move to another monastery. His request was granted, but by 1191 Joachim had set out to establish his own, more austere branch of the Cistercian order. Throughout his career Joachim developed several provocative ideas. His fascination with the Trinity, however, formed the foundation of his prophecy. More specifically, Joachim's method of correlating the three persons of the Trinity to the epochs of creation, in combination with the coincidental emergence of the mendicant orders, gave his work an amazing clout.

In his reading of the Bible, Joachim found a kind of mystical insight that portrays human history as a three-part process, progressing steadily toward God. The first stage is the age of the Father. The era essentially recorded in the Old Testament, it spans the time from Adam to Jesus. By Joachim's reckoning, the age of the Father lasted for exactly forty-two generations. The incarnation marked the beginning of the second period, the age of the Son, which is recorded through the stories of the New Testament. This second age was to last as long as the first. As Joachim did the math, the second age would end in the year 1260. Joachim foretold the culmination of history in the third age, the time of the Holy Spirit. This would be the greatest of the three ages, because it amounted to the full unification of God and creation. Moving from the second to the third age would not be easy, however. In fact, the process that Joachim described was frightening. Before entering the age of the Holy Spirit, there would be a period of great suffering. The antichrist would be loosed upon the world. In short, Joachim's prediction looked a bit like the end times. The one consolation that he foresaw in the transition between ages was that a group of spiritual men would emerge to lead the faithful. The first group that Joachim described was an order of preachers. The second group was an association of humble contemplatives.

Some people naturally supposed that the Dominicans and the Franciscans were the two groups of spiritual leaders that would bring the faithful into the new age. In particular, the poor, humble servants of St. Francis appeared to fit Joachim's description. What ultimately propelled the prophecy into the general culture, however, was its popularity with several of the more zealous Franciscan friars themselves. Some of the friars had keyed in on St. Francis's lessons about poverty and supposed that strict adherence to their vows would ensure their success in actualizing Joachim's prediction. It was not, however, the entire Franciscan order that thought that Joachim's teachings were instructive. Rather, it was a range of Franciscans, including scholars and preachers, who found a fascination with the millennial fantasy. After studying Joachim's work, many of the friars became convinced that the only way to bring in the new era was to end the general laxity related to the observance of poverty within the Franciscan order. Their task was not easy. Pope Gregory IX (1227–41) had been providing tremendous support for the mendicant orders. He was even willing to alter the rule of poverty for the Franciscans in order to help ensure that their basic needs were met. Roughly four years after the death of Gregory, the order was in full possession of property. With only fifteen years left to go before the inauguration of the new age, the more literally minded friars undoubtedly realized a sense of urgency in their mission.

Then, with about six years to go before the kickoff for the new age, a young friar named Gerard of Borgo San Donnino wrote an explosive commentary on Joachim's prophecy. According to Gerard, the age of the Holy Spirit was about to begin. The Old and the New Testaments and the established church in the form of the pope and the clergy were set to fade into the annals of history. In fact, in the new age the entire decadent Christian church was to become irrelevant. It would all be placed under the careful guidance of the poor, humble servants of God, the Franciscan friars. The Spiritualist, or more zealous, Franciscans celebrated Gerard's ideas. But for nearly everyone else who considered themselves to be ministers of God's word—namely, the friars who had a more moderate view of poverty, the regular clergy, and the pope—what Gerard had to say was offensive. Gerard's interpretation was debated in both the universities and the papal court. In the end, his speculation was declared heretical, and he was disciplined. Yet the bomb that Gerard dropped made a huge impression. There were still several friars who believed in Joachim's vision, and the pope's condemnation now meant that the more zealous Franciscans found themselves in the position of having to work even harder to cultivate the impoverished life. Although the Spirituals were in the minority among Franciscans, the orthodoxy of the order had been questioned. In order to remove the taint of heresy from the larger Franciscan order, the zealots needed to be controlled.

At the time that Gerard wrote his commentary, the leader of the Franciscan order was a man named John of Parma, who, like many of his Franciscan brothers, tended to a more moderate view of Joachim's vision. He was sympathetic to the zealous followers but was a bit more circumspect in his theology. John had even punished Gerard for his errors, but he had made the mistake of letting it be known that he was open to Joachim's ideas. That admission alone was equal to sticking his head in a noose. More specifically, as the church administration began the process of purging the newly declared heretics, John was easily identified as one of the Spirituals. Rather than subject the minister general to active persecution, however, Pope Alexander IV (1254–61) suggested that he step down from his office. It was probably unfair that John was forced to resign, because he had only flirted with the Joachite ideas. The fact that he was allowed to pick his successor indicates that his dismissal was probably a matter of formality. Nevertheless, John of Parma was tarred with the heresy and, after he chose St. Bonaventure as his successor, retired to the town of Greccio.

Bonaventure took office in 1257, three years before the age of the Holy Spirit was to begin. On a very practical level, it is safe to say that he inherited a crisis. He had both to contend with angry clergy who resented the Franciscan claim of religious superiority and to sort out the squabbling within the Franciscan order. That is, he had to deal with the tension between the friars who recognized the value of owning property and those who saw possession as a direct violation of their oaths to God. All of that had to be reckoned with under the cloud of the Joachite heresy that would be tested out in a very short period of time. Suffice to say that Bonaventure made some amazing inroads. In dealing with the issue of poverty, he chose to split the difference by putting all Franciscan held property in the name of the church. Thus the friars were allowed to use their possessions, but they never actually owned anything. The strategy was absolutely brilliant, but it did not satisfy everyone. In fact, the debate among the Franciscan friars regarding the proper place of poverty continued to fester well into the fourteenth century. About 1325, when the papacy tried to quash the Spirituals once and for all, the Franciscan order went into schism and gave birth to a theological ideology that would ultimately open the path to the Protestant Reformation.

QUESTIONS FOR DISCUSSION

1. Can religious belief in the Holy Spirit be balanced against the historical development of the doctrine of the Holy Spirit?
2. In your judgment, did medieval theologians fail to grasp the underlying problem of the struggle for political power as the reason for the division of the church?
3. The prophecies of Joachim of Fiore and the Spiritual Franciscan movement were both expressions of devotion to the Holy Spirit. Are there any modern religious developments that are equivalent to the medieval enthusiasm for the Spirit?

8

The Road to the Reformation

The fourteenth century is, in a sense, a period that is marked by the unraveling of reason. The intellectual movements from within the mendicant orders created an undertow that began to whittle away at the teaching office of the church. Where scholars like St. Anselm, St. Thomas, and St. Bonaventure had tried to apply reason to church dogma in order to make the truth of the Christian faith absolutely clear, a new generation was busy developing a system of thought that unhooked faith and reason. There were several scholars who worked to advance the new mindset. For instance, the Dominican Robert Holcot (d. 1349) taught that since all knowledge comes from sense experience, it would be impossible to prove the existence of either the soul or God. The intangible things in the universe would have to be considered as objects of faith. So too, a Cistercian named John of Mirecourt (fl. 1345) argued that certainty could only come only through the senses. Everything else was merely probable.

It was not just the shift in theological method that made the latter Middle Ages an unhappy time. The fourteenth century in particular was a period of intense crises on several fronts. Most significantly, a battle for papal dominance split the church, another layer of fragmentation on top of an already splintered church. The tragedies extended to the social and economic realms too. The Black Death swept though the rapidly growing cities of the mid-fourteenth century. To make matters worse, as people left the villages and farms to take up residence in more urban areas, western Europe suffered an economic depression. From about 1450, wheat held a virtually worthless market value, so the nobility had difficulty paying their subjects, and the levels of poverty increased. The one steady voice of the church during this period of chaos was that of the Franciscan friars, who had become the ministers to the people in the cities. Their zeal for poverty enabled them to connect more readily with the general populace, and their insistence on poverty as a moral virtue became a powerful tool in the call for a reformation of the leadership as a remedy for the social and economic challenges.

INTRODUCING OCKHAM

Unquestionably the central figure in the rise of the more skeptical approach to faith and reason was an English Franciscan named William of Ockham. His method of questioning the limits of human reason planted a seed of uncertainty that eventually grew into a form of faith that was aided only by Scripture. In fact Martin Luther, the sixteenth-century Protestant reformer, even went so far as to declare himself an Ockhamist. Strangely, we actually know very little about Ockham. Born at Ockham in Surrey in 1285, he was ordained a subdeacon and in 1318 was presented to the bishop of Lincoln for the license to hear confessions. By 1317 Ockham was studying theology at Oxford. For a while, some modern historians thought that Ockham might have studied under John Duns Scotus, but this was not the case. Nevertheless, the subtle doctor's ideas were in vogue at the time, and Ockham certainly was exposed to them. Around 1319, Ockham began to circulate copies of his lectures on Lombard's *Sentences*. During this period his life story becomes much more interesting. What Ockham had to say in his lectures was quite controversial. When the chancellor of the university, John Lutterell, read Ockham's theories, he drew up a list of fifty-six points that illustrated where the young friar appeared to contradict Christian teaching. The chancellor then traveled to Avignon and accused Ockham of heresy. In other words, John went all the way to the pope in order to file his charges against Ockham.

Ockham was summoned to answer for his theology. When he arrived in Avignon, six theologians, including John Lutterell, examined his works and questioned the young friar. Not too surprisingly, they found problems with Ockham's ideas, and although he was not formally condemned, he was forced to stay in Avignon under a kind of house arrest. At the end of the proceedings, John Lutterell probably had no idea that the discomfort that Ockham had caused with his lectures was nothing compared to the anxiety that he was about to create. The Franciscan fight over the ideal expression of poverty was at a rolling boil. Zealous friars in southern France were being imprisoned and harassed for their radical insistence on adhering to the vow of poverty. To make matters worse, some Dominicans were stirring the pot by alleging that the Franciscan view of poverty was hypocritical, some going so far as to claim that the Franciscans accepted money just like everybody else. In order to quell the dispute, Pope John XXII (1316–34) was obliged to intervene. His approach to the matter, however, was too heavy-handed. Pope John hunted down the Spirituals. He condemned the Franciscan teaching of apostolic poverty and actually burned at the stake four friars who refused to submit to the orders of the papacy. When Michael Cesena, the minister general of the Franciscan order, protested the papal action by stating both that it was orthodox to believe that neither Christ nor the apostles owned any property and that the pope was in error, he was arrested. While he was in detention, he met William of Ockham.

Probably with little else to do, Michael asked William to begin studying the rules that previous popes had established for the Franciscans. Within a short time, Ockham had discovered that by failing to support the Franciscan approach to poverty Pope John was contradicting both Scripture and his predecessors. The information was bad enough to create a poor perception of the pontiff, but then Pope John himself accidentally helped matters along by offering a few personal opinions about the beatific vision that ended up being condemned by the theology faculty at Paris. So, armed with plenty of spicy details of papal blunders, Michael and Ockham wrote a description of John's errors, signed the document, and escaped from Avignon in 1328. The pope, obviously not a character who took criticism well, responded to the document by excommunicating both Michael and Ockham. But, the order came too late. They had fled to Italy, and after making their way to Pisa, they met Louis of Bavaria, Pope John's greatest enemy.

The tussle between Louis and the pope was basically a disagreement about who had the right to dispense power. Louis was the rightful emperor, but Pope John refused to recognize that reality. In fact, John had gone so far as to declare that the throne was vacant and therefore it was the job of the pope to tend to imperial affairs. This hostile, not to mention strangely stubborn, approach naturally angered Louis. Taking matters into his own hands, Louis declared that John was a heretic and in 1328 the emperor-elect chose his own pope. In a rather shrewd move, Louis chose a Spiritual Franciscan named Pietro Rainalducci (Pope Nicholas V). Although Pietro was not recognized as a legitimate pope and reigned only two years, Louis was clearly allying himself with the Franciscan order and their battle against John. Then, as a matter of luck, Louis's rival for the throne, Frederick of Austria, died in 1330. With a newfound pack of allies and one less obstacle between himself and the throne, Emperor Louis, accompanied by Michael Cesena and William of Ockham, left Italy, crossed the Alps, and arrived in Munich. From there, they began to wage a kind of paper battle against Pope John that did much to undermine the office of the papacy.

Living under the protection of the emperor, Ockham spent virtually the rest of his life writing in support of the emperor. Thus much of Ockham's written legacy is political. Ockham, however, was quite different from other political writers who disagreed with papal policies. Like many others, he defended the right of the empire to be independent of the church. When Ockham applied his brand of philosophy to the ideological structures of the church, his arguments were absolutely devastating. At its bare bones, Ockham managed to strictly isolate the various components of church governance; his conclusion was that any one body could be in error. That is, neither the pope, nor a church council, nor the laity was ever completely infallible. In Ockham's world, the only assurance that a believing Christian has is that during a controversy at least one group must be right. As a matter of practicality, what Ockham was doing in crafting his argument was preserving the authority of the church as an institution while still allowing for error. The church itself would always be in possession of the truth, but what is right would never be the sole prerogative of one group or person within the church hierarchy.

What did Ockham do that led to so much skepticism? There are several answers to the question, depending upon which sections of Ockham's writings are under analysis. One of his most important tools was the distinction between intuitive and abstractive cognition that he developed from John Duns Scotus's theology. Briefly, Duns Scotus thought that intuitive cognition was when a person has a direct awareness of an object. Both the senses and the intellect are capable of such awareness. For instance, one might have a direct experience of an object through the senses, such as when holding a puppy or seeing and smelling a flower. Similarly, internal states such as thinking and doubting reveal the presence of our own minds. By contrast, abstractive cognition is much less concrete. That is, the mind undergoes a process by which the information that comes through the senses forms into a concept. It is how the mind represents things in the world to itself. The objects in abstractive cognition do not need to be present, as they do in the case of intuitive cognition. Rather, they can either exist or not exist in the real world. What matters is that they are clearly represented to the mind. To make matters simple, intuitive knowledge is concerned with facts, but abstractive knowledge is concerned with characteristics. For Scotus, this distinction between the two types of knowledge was a handy mechanism for distinguishing between experience and the processes by which we understand the world. They are the means by which we know the actual as opposed to the possible. In this way, Scotus was able to make his unique claim that human beings can have knowledge of individuals in the world—as opposed to Aristotle, who had taught that only knowledge of universals was possible.

In Ockham's hands, however, the distinction between intuitive and abstractive cognition took quite a different twist. First, Ockham wanted to use the two kinds of knowledge to separate knowing from speculating. Second, he wanted to divorce logic from metaphysics, in order to emphasize that reasoning is about terms as opposed to objects. To simplify, under the flag of intuitive knowledge Duns Scotus could claim knowledge of singulars, and under the banner of abstractive knowledge he could explain knowledge of common natures, or universals. Ockham, however, denied the existence of universals as subsistent things. Rather, he thought that universals are simply signs of individuals that exist outside of the mind. Strictly speaking, then, knowledge of a universal or common nature cannot exist, and metaphysics is an unnecessary science. With metaphysics out of the way, the next step was to find a new job for general terms which Ockham located in the field of logic. The terms that Duns Scotus thought marked out common natures were only markers that human beings can use to recall the intuition of an individual. For example, when a person says, "man is a species," the word "man" does not directly refer to a substance or real characteristic that we somehow abstracted from an individual. Rather, Ockham wants to say that man is a notion in our minds. The word "man" is simply a sign. From here, Ockham set out to reconsider the variety of signs that are available.

For Ockham, all signs are either natural or conventional. By natural signs Ockham means that when we encounter an object, an intellectual notion appears in our mind. Moreover, regardless of which spoken or written word a person uses to signify an object in the world, the thought in the mind of the person is the same for everyone. For example, a Spanish-speaking person might use the word "perro," a German-speaking person might say "Hund," and an English-speaking person would use the word "dog." Despite the differences in language, however, all three people have in mind the same basic notion of a wild or domesticated quadruped that is classed as *Canis familiaris*. Our example also illustrates what Ockham means by conventional signs, those spoken words like "hund" and "perro" that vary among the users. With the basic distinction between the kinds of signs in mind, Ockham determined that the concepts, that is, the natural signs, must be products of the mind. They are the stuff of which thoughts are made. Propositions or assertions about the world, such as "Ozzie is a dog," then are simply built up from individual concepts. Once we no longer directly perceive an object through intuitive cognition, we can formulate a proposition by thinking about the concepts. When we do that, however, we have entered the realm of abstractive cognition. Our ability to make sense of the world amounts to the activity of ordering or arranging our concepts. But there it is! That is where Ockham took off in a new direction. If the world of individuals and our experience of them is all that is available, then things like universals, species, and forms do not exist. At least they do not exist apart from our minds. Ockham invented a completely psychological theory for the theory of forms.

When Ockham proposed his world of singular things and then eliminated any connection among them through a common nature or universal, he also ended up limiting all certain knowledge to sense experience. It is precisely this point that riled other theologians. Unless one participates in the beatific vision, there is no intuitive knowledge of God. People do not have a face-to-face encounter with God in the same way that they encounter other individuals. God is known through abstract concepts. That is why Thomas Aquinas and others went to great lengths to prove the existence of God. But Ockham was now essentially saying that scholars like St. Thomas failed in his task. Thomas did not prove the existence of God. Rather, he had merely undertaken some fairly impressive logical demonstration. So too, St. Anselm's proof was merely a matter of manipulating concepts. Since Ockham's theory limited knowledge to the finite realm, it would be impossible for Anselm or anyone else to prove that God is infinite. Finally, given the limits of Ockham's approach, Duns Scotus's proof suffers the most. Scotus tried to prove the existence of God by starting with metaphysical properties. According to Ockham's view, however, this means that Scotus started with nonsense! He started with the thoughts that were already in his own mind, rather than with things out there in the world. Without any rational conclusions about the divine, faith became the only viable alternative. If fact, if abstractive cognition is less certain than intuitive cognition, it makes it hard to accept any science as credible. So Ockham planted his seed for the intellectual revolution that would call for a rejection of rational theology and eventually blossom into the Protestant Reformation.

PAPAL DECLINE

Ockham's approach to philosophy certainly undermined the ideas from the golden age of theology of the thirteenth century, but the conflict that surrounded the papacy in the fourteenth century called into question the entire power structure of the church. In order to understand what must have seemed to be a papal death spiral, however, we need to connect up a few bits from earlier chapters. When we were introducing the two-swords theory, the struggle between Pope Boniface VIII and King Philip IV served as the best example of the tension between church and state. Their story illustrated the clash between papal authority and secular authority, both of which claimed justification from God. The tit-for-tat struggle between pope and king took an interesting turn when Boniface died in 1303. At that time, the cardinals entrusted with electing a new pope were split. Some were inclined to elect a leader who would clear Pope Boniface's reputation and settle the score with King Philip. Another group of cardinals saw the election of a new pope as an opportunity to heal the rift between the papacy and the most powerful king in Europe. To make the story of a long process short, after an extended period of debate the cardinals elected Clement V.

Clement was certainly not a match for King Philip, who continued his war against the deceased Pope Boniface. Almost immediately after Clement took office, the king began lobbying for a church council to condemn the dead pope. Clement was resistant to the idea, but after six years of pressure from the French king he agreed. The pope authorized hearings to begin in 1309, but when other circumstances interfered, the inquiry was abandoned. The delay cost Clement dearly, as Clement was forced to undo many of the policies that Boniface had aimed against the French. He was also required to pay for damages to the Colonna family, who had opposed Boniface at the price of their lands and their status in the church.

Even more troublesome, Clement was made to serve the king's agenda in the process of prosecuting the Knights Templar. King Philip had been engaged in an expensive war with England. One way to pay for that war was to confiscate the property of the military religious order known as the Knights Templar. The problem, however, was that Philip could not simply take the Knights' property. The public would have viewed such an action as sacrilegious. So, Philip had all of the Templars in France arrested on charges of blasphemy and pursued a policy of torture until the Knights confessed to the crimes. With the confessions in hand, Philip then demanded that the pope formally condemn the religious order. In part, Clement did just what the king wanted: he dissolved the order. He did not, however, give the king a clear victory. Rather, Clement arranged to have the assets of the order transferred to another religious order, the Hospitallers. In short, Clement did the best that he could to deflect the royal blows against papal authority. His poor health, lack of resources, bad luck, and decision to honor the king's request to move the papal court to Avignon set the stage for a seventy-year period during which the office of the papacy became a tool of the crown. The cumulative effect of the events that followed from Clement's action ultimately weakened the structure of the Roman Church and prepared the way for the Reformation of the 1500s.

The power struggle between Pope Boniface and King Philip explains how the papacy moved from Rome to Avignon. And that also explains why the great mystic Catherine of Siena would have traveled to Avignon in order to persuade Pope Gregory XI to return to Italy (see chapter 2). When Pope Gregory did move back to Rome, the transition was not an easy one. Many of the political entanglements that snared the papacy from the time of Clement still lingered. To make matters worse, the papal court was now loaded with Frenchmen. When Gregory died in 1378, Italian people feared that the cardinals would elect a new pope who would return the papacy to France. Rather than permit the papacy to fall back into the hands of a French king, crowds of Italians began to riot, with such force that the cardinals quickly gathered and elected Bartolomeo Prignano, a native of Naples, who became Pope Urban VI. Yet it was with Urban's election that another breakdown in papal authority occurred. In the past, there had been many rival claimants to the papacy, but now, for the first time, the same group of cardinals who elected the pope would later change their minds and elect a second pope.

So what did Urban do wrong? The cardinals who elected Urban knew his earlier career as a faithful archbishop and his reputation for being conscientious and a good steward of the church. What the cardinals did not know was that Urban also had a horrible temper and at times could be obstinate. Upon discovering some of the pope's more distasteful personality traits, several cardinals began to wonder if Urban had simply lost his mind. Perhaps election to the papal office was too much for the sixty-year-old pontiff. That would at least explain Urban's uncompromising behavior toward them. More specifically, Urban had launched a reform movement aimed directly at the cardinals. He preached against their worldliness and even threatened to excommunicate the cardinals who accepted gifts. But Urban did not limit his zeal for reformation to the people in his court. He also managed to attack several dignitaries, including Queen Joanna of Naples. When finally confronted with the suggestion that the papal court should move back to Avignon, Urban became so angry that he threatened to use his power as pope to appoint more cardinals. He warned that he would flood the college with so many Italians that the French would lose their majority. Christendom probably could have survived Urban's lack of tact. There was at the time a strong popular desire to reform the church, so most people probably would have tolerated his staunch outlook. Urban's threats against the French cardinals, however, were a serious tactical error.

Pope Urban's behavior became so disagreeable that the cardinals, including the Italians, began to gather to discuss what to do about him. Several fascinating scenarios were posed. They could, for example, kill the pope. Less severe, they could imprison him. Still more realistic, some cardinals had hopes that Urban might share some of his power. Yet none of these possibilities seemed like the right approach. Ultimately the cardinals decided to issue a statement in which they claimed that Urban's election was invalid. Pointing to the riots that preceded his appointment, they claimed that because they voted out of fear of mob violence, the election was void. They even invited Pope

Urban to quit his job. Rather than wait for Urban to respond, possibly with the use of his papal army, the cardinals then fled to the protection of Queen Joanna. What they did next was hugely bizarre. The same cardinals who had elected Pope Urban VI just five months earlier chose a new pope. With the elevation of Robert of Geneva as Clement VII the cardinals began what historians have come to call the Great Schism. That is to say, the action of the cardinals divided the church and forced people to choose between two duly elected leaders. For example, St. Catherine of Sweden and St. Catherine of Siena both supported Urban. But St. Colette, the reformer of the Poor Clares, the nuns who followed St. Francis, was an advocate for Clement. The papal division and general confusion continued for the next eight papal reigns.

As soon as Robert of Geneva became pope, he immediately began to gather allies who had enough military power to help him unseat Urban. Most of the cardinals were French, and Robert did have some royal ties, as he was a cousin to the French king. Thus, the aid of powerful supporters was in reach. The hope of quickly removing Urban seemed even more plausible because Robert himself had quite a military reputation. Earlier in his career, he had led a band of mercenaries against the state of Florence, and had become quite famous for his horrifying massacres. Urban, however, proved to be a fairly tough competitor. When the two armies finally did clash in 1379, Robert's troops were crushed, along with the hope of winning the papal office by force.

Without a chance of taking the papacy by force, Robert began a new campaign of politics. For instance, his supporters wrote formal statements declaring that he was the official pope and justifying his election. Robert also started gathering large territorial support. Before long the two popes had managed to split most of Europe. Those countries that were loyal to France rallied to Robert's cause. Those who were more in favor of England sided with Urban. Despite his maneuvering Robert was unable to secure a majority. He completely failed to gain support of the Italians, which forced him to live in France. He also ran out of the money that some of his advocates required for their continued favor. But Robert was able to muster enough power to remain a viable opposition.

Eventually, the division of loyalties to the two popes equaled out in such a way that the church could find only two solutions for ending the schism. One of the popes would have to simply give up, or a church council would need to be called to determine the correct path for the church to take. Neither solution worked. Both popes were unwilling to step aside and permit the other to hold the office. Although the church council seemed like a good idea, there was no agreed-upon ruler who could express their right to call a council.

Urban died in 1388. It is not altogether clear, but he may have been poisoned. In any case, the eleven-year period of his fight with Robert of Geneva confounded the church. When Urban died, the Roman cardinals elected Boniface IX to replace the foul-tempered pope. When Robert of Geneva, Clement VII, died six years later, there was some hope that the power struggle had ended. The French cardinals, however, ignored the advice of King Charles of France and chose to elect Benedict XIII. The schism continued. Boniface died in 1404, and Innocent VII went in for the Italian team but had only a two-year reign before meeting his end. Gregory XII was quickly sent in as a replacement. It is perhaps a sign of how exasperating this pathetic situation had become that several theologians began to argue that a committee would be a better way to run the church. After roughly thirty years of schism, however, thirteen Italian cardinals crossed the line. Frustrated by Gregory's failure to renounce his title and end the schism, as he had promised upon his election, they joined forces with the French cardinals. Gathering at Pisa, the newly merged college of cardinals publicly declared their desire for church unity and called for a church council. The new problem, however, was finding a way to get the rival popes to actually attend the meeting.

After a few futile appeals for the disputing pontiffs to come to the church council, it became clear that neither pontiff intended to resign his position. So a handful of cardinals held their own council in Pisa on March 25, 1409. This was a highly unusual move. The cardinals were responsible for the administration of the government of the church but they were never permitted to act on their own. They derived their authority from the pope. To put it another way, cardinals are analogous to princes, and popes to kings. So, when the group of protesting cardinals met in Pisa and declared that both of the rival popes were heretics, they were clearly acting outside of their jurisdiction. Nevertheless the need to protect the church from the schism created by the ongoing papal rivalry justified the gathering, which deposed both Benedict and Gregory and elected a new pope, a Greek named Pietro Philarghi, who became Alexander V. On the one hand, the council at Pisa was a complete failure. Benedict and Gregory were not willing to honor the order of deposition. Nobody appeared to be prepared to accept the authority of Alexander V. That is, the council did not have enough gravity to attract the allegiance of nations that had aligned themselves with either Gregory or Benedict. Now there were three popes. To make matters worse, Alexander died unexpectedly after holding office for only one year. On the other hand, the council at Pisa was the prelude to a great success. It was the first inroad of a cooperative venture in a divided college of cardinals. Great champions such as Jean Gerson and Pierre d'Ailly emerged. And the ridiculous situation of having three popes forced the meeting of the much more successful Council of Constance.

When Alexander V died in 1410, he was replaced by Baldassare Cossa. One of the architects of the council that met at Pisa, Baldassare was a colorful personality. He had made his living as a pirate and had proven himself to be an able, and possibly irreligious, soldier. As a clergyman, he was both ambitious and ruthless. For example, when serving as Pope Benedict's treasurer, he invented a few schemes for the sale of papal favors in order to increase revenue. It is not at all surprising that his election as pope came with a degree of anxiety. More specifically, he had been accused of poisoning Pope Alexander in order to win the papal office. The allegation, though unfounded, indicates something of the general perception of Baldassare's unsavory character. The more serious concerns surrounding his election, however, came from the genuine danger of aggression if the office had gone to someone else. If Baldassare had not been chosen, there was a chance that the cardinals would have been punished by his wartime ally Louis II of Anjou. For that matter, Baldassare himself had experienced military forces that could seize the papal office if he was so inclined. Suffice to say that the cardinals correctly assessed their situation and they voted unanimously to elect Baldassare.

A CLOSER LOOK

The fact that Baldassare Cossa became Pope John XXIII may be a source of confusion, because Angelo Roncalli held that same name from 1958 to 1963. That is, there are two men in history who took the title of Pope John XXIII. The reason for this is that Baldassare was not recognized by the Roman Catholic Church as a lawfully elected pontiff. Rather, he is considered to be an antipope. There have been, in fact, roughly thirty-five antipopes in papal history. Most of them lived during the Middle Ages. For instance, there are two popes known as Celestine II. The official Celestine was elected in 1143 and reigned for one year. The antipope by the same name presided in 1124. There were two popes by the name of Innocent III who both lived in the twelfth century. The confusion caused by the large number of popes called John during the tenth and eleventh centuries is the likely reason that there has never been a Pope John XX.

Further Reading: E. Duffy, *Saints and Sinners: A History of the Popes* (New Haven 1997).

Baldassare Cossa may have been a bad man, but, in the end, as Pope John XXIII he did the right thing. In fact, there were several occasions when he tried to follow the reforming spirit of the council at Pisa. But he could not ignore the fact that there were still two other powerful individuals who held the papal title. Although he had the backing of the more powerful nations such as England and France, John was still politically vulnerable in Italy. King Ladislas, a supporter of Pope Gregory XII, was conspiring to win a handful of the southern papal states. Without losing sight of the imminent dangers, John called for a crusade against Pope Gregory. That venture included support for Louis II of Anjou in a campaign against King Ladislas. In order to help ensure the victory, John extended special privileges to those who contributed money to the war effort. The short-term outcome was worth the effort, as Louis defeated Ladislas in 1411. But Louis did not completely destroy Ladislas. Rather, after his victory Louis returned to France, and Ladislas continued both to control his lands around southern Italy and to support Gregory XII. So Pope John switched tactics. Rather than war, he tried bribery. He approached Ladislas and offered him the fiefdom of Naples in exchange for his support. Ladislas accepted. The newfound allegiance did not last long, however.

With Louis in France and too far away to help, Ladislas turned on Pope John. He attacked Rome in 1413 and forced John to flee. Without the military might to contain Ladislas, John appealed to King Sigismund of Germany for support. Sigismund had come to power only a few years prior, but he had reasonable motives for entering into the conflict. More specifically, Sigismund's estates in Bohemia were becoming unstable. Initially, Bohemia like other kingdoms issued calls for reform, aimed at the moral laxity of the clergy. By 1400, however, several of the Czech reformers had discovered the works of John Wycliffe, and the pressure increased. Despite the more conservative-minded opinion that Wycliffe was a heretic, reformers such as Jan Huss demanded absolute poverty for the clergy and punishment for priests who committed mortal sins. As the division within the clergy grew, so did the social tension. Sigismund rightly saw the need to end the papal schism in order to present a unified church against the factions that were steadily pulling his kingdom toward revolution. Rather than simply plunge into the conflict between Pope John and the other pontiffs, however, Sigismund demanded a church council in exchange for his support. John reluctantly agreed, and the Council of Constance was convened on November 5, 1414.

Pope John had hoped that the council would eliminate both Pope Benedict XIII and Pope Gregory XII. In order to hedge his bets, he brought a large group of Italian bishops to the council and immediately began campaigning for confirmation of the decisions from the council at Pisa. His effort was confounded, however, when the cardinals decided that all voting should be done according to nations, as opposed to individual ballot; that is, each nation present—England, France, Germany, Italy, and Spain—would cast one vote. To make matters worse for John, several participants at the council were calling for all three of the popes to step down, and John himself was especially vulnerable. With a reputation as a morally bankrupt individual who had been accused of several serious crimes, he could easily fall subject to a public scandal. Rather than face both humiliation and defeat, John fled in the middle of the night to the protection of Frederick, duke of Austria. His departure failed to disrupt the business of the council, however. Rather, it appears to have accelerated the processes for ending the schism. In fact, King Sigismund became the driving force for the final settlement. With regard to the council, he steadied the participants and permitted the group to formally declare superiority over the decisions of the papacy. In dealing with Pope Gregory, he found an honorable way for the pope to step down and accept the position of cardinal bishop of Porto, Portugal. Dealing with Benedict, Sigismund pushed the defiant ninety-year-old pontiff into a position of irrelevance. Finally Sigismund turned his attention to Austria and declared war on Frederick. The duke quickly submitted, but Pope John escaped. Sigismund finally caught John in Freiburg, Germany, and returned the fugitive pope to the council, this time as a prisoner. John was tried for gross misconduct and deposed.

Pope John accepted his fate gracefully. He was placed in the custody of one of his old enemies, Ludwig III of Bavaria, and remained a prisoner for a few years. Upon his release, he submitted to the new authorities and was granted the position of cardinal bishop of Tusculum. In the meantime, the Council of Constance closed, and the cardinals set out to select a new, completely legitimate, pope. Sadly, the man they chose, who became Martin V, ended up being little better than his predecessors. He found ways to increase papal authority and pursued policies to replenish his treasury after so many years of turmoil. Consequently the public expectation for a reformed church went unanswered. The pressure for rule by church council increased, and still more seeds were sown for what would grow to become the Protestant Reformation.

THE INFLUENCE OF CARDINALS

The Great Schism had an enormous impact on the church. It opened the way for people to wonder whether or not the supremacy of a church council was the better approach for governing the affairs of Christendom. Many people, including clergy, laity, and nobility, were well aware of the need to reform the administrative practices within the church hierarchy. Two cardinals, in particular, had quite an impact on the dialogue about running church affairs. More specifically, the French Cardinal Pierre D'Ailly (pronounced DIE-ee) and Nicholas of Cusa both tried to inject a more democratic ideal into the life of the church by advocating for the rule by a church council, as opposed to the supremacy of the pope. Of the two men, Cardinal D'Ailly is the lesser known but was a continual presence in the councils both before and after the Great Schism. Pierre wrote on a broad range of theological topics and had a remarkable influence on a number of later scholars, such as John Major (discussed later in this book) and Martin Luther. Although D'Ailly tended toward the ideas of William of Ockham, some elements of St. Thomas Aquinas's theology also appeared in his writings.

One of D'Ailly's most provocative theological works was *Destructiones modorum significandi*, in which he advocated for an end to a popular language theory that explained how analogies for God could be meaningful. Many medieval theologians struggled with the problem of how concepts derived from our experiences of creatures could be applied to God. That is, medieval theologians were trapped. They recognized that when a term is used of God—"good" in the phrase "God is good," for example—the word must either mean what it always means in every other statement, like "Socrates is good," or the word must mean something particular to the divine. If the word refers to some unique characteristic of God, then we should be able to say exactly what that word means. And therein lies the problem. On the one hand, theologians did not want to give the impression that God could be adequately described in common terms. On the other hand, without the ability to say how a word like "good" differed when applied to God as opposed to Socrates, theologians were forced to admit they had no idea what they were saying.

One popular solution to the problem was to argue that the word in question was expressing different ways of being or modes. For example, medieval scholars would claim that a word like "healthy" always has the same root meaning. That is to say, it always means wholesomeness or soundness. At any rate it is a much less horrifyingly complicated way to express salubriousness. But when "healthy" is used in different sentences, its signification changes, such as when one says, "vitamins are healthy," and "Socrates is healthy." So too we can map out the different modes expressed by a word like "good." For example, it might be better to say, "Socrates is $good_1$," and "God is $good_2$." The word "$good_1$" means excellence, and "$good_2$" is related to that, but the mode of signification is proper only to the divine. For Pierre D'Ailly, this entire business of multiple modes of signification is a load of rubbish. Following along the lines of William of Ockham, Pierre simply thinks that any difference between words like "$good_1$," and "$good_2$" must be either a relevant distinction or be metaphorical. Either there are two words that pick out different things in the world, or the word is being used as a figure of speech in which the meaning is transferred from one object to another for the purpose of making a comparison. But it is not the case that some metaphysical entity, that is, the good, exists in different ways.

If Pierre D'Ailly's semantic theory was complicated, his role in church politics was positively convoluted! Sometimes it appeared that Pierre had the best principles that money could buy. Nevertheless he loved the church, and his Ockhamistic bias did enable him to make an important contribution to the movement to replace the authority of the pope with the authority of church councils. For instance, in 1407 he persuasively argued that the pope's spiritual authority be recognized but that the pontiff be denied temporal authority. Two years later, however, Pierre broke with Pope Benedict XIII, who had elected him bishop, and attended the council at Pisa. In any case, Pierre's impact at the council was probably limited because he arrived late. What he did accomplish that did matter a great deal, however, was a change of allegiance. Sometime around 1409, Pierre, along with his friend William Fillastre, decided to support Pope John XXIII. For their trouble, they were both elevated to the rank of cardinal in 1411. Despite receiving his reward, Pierre D'Ailly remained firm in his conviction that only a general council could end the schism. With that in mind, he assumed a leadership role in the activities at the Council of Constance.

The second cardinal who merits a comment was Nicholas of Cusa. Nicholas came from slightly more humble stock; his father was a boat owner and merchant. Nevertheless, Nicholas managed to attend several universities and received his education in both canon law and theology. As with Pierre D'Ailly, a case can be made for Cusa putting his education forward in service of church reform. Shortly after he was ordained as a priest in 1430, he started to receive some fairly impressive church appointments, such as the deanship of St. Florin's at Coblenz. That is, Nicholas had become a fairly well-respected clergyperson. In 1433 Nicholas, acting in his capacity as a canon lawyer, went to the Council of Basle. The council had been convened two years earlier by Pope Martin V to continue work on the issues raised at the Council of Constance. Nicholas, however, was present on a completely unrelated matter. There had been a dispute as to who should be the rightful heir to the archbishopric of Trier, and Nicholas represented one of the claimants for the office. As it turned out, Nicholas lost his case. But his talents were noticed, and he ended up getting involved in the business of the council. For example, he worked to reconcile the factions from the Hussite controversy with the church.

He also started having opinions about the rights of the church councils. He outlined a complete program to reform the church. What Nicholas proposed was revolutionary for the period. He argued that the pope did not have the sole power to create the law. Rather, Nicholas noted that law is a product of a common consensus. As a matter of practicality, Nicholas noted that rulers do not receive their authority directly from God. Rather, they govern by the general consent of the people who are willing to subject themselves to an authority. When Nicholas presented this work to the council, it was well received.

At the time that Nicholas was presenting his ideas in Basle, the relationship between the council and Martin V's successor, Pope Eugene IV, was becoming strained. A definitive break came when the two parties could not agree on the new site for a council to convene and consider possible reunion with the

Eastern church. The council wanted to meet in Basle or Avignon, but the pontiff preferred a site in Italy. A minority group of moderates from the council, with Nicholas among them, left for Ferrara and joined forces with the pope. Nicholas was not selling out, however. Rather, he had developed a new understanding of what constituted unity. Basically Nicholas came to see unity not so much as a matter of subordinating everything under one roof but as a synthesis of differences. More specifically, he defined unity as a kind of harmonizing of opposites. In his theology, for example, God both transcends and unites all of the differences of the finite world. Everything that is either big or small, hot or cold, good or evil coincides in God in an incomprehensible way. So too in the affairs of the church, the issue is not one of subordinating the state to the pope or vice versa. Rather, true unity means reconciliation in the form of an ongoing, harmonious, peaceful relationship between the two bodies. With his new understanding of unity, Nicholas worked feverishly for the reform of the church. His accomplishments, too numerous to recount here, ranged from preaching to both clergy and laity to reforming financial policies in his diocese. His work was so impressive that Pope Nicholas V, Eugene's successor, elevated him to the rank of cardinal around 1448.

Both Nicholas of Cusa and Pierre D'Ailly managed to hammer away at the moral corruption of the church, by using unique combinations of talents. For Pierre, it was strategy and the influence of Ockham's philosophy that gave credence to the council. For Nicholas, it was canon law and a dash of mysticism that provided a unique path through the quagmire of papal prerogatives. In both cases, the mess of sorting out who was in charge of the church trickled down into every level of Christendom, and the cardinals were the first stop on the road to the reform that would eventually take place in the sixteenth century.

THE INFLUENCE OF CLERGY

While the two giant institutions of council and papacy struggled, the calls for reform penetrated the church hierarchy and drilled down below the level of the cardinals. In the case of the preachers, however, their activity ended up being something of a counterweight to the intellectual skepticism of Ockham and the suspicion of the ecclesiastical authority. While the institutional church struggled, the preachers offered people a voice that stressed individual personal experience and piety. Three priests in particular are commonly associated with this infusion of personal religion into medieval culture. The first of these was John Tauler. Born around 1300, he earned his fame as a preacher more than as a speculative theologian. Despite his formal education at the University of Paris, John gravitated toward the writings of the mystics like St. Augustine, St. Bonaventure, and Hugh of St. Victor. The most influential figure in his thinking was Meister Eckhart, whom John encountered while studying in Cologne. Thus Tauler's theological disposition is one in which Christians are encouraged to seek the indwelling God. Unlike his favorite teacher, Tauler was careful to balance his message and to make his points in clear, simple language. When he spoke to congregations of nuns, just as Meister Eckhart had, John was careful to urge the need for simplicity and humility. Yet he also encouraged them to continue using their talents to strive for the greater kingdom of God.

A second friar who operated in the wake of the Great Schism was also a student of Meister Eckhart. Henry Suso, born in Constance in 1295, joined the Dominican order in his hometown when he was about thirteen years old. After living a fairly normal religious life in the convent, he was sent to Cologne sometime around 1322 to begin studying theology. There he fell under the influence of Meister Eckhart. Although Henry was a strong supporter of his old teacher, he took great care to steer clear of his master's obscure language. Henry, like Eckhart and Tauler, thought that a mystical union with God takes place in the human soul. Yet Henry is very clear that the image of God resides at the center of the soul and that God's love is supernaturally infused. Moreover, Henry teaches that when mystical union takes place, the soul stops short of being fully united or absorbed into the divine. He does not accidentally suggest that there is a blurring of the line between God and creatures, a distinction that Eckhart did not make so obvious. Henry thought that human beings always remain separate from God, but despite his best attempts at clarity, he did encounter difficulty with church authorities when his ideas were allied too closely with those of Eckhart. As the result of the conflict, Henry was deprived of his teaching position. Despite the minor setback, however, he continued to follow his master in preaching to nuns, and his Christ-centered spirituality without the need for the medieval ecclesiastical structure found great favor with that audience throughout Germany.

The last friar to merit a comment was John of Ruysbroeck. He was born in 1293 in the town near Brussels, Belgium, from which his name is derived. At eleven years old, John went to live with his uncle who was the canon of St. Gudules. While there, John began taking studies that would prepare him for the priesthood, and by 1317 he was ordained. Apparently, John continued living with his uncle and became well regarded in his community. In any case, his preaching against a woman connected with the Brethren of the Free Spirit, a mystic and supposedly pantheistic group who claimed to be unfettered by church authority, gained him some notoriety. By 1349 John had retired to a hermitage with his uncle and a friend. The community that they established became quite renowned for its Christian life and devotion. John remained ensconced in his community of contemplatives, serving as the prior and writing works of theology until his death in 1381. In his theology John is a mystic who, like Tauler and Suso, followed the Neoplatonists. More specifically, his ideas were influenced by St. Augustine and Hugh of St. Victor. Meister Eckhart too played an important role in shaping his thought. John was also careful to distance himself from many of Eckhart's ideas, especially when he discussed the concept of unification with the divine. John agreed that contemplation was the highest form of religious experience, but he distinguished between the kinds of mystical experience. For example, at one point he supposed that there were three levels of mystical unity. The first was tied to the active life and involved external works. The second was a spiritual unity that related to the interior life but was expressed through an imitation of Christ. Finally, the third was a unity that came through contemplation and flows from the supernatural life.[1]

The writings of these three priests constitute another building block that would eventually form a foundation for the popular religion of the Protestant Reformation. For example, Martin Luther appreciated Tauler's concept of salvation and thought highly of the idea of righteousness as a virtue as opposed to something earned by merit.[2] Several movements became associated with the work that John of Ruysbroeck did. His hermitage became a center of religious revival during the fourteenth century that stressed the importance of the individual inner life. As consequence, his followers turned a blind eye toward the importance of the church hierarchy. So too, many of the groups of nuns who followed Henry Suso's ideas eventually joined the Common Life movements (see p. 24) and consequently grew more independent of church authority.

FROM DUNS SCOTUS TO KNOX AND CALVIN

While the political turmoil continued to rock the government of the church at virtually every level, the Franciscan friars added yet another dynamic through their exponential growth. Although they were only a small group when Pope Innocent III officially recognized them in 1210, by 1275 they had established 195 houses in France alone and had become one of the largest religious groups in Europe. Because of their great number and their mission of working among the people, they were a dominant theological force. Sometimes this fact is obscured because medieval theology is tacitly considered to be the domain of the Roman Catholic church. And when modern encyclical letters like *Fides et Ratio* indicate a clear preference for the works of St. Thomas as "a model for the right way to do theology," people wrongly assume that the Angelic Doctor's ideas were the standard against which Protestant theology developed.[3] St. Thomas was an important figure, but many medieval theologians did not agree that his thought was sound, and some of his ideas were in fact condemned by the church in 1277. Moreover, during the thirteenth and fourteenth centuries, the Dominican order had not grown as large, having only half the number of houses as their Franciscan counterparts. That is, the Dominicans did not have the personnel to get the Thomistic word out to the people. Generally speaking, much of the popular theology in the run-up to the Reformation was Franciscan. In particular, the ideas taught were those of William of Ockham and John Duns Scotus. It was the writing of these two scholars that impacted the curriculum of the universities and was transmitted to the Protestant Reformers.

One of the most important transition figures out of the Middle Ages and into the Protestant Reformation was John Major (1467–1550). Since our task is primarily to examine the thought and culture of the Middle Ages, John's story does stretch things a bit. He is an important figure for unpacking the foundations of the early modern period, but he also stood with at least one foot in the medieval period. Trained as a scholastic philosopher like Aquinas and Scotus, as a Scottish-born theologian, he was sensitive to the writings of John Duns Scotus. He edited the Subtle Doctor's works and took great pride in the fact that they were fellow countrymen. But John Major was an eclectic. For example, John was also an active logician and wrote commentaries on the works of Peter of Spain (Pope John XXI). His theology, in fact, tends more toward favoring the themes that were introduced through William of Ockham. That includes his disposition toward the power of the pope; that is, John supported the authority of the church councils.

How does the cataloging of medieval theology make John Major a transition figure into the Protestant Reformation? The answer lies with whom he taught. Major was definitely the leading intellectual figure of his day and had several students who became key players in the turmoil of the Reformation. Some believe that John Calvin studied with Major, and any good edition of Calvin's *Institutes* will show traces of John Major's influence. For example, when Calvin rails against multiple benefices held by bishops, it is clear that the shadowy influence of John Major lingers under some of the comments.[4] John Major also taught John Knox, who praised his teacher as "an oracle on matters of religion."[5] Ignatius of Loyola, the founder of the Jesuit order, also owed his education to John Major. In short, the man who became the first chancellor of St.

Andrew's University in Scotland had an enormous impact on the leaders of the church as it moved into a new era. Major was aware of the church's inability to recover from the long-standing power struggles but did not share his students' enthusiasm for separating from Rome. Indeed, he remained faithful to the Roman Catholic Church until his death.

SUMMARY

So what good were the Middle Ages? At the beginning of this book we started with the monks and friars. I claimed that they stood at the crossroads between the early church and the early modern era. Chronologically, that is exactly where they were located. But the innovations by the monks and the friars who navigated the treacherous political landscape of the medieval world provided a foundation for many of the institutions and customs that are part of modern society. The ceremony of marriage came through the church. Some of the customs surrounding the common holidays like Easter and Christmas grew out of the medieval period. Theological concerns, such as the purpose behind the incarnation, the role of angels, the struggle with evil in the world, and just plain wondering about the existence of God, all received quite a bit of shape from the intellectual activity of the monks and friars. The modern university system was a medieval contribution too. The monks and friars formed the modern church. They set up its laws, struggled with its humanity, reformed it, divided it, and healed it.

In fact, one must be careful using the term "Reformation," because the church has been in a perpetual state of reform since it started. Indeed, the penchant for reform is clearly visible since the time of Charlemagne. In short, medieval thought and culture is a central part of the Christian heritage, at the core of the modern Christian identity. Rather than standing opposed to Protestant Reformation, the medieval church is actually its complement. Thus there is a strong sense in which the medieval church is also the ideological crossroads for Christianity. It is the point at which the early church and the early modern church converge in the ongoing, yet difficult, journey to be a faithful witness to the Word of God.

QUESTIONS FOR DISCUSSION

1. How does William of Ockham's theory of knowledge affect your view of the proofs for the existence of God?
2. In what sense can we say that the rocky papal history of the fifteenth century was really a political war between France and Italy?
3. If Scripture alone is sufficient for an individual to connect with the divine, what need is there for a church council, clergy, or pope?
4. Is it possible for human beings to use normal language in order to speak meaningfully about God?

Notes

Chapter 1

1. J. A. Watt, "Spiritual and Temporal Powers," in *Cambridge History of Medieval Political Thought, c. 350–c. 1450*, ed. J. H. Burns (Cambridge: Cambridge University Press, 1991), 370–74.
2. D. E. Luscombe, "Introduction: Formation of Political Thought," in *Cambridge History of Medieval Political Thought, c. 350–c. 1450*, ed. J. H. Burns, 159–61. S. Painter, *Mediaeval Society* (Ithaca, NY: Cornell University Press, 1951), 11–42.
3. I. Wood, *The Merovingian Kingdoms, 450–751* (London: Longman, 1994), 37. Professor Wood has written perhaps the best introduction to the Merovingians. The synopses of the kings that follow are drawn mainly from his work.
4. Rosamond McKitterick has offered perhaps the best sketch of the Frankish kings and the sketch presented here follows her work. See R. McKitterick, *The Frankish Kingdoms under the Carolingians, 751–987* (New York: Longman, 1983).
5. For the life of Louis IX, see E. Hallam and J. Everard, *Capetian France 987–1328* (Harlow: Longman, 2001), 263–346.
6. For the most comprehensive treatment of Boethius, including an outstanding chapter about his contribution to the Middle Ages, see J. Marenbon, *Boethius* (Oxford: Oxford University Press, 2003).
7. M. Fakhry, *A History of Islamic Philosophy* (New York: Columbia University Press, 1983), 270–73.

Chapter 2

1. For a more detailed account of St. Bernard's life, see the introduction by G. R. Evans in *Bernard of Clairvaux, Selected Works* (New York: Paulist Press, 1987), 15–29.
2. Bernard of Clairvaux, *Bernard of Clairvaux, Selected Works* (New York: Paulist Press, 1987), 215.
3. Several editions of Julian's work are available. The Classics of Western Spirituality edition contains a useful introduction, and the translation of the short text is highly readable. For the text of the gloss that follows, see *Showings* (New York: Paulist Press, 1978), 125–70.
4. E. Gilson, *A History of Christian Philosophy in the Middle Ages* (New York: Random House, 1955), 113–128.
5. Aquinas, *Summa Theologica*, trans. Fathers of the English Dominican Province (Westminster, MD: Christian Classics, 1981), II-II, q.2, a.1.

151

6. R. Bainton, *The Medieval Church* (Malabar: Krieger Publishing Co., 1979), 61.
7. Aquinas, *Summa Theologica*, II-II, a.2, n.2.
8. G. Duby, D. Barthélemy, and C. de la Roncière, "Portraits," in *A History of Private Life* (Cambridge, MA: Belknap Press, 1988), 2:128.

Chapter 3

1. P. Schaff, *History of the Christian Church*, vol. 5 (Grand Rapids: Wm. B. Eerdmans, 1988), 598–99.
2. Anselm, *Proslogion*, *A Scholastic Miscellany: Anselm to Ockham*, ed. E. Fairweather, Library of Christian Classics (Philadelphia: Westminster, 1956), c. 1, p. 73.
3. *Proslogion*, 74.
4. Eadmer, *Vita Sancti Anselmi* [The Life of St. Anselm], trans. R.W. Southern (New York: Oxford University Press, 1962), 8.
5. Aquinas, *Summa Theologica*, trans. Fathers of the English Dominican Province (Westminster, MD: Christian Classics, 1981), I, q.2, a.2.
6. J. Duns Scotus, *Opera Omnia* (Vatican: Typis Polyglottis, 1950–), Ordinatio I, d.2, q.2, n.35.
7. Ibid.
8. W. Frank and A. Wolter, *Duns Scotus, Metaphysician* (West Lafayette, IN: Purdue University Press, 1995), 83.
9. R. Cross, *Duns Scotus* (Oxford: Oxford University Press, 1999), 17.
10. R. Wood, "Scotus's Argument for the Existence of God," *Franciscan Studies* 47 (1987): 259.
11. B. Bonansea, *Man and His Approach to God in John Duns Scotus* (New York: University Press of America, 1983), 138–39.
12. B. Bonansea, "The Proof for the Existence of God as an Infinitely Perfect and Unique Being," in *Man and His Approach to God in John Duns Scotus* (New York: University Press of America, 1983), 136.
13. R. Wood, "Scotus's Argument for the Existence of God," *Franciscan Studies* 47 (1987): 268.

Chapter 4

1. Quoted in R. North, "The Scotist Cosmic Christ," in *De doctrina Ioannis Duns Scoti* (Rome: Acta Congressus Scotistici Internationalis Oxonii et Edimburg: 11–17 Sept. 1966 Celebrati: Cura Commissionis Scotisticae, 1968), 194.
2. D. Unger, "Robert Grosseteste Bishop of Lincoln (1235–1253) on the Reasons for the Incarnation," *Franciscan Studies* 16 (1956): 27–28.
3. Et secundum hunc modum ipse homo Deus esset primogenitus omnis creaturae, quia finis prior est intentione, quam sunt illa quae sunt ad finem. In D. Unger, "Robert Grosseteste Bishop of Lincoln (1235–1253) on the Reasons for the Incarnation," *Franciscan Studies* 16 (1956): 16.
4. John Peckham, *Quodlibeta Quatuor*, ed. G. Etzkorn, Bibliotheca Franciscana Medii Aevi (Florence, 1989), q.2, n.3, p. 135.
5. Matthew of Aquasparta, *Quaestiones Selectae de Christo et Eucharistia*, q. 1, p. 195. In, *Quaestiones Disputate de Incarnatione et de Lapsu*, Bibliotheca Franciscana Scholastica Medii Aevi, Tom. II, Collegii 2. Bonaventurae, Quarecchi (Florence, 1957).
6. Ibid., 196–97.

Chapter 5

1. M. D. Grmek, *Western Medical Thought from Antiquity to the Middle Ages* (Cambridge, MA: Harvard University Press, 1998), 58.

2. F. Getz, *Medicine in the English Middle Ages* (Princeton, NJ: Princeton University Press, 1998), 52.

3. Ibid., 54.

4. M. D. Grmek, *Western Medical Thought*, 237.

5. Augustine, *Expositions on the Psalms*, in *Nicene and Post Nicene Fathers*, vol. 8 (Peabody, MA: Hendrickson Publishers, 1994), 83.

6. Augustine, *On the Merits and the Remission of Sins*, in *Nicene and Post Nicene Fathers*, vol. 8, 22.

7. H. Chadwick, *Augustine* (New York: Oxford University Press, 1986), 113.

8. In chapter 16 of *The Virgin Conception* Anselm specifically asks how Christ assumed flesh without acquiring sin. My presentation of his argument follows from that discussion. See Anselm of Canterbury, *Why God Became Man, The Virgin Conception and Original Sin* (New York: Magi Books, 1969), 143–47.

9. Henry's theory as presented here is quite simplified. A good exposition of the theory in a historical context can be found in A. Wolter and B. O'Neill, *John Duns Scotus, Mary's Architect* (Quincy, IL: Franciscan Press, 1993), 58–61.

10. Aquinas, *The Summa Theologica of St. Thomas Aquinas*, q.27, a.1, pt.3.

11. Aquinas, *Summa Theologica*, q.27, a.2, pt.3.

12. Perhaps the most accessible account of Scotus's view of original justice is found in R. Cross, *Duns Scotus*, 96–99.

Chapter 6

1. D. Burr, *The Spiritual Franciscans: From Protest to Persecution in the Century After Saint Francis* (University Park: Pennsylvania State University Press, 2001), 6–9.

2. D. Luscombe, "Anselm on the Angels," *Rivista di storia della filosofia* 3 (1993): 537.

3. G. Evans, "Why the Fall of Satan?" *Recherches de Theologie Ancienne et Medievale* 45 (1978): 138.

4. J. Evans, *Paradise Lost and the Genesis Tradition* (Oxford: Clarendon Press, 1968), 176.

5. D. P. Henry, *The Logic of St. Anselm* (Oxford: Clarendon Press, 1967), 207–21.

6. F. Copleston, *A History of Philosophy* (New York: Doubleday, 1993), 2:41.

7. *The Old Testament Pseudepigrapha*, ed. J. Charlesworth (New York: Doubleday, 1983), 2:256.

8. For the discussion that follows, I have used the text that appears in *Duns Scotus on the Will and Morality*, trans. A. Wolter (Washington, DC: Catholic University of America Press, 1987), 463–77.

9. This story is conveyed by Hastings Rashdall in *The Universities of Europe in the Middle Ages* (Oxford: Oxford University Press, 1958), 1:334–35.

10. J. Brundage, *Medieval Canon Law* (New York: Longman, 1995), 20.

11. J. Brundage, *Medieval Canon Law*, 27.

12. K. Pennington, "Law, Legislative Authority, and Theories of Government, 1150–1300," in *Cambridge History of Medieval Political Thought* (Cambridge: Cambridge University Press, 1991), 425.

13. See the general introduction by David Hugh Farmer in *Butler's Lives of the Saints* (Collegeville, MN: Liturgical Press, 1998), xiv–xv.
14. *Butler's Lives of the Saints*, 120.

Chapter 7

1. R. Southern, *The Making of the Middle Ages*, (London: St. Anthony Guild Press, 1953), 67–73.
2. E. Gilson, *The Philosophy of St. Bonaventure* (Paterson, NJ: St. Anthony Guild Press, 1965), 31.
3. D. J. Geanakoplos, "Bonaventura, the Two Mendicant Orders, and the Greeks at the Council of Lyons," in *The Orthodox Churches and the West*, ed. D. Baker, Studies in Church History 13 (Oxford: Blackwell, 1976), 183–211.
4. J. Duns Scotus, *Opera Omnia* (Vatican City: Typis Polyglottis 1950–), Ordinatio I, d.11, q.1, n.1–2.
5. My translation; see Ordinatio I, d.11, q.1, n.4.
6. My translation; see Ordinatio I, d.11, q.1, n.9.
7. Ordinatio I, d.11, q.1, n.10.
8. Augustine, *De trinitate*, Curia et Studio W. J. Mountina, Corpus Christianorum Series Latina; 50, 50A. Aurelii Augustin; Opera; pars. 16, 1–2 Typographi Brepols Editores Pontsficii, (Turnholt 1968), 15:27.
9. See Henry of Ghent, *Summae Quaestionum Ordinarium* (New York: Franciscan Institute Publications, 1953), a. 54 a. 6 B.
10. See Henry of Ghent, *Summae Quaestionum Ordinariarum*, LX q. III fo. CLXIII.
11. See J. Duns Scotus, *Opera Omnia*, Ordinatio I, d.11, q.1, n.17.
12. My translation; see Ordinatio I, d.11, q.1, n.1.
13. Ordinatio I, d.11, q.1, n.20.
14. My translation; see ibid.

Chapter 8

1. *Late Medieval Mysticism*, ed. R. C. Petry, Library of Christian Classics (Philadelphia: Westminster Press, 1968), 289.
2. B. Hägglund, *History of Theology* (St. Louis: Concordia Publishing House, 1968), 219.
3. *Encyclical Letter Fides et Ratio of the Supreme Pontiff John Paul II to the Bishops of the Catholic Church on the Relationship between Faith and Reason* (Boston: Pauline Books and Media, 1998), 43.
4. See, for example, the editor's note in *Calvin: Institutes of the Christian Religion*, vol. 2, ed. J. McNeill (Philadelphia: Westminster Press, 1960), IV, 5, 7, n. 18, p. 1091.
5. A. Broadie, *The Shadow of Scotus: Philosophy and Faith in Pre-Reformation Scotland* (Edinburgh: T. & T. Clark, 1995), 6.

Selected Bibliography

Reference Works

The Columbia History of Western Philosophy. Ed. R. Popkin. New York: MJF Books, 1999.

Dictionary of the Middle Ages. Ed. J. R. Strayer. New York: Charles Scribner's Sons, 1982–1989.

Encyclopedia of the Renaissance. Ed. P. Grendler. New York: Charles Scribner's Sons, 1999.

Harvey, Van A. *A Handbook of Theological Terms.* Collier Books. New York: Macmillan Publishing, 1964.

Kelly, J. N. D. *Oxford Dictionary of Popes.* New York: Oxford University Press, 1996.

New Catholic Encyclopedia. 2nd ed. New York: Thomson Gale, 2003.

Oxford Dictionary of the Christian Church. Ed. F. L. Cross. Oxford: Oxford University Press, 1989.

Stockhammer, M. *Thomas Aquinas Dictionary.* New York: Philosophical Library, 1965.

Selected Bibliography of English Resources

Back, A. "Anselm on Perfect Islands." *Franciscan Studies* 43 (1983): 188–204.

———. "Scotus on the Consistency of the Incarnation." *Vivarium* 36 (1998): 83–107.

Bainton, R. *The Medieval Church.* Malabar: Krieger Publishing Co., 1979.

Balic, C. *John Duns Scotus, Some Reflections on the Occasion of the Seventh Centenary of His Birth.* Rome: Scotistic Commission, 1966.

Barnette, R. "Anselm and the Fool." *International Journal for Philosophy of Religion* 6 (1975): 201–18.

Barraclough, G. *The Medieval Papacy.* New York: Norton and Co., 1968.

Beha, H. M. "Matthew of Aquasparta's Theory of Cognition I." *Franciscan Studies* 20 (1960): 161–204.

Bettoni, E. *Duns Scotus: The Basic Principles of His Philosophy.* Ed. B. Bonansea. Westport, CT: Greenwood Press, 1978.

Bonansea, B. *Man and His Approach to God in John Duns Scotus.* New York: University Press of America, 1983.

Broadie, A. *The Shadow of Scotus: Philosophy and Faith in Pre-Reformation Scotland.* Edinburgh: T. & T. Clark, 1995.

Brown, P. *Augustine of Hippo.* Berkeley: University of California Press, 1969.

Brundage, J. *Medieval Canon Law.* New York: Longman, 1995.

Cambridge History of the Bible: The West from the Fathers to the Reformation. Vol. 2. Ed. G. W. H. Lampe. New York: Cambridge University Press, 1989.

Cambridge History of Later Medieval Philosophy. Ed. N. Kretzmann, A. Kenny, J. Pinborg. Cambridge: Cambridge University Press, 1982.

Cambridge History of Medieval Political Thought, c. 350–c. 1450. Ed. J.H. Burns. Cambridge: Cambridge University Press, 1991.

Campbell, R. "Anselm's Theological Method." *Scottish Journal of Theology* 32, no. 6 (1979): 541–62.

Cantor, N. *Medieval History: The Life and Death of a Civilization.* New York: Macmillan Co., 1963.

Chadwick, H. *Augustine.* Past Masters. New York: Oxford University Press, 1986.

Collins, R. *Charlemagne.* Toronto: University of Toronto Press, 1998.

———. *Early Medieval Europe, 300–1000.* London: Macmillan, 1991.

Copleston, F. *A History of Philosophy.* Vol. 2. New York: Doubleday Image, 1993.

Cowdrey, H. E. J. *The Cluniacs and the Gregorian Reform.* Oxford: Clarendon Press, 1970.

D'Arcy, M. C., M. Blondel, et al. *St. Augustine, His Age, Life, and Thought.* New York: Meridian Books, 1958.

Davis, R. H. C. *A History of Medieval Europe, from Constantine to Saint Louis.* 2nd ed. London: Longman, 1988.

d'Avray, D. L. *The Preaching of the Friars.* Oxford: Clarendon Press, 1985.

De doctrina Ioannis Duns Scoti, acta Congressus Scotistici internationalis Oxonii et Edimburgi 11-17 sept. 1966 celebrati. Vol. 3. *Problemata Theologica.* Rome: Cura Commissionis Scotisticae, 1968.

Denton, J. *Philip the Fair and the Ecclesiastical Assemblies of 1294–1295. Transactions of the American Philosophical Society* 81 (1991).

———. "Taxation and the Conflict between Philip the Fair and Boniface VIII." *French History* 11, no. 3 (1997): 241–64.

Doyle, J. P. "Saint Bonaventure and the Ontological Argument." *The Modern Schoolman* 52 (1974): 27–48.

———. "Some Thoughts on Duns Scotus and the Ontological Argument." *The New Scholasticism* 53 (1979): 234–41.

Duffy, E. *Saints and Sinners: A History of the Popes.* New Haven, CT: Yale University Press, 1997.

Evans, G. R. "Why the Fall of Satan?" *Recherches de Theologie Ancienne et Medievale* 45 (1978): 130–46.

Fakhry, M. *A History of Islamic Philosophy.* 2nd ed. New York: Columbia University Press, 1983.

Farmer, S. and Rosenwein, B., eds. *Monks and Nuns, Saints and Outcasts: Religion in Medieval Society: Essays in Honor of Lester K. Little.* Ithaca, NY: Cornell University Press, 2000.

Frank, W. and Wolter, A. *Duns Scotus, Metaphysician.* West Lafayette, IN: Purdue University Press, 1995.

Getz, F. *Medicine in the English Middle Ages.* Princeton, NJ: Princeton University Press, 1998.

Gill, J. *Eugenius IV, Pope of Christian Union.* Westminster, MD: Newman Press, 1961.

Gilson, E. *A History of Christian Philosophy in the Middle Ages.* New York: Random House, 1955.

———. *The Philosophy of St. Bonaventure.* Paterson, NJ: St. Anthony Guild Press, 1965.

———. *The Philosophy of St. Thomas Aquinas.* Trans. E. Bullough. Salem, NH: Ayer Co., 1983.

———. *The Spirit of Mediaeval Philosophy.* Trans. A. H. C. Downs. Notre Dame, IN: University of Notre Dame Press, 1991.

Giordani, I. *Saint Catherine of Siena, Doctor of the Church.* Boston: St. Paul Editions, 1975.

González, J. *The Story of Christianity*. Vol. 1. New York: Harper Collins, 1984.

Goodman, L. *Avicenna*. London: Routledge Press, 1992.

Grant, R., and D. Tracy. *A Short History of the Interpretation of the Bible*. 2nd ed. Philadelphia: Fortress Press, 1989.

Grmek, M. D. *Western Medical Thought from Antiquity to the Middle Ages*. Trans. A. Shugaar. Cambridge, MA: Harvard University Press, 1998.

Gross, C. "The Political Influence of the University of Paris in the Middle Ages." *American Historical Review* 3 (1901): 440–45.

Hägglund, B. *History of Theology*. Trans. Gene Lund. St. Louis: Concordia Publishing House, 1968.

Hallam, E., and J. Everard. *Capetian France 987–1328*. Harlow: Longman, 2001.

Hayes, Z. "Incarnation and Creation in the Theology of St. Bonaventure." In *Studies Honoring Ignatius Charles Brady*, 309–29. St. Bonaventure, NY: Franciscan Institute, 1976.

Henry of Ghent: Proceedings of the International Colloquium on the Occasion of the 700th Anniversary of His Death (1293). Ed. W. Vanhamel. Leuven: Leuven University Press, 1996.

A History of Private Life, Revelations of the Medieval World. Ed. G. Duby. Cambridge, MA: Belknap Press, 1988.

A History of Twelfth-Century Western Philosophy. Ed. P. Dronke. Cambridge: Cambridge University Press, 1992.

Kneale, W., and M. Kneale. *The Development of Logic*. Oxford: Clarendon Press, 1984.

Knowles, D. *The Evolution of Medieval Thought*. New York: Vintage Books, 1962.

Knowles, D. and D. Obolensky. *The Christian Centuries*. Vol. 2. New York: Paulist Press, 1983.

Lawrence, C. H. *The Friars: The Impact of the Early Mendicant Movement on Western Society*. London: Longman, 1994.

Leaman, O. *An Introduction to Medieval Islamic Philosophy*. Cambridge: Cambridge University Press, 1992.

———. *Averroës and His Philosophy*. Oxford: Clarendon Press, 1988.

Leff, G. "The Changing Pattern of Thought in the Earlier Fourteenth Century." *Bulletin of John Rylands Library* (1961): 354–72.

———. *Medieval Thought: From St. Augustine to Ockham*. Chicago: Quadrangle Books, 1958.

Little, A. G. "Chronological Notes on the Life of Duns Scotus." *English Historical Review* (October 1932): 568–82.

Luscombe, D. "Anselm on the Angels." *Rivista di storia della filosofia* 3 (1993): 537–49.

———. *Medieval Thought*. Oxford: Oxford University Press, 1997.

Marenbon, J. *Boethius*. Oxford: Oxford University Press, 2003.

———. *Later Medieval Philosophy, 1150-1350*. London: Routledge & Kegan Paul, 1987.

Martinich, A. P. "Scotus and Anselm on the Existence of God." *Franciscan Studies* 37 (1977): 139–52.

McCord Adams, M. "Fides Quaerens Intellectum: St. Anselm's Method in Philosophical Theology." *Faith and Philosophy* 9, no. 4 (October 1992): 409–35.

———. *William Ockham*. Vol. 2. Notre Dame, IN: University of Notre Dame Press, 1987.

McKitterick, R. *The Frankish Kingdoms under the Carolingians*. London: Longman, 1983.

———. *The Frankish Church and the Carolingian Reforms, 789–895*. London: Royal Historical Society, 1977.

New Cambridge Medieval History. Vol. 2, 700–900. Ed. R. McKitterick. Cambridge: Cambridge University Press, 1995.

Nicholson, M. F. "Celtic Theology: Pelagius." In *An Introduction to Celtic Theology*, 386–413. Edinburgh: T. & T. Clark, 1995.

Nimmo, D. *Reform and Division in the Medieval Franciscan Order*. Rome: Capuchin Historical Institute, 1987.

Painter, S. *Mediaeval Society*. Ithaca, NY: Cornell University Press, 1951.

Pegis, A. "St. Anselm and the Argument of the Proslogion." *Mediaeval Studies* 28 (1966): 228–67.

Pelikan, J. *Mary through the Centuries: Her Place in the History of Culture*. New Haven, CT: Yale University Press, 1996.

Plantinga, A. "Aquinas on Anselm." In *God and the Good, Essays in Honor of Henry Stob*, ed. C. Orlebeke and L. Smedes, 122–39. Grand Rapids: Wm. B. Eerdmans, 1975.

Powicke, M. *The Thirteenth Century 1216–1307*. Oxford History of England. Oxford: Oxford University Press, 1998.

Rabbitte, E. "The 'Motive' of the Incarnation: Was Scotus a Scotist?" *Irish Ecclesiastical Record* 70 (1948): 878–89.

Rashdall, H. *The Universities of Europe in the Middle Ages*. Vols. 1–3. Oxford: Oxford University Press, 1958.

Richard, J. *The Crusades, 1071–1291*. Cambridge: Cambridge Medieval Textbooks, 1999.

Russell, B. *A History of Western Philosophy*. New York: Simon & Schuster, 1972.

Ryan, J. *The Nature, Structure, and Function of the Church in William of Ockham*. AAR Studies in Religion 16. Missoula, MT: Scholars Press, 1979.

Schaefer, A. "The Position and Function of Man in the Created World according to St. Bonaventure." *Franciscan Studies* 20 (1960): 261–316.

Shannon, T. *The Ethical Theory of John Duns Scotus*. Quincy, IL: Franciscan Press, 1995.

Smalley, B. *The Study of the Bible in the Middle Ages*. Notre Dame, IN: University of Notre Dame Press, 1978.

Southern, R. W. *Western Society and the Church in the Middle Ages*. London: Penguin Books, 1970.

Strayer, J. R. *The Reign of Philip the Fair*. Princeton, NJ: Princeton University Press, 1980.

Unger, D. "Franciscan Christology: Absolute and Universal Primacy." *Franciscan Studies* 2 (1942): 429–75.

Watt, W. M. *Islamic Philosophy and Theology, An Extended Survey*. Edinburgh: Edinburgh University Press, 1992.

Wieruszowski, H. *The Medieval University*. New York: D. Van Nostrand Co., 1966.

Wippel, J. *Mediaeval Reactions to the Encounter between Faith and Reason*. Milwaukee, WI: Marquette University Press, 1995.

Wolter, A., and B. O'Neill. *John Duns Scotus, Mary's Architect*. Quincy, IL: Franciscan Press, 1993.

———. "Reflections on the Life and Works of Scotus." *American Catholic Philosophical Quarterly* 57, no. 1 (1993): 1–36.

Wood, C. "The English Crises of 1297 in the Light of the French Experience." *Journal of British Studies* 18 (1979): 1–13.

Wood, I. *The Merovingian Kingdoms 470–751*. London: Longman, 1994.

Wood, R. "Scotus's Argument for the Existence of God." *Franciscan Studies* 47 (1987): 257–77.

Primary Sources in English

Anselm of Canterbury. *Why God Became Man, The Virgin Conception and Original Sin.* New York: Magi Books, 1969.

Aquinas, T. *Summa Theologica.* Trans. Fathers of the English Dominican Province. Westminster, MD: Christian Classics, 1981.

Augustine. *The Essential Augustine.* Ed. V. Bourke. Indianapolis: Hackett Pub. Co., 1974.

———. *Nicene and Post Nicene Fathers.* Vols. 5 and 8. Ed. P. Schaff. Peabody, MA: Hendrickson Publishers, 1994.

Bede. *Ecclesiastical History of the English People.* London: Penguin Books, 1990.

Bernard of Clairvaux. *Bernard of Clairvaux, Selected Works.* Trans. G. R. Evans. Classics of Western Spirituality. New York: Paulist Press, 1987.

———. *The Steps of Humility and Pride.* Kalamazoo, MI: Cistercian Publications, 1989.

Bonaventure. *The Soul's Journey into God, The Tree of Life, The Life of St. Francis.* Classics of Western Spirituality. New York: Paulist Press, 1978.

Calvin, J. *Institutes of the Christian Religion.* 2 vols. Ed. J. McNeill. Trans. Ford Lewis Battles. Library of Christian Classics. Philadelphia: Westminster Press, 1960.

Dante Alighieri. *The Inferno.* Trans. J. Ciardi. New York: New American Library, 1954.

———. *The Purgatorio.* Trans. J. Ciardi. New York: New American Library, 1961.

Duns Scotus, J. *Duns Scotus on the Will and Morality.* Trans. A. B. Wolter. Washington, DC: Catholic University of America Press, 1986.

———. *Philosophical Writings.* Indianapolis: Hackett Pub. Co., 1987.

Julian of Norwich. *Showings.* Classics of Western Spirituality. New York: Paulist Press, 1978.

Late Medieval Mysticism. Ed. R. C. Petry. Library of Christian Classics. Philadelphia: Westminster Press, 1957.

Lives of the Eighth-Century Popes [Liber Pontificalis]. Trans. R. Davis. Liverpool: Liverpool University Press, 1992.

Index of Names of Persons

Index of Subjects

LINCOLN'S
Ladies

ALSO BY H. DONALD WINKLER

LINCOLN AND BOOTH
More Light on the Conspiracy

LINCOLN'S
Ladies

The Women in the Life of the Sixteenth President

H. DONALD WINKLER

Foreword by Chief Justice FRANK J. WILLIAMS
Chairman of the Lincoln Forum

CUMBERLAND HOUSE

NASHVILLE, TENNESSEE

Lincoln's Ladies: The Women in the Life of the Sixteenth President
Published by Cumberland House Publishing, Inc.
431 Harding Industrial Drive
Nashville, Tennessee 37211

This book is a revised and expanded edition of *The Women in Lincoln's Life* (2001).

Cover design by Gore Studio, Nashville, Tennessee.

Library of Congress Cataloging-in-Publication Data

Winkler, H. Donald, 1932–
    Lincoln's ladies : the women in the life of the sixteenth president / H. Donald Winkler.
        p.   cm.
    Rev. ed. of: The women in Lincoln's life. 2001.
    Includes bibliographical references.
    ISBN 1-58182-425-4 (pbk. : alk. paper)
    1. Lincoln, Abraham, 1809–1865—Relations with women. 2. Lincoln, Abraham, 1809–1865—Psychology. 3. Lincoln, Nancy Hanks, 1784–1818. 4. Rutledge, Ann, d. 1835. 5. Lincoln, Mary Todd, 1818–1882—Marriage. I. Winkler, H. Donald, 1932– Women in Lincoln's life. II. Title.
E457.2.W78 2004
973.7'092—dc22   2004014966

Printed in the United States of America

1 2 3 4 5 6 7 8 9 10 — 08 07 06 05 04

For Azile,
my loving wife and cheerleader since 1956.

For our sons, Don and Jim,
who make us proud to be their parents.

And for our grandchildren,
Ben, Jason, Jessica, and Michelle,
whom Ann Rutledge would have enjoyed knowing
as her first cousins, seven times removed.

I want in all cases to do right, and most particularly so, in all cases with women.

Abraham Lincoln, 1837

*M*r. Lincoln had a heart [like] a woman's—filled to overflowing with sympathy for those in trouble, and ever ready to relieve them by any means in his power.

G. W. Harris, a law student in Lincoln's
office in Springfield, Illinois

CONTENTS

FOREWORD

$\mathcal{A}$BRAHAM LINCOLN'S tumultuous encounters with women are well known, but H. Donald Winkler weaves these accounts together in a highly provocative and readable way to suggest their dramatic impact on Lincoln's personality, ambition, and spirit. In *Lincoln's Ladies: The Women in the Life of the Sixteenth President* (formerly *The Women in Lincoln's Life*), Winkler asserts that Lincoln became the Lincoln of history in large measure due to the influence of a few of these women.

The author ably demonstrates that the first three women in Lincoln's life were also among his most important teachers. These were his natural mother, Nancy Hanks Lincoln; his stepmother, Sarah Bush Johnston Lincoln; and his sister, Sarah. Lincoln's later episodes of depression most likely arose from the loss of his natural mother when he was nine years old. It is clear that he maintained his equally deep relationship with his stepmother throughout his life—continually revealing a lifelong concern about her welfare. Though much less is known about his sister, her early death seems to have contributed to his tendency to a lifelong sense of melancholy. In each of these relationships, Lincoln emerges as a deeply caring person. Dealing with death at an early age led him to appreciate and empathize with the plight of others.

Winkler shows that Lincoln continually sought the company of women between the time of his leaving home and his eventual marriage, especially since his relationship with his father was less than satisfying. His short relationship with Ann Rutledge may have been his first true love, but unfortunately it ended tragically with her untimely death. The author argues that Lincoln never fully recovered from her death. The author sides with those who view this as Lincoln's most passionate relationship. At the very least this relationship suggests Lincoln's early and continued need for feminine companionship. His subsequent awkward and perhaps bumbling relationship with Mary Owens reflects a second effort on his part. His search for companionship was also noticed by the married women who knew him. Their concern for him made them want to act as matchmakers for him.

In this new edition, Winkler adds an appendix on "Evidence of the Lincoln-Rutledge Romance and Engagement" to substantiate what may have been Lincoln's first serious relationship. It includes relevant quotes from *Herndon's Informants* (edited by Douglas Wilson and Rodney O. Davis) with emphasis on statements by Robert Rutledge (Ann's brother); Will Prewitt, grandson of Ann's mother (she lived with Prewitt for several years and died at his home); statements by Jean Rutledge (Ann's oldest sister) and Elizabeth Grimsley (Mary Lincoln's cousin) as reported by journalist Ida Tarbell; and John Hill's article, "A Romance of Reality," in the *Menard Axis* of February 15, 1862. Hill was the son of Parthena Nance (Ann's best friend) and Sam Hill (Ann's second suitor). The article was the first published account of the Lincoln-Rutledge romance. Isaac Cogdal, a New Salem friend of Lincoln's, purportedly met with Lincoln in 1861 and reported Lincoln saying about Ann, "It is true—true indeed [that I loved her and courted her]. . . . I did honestly and truly love the girl, and think often, often, of her now." Winkler includes the purported recollections of Lincoln's Springfield housekeeper Mariah Vance about turmoil between Lincoln and his wife triggered by memories of Ann Rutledge. In addition to the Rutledge speculation, Winkler has uncovered more documented information about Ann's life than has previously been known as well as fresh material about the Lincoln-Rutledge romance from sources such as Ann's close friend Parthena Nance and Ann's cousins, the Camron girls, who lived next door to Ann in New Salem.

Of course the best documented woman in Lincoln's life was Mary Todd, his spouse of twenty-three years. She proved to be his most complex relationship. The pattern of his earlier relationships and particularly his relationship with Mary suggests that his motivation was to marry up, although Winkler builds a case that doing the "honorable thing" was a major factor in the Lincolns' marriage. Still, both shared a passion for politics. And if Lincoln wanted to move up socially, Mary wanted to move up politically to what she considered her rightful place. She continually promoted and encouraged his political advancement. At the same time, both were emotionally needy partners who learned at some level to deal with each other's deficits. Winkler concludes that the relationship was "Lincoln's greatest tragedy." Yet they forged an enduring relationship that, however imperfect, was enriched by the concern, love, and enjoyment they both had for their children. The turbulent marriage may have furthered Lincoln's appreciation of the complexity of human behavior.

Winkler also presents material on other women with whom Lincoln interacted, such as Caroline Meeker of Kentucky (who apparently wanted to marry him), activist Sojourner Truth, and Quaker religious counselor Eliza Gurney. Contrary to those who traditionally link leadership only to masculinity and detached objectivity, the most haunting images of Lincoln are often unmistakably feminine. For that reason alone this study becomes an important one.

Lincoln's women shaped the extent and dimension of his emotional life. Without these interactions, it is hard to imagine that he could have become the greatest American president and democratic political leader in world history. These women taught Lincoln to appreciate and value others in a profound sense. At a fairly early age he learned that others could teach him about life, just as he could later teach them, regardless of his own humble origin. These were essential lessons in his development as an individual and a politician. Even if a reader may not agree with every one of the author's conclusions, Winkler is right that, in a broad sense, it was the positive impact women had on Lincoln that helped form him—even though these relationships involved hardship, loss, rejection, and compromise. The women in Lincoln's life provided a necessary grounding that balanced him and that today makes him more accessible to us who know him only through history. This book is a great place to begin to appreciate the feminine contribution to Abraham Lincoln's historical legacy.

Frank J. Williams

FRANK J. WILLIAMS is the founding Chair of The Lincoln Forum and Chief Justice of the Rhode Island Supreme Court. His latest book, *Judging Lincoln,* was published by Southern Illinois University Press.

ACKNOWLEDGMENTS

$\mathcal{T}$HE FOLLOWING persons and institutions are respectfully acknowledged
for their important services in the development of this book:

Genealogists: Charlotte Bergevin, Peoria, Illinois; George R. Rutledge,
Hanover, Pennsylvania; Sharon Schirding, Petersburg, Illinois; Irene
Wilson, San Diego, California; and Ralph E. Winkler, Lakeside, California.

Agencies and Libraries: Betty Webb, Anna Porter Public Library, Gatlin-
burg, Tennessee; Darlene Epperson and Linda Wilson, Beaufort County
Library, Hilton Head Island, South Carolina; Joelle Bertolet, Haverford Col-
lege Library; Linda Hallmark, Henderson County Historical and Genealogi-
cal Society (KY); James T. Murphy and Iver F. Yeager of Illinois College,
Jacksonville, Illinois; New Salem Lincoln League; David Blanchette, Illinois
Historic Preservation Agency; Illinois State Historical Library; Library of
Congress; Carol Jenkins, Mary Ann Russell, and Charles Starling, Lincoln's
New Salem State Historic Site; Menard County Historical Society (IL); and
Emily Jansen, *New England Quarterly.*

Individuals: historian Webb Garrison, Lake Junaluska, North Carolina;
philanthropist Mabel Gunn, Stone Mountain, Georgia; New Salem informants Georgia Leinberger and Raymond H. Montgomery, Petersburg, Illinois;
frontier historian Susan Hatton McCoy, Peoria, Illinois; Mohamed Danawi
and Dan McGregor, Savannah College of Art and Design, Savannah, Georgia; and my wife, Azile, the 1992 Virginia DAR Outstanding Teacher of
American History.

Special thanks are due to historians Steven L. Carson and Rod Gragg,
who read the original manuscript and identified various areas for improvement; to historian Michael Burlingame, who provided recently discovered

information about Ann Rutledge; and to my editor at Cumberland House, Ed Curtis, whose support and advice made *Lincoln's Ladies* a far better book.

I am especially indebted to Chief Justice Frank J. Williams of Rhode Island, who graciously agreed to write the foreword to this edition. A Lincoln scholar, collector, and author, he is chairman of the prestigious Lincoln Forum and a member of the U.S. Lincoln Bicentennial Commission, which is planning the official nationwide observance of Lincoln's two-hundredth birthday in 2009. Williams's review of this book's first edition inspired significant changes and additions.

Finally, I thank all historians, journalists, and genealogists of present and earlier generations who have taken a special interest in Lincoln's relationships with women and have contributed informational gems that, combined, provide a treasure chest of rich resources.

INTRODUCTION

$\mathcal{I}$T TOOK a postcard to prime my interest in this subject.

I remember it falling to the ground from the pile of bills and junk mail I pulled from the mailbox. The postcard was from my brother Ralph, our family's genealogist. There was a photo of a log home on one side and a simple message on the other: "Congratulations! You are a first cousin of Ann Rutledge! More information will follow." From my school days in southern Illinois I remembered Ann Rutledge's name. She was somehow connected with Abraham Lincoln, perhaps as a girlfriend. At the time, however, I was busily engaged in a high-level administrative position at a university in central Virginia, and there was little time to ponder genealogy.

While I savored a bowl of chili in the college dining room a few days later, a history professor sat down at my table. "What do you know about Ann Rutledge?" I asked. "Oh," he said, "she was once thought to be Lincoln's sweetheart, but most historians think the story is pure nonsense. Why do you ask?" I reported my recent news. "Her paternal grandparents were my five-times great-grandparents. Should I be ecstatic?" I laughed. "Well, it's interesting," he replied, "but if it's only folklore, it's not worth talking about. I suggest you read J. G. Randall's book on Lincoln."

Randall, I learned, was an imposing Lincoln scholar of the 1940s—a scholar so respected that when he called the romance "a great myth" everyone assumed that it was. Randall repudiated the love story revealed by William H. Herndon, Lincoln's longtime law partner and early biographer. Herndon discovered the romance during his twenty-five-year search for information about the martyred president—a search that produced a voluminous collection of letters, interviews, and statements. According to Herndon, the Lincoln-Rutledge romance and her tragic death were keys to Lincoln's greatness and to his chronic melancholy. Historian Randall regarded Herndon's rambling accounts as unreliable, however, and suggested that Herndon had created his account of the romance because he disliked Mary Todd Lincoln. Who was I to question J. G. Randall's conclusions? So I forgot about my cousin Ann for the next three years. In January 1991 my wife's brother-in-law, Webb Garrison, called. He had written numerous books on the Civil War and was aware of my relationship to Ann Rutledge. "I've got two articles in front of me that I think you'll find interesting," he said. "Both were published this past year. One is in the *Journal of the Abraham Lincoln Association;* the other is in *Civil War History.* Both shed new light on the romance."

The first, by Lincoln scholar John Y. Simon of Southern Illinois University, was based on his exhaustive study of Herndon's source material. Simon acknowledged Herndon's "misuse of the romance to settle scores with Mary Lincoln," but he also noted serious problems in Randall's work. "All the primary sources—the testimony of witnesses—support the romance," Simon argued, "and the reality of the story appears certain."

The second article, by Douglas L. Wilson, director of the Center for Lincoln Studies at Knox College, added more substance. Wilson found statements from twenty-four witnesses in Herndon's documents. They included Ann's teacher, siblings, and relatives and Lincoln's friends and associates. Wilson considered these witnesses to be "straightforward and reliable" and "with no purpose to deceive."

Significantly, no witness denied Lincoln's love for Ann. Fifteen knew about the Lincoln-Rutledge engagement; twenty-two knew that Lincoln courted Ann; and seventeen knew that he grieved excessively after her death.

The reports from Simon and Wilson were so convincing that I began my own research, reading everything I could find on Lincoln and Ann Rutledge. The work intensified after my retirement in 1995. I secured and read more than one hundred books and articles and even retraced Lincoln's travels down the Mississippi River (although I chose an elegant steamboat over the kind of flatboat he used).

Research of Herndon's materials at the Library of Congress was next on my agenda, but I was spared that tedious work by the publication of *Herndon's Informants* (edited by Wilson and Rodney O. Davis) in 1998. It contained not only all of Herndon's materials but also items collected by his collaborator, Jesse W. Weik. Other recent works also reinforced the revived theory about the romance, especially *The Shadows Rise* by John E. Walsh.

Even with all these resources, the complete story of Ann's life and relationship with Abraham Lincoln remained untold. With the material I had accumulated from persistent research, I felt I could do so. In my bulging files were stories from obscure sources apparently seen by few historians—family genealogy from the New Salem community where Lincoln and Ann lived; testimony from daughters of Ann's cousin, John Miller Camron; Camron family scrapbooks of period newspaper reports; and accounts of Ann's early life in White County, Illinois, by Margaret Land, a family historian.

Further investigation into the Camron and Rutledge families uncovered a 195-page manuscript, "Camerons, Westward They Came," by Charlotte Bergevin, Daisy Sundberg, and Evelyn Berg, which provided valuable information. Of special help were the papers of descendants of Ann's siblings and relatives: James Rutledge Saunders, George Rutledge, C. Vale Mayes, Pauline Warthen, and Capt. Keith F. Brown. My brother Ralph also provided substantial information.

Culminating my search for the real Ann Rutledge, I explored Rutledge and Lincoln sites in Illinois and participated in a workshop at New Salem addressed by historian Michael Burlingame. He graciously shared with me some new research about Ann. Through New Salem volunteer Georgia Leinberger I met genealogist Sharon L. Schirding, who is a distant cousin of John Camron's wife and the niece of Julia Drake, one of Camron's biographers. Sharon Schirding provided background material used by her aunt in writing the biography. It contains interesting anecdotes about Ann and the relationship between Camron's daughters and Lincoln. The people of central Illinois were unusually hospitable to me. When I asked for directions to Ann's original gravesite, Georgia Leinberger shook her head. "It's impossible to tell you. You could never find it. But Mrs. Schirding and I will be happy to guide you there." And they did. A few miles from Petersburg they turned off a state road into a space between cornfields. It felt like a rough tractor path overgrown with weeds. About a half mile down the trail a flagpole marked the Old Concord Burial Ground. Many headstones were hidden by knee-high weeds, but near the middle of the cemetery was Ann's original grave. Here Ann lay buried for fifty-five years before her remains were reinterred at Oakland Cemetery in Petersburg, Illinois. Here, at Old Concord, Lincoln wept for days. I stood there and absorbed the historical significance of this obscure location.

I had also researched Mary Todd and found remarkably diverse opinions about her marriage to Lincoln—and about their courtship. The differences led me to look deeper into Lincoln's relationship with his wife. Especially helpful were biographies of Mary Todd and works by Burlingame (*The Inner World of Abraham Lincoln*) and Wilson (*Honor's Voice*). The more I studied, the more I discovered other women who had influenced Lincoln. I became so intrigued that I expanded my work to examine the way women affected Lincoln's life as well as the impact he had on many of them.

For me, closure on this subject finally came when I signed a contract to publish this book. Ironically, the signing occurred at a meeting in the palatial Charleston Place Hotel in Charleston, South Carolina, where the first shots of the Civil War were fired in the opening days of Lincoln's presidency. As my wife and I were homeward bound, she asked me, "Do you think Lincoln would like this book?"

No, I started to say, because he was a very private person, and this book pokes into private matters. But on further reflection, I replied, "I think he might, but only if he knew his wife would never see it!"

LINCOLN'S
Ladies

1

"All That I Am or Ever Hope to Be I Owe to Her"

𝒯HE PRETTIEST, smartest, and sweetest girl around was dead. Her name was Ann Rutledge, and she was the fiancee of Abraham Lincoln.

"He sorrowed and grieved, rambled over the hills and through the forests, day and night. . . . He slept not, he ate not, joyed not. This he did until his body became emaciated and weak. His mind wandered from its throne. . . . It has been said that Mr. Lincoln became and was totally insane at that time and place." So spoke Lincoln's friend, law partner, and biographer, William H. Herndon, in a lecture delivered the year after Lincoln's death. "Lincoln loved Ann Rutledge better than his own life," Herndon said. He loved her "with all his soul, mind, and strength," and "she loved him dearly. . . . They seemed made in heaven for each other."

The untimely death of Ann Rutledge appears to have had a phenomenal impact on Lincoln's life. Herndon claimed that "the love and death of this girl shattered Lincoln's purposes and tendencies" and that "he threw off his infinite sorrow by leaping wildly into the political arena." Had she lived and married Lincoln, would he have been content as a lawyer outside the political arena? Would he ever have become president? There are no answers to these questions, but without a doubt Lincoln's life was dramatically shaped by a succession of remarkable women—beginning with his mother.

3

Yet from all accounts, Lincoln was ashamed of his mother. In his auto-
biographical musings he said little about Nancy Hanks. He visited her
grave only once and never had it marked with a headstone. In an 1836 letter he matter-of-factly recorded a callous description of his mother's "want
of teeth [and] weather-beaten appearance." But he apparently believed that
to her noble bloodline he owed much of his success. His fierce ambition—
his driving desire to *be* someone—came, he told William Herndon, from
his mother.[1]

"My mother was the illegitimate daughter of Lucy Hanks and a well-
bred Virginia planter or farmer," Lincoln confided to Herndon. "My grandmother was poor and credulous, and she was shamefully taken advantage
of by the man. My mother inherited his qualities, and I hers." According to
Herndon, Lincoln was convinced that from this unknown grandfather he
acquired his "power of analysis, logic, mental ability, ambition, and all the
qualities that distinguished him from . . . the Hanks family."[2]

Lincoln made his comments to Herndon as the two shared a buggy ride
en route to a distant court case about 1851. As the vehicle jolted over the
country road, Lincoln added ruefully, "God bless my mother. All that I am
or ever hope to be I owe to her." He then lapsed into silence and was "sad
and absorbed," Herndon recalled. Finally Lincoln spoke again, telling Herndon: "Keep it a secret while I live."[3]

Lincoln knew that his mother, with all her limitations—including an
inability to write—was a strong woman. She was strong-minded and had
"remarkably keen perception," according to her maternal cousin, Dennis
Hanks. These were uncommon traits within the Hanks family, which was
notable for notorious philanderers and numerous cases of illegitimacy. Lincoln's grandmother, Lucy Hanks, was charged with "fornication" by a
grand jury in Mercer County, Kentucky. No wedding certificate was ever
found for her.[4]

Nancy Hanks may have continued the family's illicit tradition. An Indiana neighbor who was Lincoln's age, Laurinda Mason Lanman, told an interviewer: "My mother . . . liked [the Lincolns] but she always said that not
only was Nancy Hanks an illegitimate child herself but that Nancy was not
what she ought to have been herself. Loose." Lincoln may have known
about her disgraceful reputation, according to Herndon. He told Herndon
that "his [relatives] were lascivious—lecherous not to be trusted."[5]

In early childhood Nancy was taken from her mother—afterward married to Henry Sparrow—and sent to live with her aunt and uncle, Thomas

and Elizabeth Hanks Sparrow. In late 1805, when Nancy was twenty-two, she drifted to Elizabethtown, Kentucky, and lived briefly with her uncle Joseph Hanks.

Thomas Lincoln, described by a neighbor as "an uneducated . . . plain unpretending plodding man," walked into Hanks's carpentry shop that winter and asked to be an apprentice. The rapidly growing frontier town needed carpenters, and Hanks needed help, so he hired Thomas. Soon Hanks introduced Thomas to Nancy, and the two began courting.[6]

Like Thomas, Nancy "cared nothing for forms, etiquette, and customs," according to Herndon. He further described her as "a bold, daredevil person who stepped to the very verge of propriety." At five feet ten inches and about 140 pounds, she was tall and athletic. "In a fair wrestle, she could throw most of the men who put her powers to test," a townsman recalled. "A reliable gentleman told me he heard Jack Thomas, clerk of the Grayson Court, say he had frequently wrestled with her, and she invariably laid him on his back." Thomas Lincoln may never have wrestled with Nancy Hanks, but he did propose to her, and she accepted. He was twenty-eight, and she twenty-three. They were reportedly married on June 12, 1806, in Washington County, Kentucky, and set up housekeeping in a log cabin in Elizabethtown, where their first child, Sarah, was born on February 10, 1807.[7]

In December 1808 Thomas paid two hundred dollars for a farm on the south fork of Nolin Creek, about two miles south of Hodgenville. It was called Sinking Spring farm after a bountiful spring at the bottom of a deep cave on the property. On a knoll near the spring, Thomas built a one-room log cabin, eighteen by sixteen feet, with a dirt floor and a door that swung on leather hinges. In that little cabin on a snowy winter evening Nancy went into labor. Soon after dawn on February 12, 1809, upon a bed of poles, cornhusks, and bearskins, Abraham Lincoln was born.

Childbirth for Kentucky pioneers could be frightening as well as joyful. With few doctors in the region, a midwife was necessary but often not called until the last moment. When his wife went into labor, Thomas Lincoln hurried to fetch the midwife. He ran into Abraham Enlow, one of his neighbors. Enlow volunteered to find a midwife and advised Thomas to stay with Nancy. Enlow returned with his mother, who oversaw the birth. Enlow claimed the baby was named for him to honor his "neighborliness." In later life Lincoln acknowledged that was partly true. "The Enlows were good to us, and Mother gave them the pattern of the quilt that covered me." Abraham was also named for his grandfather, whom Thomas, at age eight, had seen killed by an Indian. There had not been a generation of Lincolns without an Abraham since the late seventeenth century.[8]

As a child, Lincoln undoubtedly heard gossip about his possible illegitimacy. When he ran for president in 1860 his political opponents zeroed in on the old stories and repeated them with vicious abandon. To counter the political damage, Lincoln wrote to Samuel Haycraft, clerk of the court in Hardin County, Kentucky, asking him to find the marriage record. Haycraft, a local historian and loyal Union supporter, had grown up in Elizabethtown and had known Thomas Lincoln. But whatever search he conducted apparently failed to turn up the requested document.

Lincoln's longtime friend Ward Hill Lamon later claimed that there was no marriage license. Thomas Lincoln's marriage was a common law agreement with "no evidence but that of mutual acknowledgment and cohabitation," Lamon wrote in his biography of Lincoln. In 1878, however, W. F. Booker, clerk of the court in Washington County, discovered two documents. While rummaging through piles of papers in the county courthouse, Booker reported that he found the marriage papers—a June 10, 1806, marriage bond signed by Thomas Lincoln and Richard Berry, guardian and uncle of Nancy Hanks, and an April 22, 1807, "marriage return" by Methodist circuit rider Jesse Head certifying he performed their marriage. Most Lincoln scholars accept the documents as genuine, even though the bond was a simple form with the signatures added. An actual marriage certificate was never found.[9]

In the nineteenth century an out-of-wedlock birth was scandalous. A worse sin was adultery, and in Lincoln's day rumors persisted that Nancy Hanks had adulterous relationships. Was someone other than Thomas Lincoln possibly the father of Abraham?[10]

Upon what were the rumors based? Thomas Lincoln was five feet ten inches tall and stout, weighing 195 pounds. He had a round face and a barrel chest. He was not likely, some suggested, to produce a slender son who would grow to a height of six feet four inches. Thomas was also said to be sterile, according to the rumors. "Nancy Hanks was a rather loose woman," observed Alfred M. Brown, a respected judge who lived most of his life in Hodgenville. According to some claims, as many as sixteen men other than Thomas Lincoln have been credited with fathering Abraham Lincoln. Prominent sources in or near Elizabethtown claimed that either George Brownfield or Abraham Enlow (the helpful neighbor) was Lincoln's father. Author William E. Barton investigated Lincoln's paternity and published a book on the subject in 1920. He concluded that all the charges were nonsense.[11]

But were they? Sometime between mid-May and early June 1808—when Abraham was conceived—Thomas, Nancy, and toddler Sarah moved to George Brownfield's farm, where they lived as tenants on the property. Thomas served as a hired laborer until that fall, when the family settled at their Sinking Spring farm. Brownfield, then a thirty-five-year-old property owner, was a good-natured intellectual who resembled Lincoln in looks, height, and temperament.

Abraham Enlow also had notable Lincoln features—long arms and ears, a large nose, and very large feet. In his old age, Enlow publicly denied the allegations that he had fathered Lincoln. However, Presley Haycraft, a staunch Lincoln supporter, reported that Enlow privately claimed Lincoln as his son throughout his life. "Enlow [was] as low a fellow as you could find," reported John B. Helm, a local merchant and lawyer. Enlow lived with his sister Polly, whom Helm referred to as "a notorious prostitute." One of Polly's granddaughters, Lizzie Murphy, claimed she often heard her mother and grandmother refer to Enlow as Lincoln's real father. Helm reported that Enlow once bragged that he was Abe's father, prompting a fight with Thomas Lincoln, who bit off a chunk of Enlow's nose. "I remember [Enlow and his maimed nose] as one of the institutions of our county for some thirty years," Helm recalled. One reason Thomas Lincoln left Kentucky, Helm claimed, was "to get clear of Abe Enlow."[12]

Skeptics argued that Enlow could not have been Abraham's father because he was only fourteen or fifteen at the time Abe was conceived. And in early May 1808 the Lincolns were still living in Elizabethtown. Enlow was big for his age, however, and could have worked or visited relatives there. Also, it's not clear where the Lincolns actually resided just before moving to George Brownfield's farm. Adding to the conjecture about Lincoln's paternity was the fact that widower Thomas Lincoln, forty-one, married a thirty-one-year-old healthy and fertile woman in 1819, yet the couple never had children—proof, some said, of Thomas Lincoln's sterility. Herndon was convinced that Thomas Lincoln was incapable of fathering a child, and that his fight with Enlow occurred after Thomas caught Enlow with Nancy.[13]

Three other Abraham Enlows are listed by various authors as Abraham's father. These Enlows were from Rutherford County, North Carolina, and LaRue and Bourbon Counties in Kentucky. No primary records exist to lend credibility to any of these claims.

In 1816 Thomas gave up on Kentucky—motivated in part by land-title problems and reportedly his dislike of slavery—and moved his family to Indiana. As little Abe grew, he became more like his mother than his father— mild, tender, and athletic, with a strong memory and acute judgment. Her face, sharp and angular like his, projected a marked expression of melancholy. The same would be said of Lincoln after the death of Ann Rutledge and for the rest of his life. As a child, Abe suffered experiences that could have emotionally scarred any youngster. He was poor. He was continuously subjected to hard work, and was often punished for talking, asking questions, or studying.

Nancy had little time for her son. She and Sarah cooked, churned, cleaned, milked cows, hoed corn, dried beans, prepared tallow for candles, and made clay lamps. From Nancy's loom came clothes for the children and woolen blankets for the beds. She washed clothes in a large kettle by adding lye soap to the water and stirring the pot with a long-handled paddle. Survival in the wilderness required endless hours of tedious labor, so men prayed for sons, and mothers prayed for daughters—the more the better— to share the workload. But Thomas would have no more children—perhaps because he could not. His family was unusually small for his day.

At age eight, Abe was given an axe and required to clear trees, grub stumps, and split rails for fences—work usually reserved for older boys and men. He also had to carry heavy pails of drinking water about a mile—from a spring to the cabin. Settlers usually built their cabins near a spring or stream, but for reasons unknown, Thomas did not do that in Indiana.

Twice Abe nearly died. And both instances may reflect the nature of his relationship with his mother.

Abe's playmate was Austin Gollaher. One day as the two boys were hunting partridges, Abe crossed Knob Creek on a narrow log, lost his footing, and fell into the swollen stream. Neither boy could swim. Austin hurriedly found a long pole and held it out to Abe, who was struggling to stay afloat in the deep water. After several attempts, he finally grabbed it, and Austin pulled him out of the creek. "I thought he was almost dead," Austin later recalled, "and I was badly scared. I rolled and pounded him in good earnest. Then I got him by the arms and shook him . . . and the water [began] pouring out of his mouth. . . . He was soon alright."

Both boys became worried about what their mothers would do to them if they came home with wet clothes. "They would have whipped us hard," Austin recounted. "We dreaded their whippings from experience, and we were determined to avoid them." So they shed their clothes and dried them in the sun before returning home. Strangely, Abe seemed more afraid of his mother than his father.[14]

The other close call of Lincoln's childhood occurred at a gristmill on a fall day in 1818. Abe hitched an old mare to the arm of the gristmill, as was customary in grinding corn. It was late and he wanted to get home before dark, so with each revolution, he yelled, "Get up, you old hussy," and applied the lash. The horse responded with a fierce kick to Abe's forehead. It sent him sprawling to the earth, bleeding and unconscious. The mill owner summoned Thomas Lincoln, who loaded the seemingly lifeless child into a wagon and took him home.

The nine-year-old lay unconscious all night, but near daybreak he awoke and blurted out the words, "You old hussy . . . !"—finishing the phrase interrupted by the horse's kick. His mother seems to have been unconcerned about the injury. It was enough for her to leave matters in God's hands. She reportedly told Abe he did not die because it was "not his time," that Providence had "other designs" for him. "Nothing can hinder the execution of the designs of Providence," she said. "What is to be will be, and we can do nothing about it." Was Nancy Lincoln's untroubled response an admirable expression of faith or a lack of interest in her son?[15]

Abraham Lincoln's lifetime preoccupation with dreams and superstitions also appears to have come from his mother. A bird flying in the window, a horse's breath on a child's head, a dog crossing a hunter's path—all meant bad luck to Nancy Lincoln and her frontier neighbors. The moon had enormous influence. Fence rails could only be cut in the light of the moon, and potatoes planted in the dark of the moon. Trees and plants that bore their fruit above ground could be planted only when the moon shone full. Soap could be made only in the light of the moon, and it had to be stirred in only one direction and by only one person. Nothing was to be started on Friday, lest an endless chain of disasters occur. When a baby was due, an axe placed under the bed and a knife under the pillow supposedly eased the pain. Listening in boyish wonder to the legends his mother told him, Abe was led to believe in the significance of dreams and visions. Throughout his life, he would be puzzled and troubled by dreams, and he would hold a conviction that he was guided by forces beyond his control.[16]

His mother also influenced him in a positive manner. She introduced him to the Bible. In the winter the family gathered around the fireplace, and Nancy recited Bible stories. Those episodes produced Lincoln's warmest memories of his mother. His personal values, Lincoln would later claim, came from Scripture. "The fundamental truths reported in the four gospels . . . that I first heard from the lips of my mother," he would say, "are settled and fixed moral concepts with me."[17]

What Nancy did not do, or was unable to do, was restrain Thomas Lincoln from what Herndon called "cold and inhuman treatment" of Abe, treatment that may have been due primarily to Thomas's doubts about Abe being his son. Thomas, for example, physically abused Abe for asking child-like questions of neighbors, sometimes striking him with blows that knocked him to the ground. The boy did not cry, according to Abe's cousin Dennis Hanks, "but dropped a kind of silent, unwelcome tear, as evidence of his . . . feelings."[18]

Abraham Lincoln's greatest childhood pain occurred in the fall of 1818 when his mother died. A year earlier, Nancy's uncle and aunt, Tom and Elizabeth Hanks Sparrow, had moved into the Lincolns' neighborhood along with Dennis Hanks, Elizabeth's eighteen-year-old talkative and likable nephew.

In the fall of 1818 the Sparrows became ill from the deadly scourge called "milk-sickness" that swept through the Little Pigeon Creek community. The illness originated with a poisonous plant known as white snakeroot, which was grazed by cows and transmitted through their milk. In humans, the disease began with dizziness, nausea, and stomach pains. Then the skin turned clammy, breathing became irregular, and victims slipped into a coma. Death quickly followed—usually within a week.

Tom and Elizabeth were among the first to die. Nancy nursed them in their last hours, and then she too became ill. Abe and his sister nursed their mother and read Bible passages to her. Near death, she called the children to her side. Placing a feeble hand on Abe's head, she told him to be good and kind to his father and sister and to worship God. Later that day she died. She was thirty-five (some historians say thirty-four). Herndon would later write: "Groping through the perplexities of life, without prospect of any betterment in her condition, she passed from earth, little dreaming of the grand future that lay in store for the ragged, hapless little boy at [her] bedside."[19]

As Abe watched his mother agonize and die, he was devastated. "I'll never forget the mizry in that cabin," Dennis Hanks recalled. As Nancy's body lay in the same room where they ate and slept, "Abe an' me helped Tom make the coffin. He took a log left over from makin' the cabin, and I helped him whipsaw it into planks an' plane 'em. Me 'n Abe held the planks together while Tom bored holes an' put 'em together with pegs Abe'd whittled. . . . Abe never got over the mizable way his mother died."

When the coffin was ready, the family placed Nancy Lincoln's body on a sled and took her to a hillside near the cabin. They buried her next to her aunt and uncle. The burial was not accompanied by a funeral because there was no church in the remote neighborhood.

Dennis Hanks, with no place to go, moved in with the Lincolns and became an extra field hand for Thomas and an "older brother" for Abe. The Lincoln children were miserable that winter. Deprived of their mother's care, they craved encouragement and compassion, but Thomas was capable of neither. Eleven-year-old Sarah cooked and kept house, but she was lonesome and sad. Dennis and Abe gave her a baby coon and a turtle and tried to get a fawn, "but we couldn't ketch any," Dennis recalled.

In a remarkable gesture for a nine-year-old, Abe wrote to the family's former pastor in Kentucky and asked him to come and conduct proper burial rites for Nancy Lincoln. In the spring of 1819 the Baptist parson, David Elkins, rode one hundred miles on horseback to conduct the service. On a bright Sunday morning two hundred people gathered around Nancy's grave. As Parson Elkins said a final prayer, all the mourners fell upon their knees. Abe's wish for a proper burial had been fulfilled.

Despite any problems and peculiarities in his relationship with his mother, the boy was left with an empty heart—a feeling his mother had abandoned him. Historian Michael Burlingame, who used the tools of psychobiography to analyze Lincoln's attitudes and feelings, concluded that the death of his mother and his relationship with her may have convinced him "that women are untrustworthy and unreliable." In the years ahead Lincoln would face more "abandonments" by women he loved. Each episode would deepen his emotional scars and perhaps make it more difficult for him to relate to women.[20]

That summer, Abe and Sarah again may have felt abandoned when Thomas Lincoln returned to Kentucky to search for a new wife. He was gone nearly six months, and the children eventually assumed that he too had died. Left to live in squalor, they became hungry, ragged, and dirty. After almost half a year without parental support, Abe reportedly feared they would soon all be dead.[21]

2

"She Was Doubtless the First Person That Ever Treated Him Like a Human Being"

*W*HILE YOUNG Abe and Sarah were barely surviving in Indiana, their father returned to Elizabethtown, Kentucky. There Thomas Lincoln eventually called upon a thirty-one-year-old widow, Sarah Bush Johnston. She was a tall, sprightly, and talkative woman who had once declined Thomas's marriage proposal before he had met Nancy Hanks. Known as Sally, she was ten years younger than Thomas. Like Thomas, she was illiterate. Her former husband, the town jailer, had died of cholera in 1816. Before his death, she had cooked for the prisoners while rearing three children. After her husband's death, Sally had moved her family to a modest cabin, where Thomas found her.[1]

"Mrs. Johnston," he told her, "I have no wife and you no husband. I came [with] a-purpose to marry you. . . . I know you from a gal and you know me from a boy. I've no time to lose; and if you're willin' let it be done straight off."[2]

She could not marry him immediately, she explained, because she had debts to pay. "Give me a list of them," he told her. She did, and he paid the debts. The following day, December 2, 1819, Thomas Lincoln and Sally Johnston obtained a license and were married.[3]

13

Back in Indiana, meanwhile, Abe, Sarah, and Dennis assumed they were on their own. But in late December a four-horse wagon arrived at their cabin with their father and four strangers. In addition to the new Mrs. Lincoln, there were her three children—Matilda, John, and Sarah Elizabeth—ranging in age from eight to thirteen, and Sarah Bush Johnston Lincoln's furniture.

The little cabin became home to a family of eight. John slept with Abe and Dennis in the loft. The three girls slept in one corner of the main floor. The newlyweds slept in another corner. "Mrs. Lincoln soaped, scrubbed, and washed the children clean, so they looked pretty [and] neat," Dennis later recollected. "She sewed and mended their clothes, and the children once more looked human."

A resourceful woman, Sally immediately began to improve her home. She cleaned it thoroughly then had Thomas add a wood floor, a door, and a window. Abe could not have hoped for a better stepmother. Warm and loving, Sally Lincoln reared him like her own child. "She was doubtless the first person that ever treated him like a human being," recalled merchant John B. Helm. She won Abe's heart by replacing his hard, lumpy cornhusk bed with a soft feather mattress. She smiled a lot, hugged him often, and offered kind words and encouragement—something Abe had never heard from his father.

"Abe was a good boy, the best boy I ever saw," she later attested. "I never gave him a cross word in all my life. His mind and mine seemed to move in the same channel. He never told me a lie, and he never quarreled, swore, or used profane language in my presence nor in others that I know of."

Lincoln described this period of his life as "a joyous, happy boyhood," a time when "there was nothing sad nor pinched, and nothing of want." He called his stepmother "Mama." And from her he received the softening influences of a mother.[4]

Through Sally's encouragement, the Lincolns enrolled their children in a newly opened school—a one-room log schoolhouse where pupils sat on rough wooden benches and repeated their lessons aloud. For two brief periods Abe had attended a school in Kentucky where, according to a relative, he was sent "more as company for his sister than with the expectation that he would learn much." At Andrew Crawford's subscription school they now learned to prepare essays. When that school closed, the children were enrolled in another that opened four miles away.

Abe, however, attended only sporadically. Thomas Lincoln wanted the boy to stay home and work the fields and tend the livestock. A year later a closer school opened, and apparently through Sally's influence, Abe was allowed to attend for six months. That school term concluded Abe's formal education. He was fifteen. He would later say that he had attended school "by littles," a little now and a little then, and that "the aggregate of all his schooling did not amount to one year."[5]

Perhaps through his stepmother's efforts he developed the ability to think creatively and became sensitive to the mistreatments that were common on the frontier. He was annoyed by the boyhood practice of placing hot coals on the shells of terrapins, for instance. "He would chide us," Nat Grigsby recalled. He would "tell us it was wrong, and would write essays against it."[6]

Abe's stepmother wanted him to make something of himself. She encouraged him to read and study. Thomas, on the other hand, continued to belittle education. "It's enough for a boy to work hard and be strong," he allegedly proclaimed.

Sally brought books with her from Kentucky, and she encouraged Abe to read them. Exciting new worlds were revealed to him in John Bunyan's *Pilgrim's Progress* and Daniel Defoe's *Robinson Crusoe*. In the *Life of Benjamin Franklin* Abe found the poor boy who became great, and in Mason Weems's *Life of Washington* he discovered the hero who fathered a republic. *Arabian Nights* was another of Abe's favorites. "Abe lay on his stummick by the fire and read out loud to me'n Sairy, an' we'd laugh when he did," Dennis Hanks recollected. "I reckon Abe read the book a dozen times, and knowed those yarns by heart."

He kept a book in his loft—stuck in a crack in the logs—to read at daybreak. When working in the field, he would rest the horse at the end of each row—while he leaned on a fence and read. When Abe came across a passage that struck him, he wrote it down on a plank and kept it until he had paper. Then he would rewrite it, look at it, repeat it. He had a copybook, a kind of scrapbook, in which he wrote things. "I never saw Abe after he was twelve that he didn't have a book in his hand or in his pocket," Dennis recalled. "It didn't seem natural to see a feller read like that."

"My best friend," Abe declared, "is the man who'll get me a book I ain't read." Sally Lincoln appears to have been the female figure who stirred Lincoln's imagination, promoted his education, and fueled the critical thinking of the man who would become the sixteenth president.[7]

As a teenager, Abe discovered the opposite sex. With male friends he pondered the biblical references to sexual activity, focusing most likely on

the Old Testament's Song of Songs, which celebrates the joys of marital intimacy. Lincoln's curiosity about the opposite sex may have been further
whetted by the presence of three teenage girls in the Lincoln cabin.

Although Lincoln certainly became interested in girls, most girls apparently were not attracted to his gaunt, lanky figure and somewhat homely
face. "Girls found him repelling," admitted Polly Richardson, a female acquaintance of young Abe. "Abe took me to church and to spelling bees," she
claimed, "and even wanted to marry me, but I refused." Her recollection of
the teenage Lincoln depicts an awkward, unpopular youth. "All the girls my
age made fun of him," she recalled. "They'd even laugh at him right before
his face."

Frontier damsels thought young Lincoln's manner of dress was odd: his
buckskin pants were always too short. "Six or more inches of Abe's shin
bone was bare and naked," one classmate remembered. "He tried to go out
with some of the girls," recalled Polly, "but no sir-ee, they'd give him the
mitten every time, just because he was so tall and gawky. It was mighty
awkward trying to keep company with a fellow as tall as Abe was."[8]

Beautiful and amiable Hannah Gentry, daughter of the community's
richest man, refused to court Abe because "he was too fond of onions, and I
could not endure them." Another girl found Abe to be "quiet and awkward
and so awful homely that girls didn't much care about him." An acquaintance of Sarah Lukens related, "Abe took me home from church once and I
could a'been his wife if I'd wanted to, but I didn't. He was just too peculiar."[9]

Abe took a special "likin'" to pretty Elizabeth Wood, who lived on a
farm about a mile and a half north of the Lincoln cabin. His opportunity to
attract her attention came after an ox that Thomas Lincoln had bought from
her father broke loose and returned to the Wood farm. Abe went to fetch
the ox—named Buck—and Mr. Wood offered him a rope to lead the animal
home. "No, thank you," said Abe, who intended to impress Elizabeth. "I'll
ride him home and make him pay for his action." As Elizabeth watched,
Abe leaped onto Buck's back and kicked him on both sides. The animal
bolted and bucked—and disappeared down the road with Abe doing his
best to stay on the beast. Elizabeth and her father laughed at the spectacle of
the lanky Lincoln boy straddling the stampeding ox. Abe somehow rode
him all the way home and proudly told his father, "I gentled him, Pap." Despite the triumph, Abe's daring feat failed to impress Elizabeth. "I know he
wanted to become better acquainted with me," she said, "but I wasn't interested in him. He was so awkward, and his feet were awful big."[10]

Elizabeth Tuley was Abe's first "regular company." According to Elizabeth, she and Abe "kept company for several months"—until she could no longer bear the "unmerciful" teasing from her friends, who joked about Lincoln's "coat sleeves and pant legs always being too short." Elizabeth broke off the relationship.

Abe also became infatuated with Julia Evans, an attractive girl who bowed to him one day as they passed on the street. At the time he was visiting Princeton, Indiana, where he had gone to have some wool carded. "My heart was in a flutter," Lincoln later confessed. "I was so thoroughly captivated by this vision of maidenly beauty that I wanted to stop in Princeton forever." But to his teenage dismay, he never saw her again.

Once Abe's sister, Sarah, scolded him for "bothering girls" when they were playing. "You ought to be ashamed of yourself, Abe. What do you expect will become of you?" He promptly responded: "I reckon I'll be president of the United States."[11]

Occasionally, Abe's interest in books and girls merged. When the schoolmaster asked Anna Roby, an attractive fifteen-year-old, to spell *defied*, she began "d-e-f" then stopped, debating whether to proceed with an *i* or a *y*. She glimpsed Abe with his index finger on his eye and a smile on his face. She took the hint and added "i-e-d."

"He was the learned boy among us unlearned folks," Anna recalled. "He took great pains to explain; he could do it so simply." On an evening stroll alongside a river, Anna and Abe sat on the bank, dangled their feet in the stream, and watched the moon slowly rise over the neighboring hills. Ignoring the romantic opportunity, Abe turned to a scientific discourse on the movement of heavenly bodies. "I did not suppose that Abe, who had seen so little of the world, would know anything about it," Anna commented, "but he proved to my satisfaction that the moon did not go down at all; that it only seemed to; that the earth revolving from west to east, carried us under, as it were." Abe explained, "We do the sinking, while to us the moon is comparatively still. The moon's sinking is only an illusion." Abe had improved Anna's intellect but had ignored her heart. "What a fool you are, Abe!" she exclaimed. Their relationship was short-lived.[12]

"As he got older, Abe seemed to develop a dislike for girls," Anna observed, "and didn't go out much with them." That view was confirmed by Abe's stepbrother John Johnston, who said Abe was so busy studying he "didn't take much truck with the girls."

Having been consistently rejected and often insulted by the fairer sex, Abe became even more bashful and uncomfortable around girls. "He wasn't very fond of them," his stepmother noted.

But he became a popular figure among the farm boys of the community due to his colorful jokes and barnyard stories. He fished, wrestled, ran races, and became the best athlete in the neighborhood. He never missed a horserace or a fox chase, a sugar boiling or a wool shearing. He excelled at cornhuskings, where men and boys were divided into two groups, each striving to shuck the most corn. Cornhuskings were often followed by an all-night dance for young people, but Abe was usually without a female partner. Participants shuffled and kicked to the sounds of a cracked fiddle and swaggered home at daybreak to the tunes of Dennis Hanks's festive lines: "Hail Columbia, happy land / If you ain't drunk, I will be damned."[13]

Once, while attending a cornhusking with his friend Green Taylor, Abe drew the red ear of corn—which entitled him to kiss the girl he liked best. Being more honest than discreet, Abe kissed Green's girlfriend. Green was furious and a fistfight erupted. The fight ended when Green hit Abe with an ear of corn, causing a deep wound. Abe learned to stay away from other boys' sweethearts.

Abe and his stepsister Tilda developed a frisky mutual interest during their teenage years. One of Tilda's chores was to take lunch to Abe when he went to the woods to cut trees. But when neighborhood gossips whispered about two young people running wild and alone in the forest, Tilda's mother ordered her to prepare Abe's lunch *before* he left for work.

One day, however, she secretly followed him for what she later called "a long chat and a wild romp." As she caught up with Abe, she darted forward and landed squarely on his back. Both fell to the ground. As they did so, Tilda struck the sharp edge of the axe blade with her foot, causing it to bleed profusely. Frantically, Abe tore pieces of cloth from his undergarment and dressed the injury. Then he looked at her in astonishment. "Tilda, what will we tell Mother as to how this happened?"

Tilda said, "I'll tell her I cut my foot on the axe. That will be the truth, won't it?"

"Yes," Abe replied. "That is the truth, but it won't be all the truth, will it, Tilda? Tell the whole truth, and trust your good mother for the rest."

Tilda confessed to her mother, who merely scolded her and warned her not to follow Abe again. This time she obeyed.[14]

Dennis Hanks, meanwhile, developed a passionate interest in Abe's other stepsister, Sarah Elizabeth. When she was fifteen, they were married and set up a homestead about half a mile from the Lincoln farm. Sarah Elizabeth's marriage reduced the male workforce on the farm to Thomas Lincoln, John Johnston, and Abe, with occasional help from John Hanks.

By then Thomas had impaired vision and depended more on his farmhands. He appeared to favor his stepson John over Abe, and Abe found himself with more work to do—farming, grubbing, hoeing, making fences, plowing, splitting rails, skinning coons, and butchering hogs.

Thomas also leased Abe and his axe to work for other farmers—at twenty-five cents a day for hard labor—and then made Abe give him the money. By law, Thomas was entitled to everything Abe earned until he became twenty-one, and Thomas took it all. Abe would later describe the arrangement as "organized robbery" and remained outraged at the idea that someone could be forced to work in the hot sun all day while someone else received all the profits.[15]

Abe's relationship with his father gradually worsened—possibly due in part to Abe's doubts that Thomas Lincoln was really his father. Abe undoubtedly had heard the gossip that mumps or an accidental castration had rendered Thomas impotent. And Thomas sometimes whipped Abe when he found him reading instead of working. There was no "break time" in Thomas Lincoln's fields—at least not for Abe.

Thomas tried hiding his son's books and sometimes even threw them away—defying both his wife and his son. "Thomas never thought much of Abraham as a boy," A. H. Chapman, Abe's cousin, admitted. They were opposites in temperament, values, abilities, motivations, and ambitions, and there appeared to have been little rapport between them.

Their sharpest exchange of words probably came over Abe's refusal to join the Little Pigeon Creek Baptist Church, where his parents worshiped. "Abe had no particular religion," his stepmother acknowledged. Perhaps to placate his father, Abe attended the church and served as a sexton—sweeping the floor and furnishing the candles—but he never became a member.[16]

In 1826 Abe's stepsister Tilda married Squire Hall. In the same year Abe's eighteen-year-old sister, Sarah, married Aaron Grigsby, who was from a leading family in nearby Gentryville. The two had met nine years earlier while fetching water from a spring, and their fondness for each other had blossomed over the years. Abe dearly loved his sister, and her marriage could have caused him to feel abandoned again. Sarah was a cheerful, attractive girl with a bright mind, and Abe surely missed her.

A year and a half later, on January 20, 1828, Sarah Lincoln Grigsby went into hard labor, but Aaron was slow to realize she was having trouble. When he finally understood her life was in danger, he bolted out of their cabin and ran through the snow to his father's home. He and his father yoked a team of oxen to a sled and went back after Sarah. They wrapped her in deerskins, placed her on the sled, and took her to her father-in-law's home. A doctor was summoned, but he arrived drunk. A midwife was called, but she arrived too late to deal with the emergency. Sarah died in childbirth, and her baby was stillborn.

Distraught and frantic, Aaron ran to Abe's cabin and found him standing in the smokehouse doorway. Abe knew something was wrong and asked what had happened. "Sarah just died," Aaron announced. Abe sat down in the doorway of the smokehouse, buried his face in his hands, and wept. The sister he loved so dearly was gone at age twenty. With her stillborn baby cradled in her arms, Sarah was buried in the church cemetery.

Abe was engulfed in a depression at first, then his grief was replaced by anger. He blamed Sarah's death on Aaron's neglect. Aaron had let her "lay too long" before getting help, Abe believed, and he set out to "get even." With the help of friends, Abe planned a trick to embarrass Aaron and his family. It would occur after the double wedding of Grigsby's brothers—Charles and Reuben. When the two Grigsby brothers and their brides returned to the family home after the wedding, their father hosted an elaborate frontier-style reception with feasting, dancing, and the grand finale—"putting the bridal party to bed."[17]

At the appropriate time, the two brides were taken upstairs to separate bedrooms. The candles were then blown out, and the brothers were escorted to their brides. Through a friend at the celebration, Abe arranged for the bridegrooms to be led to the wrong rooms. The brothers' mother discovered the error at the last moment and sprang upstairs. "O Lord, Reuben, you are in bed with Charles's wife," she yelled. Alarmed, the brothers raced from their rooms in confusion, and the party became an uproar.

After the event, Abe lampooned the men in a merciless satire called "The Chronicles of Reuben." It was circulated in the community. The drama continued when the brothers' younger sibling, Billy Grigsby, challenged Abe to a fight. Abe refused, saying he was too big for a fair fight with Grigsby. Abe's stepbrother John accepted, however, and the two young men engaged in what one witness called "a terrible fight." John got the worst of it and was bleeding and badly hurt. Abe stepped in, grabbed Grigsby, and hurled him several feet. That provoked a general fight among supporters—which became a brief but exciting frontier brawl.[18]

Snubbed so often by the opposite sex, Abe must have been ecstatic when a pretty seventeen-year-old girl asked him to accompany her to a cornhusking bee in Hancock County, Kentucky, just across the Ohio River from Indiana. This poised and well-educated girl with curly brown hair was Caroline Meeker. She lived with her uncle, magistrate Samuel Pate, in an upscale home on a hill above the river.

Caroline met Abe when he was summoned to Pate's residence to answer charges that he had illegally interfered with John Dills's ferry business. Dills was the only person licensed by Kentucky to convey passengers across that portion of the river. Thus he was upset when told that Abe had ferried a passenger from the Indiana side to a steamer stopped in the middle of the river. Since Kentucky considered the river within its boundaries, Dills brought charges against Abe.

As Caroline listened, twenty-year-old Abe argued that all he did was help a man catch a passing steamer. Dills was not in sight, Abe said, "And it was not fair to expect me to sit there in my boat and let that man miss the steamer just because Dills was not attending to his business." Squire Pate agreed with Abe and dismissed the case.

Caroline walked with Abe to the river. That's when she mentioned the cornhusking bee to be held the following week in Eli Thrasher's barn. "Won't you come?" she urged, smiling and looking into his eyes. Tongue-tied, he blurted out an awkward yes.

At the bee, Abe searched frantically for the illusive red ear of corn that would allow him to kiss Caroline. He never found one, but Caroline did, and she slipped it to him unobserved. He held it up for all to see and then demurely kissed her.

Abe's courting continued until after the winter of 1829–30 when his parents decided to move to Illinois after hearing glowing reports of rich lands available on easy terms. Thomas had moved four times since his marriage but was still not much better off.

During Abe's last visit with Caroline she pleaded, "Come back for me." But he made no promises. He concluded that it would be wrong to pursue her. She was, after all, from an aristocratic and prosperous family, and he felt he had nothing to offer her.

Meanwhile, Thomas sold his land, hogs, and corn in March 1830. And the Lincolns loaded their meager household effects into two wagons—each pulled by a pair of oxen—and began the arduous two-hundred-mile journey to Illinois. Accompanied by the families of his two stepdaughters and their husbands—Dennis Hanks and Squire Hall—Thomas Lincoln's party numbered thirteen. Abe drove one of the wagons.

They crossed the Wabash River at Vincennes and continued through the village of Decatur to a tract of land on the north bank of the Sangamon River, which Thomas Lincoln's cousin by marriage, John Hanks, had staked out for them. Abraham Lincoln had come to Illinois. All hands worked to prepare the new home, but the Illinois weather was not welcoming.

On Christmas Day 1830 the snow began to fall, and it did not stop until drifts reached depths up to twelve feet. For nine weeks temperatures hovered ten to twenty degrees below zero. The Lincolns were confined to their cabins all winter, surviving on boiled corn and pounded meal. In the spring the snow melted, and the land flooded. Just a year after arriving in Illinois, Abe was reminded of the harsh, unpredictable ways of farming.

At twenty-two years of age Abe Lincoln was ready to be on his own. The opportunity came from a person destined to shape Lincoln's future—Denton Offutt, an adventurous, colorful speculator and trader who trafficked goods up and down the Sangamon River. Offutt had come downriver in search of reliable hands to deliver a boatload of provisions to New Orleans. He first came to Lincoln's cousin John Hanks. "I hunted up Abe," Hanks recalled, "and I introduced him and John Johnston, his stepbrother, to Offutt. After some talk we made an engagement with Offutt at fifty cents a day and sixty dollars [for the trip]."[19]

Lincoln said goodbye to his family and left empty-handed, with no land, no patron, and no profession. He returned home only a few times, and then just for short visits. Whatever Lincoln's future was to be, he was determined it would not be a repetition of his father's difficult and unproductive life.

He also vowed that if he ever had children, he would give them unbounded liberty instead of parental tyranny. Love was the chain to bind a child to parents, Lincoln believed. It was a lesson he learned from his stepmother. From his mother he held a vague but strong belief in fate and providence. So Abraham Lincoln left his family and his childhood behind and faced the future with the hard-won optimism typical of the frontier. Ahead lay countless experiences—and a girl named Ann Rutledge.

Caroline Meeker never forgot Abe Lincoln, and she avoided other potential suitors for three years while waiting to hear from him. Finally she gave up and married wealthy Eli Thrasher. Two years later, on Christmas Eve, 1835, their child was born, but on Christmas morning Caroline died. Lincoln probably never learned of her fate.[20]

In 1842 Lincoln married into a prominent family—the Todds of Kentucky. Contrary to what some historians have written, he apparently did not marry for money, social advancement, or even love. It was for something more important to him.

3

"Teach Me, O Lord, to Think Well of Myself"

$\mathcal{A}$ NNA MAYES RUTLEDGE was born January 7, 1813, a few miles from the frontier village of Henderson, Kentucky, where forty houses dotted the landscape on high red bluffs overlooking the Ohio River. The third child and second daughter of James and Mary Ann Rutledge, she would be known simply as Ann Rutledge.[1]

Thirty-one-year-old James Rutledge had known Mary Ann Miller all her life, and they had been longtime sweethearts when they married in Henderson five years earlier, on January 25, 1808. She was attractive with reddish brown hair and dark eyes. They were married by their Presbyterian pastor, James McGready, and feted with a splendid feast of roast venison prepared by James's three brothers and their sisters and cousins. After dinner the newlyweds rode horses to the new log home James had built for his bride. At bedtime family members and friends stood outside and banged on pots and pans, rang cowbells, tooted whistles, and shouted raucously for thirty minutes. It was a quaint custom called a "shivaree" and was intended to proclaim good tidings. Most couples accepted it good-naturedly.[2]

Buffalo roamed nearby, and in the summer flocks of geese settled gracefully into the Green River. All types of wild game were in gunshot range of their cabin. Deer herds grazed peacefully until the first shot was fired and then fled in arching lopes.

James and Mary Ann farmed, planting corn and wheat, orchards of apples and peaches, and fields of strawberries. Their simple pleasures centered around a backwoods fiddler and his inspired renditions of "Polly, Put the Kettle On" and "Buffalo Gals."

Ann's grandparents were part of the great exodus of Scotch-Irish Presbyterians who migrated from Ireland to America in the eighteenth century. John Rutledge was only eighteen when he left his parents and his work as a Dublin shoemaker around 1757 to seek religious freedom and better times in the new land. His family came from County Tyrone in Northern Ireland. Their ancestors, originally from Scotland, were lured to Northern Ireland by English inducements to acquire cheap farmland. Later, oppressive British rule over Ireland made their life intolerable. Brutal laws banned Presbyterian services, labeled as "fornicators" anyone married in their churches, and prohibited the Scotch-Irish from holding any position higher than that of postman.[3]

John's future wife, Jane "Jennie" Officer, migrated at age eight with her parents and grandparents, who were natives of County Antrim in Northern Ireland. Her father, Thomas, was a sheep farmer; her grandfather, James, a shoemaker. Their families also dated back to Scotland. The three-thousand-mile Atlantic crossing could be challenging for immigrants. Crammed into meager quarters, passengers slept on straw mattresses or hammocks. Rations were short, food was often vermin-ridden, and water tasted putrid. Many passengers died at sea.

John Rutledge and the Officers survived the voyage and headed for Philadelphia, where established Presbyterian congregations would assist them. They looked forward to Pennsylvania's promised tolerance for all who acknowledged "one almighty God, the Creator, Upholder, and Ruler of the World."[4]

Although ten years older than Jennie Officer, John Rutledge was obviously charmed by the little girl and observed with more than a passing interest her development into an attractive young woman. They were married around 1765, when he was twenty-six and she was sixteen, probably in or near Philadelphia. Shortly thereafter they migrated southward. Following the great Pennsylvania Wagon Road through Virginia and the Carolinas, they settled briefly in Charlestown, South Carolina, which was another colonial city noted for religious tolerance. Their first child was born there in 1768.[5]

It did not take long, however, for the Rutledges to dislike Charlestown. It was America's fourth largest and wealthiest city. Aristocratic merchants and planters ruled and reveled in a pleasure-oriented society where gambling and partying were daily occurrences. Tradesmen and other workingmen were expected to know their place. High rents, high prices, and competition from slave labor gave them much to be unhappy about.[6]

By 1770 the Rutledges had made their way west to Winnsboro in what is now Fairfield County, South Carolina, taking a narrow, rough trail known as the Charleston Path. Winnsboro was a stylish town influenced by Charlestonians who moved inland and built an academy and brick and frame churches, homes, and estates.

Soon to link up with the Rutledges were two other families—the John Millers of Ireland (Ann's future maternal grandparents) and the Thomas Camrons of Scotland. The Millers and Camrons crossed the ocean together from Ireland, landing in Charlestown. They all became close friends and remained in and around Winnsboro through the Revolutionary War. Their children grew up and played together, with six Rutledges and at least four Millers and four Camrons born in Fairfield County. Two of them—James Rutledge, born May 11, 1781, and Mary Ann Miller, born October 21, 1787—would later fall in love, marry, and produce a famous daughter.[7]

The Rutledge/Miller/Camron group worked as farmers and lived modestly in log homes. They worked to the rhythm of a song: housewives as they churned butter and rocked babies—"Hush, little baby, don't say a word, Mama's gonna buy you a mocking bird"; husbands as they planted corn—"One for the blackbird, One for the crow; One for the cutworm, And one to grow." Honoring their heritage in Scotland, while not forgetting their love for Ireland before English rule, they celebrated St. Andrew's Day every November 30. They sang Scottish ballads, such as bonny "Barbara Allen" and other songs "my mither sang." And they shared memories of full pipe bands and swinging kilts and of the land of the mountains and the mist.[8]

The men wore a nightshirt called an "ebenezer." At church, when they sang "Here I raise mine Ebenezer," young couples smiled at each other. Self-confident—a Scotch-Irish trait—they prayed, "Teach me, O Lord, to think well of myself." On churchless Sundays it was common to see John Rutledge on a horse with a bed quilt or deer skin for a saddle and as many of his children as he could keep on the horse. Some rode in front and some behind him, with Jennie walking ahead, all going to spend the day with the Millers or the Camrons, four or five miles away.[9]

These Scotch-Irish folks left Ireland because of English policies, and they were strong supporters of the Revolution. In 1781 Thomas Camron supplied the Continental army with "two beefes, two muttons, and six gallons of whiskey." Son-in-law Robert McClary was among the two thousand casualties at the 1780 battle of Camden. Fought less than thirty miles from Winnsboro, it was a crushing defeat for the Americans. The war was all around the Rutledges. South Carolina recorded more battles than any other state.[10]

After the war the new American government offered free land in Georgia, and the Rutledge, Miller, and Camron families left Winnsboro to claim this favored earth. By the end of the 1790s they had migrated a hundred miles west, ferrying the Savannah River to Augusta. They settled in the nearby counties of Elbert and Wilkes, a region of rolling hills and fertile bottomlands with rich, deep-loamed soil easy to cultivate. The area's good schools and Presbyterian congregations were added incentives for the newcomers from Winnsboro, as were numerous fresh-water springs.[11]

John Rutledge set up a shoemaking shop and ran a farm. Thomas Camron Jr. married the oldest Miller daughter and established saw- and gristmills in Elbert County. John Miller Camron was born in 1790 and eventually became close to his uncle James Rutledge, who was nine years older. In time they would form a partnership that would significantly change the life of Abraham Lincoln.[12]

James Rutledge benefited from growing up in the Winnsboro and Augusta areas, which were enriched by good schools and supportive kinfolk. The boy had a keen and thoughtful mind that led him to excel in debating, an interest that would take root and grow years later in a place called New Salem. His opinion of women's roles was surely affected by his firsthand observation of a professional female, Sarah Hillhouse, Georgia's first woman newspaper editor. She took over the Wilkes County paper, the *Monitor,* after her husband's death and built it into a successful enterprise. James was probably among the paper's avid readers.

With that background and his own intellect, enhanced by his growing book collection, James undoubtedly sensed the positive difference women could make in the community if unleashed from their dawn-to-night household chores and motivated by education and opportunity. Perhaps James resolved to provide such a foundation for any daughters he might have—a conclusion supported by his later actions.

Among other Scotch-Irish families attracted to the Georgia countryside were the Mayeses, Hawthorns, Veatches, and Davidsons. From Georgia they followed or accompanied the Rutledges, Camrons, and Millers on their further migrations. They were intelligent and industrious, and most were devoutly religious. United by blood, marriage, and friendship, they would eventually populate central and southern Illinois.[13]

Most members of these Scotch-Irish families were on the road again by the fall of 1807. They headed north to Henderson, Kentucky—which would become their home until 1813. In Henderson, newlyweds James and Mary Ann Miller Rutledge visited often with James and Lucy Audubon in their log cabin and his general merchandise store. Both men were of similar age. Audubon, destined to become a famous ornithological illustrator, imitated bird calls on his flute, and his talented wife played the piano and violin. Associating with the Audubons made James and Mary Ann even more convinced of the importance of education for their children.[14]

James's brother Billy married Susannah Camron, John Miller Camron's sister, and on September 29, 1814, a son, McGrady, was born in Henderson County. McGrady and Ann Rutledge, a year and a half apart, would grow up to be close friends. Meanwhile, John Miller Camron met Polly Orendorff shortly after her family's wagon train arrived from Franklin County, Tennessee. Her great-great-grandmother was said to have been a Prussian princess, and Camron bragged of eating corn bread made by the descendant of a princess. They were married on January 12, 1811.[15]

The Rutledge group might have remained in Henderson County had it not been for two developing nightmares: vengeful Indians who provoked frequent and bloody encounters, and disputes among settlers over land titles and boundaries. In the spring of 1813, three months after the birth of Ann Rutledge, a visiting trader spoke of rich farmland soon to be opened to homesteaders in the Illinois Territory. Perhaps, Rutledge pondered, that was the promised land they sought. Neither Mary Ann Rutledge nor Polly Camron wanted to leave their beautiful setting in "God's country" for long, cold winters on the raw, wide prairie, where some said the grass was so tall a man on horseback could be lost in it. The women, however, were reconciled to follow their husbands.

That fall the seven related families were off to Illinois with thirty children and a bevy of grandparents, including John and Jennie Rutledge. John Miller Camron's father, Thomas Jr., was captain of the wagon train, and his cart led the way. Close behind were James and Mary Ann Rutledge with Ann and her two older siblings. The train of ox carts ferried the Ohio River near Shawneetown and then headed north along an old Indian trail. They all plodded along—the oxen pulling the carts, the men accompanied by their wives and their muskets. Some women, with babies in their arms, rode horseback; older family members and small children shared the carts. Boys in jeans and deerskin jackets and girls in sunbonnets and linsey-woolsey dresses led cows and coaxed pigs and sheep along the narrow path. The younger boys, dressed only in long-tailed shirts, scampered about chasing stray sheep and helping their dads look for wild game.[16]

The carts' wooden wheels and axles creaked from their loads—farming implements, pots and kettles, feather beds, homespun blankets, young fruit trees, crates of chickens and geese, and cuttings from roses and lilacs left behind in their Kentucky yards. A washtub turned upside down was the driver's seat.

For some thirty-five miles the trail took them through heavy forests of oak, maple, evergreen, and tall gum trees. Then, as they crested a hill, the pioneers saw an immense valley spread out before them. It was at least three miles wide and seven miles long, with a shaded stream—Seven Mile Creek—meandering through it.[17]

They agreed it was a good place to camp, and the whole cortege of men, women, children, cows, pigs, sheep, and horses rested and prepared to settle down for the night. According to White County historian Margaret Land, a descendant of several lines of these pioneers, the families cut evergreen branches for beds, fed the stock, roasted plump prairie chickens on sticks skewered over a fire of twigs and fallen limbs, and offered a prayer of thanksgiving. Guards kept fires burning to deter wild animals.[18]

The rays of the morning sun flowed through the crystal-clear air of the forest, adding splendor and richness to the wilderness while awakening the settlers' latent energy and ingenuity. It was time to go to work and give birth to the Seven Mile Prairie community, forerunner of the town of Enfield in White County, Illinois.

Providing shelter and food were their first tasks, and axes, augers, plows, spades, and hoes were soon put to work. Trees from their forested hill sites provided logs and fuel for their cabins and wood for fences and bridges. Underneath log floors, they dug out hiding places for women and children, lined them with beds of straw, and secured them with closely fitting trapdoors. Cabin doors were made of boards split from logs, held together by wooden pins, and fastened with wooden hinges and latches. They made their chairs, tables, and beds and added other furnishings they brought with them—cornhusk mattresses, goose-feather pillows, spinning wheels, looms, corner cupboards, and dutch ovens. Some made high beds with trundle beds underneath for children.

They planted the fruit trees they brought with them as well as seeds for flax, corn, and other crops. It was a common sight to see a woman driving horses while a man maneuvered the plow. Corn was planted in rows about six feet apart, with peas, beans, and pumpkins in between. They enclosed fields and gardens with rail fences but allowed their livestock to roam the woods. There it cost almost nothing to raise them: they would feed themselves.

Wild game supplied much of the food. Prairie chickens were so numerous they could have had chicken pie every day of the year. The area also abounded in turkeys, deer, quail, and pigeons. One settler noted that wild pigeons flew overhead in such dense clouds that the sky grew dark and chickens went to roost. Smoked pork was a common meat. It was stored in large barrels. A family was considered to be "in a desperate way" when the mother could see the bottom of the pork barrel. As a housewife noted in James Fenimore Cooper's *The Chainbearer:* "Give me the children raised on good sound pork afore all the game in the country. Game's good as a relish and so's bread; but pork is the staff of life." Pigs grew quickly from eating acorns and roots, and after December's first cold spell, neighbors came together to butcher their porkers. They cooked in iron pots hung in the fireplace, and they ate from pewter plates, using pewter spoons, knives, and forks, and wooden cups.

Two years passed, and the settlement grew as more relatives came from Kentucky and Tennessee. James Rutledge's nephew John Miller Camron arrived in 1814 or 1815, accompanied by his wife, Polly, and their baby and toddler. Apple, peach, and pear trees bore fruit, providing their main beverages—cider and brandy. James Rutledge built the first gristmill. Powered by a pair of horses, the mill was said to grind so slowly that a hungry jaybird could peck up the meal almost as fast as it fell from the stones.

Then came 1816—"the year without summer." A heavy snow fell on June 17, ruining many crops. Fall came, and there was no corn to grind at Rutledge's mill. Perhaps it was time to pack up and move farther west, Rutledge reportedly told fellow pioneers.

As they argued options, their Kentucky pastor, James McGready, arrived at Seven Mile Prairie. He was well educated and noted for eloquence. He urged patience and faith, and they listened. He established in their community the first Presbyterian church in Illinois. It was housed in a small log

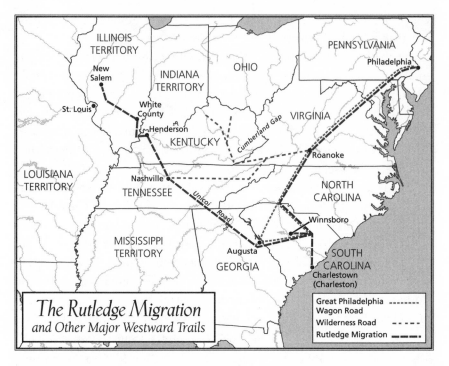

The Rutledge Migration
and Other Major Westward Trails

structure. The first three ruling elders were James Rutledge, James Mayes, and Peter Miller. Miller, who was Ann Rutledge's uncle, had a novel way of curing his wife's nervous seizures: he would draw a bucket of cold water from the well and dump it over her head.[19]

In that same year without summer, the settlers received shocking news from Georgia. A milk-sickness epidemic had taken the lives of Ann's aunt, Susan Rutledge Mayes, and her husband, Edward. They left five children, ages two to thirteen. Uncles Tommy Mayes and Billy Rutledge loaded an ox cart with cornmeal and bacon and set out for Georgia to fetch the orphaned children. They were parceled out among the Rutledge, Mayes, and Miller families. The toddler, Minerva, was taken into Ann Rutledge's family. Ann, then three years old, had a new playmate.[20]

Ann and Minerva grew up together, played together, and occasionally got into trouble together. When Ann was seven and Minerva was six, Ann's parents were preparing to entertain the new preacher. It was considered a special honor for them because he ministered to a large area and rode miles on horseback to keep appointments. On this brisk winter day, Mary Ann Rutledge had prepared a hot drink containing liberal portions of whiskey and was keeping it hot on the fireplace hearth. The Rutledges seldom used strong drink, but on this day a "sip of toddy" was prepared to warm the reverend's bones and prevent his catching a cold.

While Mrs. Rutledge was cooking dinner, Ann and Minerva decided to taste the toddy. Ann poured some into a cup, sampled it, and shared it with her cousin. Minerva gulped it and shrieked at the taste. Both took several sips, and then Minerva passed out and Ann became sick. When Mrs. Rutledge realized what had happened, she put the girls to bed, made more toddy for the preacher, and "forgot" to tell her husband about the incident. The next day Ann assured her mother she never wanted strong drink again.[21]

Ann's favorite male cousin, McGrady Rutledge, had his own encounter with whiskey. At age ten he found a jug, drank too much of it, and became sick. His mother found him flat on his belly in the loom house. She pulled him out and drenched him with sweet milk. He too swore he would never drink again. But McGrady's father had other ideas. He was confident that whiskey would prevent fever and chills and tried to make McGrady drink some. The "chills" were a common health problem. Settlers called the disease "ague." It caused periodic shakes, fevers, weakness, and sweating, but was seldom fatal. When the child refused the whiskey, his father bristled. His mother understood, however, and intervened, and the couple argued over the benefits of whiskey. After McGrady pleaded, "I would rather be sick than drink it," his father finally gave in. McGrady turned out to be the healthiest one in the family.[22]

In 1818 Ann's uncle Thomas Rutledge started the county's first school. Tuition was twenty-five cents a week, and each child brought a candle for light. Thomas believed in strict and swift discipline. When a boy suggested that maybe someday men would fly and even talk across the ocean, Thomas thrashed him soundly, using a heavy whip toughened in hot embers.

James Rutledge wanted his daughters to be educated, and Ann, being the smartest, may have been the first girl at the school. She enrolled in 1820, the same year her grandfather John Rutledge died at age eighty-one.[23]

These hardy pioneers tanned their own leather, made their own boots, and produced their own wool and linen. An acre of flax supplied enough linen to clothe a large family, with enough material left over for tablecloths and bedspreads. Making linen was an all-family project. The flax, after being thrashed, cleaned, and combed, was spun into linen thread, and the thread was then put into a hand loom. Out came linen cloth that was strong and durable, although a little rough by modern standards and nappy after worn awhile. For coloring they made dyes from sumac berries, indigo, and white-walnut bark. They also made linsey, combining wool with either linen or cotton. Five or six yards of linsey were enough for a dress.

For a while these pioneers tried raising cotton, but the climate was unfavorable. That was good news for the children who, in a frontier version of a sweatshop, had to lie before the fire at night and pick seeds from cotton bolls. The warmer the cotton, the better it picked. So everyone worked up a sweat.

One loom generally did the weaving for several families. Requiring space that could not be spared in a cabin, it was placed in a lean-to called a loom house. By the time she was ten, Ann Rutledge had learned to spin thread and work the loom. When she was older she became a superior seamstress, designing and making clothes for her siblings and parents. Like other girls her age, she also learned to cook, churn butter, keep house, do chores, and care for younger brothers and sisters—duties that were essential for pioneer women.

Wool was highly prized but rare on the Illinois frontier due to scavenging packs of sheep-killing wolves. At night, the howling of a wolf pack could be terrifying. Sometimes they even chased men on horseback. To eliminate the thieving, troublesome pests, settlers hunted, trapped, and sometimes poisoned them. In traditional wolf hunts, a large number of settlers went into the wilderness and made a large circle. Shouting and whooping, they beat the bushes and tightened the circle until the wolves were trapped. Then they killed them with clubs.

One settler who had lost sheep and had heard enough howling, vowed to "thin the wolf herd." He took his wagon-box about a mile out on the prairie, moistened a rope with a smelly solution that attracted wolves, and trailed the rope through the prairie from different points toward the wagon-box. About sunset he positioned himself under the box where he had cut portholes to shoot through. As it grew dark he heard one wolf howl, then another, and shortly the howls came from all directions and became louder and louder. Soon the wolves surrounded the wagon-box and lunged toward him with vicious snarls. The settler fired again and again and killed several. But they kept coming, and he fired until his ammunition was gone. The wolves prowled, snapped their jaws, and kept him besieged all night. Finally, at daybreak, they departed. Panic-stricken, the settler skedaddled for home.[24]

FAMILY DOGS were prized possessions in early Illinois. A good coon dog was worth more than a horse, and some could not be bought at any price.

Coonskins and whiskey were legal tender throughout southern Illinois and were traded for coffee, powder, and lead. With money scarce, and many people not knowing there was any, most business was by trade or barter. Coon hunting at night was not only profitable but also considered great sport. When a dog treed a coon, he barked loudly and everyone rushed to the scene. Sometimes the coon was shot, but often the tree was chopped down so the hunters could enjoy a dog and coon fight.[25]

Frontier fathers could be very particular about their daughters. A Rutledge neighbor, Tennessean William Davidson, promised his daughter a dowry of "a good, first-rate cow and a feather bed"—with which he hoped to attract a Presbyterian suitor. To his chagrin, his daughter eloped with an aspiring preacher of another denomination. The promised dowry was replaced by a small, spindly legged calf and a bonnet full of goose eggs. Advised the irate father: "If you want a first-rate cow, raise your own, and if you want a feather bed, make it!"[26]

In this environment Ann Rutledge spent the first twelve years of her life. Four siblings were born in White County: David in 1815, Robert in 1819, Nancy in 1821, and Margaret in 1823.

About 1817, however, families began to leave Seven Mile Prairie. They were sick of the chills and fevers that seemed to lurk behind every stump in White County, and they were lured by richer lands to the northwest. Ann's cousin, John Miller Camron, then twenty-seven, was among the first to seek greener pastures. He and his family followed a trail across the Illinois frontier to Looking Glass Prairie near St. Louis, where he staked out a farm twelve miles east of Belleville. Soon afterward, Camron and his wife, Polly, began attending camp meetings that spread through the frontier during the Second Great Awakening. At one session, Polly embraced Christianity, and soon Camron was consecrated as a Cumberland Presbyterian elder. Later he became a minister.[27]

Camron's small farm eventually proved unprofitable. When a neighbor mentioned a promising land called Sangamon Valley—"the land where there is plenty to eat"—Camron listened. It was near Springfield, in central Illinois, about ninety miles northeast of Looking Glass Prairie. Soon the Camrons packed their goods and moved again. They first settled north of Springfield then moved to Rock Creek on the west side of Sangamon County. Each time Camron moved he established a farm, set out an orchard, and hoped to prosper. The only thing that multiplied, however, was his family. By 1825 he had six daughters and one son, with five more girls yet to come.[28]

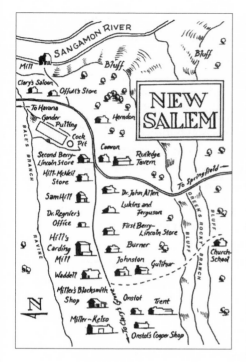

A MILLWRIGHT by trade, John Miller Camron decided his future was in saw- and gristmills, and he believed Sangamon Valley would be a perfect location for such mills. He rode down to Seven Mile Prairie to convince Ann's father, James Rutledge, to join him in a partnership. Rutledge thought highly of Miller, even though their demeanors were quite different. Rutledge, of medium height, was quiet and dignified. Camron, who had great physical strength, was aggressive and outspoken—and persuasive.[29]

Intrigued by Camron's description of the distant valley, Ann's family hitched up the oxen and "headed right out" on the 160-mile trek to Sangamon County in 1826. Others in the traveling party were Ann's uncle and aunt, Billy and Susa Rutledge, and their children—McGrady and his four brothers and sisters. At first James and Mary Ann seriously considered leaving Ann, then thirteen, with her grandmother. Finally they decided that Ann should go. Had she remained behind, Abraham Lincoln's life would have been affected dramatically.[30]

At Rock Creek in Sangamon County the Rutledges found a contented circle of friends, including Presbyterian minister John M. Berry and his brother Samuel. Samuel's son James was immediately attracted to Rutledge's oldest daughter, Jean, and would marry her two years later.

Among the region's favorite pastimes was ice skating. One of Pastor Berry's sons taught Vian Camron and Ann Rutledge how to skate. Ann became a graceful skater, but Vian kept running into snowbanks. After warming themselves in the Rutledge cabin, James Rutledge suggested that the young people dramatize scenes from Shakespeare. They chose *A Midsummer Night's Dream*. Ann enjoyed Shakespeare and had read several plays and sonnets. Now she read aloud with the style and passion of an actress.[31]

On July 19, 1828, Camron and Rutledge selected a mill site about twenty miles northwest of Springfield. It was on the Sangamon River, a powerful winding stream bounded by high bluffs and broad plains. The site was at a point where the river was navigable and the water flowed steadily. The site seemed ideal. A road on the bluff connected Springfield and Havana and provided easy access to the nearby settlements.[32]

Anticipating legislative approval to dam the river for water power, they moved in the fall of 1828 and built adjacent log homes on the high bluff above the Sangamon and in the midst of huge oak, maple, and walnut trees. Approval came in January. The construction was a massive undertaking, requiring a thousand loads of rock hauled in from nearby Green's Rocky Branch and Rocky Run. Then, on rock pillars, they built a fully enclosed gristmill, set well out in the river. On the shore they erected an open-sided primitive sawmill.[33]

Settlers in the area had been grinding their cornmeal by hand and welcomed the new mill. From as far away as fifty miles, farmers began trading at the Camron and Rutledge mill. If a farmer had four sacks of grain, he would send four boys with a two-bushel sack on each horse. On some days as many as forty horses could be found hitched to nearby trees. The operation was profitable because there were no other mills in the area, and cornmeal was the staple of the local diet. Babies ate corn bread crumbled in milk and a thick cornmeal porridge called "mush." Adults ate corn bread as well as corndodgers, which consisted of cornmeal and cold water patted into pones and baked in a greased skillet. The corndodgers sometimes came out so hard "they could split a board or fell a steer at forty feet," according to one settler. They were usually served with honey and buttermilk. Another product was "ashcake," made of cornmeal and water, wrapped in green cornhusks or cabbage leaves, and cooked on the hearth in wood ash.

On October 20, 1829, shortly after the mills opened, Rutledge's wife gave birth to their tenth and last child, Sarah. She would live to be ninety-three.

Pleased with the success of their mill, Camron and Rutledge employed a surveyor and on October 23, 1829, laid out a town on a wooded grove on the bluffs, one hundred feet above the river. They named the town New Salem and sold lots for about ten dollars. From eastern states, single men came to New Salem seeking adventure and wealth. From southern states, especially Kentucky, families came to "break prairie" or create a business. One- and two-room log houses were constructed, with split-rail fences enclosing grazing areas for horses and cattle. Attracted by the mill's growing business, bachelors Sam Hill and John McNeil came from back East and opened the first general store. They sold groceries, whiskey, and dry goods.[34]

An industrial center of sorts developed. Kentuckian Henry Onstot, in his midtwenties, built a cooper shop. He fashioned buckets and tubs for domestic use and barrels for produce and whiskey. He was vital to the community since almost all produce was shipped in barrels—wet ones for whiskey or meat products, dry ones for flour. He sold flour barrels for 40¢ and washtubs for $1.50.

Joshua Miller, a short, heavyset man, erected a blacksmith shop, forging shoes for oxen and horses and iron parts for wagons and farm implements. His shop was one of the town's busiest and noisiest places. The clanging of the anvil could be heard throughout the village from early morning until night. Miller and brother-in-law Jack Kelso built a double residence for their two families. Kelso, childless and with little incentive to accumulate property for descendants, observed the habits of fish and wild animals and became an expert hunter and fisherman. He was also adept at robbing a bee tree of its honey.

Soon a tinner, a wheelwright, a weaver, a shoemaker, and a hatter opened businesses here. Wheelwright Robert Johnson, a devout Presbyterian, made spinning wheels, looms, and furniture. Shoemaker Peter Lukins was a devoted drinker, and after a night of drunken debauchery, he was found dead in bed. Hatter Martin Waddel made caps of felt, rabbit fur, and coonskins, the last type being the most expensive at two dollars each. Later Sam Hill erected a storage building for wool and added a wool-carding treadmill. It was propelled by an ox walking endlessly on a circular inclined plane.[35]

Just above the dam, off the main street and around a bend in the road, Tennessean Bill Clary started a saloon, with liquor costing from twelve to twenty-five cents for a half-pint. Clary's saloon became the hangout of a gang of ingenious and reckless rowdies from Clary's Grove, a settlement southwest of New Salem. Night after night, the Clary's Grove boys raced down the half-mile main street, raised a ruckus, and made all good citizens shake their heads. Always up to mischief, they trimmed horses' tails and put stones under saddles to cause horses to throw their riders.

Near Clary's saloon foot- and horseraces began and ended, and men bet money, coonskins, ginseng, and other items. Gander pullings were regular attractions. An old male goose was swung head down from a tree limb, with his neck greased. Riders paid ten cents to compete. They rode full speed, and the one who grabbed the neck and pulled off the head got the bird. On Saturdays men from New Salem and nearby settlements competed in wrestlin' and shootin' matches and carried feisty roosters under their arms to fight in the cockpit, a spectacle that generated deafening shouts and raucous laughter.

North of Clary's saloon, an outcropping of stone was turned into a quarry, providing material for foundations and fireplaces. Bill Clary also initiated a ferry service to improve access from the east. He charged fifty cents for a team and wagon to cross.

More stores opened, and a young spiritually minded physician, Dr. John Allen, arrived from Vermont. He constructed a three-room log home and office across the street from the Hill-McNeil store. Dr. Allen reportedly had tuberculosis and had come west for his health. Crippled from youth, he walked with a slight limp.

A post office was established on December 25, 1829, with Samuel Hill as postmaster. Previously, settlers rode twenty miles to Springfield to get their mail.[36]

New Salem became a flourishing trading place for the surrounding area—a place where farmers could get their corn ground and walk up the hill and buy supplies, have a few drinks, and play card games such as euchre and seven-up. As the town prospered, James Rutledge converted his log home into a small tavern, where travelers could enjoy a meal and a bed for thirty-seven and a half cents per day. Between Chicago (which had a population of 150) and New Salem, inns were scarce and primitive, and few villages of any size existed. A traveler between the two towns reported stopping at a one-room inn crowded with twenty-seven lodgers. Rutledge Tavern was luxurious by comparison.

On January 7, 1830, Ann Rutledge quietly observed her seventeenth birthday. She had had several beaux but had not found one who had a mind to match hers. From her father's library she had read the works of Robert Burns, Thomas Paine, and Constantine de Volney. Not many men on the frontier wanted a woman who read and recited Shakespeare, could talk about the great philosophers, and had not yet joined a church, even though her parents were deeply religious. On the other hand, she was an excellent seamstress and dedicated to her duties, whatever they were. But would she be satisfied as a merchant's or farmer's wife whose main goals were to keep house and rear a bunch of children, with no one to share her intellectual interests? She was looking for someone special. Soon she would have four interesting choices.

4

"There's More in Abe's Head than Wit and Fun"

1830–31

*T*HE GIRLS of New Salem chose their mates at an early age—thirteen or fourteen—and were usually "hitched" by fifteen or sixteen. Most girls on the prairie planned to be homemakers, and there was no reason to delay marriage. Once married, few of them continued whatever schooling they may have begun. They were too busy fixin' meals, keepin' house, and raisin' kids.

So when Mentor Graham started a school about a half-mile southwest of town, only a few older girls were among the thirty to forty students from ages six to eighteen in the small log church building loaned by the Baptists for school use. This subscription school wasn't cheap, especially for large families—thirty to eighty-five cents a month per child, based on age. With money scarce, most families paid tuitions with commodities, such as corn, pork, chickens, butter, eggs, and whiskey. Corn was worth only twenty cents a bushel; hogs, $1.25 per hundred pounds, dressed; butter, five to eight cents a pound; and eggs, three to five cents a dozen. Thus a full school meant a full stomach for Mentor Graham and his family. A teetotaler, Graham accepted whiskey but traded it for sugar and coffee or calico fabric for his wife, Sarah.[1]

Thirty-year-old Mentor Graham was an anti-slavery Kentuckian of Scotch-Irish origin. Tall, lithe, and strong muscled, he walked with a swift, determined gait. A stylish dresser, he usually wore a black velvet vest, cut-away coat, and stovepipe hat. His curly red hair and freckled face were matched by his rough, red hands, calloused from cutting brush to feed his livestock and from making bricks for the fireplaces and chimneys of "stuck-up folkes' houses."[2]

Graham's proposed contract with parents called for reading, writing, arithmetic, geography, and grammar, but many parents objected to the last two. "Nobody needs no grammar," some said. Nevertheless, Graham taught grammar to every child; he just did not refer to it by that name. He taught his pupils to think and to say what they thought—audibly, clearly, and well.[3]

His students were a mixture of youngsters just starting to school and older students in various stages of literacy or, as one put it, "jest ketchin' up a bit." Some were sincere learners; others were there because they preferred school to farm work.

Graham's endless energy, powerful voice, and forceful gestures commanded their attention. Strict and stern, he kept large hickory switches beside his desk and, as some of the boys remembered, was "apt to whip mighty hard" or to "thump y' on the gourd."

Graham taught by the "blab" method. Students recited their lessons aloud, over and over, and Graham listened through the din for errors. But when a student had mastered a lesson, he or she had to stand before the others and recite. Then all became quiet.[4]

Ann Rutledge was one of the best students in Graham's school. She had attended since the age of fourteen with strong support from her parents. Graham admired her "quick mind" and her scholarship "in all the common branches, including grammar." Billy Greene, himself bright and college-bound, noted her "sharp intellect." Ann's younger brother Robert acknowledged she had "the brightest mind of the family" and was "devoted to her duties of whatever character."[5]

Ann and her brothers walked to the one-room school from Rutledge Tavern, their parents' home and boarding house. They took a wooded path down a bluff, crossed Green's Rocky Branch, and climbed another bluff to reach the school. From time to time Ann shopped for her family at the Hill-McNeil store, across the street from Rutledge Tavern. It carried groceries and dry goods ranging from coffee, sugar, salt, and whiskey to blue calico, brown muslin, homemade jeans, and bonnets. Ann often traded butter for a few yards of calico.

On her rounds, and in the Rutledge Tavern, Ann could not go unnoticed, whether alone or in a crowd, even in her plain green calico dress, sturdy calfskin shoes, and straw sunbonnet. At eighteen, she had blossomed like a lily of the valley, bringing beauty and color to the New Salem landscape. She was slender, pretty, and graceful, with a pink rosebud complexion, a good figure, large blue eyes, and cherry red lips. Her long curly hair was described by some as light sandy and others as reddish blonde. Her mouth was "well-made, beautiful," with good teeth. She stood about five foot four and weighed around 125 pounds. Everyone knew her to be vivacious yet gentle and tender-hearted. She was amiable and loving. She was not sophisticated in the traditional sense, as one could not expect her to be, given her circumstances, but she stood out as "cultured" in contrast to those around her.

Billy Greene said she was "full of love, kindness, and sympathy" and that her character was "positively noted throughout the county." Ann's cousin, McGrady Rutledge, recalled that he never knew her to complain. "She's always cheerful," he observed, "and a good conversationalist."[6]

William F. "Bill" Berry, son of the Presbyterian minister at Rock Creek, was the first New Salem bachelor to seek Ann's affection. They had known each other since she was thirteen and had skated together on Rock Creek. In December, Bill Berry and Ann were invited to a goose dinner celebrating Vian Camron's sixteenth birthday. Her father, John Miller Camron, being a Presbyterian minister, took down the Bible after dinner and asked each guest to read a favorite passage. Ann chose the opening of Psalm 24: "The earth is the Lord's and the fulness thereof. . . . Who shall stand in his holy place? He that hath clean hands and a pure heart; who hath not lifted up his soul unto vanity, nor sworn deceitfully." As the party drew to a close, Ann reached for her cape. Bill helped her put it on and offered to accompany her home. She consented.[7]

But Bill developed a taste for whiskey, and the taste turned into an addiction, which irritated his father, who preached abstinence. Ann was a teetotaler, and when Bill called on her one evening and was visibly groggy from too much whiskey, she broke off the relationship. Clearly Bill had neither "clean hands nor a pure heart," as the Scriptures advised.

Next came Samuel Hill, co-owner of the successful Hill-McNeil store. He had migrated from his native New Jersey to Cincinnati, Ohio, at age twenty and to New Salem at age twenty-eight. A shrewd businessman, he cultivated the drinking crowd, and his store profited greatly as a result. Hill was New Salem's Ebenezer Scrooge—hot-tempered, irritable, rash, and thrifty to the point of stinginess. He disliked "loud-mouth yellin' preachers" and let them know it.[8]

Methodist circuit rider Peter Cartwright fit that description in Hill's opinion. Of gigantic build and not easily intimidated, Cartwright was both a preacher and a politician. The Hill-McNeil store was the gathering place for the gossipers, gabbers, and loafers. Cartwright hoped to convert them, so he would sit on Hill's porch, wearing his broad-rimmed white hat, and entertain them with his keen wit and spunky conversation. At one point Cartwright ridiculed Hill in front of his own store, exclaiming: "I always thought that Hill had no soul until he put a quarter to his lips and his soul 'came up to get it.'" A slender man of average height, Hill often got even with his enemies by hiring ruffians to beat them up, but Cartwright was a match for most frontier bullies, and none wanted to fight him. Hill had to find another way to retaliate.[9]

Women seldom saw Hill's vicious disposition. To them he was polite and attentive. So when he asked Ann out, she accepted, and they courted. Believing he had captured Ann's heart, Hill requested her hand in marriage. To his surprise, she said no. Ann had become interested in Hill's handsome, urbane partner, New Yorker John McNeil. McNeil eventually began courting Ann—an action destined to detonate Hill's explosive temper.

The winter of 1830–31 was known in New Salem as "the winter of the deep snow." Under the top surface of four feet of snow was a layer of ice from freezing rain that came between blizzards. Fifteen-year-old David Rutledge and sixteen-year-old Tom Camron worked long hours in below-zero temperatures to keep the paths open between their homes. For days they skated from one house to the other. With drifts up to twelve feet, families had to cut trees high off the ground to get wood for the fireplace. They melted ice to make coffee and heated bricks to warm the sheets. Chest colds were common. Constant applications of bear oil helped them survive.

The deep snow starved the deer, turkeys, and prairie chickens. Some animals froze to death and were eaten by wolves. McGrady Rutledge recalled that two deer came to his father's feed lot "and were fed with the cattle and sheep."

Finally, the spring of 1831 brought welcome relief. On April 19, 1831, the residents of New Salem, including Ann Rutledge, were drawn to the river bluff to witness a bizarre sight. A large flatboat—eighty feet long and eighteen feet wide—had come around the bend of the river and was stuck on the milldam. Loaded with hogs and barrels of bacon, wheat, and corn, the boat could not negotiate the receding river. Its bow hung over the dam, and its down-tilting stern was taking on water at a perilous rate.[10]

Four men were aboard. One of them, noticeably taller than the others, was taking charge. He directed the others to transfer cargo from the stern to a ferry boat just below them. They then rolled the remaining barrels forward toward the bow. Next the tall stranger waded ashore, introduced himself as Abraham Lincoln, and inquired about a cooper shop. He needed an auger. He was directed to Henry Onstot's shop about a quarter mile down the road.

Onstot thought the boatman strange-looking. He had a "rather singular grotesque appearance," Onstot noted, with a long, scraggy neck and a narrow, thin chest that appeared to have been stretched by his towering six-foot-four body. His head, with long hollow cheeks, seemed much too small for his stature, while his nose and ears seemed much too large for his head. Feeling sorry for him, Onstot loaned him an auger. Lincoln thanked him, and while returning to the boat, he cut a limb and fashioned a plug the diameter of the auger bit.[11]

Back on the riverbank the villagers awaited his next move. He did not disappoint them as he worked in the water, with his "boots off, hat, coat, and vest off; pants rolled up to his knees and shirt wet with sweat and combing his fuzzie hair with his fingers as he pounded away on the boat." With the auger he bored a hole in the bow to release the accumulated water. Next he called for volunteers to stand in the bow to weigh it down. The stern lifted, the water drained, he plugged the hole, and the boat floated over the dam. The villagers cheered.[12]

Ann Rutledge undoubtedly shared Onstot's analysis of the stranger. To this "lily of the valley," Abraham Lincoln must have looked like "the ragweed of the prairie." It certainly was not love at first sight, at least not on her part. But while she was not charmed by his appearance, she was surely intrigued by his ingenuity.

Meanwhile, the crew reloaded the boat and passed on down the river. Villagers learned that the other voyagers were Lincoln's cousin and stepbrother, John Hanks and John Johnston, respectively, and their employer, Denton Offutt. They were headed for New Orleans, a thousand-mile river trip, with stops along the way to deliver produce to southern markets. From New Salem the crew piloted the boat northward to the Illinois River and then south to the Mississippi. They glided past Alton, St. Louis, and Cairo in rapid succession, tied up for a day at Memphis, and made brief stops at Vicksburg and Natchez. Early in May they reached New Orleans, where they disposed of their cargo and lingered a month.

In New Orleans, Lincoln beheld the true horrors of American slavery. He saw "Negroes chained—maltreated—whipped and scourged," John Hanks later told Herndon. At a slave auction, Lincoln observed "a vigorous and comely mulatto girl" being sold. "She underwent a thorough examination at the hands of the bidders; they pinched her flesh and made her trot up and down the room like a horse [so] that the bidders might satisfy themselves whether [she] was sound or not." Lincoln moved away from the scene "with a deep feeling of unconquerable hate." Herndon said the information was furnished not just by John Hanks but that he also "heard Mr. Lincoln refer to it himself." Having had enough of New Orleans, Lincoln and his colleagues boarded a steamboat for the return trip. They disembarked in St. Louis.[13]

Offutt was profoundly impressed with Lincoln's abilities and with New Salem's potential boom-town profits. So he decided to establish a store there and employed Lincoln to operate it. Offutt remained in St. Louis to secure merchandise, and Lincoln visited his parents in their new home in Coles County. He then walked to New Salem, arriving there in late July. This time his unrolled pants attracted even more attention because they were several inches too short. William Butler, a Kentuckian who later became a friend of Lincoln's, described him "as ruff a specimen of humanity as could be found."[14]

The bad impressions soon changed, however, when villagers found him to be articulate and intelligent. "He's no green horn," one said. Waiting for Offutt to return, Lincoln loafed about, spinning out Indiana yarns, such as this one:

> An itinerant preacher stepped into the pulpit and announced as his text, "I am the Christ, whom I shall represent today." Just as he started his sermon, a green lizard crept up his baggy pant leg. With one hand, he gestured the strong points of his sermon; with the other he tried to stop the upward advance of the lizard. Finally, he opened the button of his pantaloons and, with one sweep and a kick, he freed himself of his jeans while continuing his sermon without missing a word. However, the lizard was now making its way up his back, and the preacher unfastened the button holding his shirt and divested himself of that garment too, with

the flow of his eloquence uninterruptedly marching on. The congregation was stunned, and one elderly woman rose, pointed an accusing finger at the preacher, and shouted: "If you represent Jesus Christ, then I am done with the Bible."[15]

When Denton Offutt returned to New Salem with supplies, Lincoln helped him build the small log store he would manage. It opened for business in early September 1831. Offutt's store was adjacent to Clary's saloon, just above the milldam, and across from the cockpit. In that location Offutt anticipated the patronage of those bringing grist to the mill from both sides of the river. It was also convenient for loading flatboats with products he accepted in exchange for the goods he sold.

But the site placed Lincoln side-by-side with the rowdies. The challenge he would soon be forced to meet was how to walk untouched by their excesses and meanness and yet win their admiration and respect. To their disappointment, he refused to join them in their drinking bouts and carousals. He reportedly abstained from intoxicating liquors and never smoked or chewed tobacco. Lincoln said he used to drink some, but it had threatened his self-control. He said he could not allow that to happen.[16]

Offutt expanded his enterprise by renting the mill from Camron and Rutledge, and Lincoln ran from the store to the mill, where he unloaded, measured, and settled for sacks of grains brought in by farmers. To assist Lincoln at the store, Offutt hired Charles Maltby as his chief assistant and Billy Greene as the credit checker. Greene knew the financial standing of people in the community and could tell Lincoln whose credit was good. Most settlers bought on credit and paid with produce. Greene had an exceptionally keen mind, especially in financial matters. Some called him "Slicky Bill." He lived with his father, a drinking and illiterate man, on a farm two miles from town, but he often stayed overnight at the store, sharing a bed with Lincoln. They developed a lifelong friendship.[17]

Lincoln paid village cofounder John Miller Camron one dollar a week to dine with his large family of eight girls and one boy, with another girl on the way. Lincoln's main love at the Camrons turned out to be Polly's pies, although he was fascinated by the girls. Solena and Sorena, four-year-old twins, were especially amused by the tall stranger who told them stories. Eleven-year-old Mary, nine-year-old Martha, and seven-year-old Sarah teased him about his long legs, long arms, and horsy "ways." And he admitted he was not much "to look at."

Thirteen-year-old Nancy ignored him. Sixteen-year-old Vian made fun of his appearance: "He's as thin as a beanpole and as ugly as a scarecrow!" Vian piqued Lincoln's interest with her coal black hair, flashing brown eyes, keen wit, and frisky, frolicsome ways. "You're full of spice and vinegar," he said to her. "I'll call you 'Quinine.'" Her beau was William Prosise, a prosperous farmer. "I'd not bother with him," Lincoln teased her. "A lawyer's who you want." She remembered thinking, "How dare he talk to me like that!"[18]

The oldest daughter, eighteen-year-old Betsy, was a dark-haired beauty, well poised and courteous, with a regal manner like that of her mother. Lincoln called her "Queen Isabella." Her father warned her not to get too interested in Lincoln, declaring that "he's poor and won't amount to much."

On one occasion when Lincoln was visiting the Camrons, he saw one of Betsy's suitors, Billy Greene—whom she did not like—coming toward the house. Roguishly, Lincoln told Betsy that her favorite beau was headed their way. Not wanting anything to do with "Slicky Bill," she slipped into a rocking chair on the far side of the room. Greene came in, and then Lincoln saw Betsy's true love, Baxter Berry, approaching on the path. As Berry knocked at the door, Lincoln pushed Greene onto Betsy's lap, and Greene tried to kiss her as Berry entered the room. Betsy reacted with a strong uppercut to Greene's head, knocking him off the chair. She then rose with a vengeance and slapped Lincoln, who was laughing hysterically. Berry sized up the situation. He took Betsy's arm and led her outside. A year later Betsy married Berry, with Lincoln acting as best man. When he delivered his gift—matching berry bowls decorated with roses—Vian met him at the door. "These are for Queen Isabella to dine with in fine style," he reportedly said.[19]

Twice a day, after meals, Camron conducted devotions. Some of the girls would read from the Psalms or the Epistles, and then he would pray for fifteen to twenty minutes or longer. Lincoln, during his first day of dining with the Camrons, was not aware of the ritual and had stretched out by the fire after supper. Camron quickly advised him to kneel for Bible readings and prayer. Lincoln apologized as he assumed the proper position. After Camron closed his eyes and began praying, Lincoln procured a pillow from Vian for his knees. Then, as the prayer ended, he pushed it away. He repeated the procedure daily.[20]

OFFUTT'S GROCERY store offered varied goods, including calico prints from Massachusetts, teas from China, coffee from Brazil, stoneware from Pennsylvania, and gloves and mittens made by New Salem women from tanned deerskins. Lincoln showed a pair of dogskin gloves to a customer one day. "I ain't never heard of dogskin gloves," said the farmer dryly. "How do you know that's what they are?" Said Lincoln, "Well, I reckon I can recollect how that came 'bout. Jack Clary's dog killed Tom Watkin's sheep. Then, Tom Watkin's boy killed the dog, and old John Mounts tanned the dogskin, and Sally Spears made the gloves. That's how I know." The man bought the gloves for seventy-five cents.[21]

In making change for another customer, Lincoln accidentally took out six and a quarter cents too much. He discovered the error at closing time and reportedly walked six miles to return the money. In New Salem he became known as "Honest Abe."[22]

Lincoln's respect for New Salem women was demonstrated by his reaction when Charlie Reavis cursed around women shoppers. Lincoln demanded that Reavis desist, saying he would not tolerate such language in his store when ladies were present. When Reavis continued the vulgarity, Lincoln admonished him: "I have spoken to you a number of times about swearing in the presence of ladies, and you have not heeded. Now I am going to rub the lesson into you so that you will not forget again." Thereupon he seized Reavis by the arm and led him out of the store to the side of the street where there was a patch of smartweed. Throwing Reavis on his back and putting his foot on his chest, Lincoln grabbed a handful of the stinging weeds and rubbed Reavis's face, mouth, and eyes with them until he yelled for mercy. Reavis begged Lincoln to stop and swore he would never again swear around ladies if Lincoln would let him up. But Lincoln told him that was not sufficient; he would have to quit swearing altogether. Having little choice, Reavis agreed.[23]

Frequently Lincoln would stop at the homes of widows and ask if they needed any wood chopped. If so, he would chop it at no charge. When Lincoln saw a barefooted boy chopping wood one cold winter day, he asked what he would get paid for the job and what he would do with the money. The boy replied, "One dollar." And pointing to his naked feet added, "A pair of shoes." Lincoln sent him inside to get warm and said he would chop for a while. He finished the job and told the boy to collect his pay and buy the shoes.

If a traveler got stuck in the mud in New Salem's main street, Lincoln was always the first to help pull out the wheel. "Abe will do anything to help anyone," a merchant said. Lincoln's spontaneous, unobtrusive helpfulness endeared him to everybody and inspired them to help him when he needed it. "All loved him," said Mentor Graham, because he was one of "the most companionable persons you will ever see in this world." He would even stop reading to play marbles with children.[24]

When a merchant was wrongly informed that Lincoln had spoken unkindly of his wife, he tore into Lincoln with foul and abusive language. Lincoln kept his temper and denied the accusation. "In fact," said Lincoln, "I have a very high opinion of her, and the only thing I know against her is the fact of her being your wife!" The merchant laughed and apologized.[25]

In Lincoln's day New Salem was a man's world. For an hour at the close of most days Lincoln sought out athletic activities—wrestling, jumping, and lifting heavy weights. He would lift heavy timbers and pile one upon another, and he would take a barrel of whiskey and hoist it up to his head, a difficult feat he accomplished easily.

He once wrestled the town bully, Jack Armstrong, and was about to win when Armstrong made an unfair move, grabbing Lincoln by the thigh. Reacting, Lincoln seized him by the throat and thrust him at arm's length from him. "If you want to 'wrastle' fair, I am ready," he said calmly. "But if you want to fight, I will try that." Armstrong preferred to call it a draw. "Boys," said Armstrong, "Abe Lincoln is the best fellow that ever broke into this settlement. He shall be one of us."[26]

Armstrong was the leader of a gang of ingenious and reckless rowdies from Clary's Grove. Despite the gang's mischievous ways, Lincoln's fair play and his good-natured attitude in the wrestling match won the gang's admiration. From that time on, the Clary's Grove Boys were Lincoln supporters.

After the wrestling match, Lincoln was often called to judge contests because he was regarded as the most impartial man in town. He once refereed a cockfight between Babb McNabb's bird and a fighting veteran. McNabb had bragged incessantly about his bird's abilities. Bets ran high. When the two birds were thrown into the pit, McNabb's rooster "turned tail and ran." At a safe distance he mounted a fence, spread his feathers, and crowed. Babb paid his wager and addressed his bird: "Yes, you little cuss, you're great on dress parade, but not worth a damn in a fight." Years later, during the Civil War, Lincoln remembered the incident while dealing with Gen. George B. McClellan and compared the general to McNabb's rooster. McClellan would exhaust Lincoln's patience by endlessly drilling and reviewing the Army of the Potomac while persistently refusing to fight.[27]

Adding further diversity to New Salem events, a temperance society was organized in December 1831. The group hoped to reform its hard-drinking neighbors but had little success. T. G. Onstot, the cooper's son, complained that the worst opponents of temperance were "the church members, most of whom had barrels of whiskey at home."[28]

When Mentor Graham joined the society and signed a temperance pledge, the local hard-shell Baptists threw him out. At the same time, another member was expelled for getting drunk. These activities prompted still another member to ask: "I should like to have someone tell me just how much whiskey a man has to drink to be in full fellowship and good standing in this church." No one responded. However, some predestinarian Baptists rationalized that temperance societies were bad because they tried to alter matters predestined by God. That would explain why the Baptists re-admitted Graham after the temperance society expelled him for breaking his pledge.[29]

Lincoln enjoyed male company, and he entertained the men and himself. He swapped stories and opinions with the blacksmith, the saloon keeper, the cobbler, and others. Lincoln's knack for storytelling attracted the fun-loving men of New Salem, while his range of knowledge caught the attention of more prominent citizens, such as Mentor Graham and James Rutledge. Lincoln knew their intellectual and literary resources, and he drew upon them. He borrowed books from Graham, Rutledge, Bennett Abell, John McNeil, and folks in Springfield, walking there or riding on farmers' wagons. He read everything he could find. And he wrote down everything he wanted to remember. History held a special fascination for him. Lincoln read and reread William Grimshaw's *History of the United States*. Denouncing slavery and stressing the significance of the American Revolution, it exhorted readers: "Let us not only declare by words, but demonstrate by our actions, that 'all men are created equal.'"

Lincoln borrowed Shakespeare's works from an unlikely source, Jack Kelso, a lazy fisherman and jack-of-all-trades who had the gifts of a poet. When others got drunk, they fought, but when Kelso got drunk he astonished the rustic community with lengthy, memorized quotations from Robert Burns and William Shakespeare.

Although Lincoln hated fishing, he loitered away whole days talking with Kelso along the banks of quiet streams where Kelso expounded on "our divine William" and "Scotia's Bard" between intervals of fixing bait and dropping line. From Kelso, Lincoln learned to appreciate the finer sentiments of poetic expression. Some folks said Lincoln seemed to read more than he worked, and they wondered if he was shiftless. "My father considered me lazy," Lincoln told Billy Greene. "When he caught me reading when he thought I should have been doing chores, he gave me a good thrashing. . . . He taught me to work, but he never taught me to love it." Lincoln readily admitted he didn't like physical labor and thought there were better ways to make a living.[30]

While intellectual pursuits were not commonplace on the Illinois prairie, New Salem was by contrast an intellectual center. Debating societies were the vehicle, and Ann Rutledge's father was the primary mover. In 1831 he organized what was probably the first debating society. Lincoln's first speech in the region was at Rutledge's debating club. Dr. John Allen said he delivered a strong argument "pretty well." Lincoln spoke in the high-pitched voice that became his trademark, but he did not know what to do with his hands. After waving them about, he finally placed them in his pockets.

Another debating club was started by Thomas J. Nance, a well-educated Kentuckian and future legislator. Lincoln walked six miles to participate. Topics included: Should females be educated and have the right to vote? Should people join temperance societies? Should a wife promise to obey her husband? David Rutledge, who wanted to be a lawyer, debated and argued questions with Lincoln. So did Mentor Graham.

James Rutledge, who owned a library of thirty books, was impressed with Lincoln's debating skills. He remarked to his wife, "There's more in Abe's head than wit and fun. All he lacks is culture." Rutledge took a deeper interest in Lincoln and urged him to announce himself as a candidate for the legislature. "In time it will do you good," Rutledge advised.

Rutledge's daughter Ann had read many of her father's books and was especially fond of Shakespeare and Burns. Her literary interests were similar to those of Lincoln. Through such intellectual activity Lincoln built up a following. Eventually, he was viewed by his New Salem neighbors as everybody's friend. He had won his own way—with his fists and his wits.[31]

During his years in New Salem, Lincoln never had his own home. He slept anywhere and everywhere there was a vacant bed. Since everyone liked him, he never had any trouble finding a place to stay. Almost any villager could have posted a sign, "Abe Lincoln slept here." Lincoln frequently visited Armstrong's home where Jack's wife, Hannah, "took a likin'" to him, washed and patched his clothes, and made shirts for him. Although she was about the same age as Lincoln, he called her "Aunt Hannah." She often chopped her own stove wood, but when Lincoln visited, he chopped it for her. "Abe would come out to our house," she would later recall, "drink milk, eat mush, cornbread and butter, bring the children candy, chop wood, and rock the cradles of our twin sons, Duff and Boger, while I got him something to eat." One of Lincoln's favorite snacks was bread with honey.[32]

Lincoln related well to the young married women of New Salem, and Aunt Hannah and others became surrogate mothers or sisters to him. While he was shy and bashful around available single women, he was completely at ease around women who were not potential mates. Lincoln was such good company that the Armstrongs wanted him to visit often. If either Jack or Aunt Hannah needed help or knew that Lincoln was idle, they would send for him. "Do stay to supper, Abe," they would implore. "Stay all night, might as well." He usually did.

Some twenty years later, Aunt Hannah needed Lincoln's help twice, and she got it. Her son Duff was charged with murder in a late-night drunken brawl with James Metzger in 1857. Jack had died, and Hannah offered Lincoln her farm to defend him. Lincoln refused any payment and took the case. The prosecutor's star witness said he clearly saw Duff strike Metzger because a full moon was shining directly overhead. Lincoln opened a copy of the 1857 almanac and read a page to the jury; at the time of the incident, the moon was not directly overhead. It was low in the sky. Duff was acquitted.

During the Civil War, Lincoln received another request from Hannah—to discharge Duff from the Union army because he was needed to run the farm. Lincoln honored the request.[33]

IN ADDITION to the uncultured Armstrongs, Lincoln developed a close relationship with a couple at the opposite end of the cultural spectrum: Elizabeth and Bennett Abell. Well-to-do Kentuckians, they owned one of the area's finest farms, about two miles north of the village.

Elizabeth, in her late twenties, was smart and cultivated. She was attracted to Lincoln, and he to her. She washed clothes for him, they had many long talks, and she urged him to seek a "higher plane of life." Lincoln lived luxuriously with the Abells for several months and dined on such scrumptious delicacies as roast duck and gooseberry pie.

Row Herndon, a village resident, noted that young married women "all liked Lincoln and he liked them as well." Herndon then added a shocker that gave his statement new meaning: "Elizabeth Abell has a daughter that is thought to be Lincoln's child. They favor very much."

"Lincoln did live with the Abells in a sort of home intimacy," acknowledged William Butler, another Kentuckian and close friend of Lincoln. Elizabeth later described Lincoln admiringly: "He was very sensitive . . . [never rash], and . . . the best-natured man I ever got acquainted with. . . . He was always doing good."[34]

Lincoln also enjoyed the company of Mentor Graham's wife, Sarah, who was in her early twenties. He often sought her advice about boy-girl relationships, love, and other personal matters.

While he liked being around married folks, Lincoln found young single women to be as antagonistic toward him as they were in his Indiana neighborhood. They made fun of him, but on occasion he used his sharp wit to retaliate.

Taking odd jobs to earn money, he once served food at a party where, as one guest recalled, "a girl there who thought herself pretty smart" protested when he filled her plate with an exceptionally generous portion. She said sharply, "Well, Mr. Lincoln, I didn't want a cart-load." A little later when she asked for more food, he announced in a loud voice, "All right, Miss Liddy, back up your cart and I'll fill it again." Everyone laughed, except for Miss Liddy, who "went off by herself and cried the whole evening."[35]

SEXUAL GOSSIP spiced up conversations around New Salem, and some of it centered on Lincoln. Nancy Burner was an attractive woman with strong passions, weak will, little sense, and a "strong desire to please and gratify friends." When she became pregnant, the gossips said it was either Lincoln's or Dr. Jason Duncan's child. "Yes, Lincoln knew the girl," Billy Greene said, "but [he] never touched her." Billy's younger brother, Gaines, however, suggested otherwise: "I really don't know who the father is. . . . Billy and Lincoln do as they please."

John McNeil later pointed a finger at Billy. Once, McNeil said, when a group of New Salem young people were walking home from an outing, Billy was "trudging along in silence" because Dr. Duncan had taken Nancy away from him. "Then, Billy came alongside Nancy, who was with Dr. Duncan, and pleaded his lost cause with her. The girls in the rear moved up to hear. After many arguments . . . Billy finally put in a clincher: 'You know, we have done things we ought not if we are going to separate.' The girls wilted and fell back."

According to both Greene brothers, Billy Greene and Lincoln persuaded Duncan to marry Nancy and move away. Before leaving, Duncan gave Lincoln a copy of the poem "Mortality" by Scotsman William Knox. Lincoln later memorized it—all fourteen quatrains—and recited it often. The first stanza reads:

> Oh, why should the spirit of mortal be proud?
> Like a swift-fleeting meteor, a fast-flying cloud,
> A flash of the lightning, a break of the wave,
> He passes from life to his rest in the grave.[36]

That fall of 1831 John McNeil initiated a courtship with Ann Rutledge. McNeil had boarded briefly at Rutledge Tavern, where he first noticed her. He was cultured, erudite, and debonair. Ann's father was less than enthusiastic, however, because McNeil was twelve years older than Ann and seemed cold and unfriendly. McNeil had come from New York and had formed a partnership with Sam Hill. Plucky and industrious, McNeil made high-interest loans and purchased low-cost land from distressed farmers. He acquired considerable property and was believed to be worth about twelve thousand dollars. His wealth and standing placed him at the top of the social ladder. And Ann's brother Robert regarded him as "high-toned, honest, and moral."

McNeil supposedly fell in love with the "gentle, amiable maiden with the bonny blue eyes." Ann doesn't have "any of the airs of the city belles," he told a New Salem friend, "and I like that."[37]

5

"He Has Dumped Her— Ho, Ho, Ho"

1832–33

$\mathcal{A}$ s LINCOLN measured calico prints for fewer and fewer customers, he surely suspected that Offutt's store was about to collapse. Ann Rutledge came in occasionally when she could not find what she wanted at the Hill-McNeil store. Lincoln always enjoyed seeing her, but it was good to see anyone at the store. Offutt was near bankruptcy, and soon, in Lincoln's words, his enterprises "petered out."

Pondering his future, Lincoln decided to follow James Rutledge's advice and run for the state legislature. On March 9, 1832, the twenty-three-year-old merchant announced his candidacy in a statement published in the *Sangamon Journal* in Springfield. He had asked the lettered John McNeil to correct the grammar. McNeil, who was courting Ann Rutledge, was an avid reader and had an extensive library for that time and place.[1]

Lincoln's decision to seek political office was an adventurous step for a young man who just a year earlier was, in his own words, a "friendless, uneducated, penniless boy, working on a flatboat—at ten dollars per month." His credentials for public office were nonexistent. He "had nothing only plenty of friends," as one contemporary phrased it.[2]

Lincoln's campaign was interrupted in mid-April. As redbuds and dandelions colored the landscape, a rider on a muddy, sweating horse stopped in New Salem and distributed handbills conveying terrible news: Indians were on the warpath in northwestern Illinois, and the governor urgently sought volunteers to help federal troops repel them. By early May some two thousand men had volunteered for one-month enlistments and were off to become heroes and make some extra money. Lincoln signed up in New Salem, as did his fellow store clerk Billy Greene, the Clary's Grove Boys, and two of Ann Rutledge's brothers, John and David. Lincoln reenlisted twice, serving a total of three months—time spent fighting mosquitoes and trying to survive in the sweltering heat and swampy wilderness.

At Beardstown, where several companies bivouacked, Lincoln met Maj. John Todd Stuart of Springfield. A well-connected Kentuckian, Stuart was a young, college-educated attorney and the son of a college professor and Presbyterian minister. Like Lincoln, he was a Whig candidate for a seat in the Illinois legislature. The two became close friends. Stuart, a worldly man with a reputation for pursuing and seducing women, apparently coaxed Lincoln to accompany him to a brothel in Galena, Illinois. "We went purely for fun and devilment, nothing else," said Stuart, without elaborating on what those words meant.[3]

Lincoln returned to New Salem two weeks before the election. He campaigned by horseback, from house to house and farm to farm. As he talked to farmers in the fields, he helped them pitch hay, feed hogs, or shuck corn. In one speech, he said: "Fellow citizens, I presume you all know who I am—I am humble Abraham Lincoln. I have been solicited by many friends to become a candidate for the legislature. My politics are short and sweet, like the old woman's dance. I am in favor of a national bank. I am in favor of the internal improvement system and a high protective tariff. These are my sentiments and political principles. If elected I shall be thankful; if not, it will be all the same."

He was not elected. However, where he was best known, in his own precinct, he received 277 of the 300 votes cast. Stuart, who was elected in his district, noted that even though Lincoln lost, he gained a reputation for candor, honesty, and effective speechmaking. "He made friends everywhere he went," Stuart recalled, "and thereby acquired the respect and confidence of everybody."

After the election, Lincoln debated what to do next. His resources totaled $124—compensation for his military service in the Black Hawk War. He wanted to stay in New Salem, however, because—he would later admit—he "was anxious to remain with his friends who had treated him with so much generosity, especially as he had nothing elsewhere to go to."[4]

While Lincoln was running for the legislature and serving in the war, John McNeil was courting Ann Rutledge. They went to barbecues, corn-huskings, dances, house raisings, and just about anywhere it was proper for a young couple to be seen together. At square dances she danced every set and never appeared tired. Finally he asked her to marry him, and she agreed. In money and looks, McNeil was considered "a good catch."

But the engagement broke up the Hill-McNeil partnership. Hill, jealous and distraught over McNeil's success with the village belle, wrote McNeil an angry, abusive letter demanding, "You either buy me out or sell out to me at the inventory price." McNeil agreed to sell.[5]

Around late June, McNeil revealed a long-held secret to his betrothed. Telling her he desired to keep nothing from her, he declared that the name McNeil was an assumed one; that his real name was McNamar. "I left be-hind me in New York," he said, "my parents and brothers and sisters. They are poor, and were in more or less need when I left them in 1829. I vowed that I would come West, make a fortune, and go back to help them. I am going to start now and intend, if I can, to bring them back with me on my return to Illinois and place them on my farm."

He changed his name, he said, because he feared that if the family in New York had known where he was, they "would have settled down on him, and before he could have accumulated any property would have sunk him beyond recovery." Now he believed he was in a position to help them. He told Ann he would return to New Salem as soon as possible and then they "could consummate the great event to which they looked forward with undisguised joy and unbounded hope."[6]

Ann believed his story because she loved him. "She would have be-lieved it all the same if it had been ten times as incredible," wrote Ward Hill Lamon years later. Whether he really loved her is a matter for speculation. McNeil/McNamar's decision to return to New York came after he learned that Ann's father desperately needed money. He capitalized on Rutledge's problem by purchasing half of the eighty-acre farm in Sandridge for the meager sum of fifty dollars. Rutledge perhaps settled for the small amount as a favor to his anticipated son-in-law. (Rutledge sold the remaining half of his farm to John Jones for three hundred dollars.) The acreage McNamar bought was adjacent to his own farm, which he had acquired earlier from John Miller Camron.[7]

After extensive research in the 1920s, author William E. Barton con-cluded that Rutledge and Camron sold their farms because they were "on the brink of a financial precipice." They had staked everything they had on the New Salem venture, and they were losing money. Even Rutledge Tavern was a financial failure. Barton speculated that McNamar left New Salem sensing that Rutledge was close to bankruptcy and realizing that Ann was no longer "the prospective heiress of the great fortunes of one of the founders of New Salem."[8]

In August, shortly after Lincoln's return from the Black Hawk War, McNamar began his trip to New York. It was only after he was gone that Ann told his story to her family. They were skeptical and had several questions: Why would anyone desert his family in order to save it? Did he change his name because he had a lurid past? Was he really jilting Ann? "I never really trusted the man," said Ann's cousin Mary Mayes Miller. "I don't know why, but I always thought he wasn't all he was cracked up to be." But the family kept their concerns to themselves, not wanting to cause Ann public embarrassment. Spurned women were objects of scorn.[9]

BUYING AND selling real estate in New Salem hit rampage proportions in the summer and fall of 1832. Camron and Rutledge sold their mills to entrepreneur Jacob Bale. Camron then unloaded his other properties and moved north to the Spoon River country, where his father had settled. Lincoln would miss his "fun and games" with the Camron girls.

In late November, Lincoln moved into Rutledge Tavern and stayed about four months. The tavern was New Salem's biggest home. It had two large rooms on the ground floor—a kitchen-dining-living area and a sleeping-sitting room with several beds. An upstairs loft accommodated twelve boarders on hay mattresses. Guests and family ate and talked around a long table. Afterward they sat by the fireplace, told stories, and related the day's gossip. Stools, baskets, and wooden boxes lined the walls, and jugs, crocks, and platters covered the mantle. A heavy walnut china cupboard was filled with delicately patterned blue-and-white dishes. Kettles over the flames in the fireplace released savory whiffs of delicious country cooking. Filled with people, furniture, and utensils, the home radiated a homey and lively ambiance.

Earlier Lincoln had boarded with the Rutledges while sleeping elsewhere. He also "dropped in," as was the custom with other villagers, sometimes bringing a watermelon and placing it in a tub of cold water, ready for the next meal or afternoon snack. He retrieved potatoes, beans, and turnips from the root cellar where they were stored for the winter.

While he was being neighborly, he was also satisfying his desire to be near Ann Rutledge.

Ann's parents were serious and pious, forthright and down-to-earth. They called a spade a spade. As Cumberland Presbyterians they took the Bible seriously. In contrast to her quiet, reserved parents, Ann was vivacious and cheerful. When Lincoln came to live at the tavern, there were eight Rutledge children at home. The oldest, Jean, had married James Berry in 1828. Ann, now nineteen, helped her mother run the inn.

At the tavern, Ann was surrounded by protective brothers close to her age—twenty-one-year-old John, seventeen-year-old David, and thirteen-year-old Robert. Then there was eleven-year-old Nancy, nine-year-old Margaret, six-year-old William, and three-year-old Sarah. The older children shared the household duties: preparing and serving food, churning butter, making soap and candles, and scrubbing utensils and floors.

Ann was the family's seamstress, perhaps the best in the village. It was said that she performed magic with her spinning wheel. Her styles were notable for tiny buttons of contrasting colors produced from bits of cloth.[10]

Strangers popped in and out for stays ranging from overnight to a few days. On one occasion the visitors included a lady from Virginia with three stylish teenage daughters, and they stayed for about two weeks. Lincoln, who was often tongue-tied and awkward around teenage girls, refused to eat at the same table with them during their visit. He had been mocked so often by attractive, eligible girls that he ignored them when possible.

But just as Lincoln was comfortable around married women, he also was at ease around "spoken-for" women. He felt he could be himself, with no need to put on "airs" to attract their interest. Consequently, after Ann Rutledge became engaged to John McNamar, Lincoln developed a rapport with her. She treated him with kindness and respect, and he admired her lively and inquisitive spirit, which was akin to his. Although she was four years younger than he, she was a mature woman by prairie standards. Ann had also become comfortable with him and enjoyed their conversations, which she considered stimulating. He was someone whose mind she enjoyed probing. It was therefore easy for the couple to have a warm and tender friendship.[11]

Among their common interests was a love for animals and a hatred for those who mistreated them. Lincoln's attitude dated back to his childhood in Indiana. Abe's father was a good hunter, and he taught his son to shoot to kill. Game meant food and skins, and skins meant clothes and a trading commodity. When a flock of wild turkeys approached their cabin one day, seven-year-old Abe picked up a gun, shot through a crack between the logs, and killed one. But Abe's momentary joy quickly turned to grief as he watched the turkey squirm, bleed, and die. The sight made him sick, and he vowed he would never kill another animal. He would not be a hunter or a fisherman.

Just as Lincoln respected all life, so did Ann Rutledge. She cared for lame dogs and birds with broken wings and other critters in need of help. John McNamar thought she was wasting her time. He could see no financial profit in it. Ann also raised pigs and chickens. Her father gave her a pig from each litter; any profits she made were set aside for her education. When Lincoln found three baby rabbits whose mother had been killed, he put them in his pockets and took them to Rutledge Tavern. He asked Ann if she would like to take care of them, and she happily agreed.[12]

Ann's homework in grammar also caught Lincoln's attention. One morning while having a breakfast of flapjacks with Mentor and Sarah Graham, he mentioned a desire for a grammar textbook. Graham responded, "If you expect to be before the public in any capacity, I think it is the best thing you can do." Lincoln agreed. "If I had a grammar, I would commence now," he vowed. Graham said there was none in the village, but he knew of a grammar at the Vances, about six miles from New Salem, which he thought Lincoln could get. When Lincoln had finished eating, he walked to the Vances and got the book, *Kirkham's Grammar,* which Graham described as "the hardest grammar I think anybody ever studied." Lincoln gave the book his full attention, however, and in Graham's words, "mastered it in an astonishing manner."[13]

Back at Rutledge Tavern, Lincoln came and went as one of the family. One evening, while seemingly engrossed in study, he picked up Ann's youngest brother, six-year-old William, tucked him under an arm, and with *Kirkham's Grammar* in the other hand, he walked along with William yelling and kicking. Then Lincoln pretended he had just discovered he was toting a boy and released him. Lincoln was like that around all children, and most seemed to enjoy his pranks and never-failing humor.

Lincoln watched as Ann gave her youngest sister, three-year-old Sarah, her first sewing lesson. Sarah sat on a low stool beside Ann; Ann stopped her work, threaded a needle for Sarah, and taught her to make a stitch. Later Sarah tried pulling Lincoln's "big ears and mouth," and he laughed. "He's so good-natured everybody loves him," Nancy Rutledge told her friends.[14]

Lincoln and Ann studied grammar together. He laughed when she had difficulties with the lesson, and one day, in a spirit of fun, he wrote below her name on the title page, "is now learning grammar." Lincoln gave her the book, and from her it was passed to her siblings.[15]

In relaxing moments at Rutledge Tavern, Lincoln would stretch out his long legs from a chair by the fireplace and tell funny stories to the children. Once, when Nancy was sitting alone by the fire, Lincoln came in, sat down beside her, looked at her teasingly, and sang softly:

> When in death I shall calmly recline,
> Oh bear my heart to my mistress dear
> Tell her it lived on smiles and wine
> Of brightest hue while it lingered here
> Bid her not to shed one tear of sorrow
> To sully a heart so brilliant and light,
> But balmy drops of the red grape borrow
> To bathe the relic from morn till night.

Nancy did not understand the intent of his action and failed to realize it was a prank. His look and manner so distressed her that she left the room.[16]

On January 7, 1833, Ann turned twenty. A few days later a neighborhood tragedy occurred. On the night of January 17, Lincoln and Ann's older brother John had gotten into a friendly "romp and scuffle" and had broken a bed board. The next morning Ann started to repair it, and Lincoln told her he "must" help her. Needing a wrench, they sent Ann's sister Nancy to Row Herndon's cabin, their nearest neighbor, to borrow one.

When Nancy arrived, Herndon was loading his gun, and suddenly it discharged. His wife, who was talking to Nancy, was shot through the neck and mortally wounded. Nancy saw blood spurt out of each side of the woman's neck. Frightened, Nancy hurried home and told Ann and Lincoln what had happened. "I can never forget how sad and shocked they looked, after having been so merry just a moment before," she later recalled. The loss of this well-liked woman, Mentor Graham's sister, was mourned throughout the region. Soon afterward, her husband left New Salem.[17]

A business opportunity came Lincoln's way when Row and James Herndon decided to sell their general store. Lincoln signed a note for a half-interest, and Bill Berry bought the remaining interest. Berry, Ann's first suitor, had been a corporal in Lincoln's company during the Black Hawk

War. This first Berry-Lincoln store was soon replaced with one more centrally situated—across the street from Rutledge Tavern. Lincoln and Berry
acquired it from Billy Greene, who had gotten it from Reuben Radford after
the Clary's Grove Boys trashed it.

This newer store was the town's only frame structure. It had a covered
porch, with a bench along the front wall. Under a nearby maple tree Lincoln often stretched out with his books in the cool, inviting shade, with his
feet propped up against the tree. Directly across the street, when Ann sat at
her spinning wheel by the window, he could call out to her and run across
and visit. He did that many times.[18]

With their new store, Berry and Lincoln had assumed a major debt.
Unfortunately for both the store did not prosper. It was said they weren't
"gee-hawing" well together: Berry loved liquor as much as Lincoln loved
books. Now, more and more, Berry devoted himself to consuming the
store's whiskey while Lincoln talked, joked, and read. It was not a recipe
for success.

Stores were permitted to sell liquor without a license if they sold it only
in quantities greater than a quart and for consumption off premises. Unknown to Lincoln, Berry secured a license in April 1833 to sell liquor by the
drink. Lincoln was so upset that he withdrew as an active participant in the
store. Soon, in Lincoln's words, the store "winked out."[19]

On May 7, 1833, Lincoln was unexpectedly appointed postmaster at a
salary of fifty dollars a year. His predecessor, Sam Hill, had operated the
post office from his store, which had done a brisk trade in liquor sales. It
was customary for women to pick up the family mail, and they were often
compelled to wait while Hill was selling whiskey. In protest, the women
successfully petitioned the government for his removal.

As postmaster, Lincoln became aware of letters exchanged between Ann
Rutledge and John McNamar. Ann told close friends that McNamar's first
letter was loving and kind but succeeding ones grew less ardent and more
formal. He wrote that there was sickness in the family and he could not return as quickly as he had hoped. Then there were other postponements—
all due to circumstances beyond his control, but he did not elaborate. After
a few months the correspondence ceased altogether. Twice each week Ann
checked with Lincoln for mail from McNamar. But there was none. The absence of letters cast a shadow across her happiness.[20]

Ann's friend Parthena Nance later wrote that "some of the girls lorded it
over Ann who sat at home alone while we other young people walked and

visited." They whispered in her ear that McNamar had deceived her and deserted her and that she had a rival in her affections. These girls were jealous and resentful of Ann's engagement to the town's most eligible bachelor. Now they talked about her behind her back, saying such things as, "He has dumped her—ho, ho, ho." Ann was socially ostracized. Her heart was broken, and more than that, she was humiliated. Her mind was tortured by suspense and disappointment. She doubted he had ever loved her.[21]

Lincoln sensed the situation and felt sorry for her. First, he asked her to walk with him in the evenings, and she consented to do so. Then they started hiking over the hills. They sometimes sat on the bluff above the river and read to each other. Both enjoyed Shakespeare and took turns reading or reciting sonnets or passages from *Macbeth* and *King Lear.*[22]

Lincoln reportedly asked Ann if she wanted him to find McNamar. "No," she replied. "He knows where I am, and if he doesn't care enough to write to me, I'm sure I don't care enough about him to try to find him." By revealing to Lincoln her fast-ebbing feelings for McNamar, she was motivating Lincoln to pursue a long-repressed passion for her. He understood and acted upon it.[23]

At every opportunity Lincoln sought to be with her—on her way to and from Sunday school, in frequent strolls along the winding paths of the village, and in cold and wet weather in nightly gatherings around the fireplace in Rutledge Tavern.

Ann loved horseback riding, and the couple sometimes rode through the fields around New Salem, occasionally stopping for a picnic beside a shady brook or on a hillside overlooking the river. They picked bucketfuls of crab apples, grapes, and persimmons, and gathered walnuts, pecans, and hazelnuts. For the first time in his life, Abraham Lincoln was deeply in love.[24]

The postmaster's pay was low, so Lincoln did odd jobs, from making rails to harvesting hay and grain. Then he experienced another windfall. Friends learned that county surveyor John Calhoun needed an assistant. They advised Calhoun of Lincoln's intelligence, honesty, and trustworthiness. "Let him lay out the roads and towns and farms," one said, "and they will be done right." Calhoun offered the job to Lincoln.

It surprised him: Calhoun was a Democrat and a "Jackson man," while Lincoln was a Whig and a "Clay man." "If I can be perfectly free in my political action I will take the office," Lincoln remarked. "But if my sentiments or even expression of them is to be abridged in any way I would not have it or any other office." Calhoun assured him that he would not be expected to compromise his principles. "That being the case, I accept," replied Lincoln.

Lincoln had studied surveying while clerking at Offutt's store in 1831, and Mentor Graham had advised him. Now Lincoln borrowed more books on surveying and in six weeks mastered the subject.[25]

NEEDING MONEY, James Rutledge sold his tavern in May 1833. His wife moved to the farm of her relative, James Short, to keep house for him until he married on September 10. Ann Rutledge took over management of the tavern in an arrangement allowing her father and siblings to remain there until midsummer. Ann also assisted her mother at Short's home. Then, at the urging of Dr. Allen, the Rutledges moved to McNamar's farm, eight miles from town, down a dusty road bordered by tall prairie grass.

IN THE fall of 1833, the men of New Salem noticed an unusual female visitor. "She wore the finest trimmings I ever saw," one said. Talk in town changed from politics to Mary Owens, who was in town for a four-week visit with her sister, Elizabeth Abell.

Mary was the cultured, well-spoken daughter of a wealthy Kentucky landowner. Her silk dresses, leghorn hat, and kid shoes and gloves contrasted sharply with the simple sunbonnets and homespun attire of local women. Pleasingly plump and refined, she was described by one New Salem resident as "fair as the moon, clear as the sun, and terrible as an army with banners." She was sharp, shrewd, and intellectual, "decidedly the most intellectual woman I ever knew," said Gaines Greene.

Mary was twenty-five—an old maid by prairie standards—and Elizabeth thought it was time for her to marry. She and other young married women of the village also agreed that Abe Lincoln needed a wife. So, being the good matchmaker that she was, Elizabeth made sure that Mary and Lincoln met. During Mary's four-week visit, Lincoln saw her several times. He described her as "intelligent and agreeable," and he found her to be jovial and responsive to his wit and humor. However, she was no Ann Rutledge.[26]

6

"My Comfort by Day, and My Song in the Night"

1834

$\mathcal{W}$HILE ANN turned yarn into clothes for the family, Lincoln surveyed the territory around New Salem, laying out roads, school sections, and town sites. He earned three dollars a day—good pay for the times, with board and lodging costing only one dollar a week. His travels and work also enabled him to extend his acquaintances and to sound out public opinion. One assignment was to survey the hills between New Salem and Petersburg—frontier land full of brush, briars, and snakes.

He was often an overnight guest with close friends Bennett and Elizabeth Abell, whose home was midway between the two villages. It was not unusual for Lincoln to come in at night, Elizabeth recalled, "all ragged and scratched up with the briars." He laughed about it and said that was "a poor man's lot." Elizabeth advised him to "get a buckskin" and she would fix his pants so that "the briars would not scratch [him]." He got the buckskin, and she sewed it on the trouser's legs. It made his work much less painful, and he was grateful.[1]

Surveying enabled Lincoln to exercise his passion for precision, but occasionally his heart overruled compass and chain. In his tale, "Mitch Miller," Edgar Lee Masters described a surveying incident involving Lincoln:

Look at this house partly in the street and look at the street how it jigs. Well, Linkern [Lincoln] did that. You see he surveyed this whole town of Petersburg. . . . It was after the Black Hawk War . . . and when Linkern came here to survey, he found that Jemina Elmore, which was a widow of Linkern's friend in the war, had a piece of land, and had built a house on it and was livin' here with her children. And Linkern saw if the street run straight north and south, a part of her house would be in the street. So to save Jemina's house, he set his compass to make the line run a little furder south. And so this is how the line got skewed. . . . This is what I call makin' a mistake that is all right, bein' good and bad at the same time.[2]

Lincoln was still postmaster of New Salem. And when he went survey-ing, he often delivered the mail too—carrying letters in his hat.

When his surveying took him several miles from the Abells, he lodged with other families. In the two-room houses common on the frontier, family members of all sexes, along with any strangers, often slept in the same room. Undergarments were never removed, and no one seemed concerned about the arrangement.

Lincoln spent one night with the Cottenbarger family, whose bedsteads were arranged so that the foot of one bed was against the head of the other. During the night, the feet of the family's teenage daughter somehow ended up on Lincoln's pillow. Lincoln reached up and tickled the girl's leg. The girl awoke and went to her mother's bed to tell what had happened. "For God's sake," her mother said, "say no more and go to bed, the man means noth-ing. If your father hears of this, the deuce will be to pay." Lincoln was re-portedly mortified at what he or "the devil in him" had done. Early in the morning, when Cottenbarger went to the woods, his wife hustled Lincoln off as quickly as she could. And Lincoln sometimes spun a different version of the story:

Once, when surveying, I was put to bed in the same room with two girls, the head of my bed being next to the foot of the girls' bed. In the night I commenced tickling the feet of one of the girls with my fingers. As she seemed to enjoy it as much as I did, I then tickled a little higher up; and as I would tickle higher the girl would shove down lower and the higher I tick-led the lower she moved.

He never said how this version of the story ended.[3]

Lincoln's surveying territory included Sandridge, where his friend "Uncle Jimmy" Short and the Rutledges lived a half mile apart. Lincoln visited the Shorts at least four times a week, usually overnight, and then rode over to the Rutledges to be with Ann, whom he affectionately referred to as "Annie."

While not secretive about their love, they seldom showed it in public, preferring to be discreet until there was closure on the McNamar problem. The Rutledge farm was near the Sangamon River, and Lincoln and Annie found a special place on a high, flat rock with a wide view of the river and valley below. They would ride their horses across the meadow and into the woodlands, where they dismounted, tied their animals to a tree, and climbed the rock to their majestic spot.

These private moments of chatting and laughing refreshed their souls and deepened their love for each other. Often they talked about the future and what it might hold. Annie, picking up where her father had left off, encouraged Lincoln to run again for the legislature. One day she told him that if women could vote, he would win in a landslide. How he responded is unknown, but two years later, on June 13, 1836, he endorsed women's suffrage in a letter to the editor of the *Sangamo Journal*.[4]

Annie, who had attended weekend "singing schools" taught by itinerant singing masters, often sang for Abe's benefit. The two sang together from a hymnal, *The Missouri Harmony*, which contained such songs as "We're Marching to Zion" and "While Shepherds Watched Their Flocks by Night." The song Lincoln had sung earlier for Annie's sister Nancy came from this book.

The hymnal also offered advice: "Let us live so in youth that we blush not in age. . . . All kinds of spirituous liquors . . . are destructive to the voice." A good voice may be "much injured by singing too loud." Browsing through the book, Lincoln and Annie found a hymn titled, "New Salem":

> O Thou in whose presence my soul takes delight
> On whom in affliction I call
> My comfort by day, and my song in the night
> My hope, my salvation, my all.[5]

The song reflected their feelings for each other. She would sing it to him flirtatiously, and he is believed to have whispered it in her ear in public settings, which often made her blush. Although Lincoln had many talents, singing was not one of them. When Short was asked if Lincoln could sing, he replied, "Can a pig whistle?"[6]

Lincoln escorted Annie to and from quilting bees, where a dozen or so thimbled hands stitched patterns from scraps of leftover cloth, producing magnificent quilts. They did not name the patterns but referred to them as copies of "Grandma Brown's quilt" or "my neighbor Mrs. Owen's quilt." They lined them with goose down or layers of homespun. Bees lasted about six hours, starting before breakfast and ending around two o'clock.

When Lincoln took Annie to Fanny Bale's bee, he even went inside, where men were considered out of place, and sat by Annie's side as she worked on a quilt. Fanny was fond of Lincoln and had her eye on him, but he had his eye on Annie. To make Annie more attentive, he winked at Fanny, and Fanny stuck a needle in her finger; Lincoln pulled it out.

Moments later Lincoln supposedly whispered to Annie, "You are my comfort by day and my song in the night, my hope, my salvation, my all." Her stitches suddenly became irregular and uneven. The other women noticed it. Years later the quilt's owner proudly pointed out the bad stitches and told their history. These handmade quilts were part of the proud dowry of many frontier brides and were passed down as family treasures. Women also valued their quilt pieces and were quick to tell visiting friends where every piece came from: "This one is from grandmother's dress; this is from my aunt in Kentucky; this came from my first dress."[7]

THE FOURTH of July was the single most important holiday in New Salem. Patriotism was second only to God. But it was not a day for fireworks, loud parties, or noisy parades. It was primarily a day for solitude and for reflection, inspiration, and renewal—a day to remember the men who signed the Declaration of Independence and pledged a willingness to risk "our lives, our fortunes, and our sacred honor."

It was more like a memorial day, with quiet flag waving, chest pounding, and pulse-beating oratory on the greatness of the Founding Fathers and the blessings of this noble land. Although no record exists of Lincoln's involvement in the festivities, no rising politician—especially one whose political guide and inspiration was the Declaration of Independence— would have avoided the celebration. The Rutledges would probably have participated also and may even have helped plan the activities. Annie's father was born just five years after the Declaration was signed and had grown up in battle-torn South Carolina during and after the Revolutionary

War. In all likelihood, Lincoln and Annie joined the New Salem residents for the observance.

Englishman William Oliver toured the United States in the early 1840s and recorded an account of Independence Day "at a small town in Illinois" in his book *Eight Months in Illinois*. His description was probably typical of events in New Salem. About noon, he said, a crowd assembled in the street. Soon three men with fiddles and a flute appeared, playing "Hail! Columbia," and were followed by ladies marching in pairs. After the ladies had passed, the gentlemen followed in similar style.

"All was done with the most profound gravity," Oliver observed. "There was no hurrying, no laughing nor talking, nor indeed any sounds save those proceeding from two very bad fiddles and a flute, and the [chirping of birds] overhead. It would have been considered the very height of indecorum had one of the beaus offered his arm to any of the ladies. . . . [This] demeanor prevails at all public meetings of the sexes and is a national trait."

The procession left the town and entered the forest, where "among the tall stems, stood a wagon, onto which mounted the orator and another gentlemen who introduced him. The oration consisted of . . . reminiscences of previous and similar occasions and was delivered in a hesitating, unanimated style, which contrasted strangely with the [fine-sounding] language.

"The audience sat or lay at full length on the ground, the ladies on one side of the wagon, and the gentlemen on the other, whilst some boys . . . were overlooking the whole from bushy trees. There was no drunkenness or riot consequent on this occasion; indeed, the first example of drunkenness I saw in this neighborhood was in a grocery to which I was attracted by the sound of a fiddle, where, on entering, I found the barkeeper playing 'Old Coon' to a tipsy man who was dancing."[8]

NEW SALEM'S gander pullings and wrestling matches were no competition for one of the great events of the early nineteenth century—religious camp meetings. The Rutledge family regularly attended the meetings at Concord Creek. They wanted their children to find salvation. If Annie were there, then Lincoln must have been also—not only to be with Annie but also to further his political career.

Methodist Peter Cartwright conducted camp meetings each summer; Baptists and Presbyterians did so annually after the harvest. At Concord, under a large shed in a grove of walnut trees, evangelists preached electrifying two-hour sermons. They had to contend with ornery boys who set fire rings in the woods and made ghost shrieks to rattle worshipers.[9]

"At the close of one meeting," Cartwright wrote, "we had many seekers who had not obtained comfort. Twelve got into a two-horse wagon, and myself with them. We had to go about fifteen miles, but before we reached our home every one of them got powerfully converted, and we sung and shouted aloud along the road, to the very astonishment of those who lived along the way." Annie's sister Nancy was converted at the Concord Camp Meeting; her brother John was converted on the road home from Round Prairie Camp Meeting.[10]

Lincoln and Annie were apparently never converted; neither of them ever joined a church. Yet Annie was a devoted worker in her parents' church, and both Lincoln and Annie believed in God and were kind, compassionate, and moral. Both shared a common inquisitiveness about religion and a common belief in universal salvation.

Lincoln believed in the Doctrine of Necessity—that the human mind is impelled to action by some power over which the mind itself has no control. "What is to be will be," he once declared, "and no cares of ours can arrest nor reverse the decree." He would come to see himself as "the means" for certain results—as an "instrument fore-ordained by God to aid in accomplishing great works" and as one "deeply sensitive of the need for Divine assistance." Quoting Hamlet, he once said: "There's a divinity that shapes our ends, rough-hew them how we will."[11]

Lincoln, and perhaps Annie, was greatly influenced by Scotland's national poet, Robert Burns. He had reportedly rebelled against his family's religion, and Lincoln found in him "a like thinker and feeler." Billy Greene told friends that Lincoln "knew all of Burns by heart" and could quote him with a Scottish accent. Burns's *Holy Willie's Prayer* was a Lincoln favorite. It was about a hypocritical church elder who was held up to scorn. Row Herndon related one of Lincoln's practical pranks inspired by Burns's poem, *Tam o'Shanter:*

> There was a man who used to come to New Salem, and [got drunk], and stayed until dark. He was afraid of ghosts and someone had to go home with him. Well, Lincoln persuaded a fellow to take a sheet and go in the road and [pretend to be a] ghost. The ghost made his appearance, and the man became much frightened. Lincoln also had sent another

ghost. [When he] made his appearance he frightened the first ghost half to death. That broke the fellow from staying until dark anymore.[12]

Over the years Annie's well-educated father and teachers had given her a broad knowledge of literature and philosophy. She had read many of the books in her father's library and was evolving her own philosophy of life. She may have explored Burns's unorthodox views as well as his use of verse to express emotions of love, friendship, or amusement at his ironical contemplation of the social scene. Did she discuss these matters with Lincoln? Besides her beloved brother David and her friend Parthena Nance, he was just about the only other person with whom she could have comfortably pondered such controversial issues.

Two other books that may have influenced Lincoln and Ann Rutledge were *The Age of Reason* by Thomas Paine and *Ruins* by Constantin de Volney, which were passed among New Salem's freethinkers. They became part of Lincoln's self-education and motivated his lifelong intellectual inquiry.[13]

Years later when asked why he had not joined a church, Lincoln responded by paraphrasing Jesus in Mark 12:30–31. Lincoln said he would join one only if it had for its creed, "Thou shalt love the Lord thy God with all thy heart, and with all thy soul, and with all thy mind, and with all they strength. . . . and thy neighbor as thyself." Ann Rutledge might have given the same response. Put simply, they both believed in the Fatherhood of God and the brotherhood of man.[14]

Lincoln and Annie's religious positions ran counter to those of the rigidly orthodox frontier community of New Salem, a place where arguments about religion were as common as whiskey and corn bread. Lincoln joined in frequent discussions on store porches and around potbelly stoves.

As if begging to be persecuted, Lincoln wrote an essay suggesting that certain parts of the Bible did not represent divine revelation. He questioned the virgin birth, the divinity of Christ, and the immortality of the soul. He showed the essay to Sam Hill and said he planned to publish it. Hill read it, advised Lincoln it would ruin him politically, and threw it into the fire.

Annie's friend Parthena Nance once asked Lincoln: "Do you really believe there isn't any future state?" "I'm afraid there isn't," he replied. "It isn't a pleasant thing to think that when we die that is the last of us." A few years later, while lingering in the office of the clerk of the court in Springfield, Lincoln picked up a Bible, read a passage, made a critical comment, then ridiculed the Scripture. He shocked many people, including his friend

John T. Stuart, who said, "Lincoln went further against Christian beliefs, doctrines, and principles than any man I ever heard."[15]

Lincoln later modified his position, either from religious growth or political expediency or both. In a campaign handbill, he wrote: "I have never denied the truth of the Scriptures; and I have never spoken with intentional disrespect of religion in general, or of any denomination of Christians in particular." Describing himself as a "religious seeker," Lincoln was always questioning, always demanding proof—not just about the Bible but about everything he encountered.

Some thirty years later, shaped perhaps by the burden of leadership in the Civil War, his position had changed to a point where he told a friend: "Take all of the Bible upon reason that you can, and the balance on faith, and you'll live and die a happier and better man."[16]

Lincoln's belief in an omnipotent, omniscient Creator was due in no small part to his belief in the "order and harmony of all nature." "It would have been more miraculous for this order and harmony to have come about by chance than to have been created and arranged by some great thinking power," he told friends. Looking up at the starlit sky one night, he said: "I never behold the stars that I do not feel that I am looking in the face of God. I can see how it might be possible for a man to look down upon the earth and be an atheist, but I cannot conceive how he could look up into the heavens and say there is no God."[17]

Annie and Lincoln's friend from the Black Hawk War, John Stuart, persisted in encouraging him to study law and to run for the legislature again. And he committed himself to it. Lincoln finally agreed with them that law could be his passport out of poverty and into national politics. Stuart, a legislative "veteran" with one term behind him, became Lincoln's political mentor. A symbol of urbanity in the boondocks, Stuart helped the uncultivated Lincoln to become more socially and politically sophisticated. Both men were about the same age, and both were Whigs.

Lincoln gained support from the Whigs and the Democrats, thanks to Stuart and Bowling Green, a powerful Democrat who was New Salem's justice of the peace. Green urged his party's faithful to back Lincoln. Since Democrats were in the majority, Green's support was significant. His wife, Nancy, was among the more mature women of New Salem who were, in effect, Lincoln's surrogate mothers. Nancy was aware of Lincoln's courtship of Ann Rutledge and acknowledged it after Lincoln's death. In his court, Green observed Lincoln as an amateur lawyer. The two became friends, and Lincoln viewed Green as a second father. Lincoln later said he "owed more to Mr. Green for his advancement than any other man." The two enjoyed each others' wit and humor. When they were together, they looked like strange opposites—Green with his peaches-and-cream complexion, Lincoln with his leathery, weather-beaten skin. Lincoln was tall and thin; Green was of average height and weighed 250 pounds. He was nicknamed "Pot" for his protruding belly, which, like St. Nick's, "shook when he laughed, like a bowl full of jelly." His bulging trousers were held up by one linen suspender.[18]

Lincoln stumped the countryside, talked to farmers while on surveying trips, solicited votes as he delivered the mail, and attended numerous barbecues where each candidate spoke. He campaigned at horseshoe pits, cockfights, and wolf hunts. His popularity was enhanced by his advocacy of a forty-mile canal from the Sangamon River below Petersburg to Beardstown, on the Illinois River. The canal would expedite the shipment of farm produce. During the campaign Lincoln frequently stopped at the Shorts' farm for overnight lodging and visits with Annie, who lived a half mile down the road. Lincoln won the election handily. He was twenty-five.

On a cold November morning supporters gathered at dawn to see him off for the state capital. "Do right by us, Abe. Good luck, Abe," they yelled. "Our prayers go with you." He thanked them and stepped into the Yellow Bank stagecoach for the ninety-five-mile, two-day ride to Vandalia.

Lincoln gained a reputation as one whose vote could not be bought. He grew in his understanding of the political process and of the importance of legal knowledge. His style was to avoid any posturing and to know the issues, understand the system, and study matters carefully before putting himself forward. The assembly did focus on one of Lincoln's major concerns—internal improvements—and provided for clearing and deepening rivers and building canals and railroads. The assembly also granted charters for private undertakings such as toll bridges. Lincoln introduced a bill for one of these bridges—Musick's bridge across Salt Creek—to replace a ferry. It would be long remembered by Illinois travelers.[19]

During his nearly three months away from New Salem, he and Annie undoubtedly wrote often to each other although no letters now exist. The session ended February 13, 1835, the day after his birthday, and Lincoln returned to New Salem in subzero temperatures with his legislative earnings of $258. He was more ambitious than ever but not without problems.

On January 10 his store partner, William Berry, had died from chronic alcoholism. His death saddled Lincoln with the store's notes and debts totaling

$1,100—a huge obligation for a person earning only a few dollars a month. Lincoln referred to it as his "national debt." He assumed the liability and paid on it for at least fifteen years before finally clearing it.

Pursuing his political ambitions while continuing as a surveyor and postmaster, he borrowed law books from Stuart, bought others at auctions in Springfield, and studied so intensely that people became concerned about his health. "He became wholly engrossed [in the study of law]," noted Robert Rutledge. It wasn't unusual to see Lincoln studying barefooted while sitting on the ground in the shade of a tree.

Russell Godbey saw him on a woodpile absorbed in a hefty book. "What on earth are you reading, Abe?" he asked. "I'm not reading," Lincoln replied, "I'm studying law." "Law!" Godbey exclaimed, 'Good God Almighty!'"[20]

7

"Annie's Whole Soul Seemed Wrapped Up in Lincoln"

1835

$\mathcal{L}$AW AND love dominated Abe Lincoln's life in the spring and summer of 1835. For nearly two years he had loved Ann Rutledge, but he did not know if her ties with John McNamar had been permanently severed. Finally that spring the scrupulous Lincoln concluded that the "insurmountable barrier" had been removed, and he decided to act.

While the exact scenario is unknown, it is likely that after one of his frequent overnight stays with "Uncle Jimmy" Short, Lincoln rode to the Rutledge farm. Constant rain showers had produced a kaleidoscope of spring colors on nearby fields and hills—red clover, Virginia bluebells, sunshine roses, purple nettle, and golden buttercups.

Somewhere in that setting or a similar one, he apparently found the courage to propose to Ann Rutledge. She responded positively, according to at least fifteen sources. "There is no kind of doubt as to the existence of this engagement," wrote Robert Rutledge years later. "Annie's whole soul seemed wrapped up in Lincoln," said her sister Jean.[1]

But both Lincoln and Annie were concerned about propriety. Before announcing marriage plans, Annie wanted to contact McNamar, inform him "of the change in her feelings," and "seek an honorable release." She wrote the letter and mailed it. Several months passed and there was no response.

Annie's brother David, in whom she often confided, urged her to marry Lincoln immediately, without regard to anything but her own happiness. She had no obligation to the long-silent McNamar, he insisted.

But some of the Rutledges thought Lincoln was undeserving of Annie. Her cousin Mary Mayes Miller said a few family members were concerned that Annie would pass up prosperous suitors for one plagued with poverty and riddled with debt. It bothered them that her "prince charming" was, if not an ugly duckling, a peculiar specimen of humanity.[2]

Annie, however, was not swayed by their attitudes. She loved Abe Lincoln. That was all that mattered. She knew that no one else could match his remarkable qualities—his probing mind and kind heart, his good-natured and openhanded style, his wit and intelligence, his rock-solid character, his unselfish nature, and his enjoyment of life. He was fun to be with. She did not focus on his homely face and lanky physique. She knew him as a man of purpose, a man with powerful potential.

Thus, with no word from McNamar, Annie and Lincoln apparently proceeded with wedding plans. She was twenty-two, he was twenty-six. They reportedly set a date for the fall of 1836—one year away. "Both wished to better equip themselves for the positions they would eventually occupy," Nancy Rutledge commented. That view was confirmed by both Annie's brother Robert and her cousin McGrady Rutledge. McGrady, who was in her confidence, said, "Ann gave me to understand, that as soon as certain studies were completed, she and Lincoln would be married."[3]

By the next fall Lincoln expected to complete his law studies and gain admission to the bar. He would then be able to support a family. Annie would attend the Jacksonville Female Academy for a year. It was about thirty-five miles southwest of New Salem. "I must prepare myself to be the wife of a senator or governor," she told her family. They encouraged her. The importance of knowledge and education was deeply instilled in the Rutledge clan.

To bolster her preparation, Annie was being tutored by Arminda Rogers Rankin in rhetoric, grammar, and elementary studies. Her tutor was from a well-educated family in Athens, seven miles east of New Salem. Lincoln had borrowed books and newspapers from Arminda's father, Col. Matthew Rogers.[4]

Arminda had observed Annie "passing out of and above the depression and anxiety she had shown over McNamar's absence and neglect" and was fully aware of the "new love" in her life. Annie "manifested no regret or wavering in the choice she had made," Arminda said. "On the contrary, there was a decided spirit of offended maidenly dignity manifested in all the references she made to McNamar, such as could be expected of a well-bred Southern girl under circumstances showing such unaccountable neglect."[5]

Lincoln and Annie also shared their plans with Mentor Graham, Billy Greene, other close friends, and members of the Rutledge family. Annie was buoyant and happy. As she worked she often sang one of Lincoln's favorite songs. While the words were not exactly cheerful, they had a playful meaning:

> Vain man thy fond pursuits forbear;
> Repent, thy end is nigh;
> Death at the farthest can't be far;
> Oh, think before thou die.

In the evenings, when Lincoln came by, they joyfully imagined the wonders ahead. "The earth was their footstool," Carl Sandburg would later write. "The sky was a sheaf of blue dreams."[6]

Annie's education at Jacksonville Female Academy would have been comparable to her brother David's at Illinois College in the same community. Illinois College was founded by a Presbyterian minister and a group of Congregational students at Yale University in 1829 as a frontier "seminary of learning" connected with the intellectual life of New England. College president Edward Beecher had given up his church on Boston Common to train youth in the new state of Illinois. He was the brother of Harriet Beecher Stowe, the abolitionist author of *Uncle Tom's Cabin,* and of Henry Ward Beecher, the liberal Congregational minister who was one of the most influential Protestant clergymen of his time.

On July 27, 1835, David wrote to Annie from Jacksonville: "I am glad to hear that you have a notion of coming to school, and I earnestly recommend to you that you would spare no time from improving your education and mind. Remember that Time is worth more than all gold, therefore throw away none of your golden moments."[7]

In late July another letter came for Annie. This one was from John McNamar—the first letter from him in more than a year. He either had not received her letter of withdrawal from the engagement or pretended ignorance of it in order to try to re-win her affections. He told her to "be ready" to marry him soon; he was on the way back to New Salem. He would buy furniture for them in Cincinnati. He wanted to get married as soon as he arrived and set up housekeeping. He never explained his delay to her nor why he had not written.[8]

Years later McNamar said it was the illness and death of his father that caused his continued absence. But in a letter to William H. Herndon he explained that other hardships and tragedies were involved: "One of those long interminable fevers . . . came into my father's family and prostrated every member, that is except myself, and continued for months, making victims of three of them, one of whom was my father." Medical records of the attending physician, Dr. Timothy Bancroft of Colesville, New York, indicate he treated the McNamar family for nearly three months in early 1833, making eighty-one house calls. Two of McNamar's brothers died in March and April, and his father died on April 10. Settling family matters could have taken a few months. But McNamar waited another two years before returning to New Salem. Perhaps his mother did not want to leave New York, or perhaps McNamar had second thoughts about marrying a frontier woman.[9]

Regardless, he was now returning to marry Ann Rutledge, and her worst nightmare had become real. She had no way to communicate with McNamar until his arrival, and she feared his reaction. What would she say to him? How would she handle it? In her conflicts of honor, duty, love, and promises, she struggled through sleepless nights. Lincoln was surveying, and Annie could not reach him immediately to discuss the pending crisis.

She did share the letter with Parthena Nance Hill. Parthena had just married Annie's former suitor, Sam Hill, on July 28. Annie and Parthena were so close they wore duplicate riding habits made from bottle green flannel. Parthena read the letter, shook her head in dismay, and suggested that Annie should tell McNamar that their relationship was over. Critical events intervened, however, before Annie could confront McNamar.[10]

The weather in Illinois that spring and summer was consistently bad. From the first of March to the middle of July it rained almost every day, and the whole country was literally covered with water. Then the rain ceased, a tornado whipped through the area, and the weather became excessively hot and dry from late July through much of August. There were endless swarms of horseflies "as big as bats" and "skeeters as fat as birds." Crops suffered. Wheat was ruined. In early August, people began falling ill. Soon many began dying. In Springfield, which had a population of fifteen hundred, twelve practicing physicians were almost continually engaged day and night. Lincoln suffered with chills and aching bones. Some of his acquaintances died, and he made their coffins.[11]

In early August, Annie felt ill. At first she had no pain, just fatigue. She tried to continue her household duties, but one morning she was unable to get out of bed. That day her fever shot up, and one of her brothers rode to New Salem for Dr. Allen, a Dartmouth-educated physician. He said she had "brain fever." It apparently was typhoid fever, caused when the heavy rains and floods had contaminated the Rutledge's well. She "burned" all over, she said, except for her feet. They were so cold they had to be warmed with hot stones.[12]

While no record exists of her treatment, Dr. Allen and other doctors relied on a system of medical knowledge that dated back to the Dark Ages. Sickness meant bad elements were in the body, and to get well, a person had to be purged of these elements. So doctors prescribed grains of calomel (a toxic powder used as a strong laxative). They raised blisters to draw out the poison. And they practiced bloodletting, frequently puncturing the jugular vein behind the ear to collect a few ounces of blood.

Some or all of these treatments probably were used on Annie, and any of them would have weakened her and contributed to her death. But Dr. Allen did what he was taught to do at medical school. He ordered "absolute quiet" and no visitors.[13]

Many times Lincoln sought to visit her but was turned away. Days dragged by, the fever stayed high, she was unable to eat, and her situation deteriorated to the point where she could not even raise her hands. Some said her stress over McNamar's pending return had sapped her energy and weakened her resistance, making recovery difficult, if not unlikely.

When Annie realized she would not get well, she pleaded that she be allowed to see Lincoln and her brother David, who was in college at Jacksonville. At first her parents refused, following the doctor's orders. Annie kept asking for Lincoln and David, prayed for them to come, and then demanded to see them. Finally, Lincoln's friend Bowling Green was asked to notify Lincoln, who was surveying in an adjoining county, and McGrady Rutledge was sent to Jacksonville to get David.[14]

Lincoln received word late in the day. He immediately raced back despite a menacing electrical storm. Great lightning flashes pierced the darkness, booming thunder roared across the heavens, and strong winds uprooted trees and plants. Seeking a safe haven until the storm passed, Lincoln stopped at the home of the Reverend John Berry at Rock Creek. As the candlelight shone on Lincoln's face, Berry saw that he was distraught and insisted that he spend the night. Lincoln agreed to stay but was restless. Berry read from the Scriptures, and both men knelt as the pastor prayed for Ann's recovery. Unable to sleep, Lincoln walked the floor all night. Very early in the morning, the storm subsided, and he struck out for Sandridge and Annie.[15]

Her sickbed was in the Rutledges' living room. Several family members were there when Lincoln arrived. John Miller Camron had come down from Fulton County and was leading long, fervent prayers. Lincoln went to Annie, and the others left the room and closed the door. He was alone with her for about an hour. No one knows what they said to each other. But William H. Herndon, Lincoln's biographer, described it in his lecture on Ann Rutledge in 1866: "The meeting was quite as much as either could bear and more than Lincoln, with all his coolness and philosophy, could endure. The voice, the face, the features of her; the love, sympathy, and talk fastened themselves on his heart and soul forever."

As he left the room Lincoln "stopped at the door and looked back. Both of them were crying." Annie's fifteen-year-old sister Nancy was sitting on the porch when he came out. His head was bowed as tears streamed down his cheeks. He passed her without a word. "I can never forget how broken-hearted he looked," Nancy recalled. Lincoln confided to a friend: "Annie told me always to live an honest and upright life."[16]

Dr. Allen became so concerned about Lincoln's emotional state that he took him to his home for the night. A few days afterward Annie lost consciousness and remained so until her death on August 25, 1835. She was twenty-two. Ironically, her death occurred in the house owned by her first fiancé, who had purchased it from her cousin, John Miller Camron, co-founder of New Salem with her father. Lincoln had lost the third major woman in his life—first, his mother, then his beloved sister, and now his future bride whom he had loved with a passion he had never known before and, many asserted, would never know again.[17]

ANN'S FUNERAL was a simple service at her grave at Concord Cemetery, a country burying ground about seven miles northwest of New Salem on the west bank of Berry's Creek. About an acre in size, it was a peaceful place. The cemetery was bordered by an extensive prairie, by a field where sheep and cattle grazed, and by forests to the north and south. John Miller Camron gave the eulogy. Everyone in New Salem was there; Lincoln's tall figure dominated the crowd.

At the end of the service, Camron took Lincoln's hand and quietly suggested, "Come up and see us any time you care to. Maybe Aunt Polly can help you." In the days ahead Camron prayed that the humor and faith that meant so much to his friends "might be restored to Lincoln's bleeding soul."[18]

Lincoln somehow kept his deep, hidden emotions under control for about a week, but then a heavy rain saturated the area, and he became unnerved and plunged into a black hole of despair. He told Bennett and Elizabeth Abell, "I cannot bear the idea of it raining on her grave." From then on rains and storms precipitated a steady drizzle of incidents of despondency. The death of the first woman he truly loved marked the tragic end of the most beautiful hopes Lincoln had entertained for his life. His whole life was affected by the blow. The shadow of her death would always hang over him.[19]

Almost daily he walked seven miles to visit her grave, sitting beside the grassy mound for hours. Many times he was found at the cemetery with one arm across her grave as if trying to communicate with her.

McGrady Rutledge became worried about him and on several occasions went to the cemetery to bring him home. Some thought Lincoln was suicidal. Billy Greene said Lincoln was watched with special vigilance "during storms, fogs, and damp, gloomy weather for fear of an accident." Dark hollows appeared beneath his deep-set eyes. He was no longer talkative and cheerful, no longer fun to be around. Henry McHenry, a Sandridge neighbor of the Rutledges, observed that Lincoln seemed "wrapped in profound thought, indifferent to transpiring events, had but little to say, but would . . . wander off in the woods by himself, away from the association of even those most esteemed."[20]

In town he was often heard repeating the sad lines from the William Knox poem that began,

> Oh, why should the spirit of mortal be proud?
> Like a swift-fleeting meteor, a fast-flying cloud,
> A flash of the lightning, a break of the wave,
> He passes from life to his rest in the grave.

HANNAH ARMSTRONG saw him "weep like a baby," and her husband, Jack, feared he "would go crazy." He hummed sad songs and wrote them with chalk on fences and barns.

On a visit to the Rutledge home, he stood by the window of the room in which Annie died and sobbed. Mrs. Rutledge went to him and put her arms around his shoulder. "Don't let your grief destroy you or spoil your life," she counseled him. "Go on and fulfill the high promise the future has in store for you."[21]

Squire Bowling Green, afraid that Lincoln might take his own life, brought him to his home, about a mile from New Salem. It was a quiet and secluded place with a tree-covered bluff behind the house and flatland in front stretching down to a creek. Dr. Allen visited Lincoln there and ministered to his sick soul and his weak body. "Give him something to occupy his mind," he advised the Greens.[22]

Lincoln was tortured by his childhood memories when he heard preachers exclaim that God sometimes took the lives of children to punish their parents for their sins or that the Lord had taken away the loved one because "it was for the best." God made no mistakes, they said. Pondering such ideas, Lincoln seemed to grow bitter and to question God's justice and mercy. The devout Dr. Allen helped Lincoln understand that God hadn't singled him out for punishment. Such ideas were "preposterous," Dr. Allen assured him.

Lincoln sat silently by the fireside one night, watching the flames dance as a driving windstorm whistled through the trees and stirred up dust and leaves. He went to the door, looked out into the black horizon, and came back, clenching his hands and mumbling, "I can't stand to think of her out there alone."[23]

For several days Lincoln rested. The Greens, who were "salt of the earth" people, nursed him as if he was their son. Then they had him doing chores—cutting wood, digging potatoes, picking apples, and milking cows.

Neighborly kindnesses showed up everywhere. Friends visited daily. They brought cakes and pies, and they lingered to talk and share stories, jokes, and witticisms. Their compassion helped to soften his grief. Within two weeks he was much improved, and he went back to New Salem. His joyous feeling for life was gone, however, replaced by fits of melancholy and moody silence that haunted him the rest of his life.

Those who knew them both said that Ann's death taught him compassion and gave him the strength to endure all the sorrow he would later face. Others said he became obsessed with death and the meaning of his life and with related questions to which his reasoning mind could find no final answers.[24]

After Ann's death Lincoln erected an emotional barrier between himself and others, especially women. More than ever he avoided intimacy and became abstracted and cool. Having loved deeply and passionately, having been traumatized by his tragic loss, he was unable to allow himself to love another woman the same way he had loved Ann. He erected a defensive wall of passivity around himself—a wall that antagonized other women who sought to be close to him.

The word *love* all but vanished from his vocabulary. He no longer wanted to be called Abe. "It seems too familiar," he said, "and familiarity breeds contempt."

For a few weeks he became careless in his work. Young Matthew Marsh, eagerly awaiting money from home, dropped by the post office to check his mail. But postmaster Lincoln was not there. Marsh glanced at the mail cabinet; it was open, the letters exposed. He fingered through them and found the one he expected, but twenty-five cents was due. Needing the money order that accompanied it, he took it and left a note for Lincoln. Marsh returned the next day to pay the postage. This time Lincoln was there, but he marked the bulky letter "Free." That was not the normal character of "Honest Abe."

Months after Ann's death, Billy Greene remembered Lincoln's continuing grief: "Abe and I would be alone . . . and Abe would sit there, his face in his hands, the tears dripping through his fingers."[25]

Looking for solace in his heartbreak, Lincoln made a rare visit to his parents in their poor, desolate log cabin near Charleston in Coles County, Illinois. He especially wanted to see his stepmother, who loved him and could sympathize with him. Her sensibilities always "seemed to run together" with his, she once said.

In a small Charleston hotel, Lincoln met Usher Linder, who would become a longtime political friend. Among other things, they talked about familiar acquaintances, such as Lincoln's Uncle Mordecai, Thomas's brother, who had prospered. Uncle Mordecai was "wonderfully humorous," Linder said, and Lincoln noted that he had "run off with all the talents" of the family. To Linder, Lincoln seemed "modest and retiring," totally unlike what Linder had heard about his high spirits and homey charm, a man supposedly "out of the ordinary." But to Linder he seemed very ordinary. "He told me no stories and perpetrated no jokes. . . . He had the appearance of an unambitious man." Linder was not aware of Lincoln's love for Ann Rutledge or her death. Thus he was seeing a man in mourning, not the person he had anticipated.[26]

Downcast, Lincoln later moaned to a friend that "he had done nothing to make any human being remember that he had lived." Time and time again, Ann had urged him to pursue a higher calling, to achieve distinction, and to fulfill his noble destiny. Now he resolved to respond to her supplications. Nothing mattered more to him than to please her and to reach these goals. He was a changed man: quieter, more determined, and decidedly more serious in manner and intellect.

In six years at New Salem, he had developed from a self-admitted "aimless piece of driftwood" to a merchant, surveyor, militia captain, postmaster, and first-time legislator. In this small frontier village he had mastered mathematics and studied grammar and the works of Shakespeare and the poetry of Burns. He had made friendships and fallen in love. In a very real sense, New Salem was the turning point in his life. Somehow the place and its people, especially Ann Rutledge, changed Lincoln and the course of history.

McNAMAR'S SURPRISE AND REVENGE

John McNamar, Ann Rutledge's first fiance, returned to New Salem in October 1835 after an absence of three years. With him, from New York, were his mother and siblings. Expecting to marry Ann within the week, or so he had written to her, he was shocked to hear of her death. He rode to his farm, which the Rutledges managed, to see Mrs. Rutledge, who gave him a lock of Ann's hair. He made a wooden cross for Ann's grave.

On December 3, Ann's father, James Rutledge, died at age fifty-four, apparently from the same disease that took Ann's life.

On February 23, with apparently no concern for the grief-stricken Rutledge family, McNamar returned to the farm with an eviction notice effective one week later, March 1. Mrs. Rutledge pleaded for more time. They had no place to go. And it was the middle of winter, with brisk winds and high temperatures only in the teens. Despite the fact that McNamar owned considerable property, he was determined to remove the Rutledges and refused to extend their occupancy. Ann's brother David, just back from college in Jacksonville, volunteered to ride thirty miles to Fulton County to see their cousin John Miller Camron, who had cofounded New Salem with Ann's father. David returned in three days with the good news that Camron had found a farm where they could live temporarily. Two days later Mrs. Rutledge and five of her children loaded their belongings onto a wagon and moved in near-blizzard conditions. From there they eventually settled in Iowa. David, however, remained in

Illinois and practiced law in Petersburg until his untimely death at age twenty-six. He was buried next to Ann.

McNamar married in 1838 and had four children. After his wife's death, he married again in 1855, and they had one child. After Lincoln's death, William H. Herndon attempted to talk with McNamar about Ann Rutledge. He said little, denied hearing anyone speak of the Lincoln-Rutledge romance, acknowledged learning that Lincoln had grieved excessively at her death (but expressed no curiosity about it), and refused to say anything about his own relationship with Ann. He never explained why he had not written to her for more than a year before telling her he was coming back to marry her. And he made no reference to Ann's "Dear John" letter to him breaking off their engagement.

Neighbors regarded McNamar as "cold and unsocial." His second wife said, "There was no more poetry or sentiment in him than in the multiplication table." He died in 1879 at age seventy-three.

8

"I Want in All Cases to Do Right"

1836—43

*A*FTER ANN RUTLEDGE'S death, Lincoln seemed unable to love any woman the way he had loved her. He tried, however—at least four times. Two were named Mary; the others, Matilda and Sarah. Three were introduced to Lincoln by their sisters. Two were also aggressively pursued by Lincoln's best friend. All had Kentucky roots in well-to-do families. The two Marys expected Lincoln to marry them. With both he wavered and wept, and while he did so, they surprised him by gaining weight. Not feeling the genuine, mutual love he had known with Ann Rutledge and not certain he could make either Mary happy, he had second thoughts about each and tried to walk away. But after he did, he felt his actions were dishonorable. Finally, one Mary aggressively cornered him, perhaps through unbridled passion, and they suddenly rushed into marriage. It was the honorable thing to do, he said. The first woman was Mary Owens. The others were Matilda Edwards, Sarah Rickard, and Mary Todd.

Lincoln first met Kentuckian Mary Owens in 1833 when she visited her sister and brother-in-law, Elizabeth and Bennett Abell. He remembered she was witty, jovial, and noble-looking, but a little stout and a bit flirtatious and outspoken. About a year after Ann Rutledge's death, in the autumn of 1836, Elizabeth mentioned to Lincoln that she was going to Kentucky and would bring back Mary if he would marry her. Surprisingly, Lincoln accepted the offer. As he later wrote, he was "most confoundedly well pleased with the project," and "saw no good objection to plodding life through hand in hand with her."[1]

But when Mary Owens returned to New Salem, Lincoln was astonished and chagrined. He immediately regretted his promise. He felt "that her coming so readily showed that she was a trifle too willing." Among other things, he was concerned about her appearance. She had put on some weight. "I knew she was over-size," he wrote, "but she now appeared a fair match for Falstaff" and had such a "weather-beaten appearance" that she looked ten years older than her age of twenty-eight—an age approaching "old maid" status at that time. Yet Lincoln wrote that he "had told her sister that [he] would take her for better or worse." "I made a point of honor and conscience in all things," he said, "to stick to my word, especially if others had been induced to act on it, which in this case, I doubted not they had, for I was now fairly convinced that no other man on earth would have her, and hence the conclusion that they were bent on holding me to my bargain." He said he planned "how I might procrastinate the evil day for a time, which I really dreaded as much—perhaps more—than an Irishman does the halter."[2]

Nevertheless, Lincoln had made up his mind to make the best of it and to focus on Mary's good qualities: she was witty, wealthy, and polished in her manners. "I also tried to convince myself that the mind was much more to be valued than the person; and, in this, she was not inferior . . . to any with whom I had been acquainted." So he courted her for several months. But their time together was strained, overly formal, and about as passionate as Lincoln's father's expression of love for him.

The townspeople of New Salem took notice, for Ann had been in her grave just a few months and Miss Owens "dressed much finer than any lady" in the area. She even had a fashionable silk dress, a striking contrast to the calico dresses Ann had worn.[3]

Mary admired Lincoln but realized "his training had been different from mine, hence there was not that congeniality which would otherwise have existed." To her, he seemed deficient in the nicer attentions she felt to be due from the man she pictured as an ideal husband. He seldom spoke and said nothing funny or romantic.

Further, Mary was troubled by his lack of manners. She wondered why he failed to show her the common courtesies he had demonstrated earlier.

For example, when she and Lincoln and other young couples crossed a deep stream on horses, he went ahead without assisting her. Mary recalled: "The other gentlemen were very officious in seeing that their partners got over safely, [but he never looked back] to see how I got along. When I rode up beside him, I remarked . . . 'I suppose you did not care whether my neck was broken or not.' He laughingly replied (I suppose by way of compliment) that he knew I was plenty smart to take care of myself."[4]

Mary decided to test Lincoln's love. He had arranged to visit her at her sister's home. He arrived on schedule and asked for her. Elizabeth replied that Mary had gone to Mentor Graham's residence. Puzzled, Lincoln asked if she did not realize he was coming to see her. Elizabeth said no, but one of the children blurted out, "Yes, Ma, she did, for I heard her tell someone." Lincoln sat for a short time and then returned to his boarding house without going to the Grahams' cabin.

He had failed the test. Lincoln assumed Mary regarded herself as his superior and was trying to put him in his place. Mary in later life told her cousin Gaines Greene she "regretted her course" and should have played her cards differently. Still, they continued to see each other, and when Lincoln left for the legislature in Vandalia in December 1836, they agreed to write. Vandalia was so cold, wet, and windy that Lincoln was ill, and he wrote to Mary he would "rather be any place in the world than here. . . . Write back as soon as you get this, and if possible say something that will please me, for really I have not [been] pleased since I left you."[5]

To reenergize himself, Lincoln plunged into Whig politics, helped enact an internal improvements bill appropriating ten million dollars for railroads, canals, and turnpikes, and pushed through legislation transferring the capital from Vandalia to more centrally situated Springfield. On March 1, 1837, as the legislature neared adjournment, Lincoln attained a longtime goal—he was now officially an attorney, and he accepted an invitation from John Todd Stuart to join his Springfield law firm. At the age of twenty-eight, Lincoln had lived half his life.

IN NEW SALEM, on April 15, 1837, Lincoln borrowed a horse from Bowling Green, placed all his belongings in the saddlebags, and rode twenty miles to Springfield, his new home and soon to be the new state capital. He had seven dollars in his pocket. A growing frontier town, Springfield had fifteen hundred inhabitants, nineteen dry-goods stores, four hotels, two politically opposite newspapers, and six retail groceries. A dozen eggs cost six cents, and beef was three cents a pound. On rainy days, pigs wallowed freely in the town's muddy streets and rooted out garbage.

A month after his arrival, Lincoln wrote a carefully crafted letter to Mary Owens. It was one of many attempts to get out of the liaison without hurting her feelings or betraying his honor. His goal was to diplomatically persuade her to be the one to break it off. He began this letter as he would all others, "Friend Mary," with no mention of love.

The gist of the letter was that she would probably never be happy as his wife in Springfield—she would have to live in unaccustomed poverty while others lived more luxuriously. He asked her to think about that because he wanted her to be happy. "Whatever woman may cast her lot with mine, should any ever do so," he wrote, "it is my intention to do all in my power to make her happy and contented; and there is nothing I can imagine, that would make me more unhappy than to fail in the effort. . . . My opinion is that you had better not [marry me]. You have not been accustomed to hardship, and it may be more severe than you now imagine. I know you are capable of thinking correctly on any subject; and if you deliberate maturely upon this, before you decide, then I am willing to abide your decision."[6]

Three months later Mary visited Springfield. Nothing had been resolved, however, and she left confused. Preferring letters to face-to-face discussion, and attempting to force a decision, Lincoln wrote to her again:

> I want in all cases to do right, and most particularly so, in all cases with women. I want, at this particular time, more than any thing else, to do right with you, and if I knew it would be doing right, as I rather suspect it would, to let you alone, I would do it. And for the purpose of making the matter as plain as possible, I now say, that you can now drop the subject, dismiss your thoughts (if you ever had any) from me forever, and leave this letter unanswered, without calling forth one accusing murmur from me. And I will even go further, and say, that if it will add any thing to your comfort, or peace of mind, to do so, it is my sincere wish that you should.
>
> Do not understand by this, that I wish to cut your acquaintance. I mean no such thing. What I do wish is, that our further acquaintance shall depend upon yourself. If such further acquaintance would contribute nothing to your happiness, I am sure it would not to mine. If you feel yourself in any degree bound to me, I am now willing to release you,

provided you wish it; while, on the other hand, I am willing, and even anxious to bind you faster, if I can be convinced that it will, in any considerable degree, add to your happiness. This, indeed, is the whole question with me. Nothing would make me more miserable than to believe you miserable—nothing more happy, than to know you are.[7]

Offended, Mary Owens finally terminated their relationship. A year later Lincoln admitted he had "made a fool of himself," but he would try "to outlive it." "I have now come to the conclusion never again to think of marrying," he wrote, "and for this reason: I can never be satisfied with anyone who would be blockhead enough to have me."[8]

Mary Owens did not court anyone else for several years. She returned to Kentucky in early 1838 and eventually married Jesse Vineyard of Weston, Missouri. Two of their sons served in the Confederate army. In 1839, when Mary's sister Elizabeth Abell planned to visit her, Lincoln asked Elizabeth to tell Mary "that I think she was a great fool because she did not stay here and marry me." That was "characteristic of the man," Mary wrote to William H. Herndon in later life.[9]

A Springfield woman who also regarded Lincoln as tactless was Rosanna Schmink. She consented to go to a "wool picking" with him, but he failed to provide her with a horse. She had to ride on the same horse with Lincoln—something that proud southern girls did not do. It was the last time she went any place with Lincoln.[10]

THE CLOSEST friend Lincoln ever had was Joshua Speed, a well-educated, wealthy Kentuckian with dark curly hair and an air of elegance. Five years younger than Lincoln, he was a handsome man who was well liked by the ladies of Springfield.

They first met when Lincoln walked into Speed's general store shortly after arriving in Springfield. Lincoln said he wanted to buy furniture, mattresses, sheets, and blankets for a single bed. Speed calculated the cost at seventeen dollars. Lincoln said that was perhaps cheap enough, but small as the sum was, he was unable to pay it. "But," Lincoln said, "if you will credit me until Christmas and my experiment here as a lawyer is a success, I will pay you then. If I fail in that, I will probably never pay you at all."[11]

Speed recalled that "the tone of his voice was so melancholy that I felt for him. I looked up at him and I thought then, as I think now, that I never saw so gloomy and melancholy a face in my life. I said to him, 'So small a debt seems to affect you so deeply, I think I can suggest a plan by which you will be able to attain your end without incurring any debt. I have a very large room and a very large double bed in it, which you are perfectly welcome to share with me if you choose.'"

"Where is the room?" Lincoln asked.

"Upstairs," said Speed.

Without saying a word, Lincoln took his saddlebags on his arm, went upstairs, set them down on the floor, came down again, and with a face beaming with a smile, exclaimed, "Well, Speed, I'm moved."

For the next four years they shared the bed—it was customary for two or three men to sleep in the same bed—and they also shared their innermost thoughts. Lincoln apparently was not charged any rent.[12]

Speed and Lincoln organized a private young men's literary society of Springfield. It met around the fireplace in their room, where they read spicy poems and amusing papers they had written. One of Lincoln's creations reflected his sense of injustice about seduction and the double standard applied to extramarital sex—considered immoral for both sexes but doubly shameful for women. He wrote:

> Whatever Spiteful fools may Say
> Each jealous, ranting yelper
> No woman ever went astray
> Without a man to help her.[13]

"Lincoln and Speed were quite familiar with the women," wrote William H. Herndon. "I cannot tell you what I know, especially in ink. Speed was a lady's man in a good and true sense. Lincoln only went to see a few women of the first class, women of sense. Fools ridiculed him; he was on this point tenderfooted."

Lincoln was unsure of himself in his encounters with young, fashionable women of the class he aspired to, Herndon said. Consequently, "Lincoln wasn't much for society," one Springfield woman noticed. "I don't think he [was] bashful. He was never embarrassed, and he seemed to enjoy the ladies' company. But he didn't go out much, as some young men did." He knew that women saw him as homely, simple, peculiar, and paradoxical—as a man who drifted from funny street-corner stories to a granitelike calm. They did not realize his long-silent reveries stemmed from the tragic loss of one he dearly loved, a loss that made it all the more difficult for him to ever love again because he associated deep love with untimely death and personal grief.[14]

Not having a way with the women of society but reportedly endowed with a strong sexual appetite, Lincoln apparently sought other outlets. In the fall of 1839 he learned that Speed was "keeping a pretty woman."

"Speed," Lincoln asked, "do you know where I can get [someone like her]?"

"Yes, I do," replied Speed. "I will send you to the place with a note. You cannot see her without a note or by my appearance."

He wrote the note, and Lincoln took it and went to see the young woman. Before anything happened, Lincoln asked how much she charged.

"Five dollars," she replied.

"I only have three dollars," he said regretfully.

The lady said that she would trust him for the two dollars. But Lincoln thought a moment and said, "I do not wish to go on credit. I'm poor, and I don't know where my next dollar will come from, and I cannot afford to cheat you." After some words of encouragement from the woman, Lincoln got out of bed, buttoned up his pants, and offered her three dollars for her time.

She would not take it and said: "Mr. Lincoln, you are the most conscientious man I ever saw."

Lincoln bid her goodbye. Speed asked him no questions about the evening, but the woman later told Speed what was said and done.[15]

In an 1835 or 1836 escapade, several months after Ann's death, Lincoln reportedly feared he had contracted syphilis, presumably from a prostitute, "during a devilish passion" in Beardstown, Illinois. Lincoln was there to help a fellow Whig promote the Beardstown canal and gain a charter for the developer. (Lincoln invested in it himself.) He may not actually have had syphilis, but he was concerned about the possibility. The disease—and the fear of it—was widespread in Illinois in the 1830s, partly because of the army's presence and the easily found houses of prostitution.[16]

Four years later, in December 1840 or January 1841, Lincoln wrote to a distinguished physician, Dr. Daniel Drake of Cincinnati. Lincoln read most of the letter to Joshua Speed. It dealt with hypochondria. But Speed said that "there was a part of the letter he would not read." It could have been about the syphilis question. Speed said he remembered the doctor's reply, "which was that he would not undertake to prescribe for him without a personal interview."[17]

Dr. Anson Henry of Springfield probably referred Lincoln to Drake. Dr. Henry later said that Lincoln told him things he had never discussed with anyone else. Whatever those matters were, they remained confidential. Henry drowned in a shipwreck off the California coast in 1865.[18]

WEARING HIS black stovepipe hat, a "boiled" shirt, baggy trousers, and a wrinkled black satin waistcoat, Lincoln knocked on the front door of one of Springfield's most luxurious mansions—the hilltop home of Ninian and Elizabeth Todd Edwards.

Ninian Edwards was a state legislator and the son of Illinois's first territorial governor. He was also renowned as "a fashion plate in black broadcloth, with a gold-headed cane" and known as an aristocrat who "hated democracy . . . as the devil is said to hate holy water."[19]

His stunning young wife was the queen of the social elite. She regularly arranged outings, teas, games, and dances for Springfield society—a roster of the brightest young men that any state could produce, men whose names hold a prominent place in history, as well as a galaxy of beautiful, intelligent young women.

Lincoln, then thirty years old, was invited to the Edwardses' exclusive soirees because he was the undisputed leader of the Whigs in the Illinois General Assembly, having been reelected in 1836 and 1838 and chosen as a presidential elector at the Whig convention in October 1839. He was also an up-and-coming Springfield lawyer. This gathering in December 1839 celebrated the first session of the state legislature to be held in Springfield, now that the capital had been moved from Vandalia through Lincoln's leadership.

Another regular guest was Elizabeth Edwards's youngest sister, twenty-one-year-old Mary Todd, who had moved into their home in the fall of 1839. "Come out and make our home your home," Elizabeth had written to Mary, whose constant quarrels with her stepmother in Lexington, Kentucky, necessitated a change. In Springfield, Mary enchanted everyone with her engaging personality, graceful demeanor, and cultivated chatter. She was "capable of making herself quite attractive to young gentlemen," a friend remembered.[20]

Lincoln removed his hat as Elizabeth opened the front door. She had grown accustomed to his appearance and welcomed him warmly. Escorting him into the parlor, where the other guests were assembled, she introduced him to Mary Todd. Wearing a pink organdy-and-lace gown cut low at the neck, with the skirt fluffed out in a slightly balloonish hoop, Mary was about thirteen inches shorter than Lincoln and almost ten years younger.

Her vivid blue eyes sparkled from beneath a mass of soft brown hair. Her complexion—always lovely—contrasted vividly with Lincoln's weather-beaten face.[21]

Soon the guests were dancing, and Lincoln, shy and nervous, allegedly said to Mary: "Miss Todd, I want to dance with you in the worst way." She accepted and later joked about his lack of dancing skills. "Worst, indeed," she later commented—he could not dance a lick. Later, as Ninian Edwards watched his sister-in-law mimic Lincoln dancing the Virginia reel, he whispered, "Mary could make a bishop forget his prayers."

Mary had mastered ballroom dances in private boarding schools where students conversed only in French. Her hometown of Lexington was called the "Athens of America," celebrated for its culture and refinement. There she was pampered by her parents and their slaves. Yet this belle of the aristocracy seemed charmed by her new acquaintance of log-cabin origin. So when Lincoln asked if he might call on her the following evening, she responded in the positive.

On that occasion they sat on a horsehair couch in the Edwardses' parlor and talked about politics and poetry—two common interests of two otherwise opposite persons from very different social, financial, and educational planes. Both had lost mothers at an early age, Mary's mother having died when Mary was six. Her father was an eminent Whig banker who had served in both houses of the Kentucky legislature. He remarried and had nine more children. While Lincoln loved his stepmother, Mary hated hers. Growing up, Mary felt lost in the crowd of children, and when she could not cope, she threw temper tantrums and wept uncontrollably. Once Mary put salt in her stepmother's coffee, and her stepmother called her "a limb of Satan."

Mary was now the picture of culture and refinement, and she smiled and chatted with the tall politician seated beside her. In fact, during their times together, Mary dominated their conversations. Lincoln listened and gazed at her, intrigued by her turned-up nose and dazzled by her wit and intelligence and her outspoken views on almost any topic. To him, she was "a very creature of excitement."[22]

Mary believed Lincoln had "the most congenial mind she had ever met." Both were fans of Robert Burns, both were Whigs, and both were fond of reciting poetry. Mary could recite "page after page of classic poetry, and liked nothing better." Further, Mary had known Lincoln's ideal statesman, Henry Clay, from childhood and as a family friend. "He was the handsomest man in Lexington," she said. Mary's acquaintance with Clay impressed Lincoln, as did Mary's relationship to other Whig leaders—first cousin and U.S. Congressman John T. Stuart, also Lincoln's law partner; cousin Stephen T. Logan, an elected circuit judge; and still another cousin, state legislator John J. Hardin.[23]

Mary was politically astute and would take an active role in the presidential campaign of 1840—the rowdiest, noisiest one in the nation's history up to that time. It was between the incumbent Democrat Martin Van Buren (allegedly an aristocrat who ate his meals from gold plates) and his Whig opponent—and eventual winner—William Henry Harrison, Old Tippecanoe (the poor man's friend, the farmer's champion, and the hard-cider candidate, although he had been born in a plantation mansion to a signer of the Declaration of Independence).

Women across the nation supported Harrison. They rode on floats, distributed pamphlets, and stood on balconies, waving handkerchiefs and banners and exhibiting flags and garlands. Vice President Richard Johnson claimed to be shocked to see ladies "wearing ribbons across their breasts with two names printed on them." Johnson reportedly lived "in sin" with a black woman, but he admonished ministers of the gospel for showing up at Harrison rallies sponsored by women.[24]

Politics was very much on Lincoln's mind. He was the Whig floor leader in the state legislature, he was running for reelection, he had accepted new responsibilities for organizing Whigs across the state, and he was a leader of the Young Whigs who held running debates with the Young Democrats led by Stephen A. Douglas. And Lincoln was also highly active on the legal circuit, attending to duties in the Illinois Supreme Court and the Sangamon Circuit Court, where he had more than fifty cases.

So while Lincoln and Mary were attracted to each other, they could not have actively courted over the course of a year—contrary to the standard account of their relationship. Their schedules kept them apart, and no record exists of a courtship in progress during the next seven or eight months. In fact, from the first of April until the November election, Lincoln was out of town at least half the time, including two weeks in April and nearly all of May.[25]

Mary Todd left Springfield in early June to visit relatives in Missouri. She did not return until mid-September. Her correspondence with her closest friends offered no evidence of a romance in progress.

On August 18 Lincoln went on an extended speaking trip. He stumped across the middle and lower part of the state, traveling from the Wabash to the Mississippi. He was not back in Springfield until late September. A few days later he was off again—for six weeks, until November 2—to represent his clients on the circuit. Thus Mary Todd and Abraham Lincoln could not have seen each other from sometime in June until he returned in September, and then just briefly.[26]

Further, in late November, Mary was entertaining the attentions of Joseph Gillespie, the traveling companion of an Illinois legislator. Surely she would not have done so had she been romantically attached to Lincoln.

Joshua Speed later reported that during the latter part of Lincoln's August-September trip, he did indeed make romantic overtures to Mary by mail, and she is said to have responded eagerly. As their correspondence heated up, it sparked a love affair—one with no face-to-face encounters. Apparently they reached an "understanding" by mail. She regarded it as a commitment. But an engagement was never announced, and only Mary and her family referred to it as such. No one else was aware of it.[27]

Upon his return Lincoln had only a couple of days before leaving for his legal travels. He did see Mary briefly then, but he saw a person physically different from the person he had met the previous winter. Mary had gained considerable weight while she was in Missouri. A friend wrote in jest: "Verily, I believe the further West a young lady goes the better her health becomes. If she comes here she is sure to grow—if she visits Missouri she will soon grow out of our recollection and if she should visit the Rocky Mountains I know not what would become of her." It must have reminded Lincoln of Mary Owens's similar weight problem.[28]

While away through October until early November, Lincoln apparently developed second thoughts about his relationship with Mary Todd. Had he moved too quickly in expressing his love for her? Had he been tricked? Within days of his return to Springfield in November, he realized he had made a mistake. It hit him around November 15 as the legislators began arriving for the special session.

Among the arriving lawmakers was Cyrus Edwards of Alton, a prominent Whig. With him was his strikingly beautiful eighteen-year-old daughter, Matilda, a poised and polished student of the fashionable Monticello Female Seminary near Alton. She would lodge for the winter with her cousins, Ninian and Elizabeth Todd Edwards—the same home in which Mary Todd stayed. The two visiting women were probably bedmates. Ready for the social season, they had filled their closets with new dresses and "many party frocks."[29]

At a party in honor of legislators, Lincoln met the tall, blonde newcomer and was instantly "in love" or at least totally infatuated with her. He said if he had it in his power, he would not alter any feature in her face. "She is perfect!" His moments with Matilda confirmed his ever-present doubts: he did not love Mary Todd. And even more startling: he loved Matilda.

Now he wondered how he could end the relationship with Mary. He asked for Joshua Speed's help. Having started the affair with Mary by mail, Lincoln resolved to end it the same way. He showed a letter to Speed that he planned to send to Mary. In it he stated his feelings, telling her he had thought the matter over with great deliberation and felt he did not love her sufficiently to warrant her marrying him.

"Speed, I want you to deliver this letter," he said.

Speed read it and shook his head. "No, let's think about it," he counseled. "It would give her an advantage. Words are forgotten in a private conversation, but once put in writing they stand as an eternal monument against you."

"Speed, I always knew you were obstinate," Lincoln said icily. "If you won't deliver it, I'll get someone else to do it."

Speed frowned, threw the letter in the fire, and then admonished Lincoln: "Now if you have the courage of manhood, go see Mary yourself; tell her, if you do not love her, the facts, and that you will not marry her. Be careful not to say too much, and then leave at your earliest opportunity."[30]

Lincoln bristled, buttoned his coat, and walked to the Edwardses' mansion. After a few pleasantries with Mary, he became startlingly blunt. He told her he did not love her and wanted to be released from his "commitment."

She gasped and burst into tears while wringing her hands. "The deceiver [has been] deceived, woe is me," she cried, alluding to the man she had been attentive to in recent weeks to make Lincoln jealous. The scene was too much for Lincoln, and tears trickled down his own cheeks. He held her in his arms, kissed her, and then parted, doubtful that his mission had been accomplished.[31]

Lincoln reported the meeting to Speed. "And that's how you broke the engagement," sneered Speed. "You kissed her! That was 'a bad lick.' You not only acted the fool, but your conduct was tantamount to a renewal of the engagement, and in decency you cannot back down now."

"Well," drawled Lincoln, "if I am in again, so be it."[32]

With the social season at its height, Lincoln persisted in being seen with Matilda Edwards. A well-placed observer said Lincoln "couldn't bear to leave Miss Edwards' side." Ninian Edwards's sister-in-law, Mrs. Benjamin S. Edwards, noted, "He was deeply in love with her." But some of Lincoln's friends thought he was acting wrongly and imprudently and told him so.[33]

Not to be outdone, however, Mary cavorted and danced with other "marriageable gentlemen," especially Stephen A. Douglas, the state's leading Democrat, with whom she flirted boldly and conspicuously, sometimes looking over her shoulder to see Lincoln's reaction. But Lincoln was not looking at her; he was occupied with Matilda.

Mary's companion, five-foot-four Stephen Douglas, was called the "Little Giant" because his power belied his stature. He promenaded the streets arm-in-arm with Mary—frequently passing Lincoln—and in every way made plain his intention to become Lincoln's rival.

Apparently Mary's courtship strategy was to play one suitor against another. "She was the most ambitious woman I ever knew," her sister said later, and "Mary often contended that she was destined to be the wife of some future president. . . . She loved pomp and power."[34]

Just before the close of the special legislative session, December 5, Lincoln forced a second encounter with Mary. He expressed in no uncertain terms his concern about her flagrant attentions to other suitors, and he again asserted that he did not love her and that he wanted to dissolve their relationship.

With her world reeling, Mary attacked him for his interest in Matilda and for "behaving dishonorably." She scathingly remarked, "I know you love her, [but] you are honor-bound to marry me . . . honor-bound!"[35]

Her angry charge cut Lincoln like a Damascus blade. He left. Fifteen months would pass before he would call on her again. Their breakup was now official. But it and other stresses in Lincoln's life plummeted him into a brief but painful breakdown. He had endured a solid year of hard campaigning, he had traveled dirt roads on horseback in all kinds of weather, and he had given stump speeches almost daily, sometimes to hostile crowds.

Despite all his efforts, 1840 was politically painful for him. Democrats maintained control of the Illinois legislature, and in Sangamon County he barely won reelection for a fourth term, placing last of five Whigs sent to the House. It was his worst political showing since his first race in 1832.

Furthermore, on July 20 he received the first public chastisement of his career. A well-connected young lawyer and politician, Jesse B. Thomas Jr., called Lincoln and his associates to task for a political dirty trick—attributing a letter to him that they had written themselves.

On the dais with Thomas, Lincoln replied with a relentless assault. "He imitated Thomas in gesture and voice," Herndon reported, "at times caricaturing his walk and the very motion of his body. Thomas, like everybody else, had some peculiarities of expression and gesture, and these Lincoln succeeded in rendering more prominent than ever. The crowd yelled and cheered as he continued. Encouraged by these demonstrations, the ludicrous features of the speaker's performance gave way to intense and scathing ridicule." Thomas, a former circuit judge, broke down, cried, and fled the platform.

Lincoln's assault became known as "the skinning of Thomas." It surprised even Lincoln's closest friends. While he had made fun of antagonists in written material, it was totally unlike him to personally abuse them on the platform. The *Illinois State Register* criticized him editorially for his "game of buffoonery" and "an assumed clownishness in his manner that does not become him, and which does not truly belong to him. . . . We seriously advise Mr. Lincoln to correct his clownish fault before it grows on him." Lincoln realized he had gone too far, and he hunted down Thomas and apologized to him.[36]

The final political blow of the year came during the special legislative session in December to deal with the skyrocketing state debt—a debt built by internal improvements bills pushed through in 1837 by Lincoln and fellow Whigs. The public works program was halted, and unfinished projects such as railroads were canceled. Lincoln was devastated.

Finally, on the session's last day, December 5, the Whigs sought unsuccessfully to block an anti-bank measure by boycotting the session to prevent a quorum. Only a handful of Whigs took their seats. But to their surprise, a quorum was achieved and then the doors were barred to keep anyone from leaving. Lincoln and two other Whigs quickly jumped out a window. Their departure was to no avail. The state bank was dissolved.[37]

Lincoln's nerves were frazzled. Enough was enough. He rested several days, returned for the legislature's general session, and continued to see Matilda, who showed no mercy to Mary. She declared that if Mary could not keep her lover, she need not expect any help from other girls.

So Mary found an older man. On December 15 she wrote to her best friend and closest confidante, Mercy Levering, without mentioning Lincoln. She referred to her "present companion, a congenial spirit." Later in the letter she identified him: "Mr. [Edwin B.] Webb, a widower of modest merit, is [my] principal lion, dancing [with me frequently]."

Webb was twenty years older than Mary and had two children whom Mary referred to as those "two sweet little objections." Mary's letter to Mercy continued: "You would be pleased with Matilda Edwards, a lovelier girl I never saw. Mr. Speed's ever-changing heart . . . is offering [his] young affections at her shrine, with some others." The "others," according to various informants and witnesses, included Lincoln.

Mary also referred to a prospective late-December outing: "We have a pleasant jaunt, in contemplation, to Jacksonville next week, there to spend a day or two. Mr. Hardin & Mr. Browning [married men] are our leaders [chaperones], the van brought up by Miss Edwards, my humble self, Webb, Lincoln, and two or three others whom you know not."[38]

Since Webb's attention would obviously be directed toward Mary, she apparently assumed the prospective pairing of Lincoln and Matilda. The letter, however, named Speed as a contender for Matilda's love—Speed was the most prosperous young bachelor in Springfield. Thus Lincoln had a double predicament. He was desperately trying to free himself from Mary Todd so he could profess his love to Matilda Edwards. But his best friend, Joshua Speed, was observed offering his own affections to Matilda. Lincoln's knowledge of it in December 1840 undoubtedly sidetracked him and kept him from addressing Matilda romantically. What a revolting development this must have been for Lincoln. His best friend was his rival for the girl he loved.[39]

Speed's "ever-changing" heart was also flirting with sixteen-year-old Sarah Rickard. But on January 1, 1841, he apparently did an "unknown something" that infuriated Sarah and ended their relationship. Perhaps they had a repeat performance of the Lincoln-Todd encounter, with Speed declaring his love for Matilda. The situation was so explosive that in later years Speed had all references to Sarah erased from letters he forwarded to historian William H. Herndon.

Showing an obvious concern about Sarah's unhappiness, Speed wrote to her brother-in-law, William Butler, that "[I am] much happier than I deserve to be." With Sarah out of the picture, Speed professed his love to Matilda and asked her to marry him. She turned him down. Both events possibly occurred on the same date—January 1, 1841.[40]

Lincoln, meanwhile, apparently had a quiet New Year's Day, contrary to views shared by many historians that he was supposed to have been married on that date but didn't show up. That opinion was based on comments made by Elizabeth Edwards at age seventy-five, five years before her death.

She told interviewer Jesse W. Weik that wedding arrangements had been made "but Lincoln failed to appear" and "Mary was greatly mortified."

Ninian Edwards, however, disagreed with his wife's recollection. "No such thing had ever taken place," he told Judge Broadwell, who shared the comment with Mrs. John T. Stuart, who in turn told journalist Ida M. Tarbell. Mrs. Benjamin S. Edwards, a member of the family circle, agreed. Furthermore, after extensive study, historian Douglas L. Wilson found "no signs of anything unusual" in Lincoln's life on January 1, 1841. Wilson said there was evidence to suggest that Mary Todd was not even in Springfield on that date.[41]

But something on that date prompted Lincoln to refer to it as "that fatal first of January" in his correspondence with Speed. If the aborted wedding ceremony never occurred, as now appears to be the case—based on the known sequence of events in the Lincoln-Todd relationship—then that fateful "something" probably related not to Lincoln's life but to developments in Speed's life—possibly Speed's rejection by Sarah Rickard and/or Matilda Edwards.

Whatever happened, Speed disposed of his business interests on the very same day—January 1, 1841. He returned to his family home in Louisville that spring. "I endeavor to persuade myself there is more pleasure in pursuit of an object than there is in its possession," Speed wrote to his younger sister. "This rule I wish now to most particularly apply to women. I have been most anxiously in pursuit of one—and from all present appearances . . . I may have as much of the anticipation and pursuit as I please, but the possession I can hardly ever hope to realize."[42]

By terminating his partnership in James Bell and Company, Speed was also ending his longtime living arrangement with Lincoln in the large room over the store—a room where they and their friends had gathered by the fireplace on winter nights to tell stories and anecdotes. Lincoln would sorely miss these associations while surely having mixed feelings about Speed as a rival for Matilda.

Just when Lincoln thought he had Matilda to himself, he proposed to her, and she rejected him, according to Orville H. Browning, a well-educated Whig legislator and friend of Lincoln. Matilda, as it turned out, was not seriously interested in any Springfield beaux; she was having fun playing the field. A pious woman, she is said to have rejected Stephen A. Douglas because of "bad morals" (something Mary Todd never complained about in her relationship with him). Matilda did not really dislike Lincoln; he was just a little fling.[43]

But Lincoln was crushed. He had loved and lost and was discarded abruptly. He collapsed. An acquaintance said he had thrown "two cat fits and a duck fit." It was January 13, 1841, and he went into seclusion for a week at the home of Mr. and Mrs. William Butler, where he boarded. He lay there, shrouded in gloom, unable to sleep, tossing and turning every night as winter storms pelted the window with snow and freezing rain.[44]

He ventured out only to vote once in the legislature and to see his physician, Dr. Anson Henry. Hypochondria was the doctor's diagnosis, brought on by extreme anxiety, overwork, and exhaustion.

Dr. Henry, concerned about Lincoln's debilitating condition, encouraged Mary to write him an official letter of release, thinking she might be partly responsible. She finally did so but added: "I have not changed my mind, but feel as always."

Mrs. Butler, who helped care for Lincoln, went into his room on January 17, closed the door, and said: "Now, Abraham, what is the matter? Tell me all about it." He did. Mrs. Butler's sister, Sarah Rickard (Speed's former girlfriend), later told a reporter: "Suffering under the thought that he had treated Mary badly, knowing that she loved him and that he did not love her, Mr. Lincoln was wearing his very life away in an agony of remorse. He made no excuse for breaking with Mary, but said, sadly, to my sister: 'Mrs. Butler, it would just kill me to marry Mary Todd.'"[45]

Aside from his feelings toward Mary, he resented the Edwardses' perception of him as a gangly, quirky country bumpkin no longer welcome in their home, a person no longer suitable for a lady from the proud and educated Todd family. Commenting on the two *d*'s in the Todd name, Lincoln said, "One *d* is enough for God, but the Todds need two."

On January 23 Lincoln wrote to his law partner, John Todd Stuart: "I am now the most miserable man living. If what I feel were equally distributed to the whole human family, there would not be one cheerful face on the earth. Whether I shall ever be better I can not tell; I awfully forebode I shall not. To remain as I am is impossible; I must die or be better, it appears to me."[46]

Lincoln's friend Orville H. Browning also lodged at the Butlers. He had spoken often to Mary and made this judgment: "I think that Mr. Lincoln's aberration of mind resulted entirely from the situation he thus got himself into—he was engaged to Miss Todd, and in love with Miss Edwards, and his conscience troubled him dreadfully for the supposed injustice he had done, and the supposed violation of his word which he had committed."

Mary's good friend Mercy Levering, who was kept well informed, wrote to her future spouse, James Conkling, on January 24: "Poor Lincoln! How are the mighty fallen! He was confined about a week, but though he now appears again he is reduced and emaciated in appearance and seems scarcely to possess enough strength to speak above a whisper. His case is truly deplorable. . . . He can declare 'That loving is a painful thrill, and not to love more painful still' [referring to his breakup with Mary Todd]. . . . He has experienced 'That surely 'tis the worst of pain to love and not to be loved again' [an obvious reference to his romance with Matilda]. . . . And Joshua [Speed] too is about to leave."[47]

Three days later another letter shared similar sentiments. This missive was from Jane Bell, who was related by marriage to Speed's business partner, James Bell. Part of the Springfield "in-crowd," she wrote to Ann Bell of Danville, Kentucky: "Miss Todd is flourishing largely. She has a great many beaus. You ask me how she and Mr. Lincoln are getting along. Poor fellow, he is in a bad way. . . . He is on the mend now. . . . The doctors say he came within an inch of being a perfect lunatic for life. . . . It seems he had addressed Mary Todd and she accepted him and they had been engaged some time when a Miss Edwards of Alton came here, and he fell desperately in love with her and found he was not so much attracted to Mary as he thought."[48]

Elizabeth Todd Edwards, furious with Lincoln for hurting her sister's feelings, said he was grieving over making Mary unhappy. But Ninian Edwards had a different theory: Lincoln loved Matilda, he said, and his conflicts of love and honor made him "crazy as a loon."

For several months Lincoln moped and coped, dropping out of social circles while attending legislative proceedings in Springfield and venturing into a new law partnership with the town's most knowledgeable practitioner, Stephen T. Logan.

If Mary was upset, she did not show it. She socialized gaily and flirted and accepted the attentions of other men. The correspondence between lovers Mercy Levering and James Conkling continued with the following note from James to Mercy on March 7, 1841:

The Legislature has dispersed. . . . Miss Todd and her cousin Miss [Matilda] Edwards seemed to form the grand center of attraction. Swarms of strangers . . . hovered around them, to catch a passing smile. By the way, I do not think they were received, with even ordinary attention, if they did not obtain a broad grin or an obstreperous laugh. And Lincoln, poor hapless simple swain who loved most true but was not loved again—I suppose he will now endeavor to drown his cares among the intricacies and perplexities of the law.[49]

Eligible bachelors in Springfield outnumbered marriageable young ladies by ten to one. Mary and Matilda were obviously making the rounds, and Mary, who previously "had very bitter feelings toward her rival," now seemed less resentful.

As Lincoln sulked and Mary seethed privately, Matilda ended her one-year social swirl in Springfield in the autumn of 1841. It was said that she broke more hearts, male and female, than any girl in Springfield's history. "Well," she reportedly said, "if the young men liked me, it is of no fault of mine!"[50]

Waiting for Matilda in Alton was handsome, straight-laced Newton Strong, a Connecticut Yankee and Phi Beta Kappa graduate of Yale University. He had come to the bustling town on the banks of the Mississippi in 1839 to begin his professional career as a law partner with college roommate Junius Hall. Strong had met Matilda just before her departure to Springfield and was overjoyed when she returned to Alton unattached. He had learned of her flirtations from Springfield attorneys, including Lincoln himself. Strong and Lincoln argued various cases before the Illinois Supreme Court, sometimes on opposite sides, at other times jointly representing a client. Good friends, Strong even nominated Lincoln for governor in 1841. Both were Whigs and of the same age.

Matilda, however, was not easy to win over. It took Strong three years to convince her to marry him. When asked why she married such "an old Buck" (he was thirty-four, she was twenty-two), she said, "he has lots of horses and gold."[51]

Meanwhile, in Springfield in 1841 the legislature's adjournment marked the end of Lincoln's legislative career. He was not renominated, but he did not seem to care. By then he preferred to practice law.

In early August Lincoln accepted Speed's invitation to visit him for several weeks at the stately family mansion known as Farmington, near Louisville. Their mutual failure to gain Matilda's love appeared to strengthen their friendship. In Kentucky Lincoln experienced a life of leisure and luxury he had never known. He occupied an elegant room and was assigned his own servant from among the plantation's slaves. Speed's mother, whose family had been Thomas Jefferson's neighbors in Virginia, gave him an Oxford Bible and scrumptious dishes of peaches and cream to accelerate his emotional convalescence.[52]

Long walks with Speed and romps with his half-sister, Mary, regenerated Lincoln's mind and soul. He playfully locked Mary in a room to keep her "from committing assault and battery on me." He later wrote her a long, gracious letter saying they were "something of cronies" at Farmington and that he was "subsisting on savory memories." Lincoln improved gradually, day by day gaining strength and confidence in himself until at last the black cloud had lifted and passed away.[53]

Lincoln and Speed both possessed poetic tenderness and keen minds. Both also supported and were sympathetic to the other's anxieties and decision-making hurdles. They shared their innermost thoughts.

During Lincoln's visit, Speed courted and proposed to beautiful, vivacious Fanny Henning, who lived on a nearby farm. Fanny accepted. Lincoln was partly responsible. He distracted Fanny's guardian-uncle so Speed could pop the question. Then Speed, like Lincoln, was consumed with self-doubt. Their roles reversed, and Lincoln counseled Speed on matters of the heart.[54]

Speed accompanied Lincoln back to Springfield and then returned to Kentucky in January 1842. He and Lincoln maintained a regular correspondence. Lincoln asked: "Are you afraid you don't love her enough? What nonsense! Remember . . . that you love her as ardently as you are capable of loving." Everybody worries about marriage, Lincoln said, but "you are naturally of a nervous temperament." In time, that feeling will go away, he counseled, if you "avoid bad weather," which "my experience clearly proves to be very severe on defective nerves. . . . In two or three months . . . you will be the happiest of men."

Speed finally relented and married Fanny on February 15, 1842. Upon hearing the news, Lincoln wrote his friend: "I have no way of telling you how much happiness I wish you both. I feel somewhat jealous of you both now." Speed replied that he was "far happier than I ever expected to be." Lincoln responded in a March 27 letter: "It now thrills me with joy [to learn of your happiness]. . . . Your last letter gave me more pleasure than the total sum of all I have enjoyed since that fatal first of January, '41."[55]

Lincoln noted he had seen Sarah Rickard "and am fully convinced she is far happier now than she has been for the last fifteen months past" (which would date her unhappiness back to early January 1841). Lincoln said he "should [be] entirely happy, but for the never-absent idea, that there is one still unhappy whom I have contributed to make so. That still kills my soul. I can not but reproach myself, for even wishing to be happy while she is otherwise." He, of course, referred to Mary Todd.

Speed, again advising Lincoln, pleaded with him to either wed Mary or forget her. Lincoln agreed. "But before I resolve to do one thing or the other, I must regain my confidence in my own ability to keep my resolves when they are made. . . . I have not regained it; and until I do, I can not trust myself in any matter of much importance."

Reasserting that destiny was controlled by a higher power, Lincoln wrote: "I believe God made me one of the instruments of bringing Fanny and you together, which union I have no doubt he had fore-ordained. Whatever he designs he will do for me yet. 'Stand still and see the salvation of the Lord' is my text just now."[56]

Meanwhile, politics took over Lincoln's mind that summer and early fall of 1842. State auditor James Shields, a Democrat, announced and enforced an unpopular order prohibiting the use of state bank currency to pay state taxes. The currency was depressed because the bank was near collapse. The action was a political windfall for the Whigs and a nightmare for Shields and the Democrats.

A fictitious farm woman named Rebecca, from the "Lost Townships," entered the fray with a series of scurrilous letters in the *Sangamo Journal*. The first, published on August 19, was a relatively mild attempt at political humor. It was probably written by the editor. But the second letter was nasty. It attacked Shields and the Democrats with a vengeance. Full of satire, political insults, and racy metaphors about married women in tight clothing, it lampooned the vain Irish bachelor (Shields) and called him "a conceity dunce" and "a liar as well as a fool." Lincoln wrote the letter but signed it "Rebecca."[57]

In one passage Lincoln drew upon Shields's reputation as a handsome man who fancied himself irresistible to women. The letter spoke of Shields "floatin' about on the air, without heft or earthly substance, just like a lock of cat fur where cats had been fightin'" and of the "sweet distress" he seemed to be in because he could not marry all the girls around him. "Too well I know how much you suffer," Shields exclaims in the parody, "but do, do remember it is not my fault that I am so handsome and so interesting."

More letters from Rebecca appeared in September, baffling Lincoln. Someone else had written them. By now, Shields was outraged. "I am the victim of slander, vituperation, and personal abuse," he complained. "Tell

me the writer's name," he demanded of editor Simeon Francis. Francis
sought Lincoln's advice. Covering for the other writers, Lincoln replied,
"Oh, just tell Shields I am responsible."[58]

Lincoln later learned that three of the letters were from Mary Todd and
her friend Julia Jayne, the daughter of a Springfield physician. Shields had
squeezed Julia's hand, much to her dislike, at a party at the Edwards mansion, and she and Mary took revenge by writing the letters.

Unaware of their involvement, Shields blamed Lincoln and demanded
"a full, positive, and absolute retraction of all offensive allusions" or suffer
"consequences which no one will regret more than myself." When negotiations failed to resolve the conflict, Shields, an expert marksman, challenged
Lincoln to a duel. As the one challenged, Lincoln could name the weapons
and chose "cavalry broadswords of the largest size"—weapons advantageous to him as a tall man with long arms. Shields was only five foot nine.

"I did not want to kill Shields," Lincoln later told his friend Usher Linder. "[I] felt sure I could disarm him, having had about a month to learn the
broadsword exercise; and furthermore, I did not want the darned fellow to
kill me, which I rather think he would have done if I had selected pistols."[59]

Since duels were illegal in Illinois, on September 27 the parties traveled
a hundred miles to "Bloody Island" on the Missouri side of the Mississippi.
Lincoln arrived first and killed time by trimming underbrush while hum-
ming "Yankee Doodle."

As the duel was about to begin, Whig leader John J. Hardin (Mary
Todd's cousin) and Democrat Revel English interrupted the proceedings
and offered to submit the case to impartial judges. Their plan was not followed, but it steered Shields away from dueling. Shields's friends, without
his knowledge, declared his offending note withdrawn. Lincoln responded
by admitting he had written "solely for political effect" with no intent of "injuring your personal or private character."

Shields's supporters convinced the state auditor that the "apology" was
sufficient, and all parties agreed to cancel the duel. Maj. J. M. Lucas, a friend
of Lincoln, said he had no doubt Lincoln meant to fight. Lincoln told him,
"I did not intend to hurt Shields unless I did so clearly in self-defense. If it
had been necessary, I could have split him from the crown of his head to the
end of his backbone."[60]

Privately, Lincoln was ashamed. Guided as he was by unimpassioned
reason, it was totally out of character for him to act on boisterous emotions.
And Mary, touched by his chivalry, must have regretted her role in putting

his life on the line. Both of them agreed never to speak of it. When years later an army officer teased Lincoln about fighting a duel "for the sake of the lady by your side," Lincoln's face flushed. "I do not deny it. But if you desire my friendship," he warned the officer, "you will never mention it again."[61]

Shields was later a Union general in the war and the only person in American history to serve three different states in the U.S. Senate: Illinois, Minnesota, and Missouri.

Five days after the duel, John J. Hardin's eighteen-year-old sister Martinette married Alexander McKee of Kentucky. Both Lincoln and Mary attended the ceremony but not together. Lincoln was with a young woman about half his age, eighteen-year-old Sarah Rickard, a close friend of Martinette and former sweetheart of Joshua Speed. Lincoln and Sarah had been seen together frequently.[62]

Six years earlier Lincoln met Sarah at the dining table in the home of her sister and brother-in-law, the William Butlers. Lincoln teased the young twelve-year-old and grew fond of her. In a couple of years he starting taking her to "little entertainments," including the first theater to play in Springfield. She liked him too but thought of him as a big brother and a friend of the family.[63]

When Sarah was sixteen, Lincoln became even more attentive and teasingly proposed marriage, citing the biblical Sarah becoming Abraham's wife. Sarah considered herself too young to think much about matrimony. In later life she said, "I always liked him as a friend, but . . . his peculiar manner and his general deportment would not be likely to fascinate a young girl just entering the society world." She eventually married Richard F. Barret, son of a well-known Springfield family. She found him "much more graceful and attractive" than Mr. Lincoln.[64]

At the McKees' wedding dinner, Mary Todd sat directly across the table from Sarah and Lincoln. "They [Mary and Lincoln] spoke to each other [for the first time in months], and that was the beginning of the reconciliation," Sarah reported.

Shortly thereafter, Eliza Francis, wife of the editor of the *Sangamo Journal,* stepped in. She invited both Mary and Lincoln to a social affair without telling either that the other would be coming. Once there, Eliza brought them together and advised, "Be friends again."[65]

John J. Hardin took a further step to unite the pair. He and his wife, Sarah, invited Mary and several other young people from Springfield to Jacksonville for a visit. All but Mary were told to go for a carriage ride, and she was chagrined when they departed without her. Then, as if on cue, Lincoln drove up and asked for her. He said he had come to escort her to the party. She smiled triumphantly.[66]

In the span of just two months, Hardin had affected Lincoln's life dramatically. He had saved him from possible death in a duel, and he had lured him back into a relationship with Mary Todd. For her part, Mary had used every tactic at her disposal to encourage him to do so. A year younger than Lincoln, Hardin was one of the most admired men in Illinois. He served in the state legislature and would succeed John T. Stuart in Congress at the next election. Hardin seemed destined for greatness, possibly even the presidency. Tragically, he died in the Mexican War in 1847. Had Hardin lived, Lincoln's political future might have taken a different course.

What definitely did change in the fall of 1842 was Lincoln's long and severe inner struggle. He could not live down his guilty feelings. So he gave up. He again courted Mary Todd even if his heart was not in it. By doing so he saved his honor, but he sacrificed his domestic happiness. So Lincoln proposed to Mary, and she was ecstatic.

Orville H. Browning, closely connected with both Mary and Lincoln, said, "There is no doubt of her exceeding anxiety to marry him." He added: "In this courtship, [Lincoln] undoubtedly felt that he had made [a mistake] in having engaged himself to Miss Todd. But having done so, he felt himself . . . honor-bound to act in perfect good faith towards her—and that good faith compelled him to fulfill his engagement with her, if she persisted in claiming the fulfillment of his word. . . . Had circumstances left him entirely free to act upon his own impulses, [I doubt] he would have voluntarily [proposed] to Miss Todd."

Joshua Speed emphasized: "Lincoln [decided to marry] for honor—feeling his honor bound to her." Mary's cousin Elizabeth Grimsley cautiously acknowledged that Lincoln's feelings for Mary "had not the overmastering depth of an early love"—his love for Ann Rutledge.[67]

Mary apparently wanted to keep their engagement secret. Thus if it did not work out, no one would know, and she would not be embarrassed. Further, she wanted to avoid a confrontation with her sister. Elizabeth Todd Edwards was angry with Lincoln and had bluntly told Mary that she and Lincoln "could not live happily as husband and wife." So Mary and Lincoln met secretly for about three weeks at the home of their friends, Simeon and Eliza Francis, who had no children and plenty of room for Mary and Lincoln to be together, alone and undisturbed.[68]

While Mary may have wanted to keep the engagement secret, the ensuing chain of events seemed to carry secrecy far beyond what normal circumstances would dictate.

Early on the morning of November 4, 1842, Lincoln dropped by the Reverend Charles Dresser's home. The Dresser family was eating breakfast when Lincoln announced, "I want to get hitched tonight." The surprised Episcopal minister checked his schedule and said he would be available.

After the stores opened, Lincoln dashed into Chatterton's jewelry shop and ordered a wide-band gold ring—perhaps according to Mary's instructions. It was to be inscribed: "A.L. To Mary, Nov. 4, 1842. Love Is Eternal."

At noon Lincoln visited James H. Matheny, a friend who was the son of the county clerk. "Jim, I shall have to marry that girl this evening. Will you be my best man?" Matheny agreed and thought that "Lincoln looked and acted as if he was going to the slaughter." Lincoln told Matheny he was "driven into the marriage."

Meanwhile, Mary Todd called on Julia Jayne, coauthor of the "Lost Townships" letters, and asked her to be a bridesmaid. At about the same time, the couple's closest friends and relatives were notified.

Mary broke the news to her sister Elizabeth Edwards, fueling the most memorable of the day's unforgettable exchanges: "How could you marry someone who humiliated you? He's white trash, a common person, a plebeian."

But Mary would not back down. Elizabeth finally gave in but then attacked the timing: "You've only given me two-hours notice. I don't have time to prepare a suitable wedding feast . . . I guess I'll have to send out for gingerbread and beer."

"Well," Mary replied sarcastically, "that will be good enough for plebeians, I suppose!"

As Lincoln was dressing for the ceremony, his landlord's son asked him where he was going. Lincoln replied, "To hell, I suppose."[69]

On that cool November night, rain fell in torrents as twenty-three-year-old Mary Todd and thirty-three-year-old Abraham Lincoln exchanged marriage vows at the Edwards mansion. Thirty friends attended the ceremony. Among those present was Thomas C. Brown, a supreme court judge who tended to say what he thought without regard to place or surrounding.

When Lincoln placed the ring on Mary's finger and repeated the vow, "With this ring I thee endow with all my goods and chattels, lands and tenements," Brown blurted out, "God Almighty, Lincoln! The statute fixes that!"[70]

The flustered parson hastily pronounced them husband and wife.

The newlyweds left to live in the Globe Tavern, a very ordinary Springfield boarding house that was a stopover for two stagecoach lines. They occupied a furnished second-floor room, eight by fourteen feet, and ate their meals in the common dining room. The total cost for room and board was four dollars a week.

At bedtime, Lincoln would often go downstairs to fill a pitcher of water and then "sit on the steps of the porch and tell stories to whoever happened to be near." Mary would cough to signal that she wanted him; sometimes he "kept her coughing until midnight or after."

One morning, in a rage, Mary flung hot coffee in her husband's face. Another renter cleaned him up and treated the burns. A year later the Lincolns left the Globe and rented a three-room cottage.[71]

It is not known why the marriage announcement was so abrupt and the wedding so urgent. Perhaps they planned it that way to avoid opposition, or perhaps something significant occurred the night before to spur Lincoln into action.

Mary was aggressive and determined to marry Lincoln. Did she lure him into bed, thereby forcing his commitment? Mary later admitted that during their courtship she had "trespassed, many times and oft, upon his great tenderness and amiability of character" and that she had used "all my friends and every art given to me."[72]

A week after the wedding, Lincoln wrote to a friend: "Nothing new here, except my marrying, which to me, is a matter of profound wonder." Indeed, it was profound. He had lost his one true love in New Salem. He had been rejected three times in Springfield—by Mary Owens, by Matilda Edwards, and by Sarah Rickard. He had agonized for months over the Mary Todd situation. Then, suddenly, he had married Mary Todd.[73]

Their first son, Robert Todd Lincoln, was born on August 1, 1843, just three days short of nine months after the wedding. Lincoln later wrote to Speed: "[Robert] has a great deal of that sort of mischief that is the offspring of much animal spirits."

Some historians insist Lincoln married to foster his political fortunes. Mary Todd was part of the Edwards-Stuart-Todd aristocracy. In marrying into this group, however, Lincoln had to constantly reassure his political base—the common people—that he was still one of them. His political opponents labeled him "the candidate of pride, wealth, and aristocratic family distinction"—a charge that prompted Lincoln to counter: "I am now and always shall be the same Abe Lincoln that I always was."[74]

Mary, on the other hand, soon felt she had tumbled from the aristocracy to the bourgeoisie or lower. Always afraid of poverty, she believed she was now experiencing it.

Lincoln was still paying off his New Salem debts, so the newlyweds had to pinch every penny. Mary had to cook, clean, and scrub—tasks slaves had done for her in the past. She believed her wealthy friends were snickering. It was a difficult time for this well-bred, sophisticated "creature of excitement."

9

"Lincoln's Wife Was
a Hellion"

1844–61

*B*Y EARLY 1844 Abraham Lincoln was earning a modest but respectable $1,500 to $2,000 a year from his law practice. From the Reverend Charles Dresser, who had presided over their marriage, he purchased a one-and-a-half-story frame house in Springfield—with a stable and privies in back—for $1,200. With a house of their own, the Lincolns could enjoy family life.

Mary read reports and verse to him by lamplight, and on starry nights they sat on the porch and she pointed out planets and constellations. He chopped wood for the fireplace and stove, and she drew their water from a backyard pump and toted it into the house. She mended his clothes, sewed fine tucks in his shirts, and nagged him about his rumpled attire and untidy ways—sprawling around on the floor, wiping his mouth on his sleeves, and raking food from the meat plate with his knife. She was determined to improve his manners.

Coping with household chores, tending to baby Bobbie, making ends meet, and adjusting meals to Lincoln's irregular hours became more than Mary could handle. To get relief she finally hired a maid, one of the lazy "wild Irish," as she called her. Even with help, Mary seemed overworked and exhausted. She suffered excruciating headaches that sent her to bed for days at a time, and she became anxious and had swift mood changes that were marked by vitriolic outbursts followed by dazzling charm and gaiety.

The Lincoln-Todd "marriage of opposites" was soon referred to by friends and acquaintances as "a state of mutual abuse." And their home was viewed by some as a suburb of Hades, where Mary served up steaming platefuls of invectives.[1]

The tongue-lashings that she dished out to maids, workmen, and her husband were widely discussed in Springfield. Turner R. King, register of the Springfield land office, observed, "Lincoln's wife was a hellion—a she devil [who] vexed and harrowed the soul out of that good man [and] drove him from home, often and often."

On at least two occasions Mary was seen chasing Lincoln from the house with a broomstick. He was half-dressed during one of these incidents, and their Irish house servant, Meg Ryan, had to bring him his clothes. He dressed in the yard and told Meg not to be scared, that Mrs. Lincoln would get over it.

Another time Lincoln was observed fleeing out the door as Mary threw potatoes at him. On other occasions she threw books. One Sunday morning, Mary chased him through the yard with a knife. When Lincoln realized that passers-by were witnessing the scene, he abruptly wheeled on his wife and said, "You make the house intolerable, damn you, get out of it!"[2]

Servants were also harshly treated. When one threatened to leave unless her meager pay was raised by twenty-five cents to a dollar-fifty a week, Mary refused.

"But Mother," Lincoln implored her, "I don't want her to leave. Pay the twenty-five cents. We can afford it."

"No!" Mary defiantly resisted," I won't do it!"

Lincoln secretly told the servant, "Don't leave. Tell Mrs. Lincoln you've decided to stay, and I'll pay the extra twenty-five cents."

Mary overheard them and stormed into the room: "What are you doing! I'm not going to be deceived. Miss, you can leave! And as for you, Mr. Lincoln, I'd be ashamed of myself!"[3]

With the rapid turnover of domestics, a friend, Jacob Taggart, volunteered his niece: "a fine girl, intelligent and industrious, who could satisfy anybody on earth." Mary hired her, and all went well for a while. Then Mary insulted and slapped her one day, and she quit. Taggart went to see Mary and offered to make amends.

"Mr. Taggart, how dare you bother me!" Mary raged. "You're a dirty villain, a vile creature!" Then she struck him with a broom several times.

Taggart looked up Lincoln in town. "You must punish your wife," he demanded. "She has insulted me and my niece. I demand an apology, and if I don't get it, I'll—" Lincoln interrupted, put his hand on Taggart's shoulder, and said mournfully: "Friend, can't you endure this one wrong done to you by a mad woman for our friendship's sake while I have had to bear it without complaint and without a murmur for lo these many years."

Taggart immediately felt sorry for Lincoln, assured him of his continued friendship, shook hands, and left.[4]

On another day Mary angrily dismissed a servant boy and threw his suitcase out the window. Then she hired a woman to help the two servants she already had—"but fired them all the next day."

Her actions were consistent with two incidents reported by a local official, John B. Weber: "Once I heard a scream of 'Mr. Weber! Mr. Weber!' It was the voice of distress. I looked back and saw Mrs. Lincoln. She said, 'Keep this dog from biting me!' The dog was small and good natured and was doing nothing. . . . Another day I heard her scream, 'Murder! Murder! Murder!' and saw her up on the fence. I went to her. She said a big ferocious man had entered her home. I saw an umbrella man come out. I suppose he had entered to ask for old umbrellas to mend. He came out and said, 'Should be sorry to have such a wife.'"[5]

Neighbor Elizabeth A. Capps remembered that when Robert was a toddler, Mrs. Lincoln appeared in her front yard yelling, "Bobbie will die! Bobbie will die!" Elizabeth's father ran over to see what had happened. He found Bobbie "sitting by a lime box with a little lime in his mouth." He washed his mouth out, and "that's all there was to it."

Jesse K. Dubois, a political friend of Lincoln's, stopped by Lincoln's office one morning just as he was leaving to go home with a package of meat for breakfast. "Walk with me, Jesse, we can talk on the way." Mary met them at the door, opened the package, and screamed at Lincoln: "You've brought the wrong kind of meat! I can't use this! I don't want this!" Then she struck Lincoln in the face. He wiped off the blood, motioned to Dubois, and they left.[6]

Vexed and harassed, Lincoln equipped his office with a six-and-a-half-foot-long couch and slept there on nights of domestic discord. He would often dine on cheese and crackers rather than go home. Chased out of his home one morning, he took Bobbie to a restaurant. After they finished breakfast, Lincoln said: "Well, Bobbie, this ain't so bad after all, is it? If Ma don't conclude to let us come back, we will board here all summer."[7]

Turmoil often followed dinner parties. Mary would invite local aristocrats, but Lincoln would lead the men into a corner and swap stories until the party ended. After the guests left, Mary "would be as mad as a disturbed hornet," according to William H. Herndon. She would lecture Lincoln "all night, till he got up out of bed in despair and went whistling through the streets and alleys till daybreak."

While Mary was hosting a party for society women one evening, Lincoln answered the door in his shirtsleeves. The two callers asked for Mary, and he told them he would "trot the women folks out." Mary cursed him when her guests departed, and he left the house until early the next morning.[8]

Sometimes he did not come home for days. One evening he dropped by a neighbor's house with "a prodigious carpet bag" in hand. He said: "Mary is having one of her spells, and I think I had better leave her for a few days. I didn't want to bother her, and I thought as you and I are about the same size, you might be kind enough to loan me one of your clean shirts! I have found that when Mrs. Lincoln gets one of these nervous spells, it is better for me to go away for a day or two."

The postmaster reported that Lincoln tarried at the post office one evening, swapping stories until eleven. "Well, I hate to go home," he finally admitted. "You can spend the night at my house, if you wish," Ellis offered, and Lincoln accepted.[9]

Mary's actions, regardless of their cause, were counter to the accepted rules for a wife's behavior in that period. Submissiveness, purity, and piety were expected. Mary's friend, Kentucky Senator John Crittenden, advised his newlywed daughter accordingly: "I have never seen a wife who made her husband happy that was not happy herself. Remember this. Kindness and gentleness are the natural and proper means of the wife. There are wives who seek to rule, to make points with their husbands and complain—ay, scold. To love such a woman long is more than a mortal can do."

In 1844 Lincoln formed a law partnership with William H. Herndon. He was part of a small group of men whose company Lincoln enjoyed. They would sit around the potbelly stove at the drugstore, swap stories, and talk politics.

"I don't like that man," Mary complained. "He's a drunkard, a 'dandy,' and a ladies' man. Your partnership with him will be a disaster!" The partnership lasted twenty years—and was still in effect at the time of Lincoln's assassination—but Mary remained spiteful toward Herndon.

Her hatred dated to 1837. As a visiting belle from Kentucky that year, she attended a ball at which Herndon asked her to dance. Intending to compliment her, he observed that she seemed to glide through the waltz "with the ease of a serpent." Mary was never known for her sense of humor, and she bristled at the reference to a serpent and stomped away.[10]

Matilda Edwards and Newton Strong reentered the Lincolns' life as newlyweds during the winter of 1844–45, after Strong's election to the legislature. They dined with the Lincolns and saw them at levees and soirees. Mary kept a close eye on twenty-three-year-old Matilda, not wanting to see her alone with Lincoln. From Mary's standpoint it was "good riddance" when the Strongs moved to Pennsylvania.

LINCOLN RODE the legal circuit in Illinois twice a year, traveling from courthouse to courthouse for three months in the spring and three months in the fall. His absences caused Mary to fret even though she knew it was financially necessary. While on the circuit he seldom wrote to her, and her letters to him were often more than a month apart. On weekends other lawyers would go home, but Lincoln would often be away from home for as long as six weeks. In 1851, for instance, he was out of town from April 2 to June 4. Lincoln "would refuse to go home," said Illinois judge David Davis. Lincoln preferred to spend his weekends with "tavern loungers."[11]

At a week's end on the circuit, Lincoln would frequently quote his favorite poem, "Mortality," by Scotsman William Knox. He had learned it in New Salem and was said to have recited it often after Ann Rutledge's death. "I would give all I am worth, and go into debt," he would say, "to be able to write so fine a piece as I think that is." The fourth stanza may have reminded him of Ann:

> The maid on whose cheek, on whose brow, in whose eye
> Shone beauty and pleasure—her triumphs are by;
> And the memory of those who loved her and praised,
> Are alike from the minds of the living erased.[12]

Another poem Lincoln often recited, "The Last Leaf" by Oliver Wendell Holmes, may also have reminded him of Ann and her grave near New Salem:

The mossy marbles rest
On lips that he has pressed
In their bloom
And the names he loved to hear
Have been carved for many a year
On the tomb.

According to Herndon, Lincoln would "recite it, praise it, laud it, and swear by it" and "tears would come unbidden to his eyes."[13]

Judge Davis. a powerful man who on the circuit shared more beds with Lincoln than any other judge, said, "Lincoln was a man of strong passion for women, but his conscience kept him from seduction. His [morals] saved many a woman."

Lois Hillis, an itinerant performer with the Newhall Singers, was among the women who exhibited a special interest in Lincoln. She showed up in the country hotels on the circuit, and when she saw Lincoln, she greeted him warmly. "The emotions of his heart were deep and strong," observed Charles S. Zane, a Springfield attorney. "But they had the benefit of the light and wisdom of a great intellect, and the admonitions of a great conscience. He felt [obligated] to do what his conscience approved. He measured the morality of every action." He was never known to be unfaithful to his wife.[14]

Were his absences due to Mary's vitriolic outbursts and an unhappy married life, or were her outbursts due to his long absences? Historians differ. Mary told neighbor James Gourley, "If [my] husband had stayed at home as he ought to, [I] would love him better." Gourley, a deputy U.S. marshal, called Mary "a good friend" who "dared me once or twice to kiss her," but "I refused."

Lincoln claimed that weekends on the road gave him time to think without family interruptions. On the circuit he was "as happy as he could be," said Judge Davis, "and happy no other place."[15]

Even when he was in Springfield, Lincoln seldom spent his evenings at home. To reduce domestic conflicts, he often left for work around seven or eight in the morning and would not return until midnight or later. He read widely at the state library, broadening his knowledge of history, the Constitution, and the laws of government. Thus his terrible domestic situation diverted him to studious pursuits that helped him to succeed in law and in politics.

On those rare occasions when Lincoln returned home early in the evening, he preferred to sit quietly by the fire and read. As he sat reading one evening while Mary cooked dinner, she warned him that the fire was about to go out. Absorbed in his reading, he did not respond. She called out again. No response. Furious, she grabbed a piece of firewood and struck him on the face, cutting his nose.

Did her fits of violent anger cause Lincoln to wonder what might have been had Ann Rutledge lived? Reflecting on earlier times in Indiana and on his grandest love and most gripping tragedy, he penned a poem a decade after Ann's death. It read in part:

> O Memory! thou midway world
> 'Twixt earth and Paradise,
> Where things decayed and loved ones lost
> In dreamy shadows rise,
> And, freed from all that's earthly vile,
> Seem hallowed, pure, and bright,
> Like scenes in some enchanted isle,
> All bathed in liquid light.[16]

In 1847 Lincoln was off to Washington, D.C., as a newly elected member of the U.S. House of Representatives. He, Mary, four-year-old Robert, and a new baby, Eddie, moved into a Washington boarding house. Throwing himself into his work, Lincoln spent very little time with Mary. She hindered him "in attending to business," he confided to a colleague.

Most congressmen did not bring their wives to Washington, so Mary had few female friends. Further, she was appalled to discover that many legislators frequented saloons and brothels. Although Lincoln was a passionate man with a strong attraction to the opposite sex, he also possessed extraordinary self-control. He was something of an exception in prewar Washington. Prostitution was tolerated, and sexual escapades attracted little public attention in the press.[17]

Near the Capitol, at 349 Maryland Avenue, a twenty-something entrepreneur named Mary Ann Hall built and managed a top-of-the-line brothel, which offered fine food, expensive carpets, and plush red furniture. It was a place where men of wealth and distinction were wined and dined and sexually served by women noted for their youth, beauty, and social refinement.

Lobbyists employed Madam Hall's lovelies and other prostitutes to influence legislators. During the Civil War, Gen. Joseph Hooker's troops bivouacked nearby and patronized a substantial number of the city's estimated five thousand prostitutes. The area was known thereafter as "Hooker's Division." When Madam Hall retired in 1876, she rented her property to a women's health clinic. After her death in 1886 the *Washington Evening Star* praised her civic character and "a heart ever open to appeals of distress."[18]

Mary Lincoln, however, found few pleasures in the nation's capital. She felt snubbed as the wife of a freshman congressman. She resented the complaints of other boarders about her noisy, undisciplined children. She was concerned about Eddie, who was sick much of the time. After three months of loneliness and boredom, she packed her boys and her bags and fled to her family home in Kentucky for the remainder of the congressional session.

Lincoln missed them. "I hate to stay in this old room by myself," he wrote to Mary. "Having nothing but business—no variety—has grown exceedingly tasteless to me." He worried about the children and enjoined his wife, "Don't let the blessed fellows forget father." She responded: "How much, I wish instead of writing, we were together this evening. I feel very sad away from you."

Mary's health improved in Kentucky, and for the first time since their wedding, she was free from headaches. "That is good—good," wrote Lincoln. Teasing her, he added: "I am afraid you will get so well, and fat . . . as to be wanting to marry again. . . . Get weighed, and write me how much you weigh." If that did not irritate Mary, another situation certainly did.[19]

In his seat in the House of Representatives, Lincoln was just across the aisle from William Strong of Pennsylvania, the brother-in-law of Matilda Edwards, Lincoln's lost love from Springfield. Lincoln and Strong met at a congressional reception, where Lincoln asked about Newton and Matilda Strong. Later, after Congressman Strong mentioned to Lincoln that Matilda was planning a trip to Washington, Lincoln dashed off a letter to Mary: "A day or two ago Mr. Strong, here in Congress, said to me that Matilda would visit here within two or three weeks. Suppose you write her a letter, and enclose it in one of mine; and if she comes I will deliver it to her, and if she does not, I will send it to her."[20]

Mary ignored her lonely husband's request while intimating she wanted to return to Washington. Mindful of her tantrums and extravagances, Lin-

An idealized portrait of Nancy Hanks Lincoln, Abraham's mother. Lincoln believed that from her unknown father he acquired his mental abilities and ambition. From her he learned the fundamental truths of the four gospels, and they became fixed moral concepts with him.

Lincoln's stepmother, Sarah Bush Johnston Lincoln, may have been the first person who ever treated him like a human being. She encouraged Abe to study and make something of himself, but she opposed his run for the presidency, fearing he would be killed.

Lincoln adored his sister, Sarah, a cheerful, attractive girl with a bright mind. When she died during childbirth at age twenty, Abe was engulfed in depression, followed by anger against her husband for neglecting her.

Ann Rutledge encouraged Lincoln to study law and to run for political office. Deeply in love, they were engaged in the spring of 1835 and planned to be married a year later. After she died that fall, Lincoln was devastated and suicidal.

Right: Ann Rutledge and other New Salem residents gathered on the river bank to watch four strangers, including Abe Lincoln, struggle with a stranded flatboat. The incident led Lincoln to return to New Salem three months later.

Left: Ann Rutledge and Abe Lincoln share a few moments near Rutledge Tavern.

Rutledge Tavern (*below*) was erected by Ann's father, James Rutledge, in 1828 for his family. When New Salem prospered, he converted it into an inn. Lincoln stayed there about four months in the winter of 1832–33 and became friends with Ann Rutledge, then nineteen.

The second Berry-Lincoln store was directly across the street from Rutledge Tavern. Under a nearby maple tree Lincoln often stretched out with his books. When he saw Ann Rutledge through her window he would call out to her and run across and visit.

The interior of the Berry-Lincoln store. Ann Rutledge shopped here occasionally when she couldn't find what she wanted at the Hill-McNeil store.

Abolitionist Harriet Beecher Stowe strongly supported Lincoln. Her anti-slavery novel *Uncle Tom's Cabin* was a potent abolitionist weapon in the North.

Sojourner Truth, reared as a slave, became a national figure in anti-slavery and women's rights causes. She told Lincoln that he was "the best president" ever.

Anna Ella Carroll wrote and distributed eloquent and persuasive pamphlets that supported Lincoln's policies and helped keep Maryland in the Union. She claimed she suggested successful military strategies to Lincoln.

Eliza Gurney strengthened Lincoln's faith and was one of the most important women in his life during the war years. They exchanged beautiful and revelatory letters.

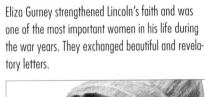

Rebecca Wright, a young Quaker schoolteacher, bravely contributed to Gen. Philip H. Sheridan's success in the Shenandoah Valley in 1864, which helped to assure Lincoln's reelection.

Vinnie Ream was a seventeen-year-old art prodigy who also composed poetry and music. After Lincoln's death she was chosen to create a life-size marble statue of him for the U.S. Capitol (below right).

Elizabeth "Lizzie" Keckley was the First Lady's stately mulatto dressmaker and confidante. They spent hours together as Mary welcomed the advice of this "remarkable woman." Her autobiography, *Behind the Scenes,* reveals Mary's innermost thoughts and interesting interactions between the president and his wife.

Mary Ord accompanied her husband, Gen. Edward O. C. Ord, during a March 1865 military review at City Point. But her close proximity to the president riled Mary Lincoln, and the First Lady verbally assaulted her.

After Mary Lincoln's escapade at City Point, Julia Grant persuaded her husband not to go to Ford's Theatre with the Lincolns. She did not want to be confined in a theater box with "that crazy woman."

Actress Laura Keene, star of the play *Our American Cousin* at Ford's Theatre, rushed to the presidential box where she cradled Lincoln's bloody head on her lap and dabbed cool water on his forehead.

Social reformer Dorothea Dix alerted authorities about a plot to kill Lincoln in Baltimore in February 1861. During the war she served as head of women nurses for the Union army.

coln replied: "Will you be a good girl in all things, if I consent? Then come along . . . as soon as possible. . . . I want to see you, and our dear, dear boys very much."

It has never been determined if Matilda came to Washington that year or if she ever saw Lincoln again. Three years later, in Philadelphia, Matilda died suddenly from an undisclosed illness. She was only twenty-nine. Although she had lived in Reading just four years, the editor of the local newspaper wrote this unusual tribute:

> The sudden death of this most esteemed lady has awakened an unusual degree of sorrow in the circle of her friends. Her gentle temper, her conciliatory manners, and the sweetness of her heart made her dear to all who knew her. The memory of such as she cannot perish and it will be long ere her many friends shall cease to think of her virtues and grieve for her early death.[21]

In December 1848 Lincoln jumped into the congressional debates over slavery in the territories—and in the nation's capital. From Capitol Hill he could see the notorious "Georgia pen," which he described as "a sort of Negro livery-stable"—where "Negroes were collected, temporarily kept, and finally taken to Southern markets, precisely like droves of horses." He proposed a bill to free all slave children in the District and to compensate their owners, but when Southerners threatened to boycott Congress, Lincoln's backers abandoned him and he withdrew the bill.[22]

During his term in Congress, Lincoln's outspoken stand against President James K. Polk's support for the Mexican War alienated both friends and foes. The president, said Lincoln, provoked the war by announcing that Mexican troops had shed American blood on American soil in a border dispute. "Reveal the exact spot," demanded Lincoln, but Polk did not do so. Other Whigs failed to support Lincoln's efforts, and even in Illinois Lincoln was termed "misguided." Some critics even labeled him a "second Benedict Arnold." To a friend, Lincoln confided, "I neither seek, expect, or deserve" a seat in the next Congress.

With Gen. Zachary Taylor's election to the presidency in 1848, Lincoln expected to be rewarded with a cabinet post for his strong support of Taylor's candidacy. "Old Rough and Ready" ignored him, however, and Lincoln also lost a bid to become commissioner of the U.S. Land Office. The interior secretary offered to nominate him for governor of the Oregon Territory, but

Mary adamantly opposed accepting the offer. She had had enough of frontier life; she feared Indians, and she was concerned about Eddie's health. Lincoln concluded that the position led nowhere and rejected it.

With his public career stalled, Lincoln brooded. "How hard it is to die and leave one's country no better than if one had never lived," he told Herndon. When an autograph collector requested his "signature with a sentiment," he wrote, "If you collect the signatures of all persons who are no less distinguished than I, you will have a very undistinguishing mass of names."[23]

In 1849, at age forty, Lincoln returned to full-time legal practice in Springfield. Haunted by his failure to achieve his political goals, he zealously focused on the law and intellectual pursuits. He mastered the abstract mathematical propositions in the first six books of Euclid and also resumed his study of Shakespeare. For five years he avoided politics. By age forty-five his disciplined approach had produced a new maturity. He had become a statesman—while also facing personal tragedies.

In December 1849 three-year-old Eddie fell gravely ill. He was nursed day and night for nearly two months, but his condition was hopeless. On February 1 he died, probably of pulmonary tuberculosis. Lincoln was anguished, and Mary collapsed. She remained in her bedroom for weeks, crying much of the time. Lincoln tried to comfort her and tended to her every need. When she finally emerged, she was more temperamental and unstable than ever.

Dr. James Smith, pastor of Springfield's First Presbyterian Church, was the only person who seemed able to comfort her. He reassured her that God loved and cared for Eddie in heaven. Lincoln rented a family pew in the church so Mary could attend regularly. He occasionally accompanied her but refused to become a church member.

Eleven months after Eddie's death, on December 21, 1850, Mary gave birth to William Wallace "Willie" Lincoln. He was named after Mary's brother-in-law.

That December Lincoln also learned from his stepbrother, John Johnston, that his father was terminally ill, but Lincoln made no effort to contact him. "Why haven't we heard from you?" Johnston wrote. "Because," replied Lincoln, "it appeared to me I could write nothing which could do any good." He also claimed he could not visit his father because of Mary's illness and other commitments. Finally, Lincoln sent a message:

Tell him to remember to call upon, and confide in, our great, and good, and merciful Maker; who will not turn away from him in any extremity. He notes the fall of a sparrow, and numbers the hairs of our heads; and He will not forget the dying man who puts his trust in Him. Say to him that if we could meet now, it is doubtful whether it would not be more painful than pleasant; but that if it be his lot to go now, he will soon have a joyous [meeting] with many loved ones gone before; and where [the rest] of us, through the help of God, hope ere-long [to join] them.[24]

Seventy-three-year-old Thomas Lincoln died on January 17, 1851. He had never seen his grandchildren or his daughter-in-law, Mary. He had sent a letter saying he "craved" to see his "only child," but Lincoln said he was too busy. A trip by buggy would take three days each way, and he had court cases daily. For the same reason, he did not attend the funeral.[25]

Mary gave birth to another baby boy on April 4, 1853, and they named him Thomas after Abraham's father. But they never called him by that name. Instead, he became Tad because he was born with an unusually large head and squirmed like a tadpole. The delivery was difficult, and for the rest of her life Mary suffered from what she called, with Victorian propriety, troubles "of a womanly nature."

Still traveling the circuit at the time, Lincoln began to spend most weekends at home. The expansion of the railroads made the journey easier. Lincoln even helped with the baby-sitting—although it was an activity Mary apparently forced upon him.

A neighbor claimed that Mary compelled Lincoln "to get up and get the breakfast and then dress the children, after which she would join the family at the table, or lie in bed an hour or two longer as she might choose. . . . It was [also his duty] to wash the dishes before going to his office." Another neighbor said she made him "take care of the baby," whom "he rolled . . . up and down in [the] baby carriage." He romped with the older children and chuckled at their misbehavior.[26]

The Lincolns allowed their children considerable freedom, encouraged them to ask questions, and held lavish birthday parties for them—all in stark contrast to Lincoln's childhood. He kept a promise he made to himself when he left his father's house—that his own children would be "free, happy, and unrestrained by parental tyranny" and that "love would be the chain to bind a child to its parents."

He pulled Willie and Tad around in a little wagon, and when they were older he took them to his law office on Sundays, much to the displeasure of Lincoln's law partner William Herndon. "These children would take down the books and empty ash buckets, ink stands, papers, gold pens, and letters in a pile and then dance on the pile. Lincoln would say nothing, [being] so . . . blinded to his children's faults. Had they s—t in Lincoln's hat and rubbed it on his boots, he would have laughed and thought it smart. I have felt many a time that I wanted to wring their little necks and yet out of respect for Lincoln I kept my mouth shut."[27]

Lincoln never had the daughter he hoped for. Perhaps to fill that void, he developed a special fondness for Josie Remann, a little girl in his neighborhood. He carried her on his shoulders and took her to the circus with other children whose parents could not afford tickets.

Willie was a near replica of his father. He was bright, articulate, compassionate, and gentle-mannered. He liked to read, and he memorized railroad timetables. He solved problems the way his father did. Lincoln told a visitor: "I know every step of the process by which [he] arrived at his satisfactory solution of the question before him, as it is by just such slow methods I attain results."

Tad was like his mother—nervous, hyperactive, and affectionate. He was mentally challenged—he had trouble dressing himself and learning to read—and he had a cleft palate and a speech impediment. "Papa dear" sounded like "Pappy-day."

Robert, the oldest, was never close to his father. During his childhood Lincoln was away much of the time, and Robert's main recollection of his father was watching him load his saddlebags in preparation for going on the circuit. As he grew older he was jealous of his father's attention to Willie and Tad. "Robert is a Todd, not a Lincoln," said Herndon. "Robert is proud, aristocratic, and haughty." Lincoln had wanted to name him Joshua after his friend Joshua Speed but instead chose the name of Mary's father.[28]

To obtain the discipline unavailable at home, Robert was placed in a private school in Springfield. Even so, he failed fifteen out of sixteen entrance exams at Harvard. The Lincolns then sent him to Phillips Exeter Academy in New Hampshire for a year, where he apparently matured, excelling academically and in athletics. He was known as "a gentleman in every sense of the word, quiet in manner, with a certain dignity of his own." From there, he went to Harvard.[29]

By the early 1850s Lincoln was one of the most successful attorneys in central Illinois. It was a happy time for Mary. And he pampered her more and more.

As an attorney Lincoln was at his best when he felt his client was oppressed. "When Lincoln attacked meanness, fraud, or vice, he was powerful and merciless in his castigation," said Herndon.

No case stirred him more than that of Rebecca Thomas, an elderly crippled woman who hobbled into their law office and told her story. She was the widow of a Revolutionary War soldier, and a pension agent had withheld half of her four-hundred-dollar pension as his fee. "Can you help me get what is due to me?" she asked Lincoln. He assured her he would do his best. Lincoln went to the agent's office and demanded that the money be returned to the widow. Agent Erastus Wright refused, so Lincoln filed a lawsuit. He told Herndon, "I'm going to skin Wright and get that money back."[30]

In court the only witness Lincoln called was the widow, who told her story through her tears. In his summation to the jury, Lincoln recounted the causes of the Revolution and drew a vivid picture of the hardships of Washington's army at Valley Forge. In minute detail he described the men, barefooted, leaving bloody footprints in the snow. Then he accused the defendant of fleecing the woman of her pension. His eyes flashed as he launched into Wright. "Never," said Herndon, "did I see Lincoln so wrought up."

Before Lincoln closed, he drew an ideal picture of the plaintiff's husband, the deceased soldier, parting with his wife at the threshold of their home, and kissing their baby in the cradle, as he started for the war. "Time rolls by," he said in conclusion:

> The heroes of '76 have passed away and are encamped on the other shore. The soldier has gone to rest, and now, crippled, blind, and broken, his widow comes to you and to me, gentlemen of the jury, to right her wrongs. . . . Out here on the prairies of Illinois, many hundreds of miles away from the scenes of her childhood, she appeals to us, who enjoy the privileges achieved for us by the patriots of the Revolution, for our sympathetic aid and manly protection. All I ask is, shall we befriend her?

The jury responded by awarding his client full restitution. Half of them were in tears, while the defendant sat writhing under Lincoln's scathing attack. Lincoln's interest in the widow did not stop there, however. He also paid her hotel bill and travel expenses—and charged nothing for his services.[31]

In another case Lincoln was sitting in the Clinton, Illinois, courtroom when fifteen ladies were charged with trespassing. Objecting to a newly opened saloon, they had called upon the owner, known now only as Tanner, and requested that he cease selling liquor. When he refused, they dumped his liquor upon the ground. He filed a complaint. The ladies' attorney was less than convincing, and one of the women asked Lincoln to speak to the jury if he thought he could aid their cause. He was too gallant to refuse.

Lincoln said he would "change the order of indictment and have it read 'The State versus Mr. Whiskey' instead of 'The State versus The Ladies.'" He spoke of the ruinous effects of whiskey on society and compared their act to that of "our forefathers in casting the tea overboard and asserting their right to life, liberty, and happiness." Lincoln then accused the saloon keeper of violating the moral law—"a law for the violation of which the jury can fix no punishment."

After Lincoln had concluded, the judge, without awaiting the jury's return, dismissed the women, saying: "Ladies, go home. I will require no bond of you, and if any fine is ever wanted of you, we will let you know." The jury found them guilty, but the court fined them only two dollars. "Huzzah for the ladies," wrote the *Decatur Gazette*.[32]

After a day in court in Danville, Illinois, in 1854, Lincoln was informed that an elderly black woman who had known him in Kentucky wished to see him. Lincoln found her sick and destitute in a wretched hovel on the outskirts of town. He gave her money and also engaged a physician to provide medical attention.[33]

In the fall of 1854 Lincoln charged back into politics after Congress passed the Kansas-Nebraska Act. Voiding a section of the Missouri Compromise banning slavery from these territories, the Kansas-Nebraska Act provided for "popular sovereignty"—leaving it to the people to choose for or against slavery.

Opposing any extension of slavery, Lincoln ran for the Illinois legislature and was elected—but then he resigned to seek election to the U.S. Senate. That election was determined by legislative vote, and in a close contest Lincoln gave up on the tenth ballot and endorsed Lyman Trumbull, an antislavery Democrat. Trumbull was elected.

Meanwhile, popular sovereignty turned Kansas into a killing field as proslavers and abolitionists battled each other. In March 1855 five thousand heavily armed "Border Ruffians" from Missouri rode into Kansas, seized the polling places, voted into legislative office a slate of proslavery candidates, and imprisoned anyone who spoke against slavery.

Abolitionist John Brown was infuriated by these events. He stormed into Kansas and in May 1856 led a company of eight men toward the proslavery settlement on Pottawatomie Creek. In the middle of the night they banged on doors, seized five men at gunpoint, dismembered them with heavy artillery swords, and threw their mangled bodies into the bushes. The massacre ignited a war that lasted six months.

Amid these extraordinary events Lincoln decided to abandon the Whig Party and became the principal architect of the new Republican Party in Illinois—a party with one major goal: opposition to the spread of slavery. At the national convention in 1856 Lincoln received 110 votes for the vice presidential nomination, but the post went to William L. Dayton, a former New Jersey senator. The ticket was headed by John C. Frémont, a famous explorer and a national hero. Lincoln campaigned wholeheartedly for the Republican ticket, but Democrat James Buchanan, the former secretary of state, was elected president.

Despite his loss, Lincoln radiated a new enthusiasm for politics. No longer did he lament to anyone about his future or grieve that he had done nothing to improve his country. He was focused and moving forward boldly.

In 1856, with assistance from her father, Mary Lincoln transformed the family's Springfield cottage into a handsome two-story Greek Revival home. She had it tastefully painted Quaker brown and equipped with dark green shutters. Construction was completed while Lincoln was on the circuit. When he returned he pretended to be puzzled. "Do you know where Lincoln lives?" he asked a neighbor. "He used to live here!"

Their home was now one of Springfield's finest. It had a parlor, a large sitting room where the boys could play, a dining room, a library, and separate but connecting bedrooms for Lincoln and Mary—a fashionable arrangement that may have reflected their complex relationship. It also enabled Mary to indulge her favorite pastime—reading romantic novels in bed into the wee hours of the morning. "An air of quiet refinement pervaded the place," a visitor reported. "You would have known instantly that she who presided over [it] was a true type of American lady."[34]

Mary's behavior, however, continued to be unpredictable. When she got "the devil in her," James Gourley recalled, "Lincoln would pick up one of the children and walk off—would laugh at her, and go to his office until she calmed down." When she was feeling well, she was an excellent neighbor. Shortly after Tad's birth she even breast-fed a sick neighbor's baby along with her own.

To show off her "new" home—and perhaps to also enhance her husband's image—Mary entertained extravagantly. She hosted after-church strawberry and ice-cream parties and organized buffet suppers for as many as three hundred guests. She was a charming hostess, and her parties unquestionably helped Lincoln climb the steep passages through social classes.[35]

Circumstances brought an even better life a notch closer when the U.S. Supreme Court announced the Dred Scott decision in 1857. Confirming Northern fears, the decision proclaimed the constitutionality of slavery and guaranteed slave owners the right take their slaves into free states as well. The decision riled Lincoln and intensified his political drive.

On June 16, 1858, his efforts paid off. It was to be the single most important day in his career—the day he was nominated by the Illinois Republican Convention to run against Senator Stephen A. Douglas. Lincoln prepared his keynote speech and read a draft to a gathering of friends. All but one advised him to change it because it was "in advance of the times," but William Herndon, who had been sitting silently, sprang to his feet: "Lincoln, by God," he exclaimed, "deliver it just as it reads. If it is in advance of the times, let us lift the people to the level of this speech now, and higher hereafter. . . . It will aid you. . . . It will make you president of the United States."

A key paragraph in the speech read: "A house divided against itself cannot stand. I believe this government cannot endure permanently half slave and half free. I do not expect the Union to be dissolved. I do not expect the house to fall, but I do expect it will cease to be divided. It will become all one thing or all the other."[36]

He gave the speech, and it sparked an explosion of controversy. A few days later an associate told him it would defeat him "for all offices for all times to come. . . . I wish it was wiped out of existence. Don't you now wish so?" Lincoln frowned, raised up his spectacles, and replied: "Well, if I had to draw a pen across and erase my whole life . . . and I had but one poor gift or choice left as to what I should save from the wreck, I should choose that speech and leave it to the world un-erased!"[37]

Lincoln engaged Douglas in a series of seven debates that left an indelible impression across the nation. "The prairies are on fire," wrote a New York reporter. At every place large crowds turned out to hear "the Tall Sucker and the Little Giant"—ten thousand at Ottawa and fifteen thousand at Freeport, sites of the first two debates. The sole topic was slavery and its effect on the nation's future.

The well-dressed Douglas, who through marriage owned a Mississippi plantation with 140 slaves, repeatedly quoted Lincoln's House Divided speech and asserted that Lincoln was advocating war between the North and South. Why can't the nation exist "forever divided" on this issue? Douglas asked. He claimed the signers of the Declaration of Independence made "no reference to Negroes when they declared all men to be created equal. . . . They were speaking of white men." Injecting the female factor, Douglas thundered: "If you think that the Negro ought to be on a social equality with your wives and daughters, then support Mr. Lincoln!"

Lincoln responded by stating his opposition to racial equality and intermarriage. But he made it clear that he believed slavery was "a moral, a social, and a political wrong" that was incompatible with America's ideals of freedom.[38]

Mary stayed home and rarely saw her husband that summer and fall. Lincoln gave sixty-three speeches and covered forty-two hundred miles, usually wearing a shabby old top hat, an ill-fitting frock coat, and unpolished boots. In the election, Lincoln outpolled Douglas by 4,085 popular votes, but the final outcome lay with the Democratically controlled legislature. There Douglas had the upper hand. The final tally: Douglas, 54; Lincoln, 41. Lincoln said he felt like the Kentucky boy who stubbed his toe: "I am too big to cry about it, but it hurts too awful bad to laugh."[39]

The debates, however, propelled Lincoln into national prominence. As the state's leading Republican, he felt a huge obligation to keep the party's fragile coalition together and to plan for a Republican victory in 1860. Although "absolutely without money" he spoke to far-flung crowds throughout the Midwest, frequently traveling alone in an open buggy across the windy plains. "Never forget," he said often, "we have before us this whole matter of right or wrong."[40]

In Springfield, Mary shopped on credit and spent lavishly. The amount she paid for one dress was equivalent to two months' pay for a typical Springfield family. Fearful of robbers and storms, Mary paid a neighbor's child to sleep in a backroom or the loft of the home. At various times all of her boys slept in her bed. She also solicited male neighbors, including James Gourley, to share a bed with her and Robert. She wanted companionship and protection even though her actions were a shameful impropriety.[41]

Wherever Lincoln went, he rose in political stature. "I suppose I am not the first choice of a great many," he said, but he suspected he could become an attractive compromise figure. Senator William H. Seward of New York was the odds-on favorite, but Lincoln was touted by major newspapers as a possible vice president. "No, No," exclaimed Mary in a hard, bitter manner. "If you can't have the first place, you shall not have the second!"[42]

Lincoln received numerous invitations to speak, but none boosted his career more than the invitation to speak at New York's Cooper Union on February 27, 1860. The telegram excited him, noted his friend Ward Hill Lamon, and gave him "more heartfelt pleasure" than any other event in his life. The proposition was an opportunity to become known in a major section of the country where he had not been seen or heard before. But it was also a make-or-break moment for him politically.

He did not take Mary with him, but she did not seem to mind. She even approved that another woman—Elizabeth Dorlan Smith of Springfield, whose brother was married to one of Mary's sisters—would accompany him and packed baskets of food for the journey. Smith had planned to take her toddler to visit relatives in Philadelphia but rescheduled her journey to coincide with Lincoln's when she learned of his trip to New York. He would be her escort and help take care of the child.

In her memoir, written thirty-five years later, Smith made certain that no one suspected the traveling companions of any impropriety: "There were no arrangements in those days to accommodate the traveling public in the matter of eating and sleeping. We relied upon our lunch baskets for meals and sat up in a very crowded car all the way and obtained very little sleep." The three-day, twelve-hundred-mile trip involved five different trains and three middle-of-the-night transfers.[43]

Lincoln's enthusiasm to go east was also based in part on a desire to see Robert at Phillips Exeter Academy in New Hampshire. Not only did the visit serve as a happy reunion for father and son, but it would later prove beneficial to Robert's roommate, George C. Latham, who was from Springfield. Lincoln befriended the young man and a few years later wrote him a noteworthy letter about perseverance when he failed his entrance exams to Harvard:

I have scarcely felt greater pain in my life than on learning yesterday from Bob's letter that you had failed to enter Harvard University. And yet there is very little in it, if you will allow no feeling of discouragement to seize, and prey upon you. It is a certain truth, that you can enter, and graduate in, Harvard University; and having made the attempt, you must succeed in it. "Must" is the word.

I know not how to aid you, save in the assurance of one of mature age, and much severe experience, that you can not fail, if you resolutely determine, that you will not.

The president of the institution, can scarcely be other than a kind man; and doubtless he would grant you an interview, and point out the readiest way to remove, or overcome, the obstacles which have thwarted you.

In your temporary failure there is no evidence that you may not yet be a better scholar, and a more successful man in the great struggle of life, than many others, who have entered college more easily.

Again I say let no feeling of discouragement prey upon you, and in the end you are sure to succeed.[44]

For his Cooper Union address Lincoln devoted more time for research and preparation than he had for any other speech in his life up to that time. He even purchased a one-hundred-dollar black suit for the occasion. The audience of fifteen hundred braved the slush, snow, and mud from recent storms to see what one observer predicted would be "something weird, rough, and uncultivated" from Illinois.

After Lincoln spoke, he was proclaimed as better than New York's best. He was "the greatest man since St. Paul," an eyewitness told Noah Brooks, a *New York Tribune* writer. "His face lighted as with an inward fire. Forgetting myself, I was on my feet with the rest, yelling like a wild Indian, cheering this wonderful man." Brooks reported, "No man ever made such an impression on his first appeal to a New York audience."[45]

In a ninety-minute address unlike any he had ever delivered, Lincoln buttressed his political position on slavery with powerful statesmanlike logic and massive historical data supporting the power of the federal government to restrict the spread of slavery. While bristling with indignation over the moral outrage of slavery, he noted there was no legal basis for abolishing it where it already existed. Nevertheless, the Republican Party should work fearlessly to exclude slavery from the territories.

Rallying party members, he concluded in spine-tingling form: "Let us have faith that right makes might, and in that faith, let us, to the end, dare to do our duty as we understand it." As he finished, the audience stood, applauded thunderously, and waved hats and handkerchiefs all over the huge auditorium.

Lincoln restated his position later to a questioner from the South: "There's only one difference between us. You think slavery is right and ought to be extended. I think it is wrong and ought to be restricted. For this, neither of us has any just cause to be angry with the other."

After the Cooper Union speech Lincoln was known to the entire nation. In New England he gave eleven speeches in as many days and won support everywhere. At the Republican National Convention in Chicago, the primary objective of Lincoln's campaign manager, Judge David Davis, was to secure at least a hundred votes on the first ballot as well as commitments from other delegates for support on the second ballot. If it worked, Lincoln would appear to be gaining momentum and still others would swing to him. Davis also arranged for Illinois railroads to offer special rates so thousands of Lincoln men could come to Chicago.

Seward continued to be the favorite, and his supporters packed the hall on the day of the first ballot. Then something strange occurred. The tally sheets failed to arrive from the printer, and the delegates could not vote. The convention was adjourned until Friday. Lincoln's managers hailed the delay as an act of God. With thousands of Lincoln's supporters in Chicago, Davis's staff made bogus tickets for them and told them to come early to the convention hall, a large wooden structure known as the Wigwam.

On Friday morning Seward's confident and jubilant followers marched in the streets, complete with a brass band. When they returned to the Wigwam, there was no place for them. The hall was already packed with Lincoln's people.

A total of 233 votes was needed to win the nomination. On the first ballot, Seward had 173½, Lincoln had 102, and the other candidates trailed far behind. On the second ballot the promised votes switched to Lincoln, and except for Seward, other candidates lost strength. Seward had 184½; Lincoln had 181. On the third ballot, Seward retained his position, but nearly all other delegates flocked to Lincoln, and he had 231½, needing only 1½ votes for the nomination. Ohio then switched four votes to Lincoln, and others followed. Seward's men moved to make it unanimous. A tally official shouted: "Fire the salute! Abe Lincoln is nominated."

Lincoln was not in Chicago for the convention. So a delegate wired to Springfield: "Abe, we did it. Glory to God!" Thus a former one-term congressman who had not held office for a dozen years snatched the nomination from the clear front-runner.

Was it Providence, strategic planning, or backroom politics? Lincoln simply said it was meant to be. In Springfield the news reached him at the office of the *Illinois State Journal.* His supporters danced and sang, shouted and cheered. "Well, gentlemen," the nominee said with a twinkle in his eye, "there's a little woman at our house who is probably more interested in this dispatch than I am, and if you will excuse me, I will take it up and let her see it."[46]

On May 19 a delegation headed to Springfield with the official notification. Mary prepared a fashionable table of cakes and sandwiches, two decanters of brandy, and a bottle of champagne. As soon as Lincoln saw the table, he objected to the liquor, knowing that several members of the delegation favored temperance. An argument ensued. Mary adamantly stressed that the delegates would expect liquor; Lincoln insisted that only ice water should be served. Mary yelled and screamed, and Lincoln left the house and walked around the block. He returned just as the delegation arrived.[47]

He introduced Mary, who now radiated Southern charm. She so wowed them with her conversation and poise that the head of the delegation, George Ashmun of Massachusetts, reported: "I shall be proud, as an American citizen, when the day brings her to grace the White House."

Lincoln had three major opponents. A split in the Democratic Party resulted in the Northern wing nominating Douglas, while the Southern wing chose John C. Breckinridge of Kentucky, who was the current vice president under James Buchanan. A new National Unity Party—a reincarnation of the Whig and American parties—nominated John Bell of Tennessee. In one of the ironies of history, Mary Todd Lincoln had been courted by three of the four candidates—all except Bell. If she had been a little older she might also have had Jefferson Davis as a beau when he studied at Transylvania College in Lexington.

On election night—November 6, 1860—Lincoln joined fellow Republicans at the state capitol to hear the returns, which were relayed from the telegraph office. About two o'clock in the morning, the long-awaited news came over the wire: Lincoln had won. He hurried home to tell Mary, who had peevishly locked him out of the house. He used a spare key to let himself inside. He woke her, saying, "Mary, Mary! WE are elected!" The next day, when he told callers his wife had locked him out, she admonished him, "Shut your mouth. Never tell that again!"[48]

Tired and weary the day after the election, Lincoln stretched out on a sofa at home. Glancing into a mirror across the room—as he later told the story—he had two faces instead of one. Puzzled, he looked two more times; both times seeing two faces, one very pale. To Lincoln, it was an omen: he would be elected twice as president, he believed, but would not live through a second term.

Lincoln's election to the presidency was highly gratifying to Mary, who was—said a Lincoln friend—"an ambitious little woman." Mary now became "pleasant and talkative and entertaining." To prepare for her new role, she traveled to New York in January and incurred a huge debt while buying expensive clothes with which she hoped to impress Washington society. She concealed the staggering debt from her husband.[49]

At the end of January, after Mary returned from her New York shopping spree, Lincoln left for Farmington in Coles County to visit his seventy-three-year-old stepmother and his father's grave. As the short visit ended, Sarah Bush Johnston Lincoln was in tears. "I didn't want Abe to run for president," she recalled later. "Didn't want him elected—was afraid somehow or other that something would happen [to] him and that I should see him no more."

"No, no, Mama," he comforted her. "Trust in the Lord and all will be well. We will see each other again."[50]

Back in Springfield, Lincoln ran into an old friend from New Salem, Isaac Cogdal. A fellow Kentuckian and a former Whig, Cogdal was now a leading Republican. Feeling unusually nostalgic, Lincoln invited him to drop in at the statehouse that evening to talk over old times.

A tall, good-looking man, Cogdal had been a farmer and stonemason in New Salem before Lincoln encouraged him to study law. Recently admitted to the Illinois bar, he was destined to become a respected attorney. That evening Lincoln immediately began reminiscing about New Salem families—the Greens, Potters, Armstrongs, and Rutledges, among others. Lincoln asked about them all, and Cogdal reported what he knew.

Lincoln was clearly in a retrospective mood, and Cogdal—he later claimed—asked if it was true that Lincoln had loved and courted Ann Rutledge. "It is true—true indeed, I did," Lincoln reportedly replied without hesitating. "I have loved the name of Rutledge to this day. I have kept my mind on their movements ever since." He then discussed his reaction to Ann's death, according to Cogdal. "I ran off the track," the president-elect reportedly admitted. "It was my first. I loved the woman dearly. She was a handsome girl; would have made a good, loving wife; was natural and quite intellectual, though not highly educated. I did honestly and truly love the girl, and think often, often, of her now."[51]

ELEVEN-YEAR-OLD Grace Bedell of Westfield, New York, set in motion a transformation of Lincoln's appearance that produced a new, lasting image for the new president. "You ought to grow a beard," she wrote on October 15. "All the ladies like whiskers, and they would tease their husbands to vote for you, and then you would be president. I have got four brothers, and part of them will vote for you any way, and if you will let your whiskers grow, I will try and get the rest of them to vote for you; you would look a great deal better for your face is so thin."

He responded in his own handwriting: "My dear little Miss, Your very agreeable letter of the 15th is received. I regret the necessity of saying I have no daughters. I have three sons—one seventeen, one nine, and one seven years of age. They, with their mother, constitute my whole family. As to the whiskers, having never worn any, do you not think people would call it a piece of silly affectation if I were to begin to now? Yours very sincerely, A. Lincoln."

A month later Lincoln's chin sprouted stubble. Two days before his departure to the capital, his beard was fully grown. It gave him a more distinguished look, and be became the first president to have a beard.[52]

A CROWD of Springfield residents gathered at the Great Western Railroad Depot to see Lincoln off on February 11, 1861. It was a cold, rainy morning as the president-elect climbed the steps to his private car and paused for a final goodbye to his neighbors—people from Springfield he had seen every day for years as well as friends from the old days in New Salem. Did Ann Rutledge come into his mind as he pondered this dramatic departure from the people and places of his past?

"My friends—No one, not in my situation, can appreciate my feeling of sadness at this parting," he told the crowd. "To this place, and the kindness of these people, I owe every thing. Here I have lived a quarter of a century, and have passed from a young to an old man. Here my children have been born, and one is buried."

Despite his reference to being "old" he would observe his fifty-second birthday the following day: he was one of the youngest presidents in American history at that time, and he was a generation younger than his predecessor.

"I now leave," he continued, "not knowing when, or whether ever, I may return, with a task before me greater than that which rested upon [George] Washington. Without the assistance of that Divine Being . . . I cannot succeed. With that assistance I cannot fail. . . . Let us confidently hope that all will yet be well. To His care commending you, as I hope in your prayers you will commend me, I bid you an affectionate farewell."[53]

As the train passed through New York, it was delayed at Westfield, and Lincoln was called out by a crowd. In his remarks he noted that shortly before the election he had received a letter from a little girl in Westfield, suggesting he would be better looking if he would grow a beard. Then, stroking his face, he added, "I am following her advice." He asked if she were present, and if so, he would like to meet her. She came forward, and he looked down at her. "You see," he said, "I have let these whiskers grow for you, Grace." Then he leaned over and kissed her.[54]

As Lincoln's train headed for Washington, an assassination plot was unfolding in Baltimore. Information about a possible plot was volunteered by a woman—social reformer Dorothea Lynde Dix—who alerted railroad officials of the threat. She said friends from the South had warned her of "an extensive and organized conspiracy to prevent Lincoln's inauguration." In response, the Pinkerton Agency was hired to protect Lincoln.

Allan Pinkerton assigned agents to infiltrate radical groups. One agent, Kate Warne, was assigned to get to know the wives and daughters of known Secessionists. Intelligence she and other agents gathered enabled Pinkerton to identify the potential assassins and to establish the time and place of the ambush.[55]

Pinkerton and Warne rushed to New York City, where the presidential train had arrived, and urged the Lincoln party to alter plans and travel to Washington immediately. Despite the dangers of delay, Lincoln insisted on a scheduled stop in Philadelphia.

"I cannot go tonight," he declared. "I have promised to raise the flag over Independence Hall tomorrow morning and to visit the legislature at Harrisburg in the afternoon. Any plan that may be adopted that will enable me to fulfill these promises I will accede to, and you can inform me what is concluded upon tomorrow."[56]

At Independence Hall on February 22 he declared that all his political sentiments were drawn from the Declaration of Independence. Believing that threats of secession originated in opposition to its principles of equality, he stated fearlessly: "I would rather be assassinated on the spot than surrender those principles so dear to me."

Just two nights earlier thirty conspirators had reportedly met in Baltimore and drawn lots to determine who would kill the president-elect. Whoever drew the red ballot was committed to do the deed. But the group's leaders placed eight red ballots in the hat, rather than one. Thus there would be eight killers waiting for Lincoln in Baltimore.

Lincoln, pushed by his advisers, turned himself over to the Pinkerton Agency. Pinkerton's revised plans called for Lincoln and one companion to depart Harrisburg for Philadelphia in a special two-car train, ostensibly arranged to transport railroad officials back home. In Philadelphia, Lincoln would transfer to a sleeping car on the regular train leaving for Baltimore at 11:00 p.m. Kate Warne would reserve the rear half of the Pullman to accommodate herself and Lincoln—who was passed off as an "invalid brother." A curtain would separate them from other passengers.[57]

The strategy called for Mary Lincoln and the rest of the presidential party to follow the next day as scheduled. When Mary learned of the changes, however, she became unruly. She loudly insisted that she must accompany her husband and ignored all appeals to keep silent. Concerned for the president-elect's safety, officials finally hustled her into a locked room. One official—disgusted with her conduct—called her a "helpless fool."

With telegraph wires disabled to prevent leaks to conspirators, Lincoln left his Harrisburg hotel at 5:45 p.m. wearing an unfamiliar soft felt hat positioned low on his head. A large overcoat thrown over his shoulders concealed his long arms. He stepped into a carriage and was whisked to the special train, accompanied by his friend Ward Hill Lamon, who carried a personal arsenal with him.

Pinkerton met them in Philadelphia at 10:00 p.m. and drove them in his carriage to the railroad depot. As they approached the train, Kate Warne greeted the president-elect as if he were her brother, and they entered the sleeping car. Several disguised guards also boarded the sleeper, but it was Warne who was posted near the door to Lincoln's compartment. She carried a revolver under her cloak.[58]

Soon the train was in motion and rolled unmolested to Baltimore's Calvert Street Station, where Lincoln was to have been assassinated. At 3:30 a.m. the station was nearly deserted. Lincoln's Pullman car was hitched to a team of horses and pulled across town to the Camden Station—where it connected with the Baltimore & Ohio for the trip to the nation's capital. Waiting almost two hours in his berth, Lincoln regaled his tense, silent companions with homespun humor. Outside, a drunkard sang "Dixie." The deception worked perfectly, and Lincoln arrived in Washington around six o'clock in the morning.

ABRAHAM AND MARY UNCENSORED

No memoir of the Lincolns' private life is more sensational or more controversial than that of Mariah Vance, their black housekeeper in Springfield, Illinois, from 1850 to 1860, the ten years before his election to the presidency. Both Lincoln and Mary confided in this religious, warmhearted woman who could neither read nor write. After Lincoln's death she related her experiences to anyone who would listen. She did not profit from her recollections, and there is no indication that she tried to deceive anyone. When seventeen-year-old Adah Sutton, a secretary, heard Vance's stories, she wrote them down in shorthand over a four-year period. Her original notes and a transcribed version were eventually acquired by Lloyd Ostendorf, a noted Lincoln artist and collector. He published them in 1995 in a book titled *Lincoln's Unknown Private Life,* which he edited with Walter Oleksy, an award-winning feature writer for the *Chicago Tribune.* Some historians question the validity of the memoirs, since they cannot verify Sutton's reliability. However, Vance and Sutton were close, lifelong friends, and Vance witnessed the Lincolns' home life as no other person outside the family. The following extracts from the Ostendorf-Oleksy edition are reprinted with permission.

How Mary persuaded Lincoln to marry her after he told her he didn't love her:

"I made a vow he would yet crawl to me. I tried every approach, using all my friends. At last I cornered him where he had to reconsider me, if he was at all honorable. I cried not from shame or remorse but because men can't stand tears. His great, good heart responded in sympathy. . . . After our marriage, often I would feel I couldn't bear him another minute in my sight. I'll not repeat all the cruel things I said and did."

Mary questioned his love for her after their marriage:

"He hates me. I can see it in the sly looks he gives me. I don't think he ever loved me. He loved some common girl back in New Salem. [NOTE:

Ann Rutledge was not 'common,' but rather the daughter of a prominent resident.] One time [before our marriage] I received an anonymous letter telling me that Mr. Lincoln was and would always be in love with [this] girl in New Salem. . . . When I approached him about [it], he didn't deny it. He only asked that we not dwell on it."

Mariah responded to Mary's remarks as Mary took swigs from a bottle of paregoric:

"I don't know about that girl, but I know that all that paregoric and wine you drink is bad for you, Missy. And I knows that Mr. Lincoln has always been kind to you and given you everything you need. He don't hate you. He's plumb scared of you. You need to make yourself the kind of woman he expected you to be. You better get down on your knees and pray for the good God to root out that ole devil in you before that devil pulls you clean down to Hell."

Mariah asked Lincoln if he ever longed for earlier times:

"Yes, Mariah, I hardly believe there is a person living who hasn't wanted to be a child again. . . . I often [think of] my life in New Salem. Especially my association with a young woman some five years younger than [I am]. . . . We often talked about what was the best thing for me to start out in, as a trade or profession. . . . She encouraged me to study law. Had I not had great respect for her, for her sincere interest in me, and her intelligent judgment, I would never be where I am today. When God saw fit to take her, for a while the bottom seemed to drop out of everything. Only knowing that I wanted to do what she wished forged me ahead. I have had setbacks, but I have never doubted that I was led by her right advice and warm encouragement."

When Lincoln brought home and showed to Mary a tintype of a young girl who resembled Ann Rutledge, Mary grabbed it and headed for the stove. Lincoln lunged after her and pulled the picture from her hand. Mariah described what happened next:

"That woman plumb acted wild. Mrs. Lincoln scratched at his face [and] picked up a fork, and I believe she would of dug his eyes out with it. But Mistah Abe grabbed her hand and got the fork away. Lincoln sat Mary in a chair and looked her right smack in the eyes. 'If you try, you can stop this silly jealousy that has ruined what could be a loving disposition. But you've let yourself go unchecked until it has become an obsession. No man can go on and up shouldering such. You must make up your mind.' He started for the door. She screamed. Ran at him. Throwed her arms 'round his neck . . . drew back one hand and struck Mistah Abe with a Gawd-awful slap in the face. Then she ran to the door, locked it, and told him if he left, she would kill herself. Then we heard pounding at the door. Taddie [their son] was trying to come in. Mrs. Lincoln threw the key on the floor at Mistah Abe's feet, and when he stooped for it, she jumped on his back and pulled his hair and tried to choke him. He straightened up quick and she landed hard on the floor. He opened the door and in rushed Tad. Mistah Abe sat with his chair leaned back against the wall, with his head down and his arms wrapped around his knees."

The tintype reappeared in 1860 as the Lincolns prepared to move to Washington. As Lincoln looked long and intently at the image of the Ann Rutledge look-alike, he and Mary exchanged words:

"Have you never put her out of your life?"

"No, I haven't. But God has. Years ago. And I can't question His ways. He helps us to work out our own destiny. . . . Ann Rutledge was among those who instilled ambition in me and helped me climb. At that time, we needed each other in our lives. She was most dear to me, and her memory has been . . . a lingering part of my existence. But tonight she seems strangely far away and going out farther and farther."

"And just where do I fit in that scenario?"

"You, too, have helped me climb, and you are still helping me. Ann is a memory. You are a living reality. Let's let the past remain the past. It has played its part, and played it well, to make today for you and me. To you I now owe my devotion."

10

"Mrs. Lincoln Is Involved a in Corrupt Traffic"

$\mathcal{I}$N THE White House, Mary Todd Lincoln sought to be the president's chief adviser on appointments. She would later boast, "My husband placed great confidence in my knowledge of human nature."

Shortly after the election, Mary began accepting gifts from people hoping to influence Lincoln. One of these was Isaac Henderson, publisher of the *New York Evening Post,* who sent a diamond brooch to a Springfield jeweler to hold until Mary secured a post for him in the New York customhouse. When Lincoln objected, she lay on the floor in an hysterical fit until he finally relented. Henderson, an unsavory man, was later dismissed for accepting commissions from government contracts.[1]

While Lincoln debated cabinet appointments, Mary nagged him endlessly. She was especially severe on William H. Seward—Lincoln's main rival for the nomination and his preference for secretary of state. "He cannot be trusted," she said emphatically. "He has no principle."

"Mother, you are mistaken," Lincoln replied. "Your prejudices are so violent that you do not stop to reason. Seward is an able man, and the country as well as myself can trust him."

Mary was adamant: "It makes me mad to see you sit still and let that hypocrite twine you around his finger as if you were a skein of thread."

"It is useless to argue the question, mother," said Lincoln impatiently. "You cannot change my opinion!"

Mary's hostility toward Salmon P. Chase was equally bitter, and she urged Lincoln not to appoint him as secretary of the treasury. She claimed that "he was a selfish politician instead of a true patriot," according to Elizabeth Keckley, Mary's seamstress and confidante. Mary warned Lincoln not to trust Chase. "I do wish that you would inquire into [his] motives," she asserted.[2]

Mary apparently expressed no opinion about Lincoln's most questionable cabinet appointment, Simon Cameron, who was initially appointed as secretary of war. Even vice president–elect Hannibal Hamlin observed: "This appointment has an odor about it." Cameron had become a political boss through bribery and intimidation and had allegedly defrauded the Winnebago Indians of sixty-six thousand dollars during the Van Buren administration. Yet he was the key to delivering Pennsylvania for Lincoln. Lincoln's campaign chairman had vaguely promised Cameron a cabinet post if his delegates would vote for Lincoln after the first ballot, which they did.

Lincoln never listened to Mary about major appointments, but—according to Herndon—he gave in on lesser positions. One he refused to move on was Mary's cousin, Elizabeth Todd Grimsley. Concerned about nepotism, he turned her down for the job of postmistress of Springfield. Mary stomped her feet and screamed but to no avail.[3]

Many residents of the District of Columbia regarded Lincoln with violent animosity—an odious embodiment of the abhorred principles of abolitionism. In one instance, a proud, aristocratic South Carolina lady, a Mrs. Howard—the widow of a Northern scholar—was curious to see the man represented to her as a monster. She arranged with Seward, whom she knew, to be presented to the president-elect.

"I am a South Carolinian," she announced. Lincoln addressed her with gentlemanly courtesy. Astonished, she said, "Why, Mr. Lincoln, you look, act, and speak like a kind, good-hearted, generous man." Lincoln asked if she had expected to meet a savage. "Certainly, I did, or even something worse," she admitted. "I'm glad I've met you, and now the best way to preserve peace is for you to go to Charleston and show the people what you are and tell them you have no intention of injuring them." Lincoln thanked her for her advice, and she returned home, where she found a group of Secessionists. She told them: "I've seen him! I've seen him—the person you call a terrible monster. And I found him to be a gentleman, and I'm going to his first reception after his inauguration." They shook their heads in disbelief and left the house.[4]

At Lincoln's first reception, Mrs. Howard arrived dressed in black velvet, with two long white plumes in her black hair. She looked striking and majestic. The president recognized her immediately. "Here I am again," she said. "That South Carolinian."

"I am glad to see you," Lincoln said. "And I want to again assure you that the first objective of my heart is to preserve peace, and I wish that not only you but every son and daughter of South Carolina were here, that I might tell them so."

In his inaugural address on March 4, Lincoln indeed attempted to tell them so as he appealed to the South and held out a peaceful hand: "I have no purpose, directly or indirectly, to interfere with the institution of slavery . . . where it exists I believe I have no lawful right to do so." He ended with this passage: "I am loathe to close. We are not enemies, but friends. We must not be enemies. Though passion may have strained, it must not break our bonds of affection. The mystic chords of memory, stretching from every battlefield and patriot grave to every living heart and hearthstone all over this broad land, will yet swell the chorus of the Union, when again touched, as surely they will be, by the better angels of our nature." His consuming goal was to preserve the Union. A month later, on Friday, April 12, Confederates bombarded Fort Sumter in Charleston Harbor, sparking the Civil War.[5]

But while the country swirled in turmoil, Mary Lincoln shopped and partied for two weeks in Philadelphia and New York. She was accompanied by her cousin, Elizabeth Todd Grimsley, and William S. Wood, who supervised White House purchases. Mary, in fact, had secured Wood's appointment by locking herself in her room until Lincoln yielded. Wood supposedly rewarded Mary with a pair of fine horses, according to the *Washington Sunday Gazette*. The day after Mary returned from her shopping spree, she confronted the realities of war for the first time and responded poorly.[6]

With enemy territory just across the Potomac, Lincoln had ordered the occupation of neighboring Alexandria and Arlington Heights. Twenty-four-year-old Col. Elmer Ellsworth, a former clerk in Lincoln's Springfield law office, led one of the regiments across the river.

Ellsworth saw a huge Confederate flag atop the Marshall House and said, "I'll take care of that." He entered the building with a handful of his men. They climbed to the roof, cut down the flag, and proudly waved it over their heads. As Ellsworth came down the stairs with the flag, the Secessionist proprietor killed him with a shotgun blast—and was killed in turn by one of Ellsworth's men.

When news of Ellsworth's death reached Lincoln, he burst into tears. Ellsworth had accompanied him on his trip to Washington, and Lincoln was especially fond of the man. When Mary heard the news she collapsed and was forced to bed for two days.[7]

To command the Union forces in and around Washington, Lincoln turned to Gen. Irvin McDowell. Paris-educated, the general spoke fluent French and played Mozart sonatas with the style of a professional pianist. To protect Washington against assault from the south or west, Lincoln ordered McDowell to secure the important railroads at Manassas Junction, Virginia, about twenty-five miles from the capital. McDowell's invading army was joined by a jubilant party-minded group of Washington celebrities and their wives, many of whom brought picnic baskets in their buggies.

On July 21, 1861, the Federals forded Bull Run near Manassas and assaulted a Confederate army commanded by Gen. P. G. T. Beauregard. The Southerners fell back, and the Federals appeared to be on the verge of victory. But the tide of battle shifted, and McDowell's army was turned back in a panicky retreat.

In Washington, Seward delivered the War Department dispatch to Lincoln: "The day is lost! Save Washington and the remnants of the army!" The president said, "If hell is [not] any worse than this, it has no terror for me." But Washington wasn't attacked, and McDowell's shattered army streamed back into the capital.[8]

After Bull Run, Lincoln replaced McDowell with the confident George B. McClellan, a superb organizer of troops. McClellan was a popular choice among the people and the soldiers but not with Mary Lincoln. "He is a humbug," she told her husband. "McClellan can make plenty of excuses for himself. . . . You will have to find some man to take his place if you wish to conquer the South." She proved to be right.[9]

Needing fresh air and pampering, Mary decided to take a vacation. So she, Willie, and Tad left war-conscious Washington to spend much of August at Niagara Falls and some ocean resorts in the Northeast. As she and the children waited for a connecting train at Reading, Pennsylvania, a carload of miserably clad Confederate prisoners rolled into the station while well-dressed Federal troops passed through, heading south. On a nearby newsstand an issue of the *Reading Gazette* carried the news of the unexpected death of Senator Stephen A. Douglas, Mary's old beau and Lincoln's political opponent. Forty-eight-year-old Douglas had died on June 3 almost penniless, and the article solicited contributions for his widow and child. Mary likely never saw the newspaper, nor contemplated the significance of what was happening around her nor what had happened in this red-brick village surrounded by picturesque mountains—a village to which Newton and Matilda Strong had moved from Alton, Illinois, and where young, beautiful Matilda lay buried under the maples at Charles Evans Cemetery.

In Washington on that same August morning, Lincoln signed a proclamation declaring that "the inhabitants of the seceded states are in a state of insurrection against the United States and that all commercial intercourse between [them] and the citizens of other parts of the United States is unlawful and forbidden." A journalist wrote: "[While her husband], a lonely man, sorrowful at heart, and weighted down by mighty burdens, bearing the Nation's fate upon his shoulders, lived and toiled and suffered alone, [Mary Lincoln relaxed] at the hotels of fashionable watering places. [She] seemed chiefly intent upon pleasure, personal flattery . . . and ceaseless self-gratification."[10]

BY THE fall of 1861 McClellan was being hounded by critics who complained he had not yet launched an offensive against the Confederates. "March on to Richmond!" demanded Horace Greeley, editor of the *New York Tribune.*

In answer to these clamorings McClellan on October 21 sent part of his army across the Potomac River to Leesburg. It was a poorly planned affair, and the Federals met fierce Confederate opposition and were thrown back with heavy losses. Among the dead was another of Lincoln's longtime Illinois friends, Col. Edward D. Baker, a former senator from Oregon. When Lincoln heard the news, he wept uncontrollably. His second son, Eddie, was named after Baker. Ten-year-old Willie, who had inherited his father's literary talent, poured out his grief in a poem published in a Washington newspaper.

At the funeral, Mary shocked Washingtonians and her husband by wearing a lilac silk dress, with bonnet and gloves to match. The next day a member of her social circle visited her, and Mary greeted her by saying: "I am so glad you have come. I am just as mad as I can be. Mrs. [John J.] Crittenden has just been here to remonstrate with me for wearing my lilac suit to Colonel Baker's funeral. I wonder if the women of Washington expect me to muffle myself up in mourning for every soldier killed in this great war?"

"But Mrs. Lincoln," the woman replied, "don't you think black more suitable to wear at a funeral?"

"No, I do not," Mary said indignantly. "I want the women to mind their own business; I intend to wear what I please."[11]

That same month Mary was back on the train to New York to buy china and glassware. This time her escort was John Watt, the White House gardener. A journalist wrote: "While her sister-women scraped lint, sewed bandages, and put on nurses' caps, and gave their all to country and to death, the wife of the president spent her time in rolling to an fro between Washington and New York, intent on extravagant purchases for herself and the White House. Mrs. Lincoln seemed to have nothing to do but to shop."[12]

ADDING TO his woes, the president received an anonymous letter about "the scandal of your wife and William S. Wood," the commissioner who had traveled occasionally with Mary to Manhattan. "If he continues as commissioner, he will stab you in your most vital part," the unknown correspondent warned.

An Iowa dignitary later claimed that Mary "used to often go from the White House to the Astor House in New York to pass the night with a man [presumably Wood] who held a high government office in Washington." Lincoln spoke sharply to Mary about it. The Speaker of the House, Schuyler Colfax, called it "the war she had with Mr. Lincoln." Colfax observed that the Lincolns "scarcely spoke [to each other] for several days." Wood later resigned under fire.[13]

Mary's alleged dalliances were apparently not limited to Wood. Two White House staffers—doorkeeper Edward McManus and gardener John Watt—both reported that "Mrs. Lincoln's relations with certain men were indecently improper." There were also rumors about an "Hungarian adventurer who very nearly succeeded in eloping with Mrs. Lincoln from the White House." Mary purportedly wrote to confidant Abram Wakeman, "I have taken your excellent advice and decided not to leave my husband while he is [president]."[14]

Wakeman, an ambitious lawyer who was Lincoln's postmaster in New York City, craved the more prestigious post of port collector. He impressed Mary with his intelligence and his spiritualism, and she invited him to the White House frequently. A careful politician, he asked Lincoln's permission to "serve [Mary] in any way" when she was in New York. Soon Mary shared secrets with him.

Another confidant was known as Mr. Dennison (either William D. Dennison, postmaster general in New York in 1864 and 1865, or George D. Dennison, a naval officer in the New York customhouse). Something unsavory was going on between Dennison and Mary Lincoln, according to Sam Ward, a knowledgeable Washington insider.[15]

MARY'S MAIN project upon arriving in Washington was refurbishing the White House. It resembled a run-down hotel with broken furniture, worn carpets, and peeling wallpaper. Delighted when Congress appropriated twenty thousand dollars to be expended over four years, Mary, of course, had to go to Philadelphia and New York to acquire suitable furnishings. Spending recklessly and compulsively, she bought everything she liked, including wallpaper imported from France, crimson Wilton carpet for the Red Room, and imported Brussels velvet green carpet for the East Room. When finished she transformed the White House into a stunning mansion.

Guests at state dinners marveled at the elaborate Parisian upholstery, the French drapes and gold tassels, the Swiss lace curtains, and the expensive furniture. But when the bills came, Mary panicked. In less than a year she had spent sixty-seven hundred dollars more that the four-year appropriation. She knew Lincoln would be angry if he found out, so she launched a coverup.

As a first step she authorized the sale of used furniture and of manure from the White House stables at ten cents a wagon load. John Watt advised her to pad the household bills and to present vouchers for nonexistent purchases. Watt himself had accumulated a small fortune by stealing from the mansion.

Mary's mind went to work. She discharged the White House steward while on paper securing the job for Watt's wife and performing the duties herself and keeping the salary. Watt padded his accounts and kicked back funds to Mary to help pay her bills. He also made out fake bills for plants, pots, and services, and Mary certified them and drew the money. Included were bills for 517 loads of manure never delivered and the cost of a horse and cart for twenty-seven days to haul the manure to the White House. Newspapers reported that Mary also persuaded Watt to buy two cows and charge them to a fund to provide manure for the public lands. The Interior Department rejected the bill.[16]

Mary's dishonest financial manipulations were scandalous. In the summer of 1861 she claimed nine hundred dollars for a three-hundred-dollar dinner for a visiting French dignitary. Interior Secretary Caleb Smith rejected it after consulting with Secretary Seward, who knew the dinner's actual cost. White House gatekeeper James H. Upperman complained to Smith about Mary's "deliberate collusion" and "flagrant frauds on the public treasury." Officials subsequently informed the president that "Mrs. Lincoln is involved in ethically insensitive conduct." Lincoln hung his head and said he was convinced "her peculiar behavior is the result of partial insanity."[17]

To relieve Mary "from the anxiety under which she is suffering" and out of respect for the president, the Interior Department "measurably suppressed" the story, and Lincoln reimbursed the government from his own pocket. Nevertheless, gossip circulated throughout Washington's social circles. "I hope this calamity will be a lesson to her," Lincoln's friend David Davis said to his wife, "but I am afraid it won't." He was correct. Mary's extravagant behavior continued.

The New York World reported that Mary ordered $800 worth of china but apparently tried to hide other purchases of $1,400 by having the total bill of $2,200 applied just to the china. A $6,000 bill for silverware was paid for by a bill charged against gas fixtures, and she attempted to disguise $500 in jewelry purchases by asking a New York merchant to charge $1,000 for a $500 chandelier for the White House.[18]

Mary cornered Isaac Newton of the Interior Department and implored him to pay her personal debts that were unknown to the president. Newton had been instrumental in efforts to prevent disclosures of her illegal dealings with Watt. She thought she could wring more help out of him, but Newton had no intention of getting involved. "She sat here on this sofa and shed tears by the pint," Newton said to Lincoln's secretary John Hay in 1867. "There was one big bill for furs which gave her a heap of trouble, and she got it paid eventually by some of her friends."[19]

Still, the debt for White House furnishings had not been covered. So Mary called in Benjamin B. French, the commissioner of public buildings who kept the White House accounts. She pleaded with him: "I have sent for you to get me out of trouble. If you will do it, I will never get into such a difficulty again. I want you to see Mr. Lincoln and tell him that it is common to overrun appropriations." Weeping, she begged, "Now do go to him and try and persuade him to approve the bill. Do it for my sake, but do not let him know that you have seen me." French reluctantly agreed to see the president, sensing that he would be upset.[20]

He was right. Lincoln was furious. He stormed back at the embarrassed French: "It can never have my approval. . . . It would stink in the nostrils of the American people to have it said that the president of the United States had approved a bill over-running an appropriation of $20,000 for flub dubs for this damned old house, when the poor freezing soldiers cannot have blankets!" The president said he would pay for the overrun himself before requesting more funds.

Congress, however, rescued Mary by burying two deficiency appropriations in the White House budget the following year, and Mary rescued Watt by securing an army commission for him. Lincoln forced his reluctant cabinet to approve it after Mary slept in a separate apartment for three nights.

Watt's commission was revoked shortly afterward. He tried to blackmail the president, demanding twenty thousand dollars for three letters in which Mary evidently asked Watt "to commit forgery and perjury for purposes of defrauding the Government." Watt was warned to desist or be imprisoned. He panicked, gave up the letters, and settled for fifteen hundred dollars.[21]

Washingtonians sneered at Mary's wartime extravagance and maliciously accused her of being a Southern sympathizer. Newspapers ignored her good works, such as distributing fruit to the Union wounded—a thousand pounds of grapes in one week—and her compassion toward fugitive slaves. Instead, they publicized her excesses and her Confederate ties in Kentucky.

Lincoln was further embarrassed by information he received from William P. Wood, the superintendent of the Old Capitol Prison. He reported, "Mrs. Lincoln is involved in a corrupt traffic in trading permits, favors, and Government secrets." The superintendent described numerous shady practices. Among them, he claimed that Thomas Stackpole, a partisan Yankee Democrat, had won the confidence of Mrs. Lincoln and used her to gain trading permits, which he sold to rabid Secessionist and restaurateur John Hammack, who peddled them to others. Wood noted that the president "exhibited more feeling than I believed he possessed."[22]

Mary's mischief was almost more than Lincoln could endure. Some historians suggest that dealing with his tempestuous wife prepared him for handling the troublesome people he confronted as president. Historian Benjamin Thomas concluded that "over the slow fires of misery that he learned to keep banked and under heavy pressure deep within him, his innate qualities of patience, tolerance, forbearance, and forgiveness were tempered and refined."

Over time Mary's temper tantrums increased in frequency, and Lincoln became more distant. She flirted with other men but flew into a rage when other women were around the president. Women of all ages vied to be close to him, to hear him talk, and to be stared at by those tender gray eyes. He, in turn, wanted their opinions and found it thrilling to be acquainted with some of the most beautiful women of the time. Mary scolded him: "I do not approve of your flirtations with silly women." To others, she expressed "great terror of strong-minded women" and said she would "never allow the president to see any woman alone."[23]

AMONG THOSE on Mary's list of suspicious women was the twenty-one-year-old daughter of Lincoln's treasury secretary, the lovely and bewitching Kate Chase. The *Boston Herald* described her face as "an enchanting and dangerous study to most men, who are pretty certain to fall in love with it." The wife of Congressman Roger A. Pryor wrote of Kate:

> She was extremely beautiful. Her complexion was marvelously delicate; her fine features seeming to be cut from fine bisque, her eyes bright, soft, sweet, were of exquisite blue, and her hair a wonderful [red-gold] color like the ripe corn tassels in full sunlight. Poets sang then, and still sing, to the turn of her beautiful neck and the regal carriage of her head. She was as intellectual as she was beautiful. From her teens she was initiated into political questions, for which her genius, and her calm, thoughtful nature eminently fitted her.[24]

"Miss Kate," as Lincoln called her, loved the stir of life, from learning new games and sailing riverboats to traveling widely and dabbling in politics. Coy and ambitious, with style and brains, Kate Chase became the social hostess for her widowed father at age seventeen while he was governor of Ohio. Swept into the whirl of receptions, dinners, and balls, she mastered the art of seducing men's minds—and of steering social conversation into support for her father's causes and interests.

In Washington, when illness removed the wife of the secretary of state from the social scene, the honor of First Lady of the cabinet went to the wife or hostess of the second highest-ranking cabinet officer, the secretary of the treasury: Kate Chase. She relished this new role and entertained diplomats and celebrities in lavish get-togethers.

Prettier, slimmer, younger, and taller than Mary Lincoln, Kate was one of the most remarkable women ever known to Washington society. No one outshone her, and everything she did was done perfectly and splendidly.

But Mary Lincoln would not tolerate being upstaged. She instructed her husband not to talk to Kate Chase and other attractive women at a White House reception. Lincoln, with a mocked expression of gravity, asked: "Well, mother, who must I talk with tonight—shall it be Mrs. D?"

Mary responded: "That deceitful woman! No, you shall not listen to her flattery."

"Well, then," said Lincoln, "what do you say to Miss C? She is too young and handsome to practice deceit."

"No," said Mary. "She is in league with Mrs. D, and you shall not talk with her."

"Well, mother," said Lincoln exasperated, "I insist that I must talk with somebody. I cannot stand around like a simpleton and say nothing. If you will not tell me who I may talk with, please tell me who I may not talk with."

Mary named Mrs. D and Miss C, saying she detested both of them. "Mrs. B also will come around you," she warned. "But you need not listen to her flattery. These are the ones in particular."

"Very well, mother," said Lincoln. "Now that we have settled the question to your satisfaction, we will go downstairs."

With "stately dignity, he proffered his arm and led the way," reported Mary's seamstress, Elizabeth Keckley. Lincoln, however, continued to speak to all guests, including Kate Chase. Her sparkling conversation was a sweet diversion from the sour battlefield dispatches.[25]

At Kate Chase's wedding in November 1863 to New England's richest bachelor—former "boy" governor, now thirty-three-year-old Senator William Sprague of Rhode Island—all of Washington's elite were present, including Lincoln. Mary remained at home with a convenient chill and begged her husband to boycott the event. They argued, and her voice "penetrated the utmost end of the White House." As he left she charged after him and pulled out some of his whiskers.[26]

Sprague's wedding gift to his wife was a crown of matched pearls and diamonds costing more than fifty thousand dollars. Lincoln gave them an ivory fan. "I picked it out myself," he told Kate. "I like it. It is very beautiful," she said appreciatively. Lincoln kissed Kate on the cheek. He lingered at the reception an unusually long time for a busy president. When he returned to the White House he could not get into his bedroom. Mary had locked him out.[27]

Kate Chase Sprague's goal in life was to get her widowed father elected president so she could be White House hostess. Washington gossips claimed she had married Sprague for his money and political influence and was scheming to have her father replace Lincoln as the Republican candidate in 1864. Kate, the gossips concluded, never loved anyone except her father.

Ironically, two of the men closest to Kate—her husband and Senator Charles Sumner—both liked, and were liked by, Mary Lincoln. Yet both men were aware of the deadly dislike Kate and Mary had for each other. Such was the nature of Washington society. Mary was always suspicious of Kate's intentions and snubbed her at every chance, but Lincoln ignored Kate's political mischief and appreciated her quiet, contemplative demeanor. When Mary tried to prove to Lincoln that Kate and her father were their political enemies, he replied: "Be good to them who hate you . . . and turn their ill-will into friendship."

Mary's suspicions were valid. In February 1864 the Chase campaign issued a pamphlet charging that the failures of the Union armies were due to "the feebleness of [Lincoln's] will" and his "want of intellectual grasp." The people "have lost all confidence in his ability to suppress the rebellion and restore the Union," it stated. A second publication, known as the Pomeroy Circular, declared that Lincoln's reelection was "practically impossible" and that Chase possessed "more of the qualities needed in a president." It was copied in newspapers throughout the country.

Kate apparently was the queen bee in the nest of Chase supporters behind the strategy, but instead of producing political honey they created political turmoil leading to political suicide. The publications placed Chase in an embarrassing dilemma. He appeared to be responsible for attacking an administration he was part of and a president he was obligated by his position to support. He apologized to Lincoln by letter and denied knowledge of the Pomeroy Circular before its publication—which is plausible, although the document's author said Chase fully approved its release. Chase then offered his resignation.

Lincoln formally acknowledged the letter, promising to answer fully when time permitted. A week later Lincoln wrote that he did not "perceive occasion for a change."[28]

As support for Lincoln's reelection soared, Maj. Gen. Frank P. Blair—a Missouri congressman on leave from his army command—fired back at Chase. Blair blamed him for corruption in the Treasury Department and criticized him for the Pomeroy Circular. Blair remarked: "It is a matter of surprise that a man having the instincts of a gentleman should remain in the cabinet after the disclosure of such an intrigue against the one to whom he owes his portfolio. . . . I presume the president is well content that he should stay; for every hour that he remains sinks him deeper in the contempt of every honorable mind."

Much to Kate's displeasure, her father withdrew from the presidential contest on March 5. Chase too was miserable. He seldom spoke to Lincoln and skipped most cabinet meetings. Lincoln observed that Chase was "irritable" and "uncomfortable." As for Kate, Chase's "earnest wish" was that she should "keep entirely aloof from everything connected with politics." But that was like asking a cat to stop chasing mice. She was not about to follow her father's advice.[29]

Shortly after Lincoln was renominated in June, Chase precipitated another crisis. He attempted to fill the important position of assistant treasurer of the United States in New York City with one of his cronies. Lincoln disapproved of the selection. Chase reluctantly had the nomination withdrawn and then submitted again his own resignation, expecting the president to reject it. This time Lincoln accepted it, "having reached a point of mutual embarrassment in our official relation."

Kate, incensed by Lincoln's action, fantasized that her father should run for president as an independent candidate. He did not do so, and both father and daughter had spells of illness off and on for weeks. Senator Sprague took her on a cruise of the upper Atlantic to help her recover.

By October Chase had reversed himself and was actively supporting Lincoln's reelection. In December, after the election, Lincoln nominated him for chief justice of the U.S. Supreme Court, and Chase proudly accepted the position.

To Kate it was Lincoln's way of getting her father out of politics, and nothing could have angered her more. After her father's confirmation, Kate confronted Chase's dear friend Senator Sumner with a comment reminiscent of Julius Caesar's retort to Brutus: "You, too, Mr. Sumner! You, too, in this business of shelving Papa! But never mind! I will defeat you all." When Chief Justice Chase administered the oath of office to Lincoln at his second inaugural, Kate's emotions veered from pride in her father to intense jealousy of

Lincoln and a boiling frustration at her failure to make herself mistress of the White House.[30]

Kate and her husband continued as social leaders after the war. In 1868 she again led her father's campaign to become president. Proclaimed by Kate and his admirers as "the only man who can beat General Grant," Chase sought the Democratic nomination, but he did not come close.

Kate's marriage to Sprague soon deteriorated. He drank too much and frequently put her to shame in social functions at home, in society, and even at a state dinner during the Andrew Johnson administration. There a guest advised Sprague he should not drink any more wine. Referring to Kate, the guest said, "There are a pair of bright eyes looking at you."

"Damn them!" the excited man exclaimed as he refilled his glass.

Kate fixed her eyes steadily on her husband and said earnestly, "Yes, they can see you, and they are heartily ashamed of you."[31]

By the early 1870s Chase's energy was gone, and in May 1873 he died. With his death, Kate lost her beloved father, adviser, and hero. She turned to alcohol and carried on a scandalous affair with Senator Roscoe Conkling of New York. Sprague discovered it, and his marriage to Kate dissolved in 1882.

Kate withered as a lonely recluse and an eccentric and disappointed woman. Ironically, before marrying Sprague, Kate had been courted by Gen. James A. Garfield, who would become president in 1881. Kate could have been First Lady. But Garfield's wealth was only a tenth of Sprague's, and to her that was not enough.

ANOTHER CAPTIVATING young woman despised by Mary Lincoln was Princess Agnes Salm-Salm, the adopted, foreign-born daughter of an American diplomat. Calling herself Agnes Leclercq before her marriage, the high-spirited girl briefly pursued a career as a circus acrobat, but then she moved to Washington to meet prominent politicians.

Making it her business to know the right people, she moved from one influential circle to the next. Men loved her; women despised her daredevil spirit. The "Young Bohemienne," as she was called, cavorted with two female companions about the streets of the capital, took wild horseback rides past the White House, and visited soldiers at their campgrounds by the Potomac. Her shapely figure, wavy dark hair, and winsome smile caught the attention of Union officer Prince Felix Salm-Salm of Prussia, and he married her in August 1862. She stayed with him at military encampments and tended to the sick and wounded, even tearing up his sheets to use as bandages.

At a reception in Washington, Princess Agnes wrangled her way into a dance with Illinois Governor Richard Yates. He found her so brilliant and bewitching that he commissioned her an honorary captain. Always plotting mischief, she once bet an officer a bottle of champagne that she could place a kiss on Lincoln's lips.

According to the story, when the president was seated at a luncheon, she sauntered over to him and kissed him on the mouth. Lincoln reacted with a reserved smile. Other female guests, inspired by the princess, repeated her performance, bringing rounds of laughter from all. Fortunately for everyone in the room, Mary Lincoln was not in town.

Princess Agnes earlier had antagonized Mary at a military procession by bolting ahead of the First Lady's carriage and cutting in front of her. Mary spoke to Gen. Joseph Hooker about it and urged him to remind the princess of her manners. With no patience for pettiness, the general ordered all women out of the camp, including the First Lady.

EXCEPT FOR social functions, Lincoln seldom saw Mary. He was running a war and working late into the night. Seeking companions, she entertained male friends in her Blue Room salon.

She chose "interesting men" no matter what their pasts—men who could talk engagingly about books, politics, war, and the latest gossip. Among these men was Daniel E. Sickles, a bawdy, rambunctious adventurer who escaped conviction for murdering his wife's lover on the then novel grounds of temporary insanity.

Perhaps Mary's most notorious acquaintance was Henry Wikoff, a womanizer whose kidnapping of an American woman in Europe had landed him in jail on a charge of seduction. A flashy and cosmopolitan character, Wikoff once served as a secret agent in Paris for the British. Worming his way into the White House, he cultivated a relationship with Mary Lincoln by conversing in French. She responded by taking him on long carriage rides.

Wikoff made himself very much at home in the Executive Mansion, lounging in the conservatory, smoking on the grounds, and spending long hours cozily seated wherever he pleased. Washington society was distressed by their closeness. A reporter told his editor: "Mrs. Lincoln is making herself both a fool and a nuisance. Chevalier Wikoff is her gallant, and I have within the week seen two notes signed by him in her name sending compliments and invitations."

Lincoln's secretary John Hay called Wikoff a "branded social Pariah" and said it was disgraceful for him to be at large. Lincoln scolded Mary for her closeness to Wikoff, prompting the rogue to assure Lincoln he was just "teaching the madame a little European Court Etiquette."[32]

More trouble was brewing. Lincoln's first State of the Union message was scheduled to be read to Congress by a clerk on December 3, 1861. Someone, however, leaked the document to the *New York Herald,* which published excerpts. Other newspapers and the Congress were angry. The *Herald's* source proved to be none other than its secret Washington reporter, Henry Wikoff.

When the ever-alert *New York Tribune* accused Mary of giving Wikoff her husband's message, the House Judiciary Committee decided to investigate. The committee subpoenaed Wikoff, but he refused to disclose his source and was jailed overnight. The next morning he agreed to testify.

"Who gave you the president's message?" asked a congressman.

Without flinching, Wikoff said resolutely: "It was John Watt, the head White House gardener!" That was the same John Watt who had advised Mary on how to illegally secure funds and had been "repaid" by Mary with an army commission.

The shocked committee came dreadfully close to investigating the White House. Lincoln, deeply embarrassed, appealed to Republicans to spare him from disgrace, and the committee dropped its inquiry.

In February 1862 the New York correspondent for the *Boston Journal,* Matthew Hale Smith, brought documented information to the president about Wikoff's scandalous activities. Lincoln learned that Wikoff had been hired by certain parties in New York to plant himself in the White House and wield influence that his backers might find useful. Wikoff was to "make himself agreeable to the ladies, insinuate himself into the White House, attend levees, show that he had power to come and go, and, if possible, open a correspondence with the ladies of the Mansion." He had succeeded far beyond his backers' expectations, thanks to Mary's support and close friendship.

While Smith talked with the president, Wikoff was downstairs in the White House. "Give me those documents, and wait here until I return," demanded the incensed president as he "started out of the room with strides that showed an energy of purpose." Shortly, Lincoln returned, shook Smith's hand, and had Wikoff "driven from the Mansion that night."[33]

Another of Mary's companions was the handsome bachelor senator from Massachusetts, Charles Sumner, who once called Lincoln a dictator. A brilliant orator with a sharp tongue, Sumner believed the greatest task on earth was not only to free the slaves but to punish their former masters. Some historians have suggested that Sumner brought on the Civil War in an 1856 speech in which he cast dishonor on Senator Andrew Pickens Butler of South Carolina. Butler's enraged cousin, Congressman Preston Brooks, approached Sumner in a nearly empty Senate chamber and thrashed his head mercilessly with a cane. Sumner fell to the floor bleeding and unconscious, but Brooks continued to flail away until the cane broke. Plagued by severe wounds and posttraumatic shock, Sumner was absent from the Senate for three years while undergoing painful cures. Nerve damage from the caning left a perpetual smile on his face, but no one knew what it meant since Sumner had no sense of humor.

Sumner escorted Mary to the opera or the theater when Lincoln was unable or unwilling to go. The Lincolns had different theatrical tastes and often went to the theater with other companions. He preferred Shakespeare; she preferred Italian operas and German operettas. His musical tastes were simple and uncultivated, with a preference for old airs, songs, and ballads. He liked best the plaintive Scottish songs—the ones Ann Rutledge had often sung for him—"Annie Laurie," "Mary of Argyle," and "Auld Robin Gray." Newspaper correspondent Noah Brooks wrote:

> I remember that, one night at the White House, when a few ladies were with the family, singing at the piano-forte, he asked for a little song in which the writer describes his sensations when revisiting the scenes of his boyhood, dwelling mournfully on the vanished joys and the delightful associations of forty years ago. . . . There was a certain melancholy and half-morbid strain in that song which struck a responsive chord in his heart. The lines sunk into his memory, and I remember that he quoted them, as if to himself, long afterward.

Perhaps Lincoln was reflecting on his first true love, and as he repeated the lines in the song, tears came to his eyes.[34]

LINCOLN BROUGHT to the White House its first guest artists. His choices suggested a partiality for young women: an American Indian singer named Larooqua, known as the "aboriginal Jenny Lind"; Teresa Carreno, the temperamental nine-year-old Venezuelan piano prodigy; and a beautiful twenty-year-old opera star, Spanish-born Adelina Patti, who was destined to become the world's most celebrated soprano and the most highly paid performer of her day. Patti, singing to the Lincolns after tea, had everyone in tears with "The Last Rose of Summer." When informed on one of her American tours that she made more money in one night than did the president in one year, she suggested, "Well, let him sing!"[35]

AMONG WILLIE and Tad's favorite playmates were Bud and Holly Taft, children of the chief examiner of the federal patent office. In 1861 their older sister, sixteen-year-old Julia, often accompanied them to the White House to supervise their behavior. In Julia's memoir, titled *Tad Lincoln's Father,* she recalled the president telling stories to the children as they "perched precariously" on his knees and on the arms and back of his big chair. He held their attention with "tales of hunters and settlers attacked by Indians."

At the end of one story of frontiersmen chased by Indians, Lincoln drawled, "They galloped and galloped, with the redskins close behind."

"But they got away, Pa, they got away," interrupted Tad.

"Oh, yes, they got away." And then Lincoln stood and said, "Now I must get away."

Once Julia heard "a terrible racket" in another room, and opening the door she beheld the president lying on the floor, grinning and enjoying himself, while the four boys were trying to hold him down. They called for Julia to help.

"Come quick and sit on his stomach," Tad yelled.

But Julia would not do that. She left the room and closed the door. "It struck me too much like laying profane hands on the Lord's anointed," she wrote in her memoir.

Julia remembered going into that same sitting room one morning to look for the boys. She found Lincoln there in the big chair with an old worn Bible on his lap. She approached him, and in "an absent-minded sort of way" he clasped her hand and rested it on his knee as he stared out the window. Looking in the same direction she could not see anything but the tops of trees. Julia remained in that position for what seemed a long time. Her arm ached, and she grew restless.

Finally, Lincoln turned to her and appeared startled: "Why, Julia, have I been holding you here all this time?"

"Yes, you have, Mr. President," she responded.

He released her hand, and she went off to find the boys.

Julia was much enamored by Kate Chase's beau William Sprague. Mary Lincoln perhaps saw an opportunity to make Kate jealous or angry and had the gardener make up a special bouquet for Julia to deliver to Governor Sprague with her compliments.

Setting off for Sprague's office and rehearsing what she was going to say to him, Julia encountered Kate. Always inquisitive, Kate asked where she was taking the flowers, and Julia replied honestly that Mrs. Lincoln gave them to her to take to Governor Sprague. Kate grabbed the bouquet from Julia and said she would hand them to the governor herself. Julia went back to Mrs. Lincoln in wrath and tears.[36]

ELEVEN-YEAR-OLD Willie, the idolized, model son, came down with a severe cold and fever in early February, just a few days before a scheduled White House reception on February 5, 1862. The physician saw no cause for alarm and advised the Lincolns to proceed with the party. Determined to make the reception memorable, Mary hired one of the nation's most expensive caterers for an elaborate midnight buffet with mounds of turkey, duck, ham, terrapin, and pheasant flanking sugary models of the Ship of State, Fort Sumter, and Fort Pickens.

The Lincolns received their five hundred guests in the East Room while the Marine Band played. The music included a sprightly new piece, "The Mary Lincoln Polka," written for the event.

Mary's sartorial taste was for dresses shorter at the top and longer at the train than was customary at the time. For this special evening she wore a white satin dress decorated with hundreds of small black flowers. It exposed a remarkably low décolletage and had a very long train. As she swept through the room, Lincoln remarked to her: "Whew! Our cat has a long tail tonight." She ignored him. Lincoln then glanced at her bare arms and neck, and remarked: "If some of that tail was nearer the head, it would be in better style."

An Oregon senator, offended by the First Lady's revealing gown, told his wife that Mary "had her bosom on exhibition and a flower pot on her head." He added: "I can't help regretting that she had degenerated from the industrious and unpretending woman she was in the days when she used to cook Old Abe's dinner and milk the cows with her own hands. Now her only ambition seems to be to exhibit her own milking apparatus to the public gaze. I regret she couldn't have brought something like Republican simplicity to the White House."

Mary, however, was proud of her elegant neck and bust and unconcerned that her revealing clothes greatly grieved the president. Regardless, the party was a tremendous success. Dinner was served until three in the morning, and most guests did not leave until daybreak. The *Washington Evening-Star* called it "the most superb affair of its kind ever seen here."[37]

Upstairs, Willie ran a high fever, and both parents spent time with him. In the ensuing days nine-year-old Tad also became ill, and Willie grew weaker, gasping for breath and finally becoming delirious. It was probably typhoid fever, caused by White House water piped in directly from the sewage-infested Potomac River. On February 20 Willie died—perhaps from the same illness that had taken Ann Rutledge in 1835.

In a voice choked with emotion, Lincoln told his personal secretary: "My boy is gone—he is actually gone!" Then he burst into tears. A nurse from Massachusetts was among those who attended Willie during his illness. To her, the president said: "This is the hardest trial of my life. Why is it? Why is it?"

The nurse, who had lost her husband and two children, said she saw the hand of God in her tribulations, and she loved Him much more than she ever had.

"How is that?" asked Lincoln.

"Simply by trusting in God," she said, "and feeling that He does all things well."

"Did you submit fully after your first loss?" he asked.

"No, not wholly," she responded. "But as blow came upon blow, and all were taken, I could and did submit and then was very happy."

"I am glad to hear you say that," Lincoln said. "It is comforting to me. Your experience will help me to bear my affliction. I will try to go to God with my sorrows." Then he spoke of his mother: "I remember her prayers, and they have always followed me. They have clung to me all my life."[38]

Lincoln's growing belief in the sovereignty of God helped to cushion his sorrow. He believed that the Almighty controlled everyone's destiny and had, for His own reasons, taken Willie. More than ever, Lincoln saw himself as "an instrument of Providence" for God's own purposes. As he talked with friends, he quoted from *Hamlet* as he had in New Salem twenty-seven years earlier: "There's a divinity that shapes our ends, Rough-hew them how we will."

Mary Lincoln, however, suffered a nervous breakdown after Willie's death. She was so distraught she confined herself to her bed for three weeks and was unable to attend the funeral or to look after Tad, who was steadily improving. She screamed and moaned and acted as if she had lost all control.

After one such attack Lincoln took her by the arm, led her to a window, and pointed toward an asylum: "Mother, do you see that large white building on the hill yonder? Try and control your grief, or it will drive you mad, and we may have to send you there."

When she finally emerged from her room, she wore layers of black veils and crepes for weeks and suspended social functions for nearly a year. She spoke of seeing Willie's ghost: "He lives! He comes to me every night and stands at the foot of my bed with the same sweet, adorable smile. You cannot dream of the comfort this gives me." But Mary never again entered the room where Willie died or the Green Room where he was embalmed.[39]

The president turned to Senator Sumner and asked him to spend more time with the First Lady—to discuss issues of the day and escort her to the theater. In response, Mary dressed up and sat for hours in the Blue Room to receive his calls. They wrote each other notes in French, and she sent Sumner bouquets from the White House conservatory. Sumner made her happy, and when she was happy, Lincoln was less troubled than he otherwise would have been.

WHILE LINCOLN occasionally rebuked his wife, Mary seemed to be constantly griping about her husband's manners, even at official White House functions. When the president used official cutlery to feed a cat on a chair next to him at a dinner party, Mary asked a guest, "Don't you think it's shameful for Mr. Lincoln to feed Tabby with a gold fork?" Before he could answer, the president replied: "If the gold fork was good enough for Buchanan I think it is good enough for Tabby." He fed the cat throughout the dinner.

Working late in his office at the White House one night, Lincoln was resolving pressing business when the butler announced that dinner was ready. Lincoln ignored him. Then Mary entered the office "and in her emphatic tones of command, so characteristic of her when she was displeased," demanded that Lincoln join her for dinner. He calmly walked with her out of the room then quickly reentered and closed and locked the door before she could follow him. He then resumed his meeting.

Mary complained often that Lincoln did not doff his hat properly. She asked White House guard Ward Hill Lamon and Secretary Seward to instruct him how to do so. Despite their efforts, he never learned to do it right.[40]

One day Francis B. Carpenter, a portrait painter residing in the guest quarters next to the master bedroom, overheard a conversation between the Lincolns.

"No, Mr. Lincoln, you shan't have them!"

"Now, Mother, you know I must have them!"

"No, you can't have them until you promise me . . ." (The painter could not hear her demand.)

"But Mother, you know that I need to . . ."

"You need to be taught a lesson! Promise me what I asked for, or I won't let go of them."

"Mother, come now! Be reasonable. Look at the clock. I'm already late; let me have them—please! How do you reckon I can go to a cabinet meeting—without my pants!"[41]

They apparently compromised, and the president hurried to the cabinet meeting where newly appointed Secretary of War Edwin M. Stanton had news about the campaign in the West. Gen. Ulysses S. Grant had captured thirteen thousand Confederates at Forts Henry and Donelson and gained control of the Tennessee and Cumberland Rivers.

"Finally," rejoiced Lincoln, "we have a commander who gets things done!"

Late in the spring of 1862 Federal troops drove Confederates from Kentucky, most of Tennessee, and northern Arkansas, and took six thousand prisoners at Island Number 10 in the Mississippi River. The battle of Shiloh in Tennessee was costly for both sides, with twenty-four thousand casualties—the greatest losses in American history to that time. The war in the East had begun with a demoralizing Northern defeat at Bull Run, but Union successes in the war's western theater gave Lincoln reason for hope.

11

"Her Letter . . . Had Been Carefully Treasured by Him"

$\mathcal{F}$ROWNING AND downcast, the president wandered into a White House room where Mary was being fitted for a dress by her personal seamstress, Elizabeth "Lizzie" Keckley, a former slave who had purchased her freedom. Mary asked if Lincoln had any news from the war. "Yes, plenty of news," he replied, "but no good news. It is dark, dark everywhere."[1]

George B. McClellan's Army of the Potomac had driven up the Virginia Peninsula toward Richmond, but when the Federals were within sight of the church spires of the Confederate capital, the huge army had been ingloriously repulsed by Rebel forces under a new commander: Robert E. Lee. The Confederates then followed up on this victory on the peninsula by decisively defeating another Union army on an old battlefield, which was the battle of Second Manassas in August 1862.

Apparently dismayed by the course of the war, Lincoln picked up a small Bible and soon was absorbed in his reading. Fifteen minutes later he was more cheerful and left the room, leaving the open Bible on the table. Keckley looked at the Bible and discovered he had been reading in the book of Job. She noted the passage: "Gird up thy loins now like a man: I will demand of thee, and declare thou unto me."

Mary, disturbed by the war news, left Washington in July for New York, ostensibly to raise money for army hospitals and to get Tad out of a city ridden with smallpox and malaria. Keckley joined her a few days later. New

York was a major center of the spiritualist movement, which had become increasingly popular as Northerners sought to reach sons and husbands killed in the war. Mary spent much of her time in New York in darkened parlors trying to communicate with Willie. Lincoln, however, appeared to have no interest in spiritualism.

The president fell into a deep depression as the war appeared to go against the North in 1862. In his office, beneath the globe of a gas lamp, Lincoln wrote an informal memorandum to himself. It echoed his personal philosophy: "I am almost ready to say . . . that God wills this contest, and wills that it shall not end yet. [God could] have either saved or destroyed the Union without a human contest . . . and having begun He could give the final victory to either side any day. Yet the contest proceeds. In the present civil war it is quite possible that God's purpose is something different from the purpose of either party."[2]

A delegation of Quakers—three women and three men—visited the president on the morning of Friday, June 20, 1862, and urged a proclamation to emancipate the slaves. All six were abolitionists and supporters of the Underground Railroad that offered temporary shelter for fugitive slaves on their journey from slavery to freedom. Lincoln agreed that slavery was wrong, but he said he differed with them in regard to the ways and means of its removal. A decree of emancipation would not be effective, he said, because it could not be enforced.

"True, Mr. President," said Oliver Johnson, one of the delegates. "But we are solemnly convinced that the abolition of slavery is indispensable to your success."

Another delegate then expressed an earnest desire that Lincoln might "under Divine guidance, be led to free the slaves and thus save the nation from destruction."

Lincoln assured them he was "deeply sensible of his need of Divine assistance" in the troubles he faced. He was willing, he said, to be an instrument in God's hands for accomplishing a great work, but "perhaps . . . God's way of accomplishing the end [of slavery] . . . may be different from theirs." That afternoon, however, Lincoln signed a bill freeing slaves in the territories.[3]

Robert E. Lee's army, meanwhile, had invaded Maryland. With a major confrontation imminent, Lincoln told his cabinet: "I made a vow, a covenant, that if God gave us the victory in the approaching battle, I would consider it an indication of Divine will, and that it was my duty to move forward in the cause of emancipation."[4]

The opposing armies clashed for fourteen hours on Wednesday, September 17, 1862, along the banks of Antietam Creek near Sharpsburg, Maryland. It was the bloodiest day in American history: 4,800 dead and 18,500 wounded, of whom 3,000 more died. The South called it a stalemate, but McClellan had thwarted Lee's invasion. If McClellan had been daring, he could have smashed Lee's army and ended the war. Overly cautious again, he allowed Lee to retreat to Virginia without pursuit—a mistake that led Lincoln to remove the general after the fall elections.

Regardless, Lincoln viewed Antietam as a victory and perhaps as the omen he sought. He drafted an Emancipation Proclamation, which was scheduled to go into effect on January 1, 1863. It irrevocably notified the world that the war was being fought not just to preserve the Union but to put an end to slavery. It also secured support for the war from abolitionists and black leaders. It opened the army and navy to black volunteers. And it enabled Union armies to free thousands of slaves whenever they occupied Southern territory.[5]

As Lincoln grappled with these momentous wartime issues, no one exerted a more positive female impact on him than did Eliza Gurney, the well-to-do, attractive Quaker widow of a British banker. In 1862 she felt driven by God to meet with Lincoln immediately, she later reported. To fulfill this compulsion, Gurney drafted three close friends for the journey to Washington. Their Sunday morning appointment had been arranged by friend Isaac Newton, the commissioner of agriculture.[6]

A driving rainstorm pelted Washington that morning. Lincoln had risen early after a sleepless night and worked for two hours before breakfast—an egg and a cup of coffee. He was back at his desk when the Gurney delegation arrived around ten o'clock.

"Deep thoughtfulness and intense anxiety seemed to mark his countenance," one of the visitors later remarked. Lincoln had just returned from a visit to the Antietam battlefield, and he was troubled by what he saw. McClellan's overcautiousness had exhausted the president's patience and was playing havoc in the upcoming congressional elections. Lincoln feared a severe rebuff at the polls—one that would materialize as Democrats capitalized on what Lincoln called "the ill success of the war."

"Lincoln's introverted look and his half-staggering gait," one woman observed, "were like those of a man walking in sleep." And his face "revealed the ravages which care, anxiety, and overwork had wrought."[7]

Drawing her chair next to the president, Gurney emphasized that they came "in the love of the gospel of our Lord and Savior Jesus Christ" to express "the deep sympathy we feel for you in your arduous duties." Speaking softly and with much compassion, she said, "Earnestly have I desired that . . . whatever the trials and perplexities you may have to pass through, the peace of God, which passeth all understanding, will [fill] your heart and mind."

As she spoke, the group noted that Lincoln's anxieties appeared to vanish. He listened intently. She said she "rejoiced in the noble effort" he had made to "loose the bands of wickedness [and] to let the oppressed go free. I assuredly believe that for this magnanimous deed the children yet unborn will rise up and call you blessed in the name of the Lord. . . . May our Father in heaven guide thee . . . and bestow upon thee a double portion of [His] wisdom." After speaking for about fifteen minutes, she knelt in prayer "for her country and for the president."[8]

It was a touching scene. The others stood in reverential awe, and the president "appeared bowed in heart under the weight of his deep responsibilities." Apparently the experience deeply moved Lincoln: tears ran down his cheeks. After a pause, he responded:

> I am glad of this interview. As an humble instrument in the hands of my heavenly Father, I have desired that all my words and actions may be in accordance with His will; but if after endeavoring to do my best with the light which He affords me, I find my efforts fail, then I must believe that, for some purpose unknown to me, He wills it otherwise. If I had had my way, this war would never have been; but, nevertheless, it came. If I had had my way, the war would have ended before this; but, nevertheless, it continues. We must conclude that He permits it for some wise purpose, though we may not be able to comprehend it; for we cannot but believe that He who made the world still governs it.

It was a theme Lincoln would use in his second inaugural address. As the delegation prepared to leave, the president took Gurney's hand. He held it for a few moments in silence and then said resolutely: "I repeat that I am glad of this interview."[9]

A year later the president asked Commissioner Newton to entreat Eliza Gurney to write to him as he felt the need of her spiritual help and rein-

forcement. She wrote immediately. Dated August 18, 1863, it was the first
letter in a remarkable exchange.

Addressing him as "Esteemed Friend," she expressed thanks for his
"praiseworthy and successful attempts . . . to let the oppressed go free" and
quoted Scripture: "May the Lord hear thee in this day of trouble, the name
of the God of Jacob defend thee, send thee help from His sanctuary, and
strengthen thee." She commended his "excellent proclamation appointing a
day of thanksgiving" and his desire "that the whole nation be led through
paths of repentance and submission to the Divine Will back to the perfect
enjoyment of union and fraternal peace."[10]

In the following year, on September 4, Lincoln responded in a beautiful
and revelatory letter:

> MY ESTEEMED FRIEND,—I have not forgotten, probably never shall forget,
> the very impressive occasion when yourself and friends visited me on a Sab-
> bath forenoon two years ago. Nor has your kind letter . . . ever been forgot-
> ten. In all it has been your purpose to strengthen my reliance on God. I am
> much indebted to the good Christian people of the country for their con-
> stant prayers and consolations, and to no one of them more than to yourself.
> The purposes of the Almighty are perfect, and must prevail, though we
> erring mortals may fail to accurately perceive them in advance. We hoped for
> a happy termination of this terrible war long before this; but God knows
> best, and has ruled otherwise. We shall yet acknowledge His wisdom and
> our own error therein. Meanwhile we must work earnestly in the best light
> He gives us, trusting that so working still conduces to the great ends He or-
> dains. Surely He intends some great good to follow this mighty convulsion,
> which no mortal could make, and no mortal could stay.

He signed it, "Your sincere friend, A. Lincoln."

Gurney's response asked that God continue to sustain and strengthen
him and declared that nearly all Friends supported his reelection, believing
that he is "conscientiously endeavoring, according to his own convictions
of right, . . . to discharge the solemn duties of his high and responsible office, 'not with eye-service [or] as men-pleasers, but in singleness of heart,
fearing God.'"[11]

Seventeen years after Lincoln's assassination, Eliza Gurney's devoted
friend, Joseph Bevan Braithwaite, wrote in London's *Annual Monitor* that she

"had the mournful satisfaction of learning that her [first] letter to the president . . . had been carefully treasured by him, and was in his pocket when the fatal shot reached him."

Braithwaite was in a position to know. He had written her late husband's biography at her request and corresponded with her regularly from England. When he arrived in America in August 1865—four months after the assassination—he went directly from his boat to her home. Eliza Gurney was not a braggart or publicity seeker, and it would have been uncharacteristic of her to have promoted stories about the incident. Braithwaite's account of it was published a year after Eliza Gurney's death as part of her obituary in a Quaker yearbook. It was his way of putting it on the record although his documentation was never released. Gurney's daughter repeated the story of the letter in Lincoln's pocket in magazine articles that appeared in 1910 and 1926.[12]

Other Quakers also visited Lincoln for prayer and spiritual communion. He expressed his appreciation in a letter to two of them—Isaac and Sarah Harvey of Ohio—saying tenderly: "May the Lord comfort them as they have sustained me."

Lincoln sympathized with the Quakers, and he stretched his administrative powers to provide relief for their conscientious convictions. In early 1864 a clause was added to the enrollment bill declaring Friends to be noncombatants. It assigned all drafted Friends to hospital service or work among freedmen. It further provided for the exemption of Friends from military service on the payment of three hundred dollars into a fund for the relief of sick and wounded.

ALMOST EVERY evening Lincoln walked from the White House to the War Department to read the latest dispatches. He often found more bad news than good.

Fall and Winter 1862: Western theater—The North slowly tightened a noose around the Confederacy with five victories, including the important railroad junction at Corinth, Mississippi.

December 13, 1862: Against Lincoln's advice, Gen. Ambrose E. Burnside (McClellan's replacement) marched to Fredericksburg and suffered the worst defeat in the history of the American army up to that time—12,653 dead, wounded, or missing.

January 2, 1863: At Murfreesboro, Tennessee, both sides lost a third of their men in a three-day battle from December 31 to January 2. On the cold night before fighting started, only a few yards separated the opposing armies. Huddled around campfires the soldiers sang together to pass the time. As crickets chirped and men envisioned pain and death, they sang "Home, Sweet Home."[13]

May 6, 1863: At Chancellorsville "Fighting Joe" Hooker (Burnside's replacement) acted like "Chicken Joe" and halted his ingenious advance in three directions against Lee's encampment. Lee then attacked on two fronts, and Hooker retreated after losing seventeen thousand troops.

After Fredericksburg, Lincoln remarked to Senator Orville H. Browning, "We are on the brink of destruction. It appears to me the Almighty is against us, and I can hardly see a ray of hope." After Chancellorsville, the president appeared broken, dispirited, and ghostlike. He clasped his hands behind his back and paced up and down the room, exclaiming, "My God! My God! What will the country say! What will the country say!"[14]

It was usually near midnight when Lincoln settled down in the White House living quarters. "I consider myself fortunate if at eleven o'clock . . . my tired and weary husband is resting in the lounge to receive me—to chat over the occurrences of the day," Mary lamented.

The president, however, received little emotional support from his wife. Still grieving for Willie, she dressed in black, consorted with spiritualists, and held at least eight seances in the White House. She also traveled to Boston, where thousands of spiritualists were active. Although distraught and wallowing in self-pity, Mary remained concerned about her husband's health and poor eating habits but troubled him by stating her views publicly through letters and conversations.

From 1863 until his death, the Lincolns seem to have drifted apart. She avoided him out of fear he might raise "forbidden subjects" such as her debts and extravagance. He was afraid to confide in her because he could not trust her eccentric judgment and did not want to disturb her fragile mental health.

For a cultured woman brought up around successful politicians, she was strangely naive. She even chose as a close friend the wife of Judge James W. White, who led a petition drive to oust Seward from Lincoln's cabinet. Under such circumstances, Lincoln was not about to share sensitive information with his wife.

Lizzie Keckley wrote in her memoir: "When in one of her wayward, impulsive moods, Mrs. Lincoln was apt to say and do things that wounded him deeply. She often wounded him in unguarded moments."

For the first time Mary became critical of him around other people and called an 1864 impromptu address "the worst speech I ever listened to in my life."

Caught off-guard by the crowd's insistence that he speak while at a benefit for the Christian Commission, a wartime charity, the president paid tribute to women active in war relief. Mary, perhaps in her own harsh way, tried to goad him to do better. She chided him: "How any man could deliver such remarks to an audience is more than I can understand. I wanted the earth to sink and let me go through." He did not reply.[15]

Robert Lincoln was at Harvard College much of the year, but even when he returned to the White House during holidays, he did not provide much companionship for his father. Their conversations were stiff and awkward.

Lincoln's best support came from his private secretaries, John G. Nicolay and John Hay. They lived in the White House, and Lincoln dropped in on them at night to chat and review the day's news. Working side-by-side with them for long hours, Lincoln came to trust them with secrets of state. Hay was an especially intimate friend and was closer to Lincoln than was any other man during the war years.[16]

Occasionally, when Mary was out of town, Hay accompanied Lincoln to the theater. Hay, whose college roommate called him "a great favorite with the ladies," said it was a relaxing treat to watch "those Southern girls with their well-rounded forms, lustrous hair, and sparkling voices."[17]

Nicolay and Hay often clashed with Mary, whom Hay called "The Hellcat" or "The Madam." Their sharp conflicts were ostensibly over White House management but may have stemmed from jealousy over access to the president.

12

"The Best Abused Man of Our Nation"

$\mathcal{L}$INCOLN HAD endorsed women's suffrage during his reelection campaign to the Illinois legislature in 1836. It pained him that women in America had almost no rights and few opportunities—including the right to vote. Wanting "to do right . . . in all cases with women," as he had stated years earlier, he startled the capital city by endorsing the employment of women in Federal offices, not just as temporary "government girls," but as a permanent part of the Washington scene. U.S. Treasurer Francis Spinner appointed the first female staffers, defended them against critics, and commended them for their efficiency. With Lincoln's backing, the post office continued to appoint postmistresses, especially when soldiers' widows had "claims and qualifications" equal to male applicants. When a man and woman applied for the postal position in Rockford, Illinois, Lincoln supported the woman because she was a war widow and had the "better right" to the job.

Despite Lincoln's progressive views, he was tormented by militant women and others who boldly demanded favors, privileges, or immunities and protested alleged injustices. Generally, his manner toward them was kind and courteous, but there were exceptions. Lincoln lost his composure with Jessie Frémont, the wife of Gen. John C. Frémont. Lincoln had disagreed with the general on several issues during the general's command in Missouri. In response, Frémont sent his politically powerful wife to Washington to present his case to the president. In a long discourse she forcefully defended her husband. Lincoln finally interrupted: "You are quite a female politician." She left in anger, prompting Lincoln to write a letter to her explaining he did not question her husband's "honor or integrity."[1]

Anna Elizabeth Dickinson, an outspoken Quaker abolitionist, denounced Lincoln in 1862 as "an ass." Only twenty years old at the time, Dickinson had been writing and speaking about abolition for six years and was impatient with Lincoln's reluctance to free the slaves. Young, female, and a skilled orator, she was a popular novelty in the North. In 1863 she was invited by the Republican Party to tour on behalf of its candidates. In New York an audience of five thousand hailed her as the Joan of Arc of the abolition cause. By then she was calling Lincoln "the wisest scoundrel in the country."[2]

Her shining moment came on January 16, 1864, when she addressed the House of Representatives on behalf of the Freedmen's Aid Society. Following a highly complimentary introduction by Vice President Hamlin, she launched a lowly, uncomplimentary two-hour tirade against Lincoln, who was seated directly in front of her. Then, at the end of her speech, she reversed herself and endorsed his reelection, confusing everyone.

Visiting the president at the Executive Mansion, she urged him to do more to enforce the Emancipation Proclamation and called his reconstruction policy in Louisiana "all wrong, as radically bad as can be." He thanked her for her concerns but ended the visit by saying, "If the Radicals want me to lead, let them get out of the way and let me lead." Indignant, she stormed out of the White House.[3]

Another Anna—Anna Ella Carroll, the militant daughter of a former Maryland governor—wrote eloquent and persuasive pamphlets that supported Lincoln's policies and helped keep Maryland in the Union. Had Maryland seceded, the national capital would have been in great danger. "I am writing to aid my country," Carroll said, and no woman surpassed her as a political pamphleteer.

In one of her pamphlets, Carroll defended Lincoln's controversial assumption of broad war powers. Under these powers, Lincoln usurped what had been a congressional responsibility and suspended the writ of habeas corpus, enabling Northern military leaders to arrest anyone thought to be aiding the Confederacy—including Secessionist legislators in Maryland.

For her effective but unsolicited public relations work, Carroll demanded fifty thousand dollars. It was twice Lincoln's annual salary, and he called it "the most outrageous demand ever made to any government upon earth." While rejecting her claim as exorbitant, he paid her "a very handsome compliment" in his cabinet meeting of April 14, 1862, citing her important "usefulness to the country." The following month he allegedly told several congressmen she would "stand a good deal taller" than her father, the former governor, when "the history of this war is written."[4]

Carroll's contributions as a military strategist are not as well defined and continue to be debated. But her devotees assert she did, indeed, frame plans that led to early Union victories and that her amazing accomplishments were concealed because she was a woman. In 1870—five years after the end of the war—she claimed she originated the plan adopted by Grant in his successful Tennessee River campaign that contributed to the Confederacy's downfall. Petitioning Congress in 1870 for payment of $250,000 for the plan, she alleged that the War Department presented her proposal to Lincoln and secured his endorsement.

Her demand was not met, even though Benjamin Wade, an abolitionist senator from Ohio, believed she had proposed "some of the most successful expeditions of the war," among them "the expedition up the Tennessee River." Illinois Senator Orville H. Browning, a close friend of Lincoln, wrote that her "suggestions [for] important military movements were among the meritorious services [Lincoln and Stanton] recognized as entitled to remuneration."[5]

WANTING TO be accessible to all classes of citizens, Lincoln opened his office twice a week for those who might wish to speak with him. He was usually clad in a black broadcloth suit and neat cloth slippers and seated in an armchair beside a cloth-covered table. Each visitor was allotted a few minutes, and the president listened and decided each case.

Southern women were frequently among the petitioners, and Lincoln was sometimes brutally frank with them. To a Mississippi widow who asked for freedmen to run her farm, Lincoln replied: "I'd rather take a rope and hang myself than to do what you ask. There are a great many poor women who have never had any property who are suffering as much as you are. Your condition is a necessary consequence of the rebellion." To a Baltimore woman who wanted a parole for her Confederate son, Lincoln said: "I can do nothing for your boy." To a couple who wanted a pardon for a convicted spy, he said sternly: "He was a spy, he has been a spy, he ought to have been hanged as a spy. . . . You ought to bless your stars that he got off with a whole neck; and if you do not want to see him hanged as high as Haman, do not come to me again."[6]

Lincoln warmly welcomed antislavery crusader Harriet Beecher Stowe in November 1862. According to family stories he greeted the author of *Uncle Tom's Cabin* by jesting, "So you are the little woman who wrote the book that made this great war." Her 1852 novel about brutal treatment of slaves may, indeed, have hastened the secession crisis. During their pleasant and candid conversation, Lincoln remarked, "Whichever way [the war] ends, I have the impression that I sha'n't last long after it is over." Perhaps Lincoln reminisced about Stowe's brother Edward Beecher, who was presi-

---

Lincoln dodged a hot issue concerning a twenty-year-old woman by referring her case to Secretary of War Edwin M. Stanton. It seems that **Annie Jones** of Massachusetts wanted to be a nurse, but Dorothea Dix, the superintendent of women nurses, rejected her because she was too young and too attractive. Dix accepted only "homely looking women" who were not likely to flirt with patients. Annie sought other ways to serve the troops. She walked into camps in and around Washington and soon finagled a position as "favored guest" of Gen. Julius Stahel and his staff officers. Shortly, Stahel lost his command, and Annie attached herself to George Armstrong Custer, even accompanying him to the front as his companion. Their intimate relationship annoyed twenty-seven-year-old Gen. Hugh Judson Kilpatrick, with whom Annie had also been involved. Out of jealousy, he falsely accused Annie of espionage, and she was incarcerated.

The case drew Lincoln's attention, and after interviewing her, he referred the matter to Stanton, who imprisoned her. In the ensuing political dogfight, a congressman convinced Stanton to release the woman into his custody, assuring the war secretary that he would keep her away from the army. The governor of Massachusetts then intervened, without Stanton's knowledge, and blocked Annie's release, fearing that the congressman might use her "to the disadvantage" of the Lincoln administration in the 1864 election. It wasn't until nine months later that Stanton learned of the governor's action. Stanton then forced the matter and paroled Annie, who was never heard from again.

Lincoln clearly chose to distance himself from the delicate military debauchery and hoped for as little publicity as possible. Privately he probably blamed himself for not reversing Dix's recruitment policies. Had he done so, an enterprising young woman might have had an honorable calling instead of dishonorable escapades that made her the victim of revengeful generals.

dent of Illinois College in Jacksonville in 1835 when Ann Rutledge's brother David attended there. During his years in Springfield, Lincoln surely was aware of President Beecher and probably knew him. It was a remarkable coincidence that Beecher's sister and David Rutledge's anticipated brother-in-law were conversing twenty-seven years later in the White House.

Writing about her visit in Boston journals, Stowe compared Lincoln's "peculiar" strength to a wire cable that sways to every influence but is "tenaciously and inflexibly bound to carry its great end." Lincoln was "the best abused man of our nation," she observed. "He has seen the day when every man seemed ready to stone him, and yet, with simple, wiry, steady perseverance, he has held on, conscious of honest intentions and looking to God for help." She extolled him as "the safest leader a nation could have" in such perilous times—a leader who was "slow and careful in coming to resolutions" and "willing to talk with every person who has anything to show on any side of a disputed subject. . . . A ruthless, bold, theorizing, dashing man of genius might have wrecked our Constitution."[7]

The mother of two men imprisoned for resisting the draft in western Pennsylvania and the wife of one of them came to Lincoln for help in freeing the men. Lincoln obtained a list of all draft resistors in prison in the region and inquired if there were "any difference in the charges in degree of guilt." When he learned there were none, Lincoln said, "These fellows have suffered long enough. . . . I will turn out the flock."

The young wife ran forward and was about to kneel in thankfulness. "Do not kneel to me," said Lincoln. "Thank God and go." The older woman came forward with tears in her eyes. "Good-bye, Mr. Lincoln. I shall never see you again till we meet in Heaven." He instantly took her right hand in both of his. "I am afraid with all my troubles I shall never get there. But if I do, I will find you. That you wish me to go there is the best wish you could make for me. Good-bye."[8]

Lincoln's friend Joshua Speed had overheard the discussion from the waiting room. He approached the president and said: "Lincoln, with my knowledge of your nervous sensibility, it is a wonder that such scenes as this do not kill you."

Said Lincoln: "Things of that sort do not hurt me. For to tell you the truth, that is the only thing I have done today which has given me any pleasure. Those women were no counterfeits. The mother spoke out in all the features of her face. In doing right, I have made two people happy in one day. Speed, die when I may, I want it said of me by those who know me best that I always plucked a thistle and planted a flower when I thought a flower would grow."[9]

As LINCOLN worried about pending battles in Pennsylvania and at Vicksburg that could determine the war's outcome, his health suffered. A visitor noted "the drooping eyelids, looking almost swollen; the dark bags beneath the eyes; the deep marks about the large and expressive mouth."

In 1863 Lee invaded the North again and headed toward Pennsylvania, pursued by Gen. George G. Meade and the Army of the Potomac. Despite the grave situation in Pennsylvania, Mary took Tad with her on a shopping binge to Philadelphia. While they were away, Lincoln dreamed Tad shot himself with a pistol Lincoln had permitted him to have—the gun was big enough to snap caps but not big enough for cartridges or powder. Rising early, Lincoln wired Mary: "Think you better put Tad's pistol away."[10]

On July 2, back from Philadelphia, Mary rode alone in the presidential carriage, returning to the White House from the Soldiers' Home, which served as Lincoln's summer retreat in Washington. Hearing a strange noise from the front, Mary looked up just in time to see the driver's seat and the coachmen fly off the carriage and fall in the road. The frightened horses bolted into a fast, uncontrolled gallop, with Mary screaming for help. On a curve in the road, the carriage struck a tree, throwing Mary to the ground. Her head struck a rock, and she was taken unconscious to an army hospital.

Summoned from a White House meeting, Lincoln hurriedly drove to the hospital in his carriage. He whispered "Molly" into her ear—a nickname he often called her—but she did not respond. She did not regain consciousness until the next day. She was taken to the White House and remained bedridden for three weeks. An investigation found that the screws to the driver's seat had been removed by an unidentified culprit in an attempt to injure the president. Mary's injury may have been more than physical. Robert Lincoln later said that his mother was never the same after this incident.

Her accident occurred as a great battle bloodied the Pennsylvania fields and ridges near Gettysburg. A third of Lee's army—22,200—was lost in the three-day battle, and his crippled forces retreated southward toward Virginia. An equally important Northern victory occurred just one day after the fighting ended at Gettysburg: the mighty Confederate bastion at Vicksburg on the Mississippi surrendered to Grant's army. With the fall of Vicksburg (and Port Hudson five days later), the South was split asunder, with the Mississippi River totally under Federal control. Lincoln threw his arms around Secretary of the Navy Gideon Welles and exclaimed, "I cannot, in words, tell you my joy over this result. The Father of Waters again goes un-vexed to the sea! It is great, Mr. Welles, it is great!"[11]

As the war shifted in favor of the North, Lincoln sought relief from the intense pressures by spending more time at the Soldiers' Home. He was often alone. Meanwhile, Mary—now recovered from her accident—under-took the longest trip of her White House years. She and Tad vacationed in the White Mountains of New Hampshire. Lincoln corresponded with her by short, impersonal telegrams. On September 20, 1863, he wrote, "I wish you to stay or come just as is most agreeable to yourself." The next day he telegraphed: "I would be glad for you to come. . . . I would be glad to see you and Tad." Offended by these messages, Mary berated him, hoping "for one line to say that we are occasionally remembered."[12]

Lincoln seemed unable to resist indulging his wife and children. Ten-year-old Tad—loud, eccentric, and full of creative mischief—sprayed digni-taries with a fire hose, ran in and out of cabinet meetings, and after Lincoln created Thanksgiving Day, got his father to pardon the Thanksgiving turkey. When Tad pulled up some choice plants in the White House garden, the head gardener was irate and declared to his assistant he would tell the madam.

"But remember," the assistant said, "he is the madam's son."

Retorted the gardener: "He's the madam's wildcat."

Mary thought otherwise. "I do not have any trouble managing Tad," she bragged. "He is my little troublesome sunshine."

To briefly free himself from troubling times, the president took Mary, Mrs. Hunter Cameron, and Nicolay and Hay to Ford's Theatre on Novem-ber 9 to see John Wilkes Booth in *The Marble Heart*. Lincoln applauded the

---

Marinda Branson Moore of North Carolina perhaps best summed up the feelings of Southern women about Lincoln and the North. In a widely used geography textbook she wrote for children, she justified slavery and secession and blamed the war on the Union. The book's little readers were told that Lincoln was "a mean man" elected by abolitionists, a man "so enraged" by secession that "he declared war and exhausted nearly all the strength of the nation in a vain attempt to whip the South back into the Union." The Confederacy will win, she wrote, because "God is on our side."

actor rapturously and sent word backstage he would like to meet him. Booth declined the interview and told the messenger he would rather have "the applause of a n[—]" than that of Lincoln.[13]

Back in the White House Lincoln worked on "a few appropriate remarks" for the dedication of the National Soldiers' Cemetery at Gettysburg on November 19. On the day of his scheduled departure, family problems almost interfered. Tad was too sick to eat breakfast, and Mary screamed at her husband, demanding that he not leave her alone with the sick child. The president said that the occasion was too important for him not to be there.

He left at noon and arrived at Gettysburg around five o'clock. A telegram from Secretary of War Stanton relayed good news about Tad: "Mrs. Lincoln informed me that your son is better this evening." Lincoln was relieved, and he laughed and joked with his companions.

His short, ten-sentence speech followed a two-hour oration by Edward Everett, formerly a senator and a president of Harvard College. While Everett's remarks were consistent with the rhetoric of the era, Lincoln's masterfully phrased comments became the most memorable speech in American history.

The Gettysburg Address was a fervent affirmation of the document that shaped Lincoln's political philosophy—the Declaration of Independence. Lincoln linked the nation's birth not to the year the Constitution was ratified but to 1776, the year of the Declaration. Lincoln saw the Constitution as flawed because it protected the interests of slave owners. But the Declaration proclaimed freedom and equality, and that represented to Lincoln "a law higher than the Constitution." Lincoln was emphasizing that human equality was what the war was all about. By doing so he had changed the meaning of the war—he had placed the war on a higher moral ground.

IN SEPTEMBER the husband of Mary's youngest half-sister, Emilie Todd Helm, was killed at Chickamauga. He was a Confederate general, and Emilie was outspoken in her loyalty to the South. She buried her husband in Atlanta and, with her six-year-old daughter Katherine, headed for Washington, hoping "Brother Lincoln" would help them get home to Kentucky. But when she refused to take an oath of allegiance to the Union, the army detained her at Fort Monroe. Lincoln was notified and wired, "Send her to me."

Lincoln and Mary welcomed Emilie with "the warmest affection" and sought to comfort her in her loss, she later wrote in her diary. Knowing her presence would be troublesome, the Lincolns tried to conceal her visit, but the embarrassing news leaked out, spawning scandalous stories.

"You should not have that Rebel in your house!" exclaimed Gen. Daniel Sickles, who had lost a leg at Gettysburg.

"My wife and I are in the habit of choosing our own guests," Lincoln responded. "We do not need advice or assistance in this matter."[14]

During Emilie's stay, she and Mary dined alone and talked about old friends and wept over family tragedies. Emilie wrote in her diary: "Sister and I cannot open our hearts to each other as freely as we would like. This frightful war comes between us like a barrier of granite closing our lips but not our hearts, for though our tongues are tied, we weep over our dead together and express through our clasped hands the sympathy we feel for each other."

While the adults avoided talk about the war, Tad and little Katherine felt no constraints. Looking at newspapers on the floor of the sitting room, Tad beamed, "Oh, here's a picture of the president."

"NO, that's NOT the president. Jeff Davis is the president," Katherine asserted.

As they were about to get into a tussle, Lincoln picked them up and placed them on his knees. "Well, Tad, you know who your president is," and then, looking at Katherine, he said with a chuckle, "I will just be your Uncle Lincoln."[15]

Later in the day Lincoln said to Emilie: "Little Sister, I hope you can come up and spend the summer with us at the Soldiers' Home. You and Mary love each other. It is good for her to have you with her—I feel worried about Mary; her nerves have gone to pieces; she cannot hide from me that the strain she has been under has been too much for her mental as well as her physical health. What do you think?"

Emilie admitted that she too was concerned about Mary. "She does seem very nervous and excitable," Emilie said. "And once or twice the frightened look in her eyes has appalled me. She seems to fear that other sorrows may be added to those we already have to bear. I believe if anything were to happen to you or Robert or Tad it would kill her."

Lincoln, shaking his head sorrowfully, said: "Stay with her as long as you can."[16]

Emilie stayed only a week. With a pass from Lincoln to cross army lines, she returned to Kentucky, where she resumed her pro-South behavior. Lincoln reacted by revoking a previous order to shield her from arrest. In a message to the Federal commander of the District of Kentucky, he wrote: "If the papers given her by me can be construed to give her protection from [disloyal] words or acts, it is hereby revoked *pro tanto*. Deal with her for her current conduct just as you would with any other."

Emilie's visit, however, helped to bring Mary out of her shell and her mourning clothing. At the 1864 New Year's Day reception in the White House, Mary appeared in a purple dress trimmed with black velvet. Both the president and the First Lady showed more enthusiasm than had been evident in months. For the first time in American history the guests presented to the president at the reception included what one newspaper described as "four colored men of genteel exterior, and with the manners of gentlemen."[17]

When Lincoln's secretary John G. Nicolay produced the guest list for the annual cabinet dinner on January 14, Mary struck off the names of Treasury Secretary Salmon P. Chase, whom she regarded as a political enemy, as well as his daughter Kate and his son-in-law, Senator William Sprague. Lincoln ordered the names restored, and "her Satanic Majesty," as Nicolay once called Mary, went on a rampage.

Mary attempted to handle the dinner arrangements herself, but on the afternoon of the dinner she realized she was unable to do so. She apologized to Nicolay and requested his help. "I think," reported Nicolay, "she has felt happier since she cast out that devil of stubbornness."[18]

On a frosty winter day a young woman petitioned Lincoln for a pass to go to her father who had been badly wounded in a recent battle. "I can't let you go down there," said the president sadly as he looked up at the sweet face, so earnest and truthful. "I can't let you go, and I can't refuse you. What shall I do?"

"Let me go there," she pleaded. "God will take care of me."

"Your faith is beautiful, but I don't know. There are no women down there."

"I know that," she answered thoughtfully.

"Aren't you afraid?"

"No sir, I am not afraid. I have trusted our heavenly Father many times before, and He has never forsaken me."

"And He never will!" exclaimed the president, springing to his feet. "No, my dear, He never will!" Drawing a chair closer to the fireplace, he went on: "Come, sit here, until you are quite warm. I will write you a pass. You shall go to your father."

THROUGHOUT THE war years Lincoln apparently continued to occasionally dwell on the memory of Ann Rutledge. One who noticed the president's nostalgia was artist Francis B. Carpenter, who lived in the White House for six months while working on portraits of Lincoln. He sometimes shared evenings with the president.

On one occasion in 1864 Lincoln leaned back in his armchair and discussed poetry with Carpenter. "There are some quaint, queer verses written, I think, by Oliver Wendell Holmes," Lincoln began. He named "The Last Leaf" as one he found "inexpressibly touching." He recited part of it:

> The mossy marbles rest
> On the lips that he had pressed
> in their bloom
> And the names he loved to hear
> Have been carved for many a year
> On the tomb.

As he finished the verse, Lincoln said in his emphatic way: "For pure pathos, in my judgment, there is nothing finer than those six lines in the English language!"

Memories haunted Lincoln. Did he think of Ann Rutledge when he quoted romantic poetry to Carpenter? Was it Ann Rutledge whose lips he "pressed in their bloom" and whose name he "loved to hear"?

MARY DISLIKED Ulysses S. Grant, whom Lincoln named as general in chief of the Union armies in 1864. Engaging Robert E. Lee in a bloody campaign in northern Virginia during the dreadful summer of that year, Grant was relentless despite severe losses.

At the battle of the Wilderness, he lost 17,000 to Lee's 11,000. At Spotsylvania, 11,000 fell compared to 4,000 Southern casualties. At Cold Harbor, near Richmond, Grant sustained his worst defeat of the war, losing 7,000 men in a controversial assault. In six weeks of incessant fighting, Grant incurred almost 100,000 casualties—a number greater than the total strength of Lee's Army of Northern Virginia.

Grant had literally marched in blood and agony from northern Virginia to the James River and had few victories to show for it. However, he had forced Lee to fall back step by step to a line near the Confederate capital. Weary Johnny Rebs pondered the superior numbers of Grant's army: "What's the use of killing those fellows? Kill one and half a dozen take his place." Grant remained determined despite his horrendous losses. "I propose to fight it out on this line if it takes all summer," he wired Washington.

"He has the grit of a bulldog!" Lincoln said admiringly. "Once let him get his 'teeth' in, and nothing can shake him off."

Grant eventually besieged Lee at Petersburg, and the campaign fell into bloody, prolonged trench warfare. Inflamed at the heavy loss of life, Democrats began calling Grant and Lincoln "widow-makers."

Grant was "a butcher [who] is not fit to be at the head of an army," proclaimed Mary Lincoln.

"Well, Mother, suppose we give you command of the army," Lincoln replied. "No doubt you would do better than any generals I have tried."

The awful bloodshed troubled Lincoln as much as anyone. He and Mary often visited hospitals together. She brought delicacies from the White House kitchen, talked to the men, read to them, wrote letters for them, and endured the blood, the smells, and the groans of the wounded. Somehow she got through it, and so did Lincoln.

"I cannot pretend to advise," the president told Grant at one point, "but I do sincerely hope that all may be accomplished with as little bloodshed as possible."[19]

In July 1864 Confederate Gen. Jubal A. Early crossed the Potomac with twenty thousand men and advanced on Washington. Early's army damaged railroads, destroyed telegraph lines, and stripped the countryside of food and military equipment. In Washington some frightened residents fled to Georgetown and slept in the streets. Lincoln, Mary, and Tad were hustled back to the White House from the Soldiers' Home, and a naval vessel stood by in the Potomac to evacuate them if necessary.

On July 11 Early's forces marched through Silver Spring, Maryland, and approached Fort Stevens on the outskirts of the capital. Smoke darkened the sky as Lincoln arrived at the fort to assess the situation. The next day Lincoln returned to the fort with Mary, who thought a military outing would clear her aching head.

On Gen. Horatio Wright's reckless suggestion, the president mounted a parapet for a clearer view, and a surgeon standing near him was shot.

"Get down, Mr. President!" Wright exclaimed.

"But I want to watch the action," Lincoln countered.

"Step down, now, or I will have you forcibly removed," Wright said in exasperation.

"All right," Lincoln conceded, "I will stand behind the parapet." Moments later, as the president turned to speak to a nearby officer, a bullet smashed the man's face, and he fell dead beside the president. Another soldier shoved Lincoln to the ground. As the day ended, the reinforced Federals prevailed, and Early's army retreated. Wright made a lackadaisical move to chase them but stopped "for fear he might come across the Rebels and catch some of them," Lincoln observed angrily. Lincoln's encounter at Fort Stevens was the only time a sitting American president and First Lady were together while under enemy fire.[20]

MARY STILL spent lavishly to ornament herself and told Lizzie Keckley that she was terribly worried that Lincoln might not be reelected. "To me, to him, there is more at stake in this election than he dreams of."

"What can you mean, Mrs. Lincoln?" asked Keckley. "I don't comprehend."

"Simply this," responded Mary. "I have contracted large debts of which he knows nothing, and which he will be unable to pay if he is defeated. They consist chiefly of store bills. I owe altogether about $27,000. You understand, Lizabeth, that Mr. Lincoln has but little idea of the expense of a woman's wardrobe. He glances at my rich dresses and is happy in the belief that the few hundred dollars that I obtain from him supply all my wants."

Justifying her debt, Mary said that she "must dress in costly materials" because, being from the West, she is subjected to "more searching observation. . . . To keep up appearances, I must have money—more than Mr. Lincoln can spare for me."

"He does not suspect how much you owe?" Keckley asked.

"God, no! And I would not have him suspect," Mary exclaimed. "He does not know a thing about any debts, and I value his happiness too much to allow him to know anything. This is what troubles me so much. If he is

---

Jane Grey Swisshelm, a spellbinding lecturer noted for sarcasm and negative criticism, wanted Lincoln to punish the Sioux in Minnesota. "Their fangs are dripping with the blood of the innocents," she argued. She entered Lincoln's office with a feeling of scorn for him but was then "startled to find a chill of awe pass over me as my eyes rested upon him. . . . I have never [experienced such awe before], and I know no word save 'grandeur' [to] express the quality of that atmosphere."

reelected, I can keep him in ignorance of my affairs; but if he is defeated, then the bills will be sent in, and he will know all."[21]

Mary had ample reason to be worried. Lincoln himself had all but conceded defeat. The country was war-weary. "Negotiate to end the killing" was a common cry. The Union armies appeared stalemated, and the Republicans were badly divided. It was no wonder that a visitor found Lincoln deeply depressed, "indeed quite paralyzed and wilted down." Grant wrote to a friend: "I think . . . for [Lincoln] to attempt to answer all the charges the opposition will bring against him will be like setting a maiden to work to prove her chastity."[22]

Early's advance on Washington in the summer of 1864 had alarmed politicians and citizens throughout the North. To prevent further assaults by Early on the capital, Lincoln pressured Grant to send Gen. Philip H. Sheridan's cavalry corps to the Shenandoah Valley in August 1864. Sheridan was ordered to destroy Early's army and render the region unfit to supply any Confederate operations.

Sheridan's success, combined with William T. Sherman's conquest of Atlanta, turned the electorate around and assured Lincoln's reelection. Sheridan's victory (and Lincoln's) was due in part to a young Quaker woman, Rebecca Wright.

Living in Confederate-occupied Winchester, Virginia, Wright bravely notified Sheridan, through an elderly black man, of Rebel movements and strengths in the area. The courier delivered her message, which had been written on tissue paper, compressed into a small pellet, wrapped in tinfoil, and carried in his mouth. Acting on Wright's information, Sheridan attacked Early's army three days later and won a hard-fought battle. Wright's courage not only helped Sheridan sweep the Confederates out of the Shenandoah, but also to turn the fertile valley into a barren wasteland. After the war, Sheridan secured an appointment for her in the Treasury Department, where she worked for forty-seven years.[23]

A FORMER slave, bought and sold three times on the auction block, visited Lincoln on October 29, 1864, to thank him for the Emancipation Proclamation. This tall, slender woman was an illiterate but intelligent grandmother who had risen magnificently to become a legend in her own time. Legally freed with all slaves in New York State in 1827, she announced one night at a prayer meeting: "I am no longer Isabella [her name as a slave]. I am Sojourner Truth, an instrument for the Lord's bidding."

Traveling throughout the land as a Methodist evangelist, the eloquent "African prophetess" moved friend and foe alike with her "heart of love and tongue of fire." Soon she was a national figure loathed and feared by Southerners and Northern conservatives for her "isms"—radicalism, abolitionism, and feminism.

At a women's rights convention, she responded to a clergyman who argued that women should not have as many rights as men "because Christ was not a woman." With her eyes piercing the preacher, she asked him: "Where did your Christ come from?" Raising her voice still louder, she repeated: "Where did your Christ come from? [He came] from God and a woman! Man had nothing to do with Him!" The entire crowd responded with deafening applause.[24]

In the war's early stages, Sojourner Truth was troubled by Lincoln's goal of preserving the Union rather than freeing the slaves. But after the Emancipation Proclamation, she felt that "God's hand is in this war, and it will end in the destruction of slavery."

In 1864, at about the age of sixty-seven, she resolved to visit Lincoln and made the long journey from her home in Battle Creek, Michigan. Lizzie Keckley helped arrange the appointment. A respected black leader, Keckley was president of the Ladies' Contraband Relief Association. It was dedicated to finding food and jobs for fugitive slaves. Mary Lincoln was among its contributors.[25]

Lincoln thanked Truth for her work against slavery and for assisting freed blacks who had rushed to Washington seeking refuge. She said she appreciated him, "for you are the best president who has ever taken the seat."[26]

Lincoln showed her an elegantly bound Bible presented to him by Baltimore's black community. Removing it from its silk-lined walnut case, he handed it to her. "It is beautiful beyond description," she said, admiring its velvet lining, banded-gold corners, and heavy gold clasps. "Isn't it ironical," she said, "that colored people gave this Holy Book to the Head of the government—a government that once sanctioned laws prohibiting them from learning enough to be able to read this Book. Indeed, it's a beautiful gesture on their part to give such a valuable book to you."

"I told them," said Lincoln, "that the Bible is the best gift God has given to man. . . . But for this book we could not know right from wrong. All things most desirable for human welfare, here and hereafter, are to be found portrayed in it. Their gift of this Book to me is one of my greatest treasures." Lincoln then autographed a book she carried. She later said: "I never was treated by anyone with more kindness and cordiality than were shown to me by that great and good man. I felt I was in the presence of a friend."

Other writers have claimed that Sojourner Truth advised Lincoln on such issues as the cruelty of slavery, freeing the slaves, and enlisting blacks in the Union army. These claims "have not been substantiated and in any case seem inherently improbable," wrote her biographer Carleton Mabee. Lincoln may have been influenced by articles he read about her, but they did not meet prior to October 1864. By that time Lincoln's positions on these issues were well established.[27]

While the blacks praised Lincoln for the Emancipation Proclamation, the Democrats attacked him for it. During the political campaign of 1864 they publicized rumors of young white women parading the streets with banners inscribed, "Fathers, Protect Us From Negro Equality," and of sixty-four white schoolteachers at Port Royal, South Carolina, giving birth to mulatto babies. The Democrats also coined a new word, *miscegenation,* and explained it with an illustration in a pamphlet showing a black man and a white woman embracing.

George B. McClellan, the Democratic candidate and former general, pledged to end the war by suspending the Emancipation Proclamation in favor of an immediate armistice. The country's future was at stake. If McClellan won, the South would have won its independence and kept its slaves. Thus the election marked the beginning of a lengthy affiliation of African Americans with the Republican Party.[28]

After the election Lincoln pressed for a constitutional amendment banning slavery. It required a two-thirds majority in the House of Representatives. Lincoln worked the Congressmen one by one, cajoling, arm-twisting, and using all of his political skills to secure the necessary votes. He was suc-

Twenty-three-year-old **Laura Jones**, an attractive Southerner, came to Lincoln on Christmas Day 1864 for a pass to Richmond, where she planned to be married. She was a close friend of the wife of Gideon Welles, secretary of the navy, and Welles personally placed a formal request on the president's desk as Laura sat in the outer office. Welles left but did not close the door. As Lincoln looked up from the papers he saw her smiling at him. He invited her in. Without questioning her, he pushed the papers aside and wrote out the pass.

cessful, but just barely. The measure passed by three votes. When the final tally was announced, "There was a moment of utter silence," wrote correspondent Noah Brooks. "Then there was an explosion, a storm of cheers, the like of which probably no Congress of the United States ever heard before. Strong men embraced each other with tears. The galleries and aisles were bristling with standing, cheering crowds . . . women's handkerchiefs waving and floating . . . arms around each other's necks, and cheer after cheer . . . burst after burst."

"The great job is ended," Lincoln exclaimed in the White House. It is a "great moral victory," he said. That night Lincoln slept better than he had in years.

Newspapers ran a popular cartoon showing a black man who said, "Now I's nobody's n[—] but my own." In mass meetings blacks sang, "Jehovah has triumphed, His people are free."

But before the Thirteenth Amendment could go into effect, it had to be ratified by twenty-seven of the thirty-six states. Lincoln's home state of Illinois began the process, and the amendment soon was well on its way to becoming the law of the land.

WHEN ROBERT LINCOLN came home for Christmas in 1864, he repeated a request he had often made: to enlist in the army. He had graduated earlier that year from Harvard and was now studying law. Critics had called him a shirker for not serving his country.

Mary was against it at first, but she now acknowledged that Robert's plea "was manly and noble, and I want him to go . . . but I am so frightened he may never come back to us."

"Many a poor mother has had to make this sacrifice," Lincoln said, "and has given up every son she had—and lost them all."

Mary's voice quivered: "Before this war is over I may be like . . . my poor mother in Kentucky with not a prop left in her old age."[29]

Lincoln asked Grant to find a place for Robert with some nominal rank and offered to pay his official expenses. The president's son became an aide to Grant. He would never be exposed to battle, but he would witness Lee's surrender.

Lincoln's heart went out to mothers who suffered multiple losses—women such as Sarah Mills of Des Moines, Iowa, who lost her husband, father, and brother at the battle of Corinth, Mississippi, and Polly Ray, a widow in North Carolina whose seven sons were killed in the war.

Lincoln had recently written a compassionate and masterful letter to a Massachusetts woman, Lydia Bixby, who claimed to have lost five sons in the war:

> I have been shown in the files of the War Department a statement of the Adjutant General of Massachusetts that you are the mother of five sons who have died gloriously on the field of battle.
>
> I feel how weak and fruitless must be any words of mine which should attempt to beguile you from the grief of a loss so overwhelming. But I cannot refrain from tendering to you the consolation that may be found in the thanks of the Republic they died to save.
>
> I pray that our Heavenly Father may assuage the anguish of your bereavement, and leave you only the cherished memory of the loved and lost, and the solemn pride that must be yours, to have laid so costly a sacrifice upon the altar of Freedom.[30]

Years later historians discovered that Lydia Bixby was a Southern sympathizer who ran a whorehouse and that she had lost two, not five, sons. She did indeed have three other sons: one had deserted the army, another may have deserted, and the third was honorably discharged. Despite the mythology of her case, Lincoln's Bixby letter is a classic example of presidential compassion from a deeply caring man who could feel the pain of those who had lost loved ones.

Less known, but equally showing empathy, was his letter to young Fanny McCullough, whose father was an old Illinois friend of the Lincolns and who had died in battle:

> It is with deep grief that I learn of the death of your kind and brave Father; and, especially, that it is affecting your young heart beyond what is common in such cases. In this sad world of ours, sorrow comes to all; and, to the young, it comes with bitterest agony, because it takes them unawares. The older have learned to ever expect it. I am anxious to afford some alleviation of your present distress. Perfect relief is not possible, except with time. You can not now realize that you will ever feel better. Is not this so? And yet it is a mistake. You are sure to be happy again. To know this, which is certainly true, will make you some less miserable now. I have had experience enough to know what I say; and you need only to believe it, to feel better at once. The memory of your dear Father, instead of an agony,

will yet be a sad sweet feeling in your heart, of a purer, and holier sort than you have known before.[31]

WHILE LINCOLN'S attention was riveted on the war and reelection, two congressional friends dropped in to ask him to pose for seventeen-year-old sculptor Vinnie Ream. He refused, saying he did not have time.

"But, Mr. President," one of them argued, "she's a poor girl from the Wisconsin Territory." They explained that Ream was struggling on her own and had done fine work for others, including a number of congressmen. They pointed out that she was being tutored by Clark Mills, a famous sculptor, who had talked about her "remarkable ability."

Mills's studio was in the Capitol basement, and congressmen could not help but notice his beautiful young apprentice. Smitten by the young woman, they willingly posed for her. To some of them she expressed an interest in doing a bust of the president. Looking at them with her sparkling brown eyes and gleaming smile, she knew they would help. Now two of them were trying.

The congressmen noted that Ream's father was a land surveyor who had brought his family to Washington in 1861 and acquired a government job. Ream, then not quite fifteen, applied at the post office and was hired as a clerk in the dead-letter office. To get the job the precocious girl swore she was at least sixteen years old.

"She feels she can do better, and she has faith in herself," said one of the congressmen. Lincoln knew that Mary would not think much of his posing for a young, single woman, but he could relate to and sympathize with a poor, struggling person from the West. He said he would try to arrange his schedule to see her.[32]

As time passed and Ream heard nothing from the White House, she began haunting the upstairs corridor near Lincoln's private office. She sat there among hordes of office-seekers and, with sketchpad in hand, captured a few details of Lincoln's face as he passed in the hallway.

One day Lincoln noticed her and paused in front of her. He asked her what brought her there. She replied that she was a sculptor. He asked if she was the young lady from Wisconsin who wanted to do a bust of him. She said that she was. He told her that they should discuss the matter in his office.

Rising to her full height of only five feet, the petite ninety-pound girl looked up and was instantly "under the spell of his kind eyes and genial presence." She followed him to his office. They made an indelible impression on each other. He was struck by her drive and determination and graceful manner and lively nature. Like him, she had resolved at an early age to take charge of her life and to make something of herself. That rang a familiar chord. She later recalled: "The great heart which vanity could not unlock opened with the sympathy that recalled to him his own youth."[33]

Lincoln also learned that Ream composed poetry and music, sang at concerts in military hospitals, helped wounded soldiers write letters, and did charity work for the blind. The president recognized that this prairie Cinderella and child genius was certainly worthy of his time. He acceded to her wishes and allowed her to work in a corner of his office during his rest periods.

Some congressional patrons escorted her on her first three visits. On the third day Lincoln quipped: "Why do you always come with Miss Ream? It is not often that I get to see a pretty woman alone?" From then on the escorts stayed away.[34]

With death threats increasing daily against the president, Ward Hill Lamon, the U.S. marshal for Washington, arranged a new passage for Lincoln to enter his office unseen. It helped to ensure his safety. It was also used by Ream, and it kept the sittings secret from Mary.

Using the sittings as a time to relax during his torturous eighteen-hour workdays, Lincoln often slouched in his chair, with head bowed in deep thought. One day he looked out the south window where he had often watched Willie and Tad play on the White House lawn, and then he dropped into a chair and sobbed. Drying his eyes, he reminisced: "I was thinking of Willie."

Ream said later:

Never was there grief like Lincoln's. He was still suffering from the blow of that child's death while great affairs convulsed the nation. . . . He seemed an absolutely heartbroken man. Sometimes at these sittings his face wore a look of anxiety and pain. . . . At other times he would have that far away dreamy look that somehow presaged the tragic fate awaiting him; and again, those quiet eyes lighting up, a radiance almost Divine would suffuse those sunken cheeks, and the whole face would be illuminated with the impulse of some Divine purpose. . . . I was modeling him in clay, but all the time his personality was sinking deeper into my soul, being engraved deeply upon my heart.[35]

The half-hour sittings continued through the cold winter months of 1864–65, and Lincoln and Ream became warm friends. The finished bust was a masterpiece that bore a striking resemblance to the president. He liked it. Others also praised it.

In 1866, after the assassination, Ream sought the ten-thousand-dollar commission offered by Congress for a life-size marble statue of Lincoln for the Capitol. She was supported by a petition signed by President Andrew Johnson, members of his cabinet, 31 senators, 110 current and former representatives, and 31 other dignitaries. The House of Representatives approved Ream by a vote of 67 to 7, but she ran into trouble in the Senate.

Mary expressed her strong disapproval, as did her longtime companion Charles Sumner, who tried to block the commission. "This candidate is not competent to produce the work," he argued in the Senate. "She may make a statue, [but] she cannot make one that you will be justified in placing in this national Capitol."

Jumping to his feet, Senator James Nesmith of Oregon disagreed vehemently. Scorning Sumner's admiration for everything European, Nesmith rallied support for Ream: "If this young lady and the works which she has produced had been brought to his notice by some near-sighted, frog-eating Frenchman, with a pair of green spectacles on his nose, the Senator would . . . vote her $50,000!" The final vote was 23 for, 9 against. Winning over distinguished male sculptors, Ream became the first woman and, at nineteen, the youngest artist ever awarded a federal commission for a statue.

Explosive reactions erupted across the country, with women reporters in the forefront, all questioning how a young girl could be awarded so important a prize. She has "never made a statue," wrote Jane Swisshelm, who

---

Cordelia Harvey, widow of the governor of Wisconsin, begged Lincoln on six occasions to establish military hospitals in the North and near the Southern battlefields. She blamed the government for the thousands of graves along the Mississippi, saying they were due to ignorance that "must not continue." Lincoln bristled at the criticism and opposed her idea, believing it would encourage desertion. "You assume to know more than I do and more than the surgeons do!" he said almost contemptuously. But she persisted, and he eventually approved her plan and named one of the hospitals after her late husband. "I never could argue with women," he said later. "They always get the best of me."

summed up Ream's professional work as a few "plaster busts on exhibition, including her own minus clothing to the waist."

Undaunted, Ream set up shop in the Capitol basement. She wanted to sculpt Lincoln in an authentic suit and asked Mary Lincoln if she could borrow the clothes he wore on the night of the assassination.

The response of September 10, 1866, was a resounding no. Assuming Ream had never met the president, Mary stated bluntly: "As every friend my husband knew was familiar to me, and as your name was not on the list, consequently you could not have become familiar with [his] expression[s]." On the same day Mary wrote to Sumner: "Nothing but a mortifying failure can be anticipated . . . and the country will never cease to regret that your wise admonitions were disregarded."

Ream eventually obtained Lincoln's daytime clothes worn on April 14 from White House doorman Alphonse Dunn, to whom Mary supposedly had given them.[36]

Three years later, in 1869, Ream completed the model and accompanied it to Italy to be rendered in marble. It was returned to Washington late in 1870 and unveiled at a Capitol ceremony on January 25, 1871. As the drape rose from the statue, the audience applauded loudly, and Ream stood and bowed as the applause continued for some time. "This is Mr. Lincoln," said Senator Lyman Trumbull of Illinois during the ceremony. Reviews were generally positive, calling the statue a remarkably true and awesome representation. But women writers, especially those who had been critical of Ream's commission, labeled the statue as "frightful" and "lifeless."[37]

Ream, whose talents included poetry, penned these stirring lines a few weeks after the unveiling:

> O, Lincoln, prophet, hero, friend!
> You clasped the hands so long estranged
> You healed the wounds—you broke the chains
> You honored all our silent slain.

She went on to sculpt more than a hundred pieces, many of them of major military and political figures. She designed the first freestanding statue of a Native American (Sequoyah) placed in the Capitol, and with the support of Gen. William T. Sherman, she won the twenty-thousand-dollar commission to sculpt the city's prestigious memorial to Adm. David Farragut. The town of Vinita, Oklahoma, was named in her honor.

13

"That Woman Is Pretending to Be Me!"

$\mathcal{O}$N MARCH 23, 1865, Lincoln, Mary, and Tad cruised down the Potomac on the *River Queen* to General Grant's headquarters at City Point. White House guard William H. Crook said Tad "studied every screw of the engine and knew and counted among his friends every man of the crew."

At City Point the First Family was warmly welcomed with luncheons, dinners, parties, and dances. Lincoln visited all the hospitals in the area and shook hands with thousands of wounded soldiers. In a strategy meeting to discuss peace terms, Lincoln emphasized to Generals Grant and Sherman and Adm. David D. Porter that his objective was more than peace. He wanted reconciliation. This requires generous terms, he said, to "get the deluded men of the Rebel armies disarmed and back to their homes. . . . Let them all go, officers and all; I want submission, and no more bloodshed. . . . I want no one punished; treat them liberally all round. We want these people to return to their allegiance to the Union and submit to the laws."[1]

This was not a view Mary supported. She blamed the South for the war—a war that had torn asunder and decimated the Todd family. Her stepmother, her brother George, all her half-sisters, and all but one of her half-brothers remained loyal to the South. Four brothers and half-brothers and four brothers-in-law fought for the Confederacy. Dead in battle were three half-brothers and the husband of her youngest sister. She wanted the South punished.

To witness a grand review of the Army of the James, now commanded by Gen. Edward O. C. Ord, Lincoln and the generals rode on horseback to the main encampment. Mary and Julia Grant followed in an ambulance over muddy, bumpy roads. They sat together on the rear bench, clutching the side of the lurching wagon. One of Grant's aides sat opposite them. Mary, not wanting to be late for the review, complained about the slow speed. "Faster!" she demanded. "We must go faster!"

The driver slapped the horses, and as they responded, the front wheels struck a felled tree barely visible in the thick mud. Both women bounced off the bench simultaneously, striking their heads against the roof. Their large, well-decorated hats cushioned the blow but knocked the wax cherries on Mary's hat to the floor. The First Lady's head throbbed. Her nerves tightened. Her hands twitched. Her anger was set to explode.

The detonation came moments after they arrived at the reviewing stand, when Mary realized the review had begun without her. Fuming over being "left out," she went berserk when she saw another woman riding along the lines with Lincoln. It was General Ord's young, attractive wife.

"Look!" Mary exclaimed to Julia Grant. "That woman is pretending to be me! The soldiers will think that vile woman *is* me!"

Julia Grant tried to reassure her: "No, no, Mrs. Lincoln, that's Mrs. Ord, and she's riding with her husband."

Shaking with anger, Mary blurted out: "Does she suppose that he wants her by his side?"

Again Julia tried to explain, but Mary turned on her.

"I suppose you think you will get to the White House yourself, don't you?!" she said accusingly.

Julia replied evenly, "No, Mrs. Lincoln. We are quite happy where we are."

Inconsolable, Mary was in a towering rage as the unsuspecting Mary Ord rode to the reviewing stand. "Welcome, Mrs. Lincoln," she said cheerfully.

"You whore!" Mary shouted, adding expletives in a vicious tirade. "How dare you follow up the president?!"

Mary Ord burst into tears.[2]

Adam Badeau, secretary to General Grant, noted that Lincoln bore it "with an expression of pain and sadness that cut one to the heart . . . and he walked away hiding that noble face that we might not catch the full expression of its misery." Badeau later said: "I never suffered greater humiliation than when I saw the Head of State, who carried all the cares of the nation at such a crisis—subjected to this inexpressible public mortification. But he bore it with supreme calmness and dignity."[3]

At dinner that night aboard the *River Queen,* Mary continued her attack, lambasting first her husband for "flirting with Mrs. Ord," and then, while seated next to General Grant, demanding that he remove General Ord from command. "He is unfit for his place, to say nothing of his wife!" Mary grumbled.

"I need him," Grant replied assuredly. "He is an excellent officer."

Lincoln, embarrassed, tried to ignore Mary, but she persisted late into the night. Feeling ill, she spent several days in her cabin. On April 1 she left suddenly for Washington. Although no one could have predicted it, her actions contributed to her husband's assassination.

ON APRIL 2, following a disastrous defeat at the battle of Five Forks, Lee abandoned Petersburg and Richmond and retreated westward. Federal forces marched into Richmond the following day. Lincoln himself was eager to visit the fallen capital of the Confederacy and entered the city on April 4.

As he walked through the streets with Tad, Adm. David D. Porter, and twelve sailors, jubilant blacks thronged around him. "Thank God I have lived to see this," Lincoln said. "It seems to me I have been dreaming a horrid nightmare for four years, and now the nightmare is over."

At the Confederate White House, he sat at Jefferson Davis's desk. Outside, Federal troops cheered.

MARY, FEELING left out of a great moment in history, rushed back on April 6 to see Richmond for herself. She was accompanied by her frequent companion, Charles Sumner, as well as Lizzie Keckley and others. Keckley, a former slave, sat in Davis's chair in the Senate chamber.

That night aboard the *River Queen* an officer casually remarked to Mary: "You should have seen the president on his triumphal entry into Richmond. . . . The ladies kissed their hands to him, and greeted him with the waving of handkerchiefs. He is quite a hero when surrounded by pretty young ladies." With eyes flashing, Mary turned to him and curtly said that his familiarity was offensive to her.

"Quite a scene followed," reported Keckley. "And I do not think the captain will ever forget [it]." Mary's dressmaker later wrote that she had never seen "a more peculiarly constituted woman" than Mary Lincoln.[4]

On the Lincoln's last night aboard the *River Queen,* the ship was decorated with multicolored lights, and a military band performed for officers and dignitaries. At about ten o'clock the president was asked to speak. He politely declined, saying he was too tired but added: "Now, by way of parting from the brave soldiers of our gallant army, I call upon the band to play 'Dixie.' That tune is now Federal property, and it's good to show the Rebels that, with us in power, they will be free to hear it again." When the music ended, everyone applauded. Then the last goodbyes were spoken, and the *River Queen* headed back to Washington.

On the return trip, Mary, still seething with jealousy and resentment, reportedly struck her husband in the face and cursed him. While driving from the wharf to the White House, a calmer Mary said, "This city is filled with our enemies."

Lincoln looked at her with surprise: "Enemies! We must never speak of that."[5]

Later that Palm Sunday night of April 9, Lincoln learned of Lee's surrender at Appomattox Court House. He was also told that Capt. Robert Lincoln was on the porch of the McLean house while Lee and Grant conducted the surrender arrangements.

The bloodiest war in American history was almost over. All that remained was for Confederate Gen. Joseph E. Johnston to surrender to General Sherman. Without a doubt, Lincoln had emerged as the grandest figure of that terrible war. Now it was Lincoln's dream that brotherhood, not bloodshed, would become the American way of life and that America would become a land fulfilling the Declaration of Independence—a land where "all men are created equal"—a Declaration that was Lincoln's political chart and inspiration. With victory, emancipation, and a restored Union, Lincoln's desire for a noble destiny was fulfilled. This plain man of the people had not only persevered. He had prevailed.

At daybreak on Monday the firing of five hundred cannon announced the news. That night throngs of people assembled around the White House and repeatedly called for the president. They cheered when little Tad appeared at a second-story window, waving a Confederate flag. Lincoln finally came out to say there would be a program the next night, and he would speak then. He asked the band to play "Dixie" and called it "a lawful prize" since "we fairly captured it" and "one of the best tunes I have ever heard."

By Tuesday night all government buildings were illuminated, and the city reverberated with fireworks, exploding rockets, and ringing bells. A banking house signaled "Glory to God" in gold stars. At the Lees' Arlington mansion across the Potomac, freedmen marched on the lawn, chanting "The Year of Jubilee."[6]

At the White House great crowds gathered to hear he president speak. He was greeted with thunderous applause but was hard to see. Voices shouted, "More light! More light!" A lamp was brought out, and Tad rushed to his father's side: "Let me hold the light, Papa! Let me hold the light!" His wish was granted.[7]

During his remarks Mary embarrassed him again. She and some female friends chatted and laughed loudly from an adjacent window, drowning out the president's voice. At first the listeners tolerated it, but several of them finally hushed the women emphatically. Lincoln at first thought something he said had caused the demonstration, but then realized that Mary again was the problem. An expression of pain and mortification came over his face, but he resumed his reading.

Lincoln's powerful statement projected his vision of a united America without slavery. He said he would not accept a policy of anger and rejection toward the South because it would be "discouraging and paralyzing" for both races.

Standing in the shadows that night was John Wilkes Booth. As Lincoln talked about suffrage for educated blacks or those who had served in the military, Booth grumbled to companions Lewis Paine and David Herold, "That means n[—] citizenship." Vowing, "That is the last speech he will ever make," Booth urged Paine to shoot Lincoln then. Paine refused, and Booth turned away in disgust and exclaimed, "By God, I'll put him through."[8]

Earlier on Tuesday Lincoln had related a dream to Mary and a few friends. In his dream he heard sobs in the East Room of the White House. He saw "a corpse wrapped in funeral vestments . . . soldiers who were acting as guards [and] a throng of people . . . weeping pitifully." Lincoln demanded of the soldiers, "Who is dead?"

"The president," was the answer. "He was killed by an assassin."

Then, Lincoln said, "A loud burst of grief [came] from the crowd, which awoke me from my dream."

The day after the dream Lincoln opened the Bible and read Jacob's dream in Genesis 28. Everywhere he turned in the Bible his eyes fell upon an account of a vision or a supernatural visitation. As the president's self-appointed bodyguard Ward Hill Lamon prepared to depart for Richmond, Lincoln told him about his dream and Bible readings, adding:

> It seems strange to me how much there is in the Bible about dreams. There are, I think, some sixteen chapters in the Old Testament and four or five in the New in which dreams are mentioned; and there are many other passages scattered throughout the book which refer to visions. If we believe in the Bible, we must accept the fact that in the old days, God and His angels came to men in their sleep and made themselves known in dreams. [The dream I had] has haunted me. Somehow the thing has got possession of me, and like Banquo's ghost, it will not let go.

It undoubtedly reminded Lincoln of election night five years earlier in Springfield, when he saw double images of himself in the mirror—one face robust, the other ghostly pale, which he had interpreted as an ominous sign if he had a second term.

Lamon, a huge and imposing Virginian, was one of Lincoln's most devoted friends. He pleaded with the president: "Promise me you won't go out after nightfall while I'm gone, particularly to the theatre." Lincoln would not fully agree. "Well, I promise to do the best I can towards it," he said.[9]

On Thursday, Mary asked General Grant to escort her to view the city's illuminated buildings. Lincoln urged him to accept, and he did. As Mary and Grant entered their coach, the crowd cheered Grant's name nine times. Mary was upset and directed the driver to let her out. Then the crowd cheered for Lincoln, and she gave orders to proceed. This routine was repeated at different stages of the drive, and Mary was angry that Grant was always lauded first.[10]

On Good Friday morning, April 14, Lincoln and Mary enjoyed a relaxing breakfast together and spoke affectionately. Earlier he had sent Mary a note about taking a carriage ride that afternoon. It was "playfully and tenderly worded," she said later. Robert joined them for breakfast, and they talked about his future. Lincoln encouraged him to finish Harvard Law School and to read law for three years. That, Lincoln said, should help them determine "whether you will make a good lawyer or not."[11]

At 11:00 a.m. Lincoln met with Grant and the cabinet. Reconstruction was the principal topic. Edwin M. Stanton, whom Lincoln had asked to draft a plan for cabinet consideration, remarked that the president was "grander, graver, more thoroughly up to the occasion than he had ever seen him." All members expressed "kindly feeling toward the vanquished . . . with as little harm as possible to the feelings or the property of the inhabitants."

"There must be no bloody work," Lincoln said. "No one need expect me to take part in hanging or killing these men, even the worst of them. If we are wise and discreet, we shall reanimate the states and get the governments in successful operation, with order prevailing and the Union established, before Congress comes together in December." He expressed concern about "men in Congress . . . who possessed feelings of hatred and vindictiveness."

Stanton proposed martial law with the South ruled by military governors until civilian rule could be reestablished. The military would preserve order while federal departments carried out their various functions. These suggestions met with general approval, but another Stanton proposal to combine Virginia and North Carolina into a single military unit under the War Department (and Stanton) was controversial. Lincoln asked all members to consider carefully the matter of reconstruction. "No greater or more important [subject] could come before us or any future cabinet," he emphasized. The discussion was to be continued at the next meeting, slated for the following Tuesday.[12]

Lincoln skipped lunch and ate an apple as he went back to his office and summoned Vice President Johnson. They talked for about half an hour. Lincoln wanted to be sure Johnson understood his wishes regarding reconstruction. Lincoln then labored over pardons and reprieves and contended with numerous callers.

Alone at his desk, he heard a ruckus outside his door. "For God's sake! Please let me see the president!" shouted a woman's voice. Lincoln opened the door and saw a guard barring a former female slave from seeing him. "Let the good woman in," Lincoln said. The distraught woman, Nancy Bushrod, told the president that she and her husband had been freed as slaves on a plantation near Richmond. He had enlisted in the Army of the Potomac, but his pay was not coming through, and they had many children to support. "Can you help us, Mr. President?" Lincoln looked at her compassionately and replied: "Come back around this time tomorrow, and the papers will be signed and ready for you."[13]

About noon on Friday, April 14, John Wilkes Booth stopped by Ford's Theatre to pick up his mail. The ticket seller, Thomas Raybold, handed him a pile of letters and told him the president was coming that night. Booth asked if he was sure, and Raybold said it had been confirmed.

At about eight o'clock, Booth met with George Atzerodt, David Herold, and Lewis Paine. Atzerodt and Paine were assigned, respectively, to kill Vice President Johnson and Secretary of State Seward. Booth would kill the president. All assassinations were to occur at 10:15 p.m. Booth later wrote in his diary that the country's troubles were caused by Lincoln and "God simply made me the instrument of his punishment. . . . I struck for my country and that alone. A country groaned beneath this tyranny and prayed for this end."[14]

Late in the afternoon Lincoln and Mary rode in an open carriage to the navy yard. He seemed "cheerful, almost joyous," she recalled.

She said to him, "You almost startle me by your great cheerfulness."

He responded: "And well I may feel so, Mary. I consider this [the] day the war has come to a close." He then offered a challenge to both of them: "We must both be more cheerful in the future—between the war and the loss of our darling Willie—we have both been very miserable."

They talked about traveling abroad. He especially wanted to visit Jerusalem and Europe. They also planned to visit the American West. Then he would resume his law practice in Illinois and argue cases before the state supreme court. He looked forward to quieter and happier times.[15]

Working into the evening Lincoln wrote the final letter of his life to Gen. James H. Van Alen, who had warned him to be more careful when going out in public. Lincoln wrote that he would use "due precaution." His final sentence was: "I thank you for the assurance you give me that I shall be supported by conservative men like yourself in the efforts I may make to re-store the Union, so as to make it, to use your language, a Union of hearts and hands as well as of States."

While the Lincolns were scheduled to attend the play at Ford's Theatre, by dinnertime Mary had developed a headache and preferred to stay home. Lincoln insisted that they go. The newspapers had announced their plans, and he could use some comedy in his life, he said. To him the theater was a refuge—a relaxing escape from the reality of war, ruthless men and women, and even the bruising bouts with his rambunctious wife. Without the the-ater Lincoln said he "could not go on." He went so often—at least twelve times—that newspapers accused him of trivializing wartime.

Together Mary and Lincoln had seen the piquant comedy of Maggie Mitchell in her signature role of *Fanchon, the Crickett* and the foremost tragedian of the time, Charlotte Cushman, in the role of Lady Macbeth. Cushman was introduced to Lincoln at the White House by Secretary Seward, her close friend. A feminist and strong supporter of the war effort, she gave five benefit performances for the Sanitary Commission, a civilian effort that mobilized women to help soldiers by knitting sweaters, folding bandages, and serving as nurses. She had played opposite both John Wilkes Booth and his brother Edwin. She described Edwin as "living proof of how short the country was of gentlemen" and Wilkes as a strange, daring man who demanded complete realism on stage. Often his sword thrusts and fisticuffs left scars and bruises—in return for which he too was cut many times and slept bandaged in steak and oysters.

Now Lincoln wanted to see Laura Keene in *Our American Cousin*. The London-born actress had been an instant success in comedies in New York and was well received wherever she went. She was the first woman to manage a theater in the United States.

Lincoln invited the Stantons and the Grants to accompany them. The secretary of war refused for several reasons: his wife did not like Mrs. Lincoln, he did not approve of the theater, and he wanted to discourage Lincoln from going. "Mr. Lincoln ought not to go," he warned. "It was too great an exposure."

General Grant initially accepted but then declined. He did not want to incur Mary's displeasure again, and Julia Grant, after her horrid experience with Mary at City Point, did not want to be confined for hours in a theater box with "that crazy woman." Seeking a valid excuse, Julia decided to visit her children in Burlington, New Jersey, and the general asked to be excused so he could be with her. If Mary's rude outbursts had not occurred, the Grants likely would have accepted, and Grant would have had a large guard for protection. Lincoln might not have been assassinated that night.[16]

That morning Lincoln had walked across the White House lawn to Stanton's office and uncharacteristically asked for special protection at the theater. He told Stanton he had seen Maj. Thomas T. Eckert, chief of the military telegraph office, break five cast-iron pokers by striking them over his arm, one after the other, "and I'm thinking he would be the kind of man to go with me this evening. May I take him?"

Stanton shrugged. "I cannot spare him. I have important work for him this evening."

"I will ask him myself," Lincoln replied. "He can do your work tomorrow." The president walked into the adjoining cipher room and extended the invitation to Eckert. "Now, Major," he cajoled, "come along. Mrs. Lincoln and I want you with us." Eckert knew Stanton's wishes and was not about to cross him. He declined the president's request, citing the pressing work he had to do for Stanton, although he had no knowledge of what it was that demanded his attention. "Very well," Lincoln said, "I will take Major Rathbone along, but I should much rather have you."

Maj. Henry R. Rathbone, slender and dapper, was a ladies man incapable of breaking a poker over his arm. But after fourteen others turned down the Lincolns, they invited him and his fiancé, Clara Harris, whose father was a senator from New York. Rathbone went unarmed, and his attentions were centered not on Lincoln but on Clara.

Shortly after the president left the War Department, Stanton told Eckert he had changed his mind about needing him to work that night. "The work can wait until tomorrow," he said.[17]

Stanton's behavior has prompted several writers to link him to the conspiracy to kill Lincoln. Most historians, however, regard that as unlikely. Stanton was a peculiar man. Grant said of him: "It seemed to be pleasanter to him to disappoint than to gratify." David Homer Bates, manager of the War Department's telegraph office, thought Stanton was by nature "haughty, severe, domineering, and often rude." Bates likened him to the characterization of Napoleon by Charles Phillips, the Irish orator: "Grand, gloomy, and peculiar." When Stanton's daughter Lucy died in 1841, he had her body exhumed and kept the coffin in his room for two years. And when his wife died in 1844, he dressed and re-dressed her in her bridal clothes. Such was the man who advised Lincoln to avoid the theater but then failed to provide adequate protection when the president chose to go. At his disposal were all the military forces in Washington, as well as the Secret Service and the provost marshals with many army police and detectives at their command. Stanton, however, did nothing. Some historians interpret this as his way of trying to discourage Lincoln from going to Ford's Theatre.[18]

White House guard William Crook, as he was about to go off duty that fateful day, begged Lincoln to avoid the theater. But the president would not hear of it. "Then let me stay on duty and accompany you," Crook insisted.

"No, Crook," Lincoln said kindly but firmly, "you have had a long, hard day's work already, and you must go home to sleep and rest. I cannot afford to have you get tired out and exhausted."

As Crook was leaving, Lincoln neglected for the first time to say good night to him. Instead, he turned to him and said, "Good-bye, Crook."[19]

At 8:15 p.m. the Lincolns climbed into the presidential carriage and went to Senator Harris's home to pick up their guests, accompanied only by the coachman and a personal attendant, Charles Forbes. Heavy fog drifted in as the group arrived late at Ford's Theatre. When they entered, the play stopped, the audience stood, and the orchestra played "Hail to the Chief." The presidential party proceeded to the State Box overlooking the stage.

One solitary man—John Parker—stood guard over their box. He was a low-life metropolitan police officer with many reprimands on his record for unbecoming conduct, insubordination, and loafing and drunkenness while on duty. He also habitually arrested streetwalkers who refused to grant him their favors gratis. Who was responsible for assigning such a man to the White House detail? Mary Lincoln.

Earlier that month Parker was eligible for the army draft and wanted to avoid it. He did, thanks to a letter Mary wrote on April 3 sponsoring his transfer to the White House guard and another letter the following day to have him "exempted from the draft." She made these requests shortly after her return from City Point. Through her own acts, Parker stood guard at the Lincolns' box at Ford's Theatre.

Shortly after the play resumed, it was obvious that the president and First Lady were enjoying the performance. Lincoln laughed heartily and Mary applauded often. During the third act she placed her hand in his and moved closer to him. "What will Miss Harris think of my hanging on to you so?" she whispered.

"She won't think anything about it," he replied.[20]

Meanwhile, guard John Parker left his post, apparently to go outside for a drink, although he later told William Crook he went to find a seat "so that he could see the play." His absence was never adequately explained. All facts related to his movements were conveniently lost in the files of the official investigation. When Mary's sponsorship of Parker came to light, nobody wanted to pursue it. Her actions, Stanton's inaction, and Parker's incompetence had made it incredibly easy for John Wilkes Booth, or anyone, to kill the president at Ford's Theatre that night.

Thus, shortly after 10:00 p.m. Booth entered the president's unguarded anteroom and barred the door behind him so as not to be disturbed. Quietly he pulled from his pocket a small single-shot derringer and waited for a line in the play he knew would draw applause and laughter.

The play was about an American bumpkin, Asa Trenchard, who goes to England to claim riches inherited from a noble relative. A fortune-hunting Englishwoman follows him, hoping he will marry her daughter. When the Englishwoman, played by Laura Keene, learns that Trenchard has given away his inheritance, she denounces him and makes a haughty exit. He responds: "Don't know the manners of good society, eh? Well, I guess I know enough to turn you inside out, old gal—you sockdologizing old man-trap." Audiences tended to roar in laughter after that line.

Booth entered the front room of the box and moved behind Lincoln, who was leaning forward with his chin in his right hand and his arm on the balustrade. At a distance of about two feet, Booth pointed his pistol at the left side of the president's head, and fired. It was 10:13 p.m.

Mary screamed in deranged, impenetrable terror. Clara Harris shouted repeatedly: "They have shot the president! They have shot the president!" Rathbone sprang toward Booth and seized him, but Booth freed himself and made a violent thrust with a razor-sharp hunting knife, striking Rathbone's arm, cutting an artery, nerves, and veins. Dramatically, Booth leaped to the stage, and Rathbone cried out: "Stop that man!"[21]

Two young physicians ran to the box and found the president paralyzed, with no pulse. They removed the blood clot, administered mouth-to-mouth resuscitation, and restored his breathing. Laura Keene, the star of Our American Cousin, was just off the stage when the shot was fired. Hoping she could be helpful, she brought a glass of water to the president's box. By this time, Lincoln had been placed on the floor, with a white handkerchief under his head. The actress reportedly received permission to place his head on her lap. She dabbed water on his forehead as blood soiled her yellow satin skirt.

Other physicians made their way into the box, and with the assistance of men from the audience, they carried Lincoln across the street, through an eerie mist, to a boarding house owned by William Petersen, a merchant-tailor. In a shabby room down a narrow hallway they laid the president on a bed that was too short for his six-foot-four-inch frame. He had to be placed diagonally, with his feet dangling on the side.

Lincoln lay there for nine hours, never regaining consciousness. Mary, distraught, sat beside him and called on him to speak to her. She showered his face with kisses and spoke words of endearment. She wanted to fetch Tad, thinking Lincoln would speak to him, but the physicians advised against it. Robert arrived with Senator Sumner, saw his mother's desperate condition, and with the help of Senator James Dixon's wife, one of Mary's closest friends, persuaded her to retire to the parlor—but she returned hourly to the president's bedside.

Stanton quickly took charge and dictated telegrams. He ordered all bridges out of the capital closed and initiated a massive manhunt. Soon he learned of the two other attempted assassinations. Atzerodt, however, had disobeyed Booth and had not attacked the vice president, but Paine had savagely assaulted Seward in his bed and left him barely alive. Both Atzerodt and Paine were captured within days. It took nearly two weeks to find Booth at a Virginia farm, where he was shot and killed.[22]

As Mary sat beside her husband, he suddenly made a heavy snoring sound, and she jumped with a piercing cry and fainted. Stanton demanded: "Take that woman out and don't let her in again!" But she was allowed to return and again seated herself by the president, kissing him and beseeching him: "Love, live but one moment to speak to me once—to speak to our children."

As he neared death, she was led back to the front room. Resting on a sofa, she recalled Lincoln's prophetic dream, cried pitifully, and begged God to take her too. Shortly after 7:22 a.m. the physicians came in and told her: "It is all over. The president is no more." Robert cried aloud and leaned on Sumner. Stanton asked the pastor of the New York Avenue Presbyterian Church to say a prayer. Then the secretary of war announced, "Now he belongs to the ages."[23]

The fog had turned to a heavy rain as Robert assisted his grieving mother into a carriage and the horses pulled them through the rough, muddy streets back to the White House. Mary wept hysterically and made unearthly shrieks. Except for her family, the only companion she wanted was her dressmaker, Lizzie Keckley. An optimistic woman of tact and poise, Keckley was the perfect companion to calm Mary's emotional imbalance. She finally arrived around eleven o'clock and bathed Mary's head with cold water and comforted her. Tad hugged his mother's neck and pleaded: "Don't cry so, Momma! Don't cry, or you will make me cry too! You will break my heart!" When he pleaded, she composed herself as best she could and clasped her child in her arms.[24]

A few hours after Andrew Johnson was sworn in as president, Radical Republicans caucused to discuss the rosy picture they now expected for their program of vengeance against the South. They had been diametrically opposed to Lincoln's "soft" peace plan and his reconstruction proposals.

They wanted Rebel property confiscated and the conquered South treated as a prize of war. Johnson, they felt, would be more supportive of their position. They had rejoiced when earlier that month he went to Lincoln with demands that Confederate leaders be executed. Representative George Julian of Indiana later wrote that "while everybody was shocked at [Lincoln's] murder, the feeling was nearly universal that the ascension of Johnson to the presidency would prove a godsend to the country." Senator Zachariah Chandler of Michigan intoned that "God had placed a better man in Lincoln's place."[25]

Mary was emotionally unable to attend the funeral in the White House on Wednesday, April 19. She remained upstairs, weeping hysterically, with Keckley at her side. In the hushed and dimmed East Room, Lincoln's casket rested on a flower-covered catafalque. Robert stood at the foot of the coffin; General Grant sat at the other end, his moist eyes focused on a cross of lilies. Some six hundred Washington dignitaries crowded into the room for the eleven o'clock service. Only seven women were among them: the bewitching Kate Chase Sprague, whom Mary regarded as a heartless wretch and who for years had belittled Lincoln behind his back; Kate's younger sister Nettie; Mary Jane Welles, who was Mary's friend and whose husband, the secretary of the navy, had sat by the head of the president's bed most of the night after the assassination; Ellen Stanton, who disliked Mary and had campaigned without success to get Lincoln to appoint her husband as chief justice; Mrs. John Palmer Usher, wife of the secretary of the interior; and Anne Eliza Dennison, wife of the postmaster general, and their daughter. The supportive women in Lincoln's life were not there—probably because they had not been invited—women such as his Eliza Gurney, Harriet Beecher Stowe, Sojourner Truth, and Vinnie Ream.

Later, while Tad was being dressed, he looked up at his nurse and said: "Pa is dead. I can hardly believe that I shall never see him again. I must learn to take care of myself now." He thought for a moment and then added: "Yes, Pa is dead, and I am only Tad Lincoln now, little Tad, like other little boys. I am not a president's son now. I won't have many presents any more. Well, I will try and be a good boy, and will hope to go some day to Pa and brother Willie, in heaven."[26]

At dawn on Friday, April 21, Lincoln's body left Washington in a nine-car funeral train decorated with Union flags and accompanied by three hundred dignitaries. Willie's coffin was exhumed from its Georgetown grave and placed beside his father for the seventeen-hundred-mile journey to

Springfield. Along the way, a million Americans in a dozen cities would look upon Lincoln's face.

"No common mortal had died," observed Lizzie Keckley. "The Moses of my people had fallen in the hour of triumph." Lincoln's stepmother sighed on hearing of his murder and said, "I know'd they'd kill him." A neighbor recalled, "She never had no heart after that to be 'chirp' and 'peart' like she used to be." Sarah, too weak to attend services in Springfield, died four years later at her Goosenest Prairie cabin.[27]

The procession from the Illinois State House in Springfield to Oak Ridge Cemetery was the largest ever seen in the West. Ann Rutledge's brother Robert was among the planners and the mourners. During the Lincoln administration he had been appointed provost marshal of the First Congressional District of Iowa.

President Andrew Johnson never expressed sympathy for Mary Lincoln's grief or the loss of her husband. He never called on her, never wrote to her, and never inquired about her welfare. When she finally left the White House forty days after the assassination, no one told her goodbye. She descended the public stairway, entered her carriage, drove to the depot, and with Lizzie Keckley, Robert, and Tad, boarded a train for Chicago. Seventeen more years of heartaches and trouble lay ahead for the last woman in Lincoln's life.

EPILOGUE

"Beloved of Abraham Lincoln"

*A*NN RUTLEDGE was reinterred in 1890, fifty-five years after her death. It was the result of a commercial venture by a local undertaker and civic-minded citizens in Petersburg, Illinois, a town situated near New Salem. Undertaker Samuel Montgomery was an investor in the newly established Oakland Cemetery. To boost the sale of cemetery lots, he proposed moving Ann Rutledge's remains to Oakland.

McGrady Rutledge, then seventy-six, was Ann's only Rutledge relative in the Petersburg area. He initially opposed the idea, as did Ann's sister Nancy, then living in Iowa. "Ann's remains should stay where those of her family were buried," Nancy declared. Montgomery persuaded McGrady to change his mind, however, arguing that the grave would receive better care at Oakland than at the cemetery where she had been buried—which was abandoned.

On May 15, 1890, Montgomery, McGrady Rutledge, two laborers, and a nine-year-old boy attempted to reinter Ann's remains. When they dug up her badly decayed wooden coffin at Old Concord Cemetery, all they reportedly found were some pearl buttons, long strands of hair, a few bones, and a small silver buckle. These items, along with a few shovelfuls of dirt from her grave, were placed in another wooden box, loaded onto a flatbed wagon, taken to Petersburg, and buried the next day at Oakland.

As mementos of his favorite cousin, McGrady kept several other items: a small button covered in cloth of faded rose, a bow four inches wide made of silky ribbon, a two-foot-long strip of black lace, and a lock of hair. He later gave these relics to his brother Jasper, who passed them down to his daughter—a namesake of Ann. Eventually, the artifacts came to Jasper's great-granddaughter Margaret Richardson. A photograph of the items appeared in an 1893 booklet, *Menard-Salem-Lincoln Souvenir Album,* which was published by a local women's club.

Eventually, an impressive granite monument was erected at Ann's gravesite in Oakland Cemetery. Engraved on it is an epitaph by Edgar Lee Masters:

> Out of me unworthy and unknown
> The vibrations of deathless music!
> "With malice toward none, with charity for all."
> Out of me forgiveness of millions toward millions,
> And the beneficent face of a nation
> Shining with justice and truth.
> I am Ann Rutledge who sleep beneath these weeds,
> Beloved in life of Abraham Lincoln,
> Wedded to him, not through union,
> But through separation.
> Bloom forever, O Republic,
> From the dust of my bosom!

For more than a century and a half the former site of Ann's grave at Old Concord was marked with a simple wooden sign. In 1996 Rutledge descendants replaced it with a granite headstone etched on both sides. The front of the stone reads: "Original Grave of Anna Mayes Rutledge, Jan. 7, 1813— Aug. 25, 1835. Where Lincoln Wept." On the opposite side: "Ann Rutledge. 'I cannot bear to think of her out there alone in the storm.' A. Lincoln."

$\mathcal{M}$ARY TODD LINCOLN lay in bed in the White House forty days after her husband's assassination and even tried to contact him through bedside seances conducted by spiritualists. Finally eased out of the Executive Mansion, she moved to Chicago. She begged friends for money, tried unsuccessfully to sell her elaborate wardrobe under a false name, and became the object of ridicule and humiliation. Her hysteria intensified when William Herndon uncovered the story of Lincoln's love for Ann Rutledge and spoke and wrote about it. Mary threatened Herndon and insisted that Lincoln's heart had not been "in any unfortunate woman's grave—but in the proper place with his beloved wife and children."

In 1868 Mary left America and traveled to Germany, taking Tad with her. They returned three years later after she was awarded a long-sought government pension. Unfortunately, the cold ocean crossing was too much for Tad, who shortly developed pleurisy or pneumonia and died at age eighteen in Chicago in 1871. Mary then moved into a spiritualist commune and claimed to communicate with her dead husband. Signs of mental instability became evident. She entered a hotel elevator half-dressed, believing it was a lavatory; she bought three hundred pairs of gloves, a hundred shawls, and yards of expensive drapery for which she had no use; and she wandered around the city with thousands of dollars in securities sewn in her dress.

In 1875 Robert Lincoln gave up on her and had her committed to a sanitarium for well-to-do women. She had been there only a short time when she was declared sane and released. As might be expected, Mary severed all ties with Robert. He is a "wicked monster," she wailed. She had now lost everyone she ever cared about.

She left the country again. For three years she lived in a dingy hotel in southern France. She developed severe arthritis, suffered from a series of crippling falls, and became partially paralyzed. Returning to Springfield, she moved into the home of her sister Elizabeth Edwards. It was the same mansion where she had married Lincoln. With her bedroom shades always drawn, she packed and unpacked her sixty-four trunks of clothing by candlelight. She slept on just one side of the bed to leave a place for her husband. On July 16, 1882, she died after suffering a stroke. She was sixty-four.

$\mathcal{R}$OBERT TODD LINCOLN was admitted to the bar in Illinois in 1867 and became a corporate lawyer. In 1868 he married Mary Harlan, daughter of U.S. Senator James Harlan of Iowa. She suffered from a nervous debility and was reclusive. They had a son, Abraham, who died of blood poisoning at sixteen, and two daughters, Mary and Jessie.

Mary married Charles B. Isham and bore him a son, Lincoln Isham, who married Leahalma Correa. They had no children.

Jessie eloped after Robert disapproved of her choice for a husband, Warren W. Beckwith. They had two children, Mary Lincoln Beckwith and Robert Lincoln Beckwith, before divorcing in 1907. Jessie remarried in 1915 and again in 1925 but had no more children. Mary Lincoln Beckwith, great-granddaughter of President Lincoln, never married. An active but shy woman, she enjoyed skiing, sculpting, and piloting her own planes. She died in 1975. Her brother, Robert Lincoln Beckwith, married twice but had no children. When he died in 1985 the Lincoln line ended.

Robert Todd Lincoln served as secretary of war under Presidents James A. Garfield and Chester Arthur (1881–85) and as minister to Great Britain (1889–93) under President Benjamin Harrison. He witnessed the fatal shooting of two presidents: Garfield, at the Washington railroad station on July 2, 1881, and William McKinley, at the Pan-American Exposition in Buffalo, New York, on September 6, 1901. Robert was twice named as a contender for the presidency, but he never ran for public office. He was the wealthy president and chairman of the board of the Pullman Company from 1897 until 1911. In his senior years he and his wife spent summers at their cherished estate, Hildene, in Manchester, Vermont, and their winters in the Georgetown section of Washington, D.C. He died at eighty-two of a cerebral hemorrhage at Hildene on July 26, 1926, and was buried at Arlington National Cemetery. His wife, Mary, died on March 31, 1937, at the age of ninety.

*T*HE BODY of Abraham Lincoln lies in an ornate granite mausoleum in Oak Ridge Cemetery in Springfield, Illinois—buried within a block of concrete eight-feet-square and fifteen feet deep. Fearful his body might be stolen, the family entombed Lincoln beneath the insurmountable obstacle. Mary Todd Lincoln and three of the four Lincoln children are also buried there.

About twenty-two miles northwest lie the remains of the first love in Lincoln's life—Ann Rutledge.

APPENDIX

Evidence of the Lincoln–Rutledge Romance and Engagement

The love story of Abe and Ann has become an indestructible part of our American folk heritage. As long as America remembers Abraham Lincoln, we will remember Ann Rutledge, and that will be for a very long time.

—Irving Stone, author of *Love Is Eternal*

Letters and Statements Collected by William H. Herndon

ℋERNDON WAS Lincoln's law partner and biographer. The following statements are compiled from the Herndon-Weik Collection in the Library of Congress. The collection was published in *Herndon's Informants,* edited by Douglas L. Wilson and Rodney O. Davis of the Center for Lincoln Studies at Knox College. Wilson's analysis of the documents reveals remarkable agreement by the people of New Salem, Illinois, about the courtship and engagement of Ann Rutledge and Abraham Lincoln. Of the twenty-four respondents, twenty-two asserted that Lincoln loved and courted Ann Rutledge (two had no opinion), and fifteen claimed they were engaged (seven had no opinion, and two said they didn't think so). Early disbelievers among historians regarded Herndon's informants as vague and their memories as "dim and misty." Not so, said Wilson, who reported that they came across as "straightforward and reliable" with "no purpose to deceive" and that the information supporting the romance was "overwhelming." Lincoln scholar John Y. Simon of Southern Illinois University came to the same conclusion in his earlier research: "All the primary sources—the testimony of witnesses—support the romance . . . and the reality of the story appears certain." Albert J. Beveridge, the only scholar to have full access to the Herndon collection before 1941, wrote: "[I went into] Herndon's credibility as if I were trying a murder case, [and there was no doubt about his] entire truthfulness and trustworthiness generally. . . . When Herndon states a fact as a fact, you can depend on it." Beveridge's book, *Abraham Lincoln 1809–1858*, is recognized as a solid source for Lincoln's early years. Here are excerpts from letters to Herndon and statements he obtained through interviews:

"[When McNamar was in New York] Mr. Lincoln courted Ann and [was] engaged to marry her, on the completion of the study of law. In this I am corroborated by James McGrady Rutledge, a cousin about her age, and who was in her confidence. He says in a letter to me just received: 'Ann told me . . . that as soon as certain studies were completed she and Lincoln would be married.' There is no kind of doubt as to the existence of this engagement. David Rutledge [Ann's brother closest to her age] urged Ann to consummate it [immediately], but Ann urged the propriety of seeing McNamar first [so that she could] inform him of the change in her feelings and seek an honorable release [from the earlier engagement to him]. . . . In August 1835 Ann sickened and died. The effect upon Mr. Lincoln's mind was terrible; he became plunged in despair, and many of his friends feared that reason would desert her throne. His extraordinary emotions were regarded as strong evidence of the existence of the tenderest relations between himself and the deceased."

—Robert B. Rutledge, Ann's brother who was federal provost marshal in Iowa during the Lincoln administration. Excerpted from letters from Oskaloosa, Iowa, November 1, 18, 21, 1866. (NOTE: The Rutledges were a prominent and highly respected family at New Salem, Illinois. They had strong moral values and were very religious. No one ever questioned their honesty, and there is no evidence that any member of the family ever tried to deceive anyone. When Herndon learned of the romance from other sources, the Rutledges were reluctant to discuss it. They regarded it as a private matter. As news of the alleged romance spread across the country, family members were besieged with requests for confirmation. Robert became the family spokesman and left no room for doubt in his letters to Herndon. Other family members, including Ann's mother and sisters, later acknowledged the reality of the romance and the engagement.)

"As to the relation existing between Mr. Lincoln and Ann Rutledge, I have every reason to believe that it was of the tenderest character, as I know of my own knowledge that he made regular visits to her. During her last illness he visited her sick chamber and on his return stopped at my house. It was very evident that he was very much distressed, and I was not surprised when it was rumored subsequently that his reason was in danger. It was generally understood that Mr. Lincoln and Ann Rutledge were engaged to be married. She was a very amiable and lovable woman and it was deemed a suitable match—one in which both parties were in every way worthy of each other."

—John A. Jones, brother of Hannah Armstrong of Clary's Grove, Illinois. She and her husband were close friends of Lincoln. Winterset, Iowa, October 22, 1866.

"You asked about him [Lincoln] as regards women. They all liked him and [he] liked them as well. There was a Miss Rutledge. I have no doubt he would have married [her] if she had lived. But death prevented."

—J. Rowan Herndon, New Salem merchant. Quincy, Illinois, July 3, 1865.

"Lincoln was woefully in love with a remarkable, handsome young lady by the name of Rutledge. Two other men were in the same fix, all three paying their address to her. . . . She died and Lincoln took it so hard that some of his friends thought he would go crazy."

—Benjamin F. Irwin, public official. Pleasant Plains, Illinois, August 27, 1866.

"He [Lincoln] fell in love with a Miss Ann Rutledge—a pretty and accomplished girl of Menard County, living in New Salem. It was said that after the death of Miss Rutledge and because of it, Lincoln was locked up by his friends . . . to prevent derangement or suicide—so hard did he take her death."

—Hardin Bale, carding mill operator, New Salem. Petersburg, Illinois, May 29, 1865.

"[Lincoln] was staying with us at the time of her [Ann's] death, it was a great shock to him, and I have never seen a man mourn for a companion more than he did for her; he made a remark one day when it was raining that he could not bear the idea of it raining on her grave."

—Elizabeth Abell, wife of Dr. Bennett Abell (close friends of Lincoln) and sister of Mary Owens (courted by Lincoln). February 15, 1867.

"He [Lincoln] . . . was in love with a young lady in New Salem by the name of Ann Rutledge. She accepted the overtures of Lincoln and they were engaged to be married. This young lady was a woman of exquisite beauty . . . her intellect was quick—sharp—deep and philosophic as well as brilliant. She had a gentle and kind a heart as an angel—full of love—kindness—sympathy. . . . Everybody respected and loved her. . . . She was a woman worthy of Lincoln's love."

—William G. Greene, Lincoln's store helper who became a successful businessman. May 30, 1865.

"He [Lincoln] was engaged to be married to Miss Ann Rutledge of New Salem, a beautiful and very amiable young woman. But before the match was consummated, she took fever and died. Lincoln took it very hard indeed."

—Lynn McNulty Greene, Dr. Bennett Abell's son-in-law. Avon, Illinois, July 30, 1865.

"Mrs. Bowling Green says that Mr. Lincoln was a regular suitor of Miss Ann Rutledge for between two and three years up to August 1835 in which month Miss Rutledge died, that Lincoln took her death very hard, so much so that some thought his mind would become impaired, and in fear of it [Mrs. Green's husband] went to New Salem after Lincoln, brought him to his house and kept him a week or two and succeeded in cheering him. [Mrs. Green] thinks they would have been married had Miss Rutledge not have died. . . . Mrs. William Rutledge who resides in Petersburg and did reside in the neighborhood at the time of said courtship and who is an aunt to Ann Rutledge and acquainted with the parties and all the circumstances of the prolonged courtship corroborates all the above. . . . Mrs. Parthena Hill [also] corroborates all the above. She thinks as Mrs. Green that Lincoln would have got her had she lived and it was so generally believed."

—George Miles, a Sangamon County resident and agent for William Herndon. Petersburg, Illinois, March 23, 1866.

"[Regarding Lincoln's reported insanity]—that his mind had been shaken—that disappointed love was the cause—Her name was Ann Rutledge—It was then talked of as a part of the history of the men of the town. The extent of his insanity was such that men were then occasionally talking of it and still remembered by them."

—Thompson Ware McNeely, lawyer and congressman. Petersburg, Illinois, November 12, 1866.

"Lincoln took advantage of McNamar's absence—courted Ann—got her confidence, and in Mr. Hill's and my opinions, as well as the opinions of others, they were engaged—Ann thought that McNamar was playing off on her."

—Parthena Nance Hill, close friend of Ann Rutledge and wife of merchant Sam Hill. March 1887.

"[I] first knew Lincoln . . . in 1831. I used to go down to the river and play cards with him. . . . I next knew Lincoln in New Salem: he boarded with me in New Salem—he was engaged to Ann Rutledge."

—Caleb Carman, a carder and shoemaker in New Salem. March 1887.

"Lincoln and she [Ann] were engaged—Lincoln told me so—She intimated to me the same."

—Mentor Graham, schoolteacher who taught Ann and helped Lincoln with grammar and surveying. Petersburg, Illinois, spring, 1866.

"Knew Lincoln well—Knew Ann Rutledge well—handsome woman—It is my opinion that they were engaged—would have been married had she lived."

—Henry Hohimer, New Salem farmer. March 7, 1887.

"I have seen Miss Rutledge a thousand times . . . a pretty woman. . . . Straight as an arrow, and as quick as a flash. Lincoln would have been happy with Miss Rutledge."

—Henry McHenry, Clary's Grove resident. Lincoln appointed him a provost marshal during the Civil War. 1866.

"[Regarding Herndon's lecture on Ann Rutledge] I believe I am not able to detect any error. . . . I am well pleased [with it]."

—John M. Rutledge, Ann's oldest brother. Birmingham, Iowa, November 25, 1866.

"Heard a conversation among the old settlers—such as Squire Short—Godby and others and it was their opinion that Lincoln and Ann Rutledge were engaged to be married."

—William Bennett, a Petersburg brick maker. March 7, 1887.

"[I am] treasurer of Menard County—am related to Ann Rutledge. She died before I was born—have heard much. My brother, James McGrady Rutledge, knows all about the story of Ann Rutledge, McNamar, and Lincoln. Ann Rutledge and McNamar were engaged to be married. In making out some deeds McNamar signed the deed as McNamar—when McNamar called himself McNeil. This opened Ann's eyes. . . . Lincoln in 1834–35 seeing the way things were tending went to see Ann—and Ann and Lincoln were engaged to be married. My brother knows this as well as he knows anything—he has told me so substantially. Ann sent for Lincoln in her last sickness."

—Jasper Rutledge, Menard County treasurer and farmer. Petersburg, Illinois, March 9, 1887.

"[You asked] Do you know anything concerning the courtship and engagement of Abraham Lincoln and Ann Rutledge? Well, I had an opportunity to know and I do know the facts. Abraham Lincoln and Ann Rutledge were engaged to be married. . . . I had a long acquaintance with him [Lincoln]. Him and I slept in the same bed while he boarded [at the tavern] with my uncle James Rutledge. While he was boarding there Lincoln became deeply in love with Ann. [She] consented to wait for their marriage . . . until Lincoln was admitted to the bar, but [she] died within the year. Had she lived until spring they were to be married. He came down and was with her during her last illness and burial. . . . Lincoln took her death very hard."

—McGrady Rutledge, Ann's first cousin and confidant. From an interview in March 1887 and from the memoirs of McGrady Rutledge.

Statements from Other Sources

"Lincoln was boarding at the tavern and fell deeply in love with Ann, and she was no less in love with him. They were engaged to be married.

—Harvey Lee Ross, a close friend of Lincoln, who delivered the mail to New Salem and slept in the same loft with Lincoln at the Rutledge Tavern. From his recollections printed in the *Fulton Democrat* at Lewiston, Illinois, 1896.

"In reply to your letter of February 1, 1929: Mary Ann Rutledge, mother of Ann Rutledge, was my maternal grandmother. She lived in our home and the home of my uncle John Rutledge from my earliest recollection, dividing her time, and died in our home December 26, 1878, in Birmingham, Iowa. Scores of times I have heard her tell of the engagement between Lincoln and her daughter Ann.

—Will S. Prewitt, grandson of Mary Ann Rutledge. From a 1929 letter to John E. Boos of Albany, New York, a collector of Lincoln memorabilia. (NOTE: Lloyd Ostendorf, a noted Lincoln artist and collector, wrote the following note to me on July 29, 1999: "People tend to forget that Ann's mother lived well into her 90s and with a sound mind. She repeatedly related the story of the romance to her own family as the letters I have prove.")

"Lincoln and Ann planned to be married in the fall of 1836 when Ann completed her year of study in Jacksonville. . . . Ann's whole soul seemed wrapped up in him. . . . Every time he was in the neighborhood after she died, he would go alone to her grave and sit there in silence for hours."

—Jean Rutledge (Ann's oldest sister), as recorded by historian R. D. Miller of Springfield, Illinois, in 1860 (about five years before Herndon revealed Ann's story to the world). Miller's notes, written in his diary, were shared with journalist Ida Tarbell around 1890.

"[Lincoln's feeling for Mary] had not the overmastering depth of an early love."

—Elizabeth Grimsley, cousin of Mary Todd, in a letter to journalist Ida Tarbell dated March 9, 1895 (from the Ida Tarbell Papers at Allegheny College). She could only be referring to his love for Ann Rutledge.

"He chanced to meet with a lady, who to him seemed lovely, angelic, and the height of perfection. . . . His feelings he soon made her acquainted with, and was delighted with a reciprocation. This to him was perfect happiness and with uneasy anxiety he awaited the arrival of the day when the twain would be made one flesh. But that day was doomed never to arrive. . . . Disease came upon this lovely beauty, and she sickened and died. The youth had wrapped his heart with hers, and this was more than he could bear. . . . Who now would the reader suppose is this awkward youth . . . this day laborer, infidel writer, surveyor, love-sick swain, hog drover, and legislator? He is none other than Abraham Lincoln, the President of the United States."

—Excerpts from "A Romance of Reality," *Menard Axis,* February 15, 1862, written by John Hill, son of Parthena Nance (Ann's best friend) and Sam Hill (Ann's second suitor). The article was the first published account of the Lincoln-Rutledge romance.

"It is true—true indeed [that I loved her and courted her]. . . . I did honestly and truly love the girl, and think often, often, of her now."

—Abraham Lincoln, in conversation with Isaac Cogdal in early 1861. Cogdal and Lincoln were old friends in New Salem. Psychologist C. A. Tripp (author of *The Homosexual Matrix*), questioned Cogdal's reliability in an article in the *Journal of the Abraham Lincoln Association* (Winter 2002). Tripp argued that Lincoln's language, as reported by Cogdal, was not characteristic of his usual style. He supported his thesis by stating that Lincoln "avoided using paired duplicates" such as: "It is true—true indeed I did [love her]" and "I think often, often of her now." Tripp also claimed that no evidence existed that Lincoln ever said that he loved any woman. But a casual reading of Lincoln's debates with Stephen A. Douglas and of his letters and speeches in the 1840s and 1850s reveals several instances of paired duplicates or grammatical usage closely related to paired duplicates. Some examples: "Now as to what I feel—I feel a desire . . ." (January 14, 1846); "that promise—that windy promise. . . . I am placed improperly—altogether improperly . . ." (September 15, 1858); "There was danger to this country—danger of . . ." (September 16, 1859); "that I believed him to be a man of veracity—that I believed him to be a man of capacity" (September 18, 1858); "This again is a heavy item—heavy at first and heavy at . . ." (September 30, 1858); "I deny—at least I deny it so far as . . ." (October 13, 1858); "That is good—good" and "I want to see you and our dear—dear boys very much" (letters to Mary from Washington). These styles are not inconsistent with the conversation reported by Cogdal. As for Tripp's comment about the lack of evidence that Lincoln ever said he loved any woman, there is strong evidence from Lincoln's closest friend, Joshua Speed, that Lincoln told Mary Todd twice that he did not love her and that he told others that he loved Matilda Edwards. And with fifteen witnesses confirming Lincoln's engagement to Ann Rutledge, one cannot logically conclude that he never told her that he loved her. If he never expressed that feeling to other women, perhaps he was just being true to himself. That was certainly characteristic of him. Several prominent historians regard Cogdal's recollections as genuine.

NOTES

Citations may be fully identified in the bibliography. The frequently cited source, Wilson and Davis, relates to their major work, *Herndon's Informants* (1998), which provides for the first time all letters, interviews, and statements about Lincoln collected by William H. Herndon (WHH) and Jesse W. Weik (JWW) for a biography of the martyred president.

CHAPTER 1: "ALL THAT I AM OR EVER HOPE TO BE I OWE TO HER"

1. Basler, 1:118 (Lincoln to Mrs. Orville H. Browning, Springfield, April 1, 1838); Herndon and Weik, 3; Boritt and Boritt, 228.
2. Herndon and Weik, 3; WHH to Ward Hill Lamon, Springfield, IL, March 6, 1870, WHH to JWW, Springfield, January 19, 1886, WHH to Charles H. Hart, Springfield, March 2, 1867, Ward Hill Lamon Papers, Henry E. Huntington Library, San Marino, CA; Hertz, *HL*, 63, 139, 411–12 (Herndon's memoir on Nancy Hanks, Greencastle, IN, August 20, 1887).
3. Herndon and Weik, 2–3.
4. See James A. Peterson, *In re Lucey Hanks* (Yorkville, IL: privately published, 1973), chap. 5.
5. J. Edward Murr to Albert J. Beveridge, New Albany, IN, November 21, 1924, Beveridge Papers, Library of Congress, Washington, DC; WHH to Charles H. Hart, Springfield, IL, December 28, 1866; and WHH to Ward Hill Lamon, Springfield, February 25, 1870, Ward Hill Lamon Papers, Henry E. Huntington Library, San Marino, CA.
6. Wilson and Davis, 67 (Samuel Haycraft to WHH, June 1865).
7. Hertz, *HL*, 204 (WHH to Truman Bartlett, September 25, 1887); Hertz, *HL*, 138–39 (WHH to JWW, January 19, 1886); Wilson and Davis, 615 (John Hanks to JWW, June 12, 1887); Wilson and Davis, 37 (Dennis F. Hanks to WHH, Chicago, IL, June 13, 1865); Linder, 39.

8. Tarbell, *Footsteps,* 93; Barton, *Paternity,* 182–83 (Robert Enlow, grandson of Abraham Enlow, to Barton, May 20, 1920).

9. Garrison, 7.

10. Hertz, *HL,* 63 (letter from WHH to Ward Hill Lamon, February 25, 1870); Herndon said he "was convinced that the weight of evidence is that Mr. Lincoln was an illegitimate. The evidence is not conclusive, but men have been hung on less evidence."

11. Herndon and Weik, 12; Wilson and Davis, 67 (Samuel Haycraft to WHH, Elizabethtown, KY, June 1865); Wilson and Davis, 675 (Charles Friend to WHH, August 20, 1889); Wilson and Davis, 612 (Judge Alfred M. Brown to JWW, March 23, 1887); Barton, *Paternity,* 20–21.

12. Wilson and Davis, 612 (Judge Alfred M. Brown to JWW, March 23, 1887); Wilson and Davis, 675 (Charles Friend to WHH, August 20, 1889). (NOTE: Charles Friend, postmaster of Sonora, KY, said he was present when "Old Uncle Abe Enlow" was asked if he was Abraham Lincoln's father, and Enlow said, "I never touched more than her hand in my life, never had carnal knowledge of her or intercourse with her in my life"); Wilson and Davis, 87 (Presley Nevil Haycraft to John B. Helm, July 19, 1865); Wilson and Davis, 82 (John B. Helm to WHH, August 1, 1865); Wilson and Davis, 613 (Lizzie Murphy to JWW, March, 1887); Wilson and Davis, 82 (John B. Helm to WHH, August 1, 1865).

13. Hertz, *HL,* 63 (WHH to Ward Hill Lamon, February 25, 1870).

14. Ibid., 18; Wilson and Davis, 235 (Charles Friend to WHH, March 19, 1866); Tarbell, *Footsteps,* 103; Burba (Austin Gollaher to Howard Burba).

15. Herndon and Weik, 51.

16. Ibid., 55–56.

17. Rankin, 325.

18. Lamon, *Life of AL,* 40n and chap. 2; Wilson and Davis, 38 (Dennis F. Hanks to WHH, June 13, 1865).

19. Hertz, *HL,* 279–81; Herndon and Weik, 27.

20. Warren, *Lincoln's Youth,* 58; Temple, 11; Browne, 59–61 (quoting Dr. J. G. Holland); Burlingame, *Inner World,* 137–39.

21. *Shelby County (IL) Leader,* March 19, 1931 (address by Clarence W. Bell in Mattoon, IL, February 11, 1931; Bell was the grandson of Elisha Linder, a friend of Lincoln and a neighbor of Thomas Lincoln in Illinois).

CHAPTER 2: "SHE WAS DOUBTLESS THE FIRST PERSON WHO EVER TREATED HIM LIKE A HUMAN BEING"

1. Herndon and Weik, 29–30 (quoting Sarah's granddaughter, Harriet Chapman).

2. Ibid., 28.

3. Ibid.
4. Wilson and Davis, 41 (Dennis Hanks to WHH, June 13, 1865); Wilson and Davis, 82 (John B. Helm to WHH, August 1, 1865); Wilson and Davis, 107–8 (Sarah Johnston Lincoln to WHH, September 8, 1865); Rice, 468.
5. Basler, 4:62.
6. Wilson and Davis, 112 (Nathaniel Grigsby to WHH, September 12, 1865).
7. Hertz, *HL,* 280–81; Herndon and Weik, 38; Hertz, *HL,* 279.
8. Murr, 57 (quoting Polly Richardson Agnew); Wilson and Davis, 113 (Nathaniel Grigsby to WHH, Gentryville, IN, September 12, 1865).
9. Conway, 87; Gridley, 136 (quoting Mrs. Samuel Chowning).
10. Conway, 76; Warren, *Lincoln's Youth,* 157.
11. Nora Bender, granddaughter of Elizabeth Tuley, to an unidentified correspondent, Papers of the Southwest Indiana Historical Society, Evansville Central Library; also *Chicago Times-Herald,* December 22, 1895 (interview with Elizabeth Tuley); Conway, 89; Wilson and Davis, 126–27 (Elizabeth Crawford to WHH, September16, 1865).
12. Wilson and Davis, 131 (Anna Roby Gentry to WHH, Rockport, IN, September 17, 1865).
13. Ibid.; *Los Angeles Times,* February 12, 1929 (statement by Dennis Franklin Johnston, son of John D. Johnston); Herndon and Weik, 49, 55.
14. Wilson and Davis, 110 (Matilda Johnston Moore to WHH, September 8, 1865); Herndon and Weik, 31.
15. Wilson and Davis, 126 (Elizabeth Crawford to WHH, September 16, 1865); Hertz, *HL,* 367.
16. Donald, 605n, 33; Wilson and Davis, 134 (A. H. Chapman to WHH, Charleston, IL, September 28, 1865); Wilson and Davis, 107 (Sarah Johnston Lincoln to WHH, September 8, 1865).
17. Wilson and Davis, 119–20 (Joseph C. Richardson to WHH, September 14, 1865).
18. Ibid.; Herndon and Weik, 44–47; Wilson and Davis, 113 (Nathaniel Grigsby to WHH, September 12, 1865); Herndon and Weik, 41.
19. Herndon and Weik, 61.
20. Barton, *Women,* 141–56.

CHAPTER 3: "TEACH ME, O LORD, TO THINK WELL OF MYSELF"

1. Ann Rutledge's birthdate is recorded in the Rutledge family Bible, now preserved at Lincoln's New Salem State Historic Site in Illinois; Wilson and Davis, 382 (Robert B. Rutledge to WHH, November 1, 1866); for information on the early history of Henderson County, KY, see Bergevin et al., 21 (as described in a letter from a traveler addressed to "Friend" and signed "C.S." in October 1807).

2. The marriage date is cited in the Henderson County (KY) Marriage Register, with certification by James McGready; 1810 Census of Henderson County.

3. Telephone conversation with genealogist George Rutledge, July 1999; a letter from Rutledge researcher C. V. Mayes to Ralph E. Winkler on August 1, 1985, states that the *History of McLean County, Illinois, 1887,* contains a biography of Robert H. Rutledge, grandson of John J. Rutledge, indicating that John J. Rutledge was "born in Ireland, reared in Dublin, where he . . . learned the trade of shoemaker." Robert H. Rutledge (born March 21, 1810, in Henderson County, KY) was the son of Thomas Officer Rutledge (born October 17, 1768, in or near Charlestown, SC).

4. In the letter cited in note 3 above, Mayes indicates, apparently from the same source, that "Rutledge's bride, formerly Jennie Officer, was a lady of [a] most excellent family of Irish descent, and highly educated and accomplished." See also George H. Rutledge, *Descendants of James Officer 1690–1980* (Hanover, PA: privately published, 1982); "James Officer Descendants," *Family Newsletter* vol. 3, no. 1, p. 2; and Kenneth A. Unico, *Family History: Lest We Forget, 1720–1800* (n.p.: privately published, n.d.), LDS Film #1035658, Item 2. Except for Jennie, the Officers spent the rest of their lives in Chester and Cumberland Counties in Pennsylvania.

5. Land, "Letter," 2; Bergevin et al., 190.

6. NOTE: While Rutledge was making shoes in Charlestown, another John Rutledge (an attorney) and his four brothers (Andrew, Edward, Hugh, and Thomas) lived luxuriously. Andrew was the largest retail merchant in the Carolinas. John would become one of the fifty-five signers of the U.S. Constitution. Edward, at age twenty-six, would become the youngest signer of the Declaration of Independence. Their father, John Rutledge Sr., a surgeon born in County Tyrone or County Cavan in Ireland, immigrated around 1735 and married fourteen-year-old Sarah Hext in Charlestown on Christmas Day, 1738. The relationship, if any, between the two Rutledge families has not been determined.

7. Bergevin et al., 4; Land, "Seven Mile Prairie," 1; Land, "Letter," 1; Bergevin et al., 4 (Thomas Camron received a land grant of 450 acres in Craven County on November 19, 1772. Fairfield County was formed from Craven County at a later date, and Craven County ceased to exist. The 1790 Census for Fairfield County lists one male under sixteen and four females in the household of Thomas Camron and a wife in the household of Thomas Camron Jr. Four other Camrons, believed to be sons of Thomas Camron Sr., were listed as heads of households); Hammand; Bergevin et al., 180; Obituary of Mary Ann (Miller) Rutledge, *Birmingham (IA) Enterprise,* January 2, 1879; further documentation appears in "The Rutledge Family of New Salem, Illinois" by James Rutledge Saunders, the oldest child of Ann Rutledge's youngest sibling, 1926.

8. Rouse, *Planters and Pioneers,* 200.

9. Rouse, *Great Wagon Road,* 53.

10. Bergevin et al., 6 (Camron appeared personally and listed a sworn claim for recompense against the state of South Carolina on February 1, 1784; the claim amounted to "Eight Pounds, Eight Shillings Sterling" and was granted to Camron and signed for by John Cook on April 12, 1785); Land, "Letter."

11. Obituary of Mary Ann (Miller) Rutledge. The exact dates each family arrived in Georgia are uncertain, but legal records show Thomas Camron Sr. there by December 7, 1793. He stated on that date that he was a resident of Elbert County when he deeded to William Richardson of Fairfield County, SC, 110 acres of land for the sum of forty-five pounds sterling. It was part of a tract of 260 acres granted to Camron by William Moultrie on February 6, 1766. In 1795 Camron purchased 1,856 acres on Beaverdam Creek, Elbert County, from his son-in-law, Robert Hawthorn, who was headed for Kentucky.

12. Bergevin et al., 26.

13. Land, "Seven Mile," 1; Bergevin et al., 3, 21, 26, 180; Brown, 30. According to Bergevin et al., in 1791, a legal document from Elbert County, GA, shows the names of John Hawthorne, John Camron, and Peter Miller, with Miller as testator to a land sale.

14. Bergevin et al., 9, 195 (They note that the 1810 Census of Henderson County, KY, lists the Camrons, Rutledges, Hawthornes, and Peter Millers. Also Mrs. Land quotes James Mayes Rutledge in her article, "Interesting Incidents of History Recalled in Account on Enfield": "There was a regular clan of us living down in Kentucky, as Scotch and Presbyterian as any parish in Scotland—the Rutledges, the Millers, the Camrons, the Mayes, the Hawthornes, the Veatches, etc. They were nearly all Aunts, Uncles, and Cousins to me. Good people they were, too, smart and well-educated"); Drake, 19–20.

15. Drake, 21–22; Hammand; Bergevin et al., 26.

16. Land, "Enfield Township," 1, Land, "Seven Mile Prairie, 2 (Mrs. Land lists the members of the traveling group).

17. Land, "Enfield Township," 1, "Seven Mile Prairie, 2; Bergevin et al., 193.

18. Land, "Seven Mile," 2.

19. Land, "Enfield Township," 2; state memorial highway marker on Illinois Route 45 in White County. According to Mrs. Land ("Seven Mile Prairie," 4), the log church was built on land belonging to Thomas Rutledge in Section 21 of what is now called Enfield Township. The history of the church is also described in an undated booklet, *Norris City and Indian Creek Township, Illinois,* by Edward Oliver, sponsored by the Norris City Lions Club.

20. Shere; Brown, 34.

21. Shere; Brown, 34; letter from Mrs. C. Land to C. Vale Mayes, December 16, 1964.

22. "Memoirs of James McGrady Rutledge"; Bergevin et al., 40–41; Pond, 87.
23. Land, "Seven Mile," 3; Bergevin et al., 193.
24. Pickard, 28–29.
25. Hay, 25.
26. Land, "Enfield Township," 2–3.
27. Bergevin et al., 26, 192; Drake, 38.
28. Bergevin et al., 26.
29. Drake, 44.
30. Allen.
31. Drake, 45.
32. Reep, 6; Thomas, *LNS*, 7.
33. Reep, 9.
34. Ibid., 9–11; Bergevin et al., 192.
35. Reep, 117–18.
36. For the early history of New Salem, see the works by Barton, Chandler, Onstot, Reep (9–17), and Thomas, *LNS* (5–17).

CHAPTER 4: "THERE'S MORE IN ABE'S HEAD THAN WIT AND FUN"

1. Thomas, *LNS*, 45–46; Hay, 24.
2. Duncan and Nickols, 100.
3. Ibid., 95, 98.
4. Ibid., 91.
5. Wilson and Davis, 242–43 (Mentor Graham to WHH, April 2, 1866); Wilson and Davis, 21 (William G. Green to WHH, May 30, 1865); Wilson and Davis, 383 (Robert B. Rutledge to WHH, November 1, 1866).
6. Wilson and Davis, 527 (Esther Summers Bale interviewed by WHH, 1866); Wilson and Davis, 374 (Caleb Carman to WHH, October 12, 1866); Wilson and Davis, 253 (John McNamar to G. U. Miles, May 5, 1866); Wilson and Davis, 242 (Mentor Graham to WHH, April 2, 1866); Wilson and Davis, 80 (Lynn McNulty Greene to WHH, July 30, 1865); Wilson and Davis, 21 (William G. Greene to WHH, May 30, 1865). For additional descriptions, see Wilson and Davis, 73, 80, 242–44, 250, 253, 374, 604; see also Donald, *Lincoln,* 56; Oates, 19; Herndon and Weik, 106–7; Walsh, 96; and Sandburg, *AL,* 140.
7. Wilson and Davis, 409 (Robert B. Rutledge to WHH, November 21,1866); Drake, 72.
8. Reep, 104.
9. Thomas, *LNS,* 24; Onstot, 114.
10. Herndon and Weik, 62–63.
11. Erastus Wright to Josiah G. Holland, July 10, 1865, Josiah G. Holland Papers, New York Public Library.
12. Miers, 1:14.

13. Herndon and Weik, 63–64; Wilson and Davis, 457–58 (John Hanks to WHH, 1865/66).

14. Mearns, 1:151 (based on interview with William Butler, May 1860).

15. Herndon and Weik, 67; Wilson and Davis, 69 (J. Rowan Herndon to WHH, July 3, 1865).

16. Wilson and Davis, 73 (James Short to WHH, Petersburg, IL, July 7, 1865); Wilson and Davis, 170 (Abner Y. Ellis to WHH, January 23, 1866); Wilson and Davis, 387 (Robert B. Rutledge to WHH, November 1, 1866).

17. Wilson and Davis, 74 (James Short to WHH, July 7, 1865).

18. Bergevin et al., 27; Drake, 52, 65, 77. (The quotes attributed to Lincoln in this section come from letters written by children and grandchildren of John Miller Camron and given to Julia Drake, Camron's biographer. Julia Drake's notes were provided by her niece, Sharon Schirding, a cousin of John Miller Camron's wife, Polly Orendorff.)

19. Drake, 60–61, 79; Bergevin et al., 29.

20. Drake, 57; Bergevin et al., 35 (from a letter from a granddaughter of John Miller Camron—Mrs. W. R. Waters, nee Olive Thompson—to an unidentified person).

21. Onstot, 77.

22. Thomas, LNS, 145.

23. Reep, 55; Onstot, 86.

24. Wilson and Davis, 385 (Robert B. Rutledge to WHH, November 1, 1866); Tarbell, Early Life, 191.

25. Wilson and Davis, 90 (N. W. Branson to WHH, August 3, 1865).

26. Wilson and Davis, 387 (Robert B. Rutledge to WHH, November 1, 1866); Wilson, Honor's Voice (see pp. 21–51 for a critical analysis of conflicting accounts of the wrestling match).

27. Wilson and Davis, 189–90 (Abner Y. Ellis to WHH, February 1, 1866); Herndon and Weik, 97

28. Thomas, LNS, 48; Wilson and Davis, 546 (John McNamar to WHH, Menard County, IL, January 20, 1867).

29. Wilson and Davis, 546 (John McNamar to WHH, Menard County, IL, January 20, 1867); Thomas, LNS, 48; Reep, 102; Duncan and Nickols, 123.

30. Reep, 54; Wilson and Davis, 374 (Caleb Carman to WHH, October 12, 1866); Thomas, LNS, 70; Herndon and Weik, 38; Wilson and Davis, 118 (John Romaine to WHH, September 14, 1865).

31. Thomas, LNS, 45; Wilson and Davis, 540 (Jason Duncan to WHH, 1866–67); Pond, "Intellectual New Salem," lecture; Wilson and Davis, 384–85 (Robert B. Rutledge to WHH, November 1, 1866).

32. Thomas, LNS, 121; Reep, 68; Tarbell, Early Life, 192.

33. Reep, 119.

34. Burlingame, *An Oral History,* 19 (William Butler to John Nicolay, June 13, 1875); Wilson and Davis, 69 (J. Rowan Herndon to WHH, Quincy, IL, July 3, 1865); Wilson and Davis, 557 (Elizabeth Abell to WHH, February 5, 1867).
35. Stevens, 8.
36. Wilson and Davis, 370, 365 (Johnson Gaines Greene to WHH, October 10, 1866, and October 5, 1866); Wilson and Davis, 367–68 (William G. Greene to WHH, October 9, 1866); Wilson and Davis, 421 (John McNamar to WHH, November 25, 1866).
37. Wilson and Davis, 383, 409 (Robert B. Rutledge to WHH, ca. November 1, 1866, and November 21, 1866).

CHAPTER 5: "HE HAS DUMPED HER—HO, HO, HO"

1. Herndon and Weik, 71; Hertz, *HL,* 314, 252–53 (McNamar to G. U. Miles, May 5, 1866).
2. Roy P. Basler, ed., "James Quay Howard's Notes on Lincoln," *Abraham Lincoln Quarterly* 4 (December 1947): 391.
3. Wilson and Davis, 481 (John T. Stuart to WHH, 1865/66).
4. Basler, 4:64–65 (from autobiography written by AL for John L. Scripps, June 1860).
5. Reep, 49.
6. Herndon and Weik, 108–9; Wilson and Davis, 383 (Robert B. Rutledge to WHH, November 1, 1866).
7. Lamon, *Life of AL,* 161; Reep, 105. The acknowledgment of the deed for half of the Rutledge farm was before Bowling Green, J.P. (Transcript Record A, p. 183, Menard County, IL). On January 20, 1833, James Rutledge and his wife sold the remaining forty acres of their farm to John Jones for three hundred dollars (Transcript A, p. 239, Menard County, IL). Thus when Ann and her father died, James Rutledge owned no land. The entire eighty acres was regarded as poor farming land.
8. Barton, *The Women Lincoln Loved,* 174–75.
9. Shere; Barton, *San Diego Sun.* Shere's lengthy feature article on Ann Rutledge was based on numerous interviews of Rutledge relatives and descendants of close friends of the family. He also reviewed letters written from New Salem between 1832 and 1835.
10. Drake, 46.
11. Wilson and Davis, 170 (A. Y. Ellis to WHH, January 23, 1866); Herndon and Weik, 95–96.
12. Based on recollections of Sarah Rutledge Saunders, as told to Bernie Babcock and reported in her book on page 48.
13. Wilson and Davis, 10 (Mentor Graham to WHH, May 29, 1865); Duncan and Nickols, 128.

14. Flindt, *Chicago Inter-Ocean*, February 12, 1899 (interview with Nancy Rutledge Prewitt, Ann's sister); Hammand (Sarah Rutledge Saunders to Jane E. Hammand, March 28, 1921), for the Decatur Lincoln Memorial Collection; Barton, *San Diego Sun*.

15. Walsh, 131–32.

16. Flindt.

17. Ibid.

18. Herndon and Weik, 89; Tarbell, *Footsteps*, 217.

19. Basler, 4:65.

20. Thomas, *Lincoln's New Salem*, 94; Herndon and Weik, 110; Carnegie, *The Unknown Lincoln*, 26.

21. I am indebted to Michael Burlingame for sharing the Parthena Nance quotation. It comes from her rare volume, *A Piece of Time*. See also Herndon and Weik, 109.

22. Nance, *A Piece of Time*, 26; Wilson and Davis, 374 (Caleb Carman to WHH, October 12, 1866); Wilson and Davis, 545–46 (McNamar to WHH, January 20, 1867, in which he says Ann "undoubtedly was about as classic a scholar as Mr. Lincoln").

23. Carnegie, *The Unknown Lincoln*, 26.

24. Wilson and Davis, 383 (Robert B. Rutledge to WHH, November 18, 1866); see also 13, 21, 25, 67, 80, 175, 325, 374, 387, 402–3, 409, 440, 520, 541; Carnegie, *The Unknown Lincoln*, 28; Walsh, 157; Chandler, 503.

25. Herndon and Weik, 98; Tarbell, *Early Life*, 181.

26. Barton, *Women*, 187–88; Wilson and Davis, 374 (Caleb Carman to WHH, October 12, 1866); Wilson and Davis, 364–65 (Johnson Gaines Greene to WHH, January 23, 1866).

CHAPTER 6: "MY COMFORT BY DAY, AND MY SONG IN THE NIGHT"

1. Wilson and Davis, 557 (Elizabeth Abell to WHH, February 15, 1867).

2. Tarbell, *Footsteps*, 199.

3. Hertz, *HL*, 233–34; Wilson and Davis, 90 (N. W. Branson to WHH, August 3, 1865).

4. Wilson and Davis, 73 (James Short to WHH, July 7, 1865); Walsh, 70–72; Drake, 90; Basler, 1:48; also see Helen Ruth Reed, "A Prophecy Lincoln Made," *Boston Herald*, February 9, 1930. The endorsement came during his reelection campaign for the Illinois legislature. He received the most votes of the seventeen Sangamon County candidates on election day, August 1.

5. Wilson and Davis, 423 (John M. Rutledge to WHH, November 25, 1866); Herndon and Weik, 112; letter from A. M. Prewitt, son of Nancy Rutledge Prewitt (Ann Rutledge's sister) to Miss J. E. Hamand.

6. Hertz, *HL*, 138.

7. Herndon and Weik, 106; Wilson and Davis, 591, 605–6 (Elizabeth Herndon Bell to JWW, August 24, 1883 and to WHH, March 1887). Elizabeth Bell was the daughter of schoolmaster Mentor Graham.

8. *The Prairie Picayune,* Lincoln's New Salem newsletter, 1996 (quoting from Englishman William Oliver's account in *Eight Months in Illinois*). I am grateful to New Salem volunteer Carol S. Jenkins for this information.

9. Onstot, 125–26.

10. Saunders, 3 (from a paper, "The Rutledge Family of New Salem, Illinois," compiled in 1926 by James Rutledge Saunders, the oldest child of Ann Rutledge's youngest sibling).

11. Saunders, 2; Wilson and Davis, 358–60 (Mary Todd Lincoln to WHH, September 1866); Basler, 1:382; Hertz, *HL,* 406; Wilson and Davis, 506 (Joseph Gillespie to WHH, December 8, 1866). In his race for Congress in 1846, Lincoln publicly stated he was "not a member of any Christian Church." His stepmother told William H. Herndon on September 8, 1865, "Abe had no particular religion."

12. Maltby, 31; Mearns, 1:154 (William G. Greene to James Q. Howard, May, 1860); Mearns, 1:74–76; Wilson and Davis, 70 (J. Rowan Herndon to WHH, July 3, 1865).

13. Drake, 82; Land, "Enfield Township," 2; Wilson and Davis, 172 (A. Y. Ellis to WHH, January 23, 1866); Herndon and Weik, 102.

14. Wilson and Davis, 578 (Jesse W. Fell to Ward Hill Lamon, September 22, 1870).

15. Wilson and Davis, 13 (Hardin Bale to WHH, May 29, 1865); Wilson and Davis, 62 (John Hill to WHH, June 27, 1865); *The Index,* 5, February 18, 1870 (WHH to Francis E. Abbot); Wilson, *Honor's Voice,* 81; Wilson and Davis, 441 (Isaac Cogdal to WHH, 1865/66); Stevens, 11–12; Wilson and Davis, 472 (James H. Matheny to WHH, 1865/66); Wilson and Davis, 576 (John T. Stuart to WHH, March 2, 1870).

16. Basler, 1:382; Speed, 32–33.

17. Wilson and Davis, 464 (James W. Keyes to WHH, 1865/66); *Bicentennial Collection of Quotes,* Salesian Missions, New Rochelle, 1976.

18. Wilson and Davis, 501 (A. Y. Ellis to WHH, December 6, 1866).

19. Duncan and Nickols, 156.

20. Wilson and Davis, 426 (Robert B. Rutledge to WHH, November 30, 1866); Herndon and Weik, 92.

CHAPTER 7: "ANNIE'S WHOLE SOUL SEEMED
WRAPPED UP IN LINCOLN"

1. Wilson and Davis, 236 (George U. Miles to WHH, March 23, 1866, quoting Mrs. Bowling Green); Wilson and Davis, 402–3 (Robert B. Rutledge to

WHH, November 18, 1866); Herndon and Weik, 112; Wilson, *Civil War History;* Wilson and Davis, 383 (Robert B. Rutledge to WHH, November 1, 1866); Tarbell, *Early Life,* 218 (quoting Jean Rutledge Berry). One cannot state precisely when and where Lincoln proposed to Ann Rutledge. Wilson (*Honor's Voice,* 117) says "the engagement was most likely agreed to sometime in the first half of 1835" after Lincoln had returned in February from his legislative session.

2. Herndon and Weik, 111; Wilson and Davis, 402–3 (Robert B. Rutledge to WHH, November 18, 1866); Sandburg, *AL,* 186; Walsh, 35–36; Wilson and Davis, 383 (Robert B. Rutledge to WHH, November 1, 1866); Flindt; Shere.

3. Flindt; Wilson and Davis, 409 (Robert B. Rutledge to WHH, November 21, 1866, corroborated by McGrady Rutledge, who reported that Ann told him "that as soon as certain studies were completed" and Lincoln "was admitted to the bar," they would be married); Herndon and Weik, 112.

4. Drake, 94, 83.

5. Rankin; Tarbell, *Footsteps,* 218; Walsh, 107.

6. Wilson and Davis, 21 (William G. Greene to WHH, May 30, 1865); Wilson and Davis, 80 (Lynn McNulty Greene to WHH, July 30, 1865); Wilson and Davis, 243 (Mentor Graham to WHH, April 2, 1866); also Harvey Ross, *Early Pioneers* (Ross carried mail between Springfield and Lewistown, passing through Lincoln's post office at New Salem four times a week); Wilson and Davis, 423 (John M. Rutledge to WHH, November 25, 1866); Herndon and Weik, 112 (Herndon reported that, according to Ann's brother John, Ann sang this hymn to Lincoln early in her illness and that it was "the last thing she ever sung"); Sandburg, *AL,* 186.

7. Barton, *The Women Lincoln Loved,* 82–83. Between the pages of the Rutledge family Bible, Ann's sister Nancy Rutledge Prewitt found this letter from David. Nancy gave the letter to her youngest sibling, Sarah, and Sarah shared it with historian William Barton when he interviewed her in California. The letter provided evidence that Ann wanted to prepare herself to be a lawyer's wife before marrying Lincoln. Barton first mentioned it in a lecture at New Salem in May 1926.

8. Wilson and Davis, 604–5 (Parthena Nance Hill to WHH, March 1887).

9. Walsh, 133–34.

10. Wilson and Davis, 604–5 (Parthena Nance Hill to WHH, March 1887); letter from John Hill to Ida M. Tarbell, February 6, 1896, original in Ida M. Tarbell Papers, Allegheny College Library.

11. Shutes, 45 (quoted from the doctoral dissertation of Lorenzo D. Matheny, a Springfield resident studying for his medical degree, 1836).

12. Donald, *Lincoln,* 57; Carnegie, *The Unknown Lincoln,* 31.

13. Thomas, *LNS,* 46–47; Herndon and Weik, 112; Herndon's lecture of November 16, 1866; Thomas, *LNS,* 123.

14. Flindt; Herndon and Weik, 112; Wilson and Davis, 606–7 (Jasper Rutledge to WHH, March 9, 1887); letter from A. M. Prewitt (son of Nancy Rutledge Prewitt) to Miss J. E. Hammand, November 7, 1921, for the Decatur Lincoln Memorial Collection.

15. Reep, 75 (based on statement from Berry's daughter, Mary, who was thirteen at the time).

16. Drake, 95; Flindt; Herndon and Weik, 112; Manfrina, *News-Press;* Cook, *Lompoc Record;* Walsh, 15–16 (quoting from WHH's lecture of November 16, 1866); *Chicago Tribune Magazine,* February 22, 1922 (Sarah Rutledge Saunders to Katherine Wheeler); undated statement by Sarah Saunders enclosed in J. R. Saunders to Mary Saunders, Sisquoc, CA, May 14, 1919, Saunders Papers, Illinois State Historical Library, Springfield (Sarah's information is based on what her mother and sister Nancy told her); Reep, 76; Flindt; A. M. Prewitt to Miss J. E. Hammand, November 7, 1921, Decatur Lincoln Memorial Collection.

17. Walsh, 136; Reep, 84 (based on information provided by Dr. Allen's daughter or granddaughter, Miranda Allen); Herndon and Weik, 112.

18. Bergevin et al., 27; Walsh, 37 (based on recollection of James McGrady Rutledge); Drake, 97.

19. Wilson and Davis, 383 (Robert B. Rutledge to WHH, November 1, 1866); Wilson and Davis, 325 (Benjamin F. Irwin to WHH, August 27, 1866); Wilson and Davis, 80 (Lynn McNulty Greene to WHH, July 30, 1865); Wilson and Davis, 13 (Hardin Bale to WHH, May 29, 1865); Wilson and Davis, 557 (Elizabeth Abell to WHH, February 15, 1867); Wilson and Davis, 21 (William G. Greene to WHH, May 30, 1865); Hertz, *HL,* 273 (John Hill to WHH, June 6, 1865).

20. Sandburg, *AL,* 190; Thomas, 124; Wilson and Davis, 21 (William G. Greene to WHH, May 30, 1865); Wilson and Davis, 155–56 (Henry McHenry to WHH, January 8, 1866).

21. *Lerna (IL) Eagle,* September 19, 1930 (based on correspondence of Eliza Armstrong Smith, daughter of Hannah Armstrong); Reep, 77 (based on letter from Sarah Rutledge Saunders and an interview with Mary Rutledge Moore; n.d.).

22. Reep, 77; Wilson and Davis, 236 (G. U. Miles to WHH, March 23, 1866); Herndon and Weik, 113.

23. Reep, 78–79; Angle, 116–17.

24. Tarbell, *Footsteps,* 220; Herndon and Weik, 113–14; Browne, 129.

25. Walsh, 123–26; Judd Stewart Collection, Henry E. Huntington Library, San Marino, CA (William G. Greene to Paul Hull, unidentified clipping, 1887).

26. Walsh, 128–29 (recorded in 1879 by Usher Linder, a longtime political friend of Lincoln; appears in Linder, *Reminiscences*).

CHAPTER 8: "I WANT IN ALL CASES TO DO RIGHT"

NOTE: Traditional versions of the Lincoln-Todd courtship are no longer supported by the available evidence. The scenario presented in this chapter is based primarily on Douglas Wilson's recent analyses of contemporary documents, such as Mary Todd's correspondence and those of her friends. For more information, see Wilson's *Honor's Voice* and his essays in *Lincoln Before Washington.*

1. Wilson and Davis, 610 (B. R. Vineyard to JWW, March 14, 1887); Basler, 1:117–19 (AL to Mrs. Orville H. Browning, April 1, 1838).
2. Basler, 1:117–19 (AL to Mrs. Orville H. Browning, April 1, 1838).
3. Onstot, 24.
4. Angle, *HL,* 119–20 (Mary Owens Vineyard to WHH, Weston, MO, May 22, 1866); Wilson and Davis, 262 (Mary Owens Vineyard to WHH, July 22, 1866).
5. Wilson and Davis, 531 (Johnson Gaines Greene to WHH, 1866).
6. Basler, 1:78 (dated May 7, 1837).
7. Ibid., 1:94 (AL to Mary Owens, August 16, 1837).
8. Basler, 1:117–19 (AL to Mrs. Orville H. Browning, April 1, 1838).
9. Wilson and Davis, 263 (Mary Owens Vineyard to WHH, July 22, 1866).
10. Edna Bell Howell to "My dear friend," Los Angeles, March 20, 1938, Clipping Collection, Lincoln Museum, Fort Wayne, IN.
11. Herndon and Weik, 148; Speed 21–22.
12. Herndon and Weik, 149.
13. Wilson and Davis, 470 (James H. Matheny to WHH, 1865/66); Herndon and Weik, 151.
14. WHH to James H. Wilson, September 23, 1889, Herndon-Weik Collection, Library of Congress; Hertz, *HL,* 112 (WHH to JWW, December 10, 1885); Sandburg, *AL,* 158; Hertz, *HL,* 263 (WHH to JWW, February 21, 1891). Herndon told Weik that "Mr. Lincoln had a double consciousness. . . . In one moment he was in a state of abstraction and then quickly in another state when he was social, talkative, and a communicative fellow."
15. Wilson and Davis, 719 (Joshua F. Speed to WHH, January 5, 1889).
16. WHH to JWW, January 1891, Herndon-Weik Collection, Library of Congress; Hertz, *HL,* 259.
17. Wilson and Davis, 431 (Joshua F. Speed to WHH, November 30, 1866).
18. Dr. Anson Henry to his wife, February 18, 1863, Illinois State Historical Library, Springfield.
19. Oates, 33.
20. Wilson and Davis, 624–25 (William Jayne to WHH, August 17, 1887).
21. Sandburg, *AL,* 159–60; Herndon and Weik, 165.

22. Wilson and Davis, 443 (Elizabeth Todd Edwards to WHH, 1865/66).

23. Helm, 32.

24. Angle, "Here I Have Lived," 110; Beveridge, 1:271.

25. The amount of time Lincoln was out of town is estimated based on Miers, *Lincoln Day by Day.*

26. Turner and Turner, 14–19, and Sandburg and Angle, 172 (Mary Todd to Mercy Ann Levering, July 23, 1840; James C. Conkling to Mercy Ann Levering, September 21, 1840); *Lincoln Day by Day* (states that AL was "still stumping the lower part of the state" on September 21 and by September 30 was appearing in court in the central part of the state); Wilson, *Honor's Voice,* 219.

27. Matilda Edwards to her brother Nelson, November 30, 1840 (in the Ruth Painter Randall Papers, Library of Congress, and in the Edwards Family Papers, Knox College Library, Galesburg, IL); Wilson and Davis, 474 (Joshua Speed to WHH, 1865/66); Wilson, *Honor's Voice,* 217.

28. Sandburg and Angle, 172 (James C. Conkling to Mercy Ann Levering, September 21, 1840).

29. Wilson, *Honor's Voice,* 220; Nolan, 19:3.

30. Jane D. Bell in Springfield to Ann Bell in Danville, KY, January 27, 1841, James G. Randall Papers, Manuscript Division, Library of Congress (Jane Bell, a Kentuckian, was related by marriage to the proprietor of James Bell and Co., and his partner and cousin was Lincoln's friend Joshua Speed); Wilson, *Lincoln Before Washington,* 110; Wilson and Davis, 474–75 (Joshua Speed to WHH, 1865/66); Herndon and Weik, 168; Wilson, *Lincoln Before Washington,* 102–3.

31. Herndon and Weik, 169; Wilson and Davis, 475 (Joshua Speed to WHH, 1865/66).

32. Wilson and Davis, 477 (Joshua Speed to WHH, 1865/66); Herndon and Weik, 169.

33. James G. Randall Papers, Library of Congress; Wilson, *Lincoln Before Washington,* 110; Mrs. Benjamin S. Edwards to Ida M. Tarbell, October 8, 1895, Ida M. Tarbell Papers, Allegheny College Library.

34. Herndon and Weik, 167; Wilson and Davis, 443 (Elizabeth Todd Edwards to WHH, 1865/66).

35. Wilson, *Honor's Voice,* 222–23, 230–31; Wilson and Davis, 251 (James H. Matheny to WHH, May 3, 1866); Wilson and Davis, 476 (Joshua Speed to WHH, 1865/66).

36. Herndon and Weik, 159.

37. Wilson and Davis, 187–88 (Joseph Gillespie to WHH, January 31, 1866).

38. Barton, *The Women Lincoln Loved,* 239; Turner and Turner, 20–22, 25–26. As noted in the manuscript, Joshua Speed, Ninian W. Edwards, Elizabeth Todd Edwards, and James Matheny all indicated Lincoln's love for Matilda Edwards, and other strong evidence can be found. A niece of Matilda's, Alice Edwards Quigley,

wrote: "Tradition tells us that Lincoln and Douglas were both in love with her" (reproduced in H. O. Knerr's "Abraham Lincoln and Matilda Edwards" in the Illinois State Historical Library). Ninian W. Edwards's son Albert said his "family thought that Lincoln was much taken with Matilda, but nothing came of it" (Stevens, *A Reporter's Lincoln,* 75). Sarah Rickard also remembered Lincoln's interest in Matilda (*St. Louis Globe-Democrat,* February 9, 1907). Also, Octavia Roberts of Springfield interviewed many Lincoln acquaintants. Writing about Lincoln's rejection of Mary Todd, he reported that his grandmother, who was Mary Lincoln's contemporary, always told her family that "it was due to Matilda Edwards, who won Lincoln's love" (Octavia Roberts, "We All Knew Abraham," *Abraham Lincoln Quarterly* 4 [March 1946]: 27).

39. Wilson and Davis, 133 (Ninian W. Edwards to WHH, September 22, 1865). Mary Todd and Ninian and Elizabeth Edwards all attested to Speed's pursuit of Matilda Edwards.

40. Wilson, *Lincoln Before Washington,* 125; Wilson and Davis, 431 (Joshua Speed to WHH, November 30, 1866); Wilson and Davis, 443 (Elizabeth Todd Edwards to WHH, 1865/66); Wilson and Davis, 133 (Ninian W. Edwards to WHH, September 22, 1865).

41. Wilson and Davis, 592 (Elizabeth Todd Edwards to JWW, December 20, 1883); Tarbell, *The Life of AL,* 1:174–80; Wilson, *Lincoln Before Washington,* 121.

42. Wilson and Davis, 342 (Joshua Speed to WHH, September 17, 1866); Joshua F. Speed to Eliza J. Speed, March 12, 1841, Joshua Speed Papers, Illinois State Historical Library.

43. Orville H. Browning to John G. Nicolay, Springfield, June 17, 1875, John Hay Papers, Brown University Library. Browning affirmed that Lincoln "fell desperately in love with [Matilda Edwards] and proposed to her, but she rejected him." See also Wilson and Davis, 133 (Ninian W. Edwards to WHH, September 22, 1865).

44. Martinette Hardin to John J. Hardin, January 22, 1841, Chicago Historical Society.

45. Wilson and Davis, 444 (Elizabeth Todd Edwards to WHH, 1865/66); Nellie Crandal Sanford, *St. Louis Globe Democrat,* February 9, 1907 (an interview with Sarah Rickard Barret; the clipping is in the Lincoln files, Illinois State Historical Library).

46. Basler, 1:228 (AL to John T. Stuart, January 20, 1841).

47. John Nicolay with Orville H. Browning, June 17, 1875, John Hay Papers, Brown University Library; Sandburg and Angle, 178–79 (James Conkling to Mercy Levering, January 24, 1841).

48. Jane D. Bell to Ann Bell, January 27, 1841, James G. Randall Papers, Library of Congress (from a copy of the letter supplied to John B. Clark of Lincoln

Memorial University by Mrs. Henry Jackson, a relative of Jane Bell, and also supplied to James G. Randall).

49. Wilson and Davis, 133 (Ninian Edwards to WHH, September 22, 1865); Sandburg and Angle, 178–79 (James Conkling to Mercy Levering, March 7, 1841).

50. Burlingame, *An Oral History* (Orville H. Browning to John J. Nicolay, June 17, 1875); Barton, *The Women Lincoln Loved,* 239.

51. Wilson and Davis, 444 (Elizabeth Todd Edwards to WHH, 1865/66).

52. Basler, 1:260–61 (AL to Mary Speed, September 27, 1841).

53. Ibid., 1:259–60.

54. Kincaid, 16.

55. Basler, 1:269 (AL to Joshua Speed, February 13, 1842); 1:282 (AL to Speed, March 27, 1842).

56. Ibid., 1:288–89 (AL to Speed, July 4, 1842).

57. Ibid., 1:292–96.

58. Browne, 185.

59. Linder, 66–67.

60. Onstot, 18; Burlingame, *An Oral History,* 25 (William Butler to John Nicolay, June, 1875); Herndon and Weik, 201; Burlingame, *An Oral History,* 185.

61. Turner and Turner, *MTL,* 296, 299.

62. Sanford, *St. Louis Globe-Democrat,* February 9, 1907 (from an interview with Sarah Rickard Barret and her husband); Sarah E. Hardin to John J. Hardin, January 26, 1841, Hardin Papers, Chicago Historical Society; Wilson and Davis, 665 (Sarah Rickard Barret to WHH, August 12, 1888).

63. Wilson and Davis, 665 (Sarah Rickard Barret to WHH, August 12, 1888).

64. Ibid.; Barton, *Women,* 259.

65. Sanford, *St. Louis Globe-Democrat,* February 9, 1907; Herndon and Weik, 179.

66. Mrs. John T. Stuart to Ida M. Tarbell, Ida M. Tarbell Papers, Allegheny College Library; *Chicago Times-Herald,* September 8, 1895, 40.

67. Burlingame, *An Oral History,* 2 (Orville H. Browning to John Nicolay, June 17, 1875); Wilson and Davis, 475 (Joshua F. Speed to WHH, 1865/66); Elizabeth Todd Grimsley to Ida M. Tarbell, Springfield, IL, March 9, 1895, Ida M. Tarbell Papers, Allegheny College Library.

68. Wilson and Davis, 444 (Elizabeth Todd Edwards to WHH, 1865/66).

69. Temple, 27; Wilson and Davis, 666 (James H. Matheny to WHH, August 21, 1888); Wilson and Davis, 251 (James H. Matheny to WHH, May 3, 1866); Mrs. Benjamin S. Edwards to Ida M. Tarbell, October 8, 1895, Ida M. Tarbell Papers, Allegheny College Library; Wilson and Davis, 444 (Elizabeth Todd Edwards to WHH, 1865/66); Beveridge, 1:355.

70. Kunhardt, Kunhardt, and Kunhardt, *Lincoln,* 64; Oates, 63; Wilson and Davis, 665 (James H. Matheny to JWW, August 21, 1888); Herndon and Weik, 181.

71. Reminiscences of a Mr. Beck, son of the proprietress, in Effie Sparks, "Stories of Abraham Lincoln," 20–21, Ida M. Tarbell Papers, Allegheny College Library; Carnegie, *Lincoln the Unknown,* 71–72 (Catherine Miles Early to her nephew Jimmy Miles to Carnegie).

72. Orville H. Browning confided to John G. Nicolay that Mary Todd was indeed the aggressor in the courtship, Browning to Nicolay, June 17, 1875, John Hay Papers, Brown University Library; Turner and Turner, 293 (Mary Todd Lincoln to Josiah Holland, December 4, 1865).

73. Basler, 1:305 (Lincoln to Samuel D. Marshall, November 11, 1842).

74. Temple, 28; Browne, 201; Wilson and Davis, 251 (James H. Matheny to WHH, May 3, 1866).

CHAPTER 9: "LINCOLN'S WIFE WAS A HELLION"

1. Baker, MTL, 107.

2. Wilson and Davis, 465 (Turner R. King to WHH, 1865/66); Wilson and Davis, 597 (Margaret Ryan to JWW, October 27, 1886); Hillary A. Gobin to Albert J. Beveridge, South Bend, IN, May 17, 1923, Albert J. Beveridge Papers, Library of Congress (Gobin's father was a minister who lived near the Lincolns); *New York Times,* February 6, 1938; Sandburg and Angle, 70–71 (based on WHH's notes of a conversation with Stephen Whitehurst in 1867; Whitehurst heard the story from a Mr. Barrett who allegedly observed it in 1856 or 1857).

3. Wilson and Davis, 445 (Elizabeth Todd Edwards to WHH, 1865/66).

4. Ibid., 713–14 (James H. Matheny to WHH, January 1887).

5. Paul M. Angle, "Notes of Interview with Mrs. Fanny Grimsley, July 27, 1926," in Angle to William E. Barton, Springfield, IL, January 10, 1927, William E. Barton Papers, University of Chicago; Wilson and Davis, 389–90 (John B. Weber to WHH, November 1, 1866).

6. Unpublished paper by Elizabeth A. Capps, niece of Jabez Capps, Springfield's first shoemaker; Wilson and Davis, 692 (Jesse K. Dubois to JWW, between 1883 and 1889).

7. *New York Times,* August 26, 1934 (based on interview with Victor Kutchin, who acquired the couch from Mason Brayman, to whom Lincoln entrusted the couch when he left Springfield in 1861); *Belvedere (IL) Standard,* April 14, 1868 (reminiscences of Page Eaton).

8. WHH to Isaac N. Arnold, Springfield, IL, October 24, 1883, Lincoln Collection, Chicago Historical Society; Harriet Chapman to JWW, undated, Jesse W. Weik Papers, Illinois State Historical Library.

9. Fiske, 494.

10. Donald, *Lincoln,* 160.

11. Wilson and Davis, 349 (David Davis to WHH, September 20, 1866). Judge Davis presided over the Eighth Judicial District in Illinois. Lincoln practiced

before him for more than ten years. Davis managed Lincoln's nomination effort for the presidency in 1860. In 1862 Lincoln appointed Davis to the U.S. Supreme Court.

12. Basler, 1:378 (AL to Andrew Johnston, April 18, 1846).

13. Whitney, 1:238; Carpenter, *Six Months,* 59.

14. Wilson and Davis, 350 (David Davis to WHH, September 20, 1866); Wilson and Davis,490 (Charles S. Zane to WHH, 1865/66).

15. Wilson and Davis, 453 (James Gourley to WHH, 1865/66); Wilson and Davis, 349 (David Davis to WHH, September 20, 1866).

16. Hertz, *HL,* 141; *Quincy (IL) Whig,* May 5, 1847 (poem by AL); Walsh, 169.

17. Basler, 1:465 (AL to Mary Todd Lincoln, April 16, 1848).

18. Clines; an archeological report by Elizabeth Barthold O'Brien and Donna J. Seifert preceding construction of the Smithsonian Institution's National Museum of the American Indian in 1999 and 2000 notes that Seifert unearthed the dregs of Hall's brothel on the construction site east of the Air and Space Museum.

19. Basler, 1:465–66 (AL to Mary Todd Lincoln, April 16, 1848); Turner and Turner, 36–38; Basler, 1:466 (AL to Mary Todd Lincoln, April 16, 1848).

20. Basler, 1:466.

21. Ibid., 1:477; John S. Richards, *Berks and Schuylkill Journal,* February 8, 1851; Nolan, 292.

22. Findley, 124.

23. Statement of John T. Stuart, n.d., Herndon-Weik Collection, Library of Congress; Stuart to John G. Nicolay, Springfield, June 24, 1875, John Hay Papers, Brown University; WHH to Ward Hill Lamon, Springfield, March 6, 1870, Ward Hill Lamon Papers, Henry E. Huntington Library, San Marino, CA; Basler, 2:19 (AL to C. U. Schlater, January 5, 1849).

24. Basler, 2:96–97 (AL to John D. Johnston, January 12, 1851).

25. John D. Johnston to AL, May 25, 1849, Abraham Lincoln Papers, Library of Congress.

26. "Anecdotes of Mrs. Lincoln" by "a neighbor of the family at the time of Lincoln's funeral," quoted in the *News,* n.p., Lincoln Museum, Fort Wayne, IN.

27. Wilson and Davis, 357, 359 (Mary Todd Lincoln to WHH, September, 1866); Donald, *Lincoln,* 109; WHH to JWW, February 18, 1887, Herndon-Weik Collection, Library of Congress.

28. Donald, *Lincoln,* 159; Gibson W. Harris to AL, November 7, 1860, Abraham Lincoln Papers, Library of Congress; Hill, 164.

29. Goff, 32; Holzer, 183.

30. Herndon and Weik, 274–75.

31. Ibid.

32. Ibid., 276; *Decatur Gazette,* clipped in *Illinois State Register,* May 27, 1854.

33. Browne, 217–18.

34. Whitney, 20; Katherine B. Menz, "Furnishings Plan . . . The Lincoln Home," National Park Service, U.S. Department of the Interior, 1983.

35. Wilson and Davis, 453 (James Gourley to WHH, 1865/66); Chenery, *Illinois State Register,* February 27, 1938; Arnold, 83.

36. Herndon and Weik, 326. Lincoln's vast knowledge of Scripture provided the source for his famous statement, "A house divided against itself cannot stand." He was paraphrasing Mark 3:24–25: "And if a kingdom be divided against itself, that kingdom cannot stand. And if a house be divided against itself, that house cannot stand."

37. Ibid., 327.

38. Sparks, *The Lincoln-Douglas Debates of 1858.*

39. Lorant, 79.

40. Kunhardt, Kunhardt, and Kunhardt, *Lincoln,* 110.

41. C. M. Smith and John Williams Account Books, 1859, Illinois State Historical Society; Wilson and Davis, 452 (James Gourley to WHH, 1865/66).

42. Kunhardt, Kunhardt, and Kunhardt, *Lincoln,* 120; *New York Tribune,* July 17, 1882.

43. Temple, "When Lincoln Left Town," 175–77, 182; Holzer, 61–63; "Friends of Lincoln: A Bloomington Lady Tells Some Interesting Incidents About That Great Man," *Bloomington (IN) Pantagraph,* February 19, 1895.

44. Basler, 4:87.

45. Putnam, 220–22; Baringer, 158; Kunhardt, Kunhardt, and Kunhardt, *Lincoln,* 116.

46. Zane, 430–38; Randall, *Lincoln the President,* 1:173–74.

47. Ashmun; Basler, 4:75. Newspaperman John Mason Haight wrote to Lincoln about this incident. Haight was an active member of a temperance society. In a letter marked "Private and Confidential," Lincoln replied on June 11, 1860: "I think it would be improper for me to write, or say anything to, or for, the public, upon the subject of which you inquire. I therefore wish the letter I do write to be held as strictly confidential. Having kept house sixteen years, and having never held the 'cup' to the lips of my friends then, my judgment was that I should not, in my new position, change my habit in this respect. What actually occurred upon the occasion of the Committee visiting me, I think it would be better for others to say." Nearly thirty years later the letter was reprinted in the *New York Voice,* a Prohibition publication.

48. Ward, 32 (recollection of Henry C. Bowen); Stevens, 60 (recollection of Judith A. Bradner).

49. Donald, *Lincoln,* 270–71 (quoting an Ohio cousin of Mary Lincoln).

50. Wilson and Davis, 137 (Augustus H. Chapman to WHH, October 8, 1865).

51. For an analysis of the reliability of Cogdal's account of his conversation with Lincoln, see Walsh, 31–32, 53–57, 82–85 and the appendix of this book.

52. Wilson and Davis, 517 (Grace Bedell to WHH, Albion, NY, December 14, 1866).

53. Herndon and Weik, 393.

54. Wilson and Davis, 517 (Grace Bedell to WHH, Albion, NY, December 14, 1866).

55. Tiffany, 333–34 (the information was based on a letter from Samuel Felton to Francis Tiffany, May 8, 1888.)

56. Pinkerton, 44, 47.

57. Ibid., 48.

58. Hertz, *AL: A New Portrait,* 1:248 (A. K. McClure to an unidentified correspondent); Pinkerton, 53; Cuthbert, 15–16 (from the Pinkerton Record Book).

CHAPTER 10: "MRS. LINCOLN IS INVOLVED IN A CORRUPT TRAFFIC"

NOTE: For an interesting and excellent summary of Lincoln's married life, including Mary's financial indiscretions, see Michael Burlingame, *The Inner World of Abraham Lincoln,* esp. pp. 268–355.

1. *Springfield (IL) Register,* January 14, 1874 (quoting WHH); Wilson and Davis, 701 (Horace White to WHH, January 26, 1891).

2. Keckley, 130–31, 128.

3. Carman and Luthin, 28–29; WHH to Horace White, Springfield, February 13, 1891, James G. Randall Papers, Library of Congress.

4. Browne, 413–14.

5. Ibid.; Basler, 4:271 (from AL's First Inaugural Address).

6. Baker, *MTL,* 184; Crawford, entry for November 3, 1861; *Washington Sunday Gazette,* January 23, 1887.

7. Basler, 4:385 (AL to Ephraim D. and Phoebe Ellsworth, May 25, 1861); "Ellsworth," *Atlantic Monthly* 8 (July 1861).

8. Nicolay and Hay, 4:352–55; statement by George P. Goff, enclosed in Goff to John G. Nicolay, Washington, DC, February 9, 1899, John G. Nicolay Papers, Library of Congress.

9. Keckley, 132–33.

10. Basler, 4:87; Nolan, 298; Ames, 237–38.

11. *New York Commercial Gazette,* January 9, 1887.

12. Ames, 237–38.

13. Baker, *MTL,* 184 ("Union" to Lincoln, Washington, June 26, 1861); *The Sky Rocket,* Primghar, IA, March 15, 1929 (the source was Lincoln King, who claimed he knew Mrs. Lincoln's lover "intimately" in New York); King to William E. Barton, Primghar, IA, August 9, 1930, William E. Barton Papers, University of Chicago; Schuyler Colfax to John G. Nicolay, South Bend, IN, July 17, 1875, John G. Nicolay Papers, Library of Congress.

14. George W. Adams to David Goodman Croly, Washington, October 7, 1867, Manton Marble Papers, Library of Congress; Turner and Turner, 202 (Edward McManus to Thurlow Weed); Oswald Garrison Villard to Isaac Markens, New York, March 26, 1927, Lincoln Collection, Brown University (Villard apparently was referring to Henry Wikoff, who was an adventurer but not of Hungarian origin); *Newark Star,* March 3, 1951 (letter to Abram Wakeman seen by his daughter, who described it to her daughter, Elizabeth M. Alexanderson of Englewood, NJ).

15. Baker, *MTL,* 234; Sam Ward to S. L. M. Barlow, Washington, November 21, 1864(?), S. L. M. Barlow Papers, Henry E. Huntington Library, San Marino, CA.

16. Letters Sent, vols. 13 and 14, Records of the Commissioner of Public Buildings, National Archives; bill from John Watt to AL, February 1, 1863, Ward Hill Lamon Papers, Henry E. Huntington Library, San Marino, CA; Randall, *MTL,* 254–58.

17. Records of the U.S. Senate, Committee on Public Buildings, 37th Congress, Record Group 46, National Archives (James H. Upperman to Caleb B. Smith, Washington, October 21, 1861).

18. Caleb B. Smith to William H. Seward, Washington, October 27, 1861, W. H. Seward Papers, University of Rochester Library, microfilm edition, reel 66; *New York Commercial Advertiser,* October 4, 1867 (based on statement by Thurlow Weed); David Davis to his wife, St. Louis, February 23, 1862, David Davis Papers, Chicago Historical Society; E. V. Haughwout & Co. to Manton Marble, September 26, 27, 28, 1864, and George W. Adams to David Goodman Croly, Washington, October 7, 1867, Manton Marble Papers, Library of Congress; *New York World,* September 26, 1864; *Boston Post,* October 11, 1867.

19. John Hay diary, February 13, 1867 (Isaac Newton to John Hay).

20. Benjamin French to Pamela French, Washington, December 24, 1861, Benjamin Brown French Papers, Library of Congress.

21. Ibid.; Cole and McDonough, 382; John Hay diary; Orville H. Browning Diary, July 3, 1873, quoting David Davis, William E. Barton Papers, University of Chicago.

22. *Washington Sunday Gazette,* January 16, 1887.

23. Burlingame, *The Inner World,* 325; Thomas, *AL,* 91; Keckley, 125.

24. Ross, *Proud Kate,* 47.

25. Keckley, 124–26.

26. "Presidential Domestic Squabbles," Washington correspondence, n.d., Judd Stewart Collection, Huntington Library, San Marino, CA; *Rochester (NY) Union,* unidentified clipping; Lincoln Scrapbooks, 5:44.

27. Ross, *Proud Kate,* 140.

28. Donald, *Lincoln,* 482; Basler, 7:212–13 (AL to Salmon P. Chase, February 29, 1864).

29. Phelps, 158–59.
30. Basler, 7:419 (AL to Salmon P. Chase, June 30, 1864); Phelps, 167–68.
31. *New York World,* February 20, 1870.
32. Baker, *MTL,* 231–33; Adam Gurowski to Horace Greeley, Washington, October 1, 1861, Horace Greeley Papers, New York Public Library; *Missouri Republican,* October 25, 1861 (John Hay's anonymous Washington dispatch); T. J. Barnett to S. L. M. Barlow, Washington, October 27, 1862, S. L. M. Barlow Papers, Henry E. Huntington Library, San Marino, CA.
33. Smith, 284–89.
34. Browne, 644–45.
35. Ross, *Proud Kate,* 151.
36. Ibid., 78–79 (based on the story in Julia Taft Bayne's memoir, *Tad Lincoln's Father*).
37. Keckley, 101; Burlingame, *The Inner World of AL* (J. W. Nesmith to his wife, Washington, DC, February 5, 1862).
38. Helen Nicolay, 132–33; Browne, 465–66.
39. Keckley, 105.
40. Reminiscences of Mary Miner Hill, daughter of the Reverend Dr. Noyes W. Miner, 1923, Illinois State Historical Library, Springfield; Rankin, 176–79.
41. MacKaye, 1:105–6 (MacKaye was told this story by his mother, who heard it from Francis B. Carpenter, an artist who lived in the Lincoln White House for six months and overheard Mary and Lincoln).

CHAPTER 11: "HER LETTER HAD BEEN CAREFULLY TREASURED BY HIM"

1. Keckley, 118.
2. Basler, 5:403–4 (from AL's Meditation on the Divine Will, September 2, 1862).
3. Segal, 171–73; Basler, 5:278–79 (from AL's remarks to Progressive Friends, June 20, 1862); *New York Herald,* June 21, 1862.
4. Welles, 1:143.
5. Basler, 7:281 (AL to A. G. Hodges, Washington, DC, April 4, 1864).
6. Braithwaite, 28–29; Mott, 307; Bullard, 10.
7. Mott, 308; Livermore, 550, 560.
8. Mott, 309.
9. Braithwaite, 31; Mott, 308, 313.
10. Mott, 313–15.
11. Ibid., 316–17; Basler, 7:535; Mott, 318–21.
12. Bullard, 12.
13. Robertson, 73.
14. Browning, 1:600–601; Brooks, 57–58.
15. Keckley, 147; Sandburg and Angle, 110–12.

16. Beveridge, 1:536–37.

17. John Hay to John G. Nicolay, Washington, DC, June 20, 1864, John Hay Papers, Library of Congress. Lincoln chose Nicolay as his chief private secretary during his presidential campaign. Born in Bavaria, Nicolay had been a newspaper editor. He recruited John Hay as junior secretary. Hay was a recent graduate of Brown University, had studied law in his uncle's office in Springfield, and was admitted to the bar two weeks before accompanying Lincoln to Washington. The two men had known each other since 1851. They performed their jobs with great ability. Hay later became ambassador to England (1897) and secretary of state (1898) and earned a reputation as one of the country's leading writers. With Nicolay, he wrote the monumental ten-volume *Abraham Lincoln: A History* (1890).

CHAPTER 12: "THE BEST ABUSED MAN OF OUR NATION"

1. Herr and Spence, 266; Basler, 4:519 (AL to Mrs. John C. Frémont, Washington, DC, September 12, 1861).

2. McPherson, 108; Anna E. Dickinson to [Elizabeth Cady Stanton?], Philadelphia, July 12, 1864, Harper Collection, Henry E. Huntington Library, San Marino, CA.

3. Massey, 157.

4. Basler, 5:382; Blackwell, 47 (Edward Bates to Anna Ella Carroll, April 15, 1862, Washington, DC); *Chicago Times-Herald* clipping dated only 1895.

5. Blackwell, 52 (Orville H. Browning to Anna Ella Carroll, September 17, 1873, Quincy, IL).

6. Browning, 1:659 (entry for February 6, 1864); John G. Nicolay's interview with Lot M. Morrill, probably September 20, 1878, John G. Nicolay Papers, Library of Congress; Livermore, 568.

7. *Littell's Living Age,* February 6, 1864.

8. Segal, 372 (Joshua F. Speed to WHH, January 12, 1866).

9. Ibid., 372–73.

10. Basler 6:256; 10:187.

11. Welles, 1:364.

12. Basler, 6:283, 471.

13. John Hay, 110; *New York World,* April 19, 1865.

14. Helm, 230–31.

15. Ibid., 225–26; Browning, 651.

16. Helm, 225–26.

17. Leonard, 89 (from U.S. War Department, *The War of the Rebellion: A Compilation of the Official Records of the Union and Confederate Armies,* ser. 2, 5:567).

18. John G. Nicolay to John Hay, Washington, January 18, 29, 1864, John G. Nicolay Papers; Helen Nicolay, 191–92.

19. Simon, *The Papers of U. S. Grant,* 10:422; Carpenter, 283; Keckley, 133–34; Porter, 216–23.

20. Cramer, 64.

21. Keckley, 149–50.

22. Ethan Allen Hitchcock to Mary Mann, July 14, 1864, Ethan Allen Hitchcock Papers, Library of Congress.

23. Sheridan, 276–78, 295–96; Massey, 103–4, 135; Anonymous, "The Loyal Girl of Winchester," Scrapbook, John Page Nicholson Military Collection, Henry E. Huntington Library, San Marino, CA; *Philadelphia Times,* February 26 and April 5, 1884.

24. Mabee, *Sojourner Truth,* 74.

25. Ibid., 116.

26. Ibid., 122 (letter from Sojourner Truth to Rowland Johnson, a New Jersey Quaker, November 17, 1864; published in the *National Anti-Slavery Standard,* December 17, 1864). NOTE: The additional quotations from the meeting with Lincoln are taken from this letter.

27. Mabee, "Sojourner Truth and President Lincoln," 527; Mabee, *Sojourner Truth,* 122–28.

28. Quarles, 256–57.

29. Keckley, 121.

30. Basler, 8:116–17.

31. Ibid., 6:16–17.

32. Eagle, 603.

33. Ibid., 604 (quoting from Vinnie Ream Hoxie's 1893 speech, "Lincoln and Farragut").

34. *The Midland Monthly,* November 1897; *Topeka State Journal,* July 4, 1903.

35. "Vinnie Ream, An Interesting Page in Her History," *Brooklyn Union,* November 8, 1872; Eagle, 603.

36. Hall, 58–59; Turner and Turner, 387.

37. *Washington Evening Star,* January 26, 1871.

CHAPTER 13: "THAT WOMAN IS PRETENDING TO BE ME!"

1. Pfanz, 4; Porter, chaps. 26–27 provide a full account of the visit; Arnold, 423 (based on William T. Sherman's recollection and statement).

2. Randall, *MTL,* 372–74; Badeau, 358–60.

3. Ibid.

4. Keckley, 166–67.

5. Ibid., 172; undated manuscript in Herndon's hand, Herndon-Weik Papers, Library of Congress; Ishbel Ross, 232.

6. Ishbel Ross, 235.

7. Keckley, 177.

8. Hanchett, *TLMC,* 37.

9. Lamon, *Recollections,* 115–18.

10. Turner and Turner, 219.

11. Ibid., 257.

12. Chase, *Diary,* 268; Storey, 464; Welles, "Lincoln and Johnson," 526–27; Thomas and Hyman, 357–58; Welles, *Diary,* 2:283; Flower, 271–72.

13. Bishop (based on Lincoln's remarks to John G. Nicolay).

14. Hanchett, "Booth's Diary," 40.

15. Wilson and Davis, 360 (Mary Lincoln to WHH, September 1866); Turner and Turner, 283–85.

16. Storey, 464; Bates, 366–67; Donald, *Lincoln,* 594.

17. Donald, *Lincoln,* 594; Bates 367; Crook, *Through Five Administrations,* 66–67; Roscoe, 21–22.

18. Grant, 380; Bates, 392; Kunhardt and Kunhardt, *Twenty Days,* 54.

19. Crook, *Memories of the White House,* 39.

20. Randall, *ML,* 382; Roscoe, 23.

21. Annie F. F. Wright, 113–14.

22. Donald, *Lincoln,* 599. NOTE: After the assassination, scores of women, many of them respectable ladies, were arrested and grilled by the army provosts on Stanton's orders, but apparently none of John Wilkes Booth's lady friends were pursued, even though numerous informants gave their names. Among them were Nellie Starr, "Jenny," several women from New York, Ella Turner, and Lucy Hale. Turner tried to kill herself on the night of the assassination by covering her face with a towel soaked in chloroform (*New York Herald Tribune,* April 17, 1865). Booth was betrothed to Hale, whose name was kept secret for sixty-five years. She was whisked to Spain soon after the assassination by her father, Republican Senator John P. Hale, who had been appointed minister to Spain. See Roscoe, 322–26.

23. Lattimer, 32; Letter of Elizabeth Dixon, dated May 1, 1865, in *Surratt Society News* 7 (March 1982), 3–4; Bryan, 189.

24. Keckley, 192.

25. Julian, 255, 257; Zachariah Chandler to Mrs. Chandler, April 22, 1865, Zachariah Chandler Papers, Library of Congress; Bryan, 383.

26. Keckley, 197.

27. Ibid., 190; Kunhardt, Kunhardt, and Kunhardt, *Lincoln,* 386.

SELECTED BIBLIOGRAPHY

Alford, Terry. "The Silken Net: Plots to Abduct Abraham Lincoln During the Civil War." Annandale, VA: unpublished paper, April 21, 1987.

Allen, John W. "Story of Ann Rutledge Has Ties in Henderson, Ky., Enfield, Ill." Carbondale: Southern Illinois University, undated.

Ames, Mary Clemmer. *Ten Years in Washington—Life and Scenes in the National Capital—As a Woman Sees Them.* Hartford: Worthington, 1874.

Angle, Paul M., ed. *The Lincoln Reader.* New Brunswick: Rutgers University Press, 1947.

———. *"Here I Have Lived": A History of Lincoln's Springfield 1821–1865.* New Brunswick: Rutgers University Press, 1950.

———, ed. *Herndon's Life of Lincoln: The History and Personal Recollections of Abraham Lincoln as Originally Written by William H. Herndon and Jesse W. Weik.* Cleveland: World, 1942.

Arnold, Isaac N. *The Life of Abraham Lincoln.* Chicago: Jansen, McClurg, & Co., 1885.

Asbury, Herbert. *A Methodist Saint: The Life of Bishop Asbury.* New York: Knopf, 1927.

Ashmun, George. "Abraham Lincoln at Home." *Springfield (MA) Daily Republican,* May 23, 1860.

Badeau, Adam. *Grant in Peace: From Appomattox to Mount McGregor.* Hartford: Scranton, 1887.

Baker, Jean H. *Mary Todd Lincoln.* New York: Norton, 1987.

———. "Not Much of Me: Abraham Lincoln as a Typical American." Louis A. Warren Lincoln Library and Museum, Fort Wayne, IN, 1988.

Baringer, William E. *Lincoln's Rise to Power.* Boston: Little, Brown & Co., 1937.

Barton, William E. "Abraham Lincoln and New Salem." *Journal of the Illinois State Historical Society* 19 (1926–27).

———. "Sister of Lincoln's Sweetheart Recalls Romance Death Ended." *San Diego Sun,* January 11, 1922.

———. *The Paternity of Abraham Lincoln.* New York: Doran, 1920.

———. *The Women Lincoln Loved.* Indianapolis: Bobbs-Merrill, 1927.

Basler, Roy P., et al., eds. *The Collected Works of Abraham Lincoln.* 8 vols. Springfield, IL: Abraham Lincoln Association, 1953.

Bates, David Homer. *Lincoln in the Telegraph Office.* New York: D. Appleton-Century Co., 1907.

Bayne, Julia Taft. *Tad Lincoln's Father.* Boston: Little, Brown & Co., 1931.

Bergevin, Charlotte, Daisy Sundberg, and Evelyn Berg. "Camerons, Westward They Came." Peoria, IL: unpublished paper, 1983.

Beveridge, Albert J. *Abraham Lincoln 1809–1858.* Boston: Houghton Mifflin, 1928.

Bigelow, John, ed. *Letters and Literary Memorials of Samuel J. Tilden.* New York: Harper & Brothers, 1908.

Bishop, Jim. *The Day Lincoln Was Shot.* New York: Harper & Brothers, 1955.

Blackwell, Sarah Ellen. *A Military Genius, Life of Anna Ella Carroll.* Washington, DC: Judd & Detweiler, 1891.

Bogue, Allan G. *The Congressman's Civil War.* New York: Cambridge University Press, 1989.

Boritt, Gabor S., and Adam Boritt. "Lincoln and the Marfan Syndrome: The Medical Diagnosis of a Historical Figure." *Civil War History* 29 (September 1983).

Bowman, John S., ed. *Who Was Who in the Civil War.* New York: Crescent Books, 1994.

Braithwaite, Joseph Bevan. *Memoirs of Eliza Paul Gurney and Others.* Philadelphia: Longstreth, 1883.

Bray, Robert. "The Cartwright-Lincoln Acquaintance." *The Old Methodist* 13 (Summer 1987).

Brockett, Linus P., and Mary C. Vaughan. *Woman's Work in the Civil War: A Record of Heroism, Patriotism, and Patience.* Philadelphia: Zeigler, McCurdy, 1867.

Brooks, Noah. *Washington in Lincoln's Time.* New York: Century, 1896.

Brown, Pearl. *"Marian": Modern Pioneer Woman.* Springfield, IL: n.p., 1957. Copies of various chapters provided by genealogist C. Vale Mayes of Shell Knob, MO, to Ralph E. Winkler about 1985.

Browne, Francis Fisher. *The Every-Day Life of Abraham Lincoln.* Minneapolis: Northwestern, 1887.

Browning, Orville H. *The Diary of Orville Hickman Browning.* Edited by Theodore Calvin Pease and James G. Randall. 2 vols. Springfield: Illinois State Historical Society, 1925, 1933.

Bryan, George S. *The Great American Myth.* New York: Carrick & Evans, 1940.

Bullard, F. Lauriston, "Lincoln and the Quaker Woman." *Lincoln Herald* 46, no. 2 (June 1944).

Burba, Howard. "A Story of Lincoln's Boyhood." *American Boy* (February 1905).

Burlingame, Michael, ed. *An Oral History of Abraham Lincoln: John G. Nicolay's Interviews and Essays.* Carbondale: Southern Illinois University Press, 1996.

————. *The Inner World of Abraham Lincoln.* Urbana: University of Illinois Press, 1994.

Burt, Silas W. "Lincoln on His Own Story Telling." *Century Magazine* 73 (February 1907).

Carman, Harry J., and Reinhard H. Luthin. *Lincoln and the Patronage.* New York: Columbia University Press, 1943.

Carnegie, Dale. *Lincoln the Unknown.* New York: Perma Giants, 1932.

————. *The Unknown Lincoln.* New York: Pocket Books, 1952.

Carpenter, Francis B. *Six Months at the White House with Abraham Lincoln.* New York: Hurd and Houghton, 1866.

Cartwright, Peter. *Autobiography of Peter Cartwright.* Nashville: Abingdon Press, 1984.

Chandler, Josephine. "New Salem: An Early Chapter in Lincoln's Life." *Journal of the Illinois State Historical Society* (January 1930).

Chenery, William. "Mary Lincoln Should Be Remembered for Many Kind Acts." *Illinois State Register,* February 27, 1938.

Clines, Francis X. "Discretion a Hallmark of Bordello in Capital." *New York Times,* April 18, 1999.

Cole, Donald B., and John J. McDonough, eds. *Witness to the Young Republic.* Hanover, NH: University Press of New England, 1989.

Coleman, Charles H. *Abraham Lincoln and Coles County, Illinois.* New Brunswick: Scarecrow, 1955.

————. "The Half-Faced Camp in Indiana—Fact or Myth?" *Abraham Lincoln Quarterly* 7 (September 1952).

Collier, Robert Laird. "Moral Heroism: Its Essentialness to the Crisis." August 3, 1862. Sermon, Wabash Avenue Methodist Episcopal Church, Chicago.

Conway, W. Fred. *Young Abe Lincoln: His Teenage Years in Indiana.* New Albany, IN: FBH, 1992.

Cook, Florita. "Ann Rutledge Figured Prominently in Life of Abraham Lincoln." *Lompoc (CA) Record,* February 12, 1967.

Coryell, Janet L. *Neither Heroine Nor Fool: Anna Ella Carroll of Maryland.* Kent, OH: Kent State University Press, 1990.

Cramer, John Henry. *Lincoln Under Enemy Fire: The Complete Account of His Experiences During Early's Attack on Washington.* Baton Rouge: Louisiana State University Press, 1948.

Crawford, Martin, ed. *William Howard Russell's Civil War: Private Diary and Letters, 1861–62.* Athens: University of Georgia Press, 1991.

Crook, William H. "Lincoln's Last Day." *Harper's* (September 1907).

———. *Memories of the White House: The Home Life of Our Presidents from Lincoln to Roosevelt.* Boston: Little, Brown, & Co., 1911.

———. *Through Five Administrations.* New York: Harper & Brothers, 1907.

Cuthbert, Norma B., ed. *Lincoln and the Baltimore Plot, 1861: From Pinkerton Records and Related Papers.* San Marino: Henry E. Huntington Library, 1949.

Davis, James E. *Frontier Illinois.* Bloomington: Indiana University Press, 1998.

Davis, J. M. "Lincoln as a Storekeeper and as a Soldier in the Black Hawk War." *McClure's* (January 1896).

Davis, Rodney O., ed. *A History of Illinois from Its Commencement as a State in 1818 to 1847.* Urbana: University of Illinois Press, 1995.

Donald, David Herbert. *Lincoln's Herndon.* New York: Knopf, 1948.

———. *Lincoln.* New York: Simon and Schuster, 1995.

Doster, William E. *Lincoln and Episodes of the Civil War.* New York: Putnam, 1915.

Drake, Julia A. *Flame O' Dawn.* New York: Vantage Press, 1959.

Duncan, Kunigunde, and D. F. Nickols. *Mentor Graham: The Man Who Taught Lincoln.* Chicago: University of Chicago Press, 1944.

Eagle, Mary, ed. *The Congress of Women.* Chicago: International Publishing Co., 1894.

Erickson, Gary. "The Graves of Ann Rutledge and the Old Concord Burial Ground." *Lincoln Herald* (Fall 1969).

Findley, Paul. *A. Lincoln: The Crucible of Congress.* New York: Crown, 1979.

Fiske, A. Longfellow. "A Neighbor of Lincoln." *Commonweal* 2 (March 1932).

Flindt, Margaret. "Lincoln As a Lover." Interview with Nancy Rutledge Prewitt (sister of Ann Rutledge). *Chicago Inter-Ocean,* February 12, 1899.

Flower, Frank Abial. *Edwin McMasters Stanton: The Autocrat of Rebellion, Emancipation, and Reconstruction.* New York: Western W. Wilson, 1905.

Foner, Philip S., ed. *The Complete Writings of Thomas Paine.* New York: Citadel Press, 1945.

Fowler, William Worthington. *Woman on the American Frontier.* Hartford: Scranton, 1877.

Freedman, Russell. *Lincoln: A Photobiography.* New York: Clarion, 1987.

Garrison, Webb. *The Lincoln No One Knows.* Nashville: Rutledge Hill, 1993.

Goff, John S. *Robert Todd Lincoln: A Man in His Own Right.* Norman: University of Oklahoma Press, 1969.

Grant, Ulysses S. *Personal Memoirs.* New York: Webster, 1885–86.

Gridley, Eleanor. *The Story of Abraham Lincoln.* Chicago: Monarch, 1902.

Hall, Gordon Langley. *Vinnie Ream: The Story of the Girl Who Sculptured Lincoln.* New York: Holt, Rinehart & Winston, 1963.

Hammand, Jane E. "Memoirs of the Rutledge Family of New Salem, Illinois." Manuscript, Collects Documents, Library of Congress. Compiled for the Decatur Lincoln Memorial Collection, 1921.

Hanchett, William. *The Lincoln Murder Conspiracies.* Urbana: University of Illinois Press, 1983.

———. "Booth's Diary." *Journal of the Illinois State Historical Society* 72 (February 1979).

Hay, John. *Inside Lincoln's White House: The Complete Civil War Diary of John Hay.* Edited by Michael Burlingame and John R. Turner Ettlinger. Carbondale: Southern Illinois University Press, 1997.

Hay, William D, ed. *"A Matter of History."* Carmi: White County Historical Society, 1996.

Helm, Katherine. *The True Story of Mary, Wife of Lincoln.* New York: Harper & Brothers, 1928.

Hendrick, Burton J. *Lincoln's War Cabinet.* Boston: Little Brown, 1946.

Herndon, William. *Lincoln and Ann Rutledge and the Pioneers of New Salem.* Herrin, IL: Trovillion, 1945.

———, and Jesse W. Weik. *Herndon's Life of Lincoln.* New York: Da Capo, 1983.

Herr, Pamela, and Mary Lee Spence, eds. *The Letters of Jessie Benton Frémont.* Urbana: University of Illinois Press, 1993.

Hertz, Emanuel. *Abraham Lincoln: A New Portrait.* 2 vols. New York: Boni and Liveright, 1931.

———, ed. *Lincoln Talks: An Oral Biography.* New York: Bramhall House, 1986.

———, ed. *The Hidden Lincoln: From the Letters and Papers of William Herndon.* New York: Viking, 1938.

Hill, Frederick T. *Lincoln the Lawyer.* New York: Century, 1906.

Holland, J. G. *The Life of Abraham Lincoln.* Springfield, MA: Gurdon Bill, 1866.

Holzer, Harold. *Lincoln at Cooper Union.* New York: Simon & Schuster, 2004.

Howells, W. D. *Life of Abraham Lincoln.* Springfield, IL: Abraham Lincoln Association, 1938.

Janney, John Jay. "Talking with the President: Four Interviews with Abraham Lincoln." *Civil War Times Illustrated* 26 (September 1987).

Jones, Lewis P. *South Carolina: A Synoptic History for Laymen*. Lexington, SC: Sandlapper Store, 1981.

Jordan, Philip D. "The Death of Nancy Hanks Lincoln." *Indiana Magazine of History* 40 (June 1944).

Julian, George W. *Political Reflections, 1840 to 1872*. Chicago: Jansen, McClurg & Co., 1884.

Kane, Harnett T. *Spies for the Blue and Gray*. Garden City: Hanover House, 1954.

Keckley, Elizabeth. *Behind the Scenes . . . or Thirty Years a Slave, and Four Years in the White House*. New York: Carleton, 1868.

Kincaid, Robert L. *Joshua Fry Speed: Lincoln's Most Intimate Friend*. Harrogate, TN: Lincoln Memorial University, 1943.

Kunhardt, Dorothy Meserve, and Philip B. Kunhardt. *Twenty Days*. New York: Harper & Row, 1965.

Kunhardt, Philip B., Jr.; Philip B. Kunhardt III; and Peter W. Kunhardt. *Lincoln*. New York: Knopf, 1991.

Lair, John. *Songs Lincoln Loved*. New York: Duel, Sloan, 1954.

Lamon, Ward Hill. *Life of Abraham Lincoln, from His Birth to His Inauguration as President*. Boston: Osgood, 1872.

———. *Recollections of Abraham Lincoln, 1847–1865*. Edited by Dorothy Lamon Teillard. Chicago: McClurg, 1895.

Land, Margaret. "The Seven Mile Prairie Settlement." Carmi (IL) Public Library. Circa 1960.

———. "Enfield Township." Carmi (IL) Public Library. Circa 1960.

———. Letter to Georgia Archives, January 12, 1954.

Lattimer, John K. *Kennedy and Lincoln: Medical and Ballistic Comparisons of Their Assassinations*. New York: Harcourt Brace Jovanovich, 1980.

Leech, Margaret. *Reveille in Washington: 1860 to 1865*. New York: Harper & Row, 1941.

Leonard, Elizabeth D. *All the Daring of the Soldier*. New York: Norton, 1999.

Leslie, Frank. *Heroic Incidents*. New York: n.p., 1862.

Lincoln, Waldo. *History of the Lincoln Family*. Worcester: Commonwealth Press, 1923.

Linder, Usher. *Reminiscences of the Early Bench and Bar of Illinois*. Chicago: Legal News Co., 1879.

Livermore, Mary A. *My Story of the War*. Hartford: Worthington, 1889.

Lomask, Milton. *Andrew Johnson: President on Trial*. New York: Farrar, Strauss and Giroux, 1960.

Lorant, Stefan. *Life of Abraham Lincoln*. New York: Harper & Brothers, 1952.

Mabee, Carleton. "Sojourner Truth and President Lincoln." *New England Quarterly* 61 (December 1988).

———. *Sojourner Truth: Slave, Prophet, Legend.* New York: New York University Press, 1993.

MacKaye, Percy. *Epoch: The Life of Steele MacKaye, Genuis of the Theater.* New York: Boni and Liveright, 1927.

Maltby, Charles. *The Life and Public Services of Abraham Lincoln.* Stockton, CA: Daily Independent Steam Power Print, 1884.

Manfrina, Myra. "Lincoln-Rutledge Romance Recalled by Memoirs of Lompoc Resident." *(Santa Barbara, CA) News-Press,* February 12, 1952.

Massey, Mary Elizabeth. *Women in the Civil War.* Lincoln: University of Nebraska Press, 1966.

Masters, Edgar Lee. *Lincoln the Man.* Columbia, SC: Foundation for American Education, 1997.

McCoy, Susan Hatton. *A Frontier Wife.* New York: Ballantine Books, 1988.

McPherson, James M. *The Struggle for Equality: Abolitionists and the Negro in the Civil War and Reconstruction.* Princeton: Princeton University Press, 1964.

Mearns, David C, ed. *The Lincoln Papers.* Garden City: Doubleday, 1948.

Miers, Earl Schenck, ed. *Lincoln Day By Day.* 3 vols. Washington, DC: Lincoln Sesquicentennial Commission, 1960.

Miller, R. D. *Past and Present of Menard County, Illinois.* Chicago: Clarke, 1905.

Milton, George F. *The Age of Hate, Andrew Johnson and the Radicals.* Hamden: Archon, 1965.

Moorhead, James H. *American Apocalypse: Yankee Protestants and the Civil War.* New Haven: Yale University Press, 1978.

Mott, Richard F., ed. *Memoir and Correspondence of Eliza P. Gurney.* Philadelphia: Lippincott, 1884.

Murphy, Alice Purvine. *The Rev. John Miller Camron and Descendants 1790–1962.* Privately published, 1962.

Murr, J. Edward. "Lincoln in Indiana." *Indiana Magazine of History* 14 (March 1918).

Nevins, Allan. *The War for the Union.* New York: Scribner, 1959.

Nicolay, Helen. *Lincoln's Secretary: A Biography of John G. Nicolay.* New York: Longmans, Green & Co., 1949.

Nicolay, John. *A Short Life of Abraham Lincoln.* New York: Century, 1902.

———, John, and John Hay. *Abraham Lincoln: A History.* New York: Century, 1891.

Nolan, J. Bennett. "Of a Tomb in the Reading Cemetery and the Long Shadow of Abraham Lincoln." *Pennsylvania History* 19, no. 3 (July 1952).

Oates, Stephen B. *With Malice Toward None.* New York: HarperPerennial, Harper-Collins, 1994.

Oldroyd, Osborn H. *The Assassination of Abraham Lincoln: Flight, Pursuit, Capture and Punishment of the Conspirators.* Washington, DC: privately published, 1901.

Onstot, T. G. *Pioneers of Menard and Mason Counties.* Peoria, IL: Franks, 1902. Reprint, Havana, IL: Members of the Church of Jesus Christ of Latter-day Saints, 1986.

Ostendorf, Lloyd. *Abraham Lincoln, the Boy, the Man.* Springfield, IL: Wagner, 1962.

———, and Walter Oleksy, eds. *Lincoln's Unknown Private Life.* Mamaroneck, NY: Hastings House, 1995.

Pfanz, Donald C. *The Petersburg Campaign, Abraham Lincoln at City Point, March 20–April 9, 1865.* Lynchburg, VA: Howard, 1989.

Phelps, Mary Merwin. *Kate Chase Dominant Daughter.* New York: Crowell, 1935.

Pickard, Samuel. *Autobiography of a Pioneer.* Chicago: Church and Goodman, 1866.

Pinkerton, Allan. *The Spy of the Rebellion: Being a True History of the Spy System of the United States Army During the Late Rebellion.* New York: Carleton, 1883; Toronto: Rose, 1884.

Pond, Fern Nance. "Abraham Lincoln and David Rutledge." *Lincoln Herald* (June 1950).

———. "Intellectual New Salem in Lincoln's Day." Address, Lincoln Memorial University, Harrogate, TN, February 12, 1938.

———. "The Memoirs of James McGrady Rutledge." *Journal of the Illinois State Historical Society* (April 1936).

Porter, David W. *Incidents and Anecdotes of the Civil War.* New York: Appleton, 1885.

Porter, Horace. *Campaigning With Grant.* New York: Century, 1897.

Pratt, Harry E. "Lincoln in the Black Hawk War." *Bulletin of the Abraham Lincoln Association,* no. 54 (December 1938).

Putnam, George Haven. "The Speech That Won the East for Lincoln." *Outlook* 130 (February 8, 1922).

Quarles, Benjamin. *The Negro in the Civil War.* Boston: Little, Brown & Co., 1953. Reprint, New York: Da Capo, 1989.

Randall, James G. "Sifting the Ann Rutledge Evidence." *Lincoln the President* New York: Dodd, Mead & Co., 1945.

———. *Lincoln the President: Springfield to Gettysburg.* New York: Dodd, Mead & Co., 1946.

Randall, Ruth. *Mary Lincoln: Biography of a Marriage.* Boston: Little, Brown, & Co., 1953.

———. *Lincoln's Sons.* Boston: Little, Brown, & Co., 1955.

Rankin, Henry. *Personal Recollections of Abraham Lincoln*. New York: Putnam, 1916.

Reep, Thomas. *Lincoln at New Salem*. Petersburg, IL: New Salem Lincoln League, 1918, 1927.

Rice, Allen Thorndike, ed. *Reminiscences of Abraham Lincoln*. New York: North American Review, 1888.

Richardson, Albert D. *The Secret Service, the Field, the Dungeon, and the Escape*. Hartford: American, 1865.

Robertson, James I., Jr. *Civil War! America Becomes One Nation*. New York: Knopf, 1992.

Roscoe, Theodore. *The Web of Conspiracy*. Englewood Cliffs: Prentice-Hall, 1959.

Ross, Harvey. *Early Pioneers and Pioneer Events in the State of Illinois*. Chicago: Eastman, 1899.

Ross, Ishbel. *The President's Wife: Mary Todd Lincoln*. New York: Putnam, 1973.

———. *Proud Kate*. New York: Harper & Brothers, 1953.

Rouse, Parke S., Jr. *The Great Wagon Road*. Richmond, VA: Dietz, 1995.

———. *Planters and Pioneers: Life in Colonial Virginia*. New York: Hastings House, 1968.

Rutledge, James McGrady. "The Memoirs of James McGrady Rutledge, 1814–1899." *Journal of the Illinois State Historical Society* 29, no. 1 (April 1936).

Sandburg, Carl. *Abraham Lincoln, the Prairie Years*. New York: Harcourt, Brace & Co., 1926.

Sandburg, Carl, and Paul M. Angle. *Mary Lincoln: Wife and Widow*. New York: Harcourt, Brace, & Co., 1932.

Saunders, James Rutledge. "The Rutledge Family of New Salem, Illinois." Sisquoc, CA, January 1922. Compiled from the Rutledge family Bible and other family records.

Segal, Charles M., ed. *Conversations with Lincoln*. New York: Putnam, 1961.

Shelton, Vaughan. *Mask for Treason: The Lincoln Murder Trial*. Harrisburg: Stackpole, 1965.

Shere, Doc. "Story of Ann Rutledge as Illinoisans Were Told It by Their Grandmothers." Unidentified clipping, circa 1940.

Sheridan, Philip H. *The Personal Memoirs of P. H. Sheridan*. New York: Webster, 1888. Reprint, New York: Da Capo, 1992.

Sherwood, Glenn V. *Labor of Love: The Life and Art of Vinnie Ream*. Hygiene, CO: Sunshine, 1997.

Shutes, Milton H. *Lincoln's Emotional Life*. Philadelphia: Dorrance, 1957.

Simon, John Y. "Abraham Lincoln and Ann Rutledge." *Journal of the Abraham Lincoln Association* 2 (1990): 13–33.

————, ed. *The Papers of Ulysses S. Grant*. Carbondale: Southern Illinois University Press, 1982.

Smith, Don. *Peculiarities of the Presidents: Strange Facts Not Usually Found in History*. Van Wert, OH: Wilkinson, 1938.

Smith, Matthew Hale. *Sunshine and Shadow in New York*. Hartford: Burr, 1868.

Sparks, Edwin E., ed. *The Lincoln-Douglas Debates of 1858*. Springfield: Illinois State Historical Library Collection, 1908.

Speed, Joshua Fry. *Reminiscences of Abraham Lincoln and Notes of a Visit to California*. Louisville: Morgan, 1884.

Stanton, Elizabeth Cady, Susan B. Anthony, and Matilda Joslyn Gage, eds. *History of Woman Suffrage*. Rochester, NY: Mann, 1889.

Stevens, Walter B. *A Reporter's Lincoln*. St. Louis: Missouri Historical Society, 1916.

Stoddard, William O. *Inside the White House in War Times*. New York: Webster, 1892.

Storey, Moorfield. "Dickens, Stanton, Sumner, and Storey." *Atlantic Monthly* 145 (April 1930).

Strozier, Charles. *Lincoln's Quest for Union: Public and Private Meanings*. New York: Basic Books, 1982.

————, and Stanley H. Cath. "Lincoln and the Fathers: Reflections on Idealization." In *Fathers and Their Families*, edited by Stanley H. Cath, Alan Gurwitt, and Linda Gunsberg. Hillsdale, NJ: Analytic Press, 1989.

Swinton, William. *Campaigns of the Army of the Potomac*. New York: Richardson, 1866.

Tarbell, Ida M. *The Early Life of Abraham Lincoln*. 1896. Reprint, New York: Barnes, 1974.

————. *The Life of Abraham Lincoln*. 2 vols. New York: Lincoln Memorial Association, 1900.

————. "Lincoln's First Love." *Collier's* 8 (February 1930).

————. "Ann Rutledge." *In the Footsteps of the Lincolns*. New York: Harper & Brothers, 1924.

Temple, Wayne C. *Abraham Lincoln: From Skeptic to Prophet*. Mahomet, IL: Mayhaven, 1995.

————. "When Lincoln Left Town with Another Woman." *Lincoln Herald* 68 (Winter 1966): 175–77, 182.

Thomas, Benjamin P. *Abraham Lincoln: A Biography*. New York: Knopf, 1952.

————. *Lincoln's New Salem*. Rev. ed. Carbondale: Southern Illinois University Press, 1987.

————, and Harold M. Hyman. *Stanton: The Life and Times of Lincoln's Secretary of War.* New York: Knopf, 1962.

Thompson, Ernest Trice. *Presbyterians in the South 1607–1871.* Richmond, VA: Knox, 1963.

Tiffany, Francis. *Life of Dorothea Lynde Dix.* Boston: Houghton Mifflin, 1890.

Townsend, William H. *Lincoln and Liquor.* New York: Press of the Pioneers, 1934.

Turner, Justin G., and Linda Levitt Turner. *Mary Todd Lincoln: Her Life and Letters.* New York: Knopf, 1972.

Verduin, Paul H. "Lincoln's Tidewater Virginia Heritage: The Hidden Legacy of Nancy Hanks Lincoln." Address, Lincoln Group of the District of Columbia, October 17, 1989.

————. "New Evidence Suggests Lincoln's Mother Born in Richmond County, Va., Giving Credibility to Planter-Grandfather Legend." *Northern Neck of Virginia Historical Magazine* 38 (December 1988): 4354–89.

Voss, Veronica. "Seven Mile Community." *Carmi (IL) Times,* February 8 1966.

Walsh, John Evangelist. *The Shadows Rise: Abraham Lincoln and the Ann Rutledge Legend.* Urbana: University of Illinois Press, 1993.

Ward, William Hayes, ed. *Abraham Lincoln: Tributes from His Associates—Reminiscences of Soldiers, Statesmen and Citizens.* New York: Crowell, 1895.

Warren, Louis A. *Lincoln's Parentage and Childhood.* New York: Century, 1926.

————. *Lincoln's Youth.* New York: Appleton, Century, Crofts, 1959.

Warren, Mary Bondurant. *Citizens and Immigrants—South Carolina, 1768.* Danielsville, GA: Heritage Papers, 1980.

Weeks, Stephen Beauregard. "Confederate Textbooks: A Preliminary Bibliography." *Report of the U.S. Commissioner of Education, 1898–99.* 2 vols. Washington, DC: Government Printing Office, 1900. 2:1139–55.

Weichmann, Louis J. *A True History of the Assassination of Abraham Lincoln and of the Conspiracy of 1865.* Edited by Floyd E. Risvold. New York: Knopf, 1975.

Weik, Jesse W. *The Real Lincoln.* Boston: Houghton Mifflin, 1922.

Welles, Gideon. *Diary of Gideon Welles.* Edited by John T. Morse Jr. Boston: Houghton Mifflin, 1911.

————. "Lincoln and Johnson." *Galaxy* 13 (April 1872).

Whipple, Wayne. *The Story of Young Abraham Lincoln.* Chicago: Goldsmith, 1934.

Whitney, Henry C. *Life on the Circuit with Lincoln.* Boston: Estes and Lauriat, 1892.

Williams, Frank J. *Judging Lincoln.* Carbondale: Southern Illinois University Press, 2002.

Wilson, Douglas, "Abraham Lincoln, Ann Rutledge, and the Evidence of Herndon's Informants." *Civil War History* (December 1990).

———. *Lincoln Before Washington: New Perspectives on the Illinois Years.* Urbana: University of Illinois Press, 1997.

———, and Rodney O. Davis, eds. *Herndon's Informants: Letters, Interviews, and Statements About Abraham Lincoln.* Urbana: University of Illinois Press, 1997.

———. *Honor's Voice: The Transformation of Abraham Lincoln.* New York: Knopf, 1998.

Winkler, H. Donald. *Lincoln and Booth.* Nashville: Cumberland House, 2003.

Wright, Annie F. F. "The Assassination of Abraham Lincoln." *Magazine of History* 9 (February 1909).

Wright, Richardson. *Forgotten Ladies: Nine Portraits from the American Family Album.* Philadelphia: Lippincott, 1928.

Zane, Charles S. "Lincoln as I Knew Him." *Sunset Magazine* 29 (October 1912).

INDEX